C++ for the Impatient

Brian Overland

Addison-Wesley

Upper Saddle River, NJ • Boston • Indianapolis • San Francisco
New York • Toronto • Montreal • London • Munich • Paris • Madrid
Capetown • Sydney • Tokyo • Singapore • Mexico City

The publisher offers excellent discounts on this book when ordered in quantity for bulk purchases or special sales, which may include electronic versions and/or custom covers and content particular to your business, training goals, marketing focus, and branding interests. For more information, please contact:

U.S. Corporate and Government Sales
(800) 382-3419
corpsales@pearsontechgroup.com

For sales outside the United States, please contact:

International Sales
international@pearsoned.com

Visit us on the Web: informit.com/aw

Library of Congress Cataloging-in-Publication Data

Overland, Brian, 1958–
C++ for the impatient / Brian Overland.
pages cm
Includes index.
ISBN-13: 978-0-321-88802-0 (alk. paper)
ISBN-10: 0-321-88802-2 (alk. paper)
1. C++ (Computer program language) I. Title.
QA76.73.C153O8348 2013
005.13'3--dc23

2013005331

ISBN-13: 978-0-321-88802-0
ISBN-10: 0-321-88802-2
Text printed in the United States on recycled paper at Edwards Brothers Malloy in Ann Arbor, Michigan.
First printing: May, 2013

Once more, for Colin.

Preface

Congratulations! With this book, *C++ for the Impatient,* you have in your hands the quickest and easiest way to learn the latest state-of-the-art features in C++, especially features in the new C++11 specification and other features added in recent years.

The new technology is not difficult to understand once it's explained clearly. But some of the concepts are at first so abstract and alien that it can take weeks of pounding your head against a wall, wondering when you're going to "get it." Too many descriptions (although written by knowledgeable experts) are unable to break through the conceptual barrier that makes it hard to learn something new.

I wrote this book in part so that you wouldn't have to go through those weeks and months of frustration. Learning this material shouldn't be difficult.

C++ for the Impatient also provides quick, ready reference to all of C++'s features (or at least the great majority of them), ranging from the most basic building blocks of the language, up to and including refined uses of the C++ library.

How This Book Is Different: Learning C++11

My statement that this book is "the quickest and easiest way to learn the latest, state-of-the-art features" is a strong claim. It's backed up by a number of techniques.

- Dozens of easy-to-follow figures. Sometimes a picture really is worth a thousand words. Or sometimes ten thousand.
- Simple, relevant examples. Many or most programming books are written in part to convince you how smart the author is. My goal is to make *you* feel smart. And that means short, easy-to-digest examples.
- Frequent use of syntax diagrams, summarizing grammar at a glance.
- Simple explanations of important concepts—but only to the extent necessary to understand why a feature was added to C++ and how it's used.

Who Should Buy This Book?

The quick answer: almost anyone serious about learning and using C++.

- For advanced beginners: If you haven't learned any programming language before, you'll need additional help from a teacher or (at minimum) a more elementary text. But Chapter 1, "C++ Fundamentals," and the Sample Apps in each chapter are intended to be especially helpful for beginners.
- For intermediate and advanced programmers: No matter how advanced you may be, it's likely you're still coming up to speed on at least some of the newer and more advanced features of C++, especially C++11. If that's the case, this book is for you.
- For all programmers: Unlike other books, *C++ for the Impatient* features a concise write-up on each operator and each individual function, class, and object in the C++ library, including
  - Syntax summaries, showing arguments and types at a glance
  - A concise description of what each function, object, or operator does
  - A short illustrative example (although longer examples are used where helpful)

Examples and Exercises

Having the right example is often what makes the difference in learning new technology. So, in addition to the short examples for each individual function and operator, I provide one or two complete programs—Sample Apps—at the end of most chapters.

Each of these programs does something entertaining, useful, or both. They include intriguing games and puzzles. I've selected these Sample Apps because they make heavy use of the major technology in the chapter while at the same time being easy to follow.

Because this book is more a reference than a primer, I don't include exercises on every other page. However, I do include them after each Sample App. These are graduated and numbered, beginning with easier ones and leading up to the more truly challenging.

The best way to learn is by doing. I challenge you to complete the exercises in the book. If you can do them all, you can consider yourself quite an expert and an accomplished C++ programmer!

To find answers to these exercises (although it's cheating to look before you've at least tried to solve them yourself), you can go to informit.com/title/9780321888020. For information on other books of mine, you can go to brianoverland.com

Requirements: Your Version of C++

C++ is probably the most popular programming language in the world today. Although there are other excellent tools available for specific platforms (such as C#, Java, and Objective C), C++ still reigns as the most important, general-purpose language for writing and maintaining serious stand-alone applications.

Within the first few years after C++'s introduction, compiler vendors added important new features. This book assumes your compiler supports all of the following current features.

- Templates: This feature helps make code reusable; freeing you from having to solve the same general problems over and over again.
- The Standard Template Library (STL), providing flexible containers and reusable searching, sorting, and data processing routines: Potentially, these can save you a significant amount of work no matter what data types you work on.
- String class: The classic C-string type is still supported, but the STL **string** class is easier, safer, and more convenient to use than the old null-terminated C-string type.
- Specialized cast operators: These help result in more reliable, easier-to-debug programs.
- Structured exception handing: This is a superior way to handle errors, although it is mainly of use to programmers writing source code thousands of lines long.

One thing I do *not* assume in this book is that your compiler supports all the new features in the C++11 specification. As of this writing, some of the new features are not supported even by the major compiler vendors such as Microsoft, although they soon will be.

In order to make this book easier to use, therefore, all the sections and chapters that make use of the C++11 specification are clearly marked as such. The code in the rest of the book should run on any professional-grade compiler produced in the past several years.

C++11

Although this book doesn't assume that your compiler supports all the features in the C++11 specification, it is particularly useful if your compiler does support some or all of the new features.

The move from previous versions of C++ to C++11 is a major jump. Although the new specification is backward-compatible with past versions of C++, it opens up exciting new possibilities in software development.

This book explores all of these major new areas in C++11.

- Move semantics: The C++ library takes advantage of new technology by replacing copy operations, whenever possible, with *moves*. The difference is analogous to moving a document from one folder on your internal drive to another instead of copying it. You may have noticed that a move between folders is practically instantaneous, while copying can take time.

  Now this same improved performance is available to data within your own programs. Sometimes copying is unnecessary, and data transfers (or moves) are much faster. *Move semantics* can often speed up your programs without any action on your part. However, you can optimize your programs even further by facilitating move semantics in your own classes as explained in Appendix A, "A Painless Introduction to Rvalue References (C++11)."
- Lambda functions: Traditional programming techniques require you to define a function in one place and call it in another; this is fine most of the time, but sometimes it's inconvenient to search through all your source code to find a definition. Using the lambda technology enables you to define a function at the very point it is used, which can be extremely convenient.
- Improved syntax for class declarations: The ability to declare classes is one of the most important parts of the C++ language. Although C++ has been around for some time, up until now some things have been more difficult than they ideally should be. C++11 provides significantly improved syntax, such as inherited constructors for derived classes and more convenient ways to specify default values.
- Extended features of the C++ library: C++11 brings many new capabilities to the standard library, including a full-featured regular-expression library, which provides powerful tools for searching, matching, and replacing patterns of text. There are many other new capabilities as well, including improved randomization techniques and unordered (hash-table) containers. Such containers—although they lose the ability to step through elements in a meaningful order—provide much faster lookup times for database applications and data dictionaries. This is another way C++11 can significantly increase program performance.
- Smart pointers: Pointers are an important part of the C++ language, and they get their full due in this book, but applications can be made more error-free and easier to manage by the use of smart pointers, which automatically release memory when they go out of scope. This book describes exactly how the new **shared_ptr** and **unique_ptr** types work.
- Improvements to the core language: Finally, C++11 provides a series of improvements to the core language, such as range-based **for**, which reduces the chance of errors and is more concise than standard **for** statements. Range-based **for** takes advantage of each container's built-in knowledge of where it begins and ends. C++11 provides other improvements as well.

As Bjarne Stroustrup has said about C++11, it's effectively "a whole new language." Learning the new capabilities will enable you to produce higher-quality, more efficient and bug-free programs. You should find that the rewards, over time, repay the effort in learning these new features many times over.

Appendix B, "Summary of New Features in C++11," describes all these new features in greater detail.

Appendix C, "ASCII Codes," presents ASCII codes according to decimal and hexidecimal values.

Learning about Object Orientation

The approach of this book is to clearly lay out the mechanics of classes and objects in C++, explaining computer science concepts where needed to understand the technology.

For a more in-depth discussion of the background to object orientation and the history of C++, I recommend Bjarne Stroustrup's *The C++ Programming Language, Fourth Edition* (Addison-Wesley, 2013), which is long but is an excellent resource.

Other texts are available that attempt to teach how to "think objects" in more depth than I do in this book—although again, I cover the basic concepts. *C++ Primer, Fifth Edition* (Addison-Wesley, 2013) by Stanley B. Lippman, Josée Lajoie, and Barbara E. Moo, is a good place to start.

If you are really starting from scratch, with no background in C, C++, or a language in the C family, I humbly recommend my own book, *C++ Without Fear, Second Edition* (Prentice Hall, 2011).

Typographic Conventions

Typographic conventions for syntax summaries, I've found, can be helpful as long as those conventions don't get out of hand. In this book, I adhere to light use of these conventions. See Table P.1.

Throughout the book, I make extensive use of bold and italics in syntax displays; but I use brackets to indicate optional items only occasionally, because these can be confused with literal brackets. But the text always clarifies how I intend to use them.

Here is an example of these syntax conventions taken from Chapter 2, "Data":

[*sign*]*digits***.***digits***E***exponent*

In this case, both the decimal point (**.**) and the **E** are intended literally and so are in bold font. Each set of *digits* is a sequence of the numerals 0 through 9. The *exponent* is likewise a series of digits. Each of these is a string of numerals that you supply. The brackets (which are not in bold in this case) indicate that the *sign* is an optional minus sign (–) that can either appear or not appear.

TABLE P.1 Typographic Conventions

Style	Description
Keyword	Keywords and punctuation in bold are meant to be typed exactly as shown. Note that C++ is case-sensitive; so for the keyword **if**, enter "if" into your programming code but not "If" or "IF."
Placeholder	Placeholders are in italics: These are items that you supply. Typically, they are function, class, or variable names that you choose, but they can be something more complex, such as an entire statement.
[optional]	Occasionally, I use brackets (not in bold!) to indicate an optional item. In this case, the brackets are not intended literally but indicate something that may or may not be included as you choose. However, brackets in bold are intended literally, and in those cases, I mention that they are intended that way.
item, item...	Ellipses indicate an item that may be repeated any number of times. (Note that the comma is intended literally, but the ellipses are not.)

A Final Word

When Alice followed the White Rabbit down the rabbit hole, she was at first bewildered by the strange people and animals she encountered. So it is when learning new concepts. You wonder if you ever should have left your quiet garden and drawing room behind with their comfortable surroundings, as you encounter characters who say odd things and use peculiar logic.

You may find yourself asking: What was wrong with the old, familiar world I left behind? But hopefully, like Alice, you'll find yourself in Wonderland.

Personally, I feel the trip should always be interesting and even fun. Because this book is a reference, there are some chapters you won't want to read from beginning to end, any more than you'd read an encyclopedia that way. But the sections on the new technology are meant to be read like articles, as well as being texts you can come back to and refer to again and again. Above all, I hope they communicate a feel for why I found the new concepts both useful and intriguing.

Like me, you may be impatient. There is so much to learn and only so much time to learn it. I know that I'm like the White Rabbit, wanting to understand all that I see at first glance so that I can use the new tools to get to my destination quickly. I don't want to stand around trying to figure out what I'm doing there.

C++11 is almost a new language, despite its being backward-compatible. And learning a new language (to continue the Wonderland analogy) is like slaying the mythical Jabberwocky. It's a strange, multiheaded, whimsical beast, and it looks like it's too big to ever conquer; but with the right sword in hand, you shouldn't be afraid. Before you know it, you'll have completed the quest. And then you can imagine me saying:

"And, hast though slain the Jabberwock?
Come to my arms, my beamish boy!
Oh frabjous day! Callooh! Callay!"
He chortled in his joy."

Acknowledgments

More than any project I've worked on, this book required the help of some very talented people. To begin with, this book is the vision of editor Peter Gordon as much as it is mine, and it wouldn't have happened without his support and encouragement.

I was fortunate in getting assistance from some of the smartest people at Microsoft. Herb Sutter and Marian Luparu provided the software I needed as well as invaluable pointers. Stephan T. Lavavej provided insights on the STL (and yes, those are really his initials as well as his area of expertise!) that improved the book a great deal. John R. Bennett, a Microsoft emeritus, patent holder, and coauthor of Word Spellchecker, raised some questions on lambdas and regular expressions that enabled me to make the corresponding chapters much better. Ken Nichols, one of Microsoft's best technical minds, provided free reviews as well. All these people gave me advice and assistance without asking for any compensation whatsoever; an acknowledgment is the least I can do, even if that repayment is meager.

I'm indebted to Daveed Vandevoorde and Seve Vinosky for supplying superb technical reviews. They had an enormous amount of material to cover, and they did a great job.

Finally, I'm grateful to the excellent editorial team that showed patience, flexibility, and kindness to a sometimes-curmudgeonly author: Kim Boedigheimer, Caroline Senay, Audrey Doyle, and Alan Clements. Alan's cover art was so exceptional that it inspired me to make changes to the text itself to match the cover-art theme, something I've never done before.

About the Author

With long experience in both technology and training people to use it, **Brian Overland** is uniquely qualified to write books that simplify difficult concepts. He began programming professionally in C in the 1980s, working on a software-driven irrigation system used all over the globe. He also taught programming and English composition at a community college while writing film and drama reviews. At Microsoft, he spent a decade rising from tester and tech-support specialist to project lead and manager. As a project lead of Visual Basic 1.0, he played a key role in bringing easy Windows programming to the world and explaining how to use it; he was also a member of the Visual C++ team. He has since written many successful books and founded his own high-tech company.

CHAPTER 1

C++ Fundamentals

Despite its huge array of features, C++ is not really more difficult to use than most programming languages. In fact, when you understand a few basic principles, it becomes relatively easy to start writing programs. (C++ is challenging primarily because there are so many features to learn later on, although many of them are optional: Sometimes there are several ways to do exactly the same thing, and you only have to learn one of them.)

This chapter outlines those principles and introduces important features—include files, namespaces, and comments—used universally throughout this book. Once you understand these, the examples in the book should be straightforward.

Most of this chapter may be a review. But if you're new to C++, then welcome to the language of the masters of the universe.

1.1 Elements of a C++ Program

Let's start by looking at the simplest C++ program that actually does something.

```
#include <iostream>
using namespace std;

int main() {
     cout << "Hello, C++!";
     return 0;
}
```

This program has three parts:

- The **#include** directive
- The **using** statement
- The definition of **main**, a function

Most programs have other features, but these three basic elements (with the possible exception of **using**) are the minimum you could expect to see in even the simplest programs. The next three sections describe these elements.

1.1.1 The #include Directive

One of the most fundamental rules in C++ is that you must declare a function, object, or class before using it—the exception being the **main** function.

The **#include** directive comes to your rescue here; it's a great time-saving device. The program makes use of the predefined object, **cout**; and to use **cout**, you must first declare it. Fortunately, the <iostream> header does this for you.

```
#include <iostream>
```

Each chapter of this book points out what header file (or files) must be included to support the objects, classes, and functions being used. Different services require different header-file support.

For example, to use any of the trig functions described in Chapter 12, "Math, Time, and Other Library Functions," you'd need to include <cmath>:

```
#include <cmath>
```

This may seem like extra work, but it saves a lot of effort in the long run. The rule is simple: Before using any part of the C/C++ library, place the appropriate **#include** directive at the beginning of the program. This book points out what **#include** is needed for each group of functions, classes, and objects in the library.

<iostream> supports the objects and classes used for console input/output (I/O); so as long as you perform console I/O, you'd include this file in every program.

1.1.2 The using Statement

The **using namespace std** statement is not strictly necessary, but it's a major convenience. You may choose to use it or not use it with your own programs, but throughout this book I sometimes use it to keep examples to the column width demanded by the book. Later in this chapter I'll discuss alternatives, as well as pros and cons of this statement.

```
using namespace std;
```

Without the **using** statement, it would be necessary to refer to **cout** by its qualified name, **std::cout**.

```
    std::cout << "Hello, C++";
```

The object **cout** is part of the **std** namespace, which is why (if the **using** statement is not present) you'd have to refer to it as **std::cout**.

If you use **cout** many times, it gets tedious to keep using the **std::** prefix, so for many programs—especially simpler ones—it's convenient to just put a **using namespace std** statement at the beginning of the program. This enables all names that are part of the **std** namespace—including **cout**, **cin**, and **endl**—to be referred to without the **std::** prefix.

However, there are some drawbacks to **using namespace**; Section 1.8, "More about Namespaces," discusses how to use this keyword more selectively.

1.1.3 The main Function

The **main** function is the part of the program that actually does something. The basic action of a C++ program is simple.

1. Allocate all the global variables, if any, declared at the beginning of program execution. In nearly all examples in this chapter, there are no global variables.
2. Execute the statements in the definition of the **main** function.

Other functions are executed only when called, as explained in Chapter 5, "Functions."

The statements between the curly braces, {}, constitute the body of the definition of **main** in this program. In this case, the definition is simple:

```
int main() {
     cout << "Hello, C++!";
     return 0;
}
```

The statement that features **cout** is the interesting one: **cout** is a predefined object meaning Console OUTput. The text string "Hello, C++!" is sent to the console object (see Figure 1.1); literally, this means to print that string on the console.

```
     cout << "Hello, C++!";
```

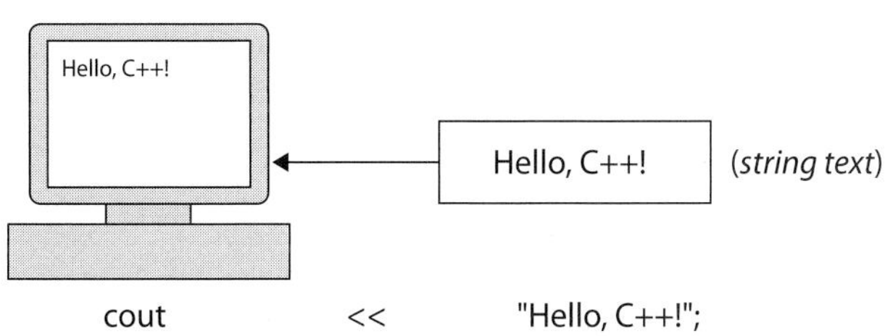

FIGURE 1.1 Sending a text string to **cout**

The **return** statement is not strictly necessary but is good programming practice. This statement terminates the program and returns a value of 0 to the operating system, meaning success; a nonzero value can be returned, as needed, to indicate failure. (But in a simple program like this, there's not much that can go wrong.)

The general pattern for the **main** function definition is:

```
int main() {
     Place_your_statements_here
     return 0;
}
```

1.2 Dealing with "Flashing Console"

If, like me, you send console input to a DOS box inside the Windows environment, you'll find that as soon as the program finishes, the DOS box goes away, preventing you from having a good look at the output. The solution is to force the program to pause.

The following statement sends a "PAUSE" command to the DOS box so that the output won't go away until the user presses ENTER.

```
system("PAUSE");
```

Here is the program from the previous section, revised to make use of the **system("PAUSE")** statement. For the sake of illustration, I've placed it in bold:

```
#include <iostream>
using namespace std;

int main() {
     cout << "Hello, C++!";
     system("PAUSE");
     return 0;
}
```

The problem with **system("PAUSE")** is that it is not platform-independent. A more universal solution—and I use it throughout this book—is the **cin.ignore()** function.

```
cin.ignore();
```

But, depending on whether or not you use the stream-input operator (>>), you may need to include this statement twice (I'll deal with those situations later, as they arise).

```
cin.ignore();
cin.ignore();
```

Therefore, if you are not compiling for a Windows/DOS environment or you want to write platform-independent programs, use the **cin.ignore**() statement instead of **system**(**"PAUSE"**). In the following code listing, I've placed the added line in bold.

```
#include <iostream>
using namespace std;

int main() {
     cout << "Hello, C++!";
     cin.ignore();
     return 0;
}
```

1.3 Working with Microsoft Visual Studio

Earlier versions of the Microsoft C++ compiler could build all the examples in this book as they are, but the current version does something a little different. This is not a problem; you can easily work with the Microsoft compiler by making a couple of small adjustments.

When you build a console application with Microsoft Visual Studio, it generates the following code, which has an extra include file (stdafx.h) and a different declaration for **main**:

```
#include "stdafx.h"

int _tmain(int argc, _TCHAR* argv[])
{
     return 0;
}
```

When working with Microsoft Visual Studio C++, make sure you leave the extra include file (stdafx.h) as the first line in the program and leave the declaration of **main** as it is. So the first example in this book becomes, with the inserted lines in bold:

```
#include "stdafx.h"
#include <iostream>
using namespace std;

int _tmain(int argc, _TCHAR* argv[])
{
     cout << "Hello there, C++!";
     system("PAUSE");
     return 0;
}
```

1.4 Doing More with C++

In general, the following should be considered a "boilerplate" for simple C++ programs.

```
#include <iostream>
using namespace std;
int main() {
     Place_your_statements_here
     return 0;
}
```

With this boilerplate in place, you can now write longer programs. For example:

```
#include <iostream>
using namespace std;
int main() {
     cout << "Was that Alice?" << endl;
     cout << "I'm afraid I'm" << endl;
     cout << "rather late!" << endl;
     cin.ignore();  // Exit when user presses ENTER.
     return 0;
}
```

This program sends three lines of text to the console, printing the following:

```
Was that Alice?
I'm afraid I'm
rather late!
```

At this point, you should note that C++ statements usually end with a semicolon (;). There are a couple of exceptions.

- A directive, such as **#include**, does not end with a semicolon (;).
- Ending (or closing) braces (}) are not, in this case, followed by a semicolon. The rule is that a closing brace (}) is not followed by a semicolon when it is terminating a statement block or function definition. (Classes are a different matter.)

All the text inside double quotation marks, including internal punctuation, constitutes a text string—or simply a *string*. A string is not part of C++ syntax, but consists of actual text to be printed.

```
"Was that Alice?"
```

The statements in this program use another predefined object, **endl**, which means END Line. (Note that the character after "end" is the letter "l", not the numeral 1.) When **endl** is sent to the console object (**cout**), it causes printing to cease on the current line and start on the next. This is also called "printing a newline." Like **cout**, **endl** is part of the **std** namespace, so without the **using** statement at the beginning of the program, the statements have to be written this way:

```
std::cout << "Was that Alice?" << std::endl;
std::cout << "I'm afraid I'm" << std::endl;
std::cout << "rather late!" << std::endl;
```

But thanks to the **using** statement, these statements can be written more succinctly.

```
cout << "Was that Alice?" << endl;
cout << "I'm afraid I'm" << endl;
cout << "rather late!" << endl;
```

This is why the **using** statement is such a convenience, at least for short programs like the ones in this book. However, there are alternatives that I discuss in Section 1.8.

You now know enough C++ syntax to write a program that prints any series of messages, on any number of lines. For example, if your name were John Doe, you could write the following statements, which print a blank line *between* the two lines of text.

```
    cout << "My name is John Doe." << endl << endl;
    cout << "Yes, that's really my name." << endl;
    return 0;
```

This prints out:

```
My name is John Doe.

Yes, that's really my name.
```

1.5 Adding Simple Variable Declarations

So far, you know how to print out lines of text, including newlines where desired, but that's still not very exciting. Programs are not especially useful unless you can, at minimum, do the following.

1. Get some information from the end user.
2. Perform some operation on that information.
3. Display the result.

We already know how to do task 3, but what about tasks 1 and 2?

Before information is operated on, it needs to be stored somewhere. That, of course, is what variables are for. A variable is a place to put information. To declare a floating-point variable (which can hold fractional quantities), use the **double** data type.

Don't let the name confuse you. The **double** keyword doesn't mean that the variable contains two values; it means "double precision," which is the standard floating-point type in C++.

The following statement uses **double** to declare a floating-point variable, x:

```
double x;
```

It's good programming practice to initialize a variable, even if it is going to be given a new value shortly thereafter. (Local variables left uninitialized contain garbage—"garbage" being a technical term for random, meaningless values.) The following declaration initializes x to 0.0:

```
double x = 0.0;
```

You can also declare a variable with the **int** data type; **int** is short for "integer"—a variable that holds no fractional portion. For example:

```
int n = 0;
```

Console output is realized in C++ through the **cout** object. You might guess, then, that console input is realized through the predefined **cin** object (Console INput). You would be right.

Just as left shift (<<) is used to display output, the right-shift operator (>>) is used to get input from the end user.

```
cin >> x;
```

If you haven't used **cin** and **cout** before, it's important to remember that the object (**cin** or **cout**) must appear as the first item in the statement. For example, you can't write the following, as reasonable as this might seem:

```
x << cin;                // ERROR! cin must be on the left!
```

Here I've used the C++ style comment symbol (//), which causes everything on its right, to the end of the line, to be interpreted as a comment. Comments are there for the programmer's benefit and are ignored by the compiler.

Remember: If you're going to use **cout** or **cin**, it must appear as the leftmost item in the statement. Once you understand that, the direction of the arrows is easy to remember. Conceptually, you can think of it as illustrated in Figure 1.2.

This helps explain why input moves to the right (>>) and output to the left (<<). Now that you know how to get input, it's easy to write a more serious program.

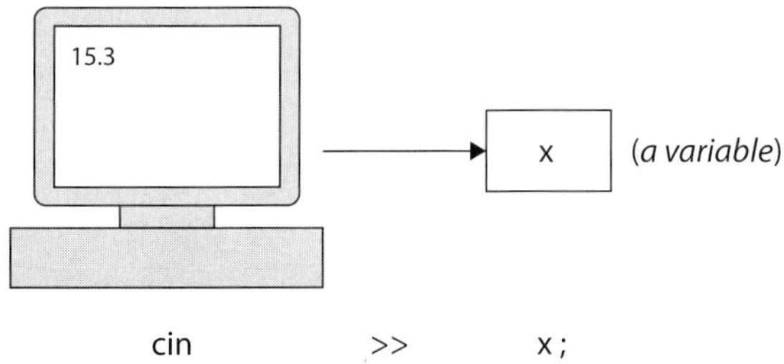

As a result of this operation, 15.3 gets placed in x.

FIGURE 1.2 Getting a number with **cin**

Again, note that each line of code is terminated by a semicolon (;) except for the directive (#include <iostream>) and the lines featuring opening and closing braces, {}.

```
#include <iostream>
using namespace std;

int main() {
     double x = 0.0;
     double y = 0.0;
     cout << "Enter value of x: ";
     cin >> x;
     cout << "Enter value of y: ";
     cin >> y;
     cout << "Average of the two numbers is: ";
     cout << (x + y) / 2;
     cout << endl;
     cout << "Press ENTER to exit.";
     cin.ignore();  // Consume last carriage-return.
     cin.ignore();  // Pause for user to press ENTER.
     return 0;
}
```

Notice that I made two uses of **cin.ignore()**. That was necessary because the >> operator was used. Remember, though: If you have a Windows/DOS system, you can use **system("PAUSE");** instead of the "Press ENTER to exit" message and the two calls to **ignore**.

This program performs an arithmetic calculation. As shown in Table 1.1, C++ provides several binary operators for arithmetic manipulation ("binary" in this case meaning that two operands are involved)—although this is a small subset of all the operators available. Chapter 3, "Operators," describes these operators and many others.

TABLE 1.1 The Four Basic Arithmetic Operators

Operator	Description	Example
+	Addition	x + y
-	Subtraction	x – y
*	Multiplication	x * y
/	Division	x / y

This next program uses multiplication (*) to perform a calculation on the number entered.

```
#include <iostream>
using namespace std;

int main() {
     double x = 0.0;
     cout << "Enter value of x: ";
     cin >> x;
     cout << "Twice that number is: ";
     cout << x * 2.0;
     cout << endl;
     cout << "Press ENTER to exit.";
     cin.ignore();  // Consume carriage-return.
     cin.ignore();  // Pause for user to press ENTER.
     return 0;
}
```

1.6 Introduction to C++ Control Structures

Adding just two critical features—the ability to make decisions and the ability to perform loops—makes a language strong enough to do some interesting things.

Chapter 4, "Control Structures," goes into much greater detail about these and other language features. But this section introduces two of the simpler control structures—enabling you to write some real programs:

- **if-else** statements
- **while** statements

1.6.1 Making Decisions with "if"

Though lacking judgment (and I'll sidestep the whole issue of artificial intelligence here), programs can make decisions as long as they are unambiguous and mathematically precise. In C++, the simplest way to make a decision at runtime is to use **if** and **else**. Those keywords have the following syntax, in which *condition* is any C++ expression producing a value, but is typically a comparison such as "n > 0":

```
if (condition) statement [else statement]
```

Here the brackets are not intended literally but indicate that the else clause is optional, so you can choose to use **if** without **else**:

```
if (condition) statement
```

It's common and recommended to always use statement-block syntax—so that each alternative can include zero or more statements, producing:

```
if (condition) {
      statements
} else {
      statements
}
```

For example, you can use **if-else** to write a program that finds the maximum of two numbers.

```
#include <iostream>
using namespace std;

int main() {
      double x = 0.0;
      double y = 0.0;
      cout << "Enter value of x: ";
      cin >> x;
      cout << "Enter value of y: ";
      cin >> y;
      if (x > y) {
            cout << "The max. is " << x << endl;
      } else {
            cout << "The max. is " << y << endl;
      }
      cout << "Press ENTER to exit.";
      cin.ignore();  // Consume carriage-return.
      cin.ignore();  // Pause for user to press ENTER.
      return 0;
}
```

TABLE 1.2 The Six Comparison Operators

Operator	Description	Example
>	Greater than	`x > y`
<	Less than	`x < y`
>=	Greater than or equal to	`x >= y`
<=	Less than or equal to	`x <= y`
==	Test for equality	`x == y`
!=	Test for inequality	`x != y`

The comparison x > y means "x is greater than y," obviously. The action is to test this condition and return the value **true** if x is greater than y. Not all the comparison operators are as obvious as this one. Table 1.2 summarizes the six comparison operators.

One of the biggest "gotchas" in the C and C++ languages is that test for equality uses double equal signs (==), not a single equal sign (=). When doing comparisons, it is critical to remember the difference. For example, to compare x to y, use a double equal sign.

```
if (x == y) {
     cout << "x and y are equal.";
}
```

A single equal sign, by contrast, performs assignment, which copies data into a variable.

```
x = y;     // Place the value of y into x.
```

The problem is that assignment inside a condition is completely legal in C++ and at times even useful, but in most cases it does something completely different from what you want.

Assignment (=) and test for equality (==) both have their place in C++ programs. In fact, assignment is probably the most common operation of all. The statements in the previous example can be revised as follows, making use of a third variable, max_val. These statements use the assignment operator (=) to assign either x or y to this variable.

```
     double max_val = 0.0;
     if (x > y) {
          max_val = x;    // max_val gets assigned value of x.
```

```
} else {
     max_val = y;    // max_val gets assigned value of y.
}
cout << "The max. is " << max_val << endl;
```

For more information on the **if** statement and other control structures, see Chapter 4. For more information on the = and == operators, see Chapter 3.

1.6.2 Looping with "while"

The term "loop" is so prevalent among programmers that it has even permeated popular culture. In programming, a loop is a construct that executes a series of statements and then goes back to the beginning where a condition is retested. Programmers say that control has *iterated* (repeated) to the *top of the loop*. The simplest loop in C and C++ is the **while** loop, which has the following syntax:

```
while (condition) {
     statements
}
```

Technically speaking, when there is only one statement in the body of the loop, the curly braces are optional; but they are recommended for clarity and because they make it easier to add statements to the loop later on.

So, for example, you can use a loop to print out all the numbers from 1 to 5:

```
int n = 1;
while (n < 6) {
     cout << n << " ";
     n = n + 1;
}
```

The increment operation (n = n + 1) is so common that languages in the C/C++ family provide a dedicated operator, ++, just to do that, making the source code a little more concise. So "n++" means nearly the same as "n = n + 1". Here I've added a comment (beginning with //) to clarify what it does.

```
while (n < 6) {
     cout << n << " ";
     n++;                  // n = n + 1
}
```

Or more concise still, embedding n++ within a statement:

```
while (n < 6) {
     cout << n++ << " ";
}
```

If you're not already familiar with the increment operator (++), you'll learn more about it in Chapter 3.

1.7 General Structure of a C++ Program

The simple programs up to this point have only featured an **#include** directive, a **using** statement, and a function definition for **main**. The following list summarizes the general structure of a C++ program, more or less in the order shown. Most of the items below are explained later in upcoming chapters.

- **#include** and other directives. Generally, you'll need one **#include** directive for each major part of the C/C++ library you use. (Chapter 8, "Preprocessor Directives.")

  ```
  #include <iostream>
  ```

- The **using** statement, to make the **std** namespace available. You don't *have* to include this statement, but without it, you must use names such as **std::cout** and **std::endl**.

  ```
  using namespace std;
  ```

- Type declarations, including classes. (Chapter 7, "Classes and Objects.")

  ```
  class EmpRec {
  public:
       string name;
       string addr;
       int level;
  };
  ```

- Global variable declarations, which are outside of all function definitions. These are visible throughout the program.

  ```
  int number_of_hits = 0;
  ```

- Function prototypes, providing type information on functions to be called in the program. (Chapter 5.)
- Function definitions, including **main**. Each definition includes curly braces {} that contain zero or more statements, telling what the function does. This chapter features simple programs that stick to using a single function, **main**, the only required function.

  ```
  int main() {
       cout << "Hello." << endl;
       return 0;
  }
  ```

1.8 More about Namespaces

Throughout this book, I occasionally include the **using namespace** statement explicitly or—in the case of short code fragments—assume that it is already in use.

```
using namespace std;
```

You're never required to take advantage of a **using** statement, but if you don't, standard objects from the C++ library, such as **cout**, **cin**, and **endl**, must be referred to with an **std::** prefix.

```
std::cout
std::cin
std::endl
```

An alternative—one strongly recommended by most C++ experts—is to make use of the **using** statement more selectively. Instead of referring to **cout**, **cin**, and **endl** with their **std** prefixes wherever they occur, you can gain access to each individual symbol (that is, name) by placing the following at the beginning of the program:

```
using std::cout;
using std::cin;
using std::endl;
```

The general form of this syntax is:

using *prefix::symbol*;

Given this statement, the specified symbol (that is, symbolic name) can subsequently be referred to without its **std::** prefix.

It's important to remember that namespaces serve an important purpose—a purpose that **using namespace std** circumvents.

In the earliest days of the C language, few software libraries were available. But as the C language became popular, and the C++ language became even more popular, the number of libraries available for C/C++ program development proliferated like crazy.

And that posed a problem. A complex program may use several libraries, and each of them may supply hundreds of class, object, and function names. The possibility of name conflicts then becomes high. The solution was to enable each library to create its own namespace. To refer to a symbol (that is, a name) within a namespace, you must either use its prefix—**std** in the case of the C++ standard library—or provide access through a **using** statement.

```
// This is safe only for simple projects.
using namespace std;
```

The **using namespace** statement is a convenient way to gain access to *all* the symbols in a library. The danger is that if you utilize multiple libraries, employing **using namespace** for all the namespaces in all the libraries is extremely likely to cause name conflicts.

For the simplest programs, **using namespace std** mostly does not cause problems (although name conflicts can still occur, so be careful). However, many C++ professionals advise even beginners to avoid **using namespace std** because—even though it is very convenient for the short programs in this book—it can become a bad habit that might hurt you later on. For this reason, they recommend employing **using** more selectively:

```
using std::cout;
using std::cin;
```

With this principle in mind, I have written this book to make few uses of **using namespace std**.

The **using** statement, it should be noted, applies only to the scope in which it is defined. So the following **using** statement grants direct access to the **std** namespace only within the function **main**, not within other functions:

```
int main() {
     using namespace std;
     cout << "Hello, C++!";
     return 0;
}
```

You can define your own namespace by using the **namespace** keyword. For example, given the following statements, the variables x and pi are declared as global variables, which are referred to as "briano::x" and "briano::pi".

```
namespace briano {
     double x = 0;
     double pi = 3.141592;
}
int main() {
     using namespace std;
     cout << "The value of pi is ";
    // pi is in the briano namespace!!
     cout << briano::pi << endl;
     cout << "Press ENTER to exit.";
     cin.ignore();
     return 0;
}
```

A **using** statement, of course, can make these variable names directly accessible by the program:

```
using namespace briano;
```

1.9 Some Comments about Comments

Technically speaking, a comment is just text embedded into a program in which the text is ignored by the compiler. What, then, is the point of a comment?

Although comments are never required in a strict technical sense, by using them you can remind yourself or another programmer what the program does, or what the purpose of a particular variable, class, or function is. You could remove every single comment from a program and (as long as you didn't alter the rest of the code) the program would do precisely what it did before. However, it would be much harder to read and maintain.

1.9.1 C++ Comments (Line Comments)

C++ comments have the following syntax. In C++, you can use this kind of comment as well as the old C-language comment syntax described in the next section.

```
// comment_text
```

This is a *line* comment. This says to the compiler, "Ignore all text from here to the end of the line." So, for example, you can place a comment on its own line.

```
// This is a full-line C++ comment.
```

You can also place a comment to the right of C++ code. The compiler ignores comment text from the double forward slashes (//) to the end of the line. But anything to the left of the slashes is compiled as usual.

```
int i;      // i is an integer variable.
double x;   // x is a floating-pt variable.
```

1.9.2 C-Language-Style Comments

Mostly for the sake of backward compatibility, C++ also supports the old-fashioned C-language comment symbols /* and */. These symbols enable comments to appear anywhere within code—even in the middle of a statement (although that would be a terrible idea). The syntax is:

```
/* comment_text */
```

The /* and */ symbols do not have to be on the same line; this enables you to write comments that span multiple lines if you choose:

```
/*comment_text
more_lines_of_text...
end_of_text */
```

For example:

```
/* Here is a multi-line comment that explains what the
   function "foobar" does.   */
```

However, the old C-style comment has some drawbacks, so it is not particularly recommended for writing new C++ source code. The major drawback is that such comments occasionally make it difficult to see what is part of the comment and what isn't. Suppose you "comment out" some portion of source code—a useful practice to temporarily prevent some code from compiling. (For example, when debugging a program, you might want to disable parts of the program in an attempt to isolate the bug.)

```
/*
if(a < b)
    cout<< "Test message.";
*/
```

This looks fine—unless there's another comment embedded in the code already. In that case, you've got a problem. The following statements look innocent enough but are a disaster waiting to happen.

```
/*
if(a < b) /* Here is a comment. */
     cout<< "Test message.";
*/
```

In this case, the compiler ignores all code from the /* symbol (begin comment) up to and including the *first* */ symbol it encounters. It then tries to compile the remaining code, resulting in a syntax error:

```
     cout<< "Test message.";
*/
```

For this reason, the C++ comment, which comments out all text to the end of the line, is generally better. And if you want to temporarily prevent a block of code from being compiled, you should use the **#if** and **#endif** preprocessor directives as explained in Chapter 8.

1.10 Sample App: Adding Machine

The following program is quite simple, but I actually had an important practical use for it: to add up the page counts for chapters in this book—enabling me to inform my editor, Peter Gordon, that I was on track to finish by deadline.

Any handheld calculator can be used to do the same thing, as can the Windows or Macintosh Calculator app; but this program has proved more reliable for me as I can type in a single line of numbers and see that I entered all of them correctly. And it's much faster than setting up a spreadsheet.

This application prompts the user for a series of numbers terminated by 0. Any non-digit input (such as "exit," "bye," or even "x") will also terminate the list. For example, to add page counts 33, 37, 22, 41, and 29, I'd type the following and press the ENTER key:

```
33  37  22  41  29  0
```

Here is the complete program listing, short though it is.

```
#include <iostream>
using std::cout;
using std::cin;
using std::endl;

int main () {
     int sum = 0;
     int n = 1;
     cout << "Enter a list of numbers, terminated with 0 ";
     cout << "or non-digit." << endl << "Enter: ";
     while (n != 0) {    // While n is not zero...
          cin >> n;      //   Attempt to read next integer.
          if (!cin) {    //   If read failed, set n to 0.
               n = 0;
          }
          sum = sum + n;
     }
     cout << "Total is: " << sum << endl;
     cout << "Press ENTER to exit.";
     cin.ignore();  // Consume carriage-return.
     cin.ignore();  // Pause for user to press ENTER.
     return 0;
}
```

This program introduces another feature of the C++ I/O stream library: You can test **cin** itself. If an input operation fails—because the end user entered a nondigit when the program tried to read an integer—**cin** evaluates to **false**. When this happens, the program sets n to 0, which in turn causes the loop to terminate as soon as the condition "n != 0" is tested again.

Exercises

1. Rewrite the example so that it accepts floating-point numbers. Remember that to give a variable floating-point type, declare it as a **double** (double-precision) rather than an **int** (integer).
2. Rewrite the program so that the list of numbers is not terminated by zero, but only by a nondigit character. Bear in mind that the expression "cin >> n" returns a reference to **cin** itself—so that "cin >> n" has the same value as **cin**. Given that insight, just how simple can you make the program? Hint: A **while** loop can test **cin** directly, just as an **if** statement can.
3. Upon conclusion of the program, print how many items were entered (not counting any term, such as 0, used to terminate it). Print the average, also. Note: To correctly calculate the average, floating-point division must be used, or else the fractional portion will be thrown away. Therefore, make sure at least one of the variables involved in the calculation of the average has floating-point type.

1.11 Sample App: Calculating Phi

The number "phi" is what the ancient Greeks called the "golden ratio": They put this ratio into much of their art and architecture. It's defined by this relationship:

phi = 1/(phi - 1)

which can also be expressed as:

phi^2 - phi = 1

By applying the quadratic formula to this equation, we can produce the value for phi, which is approximately equal to:

```
1.618033988749890
```

Mathematicians assert that if you take the *N*th Fibonacci number and divide it by its predecessor, the result should get closer to phi as *N* grows larger.

What is the Fibonacci number sequence? This sequence starts with 1, 1, and produces each subsequent number in the sequence by adding the previous two numbers, resulting in:

```
1 1 2 3 5 8 13 21 34 55 89...
```

The following program investigates whether the mathematicians are right. Does the ratio between successive Fibonacci numbers converge to phi? Here is the complete program:

```
#include <iostream>
using std::cout;
using std::cin;
using std::endl;

int main() {
     cout << endl;
     int n = 0;
     double prev1 = 1.0;
     double prev2 = 1.0;
     double current = 0.0;
     cout << "How many Fib. nums to generate? ";
     cin >> n;                 // Get input
     cout.precision(15);       // Set 15 digits of precision.
     while (n > 0) {           // While n is greater than 0...
          current = prev1 + prev2;
          prev2 = prev1;
          prev1 = current;
          cout << current << "\t";
          cout << "ratio = " << prev1/prev2 << endl;
          --n;                // Subtract 1 from n.
     }
     cout << endl;
     cout << "Press ENTER to exit.";
     cin.ignore();   // Consume carriage-return.
     cin.ignore();   // Pause for user to press ENTER.
     return 0;
}
```

When calculating integral values, it would usually make more sense to use an integer type, such as **int**. But there are a couple of problems. We are primarily interested in the ratio between two consecutive numbers rather than the numbers themselves, and this ratio needs to hold a fractional portion: Therefore, it needs to use the floating-point format.

Division between two integers causes an operation that throws away the fractional portion. Using floating-point numbers as operands forces floating-point division:

```
cout << "ratio = " << prev1/prev2 << endl;
```

Another issue is that as Fibonacci numbers grow large, they quickly exceed the range of an **int**. Therefore, I use the **double** (double-precision floating-point) type to calculate the numbers.

But **int** is still the proper type for the loop variable n—the variable used to control how many Fibonacci numbers to generate. This number never holds a fractional portion and does not need to exceed the **int** (integer) range.

This example introduces a couple of new features: output-field precision and the decrement operator (--). The following statement specifies a floating-point precision of 15 digits for console output. (Chapter 13, "C++ I/O Stream Classes," provides more information on this and other output-formatting techniques.)

```
cout.precision(15);
```

In this loop, the *condition* is "n > 0". Consequently, the following loop causes the statements within the curly braces, {}, to be executed n times. The decrement expression, --n, is basically equivalent to "n = n – 1".

```
while (n > 0) {
      current = prev1 + prev2;
      prev2 = prev1;
      prev1 = current;
      cout << current << "\t";
      cout << "ratio = " << prev1/prev2 << endl;
      --n;     // Subtract 1 from n.
}
```

The effect of the statements inside the loop is as follows.

1. Calculate the new Fibonacci number, current, by adding prev1 and prev2. This calculates the new Fibonacci by adding the previous two numbers in the sequence.
2. Promote prev2 to the previous value (prev1).
3. Promote prev1 to the new current number.
4. Print the new Fibonacci number.
5. Display the ratio between the current and previous numbers.
6. Decrement the loop counter, n, by subtracting 1 from it.

This last step, applying the decrement operator (--), can be embedded in the loop condition. Chapter 3 describes this and other operators unique to the C family of languages.

```
while (n-- > 0) {
      current = prev1 + prev2;
      prev2 = prev1;
      prev1 = current;
      cout << current << "\t";
      cout << "ratio = " << prev1/prev2 << endl;
}
```

Now, if you run the program and tell it to calculate 40 Fibonaccis, the last four lines of output are:

```
63245986        ratio = 1.6180339887499
102334155       ratio = 1.61803398874989
165580141       ratio = 1.61803398874989
267914296       ratio = 1.61803398874989
```

So the ratio of two successive Fibonacci numbers does converge to phi!

Exercises

1. Rewrite the application so that it prints only the *N*th Fibonacci number and the ratio between this number and the previous one.
2. Write another loop to verify a valid number was entered for n, which should be an integer greater than 0. If the input operation failed, query the user until acceptable input is entered. (Note: To reset the input stream's error flags, call **cin.clear()**.)
3. Would this application convince a mathematician of the truth of the idea being tested? What would it take to convince such a person?

CHAPTER 2

Data

Data is as important to a programmer as money is to a banker (and that's saying something!); it's the lifeblood of computing. The most important attribute of data is *type,* which determines what data can be stored and in what format.

C ++ has two basic kinds of types: *primitive* (or "built-in") *types,* which are inherent in the C++ language itself, and *user-defined types* (primarily classes, structures, and arrays), which are built on top of existing types. C++ recognizes almost no difference between primitive and user-defined types, except that primitive types are predefined. But once a new type is declared in the source code or a library, you can use it just as you would a primitive type. In this respect, C++ differs from most other popular languages in use today. It is more extensible.

But even as you build new data types, you need to understand the primitive types. These are the building blocks of data, which you put together just as an inventor uses little components to build larger components. This chapter describes two major kinds of information about types.

- The range of each primitive type, such as **int**, **double**, and so on.
- The formats for *literals,* which are numerals or characters that express fundamental constants, such as 1, -50, 2.5, or 3.141592. Text strings such as "Hello, C++!" are also literals. A literal is not a symbol but has a fixed value determined as soon as it is read.

In addition to summarizing primitive types and literals, this chapter also presents the rules by which C++ evaluates mixed-data expressions, as well as the complete rules for declaring data items and special data-declaration keywords—**enum**, **typedef**, **auto**, and **typedecl**—some of which are new in C++11.

2.1 Declaring Simple Variables

The basic syntax for declaring a C++ variable—whether inside a function or outside—is:

```
type  variable_decl;
```

in which *type* is the name of a primitive or user-defined type. You can also declare multiple variables in a single statement, with the variable declarations separated by commas if there is more than one:

```
type  variable_decl, variable_decl…;
```

Each *variable_decl* has one of the following two forms:

```
symbol
symbol = init_value
```

in which *symbol* is a symbolic name. See Section 2.3, "Symbolic Names ("Symbols")," for rules governing names.

For example, you can use the **int** type (integer) to declare a simple **int** variable with or without an initial value. You can also declare multiple **int** variables—each of which may or may not have initial values as you choose (although note that initialization is always recommended):

```
int  i;
int  i = 5;
int  Able = 1, Baker = 200, Charley = -30;
int  a = 0, b, c, d = 5, bug_count = i + 2;
```

The **int** data type is just one of the many primitive data types available. Integer types such as **int** cannot hold fractional values but are strongly recommended for situations that do not involve fractions: for example, a loop counter or array index.

You can declare floating-point data by using **float** or **double**. The **double** type—meaning double precision—is the preferred floating-point type and should be used in preference to **float** except where storage space is at a premium:

```
float    x, y, z = 0.0;
double   temp = 32.6, pi = 3.141592;
```

Several considerations apply to variable declarations in C++, regardless of type.

- Initialization is always recommended, even though the C++ compiler never requires it. Global variables (declared outside of functions) are automatically initialized to zero if left uninitialized. Local variables left uninitialized contain garbage: that is, random, meaningless values.
- In C++ (unlike C), the initial value does not have to be a constant. You can use any expression that can be evaluated at runtime.
- Global variables are declared outside of all function definitions. They have scope—that is, visibility—from the position they are declared forward to the end of the source file.

2.2 Primitive Data Types

The primitive data types are provided by the C++ compiler itself. The descriptions that follow give the typical range for each type. Although you need to be careful when targeting widely different platforms, the following ranges should be taken as reliable for all 32-bit systems.

Integer types cannot hold fractional portions. Some integer types are unsigned: Types cannot hold negative values but compensate by being able to hold a larger range of positive values.

- `char`

  One-byte integer: This is a data type wide enough to hold a single printable character. Typical range is -128 to 127. The **char** type is special in that if a value is printed as a **char**, a character is displayed rather than its numeric value.

  For example, the value 97 is the ASCII character code for "a". If you send the value 97 to the console as a **char** value, the character "a" is printed. If you promote the data to **int** type before displaying it, then "97" is printed.

- `unsigned char`

  Unsigned version of **char**. Unlike **char**, an **unsigned char** is always treated as its numeric value, even when printed. Range is 0 to 255.

- `short`

  Short integer, usually two bytes wide. Range is usually -32768 to 32767.

- `unsigned short`

  Unsigned short integer, usually two bytes wide. Range is usually 0 to 65535.

- `int`

  "Natural" size integer, reflecting processor size. On a 32-bit system, this type is 32 bits (four bytes) wide, making **int** equivalent to **long**. Typical range is approximately ±2 billion.

- `unsigned int`

  Same as **int**, except that it is unsigned. Typical range is approximately 0 to 4 billion.

- `long`

  Long integer, usually four bytes wide. Range is approximately ±2 billion.

- `unsigned long`

  Unsigned version of **long**. Range is approximately 0 to 4 billion.

- `long long`

  Extra-long integer, usually eight bytes (64 bits) wide. Range is approximately ±9 times 10 to the 18th. This type is mandated by the C++11 spec and is not supported by all older compilers; however, some compilers (such as Microsoft) have supported it for years.

- `unsigned long long`

  Same as **long long**, except that it is unsigned. Range is approximately 0 to 1.8 times 10 to the 19th. This type is mandated by the C++11 spec and is not supported by all older compilers.

- `float`

  Single precision floating point (four bytes wide). Seven digits of precision. Range is ±3.4 times 10 to the 38th. This type is not the default floating-point type; **double** should generally be used instead. (See guidelines in Section 2.2.2, "Floating-Point Types: Guidelines.")

  This type can store 0.0 precisely; otherwise, values can get as close to 0 as 1.175 times 10 to the -38th.

- `double`

  Double precision floating point (eight bytes wide). Fifteen digits of precision. Range is ±1.8 times 10 to the 308th. This is the natural floating type and is preferred except when storage space is at a premium. All floating-point values are converted to **double** when they appear in expressions.

  This type can store 0.0 precisely; otherwise, values can get as close to 0 as 2.225074 times 10 to the -308th.

- `long double`

  At least as wide as **double**, but compilers may use it to support a larger range and precision. See your vendor's documentation for more information.

- `bool`

  Boolean: This is an integer value that holds the value **true** or **false**; every non-negative value assigned to a **bool** variable is converted to **true**. Zero equates to **false**.

- `w_char`

  Wide character field, for holding character data for extended character sets.

2.2.1 Integer Types: Guidelines

The following guidelines apply to integer types.

- Integer data types store values precisely. For example, if you add 1 to a high value of a **long long** integer, the new value will always be distinct from the old. No rounding errors can occur. The limitation on integers is that they cannot hold fractional quantities. But they are both more accurate and more efficient for any data that doesn't involve fractions.

- The typical ranges listed earlier are nearly universal on the vast majority of computers in use today—especially personal computers. The most notable exception is the **int** type, which (unlike **short** and **long**) is the least fixed of C++ types. This type is the "natural integer" type; it matches the register size of the target platform and is therefore 16 bits wide on a 16-bit system, 32 bits wide on a 32-bit system, and so on. The advantage of this type is that it is presumably the most efficient integer size for a platform to work with (although even that is not a safe assumption in all cases).
- The **int** type has a drawback. Because its size can potentially vary, code that runs on one platform may break when ported to another. For this reason, **int** should be avoided if you intend to compile your program for a variety of different architectures; **short int** and **long int** are to be preferred where multiple platforms are involved. (These type names, by the way, are equivalent to the more abbreviated names **short** and **long**, respectively.)
- The C++ specification does not set absolute sizes even for other types—although the sizes given earlier are reliable for 32-bit systems. If your code will be ported to many platforms, the safest approach is to use header files (see Chapter 8, "Preprocessor Directives") to define precise sizes: For example, you might first define INT32 as a **long** when compiling for platforms that implement **long** as 32 bits, and then use INT32 to declare variables. (See the **#define** directive in Chapter 8 and the **typedef** keyword in Section 2.9.1, "The typedef Keyword.")

2.2.2 Floating-Point Types: Guidelines

The following guidelines apply to floating-point types (**float** and **double**).

- Floating-point types can be subject to rounding errors, because they store values as a combination of mantissa and exponent. Therefore, always use an integer type when you have a choice, as long as its range is sufficient and no fractional amounts are involved.
- During program execution, all floating-point data is promoted to type **double** (the larger of the two formats) before being evaluated in arithmetic expressions.
- For this reason, it may seem pointless to use the **float** type at all, because it is promoted to **double** when being evaluated in an expression. But when storage space is at a premium and you are using many numbers (storing them in a file or creating large arrays) you might consider using **float**; otherwise, **double** is always preferable.
- Note that in addition to storing fractional portions, floating-point types have bigger ranges than integer types. Therefore, floating-point data is often used just for

its greater range, especially in scientific applications. (However, note that the new **long long int** type also provides an exceptionally large range while also preserving the absolute precision provided by an integer type.)

2.3 Symbolic Names ("Symbols")

In C++, the term *symbol* means a symbolic name: This is a name that you create as a programmer or is defined in a library. Uses for symbols include variable, class, and function names.

(Note that words with special, predefined meaning in the C++ language itself—such as **if**, **else**, **while**, and so on—are keywords and cannot be used as symbols.)

The following rules apply to symbols. Subject to these rules, you can use any names you want for (among other things) variable, class, and function names.

- The first character must be a letter (uppercase or lowercase) or underscore. But because the underscore (_) is traditionally used to prefix names having special meaning within the C++ library, it is best to avoid using an underscore at the beginning of a name.
- The remaining characters can be any combination of letters, digits, and/or underscores.
- Uppercase and lowercase letters are freely permitted, but C++ is case-sensitive, so "myannualsalary" and "MyAnnualSalary" are two distinct symbols.
- A keyword (such as **if**) cannot be used as a symbol.
- Symbols are delimited by operators (such as + and -) and also by white spaces (blank spaces, tabs, and newlines); consequently, a symbol cannot consist of multiple words unless you use an underscore to connect them.

Here are some examples of valid symbols:

```
i
x
amount
temp
BobSalary
Bob_Salary_Amount
White_Rabbit
x1
x2
amount_999
```

Note that a decimal digit (0 through 9) can never appear at the beginning of a symbol but may appear anywhere else within the symbol.

2.4 Numeric Literals

When initializing a variable, you'll frequently use a literal, such as "5", "3.1415", or "-33.3". A literal is a text string or a number that has a self-evident meaning—that is, it isn't a name for something else. Literals have fixed values that are immediately recognized by the compiler; they are not looked up in a symbol table. Numerals are literals. So are quoted strings.

This section summarizes the formats for literals, beginning with numeric literals. In the following syntax summaries, brackets are not intended literally but indicate an optional item (in this case, an optional + or - sign).

- `[`*`sign`*`]`*`digits`*

  Specifies a literal of type **int**.

  For example: 0, 55, 1040, -33, -1, -5555.

- `[`*`sign`*`]`*`digits`*`L`

  Specifies a literal of type **long**. This is the same as an **int**, but it forces the value to be stored in the **long** format (32 bits: But by default that is the same as an **int** on 32-bit systems anyway.)

  For example: 0L, -22L, 1222000333L.

- `[`*`sign`*`]`*`digits`*`LL`

  Specifies a literal of type **long long**. This enables specification of extremely large integers in the **long long** range.

  For example: 123000123000456LL.

- *`digits`*`U`

  Specifies a literal of type **unsigned int**. The value may not be negative, but this type supports larger positive values than are possible with an ordinary **int**.

  For example: 0U, 55U, 1040U, 62000U.

- *`digits`*`UL`

  Specifies a literal of type **unsigned long**. The value may not be negative, but this type supports larger positive values than are possible with an ordinary **int**.

  For example: 0UL, 55UL, 1040UL, 3222000543UL.

- *`digits`*`ULL`

  Specifies a literal of type **unsigned long long**. Values may not be negative. This enables specification of extremely large integers in the **unsigned long long** range.

  For example: 123000123000456ULL.

- `0x`*`digits`*

  Specifies an unsigned integer in hexadecimal (base 16) format. The integer size suffixes (UL, ULL) can be applied as needed. In addition to the digits 0 through 9, hexadecimal digits can include letters A to E and their lowercase equivalents a to e, to represent digits corresponding to 10 to 15 decimal.

  For example, 0x0f represents 15 decimal, and 0xff specifies the hexadecimal value FF, equal to 255 decimal.

- `0`*`digit`*

  Specifies an unsigned integer using octal (base 8) format. Each digit must be in the range 0 to 7.

  For example: 017 (equivalent to 15 decimal).

- *`[sign]digits.digits`*

  Specifies a floating-point value of type **double**.

  For example: 0.0, 2.0, 3.141592, -100.33.

- *`[sign]digits.digits`*`F`

  Specifies a floating-point value of type **float**. Specifying a value this way reduces the range and precision of the data stored, so its use is not usually recommended; however, you might use it to initialize a **float** array or copy values to a file storing **float** values, when storage space is at a premium and must be conserved.

  For example: 0.0F, 3.14F, -100.33F.

- *`[sign]digits`*`E`*`exponent`*

  Specifies a floating-point value using scientific notation. The "E" may be uppercase or lowercase, and an optional "F" suffix indicates **float** type instead of **double** (the default).

  For example: 1e3 specifies 1000.0 as a floating-point number; 45e-17 specifies 45 times 10 to the -17th power.

- *`[sign]digits.digits`*`E`*`exponent`*

  Specifies a floating-point value using scientific notation. The "E" may be uppercase or lowercase, and an optional "F" suffix indicates **float** type instead of **double** (the default).

  For example: -1.23e15 specifies -1.23 times 10 to the 15th power.

- **`true`**

  Boolean value "true," equivalent to integer value 1. Any nonzero value assigned to a **bool** variable is converted to **true**.

- **false**

  Boolean value "false," equivalent to integer value 0.

- **'*c*'**

  A single character, *c*. Each text character has a corresponding ASCII code (for example, 'a' is decimal 97). When '*c*' appears in source code, it is normally treated as an integer value: For example, 'a' equates to the integer value 97. But when printed on the console as type **char**, *c* is displayed in its character form (in this case, "a").

- **"*text_string*"**

  Literal text string. The compiler, when reading this literal, allocates memory to store *text_string* as an array of **char** values and then adds a terminating null. See Section 2.6, "String and Character Literals," for more information on how strings are handled.

  For example: "Brian, O!", "Hello, world!"

- **L"*text_string*"**

  Wide-character text string. Similar to the standard text-string format except that it allocates two bytes for every character rather than one, thereby facilitating internationalization.

  For example: L"This is a string."

- **R"*text_string*"**

  Raw-character text string. This is the same as the standard string literal, but it ignores the escape sequences described in Section 2.6.3, "Special Characters (Escape Sequences)." This notation is supported by the C++11 spec but is not usually supported by older compilers.

  For example: R"C:\root\txt".

2.5 Mixing Numeric Types

When you combine different data types in the same expression, C++ follows specific rules. As much as possible, the compiler permits mixing of different types—providing warnings when there is a possible loss of data—and attempts to do the most reasonable thing.

Consequently, C++ usually produces the results you expect. But if you understand precisely how C++ handles mixed expressions—mixing integer and floating point, for example—you are less likely to be caught by surprise. A high-level language such as C++ is designed to free you from worrying about low-level details, yet sometimes those details are highly significant.

The next few sections consider several cases of mixing data: integer versus floating point, **bool** versus integer, and signed versus unsigned integers.

2.5.1 Integer versus Floating Point

A literal with a decimal point (such as "0.0") is stored in floating-point format whether or not it has an actual fractional portion, while a literal without decimal point or exponent is an integer (such as "0").

In mixed expressions, a data type with a smaller range is automatically promoted to the larger data type. Consider this data declaration:

```
double  x = 0;
```

In this case, the literal "0" specifies a value of 0 stored in **int** (integer format). Because it is assigned to x (which is floating point) the integer 0 is automatically promoted to **double** type before being assigned.

Going in the reverse direction is problematic. The compiler issues a warning for the following:

```
int  i = 0.0;
```

This may look innocent, but the compiler stores 0.0 in floating-point format and must then convert it to **int** type before assigning it. Converting a value to a type with a *smaller* range (downgrading it, in effect) causes the compiler to issue a warning about possible loss of data.

To avoid warning messages in these situations, use a **static_cast** operator, as described in Chapter 3, "Operators." Here is how it would be used in this situation:

```
int  i = static_cast<int>(0.0);
```

Of course, it would be far easier in this case to simply use the correct notation—using an integer literal to initialize an integer. Remember that while the literal 0.0 is stored in floating-point (**double**) format, the literal 0 is stored in **int** format.

```
int  i = 0;
```

2.5.2 bool versus Integer Types

The **bool** type is used principally to store program flags that may be set to **true** or **false**. For example, you might have a variable called power_is_on, initialized in this case to **false**.

```
bool  power_is_on = false;
```

Another statement—an assignment—might then set this flag to **true**:

```
power_is_on = true;
```

Because this variable is Boolean—it has type **bool**—you can safely use it as an **if** or **while** condition (see Chapter 4, "Control Structures"):

```
if (power_is_on) {
     start_up_factory();
}
```

The earliest versions of C and C++ had no **bool** data type, although some compiler vendors added it; it has now been mandated by the C++ standards committee for a number of years. Primitive C and C++ required the use of integer variables as flag (Boolean) variables, and this usage is still supported. But the **bool** type has the advantage of considering all "true" values to be equal, avoiding some sources of error.

For the purpose of a conditional, any nonzero value is treated as "true." But with **bool** variables, any nonzero value assigned is automatically converted to the literal value **true** (1). A zero value is considered false. Therefore, a **bool** variable will always have one of two values: **true** or **false**.

```
bool  flag = 15;   // 15 is converted to "true" (1).
```

2.5.3 Signed versus Unsigned Integers

C++ provides ten different integer types, some of which are signed and some unsigned. The signed integer types can hold negative values, but this versatility is not free; about half their range is used to represent negative numbers.

Unsigned types, by contrast, use their entire range to represent non-negative values; an unsigned type can represent about twice as many positive numbers as its signed-number counterpart.

When different integer types are combined in an expression, the compiler follows these rules.

- Integers with widths smaller than the width of an **int** are promoted in size when used in any kind of arithmetic expression. (Exception: Assigning a **char** to a **char** doesn't change its width.)
- If one of the types is smaller in number of bits than the other, the smaller type is promoted to the size of the larger. Therefore, **short** is promoted to **long**, but so is **unsigned short**.

- If two operands are the same width, but one is signed and the other unsigned, the signed is promoted to unsigned.

It's best to avoid combining signed and unsigned integers in the same expression; avoiding such combinations makes calculations more reliable and easier to predict. But if you must combine them, it's helpful to understand the format for representing signed integers.

The great majority of computers in use today—including all personal computers—use the *two's complement format* to represent signed integer values. The format is based on the idea that when a number is added to its arithmetic negation (that is, the negative of the number), the result must be 0. Therefore, the negative of 000 000 000 0001 should be 1111 1111 1111 1111, because when those two numbers are added together, the result "flips over" to produce 0. Therefore, the signed representation of -1 is defined as the bit pattern consisting of all 1's.

As a consequence, the two's complement format says that to get the negative value of a number, follow these rules.

- Take the bitwise negation of the number: This replaces each 0 bit with a 1 and vice versa.
- Add 1 to this number.

For example, to get -1, start with the bitwise representation of 1, then take its logical negation and add 1 to the result. Figure 2.1 shows how the process works starting with a bit pattern of 0000 0000 0000 0001. Applying this process arrives at the signed-integer representation of -1.

Figure 2.1 shows that -1 is represented by a bit pattern of all 1's. This is true for every signed integer: For example, the 32-bit representation of -1 has 1's in all 32 positions.

You can apply this same process for other numbers. Figure 2.2 shows how it works for 15. In its binary form, positive 15 is represented as a bit pattern of 0000 0000

0 0 0 0	0 0 0 0	0 0 0 0	0 0 0 1	Starting value: 1
1 1 1 1	1 1 1 1	1 1 1 1	1 1 1 0	Bitwise neg. of 1
1 1 1 1	1 1 1 1	1 1 1 1	1 1 1 1	Add 1

1 -> bitwise negation of 1 -> -1

FIGURE 2.1 Two's complement representation of -1

0 0 0 0	0 0 0 0	0 0 0 0	1 1 1 1	Starting value: 15
1 1 1 1	1 1 1 1	1 1 1 1	0 0 0 0	Bitwise neg. of 15
1 1 1 1	1 1 1 1	1 1 1 1	0 0 0 1	Add 1

15 -> bitwise negation of 15 -> -15

FIGURE 2.2 Two's complement representation of -15

0000 1111. (The four leftmost digits are set to 1 because each binary digit is a power of 2, and 8 + 4 + 2 + 1 = 15.) Applying the two's complement format produces the signed-integer representation of -15.

Therefore, the signed representation of -15 is 1111 1111 1111 0001. Logically enough, -15 is lower in value than -1, not higher.

For signed integers, a negative number has a 1 in its leftmost bit. A non-negative number has 0 in its leftmost bit. Each signed type therefore dedicates the upper half of its range to represent negative values. In nearly every other way, positive and negative signed values behave consistently, and—for most operations—the computer applies the exact same machine instructions to do calculations on signed and unsigned numbers alike.

You can take -1 (which, remember, has 1's in every bit position) and apply the two's complement rules to get its negative—in other words, the negative of a negative. The result produces positive 1, as demonstrated in Figure 2.3. This meets mathematical expectations, because -1 times -1 equals 1.

You can also observe that adding any positive number to its negative (such as adding 15 and -15) produces a value that is one more than 1111 1111 1111 1111; the result

1 1 1 1	1 1 1 1	1 1 1 1	1 1 1 1	Starting value: -1
0 0 0 0	0 0 0 0	0 0 0 0	0 0 0 0	Bitwise neg. of -1
0 0 0 0	0 0 0 0	0 0 0 0	0 0 0 1	Add 1

-1 -> bitwise negation of -1 -> 1

FIGURE 2.3 Taking the negative of -1

therefore "flips over" to produce 0. This fulfills the mathematical property that X added to negative X must equal 0.

Occasionally, the computer must handle signed and unsigned numbers differently. Chapter 3 explains how sign extension and zero extension are used to promote signed and unsigned numbers, respectively. But most of the time, the same machine instructions work on both.

Yet sometimes, mixing signed and unsigned numbers can yield strange results. You can copy a signed value to an unsigned number, for example, but it is interpreted as unsigned when printed.

```
unsigned short  n = -1;
cout << n;    // This prints "65535"!!
```

This prints 64K – 1 (65535), not -1. This result is surprising unless you understand the two's complement format. An unsigned **short** with 1's in all 16-bit positions is interpreted as 65535; a signed number with 1's in all bit positions is interpreted as -1.

Combining signed and unsigned integers in expressions is never recommended. Program behavior is more reliable when you stick to combining signed numbers with signed, and unsigned numbers with unsigned.

But if you must mix such numbers, remember that in a mixed **int/unsigned** expression, the **int** value is promoted to **unsigned**. For instance, consider this example:

```
unsigned usi = -1;
int si = -2;
cout << "usi => " << usi << endl;
cout << "si => " << si << endl;
cout << "usi + si => " << usi + si << endl;
cout << "usi * si => " << usi * si << endl;
```

These statements print:

```
usi => 4294967295
si => -2
usi + si => 4294967293
usi * si => 2
```

The last result may make it seem that both numbers are treated as signed, because -1 times -2 produces 2. However, what really happens is that 4294967295 is multiplied by 4294967294, and the result overflows, leaving a result of 00000002 (hexadecimal) in the 32-bit result.

2.6 String and Character Literals

Unlike some languages, C++ makes a strong distinction between single characters, placed in single quotation marks, and text strings, which are groups of characters placed in double quotation marks.

Both of these kinds of data can be used to print text to the screen or a text file, but the C++ language handles them differently. The next two sections summarize the handling of single characters and strings. Section 2.6.3 then presents the format for special characters (character escape sequences). Section 2.6.4, "Wide-Character Strings," and Section 2.6.5, "Raw String Literals (C++11)," describe the wide-character and raw-string formats.

2.6.1 Single-Quoted Characters

A single character has **char** type, which is stored internally as a one-byte integer. A character is specified with the use of single quotation marks:

```
char c = 'a';
```

This statement causes the ASCII code for lowercase "a" to be stored in the variable c. (This value is 97.)

But a **char** value is promoted to **int** type in expressions, so it is good practice to declare a single-character variable as an **int**:

```
int c = 'a';
```

This is safer programming practice because it enables the variable, c, to hold special values such as EOF (end of file) that are returned by some of the C/C++ library functions.

The general guidelines for handling characters are as follows.

- When characters are packed into an array to form a C-string, they are stored in **char** format. (Exception: Wide-character formats use **wchar_t** as the underlying type.)
- When individual characters are returned by a C++ library function, they are usually returned in the wider **int** format.
- However, to print a single character *as* a character (instead of as its integer value), you need to cast the character back to **char** form (or **wchar_t** in the case of wide characters).

For example, the **toupper** library function returns a character in **int** format. To print the results as a character (translating its ASCII value into character form), cast it back to **char** type:

```
#include <cctype>
. . .
int c = toupper('b');
cout << static_cast<char>(c);    // Print 'B'
```

You can also use a C-style cast, although this is no longer a preferred programming style.

```
cout << (char) c;
```

See Chapter 3 for more information on casts.

2.6.2 Double-Quoted Strings

The C++ compiler handles double-quoted strings differently from how it handles single characters. When the compiler reads a literal string, it allocates space for an array of **char** having enough space for the characters plus a terminating null. (A null contains a zero value.)

```
char  my_name[] = "John Doe";
```

In evaluating this statement, the compiler first allocates room for the string data "John Doe" as illustrated in Figure 2.4. It then replaces the string literal—although you never see this happen in source code—with the address of that data, as if the statement were translated into the following:

```
char  my_name[] = (address of string data)
```

Consequently, when the variable "my_name" appears subsequently in the source code, it is interpreted as the address of the string data (that is, the address of the first character). Figure 2.4 shows how the string—along with a terminating null—is allocated in memory.

Each character is stored in memory as its ASCII character code; but when the string is printed, the characters, not the codes, are displayed. (Note that the ASCII character code for a blank space is 32.) This coding system is necessary because ultimately, all data in the computer is numeric.

This format, which equates a string with a **char** address and adds a null terminator to the end of the text, is the *C-string format*. This is the traditional string format of the C language. For backward compatibility, C++ fully supports this format.

```
char my_name[] = "John Doe";
```

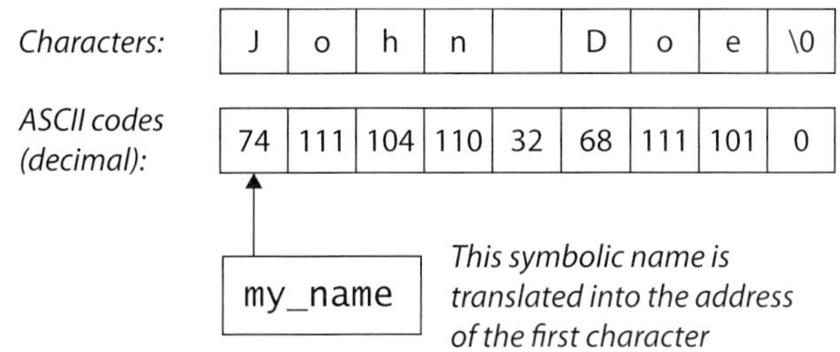

FIGURE 2.4 Allocation of a C-string

However, the C++ Standard Template Library (STL) also supports a sophisticated but highly convenient **string** class, which is easier to use and offers many advantages; but string literals have the C-string format, so it's useful to understand how that format works.

Two string literals placed next to each other are read in as one continuous string. For example, the compiler interprets:

```
"This is the " "rest of the story."
```

as if it were one long string:

```
"This is the rest of the story."
```

This syntax rule is not too useful most of the time, but there are situations that require it. In particular, it enables you to initialize strings with literals that span multiple lines.

```
char  this_is_a_long_string[] = "You see, this is just "
  "too long to place the whole thing on a single line, so "
  "I am going to have to use several lines to fit it in.";
```

Remember that a C-string is an array of **char** and conforms to the general rules of arrays. For more information on arrays, see Chapter 6, "Pointers, Arrays, and References." For more information on the handling of C-strings, see Chapter 10, "C-String Library Functions."

2.6.3 Special Characters (Escape Sequences)

C++ uses the backslash (\) as an *escape character* within quoted strings—both single-quoted and double-quoted. This means that the backslash itself, together with the character (or in some cases, characters) that follows it, are used to specify a special character such as a tab or newline. (Section 2.6.5 explains how to avoid the use of escape sequences if you have C++11.)

An obvious question that arises is: How do you specify an actual backslash? The answer is: Use two backslashes in a row. Therefore, the following statement:

```
cout << "C:\\root\\my_documents\\readme.txt\n";
```

prints the following:

```
C:\root\my_documents\readme.txt
```

Each pair of consecutive backslashes in the quoted string specifies a single backslash. The sequence "\n" specifies an embedded newline so that when the string is printed, the text following "\n" begins on the next line.

It's important to keep in mind the difference between what appears in C++ source code (which may include the escape sequences) and the actual string data used in the program. During compilation, the compiler reads string literals from source code, interprets them as necessary, and allocates the string data.

Note that printing double backslashes requires *four* backslashes in the string literal:

```
cout << "Here are two backslashes: \\\\; Here is one: \\";
```

The effect of this statement is to print the following:

```
Here are two backslashes: \\; Here is one: \;
```

The following list describes the escape sequences recognized in C++ quoted strings and characters. Some of these (such as backspace) are holdovers from a much earlier era in data processing, in which data was printed in teletype mode; the use of these special characters is now rare. Other special characters, such as newline (\n) and tab (\t), are still widely used.

- **\a**

  Bell. When this character is printed, the effect is for the computer to make a beep sound.

- **\b**

  Backspace. When this character is printed, the cursor moves back a space, and subsequent printing may erase characters already printed. Note that you cannot go farther back than the first physical column.

- **\f**

  Form feed.

- `\n`

  Newline. (This is the standard character for advancing to the next line; it contains the carriage-return effect, which moves the cursor back to column 1.)

- `\r`

  Carriage return. This has the effect of moving the cursor back to column 1.

- `\t`

  Horizontal tab: Moves rightward to the next tab position.

- `\v`

  Vertical tab.

- `\'`

  Literal single quotation mark (apostrophe). This escape sequence enables you to specify the apostrophe as an individual character, although it's not necessary inside a double-quoted string. For example:

  ```
  cout<<'\'' << "Quoted string." <<'\'';
  ```

  This prints:

  ```
  'Quoted string.'
  ```

- `\"`

  Literal double quotation mark. This escape sequence enables you to embed a double quotation mark inside a string. For example:

  ```
  cout<< "\"Quoted string.\"";
  ```

  This prints:

  ```
  "Quoted string."
  ```

- `\\`

  Literal backslash. See the examples at the beginning of this section.

- `\`*ddd*

  A numeric value specified in octal. This format reads up to three digits in the range 0 to 7. So, for example, \141 specifies the octal value 141 (decimal 97), which is the ASCII code for the letter "a".

  ```
  char  str = "\141";    // Embed ASCII 97 (octal 141).
  cout << str[0] << endl << (int) str[0] << endl;
  ```

  This source prints out the character "a" followed by its numeric (ASCII) value, 97:

  ```
  a
  97
  ```

- \x*dd*

  A numeric value specified in hexadecimal. This format reads as many hexadecimal digits as it can. So, for example, \x61 specifies the hexadecimal value 61 (decimal 97), which is the ASCII character code for the letter "a".

  ```
  char  str = "\x61";    // Embed ASCII 97 (hex 61) in string.
  cout << str[0] << endl << (int) str[0] << endl;
  ```

  This prints out the character "a" followed by its numeric (ASCII) value, 97:

  ```
  a
  97
  ```

- \x*dddd*

  A two-byte hexadecimal value, useful for entering characters into wide-character strings. The string literal should have the L prefix to indicate it is a wide string. For example:

  ```
  wchar_t  wide_str[] = L"\x10ff";
  ```

In order to understand the last three escape formats, remember that every printable character corresponds to a numeric ASCII code. When you specify an octal or hex number, you bypass the ASCII coding system and embed a numeric value directly into the string.

The numeric formats involve potential ambiguities, but these can all be resolved. In particular, the \ddd and \xdd formats can potentially involve fewer digits than permitted. For example, you can use \0 to specify 0, the null value (although you could also use \00 or \000).

```
str[length + 1] = '\0';    // Append terminating null.
```

What if—to take a problematic example—you want to embed a numeric code followed by digit characters? In other words, suppose you want to put the following three characters into a string:

- Numeric value 1
- Digit character "1" (ASCII code: 49 decimal)
- Digit character "1" (ASCII code: 49 decimal)

The **char** array will contain numeric values 01-49-49-0 (including the terminating null, which is put there automatically by C++). You can create this array with:

```
char  str[] = "\00111";
```

In this case, the leading zeroes are necessary. The following declaration would do something different:

```
char  str[] = "\111";
```

This would embed a single character (along with the terminating null) having octal value 111, or 73 decimal. The rule is: C++ will read up to three octal digits after a backslash, but if it encounters the end of the string or a character that is not an octal digit (0–7), it stops reading digits and uses what it has. Consequently:

```
char  str1[] = "\1";    // Embed numeric value 1.
char  str2[] = "\15b"; // Embed 15 octal, followed by "b".
```

If you wanted, you could specify an entire string by using numeric values rather than ASCII characters. The byte values 01-49-49-0 could be specified as follows (because 49 decimal is 61 octal):

```
char  str[] = "\1\61\61";
```

With the hexadecimal format (beginning with \x), C++ reads as long a hexadecimal number as it can and stops reading digits only when the string ends or it encounters a nondigit. (Hex digits consist of 0 to 9 and uppercase and lowercase letters A to F.) For example, C++ has no problem interpreting the following string; this string contains numeric value 0xff (decimal 255) followed by "q" (ASCII code 113):

```
char  str[] = "\xffq";
```

Because "q" is not a hex digit, the hexadecimal expression consists only of "\xff" (255). But if you wanted to embed the numeric value 0xff followed by the ASCII code for "f", the following would not work:

```
char  str[] = "\xfff";   // ERROR! Wide character needed.
```

Using leading zeroes does not solve the problem. The solution in this case is to use the split-string technique, causing C++ to read two strings joined together. This produces the desired results.

```
char  str[] = "\xff" "f";      // 255 followed by 'f'
                               //   (ASCII 102).
```

2.6.4 Wide-Character Strings

The standard approach to printing and storing characters in C++ is to use one byte (type **char**) to represent each character in a text string. This is adequate for English with its 52 uppercase and lowercase letters, plus digits, whitespaces, and punctuation; but it is insufficient for a number of other languages—some of which have hundreds or even thousands of individual characters.

When working with such languages, you need to use wide-character strings, which allocate two bytes per character; these strings are realized as arrays of **wchar_t** and are also null-terminated.

The wide-character formats are usually strict supersets of ASCII; therefore, you can rewrite any standard C-string as a wide-character string. Remember, however, to consistently use the **wchar_t** type and to use wide-character literal strings, which have this format:

```
L"text_string"
```

For example:

```
wchar_t  wstr1[] = L"This is a wide-character string.";
wchar_t  wstr2[] = L"Two bytes per character."
```

When working with such strings, you can use the \xdddd format to encode non-ASCII character codes. For example:

```
wchar_t  wstr1[] = L"\x10ff\x13e7";
```

2.6.5 Raw String Literals (C++11)

Sometimes, when working with string literals, it's inconvenient to have to deal with escape sequences. For example, if you need to store a number of backslash characters (\), it's a bother to have to type two backslashes every time you want one.

The C++11 specification gives you the option of using raw string literals by specifying an R prefix. When you use this notation, a string is stored exactly as it appears in source code. Because no escape sequences are recognized, there is no way to embed characters that are not part of the printable subset of ASCII characters.

For example, the following statement:

```
cout << R"C:\root\bin\n\readme.txt";
```

prints:

```
C:\root\bin\n\readme.txt
```

Without the raw-string feature, the C++ statement would have to be written as:

```
cout << "C:\\root\\bin\\n\\readme.txt";
```

2.7 Data Declarations: The Complete Syntax

The more complete syntax for declaring variables is:

```
[modifiers] type  variable_decl [,variable_decl] ...;
```

Here the brackets are used to indicate optional items. The *modifiers* are described in the remainder of this section. If there is more than one, they are separated by whitespace.

Each *variable_decl* has the following form:

```
variable_spec [=init_value]
```

The *variable_spec* can be a variable name or—optionally—a complex expression built on a variable name. As explained in Section 6.4, "Complex Declarations Involving Pointers," the variable name can optionally be modified by the *, &, and [] operators—to produce pointers, references, and arrays.

The *init_value* is an expression that can be calculated at runtime. It can also be a set of values (called an *aggregate*), used to initialize a container or array. Here the brackets indicate that you can include any number of values separated by commas if there is more than one.

```
{init_value [,init_value]... }
```

This is useful for initializing arrays, as described in Chapter 6.

```
int  arr[] = {1, 2, 3, 4};
```

Descriptions of the *modifiers* follow.

- **auto**

  Has two different uses, depending on whether it is a modifier or a type name. As a modifier, **auto** can be used with a local variable to specify that the variable has automatic storage class: It is created and destroyed with each invocation of the function. But since this is the default for local variables, this modifier rarely sees any use.

- **const**

  Specifies that the variable being declared has **const** type, which prevents it from being the target of an assignment, increment, or decrement. Also, such a variable cannot be passed to a reference argument that is not **const**. (As explained in Section 6.3.7, "Pointers to const Types," additional rules are imposed for pointers; in particular, a pointer to a **const** type cannot be assigned or passed to another pointer unless that pointer also points to a **const** type.)

  It's particularly important to initialize a **const** variable, because it cannot be assigned a value after it is declared. However, **const** variables can be freely assigned to other variables.

  ```
  const double pi = 3.141592;
  pi = 0.0;        // ERROR! pi is const; cannot be changed.
  double x = pi;   // But this is okay.
  ```

- **constexpr**

  C++11-specific. The variable is treated as a compile-time constant. The compiler must be able to fix the value at compile time or the declaration is not valid. Compile-time constants have the virtue of being fully computed before the program ever runs, and that improves program efficiency at run time. But unlike macro definitions (see Chapter 8), **constexpr** variables are symbols recognized by the debugger.

```
constexpr double pi = 3.14159265;
constexpr double conv_factor = 180 / pi;
. . .
double degrees = radians * conv_factor;
```

  Compile-time constants can also be used to specify array lengths and template-parameter arguments, which you cannot do with ordinary variables.

- **extern**

  Creates an external linkage for a variable; the variable may be defined in this or another module, and it is shared by all modules that include the same **extern** declaration. For example, to have an integer variable my_account_num shared by all modules, place this declaration into each and every source file in the project:

```
extern int my_account_num;     // Declaration only.
```

  In addition, one *and only one* of those modules must create the variable by defining it. That's done with a standard (non-**extern**) declaration:

```
int my_account_num = 0;        // Variable definition.
```

  You can also define a variable by using an **extern** declaration with an initial value:

```
extern int my_account_num = 0;  // This defines, and not
                                //  just declares, the var.
```

  The usual procedure is to place an **extern** declaration in a header file that is shared by all source files in the project, and then define the variable in one and only one of those source files. Note that the source file that defines the variable can have both an **extern** declaration *and* a non-**extern** declaration; the latter defines the variable, causing the compiler to actually allocate memory for it.

- **register**

  Directs the compiler to allocate a variable in a CPU register; this can only be done for automatic variables. (A local variable is automatic unless it is declared static.) If the variable is frequently accessed, placing it in a register has the potential to optimize performance. The use of **register** in no way changes any other C++ syntax; you still refer to the variable exactly the same way you would otherwise.

  But today's optimizing compilers often make sophisticated decisions about how to assign register usage themselves. In such cases, the **register** keyword is therefore no more than a suggestion to the compiler.

```
register int  i;   // Place loop variable i in a register.
```

- **`static`**

  Declares static storage class for a variable. By default, global variables have static storage class, but local variables do not. A local variable declared **static** is still local—visible only within the function or code block in which it is declared—but it is persistent the way a global variable is, and it is shared by all invocations of the function. Unlike other local variables, a static local is initialized once, at the beginning of program execution.

  For example, the following function uses a local variable, i, which is initialized to 1 at the beginning of the program. Each time the function is called it increments the value of i. If i were not static, it would be reinitialized each time the function was called; but because i is static, it retains its value in between function calls.

```
void  goofy() {
      static int i = 1;
      cout << i++ << " ";
}
. . .
goofy();
goofy();
goofy();
```

  This prints:

```
1 2 3
```

- **`thread_local`**

  C++11-specific. (Note that not all recent compilers support this keyword at the time of this writing.) This applies to global and other static variables. When a program spawns multiple threads, normally its static variables are shared by all the threads. The use of this keyword causes the program to create a separate copy of the variable for each thread; this copy is created upon thread creation and is removed from memory upon thread termination.

```
thread_local int errno;
```

- **`volatile`**

  Specifies that the data item in question is volatile, meaning that it may be changed without warning by external factors. This may be the case, for example, in a device-driver program in which a variable or array corresponds to a memory-mapped area or a hardware port.

  The compiler handles volatile data in special ways. It will not place the variable in a register or make optimizing decisions that assume the variable won't change on its own.

  Data items with the **volatile** attribute follow rules similar to those for **const**. You cannot pass a volatile variable by reference to a nonvolatile argument. And a pointer to a volatile type cannot be assigned or passed to another pointer, unless that pointer also points to a volatile type.

```
volatile int  memory_mapped;
```

2.8 Enumerated Types

In computer programming, *enumeration* is a fancy word for a list: not a sophisticated dynamic list (which is what the STL **list** class is for) but a simple list of constants. Sometimes a program needs a list of possible settings in which the actual values may not matter but are important because of what they represent.

For example, you might have a card-drawing program that records whether a card is a heart, diamond, club, or spade. One way to indicate the suit status is to define arbitrary numbers corresponding to each suit.

```
const int heart = 0;
const int diamond = 1;
const int club = 2;
const int spade = 3;
```

Given these definitions, you can assign and test the suit using meaningful names: for instance, using a symbolic name such as "heart" rather than a randomly assigned number (such as 0 or 1). For example:

```
if (my_card_suit == heart) {
     cout << "hearts";
}
```

Another approach is to use a series of **#define** directives, as explained in Chapter 8.

```
#define heart    0
#define diamond  1
#define club     2
#define spade    3
```

But a still better approach is to use the **enum** keyword to create a series of symbolic names.

In the following **enum** syntax, brackets are not intended literally but indicate you can include any number of symbols (symbolic names) separated by commas if there is more than one.

```
enum { symbol[, symbol]...};
```

For example, the four constants—heart, diamond, club, and spade—can be defined with an **enum** declaration:

```
enum {heart, diamond, club, spade};
```

As with almost all C++ syntax, newlines are not significant, but count only as another kind of whitespace. Therefore, you can optionally space an **enum** declaration across multiple lines:

```
enum {
    heart,
    diamond,
    club,
    spade
};
```

Each *symbol* can be explicitly assigned an integer value within the **enum** declaration. If a symbol is not assigned a value, it takes the value of the preceding symbol plus 1. If the first symbol is not assigned a value, it takes the value 0. Therefore, in the previous declaration, the four suit names have the values 0, 1, 2, and 3.

To instead assign the values 1, 2, 3, and 4, use this declaration:

```
enum {
     heart = 1,
     diamond,
     club,
     spade
};
```

The **enum** keyword can optionally declare a type name, and you can then use this name to declare data items, just as if the type name were a primitive type. For example:

```
enum suit {
    heart, diamond, club, spade
};

suit  my_card, card1, card2;
```

You can, as always, initialize such variables, but they can only be initialized with one of the enumerated names (in this case, heart, diamond, club, or spade). Although **enum** variables are implemented as integers, they are restricted to the range of values defined for their particular type.

You can implicitly convert from an **enum** data item to an integer, but you cannot assign an integer to a variable having an **enum** type without a cast. For example:

```
suit  this_card = heart;   // This initialization is okay.
this_card = club;          // This is okay too.
int  i = this_card;        // Okay; i gets the value 2.
i = heart;                 // Okay; i gets the value 0.
this_card = 3;             // ERROR! suit<-int not allowed.
this_card = static_cast<suit>(3);  // Okay.
```

Here is the more complete **enum** syntax. None of the brackets are intended literally but indicate optional items.

```
enum [type_name] {
     symbol_def [, symbol_def]...
} [variable_definitions];
```

Each *symbol_def* has the following syntax, in which brackets are used to indicate that the *int_value* (an integer constant whose value can be determined at compile time) is optional:

```
symbol [=int_value]
```

In C++11, you can use the **class** keyword with **enum** to create even stronger enumerated types. This syntax creates a *scoped enum type,* which places the enumerated symbols into a separate namespace. For example:

```
enum class suit {
    heart, diamond, club, spade
};

suit  this_card = suit::club;  // Scope prefix (::) needed.
```

Moreover, when you work with a scoped **enum** class, instances of the type cannot be assigned in either direction (**int** to **enum** type or **enum** type to **int**) without an explicit cast. See Chapter 3 for more information on casts.

2.9 Special Declarations (typedef, auto, decltype)

This section presents some miscellaneous keywords that, while not strictly necessary for creating data types, are frequently helpful when working with more complex types.

2.9.1 The typedef Keyword

A **typedef** declaration can be used to define a symbolic name as an alias for another type:

```
typedef  type_specification  name;
```

One way to use **typedef** is to in effect rename a primitive type:

```
typedef  unsigned long  UINT32;
```

The UINT32 type can then be used like any type name:

```
UINT32  i = 0, j = 0;
```

You might use such an alias because you choose (as programmers in large companies such as Microsoft do) to make the precise width of the type absolutely clear in source code. Although an **unsigned long** is almost always—on today's personal computers—a 32-bit unsigned integer, the C++ specification does not guarantee that for all platforms. When dealing with those platforms, you can use a **typedef** declaration to (for example) fix the meaning of INT32 for that platform, and then use the type name INT32 to declare your variables.

The **typedef** keyword also can play an important part in reducing the complexity of long declarations, and I use that technique later in this book. For example, to declare an array of pointers, you might first declare a pointer type:

```
typedef  int*  IPTR;
```

You can then use this type alias to create an array of pointers, as follows:

```
IPTR  array_of_ptrs[10];
```

See Chapter 6 for a more detailed explanation of how **typedef** can be used this way, as well as a background on the subjects of pointers and arrays.

2.9.2 The auto and decltype Keywords (C++11)

The C++11 specification provides some new keywords that can be an aid when working with complex declarations. The **auto** keyword, as a type specifier, declares a type determined from context.

(Do not confuse **auto** with a variant type; you cannot use it to declare a variable that holds different kinds of data at different times. To do that, use a union type, as described in Chapter 7, "Classes and Objects.")

For example, the following statements declare variables whose types are determined by their initial values:

```
auto n = 1;          // n has int type.
auto x = 3.141592;   // x has double type
```

The **auto** keyword is often used with the range-based **for** statement, described in Chapter 4. It also is helpful when working with lambdas, as described in Chapter 5, "Functions."

The **auto** keyword, as a type specifier, should not be confused with the use of **auto** as a data-declaration modifier. The latter usage sees essentially no use in C++ programs anyway.

The **decltype** keyword uses an argument to specify a type. For example, if n has type **int**, then the following is equivalent to the **int** keyword and can be used in any context in which you could use int:

```
decltype(n)
```

This is a trivial usage, but there are situations in very complex code in which it might be helpful to have the compiler figure out what a type is.

The following example uses **decltype** to determine the type of the expression x + y and then declares another variable of that same type. If x and y were of different types, it might not be immediately obvious how x and y are promoted in the combined expression to produce a type.

```
decltype(x + y)  z = 0;    // z has same type as "x + y"
```

2.10 Sample App: Type Promotion

The following application is a demo program more than a practical application; it reports on the effects of type promotion in C++. This application utilizes the **typeid** operator, which does not return an integer or printable value, but returns type information that can be compared to the results of other **typeid** operations. See the code that follows for clarification.

```
#include <iostream>
using std::cout;
using std::endl;

int main() {
     char c = 0;
     int si = 0;
     unsigned int ui = 0;
     double d = 0;
     d = ui = si = c;     // This avoids warning msg's.
     if (typeid(c + c) == typeid(int)) {
          cout << "type of (char + char) is int" << endl;
     }
```

```
        if (typeid(si + ui) == typeid(unsigned)) {
             cout << "type of (int + unsigned int) ";
             cout << "is unsigned" << endl;
        }
        if (typeid(si + d) == typeid(double)) {
           cout << "type of (int + double) is double" << endl;
        }
        cin.ingore();  // Wait for user to press ENTER.
        return 0;
}
```

Note that an assignment statement is included on the tenth line to avoid warnings about unreferenced variables, which most compilers will give you if you don't use the variables somehow:

```
d = ui = si = c;     // This avoids warning msg's.
```

Exercises

1. Add a test that determines what happens when two variables of type **float** (single precision floating point) are combined through addition or multiplication.
2. Add a test that determines whether an **unsigned char** added to an **int** produces **int** type or **unsigned** type. Put this test in the form of an **if-else-if** structure.

◆ ◆ ◆ CHAPTER 3

Operators

Another concept in C++ that is fundamental to all programs is the concept of *expression*. Data variables and literals—presented in Chapter 2, "Data"—form the simplest expressions. By using *operators,* you can build ever-larger expressions out of simpler ones, like an engineer building ever-more sophisticated parts and engines out of smaller ones.

A typical action in C++ is to calculate a value by evaluating a complex expression.

```
fahrenheit = (centigrade * 1.8) + 32.0;
```

The items to the right of the equal sign (=) form a complex expression joining centigrade, 1.8, and 32.0 together with the multiply and addition operators (* and +). The results are then assigned to the variable named fahrenheit. Assignment (=) is itself an expression, with this form:

```
variable = new_value
```

Terminating the assignment with a semicolon (;) turns it into a statement. In C++ grammar, assignment is not a separate kind of statement; rather, it's an expression formed by an operator (=), and it can be used as part of a larger expression. So too with nearly all C++ operators.

3.1 Precedence, Associativity, and Lvalues

To combine multiple operators within complex expressions, you need to understand precedence and associativity. Both of these concepts concern the order in which the operators are applied.

3.1.1 Precedence

Precedence determines which operators have priority over others—and so are resolved first. For example, multiplication (*) has a higher precedence than addition (+). So the following statement:

```
a * b + c * d + e
```

is evaluated as if it were written as:

```
(a * b) + (c * d) + e
```

This order is dictated because the multiplication operator (*) is applied before addition (+). Note that the asterisk here is used as a binary operator and therefore indicates multiplication rather than pointer dereference.

Of course, an expression is always clearer with parentheses than without. Sometimes it's a good idea to include parentheses even when they are not strictly necessary.

Assignment has lower priority than almost any operation, so parentheses are not really necessary in the following:

```
z = x + y;
```

This could have been written as:

```
z = (x + y);
```

But as a rule, you can generally assume that assignment (=) is carried out last. The only exceptions are the **throw** operator and the join (or "comma") operator.

3.1.2 Associativity

Associativity determines what happens when there are two or more operators at the same level of precedence. A simple example involves subtraction. Like most operators, the subtraction operator (-) associates left to right. Therefore, this expression:

```
a - 5 - 5
```

is evaluated as written this way:

```
(a - 5) - 5
```

rather than this way:

```
a - (5 - 5)
```

3.1.3 Lvalues

Many of the syntax descriptions in this chapter refer to an *lvalue*. This means "left value," an expression that can appear on the left side of an assignment. Obviously, you can't assign a value to a literal, so the following makes no sense:

```
5 = 7          // ERROR! NOT VALID!
```

In general, an lvalue is one of the following:

- A simple variable
- A fully dereferenced address expression
- An element of an array
- A member of an object
- An expression that returns a reference to an lvalue

In the last four cases, the item is an lvalue only if it directly refers to an addressable item in memory, just as a simple variable would.

The concepts of pointers, arrays, references, and objects are explained in Chapter 6, "Pointers, Arrays, and References," and Chapter 7, "Classes and Objects." If you are not yet familiar with these ideas, you can—for now— just consider an lvalue to be a variable.

3.2 Concise Summary of Operators

Table 3.1 summarizes C++ operators. Operators in the same box are at the same level of precedence. Prefix and assignment operators have right-to-left associativity (R-to-L); all other operators have left-to-right associativity (L-to-R).

The table uses the following placeholders:

- *expr*, an expression (may be a number, address, object, or other expression)
- *lvalue*, a variable name or other lvalue expression
- *ptr*, a pointer expression, containing an address
- *num*, a numeric expression, either integer or floating point, but not an address
- *int*, a numeric expression having integer type
- *obj*, an instance of a class
- *type*, a type identifier such as the name of a primitive type or class

TABLE 3.1 Summary of C++ Operators

Operator/Syntax	Description	Assoc.
class::*name*	Class-member scope.	L-to-R
namespace::*name*	Accesses symbol in a namespace.	
::*name*	Accesses global symbol.	
lvalue++	Postfix increment.	L-to-R
lvalue--	Postfix decrement.	
function(*args*)	Function call.	
ptr[*index*]	Array index through address or array name (ptr).	
obj.*member*	Member access.	
ptr->*member*	Member access through pointer.	
typeid (*expr*)	Type identification of expression.	
typeid(*type*)	Produce specified type ID.	
C++ cast operators	See Section 3.6, "Cast Operators."	
++*lvalue*	Prefix increment.	R-to-L
--*lvalue*	Prefix decrement.	
!*expr*	Logical negation.	
~*int*	Bitwise negation.	
-*num*	Arithmetic negation (take the negative of).	
*ptr	Pointer indirection ("at" operation).	
&*lvalue*	Address operator.	
sizeof(*expr*)	Get size in bytes of expression or type.	
new *type*	Dynamic memory allocation.	
new *type*[*n*]	Memory allocation of n items.	
new *type*(*args*)	Memory allocation calling constructor.	
delete *ptr*	Release memory allocated with **new**.	
delete *ptr*[]	Release memory allocated with **new** *type*[*n*].	
(*type*) *expr*	C-language cast. See Section 3.6.	
obj.**ptr_to_member*	Pointer-to-member access. (Rarely used.)	L-to-R
ptr->**ptr_to_member*	Pointer-to-member through a pointer to an object. (Rarely used.)	
num * *num*	Multiplication.	L-to-R
num / *num*	Division.	
int % *int*	Modulus (remainder from division).	

TABLE 3.1 Summary of C++ Operators (*Continued*)

<table>
<tr><th>Operator/Syntax</th><th>Description</th><th>Assoc.</th></tr>
<tr><td>expr + expr</td><td>Addition.</td><td>L-to-R</td></tr>
<tr><td>expr - expr</td><td>Subtraction.</td><td></td></tr>
<tr><td>int << int</td><td>Bitwise left shift.</td><td>L-to-R</td></tr>
<tr><td>ostream << expr</td><td>Stream output.</td><td></td></tr>
<tr><td>int >> int</td><td>Bitwise right shift.</td><td></td></tr>
<tr><td>istream >> expr</td><td>Stream input.</td><td></td></tr>
<tr><td>expr < expr</td><td>Less-than comparison.</td><td>L-to-R</td></tr>
<tr><td>expr <= expr</td><td>Less-than-or-equal comparison.</td><td></td></tr>
<tr><td>expr > expr</td><td>Greater-than comparison.</td><td></td></tr>
<tr><td>expr >= expr</td><td>Greater-than-or-equal comparison.</td><td></td></tr>
<tr><td>expr == expr</td><td>Test for equality.</td><td>L-to-R</td></tr>
<tr><td>expr != expr</td><td>Test for inequality.</td><td></td></tr>
<tr><td>int & int</td><td>Bitwise AND.</td><td>L-to-R</td></tr>
<tr><td>int ^ int</td><td>Bitwise exclusive OR.</td><td>L-to-R</td></tr>
<tr><td>int | int</td><td>Bitwise OR.</td><td>L-to-R</td></tr>
<tr><td>expr && expr</td><td>Logical AND.</td><td>L-to-R</td></tr>
<tr><td>expr || expr</td><td>Logical OR.</td><td>L-to-R</td></tr>
<tr><td>expr1 ? expr2 : expr3</td><td>Conditional operator; produces expr2 or expr3.</td><td>L-to-R</td></tr>
<tr><td>lvalue = expr</td><td>Simple assignment.</td><td>R-to-L</td></tr>
<tr><td>lvalue *= expr</td><td>Multiply and assign.</td><td></td></tr>
<tr><td>lvalue /= expr</td><td>Divide and assign.</td><td></td></tr>
<tr><td>lvalue %= int</td><td>Get modulus and assign.</td><td></td></tr>
<tr><td>lvalue += expr</td><td>Add and assign.</td><td></td></tr>
<tr><td>lvalue -= expr</td><td>Subtract and assign.</td><td></td></tr>
<tr><td>lvalue <<= int</td><td>Shift left (bitwise) and assign.</td><td></td></tr>
<tr><td>lvalue >>= int</td><td>Shift right (bitwise) and assign.</td><td></td></tr>
<tr><td>lvalue &= int</td><td>Bitwise AND and assign.</td><td></td></tr>
<tr><td>lvalue |= int</td><td>Bitwise OR and assign.</td><td></td></tr>
<tr><td>lvalue ^= int</td><td>Bitwise exclusive OR and assign.</td><td></td></tr>
<tr><td>throw expr</td><td>Throw exception object.</td><td>L-to-R</td></tr>
<tr><td>expr1, expr2</td><td>Join operator: evaluates both; produces expr2.</td><td>L-to-R</td></tr>
</table>

3.3 Operators in Detail

The following sections describe C++ operators in order of precedence and provide more information on each of the operators, along with an example. Except where noted, all the operators at the same level of precedence are described in the same section.

3.3.1 The Scope Operator (::)

The scope operator has the highest precedence of all. It has several variations.

- *namespace*::*name*

  Refers to a symbolic name declared within a separate namespace. This usage is necessary for objects in the **std** namespace unless you include a **using** statement.

  ```
  std::cout << "Welcome to the show." << std::endl;
  ```

- *class*::*name*

  Gives class scope to the *name*, clarifying that it is a member of the specified class. This usage is necessary, for example, when defining a member function outside of the class declaration. (See Chapter 7 for more information on the subjects of classes and class scope.)

  ```
  double Point::get_x() { return x; }
  ```

- ::*name*

  Specifies that the name referred to is a global name, not a class name or a name declared within a separate namespace.

  ```
  ::x++;    // Increment the global var x, not class member.
  ```

3.3.2 Data-Access and Other High-Precedence Operators

These operators have the highest level of precedence after the scope operator (::). They associate left to right. Some of these provide access to a class member, element, or function call. Postfix increment and decrement are also in this group, along with **typeid**; note that prefix increment and decrement operators are at the precedence level just below this one.

- *lvalue*++

  Increment operator (postfix). Passes along the current value of the operand and then adds 1 to it.

```
int i = 1;
int n = i++;    // Result: n  = 1, i = 2.
```

- *lvalue*--

Decrement operator (postfix). Passes along the current value of the operand and then subtracts 1 from it.

```
int i = 1;
int n = i--;    // Result: n = 1, i = 0.
```

- *function(args)*

Function-call access. Executes named function and passes arguments to it, if any. Produces the value returned by the function, unless the function's return type is **void** (in which case it cannot be part of a larger expression).

```
double x = exp(a, b);
```

- *ptr*[*int*]

Array access; *ptr* may contain any address, but it is typically the name of an array (which, in C++, is translated into the address of the first element). *int* is a zero-based index number, so 0 refers to the first element. Expression is equivalent to *(ptr + index).

```
cout << my_array[i];
cout << my_2D_array[i][j];
```

- *object*.*member*

Class member access. Accesses named member of an object.

```
MyClass  obj;
. . .
obj.x = 0;
```

- *ptr*->*member*

Class member access through a pointer. Dereferences the pointer to get an object; then accesses the named member of that object. Equivalent to (*ptr).member.

```
MyClass  obj;
MyClass *ptr_to_obj = &obj;
. . .
ptr_to_obj->x = 0.0;
```

- **typeid**(*expr*)
- **typeid**(*type*)

Produces a type ID for specified expression or type. Although they cannot be printed or compared to a number, type IDs can be compared to each other. For example, the following statements demonstrate that in a mixed signed/unsigned integer expression, the type is unsigned:

```
int si      = -1;
unsigned us = 2;
if (typeid(si + us) == typeid(unsigned)) {
     cout << "Type of (si + us) is unsigned." << endl;
}
```

Probably the most useful application of **typeid** is within class hierarchies, to determine the exact type of object pointed to by a base-class pointer. As with **dynamic_cast**, such an operation requires that the class hierarchy involve at least one virtual function. This is an example of Run-Time Type Identification (RTTI).

See Chapter 7 for more information on class hierarchies.

3.3.3 Prefix Operators

These operators have the next highest level of precedence and so are still relatively high-level.

Unlike most other operators, these operators all associate right to left. The only other operators with right-to-left associativity are the assignment operators.

- `++`*`lvalue`*

  Increment operator (prefix). Adds 1 to the operand and then produces the resultant value.

  ```
  int i = 1;
  int n = ++i;   // Result: n = 2, i = 2.
  ```

- `--`*`lvalue`*

  Decrement operator (prefix). Subtracts 1 from the operand and then produces the resultant value.

  ```
  int i = 1;
  int n = --i;   // Result: n = 0, i = 0.
  ```

- `!`*`expr`*

  Logical negation: result is **true** (1) if operand is zero; result is **false** (0) if operand is nonzero. Effect is to reverse true/false conditions.

  ```
  if (!is_file_open){
       // Respond to error condition.
  }
  ```

- `~`*`integer`*

  Bitwise negation. For each individual bit, the result contains a 0 if corresponding bit in the operand is 1, and vice versa.

  ```
  ~my_bitmask
  ```

- *-number*

  Arithmetic negation. Produces a result with a different sign from the operand, changing positive values into negative ones and vice versa.

  ```
  int i = -5;
  ```

- **ptr*

  Pointer dereference (also called "at" operator). Accesses what is at specified address; the result is an lvalue, but only if the pointer is fully dereferenced (for example, a pointer of type **int**** would need to be dereferenced twice).

  The lvalue issue is significant because only lvalues can be the target of an assignment.

  ```
  *p = 0;
  ```

- &*lvalue*

  Address operator. Takes the address of an item in memory. Result is usually assigned to a pointer or passed to a function expecting an address.

  ```
  int *p;
  int i = 0;
  p = &i;
  ```

- **sizeof(***expression***)**
- **sizeof(***type***)**

  Produces size in bytes of its operand or type specification. In the case of arrays and other complex types, it produces the overall size in bytes, not just the number of elements.

  ```
  sizeof(my_array)
  sizeof(int)
  ```

- **new** *type*

  Creates a primitive type or object from dynamic memory (called the "heap") and returns a pointer to this object. If memory allocation fails, a **bad_alloc** exception is thrown. To avoid memory leaks, the object should be deleted when you are done with it.

  ```
  int *p = new int;   // Create an integer from dyn. memory.
  *p = 5;             // Store 5 at this location.
  . . .
  delete [] p;        // We are done with it.
  ```

  With primitive data types, it's not safe to assume that the item created is initialized to zero, so it should be assigned some meaningful value. See Section 6.3.6, "Pointers and Memory Allocation," for more information on the use of the **new** operator.

▸ **new** *type*[*n*]

Performs the same action as the previous version of **new**, but this version creates any number of objects as an array; *n*, an integer value calculated at runtime, specifies the number of elements to create. If successful, **new** returns the address of the first item in the array. If memory allocation fails, a **bad_alloc** exception is thrown. To avoid memory leaks, the objects should be removed with **delete**[] when no longer needed.

For example, the following statements prompt the user for a number and then create a floating-point array of the requested size. The elements are then all set to 0.0.

```
int n = 0, i = 0;
cout << "Enter number of elements in the array: ";
cin >> n;
double *p = new double[n];   // Allocate n floating point.
while (i < n) {
    p[i] = 0.0;
    ++i;
}
. . .
delete [] p;                 // We're done with the array.
```

You should not assume that the items created are initialized to zero, even though (depending on the circumstances) they sometimes will be zero.

▸ **new** *type*(*args*)

Performs the same action as the first version of **new**, but this version passes along one or more arguments to perform initialization. If *type* is a primitive type, you can initialize the data with a single numeric argument. If *type* is a class, you can use the arguments to invoke a constructor.

```
double *p = new double(3.141592);
cout<< *p << endl;    // Print out the value.
. . .
delete p;             // We are done with the object.
```

▸ **delete** *ptr*

Removes a single data object previously created with **new**.

```
int *p = new int;
. . .
delete p;
```

▸ **delete [ ]** *ptr*

Removes data objects previously create with **new**. This is the version of delete to call if **new**[] had been used to create multiple objects.

```
int *p = new int[10];
. . .
delete [] p;
```

3.3.4 Pointer-to-Member Operators

These operators—whose use is rare for most C++ programmers—have the next highest level of precedence.

> **Note**
>
> This section requires a thorough understanding of both pointers and classes. If necessary, first read Chapters 6 and 7.

To use a pointer-to-member operator, first declare it as an offset to a particular member of a class. In the following statements, ptr_to_rank is a pointer-to-member storing the offset of rank, an integer member of MyClass; and ptr_to_name is a pointer-to-member storing the offset of name, a **string** object member of MyClass:

```
#include <string>

class MyClass {
   public:
      int rank;
      string name;
};

int     MyClass::*ptr_to_rank = &MyClass::rank;
string  MyClass::*ptr_to_name = &MyClass::name;
```

The following two operators associate left to right.

- *object.*ptr_to_member*

  Applies a pointer-to-member item to an object. For example, assume that MyClass is a class declared with a public member named rank. The following statements set obj.rank to 0.

  ```
  int  MyClass::*ptr_to_rank = &MyClass::rank;
  MyClass  obj;
  obj.*ptr_to_rank = 0;    // Set obj.rank to 0.
  ```

- *ptr->*ptr_to_member*

  Similar to the .* operator, except that it accesses the object through its address (that is, a pointer to that object). The following statements set obj.rank to 0.

  ```
  intMyClass::*ptr_to_rank = &MyClass::rank;
  MyClass  obj;
  MyClass  *p = &obj;
  p->*ptr_to_rank = 0;    // Set p->rank to 0.
  ```

These operators (.* and ->*), while perhaps interesting, are rarely necessary. A pointer-to-member item refers to a member by storing its offset within a class. This is an indirect way of referring to a member and is only occasionally of use, because there are almost always more direct ways available to do the same thing.

3.3.5 Multiply and Divide

These operators have the next highest level of precedence. They are binary operators (that is, each takes two operands) that associate left to right.

Note that the asterisk (*) has a different meaning depending on whether it is unary or binary. When applied to two operands (as done here) the asterisk is the binary multiplication operator ("binary" in this case referring to there being two operators). When applied to one operand, the asterisk is the unary "at" operator. C++ uses context to distinguish these different uses of the operator.

Syntax for the multiply and divide operators, along with description, follows.

- *num* * *num*

  Multiplication. Returns the product of two numeric operands.

  ```
  x * y
  ```

- *num* / *num*

  Division. Produces the quotient of two operands. If both are integers, the result is an integer rounded down; if either operand is a floating-point value, the result is floating point. (Therefore, to force a floating-point result and avoid loss of the fractional portion, make sure at least one of the operands has floating-point type, by casting if necessary.)

  ```
  int n = 2, m = 5;
  double ratio = n / static_cast<double>(m);
  ```

- *int* % *int*

  Modular division. Produces the remainder after performing integer division. The quotient is ignored by this operator, but remember that the quotient can be obtained separately with /. This operation, %, is supported for integers only. To perform a similar operation on floating-point numbers, see the **fmod** library function described in Chapter 12, "Math, Time, and Other Library Functions."

  For example, performing modular division by 2 returns 1 or 0. A result of 1 indicates that the left operand is odd; a result of 0 indicates that the left operand is even.

  ```
  bool  is_odd_number = (i % 2 == 1);   // Is i%2 eq. to 1?
  ```

3.3.6 Add and Subtract

The add and subtract operators have the next highest level of precedence. These are binary operators (each taking two operands) that associate left to right.

- *expr + expr*

  Addition. Produces the sum of two operands. This operator is principally used to add two numbers, but it can also be used to add an integer to an address. Adding an address uses the rules of pointer arithmetic described in Chapter 6.

  ```
  x + y
  arr + i
  ```

  Addition is also overloaded by the **string** class to perform concatenation (joining).

  ```
  #include <string>
  . . .
  string first = "White";
  string name = first + " Rabbit";
  ```

- *expr - expr*

  Subtraction. Produces the difference of its two operands. This operator is principally used to subtract one number from another, but it can also be used to subtract an integer from an address or find the distance between two addresses. These operations use the rules of pointer arithmetic described in Chapter 6.

  ```
  x - y
  ptr - 1
  p2 - p1
  ```

3.3.7 Shift Operators

These operators have the next highest level of precedence. They are binary operators (each taking two operands) associating left to right. They are also overloaded by the C++ stream I/O library. Note that when you use an operator for I/O in this way, its precedence and associativity do not change. Therefore, if you want to print the value of an expression using an operator having lower priority than <<, it's necessary to use parentheses.

- *int1 << int2*

  Left-shift operator. This operator produces the result of shifting bits in *int1* by *int2* positions. See Section 3.5, "Bitwise Operators in Detail," for more information on bitwise operations.

  ```
  unsigned short  bits1, bits2;
  bits1 = 0x0007;     // bits1 =            0000 0000 0000 0111
  bits2 = bits1 << 2; // bits2 = 0x001c = 0000 0000 0001 1100
  ```

- *ostream << expr*

  The left-shift operator is overloaded to print output to an **ostream** object such as **cout**. The operator prints output as a side effect and produces a reference to the stream itself.

```
#include <iostream>
using namespace std:
. . .
cout << "Hello, brave new world!" << endl;
```

- *int1 >> int2*

  Right-shift operator. This is a bitwise operator shifting a bit pattern to the right by the number of positions specified by int2. See Section 3.5 for more information on bitwise operations.

```
short bits1, bits2;
bits1 = 0x0070;      // bits1 =            0000 0000 0111 0000
bits2 = bits1 >> 4; // bits2 = 0x0007 = 0000 0000 0000 0111
```

- *istream >> expr*

  This operator is overloaded to read input from an **istream** object such as **cin**. The operator reads input as a side effect and produces a reference to the stream itself.

```
#include <iostream>
using namespace std:
. . .
int n = 0;
cout << "Enter new value for n: ";
cin >> n;
```

See Chapter 13, "C++ I/O Stream Classes," for more information on stream classes and objects.

3.3.8 Less Than and Greater Than

These operators have the next highest level of precedence. They are binary operators (each taking two operands) that associate left to right. These operators are all Boolean, returning a result that is either **true** (1) or **false** (0).

The most common use for these operators is for comparison of two numbers. They can also be used to compare one address to another, to determine which is higher or lower in memory, or whether the two addresses are equal. In the Standard Template Library or STL [see Chapter 15, "Introduction to STL (vector, deque)"], iterators of vectors and deques can also be compared using these operators.

- *expr* < *expr*

  Less-than comparison. Returns **true** if the first operand is less than the second.

  ```
  if (a < b) cout << "a is less than b.";
  ```

- *expr* <= *expr*

  Less-than-or-equal comparison. Returns **true** if the first operand is less than or equal to the second.

  ```
  if (a <= b) cout << "a is less than or equal to b.";
  ```

- *expr* > *expr*

  Greater-than comparison. Returns **true** if the first operand is greater than the second.

  ```
  if (a > b) cout << "a is greater than b.";
  ```

- *expr* >= *expr*

  Greater-than-or-equal-to comparison. Returns **true** if the first operand is greater than or equal to the second.

  ```
  if (a >= b) cout << "a is greater than or equal to b.";
  ```

3.3.9 Test for Equality

These operators have the next highest level of precedence. They are binary operators (taking two operands) that associate left to right. They are also Boolean (true/false) operators.

The most common use for these operators is for comparison of two numbers. They can also be used to compare addresses. Many other classes—notably the STL **string** class—overload the == and != operators so that instances of the class can be compared for equality of contents.

- *expr* == *expr*

  Test for equality. Returns **true** if the two operands are equal. Note that this operator uses two equal signs (==), not one.

  ```
  if (a == b) cout << "a and b are equal.";
  ```

  This test is often used with pointers and instances of the **string** class, as well as with numbers.

  ```
  if (p1 == p2)  cout << "p1 and p2 point to same address.";
  ```

- *expr* != *expr*

  Test for inequality. Returns **true** if the two operands are not equal.

  ```
  if (a != b) cout << "a and b are NOT equal.";
  ```

This test is often used with pointers and instances of the **string** class, as well as with numbers.

```
if (pFile != NULL) cout << "File open succeeded.";
```

3.3.10 Bitwise and Logical Conjunctions

Each of the operators in this section is at a different level of precedence. For example, & has a higher precedence than ^, and ^ has a higher precedence than |. This section lists these operators in order of precedence. All of them are binary operators associating left to right.

Logical and bitwise operations are different from each other and frequently produce different results, unless you consistently use Boolean values as operands.

Bitwise operations force evaluation of both operands. Logical operations use short-circuit logic, which means that in some cases the second operand is never evaluated. To force evaluation of both operands in a logical expression, you can use bitwise AND or bitwise OR (& and |), but in that case, make sure both operands are Boolean.

Section 3.5 provides more information on the first three of these operators.

- *int* & *int*

  Bitwise AND. Performs an AND operation between each bit in the first operand and the corresponding bit in the second operand. A bit in the result is 1 if and only if both corresponding operand bits are 1. This operator is often used to mask out specific bits.

```
short bits = 0xffff, mask = 0x000f;
bits = bits & mask;   // Turn off all but lowest four bits.
```

- *int* ^ *int*

  Bitwise exclusive OR. Performs an exclusive-OR operation between each bit in the first operand and the corresponding bit in the second operand. A bit in the result is 1 if and only if either but not both of the corresponding operand bits are 1.

```
short bits = 0x0f0f, mask = 0x000f;
bits = bits ^ mask;   // Reverse lowest four bits.
```

- *int* | *int*

  Bitwise OR. Performs an OR operation between each bit in the first operand and the corresponding bit in the second operand. A bit in the result is 1 if either or both of the corresponding operand bits are 1. This operator is often used to switch on specific bits.

```
short bits = 0x1200, mask = 0x000f;
bits = bits & mask;   // Turn on lowest four bits.
```

- *expr* **&&** *expr*

  Logical AND. Produces a result of **true** (1) if and only if both operands are nonzero. If the first operand evaluates to **false** (0), the second is not evaluated.

  ```
  if (n > 12 && n < 20)  {cout<< "n is a teen.";}
  ```

- *expr* || *expr*

  Logical OR. Produces a result of **true** (1) if and only if at least one of the operands is nonzero. If the first operand evaluates to **true** (1), the second is not evaluated.

  ```
  if (n < -5 || n > 5)  {cout<< "abs(n) > 5.";}
  ```

3.3.11 The Conditional Operator (?:)

The conditional operator (?:) is at the next level of precedence. This operator is an alternative to if/else control structures. (See Chapter 4, "Control Structures," for more information on if/else.) The conditional operator is often used with the **#define** preprocessor directive, but it can also be used just to write compact programming code. The operator has this syntax:

```
condition_expression ? true_expression : false_expression
```

The *condition_expression* is evaluated. If it is nonzero (that is, true), then *true_expression* is evaluated and its value becomes the result of the overall expression. If *condition* evaluates to zero (that is, false), then *false_expression* is evaluated and its value becomes the result of the overall expression.

This is simpler than it may sound. In the following example, x and y are compared. If x is greater than y, the result is a; otherwise, the result is b.

```
double result = ( x > y ? a : b);
```

In this next example, the string "succeeded" or "failed" is printed depending on the value of the variable file_open. If file_open contains a nonzero value, then the string "succeeded" is printed.

```
cout << (file_open ? "succeeded" : "failed");
```

3.3.12 Assignment Operators

These operators share the same level of precedence, which is low. Unlike most operators, all the assignment operators (including =) associate right to left.

All of these operators permanently change the value of the left operand—which must be an lvalue. The expression itself produces a reference to the left operand after assignment, allowing assignment expressions to be embedded within larger expressions if you choose.

For example, consider the following expression that uses simple assignment:

```
x = y
```

As a side effect, the value of x is changed. It gets the value of y. But the expression itself (x = y) also has a value, which is a reference to the left operand, x.

Since x was assigned the value of y, the effect of the assignment is to pass along x's value to a larger enclosing expression, if any, *after x is assigned the value of y*. Therefore, this rather strange-looking code is valid (and not uncommon) in C++ programs:

```
z = x = y
```

Assignment operators associate right to left. Therefore, the rightmost assignment (x = y) is performed first, evaluating y and placing the value in x. Then the value of the expression x = y is passed along to z. Consequently, the value of y is assigned to both x and z. Similarly, the following statement assigns 0 to *three* variables:

```
a = b = c = 0;
```

Because assignment returns a reference to the left operand, C++ enables some compact, refined coding techniques that can be baffling to look at if you are not intimately familiar with how assignment works. Suppose you want the variable "big" to contain 100 and you want the variable "bigger" to contain 101. You can do this with just one statement:

```
++(bigger = big = 100);
```

Hold on! What just happened here? Several things occurred.

- The subexpression "big = 100" is resolved first, putting 100 into big and producing a reference to big.
- Because big now contains 100, the effect of "bigger = big" (resolved next) is to place 100 in bigger as well.
- The subexpression "bigger = big" produces a reference to bigger, which now contains 100.
- The increment operator is resolved last. Because the expression in parentheses produces a reference to bigger, the final effect of the statement is the same as:

```
++bigger;
```

Finally, the variable named "bigger" contains 101 after everything is evaluated.

In addition to simple assignment, C++ provides ten other assignment operators. Each of these performs a binary operation, combining the two operands, and then assigns the resultant value to the left operand. For example, here's a statement employing the addition-assignment operator:

```
x += 7;
```

This has the same effect as:

```
x = x + 7;
```

Likewise, here's a statement employing the subtraction-assignment operator:

```
n -= 5;
```

This has the same effect as:

```
n = n - 5;
```

In general, the syntax for assignment operators is:

lvalue op= operand

The binary operation specified by *op* is carried out between *lvalue* and *operand*. The results are then placed into *lvalue*:

lvalue = lvalue op operand

The only difference is that with combined assignment operations (such as +=), *lvalue* is evaluated just once (rather than twice as it would be in the syntax just shown).

All the assignment operators produce a reference to the left operand.

Here are the assignment operators, starting with simple assignment.

- =

  Simple assignment. (Just place the value of the second operand into the first.)

- +=

  Addition.

- -=

  Subtraction.

- *=

  Multiplication.

- /=

  Division. (If both operands are integers, the result is an integer rounded down.)

- %=

  Modulus. (The remainder from integer division is placed in the left operand.)

- >>=

  Bitwise right shift.

- <<=

  Bitwise left shift.

- &=

  Bitwise AND.

- ^=

  Bitwise exclusive OR (each resultant bit is 1 if and only if one, but not both, of the corresponding operand bits are 1).

- |=

  Bitwise inclusive OR.

3.3.13 The throw Operator

The **throw** operator is used to raise an exception, which is an unusual occurrence—typically but not always an error condition—that must be handled or the program will abruptly terminate. See Section 4.10, "Exception Handling (try, catch)," for more information.

The operand can be any type of expression. The exception is caught (through the use of **catch** blocks) according to its type.

For example, the following statement raises an exception of type **const char** *:

```
if (!file_out) {
     throw "Unable to open file."
}
```

3.3.14 The Join Operator (,)

The operator with the lowest precedence of all is the join operator, also called the "comma operator." This operator lets you combine multiple operations within a small space without having to place them in separate statements. Its most common use is to place multiple initializations or increment actions inside a **for** or **while** statement.

The syntax is simple:

expression1, expression2

The operator causes evaluation of both subexpressions, therefore causing all side effects to happen; it then produces the value of the second operand, passing that value along to a larger expression, if any. In other words, the value of *expression1, expression2* is the same as *expression2*. The difference is that it forces side effects of *expression1* as well as *expression2*.

For example, in the following **while** loop, two expressions are evaluated: "cin >> n" and "n > 0." This causes the number n to be read from console input; then, if n is greater than 0, the body of the loop is executed. Otherwise, the loop terminates.

```
while (cin >> n, n > 0) {
. . .
}
```

3.4 The Great Controversy: Postfix or Prefix?

If you've examined the increment/decrement operators—two of which are prefix and two of which are postfix—you may have noticed that the difference between postfix and prefix matters only sometimes. In particular, the following two statements do the same thing if n is an **int**:

```
++n;     // Stand-alone prefix increment.
n++;     // Stand-alone postfix increment.
```

It might seem reasonable, then, to say the difference between these two statements is a matter of style. For many years, it was. And for decades, programmers tended to show a preference for postfix:

```
n++;     // FORMERLY, this was the preferred style.
```

Even C++ programmers showed a preference for postfix, perhaps because it reflected the name of their language.

The tide has turned in the past few years. The reason (as you'll see in Chapter 7) is that the postfix operation requires the creation of a copy of the thing being incremented. Because—thanks to the STL—increment and decrement are now often applied to objects more complex than integers or pointers, having to do this extra copying is potentially inefficient.

An objection to that argument is as follows: If an increment (++) or decrement (--) is used in a stand-alone expression, then any decent optimizing compiler ought to ignore the difference and produce the most optimal code anyway.

Among C++ gurus, however, that objection has failed to win the day. The current politically correct policy is to favor prefix increment and decrement in order to encourage programmers to develop the right habits.

```
++n;     // Favoring prefix is now politically correct.
```

I don't agree with that assessment myself, but I certainly agree it doesn't *hurt* to favor the prefix style in stand-alone expressions, so I have largely followed that style in this book.

3.5 Bitwise Operators in Detail

The bitwise operators include bitwise AND, OR, and exclusive OR (&, |, ^); bitwise negation (~); and the shift operators (<< and >>). In using these operators, bear in mind that all data is ultimately stored in the computer in individual bits, each bit containing 1 or 0. However, the C++ bitwise operators only work on integer types.

3.5.1 Bitwise AND, OR, and Exclusive OR

Let's look at bitwise operations in some concrete examples. Take the decimal value 51. This is equivalent to 0x0033 (as a 16-bit integer) or 0x00000033 (as a 32-bit integer). For simplicity, let's consider two-byte integers.

The two bytes of 0x0033 (decimal 51) look like the pattern shown in Figure 3.1 when you examine its bit pattern.

Now, consider another bit pattern. As explained in Chapter 2, the decimal value 15 is equivalent to 0x000f hexadecimal, or a bit pattern of 0000 0000 0000 1111. Figure 3.2 shows how 0x0033 and 0x000f can be combined with the binary bitwise operations AND, OR, and exclusive-OR.

You can see from Figure 3.2 that combining 0x0033 and 0x000f through bitwise AND (&) produces 0x0003, or decimal 3.

```
cout << (0x0033 & 0x000f);    // Print 3.
```

In this statement, by the way, parentheses are necessary. Bitwise AND (&) has lower precedence than the left-shift operator, <<, even though it's being used here as a

0	0	0	0	0	0	0	0	0	0	1	1	0	0	1	1	0x0033

FIGURE 3.1. Bit pattern of 0x0033 (decimal 51)

<table>
<tr><td>0000</td><td>0000</td><td>0011</td><td>0011</td><td>0x0033</td></tr>
<tr><td>0000</td><td>0000</td><td>0000</td><td>1111</td><td>0x000f</td></tr>
<tr><td>0000</td><td>0000</td><td>0000</td><td>0011</td><td>& (AND)</td></tr>
<tr><td>0000</td><td>0000</td><td>0011</td><td>1111</td><td>| (OR)</td></tr>
<tr><td>0000</td><td>0000</td><td>0011</td><td>1100</td><td>^ (Ex. OR)</td></tr>
</table>

FIGURE 3.2. AND, OR, and exclusive-OR operations

stream-output operator. In situations like these, you need to pay careful attention to precedence rules. (See Table 3.1.)

C++ also provides the unary bitwise operator, ~, which performs bitwise negation (see Figure 3.3). This is a simple operation that flips the value of each bit so that 1's are replaced with 0's and vice versa.

3.5.2 Operating on Signed and Unsigned

Bitwise operations can only be performed on integer types, which range from **char** (a signed byte integer) all the way to **long long** and **unsigned long long**. You cannot perform bitwise operations on other kinds of data without first using a cast, which is an unsafe practice that I don't generally recommend.

Smaller types are promoted to larger types as needed. For example, in the following operation, the smaller variable (us) is promoted to **unsigned long** before being combined with ul.

```
unsigned short us = 0x00ff;
unsigned long ul = 0xfff0;
cout << (us & ul) << endl;
```

0000	0000	0011	0011	0x0033
1111	1111	1100	1100	~ (neg.)

FIGURE 3.3. Bitwise negation of 0x0033

But promotion of signed values can cause unexpected results unless you thoroughly understand sign extension.

As explained in Chapter 2, signed integer formats use a bit pattern of all 1's to represent negative 1. A bit pattern for a signed number is *sign-extended* when promoted to a wider type: Sign extension checks the setting of the leftmost bit (in this case, 1) and uses that setting to pad all the bits on the left. Remember that a signed negative number has a 1 in its leftmost bit.

Figure 3.4 shows how a signed **char** value of -1 is promoted to a two-byte integer.

If a variable is an **unsigned char**, the bit pattern 1111 1111 is interpreted not as -1 but as 255. When an **unsigned char** is promoted to a wider type, it is zero-extended rather than sign-extended, preserving the unsigned value 255 (see Figure 3.5).

The upshot is that, starting from the same bit pattern (1111 1111), the following statements produce different results—because sign extension is performed for sc, a signed **char**, but not for uc, an **unsigned char**.

```
cout << (0xf00 & sc) << endl;   // Print 3840 (0xf00).
cout << (0xf00 & uc) << endl;   // Print 0.
```

The moral of the story is that you should be careful about combining different integer types in bitwise operations. In fact, it is much safer to perform bitwise operations on

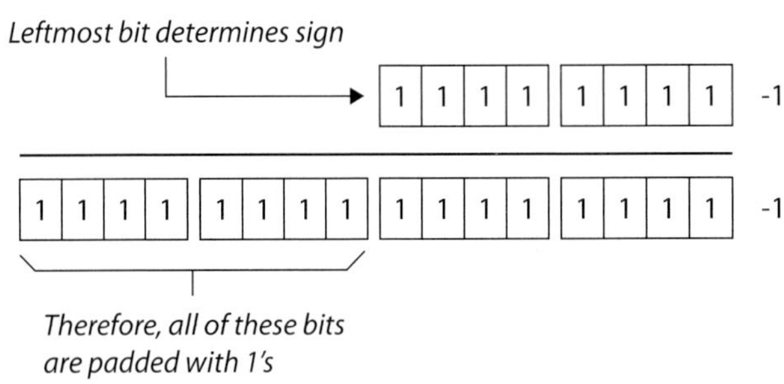

FIGURE 3.4 Sign extension of -1

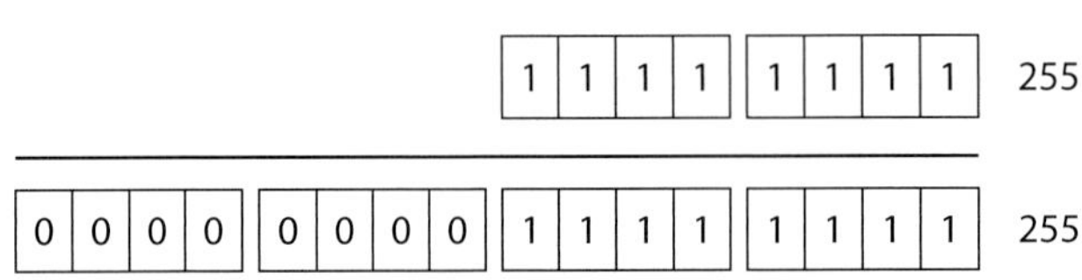

FIGURE 3.5 Zero extension of 255

unsigned integers only. Note that octal and hexadecimal literals (for example, 0xffff) always produce unsigned values.

The format for representing signed integer values was first introduced in Section 2.5.3, "Signed versus Unsigned Integers." See that section for a review of the two's complement format for representing negative values. One of the consequences of this format is that for signed integers, you can tell whether a positive or negative value is being stored by examining the leftmost (most significant) bit.

Floating-point values have another format altogether, involving an exponent, mantissa, and dedicated sign bit. The vast majority of computers in operation today—that is, virtually all—use IEEE formats for floating-point numbers. This is a complex subject unto itself. However, the **ldexp** and **frexp** functions of the C++ library safely isolate and compose parts of a floating-point number; see Chapter 12 for more information. Unless you're analyzing bit patterns as part of a programming exercise, I don't recommend attempting to ever fiddle with the bits of a floating-point number directly.

3.5.3 Bitwise Shifts

The shift operators << and >> have been overloaded in C++ to work with stream classes, performing input and output. But the shift operators were at first provided in the C language to shift bits left or right within integer fields.

When used with two integer operands rather than a stream operator, the shift operators still fulfill their original purpose.

The left-shift operator (<<) moves bits to the left—in effect, multiplying by a power of 2—and fills in 0's on the right end. Likewise, the right-shift operator (>>) moves bits to the right and fills in 0's on the left end. (Therefore, if you shift far enough to the right or left, eventually all the bits in the operand will be set to 0.) Figure 3.6 demonstrates how this works.

0 0 0 0	0 0 0 0	0 0 1 1	0 0 1 1	0x0033
0 0 0 0	0 0 0 1	1 0 0 1	1 0 0 0	<< 3
0 0 0 0	0 0 0 0	0 0 0 0	0 1 1 0	>> 3

FIGURE 3.6. Left- and right-shift operations

3.6 Cast Operators

Welcome to the casting couch.

Anytime a type conversion is needed and does not involve any conflicts or obvious risks, the C++ compiler goes ahead and does it. For example, the compiler has no problem handling this:

```
double y = 2.5;
double x = y + 1;   // Convert "1" to flt. pt. and add to y.
```

Nor does it have a problem with the following, even though 1 (as opposed to 1.0) is stored in integer format, not floating point:

```
double x = 1;
```

This is not a problem because it's clear that the integer value, 1, should be promoted to its floating-point representation, 1.0, and then assigned to x; furthermore, there is no loss of data. (Note that internally, integers and floating-point values are represented with entirely different bit patterns, so this is not a trivial issue.)

But consider this:

```
int n = 3.99997;
```

What should the compiler do? It converts to integer by dropping the fractional portion and then initializes n with the value 3. But it also issues a warning about loss of data. A good deal of information is being lost in this case.

One of the purposes of the cast operators (although far from the only purpose) is to suppress warning messages. A cast specifies a data conversion from one type to another. But a cast cannot force a conversion if no such conversion exists.

In many cases, then, a cast says to the compiler, "Yes, I really want to do this." It directs the compiler to go ahead with a data conversion even if there is a potential for loss of data or other dangers. A cast can also be used to clarify ambiguous situations.

Recent versions of C++ support four separate cast operators, each with a distinct purpose. These are strongly recommended because they are self-documenting and approved of by C++ standards committees. There is another cast operator—the old C-language cast—that is more flexible, but whose use is discouraged; I explain why in Section 3.6.5, "The C-Language Cast."

Table 3.2 provides a summary of the cast operators.

The next five sections present each of these cast operators in greater detail.

TABLE 3.2 C++ Cast Operators

Operator	Description
static_cast	Converts data to the specified type. This is a straightforward data conversion not involving pointers or the **const** attribute.
reinterpret_cast	Converts a pointer to point to a different base type.
const_cast	Can be used to remove the **const** attribute from the expression so that a **const** pointer can be assigned to a non-**const** pointer.
dynamic_cast	Enables you to cast downward through a class hierarchy, but only if the expression actually points to the type in question.
(*type*) *expr*	C-language cast, supported for backward compatibility but officially discouraged.

3.6.1 The static_cast Operator

The syntax for the **static_cast** operator is:

```
static_cast<type>(expr)
```

static_cast produces the value of *expr* but in a new data format. A conversion must exist to convert from the type of *expr* to the specified *type*, or the cast fails.

static_cast cannot reinterpret pointers or remove the **const** attribute.

The most common use for **static_cast** is to suppress warning messages as suggested earlier. For example, the following statements cause no warning message to be issued by the compiler even though a floating-point number is converted to integer type:

```
double x = 1.0;
int n = static_cast<int>(x);   // Suppress loss-of-data warning.
```

But **static_cast** does not change the way the conversion is applied or cause it to be more accurate. In the following statement, 3.997 is still rounded down to 3.

```
double x = 3.997;
int n = static_cast<int>(x);   // Suppress loss-of-data warning.
```

The **static_cast** operator is also used to clarify ambiguous situations. For example, Chapter 9, "Creating and Using Templates," describes a situation in which the compiler can take two integer arguments or two **double** arguments, but does not know how to evaluate the following. It does not know whether to convert the integer data to floating point or vice versa.

```
int n = 5;
double x = 4.89;
double x = max(n, x);
```

Application of **static_cast** resolves the situation by being specific about what data should be converted and how.

```
double x = max(static_cast<double>(n), x);
```

3.6.2 The reinterpret_cast Operator

The syntax for the **reinterpret_cast** operator is:

```
reinterpret_cast<type*>(addr)
```

reinterpret_cast produces a pointer expression with a different base type than that of *addr* (its numeric value, however, is still the same). You can also cast between pointer types and integer types:

```
reinterpret_cast<type*>(int)
reinterpret_cast<int>(addr)
```

Most of the time, however, **reinterpret_cast** is used to cast from one pointer (address) expression to another.

Except for certain special situations, use of this cast is dangerous. For example:

```
int *pInt;
double x = 3300.1;

pInt = reinterpret_cast<int*>(&x); // DANGER! double* cast
                                   //   to int*
cout<< *pInt;                      // This prints garbage.
```

This operation does nothing like **static_cast**; it does not convert 3300.1 to integer format (which **static_cast** would have done if applied to x itself). Instead, it leaves the floating-point bit pattern for 3300.1 at the address of x unchanged and interprets that data *as if it were in integer format*. There are many problems in doing that, not least of which is that **int** is four bytes wide but **double** is eight bytes wide.

And yet, **reinterpret_cast**, as dangerous as it can be, is necessary in at least two situations.

- Casting a **void*** pointer to a more specific type. Void pointers are discussed in Chapter 5.

- Reading or writing binary data. The binary I/O functions take **char*** pointer arguments even when you're reading or writing other kinds of data. It's therefore necessary to convert between **char*** and other pointer types. Chapter 11, "C I/O Library Functions," and Chapter 13 both discuss the techniques of binary I/O.

For example, suppose you're writing the value of n, an integer, to a binary file. It's necessary to get the address of n and cast that address to **char*** type, because the **write** member function takes a **char*** pointer.

```
// Get addr. of a long integer, then write it to file.
long n = 5;
char *p = reinterpret_cast<char*>(&n);
file_out.write(p, sizeof(long));
```

3.6.3 The const_cast Operator

The syntax for the **const_cast** operator is:

const_cast<*type*>(*expr*)

This operator cannot convert data to a new format or reinterpret a pointer's base type, but it can add or remove **const** or **volatile** attributes. The most common use of this cast is to remove the **const** attribute from an address so that it can be passed to a non-**const** argument.

Chapter 6 describes how, when a pointer or reference argument has the **const** attribute, it protects the value pointed to from being changed.

```
display_value(const double *x);
```

When a function is declared this way, it's safe to pass both **const** and non-**const** variables to it. The problem occurs when an argument is not declared as **const** but you need to pass a **const** variable to it:

```
display_value(double *x);
```

Normally, C++ will not allow a **const** variable to be passed to such a function.

```
const double pi = 3.141592;
display_value(&pi);     // ERROR! Cannot pass const ptr to
                        //   a non-const arg.
```

In general, this is a good rule, because it prevents functions from getting the address of a **const** variable and making changes to it. But sometimes, even though you know the risks involved (you are aware that the function has permission to change the value pointed to even though the value should not be changed), you need to call it anyway, and you want the compiler to just do what it's told. That's when **const_cast** is useful.

```
const double pi = 3.141592;
double *p = const_cast<double*>(&pi);  // Remove const.
display_value(p);    // This is okay now.
```

The expression "&pi" has type **const double***. The second line of code in this example casts from **const double*** to plain old **double***, making it legal to pass the resultant address expression to the display_value function.

3.6.4 The dynamic_cast Operator

The syntax for the **dynamic_cast** operator is:

dynamic_cast<*type>(*addr*)**

The use of **dynamic_cast** is limited to class hierarchies, a concept described in Chapter 7. This cast is provided because it's possible for a pointer of base-class type to point to an object of a derived type. For example, assume that ClassD is derived from ClassB, a base class:

```
class ClassB {
virtual int f1() {return 0;}
};

class ClassD : public ClassB {
int f1() {return 1;}
};
```

Assume that a pointer ptr_to_B is declared with base-class type (ClassB) and an object, obj_D, is declared with derived-class type (ClassD).

```
ClassD obj_D;
ClassB ptr_to_B = &obj_D;
```

Now you have a base-class pointer (ptr_to_B) of a general type (B), pointing to an object of a more specific, derived type (D). This is legal because you can always cast upward through a class hierarchy, assigning the address of an object to a pointer of more general type.

The problem occurs when going in the reverse direction. In this case, you might want to be able to cast the pointer back to ClassD type, because the object *pointed to actually has that type!* But normally, you can't do that:

```
ClassD ptr_to_D = ptr_to_B;    // ERROR! Not permitted.
```

dynamic_cast comes to the rescue. If the object pointed to has the desired type (ClassD in this case), or a type derived from that type, the cast succeeds. If not, **dynamic_cast** produces a null pointer.

```
ClassD ptr_to_D = dynamic_cast<ClassD*>(ptr_to_B);
if (ptr_to_D) {
     cout << "ptr_to_B points to a ClassD object.";
}
```

There is one caveat: **dynamic_cast** can be successfully applied only when the class hierarchy involves at least one virtual function. In this case, the virtual function is f1.

3.6.5 The C-Language Cast

This syntax for the old C-language cast is.

```
(type) expression
```

This cast can do anything that **static_cast**, **reinterpret_cast**, and **const_cast** can do—in some cases it can even perform more than one of these operations in a single step. (It slices! It dices!) In terms of the typing you have to do, it's actually easier to use than the other casts, not harder:

```
int n = (int) 3.141592;   // <- instead of static_cast

long n = 5;
char *p = (char*) &n;     // <- instead of reinterpret_cast
file_out.write(p, sizeof(long));
```

The problem with the C-language cast, as far as the C++ community is concerned, is that it is *too* easy to use. Usually that's not a problem for a language feature; but in this case, ease of use is a problem because casts are inherently dangerous and their use, it was felt, should be restricted.

For example, if you want to change an address expression's base type, you should be required to use **reinterpret_cast**. If you want to remove the **const** or **volatile** attribute, you should be required to use **const_cast**. The virtue of these new-and-improved cast operators is to make each kind of cast more self-documenting and specific. If you suspect a rogue pointer has a bad type, for example, you can scan through your source code to find a **reinterpret_cast**.

For the sake of backward compatibility, the old C-style cast is still supported, although its use is discouraged within the C++ community (in some cases, quite strongly). The ANSI C++ Committee considered deprecating all uses of this cast, which would have required compilers to issue warnings whenever it was used. But in the end, the need for backward compatibility won the day.

Promise not to tell anyone I said it was okay to use it. It's still not a bad idea, though, to use the new, more "correct" casts as long as you have enough column width in your source files.

3.7 Sample App: Binary Printout

The sample program in this section prints a 16-bit integer in binary radix (base 2). For the benefit of the user, the program inserts a space after every four digits. For example, the value of 1 is printed as:

```
0000 0000 0000 0001
```

You can use this program to verify everything stated in Chapter 2 about the two's complement format for signed numbers. (See Section 2.5.3.) If the number -1 is entered as input, the program prints:

```
1111 1111 1111 1111
```

verifying what I stated in Chapter 2 about -1 having a bit pattern of all 1's.

Here is the complete program. It uses several operators presented in this chapter.

```
#include <iostream>
using std::cout;
using std::cin;
using std::endl;

int main() {
    int n = 0;                          // Loop variable.
    unsigned short  test_num = 0;       // Number to print.
    unsigned mask = 0x8000;             // Bit mask.
    cout << "Enter a number: " << endl;
    cin >> test_num;
    while (n++ < sizeof(test_num) * 8) {
        cout << ((test_num & mask) != 0);  // Print 1 or 0.
        mask = mask >> 1;          // Then shift right.
        if (n % 4 == 0) {          // After every four digits,
             cout << " ";          //  print a space.
        }
    }
    cout << endl;
    cin.ignore();  // Consume last carriage return.
    cin.ignore();  // Wait for user to press ENTER.
    return 0;
}
```

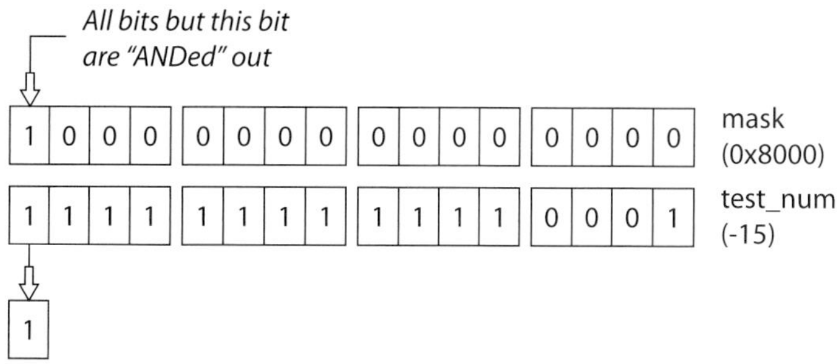

FIGURE 3.7 Testing leftmost bit using bitwise AND (&)

The program works by using a bit mask that has a 1 in its leftmost bit and 0's everywhere else: That bit-mask value is equal to hexadecimal 0x8000. Figure 3.7 shows how the mask is used. For example, suppose the user inputs -15 (which is 1111 1111 1111 0001 in binary). When the AND operation combines the bit mask with a test value, only the leftmost bit is tested; all other bits in the result are set to 0.

If the leftmost bit is equal to 1 in the test value, the bitwise AND (&) operation produces a result not equal to 0; otherwise, 0 is produced. The statement that performs this test is:

```
cout << ((test_num & mask) != 0);   // Print 1 or 0.
```

Parentheses are strictly required for the operations to be performed in the desired order. (You can refer to Table 3.1 to see that without the parentheses, the operations would be performed in the wrong order in this case, due to precedence.)

The test-for-inequality operator (!=) produces either **true** or **false**, equal to 1 or 0, respectively. That result—1 or 0—is printed on the console.

The program then needs to test the rest of the number, test_num. That's done by shifting bits in the mask one position to the right. Both operations are repeated each time through the **while** loop.

```
mask = mask >> 1;      // Then shift right.
```

The loop is repeated 16 times, which is the number of bits in a byte (eight) times the number of bytes in test_num.

Note

The **bitset** template, described in Chapter 15, does most of what this application does, although it does not insert a convenient space every four digits. Still, this application is a useful exercise.

Exercises

1. One of the statements in this program can be made more succinct by use of a single operator that combines an operation with assignment. (See Section 3.3.12, "Assignment Operators," if you need clarification.) Find that statement and revise it.
2. Rewrite the program so that it operates on a 32-bit number and prints a 32-bit display.
3. If you're already familiar with the **for** statement (described in Chapter 4), rewrite the loop using **for**.
4. You can use an even shorter program to print out the bits in reverse order, if you know the trick. Each time through the loop, compare test_num to 0 and then shift one position to the right. Write that program.
5. Write a program that prompts for and inputs a text string of binary digits, such as "1111000011110011" in the 16-bit range (or 32-bit range if you prefer), and outputs a decimal number. Hint: You will need to input a string and analyze it. I recommend using an STL **string** object. Include the <string> header:

   ```
   #include <string>
   ```

   Then declare an input string and use the input-stream operator (>>) to input data:

   ```
   string input_str;
   cin >> input_str;
   ```

   Finally, you'll need to access individual characters and compare them to the character value '1' or '0'. In C++, all indexing is zero-based; so, for example, to test the first character, use an index of 0:

   ```
   if (input_str[0] == '1') {
        // Take some action...
   }
   ```

   The value inside the brackets can be any valid integer expression, such as a variable.
6. Do the preceding exercise, but enable the end user to optionally enter blank spaces between the digits. Have the program skip over these blank spaces.

CHAPTER 4

Control Structures

A control structure determines what the program does next: make decisions, perform actions conditionally, and—critical to nearly all computing—*loop*. By looping, you direct the program to carry out repetitive actions efficiently, instead of being repetitive yourself.

This chapter begins with a concise guide to the grammar of C++ statements and then describes each control structure in detail. Finally it presents exception handling, a special kind of decision making that responds to exceptional situations at runtime. (Hence the name.)

4.1 Concise Summary of C++ Statements

The key to C++ statement syntax is that it's recursive: Each of the items described in this section is a statement; therefore, each of them can be used inside any other statement that calls for a *statement* placeholder. You can place statements inside statements to any level of complexity. An **if** statement can be placed inside a **while** statement.

In the syntax that follows, *condition* is any valid C++ expression, but ideally should be a Boolean expression that has a strict true/false value; however, any nonzero value is treated as "true."

- `;`

  Null statement. Performs no action.

- `expression;`

  Expression terminated by a semicolon (;). The only action is to evaluate *expression*. Such a statement may be useful for its side effects, such as assignment or function call.

- `{ statements }`

  Compound statement, also called a *block*. If the block is executed, all of the *statements* inside are executed (unless of course the flow of control is altered in the middle of the block). Remember that a compound statement is itself a statement and therefore is valid anywhere a single *statement* would be valid.

- *`data declaration`*

  In C++, data declarations (see Chapter 2, "Data") are also statements and can be placed inside any block.

- `if (condition) statement`

  Evaluates *condition*; if nonzero (true), *statement* is executed.

- `if (condition) statement1 else statement2`

  Evaluates *condition*; if nonzero (true), *statement1* is executed; otherwise, *statement2* is executed.

- `while (condition) statement`

  Evaluates *condition*; if nonzero (true), *statement* is executed and *condition* is reevaluated. Repeat this loop until *condition* is false.

- `do statement while(condition);`

  Executes *statement* and then evaluates *condition*. If *condition* is true (nonzero), then repeat. This control structure is the same as the standard **while** loop, except that *statement* is executed at least once.

- `for (init; condition; increment) statement`

  Traditional C/C++ **for**. Expression *init* is evaluated just once. Then *condition* is evaluated; if nonzero (true), *statement* is executed followed by evaluation of *increment*. Repeat this loop until *condition* is false.

- `for (type variable : container) statement`

  Range-based **for**. For each element of *container*, *statement* is executed, beginning with the first element and ending with the last; *variable* represents the current element during each execution of *statement* and may be accessed within *statement*. (C++11 only.)

- `switch(value) { statements }`

  Value, an expression, is evaluated. Control is then switched to a statement within the *statements*, if any, having a matching **case** label. (For example, if the *value* evaluates to 5, control is switched to a statement labeled **case 5:**.) If no case label matches, control is switched to the statement labeled **default**, if any.

- `case value: statement`

  Labels a statement so that it can be a target statement within a **switch** block. The *value* must be a literal or a constant computed at compile time.

- `default: statement`

  Labels a default statement within a **switch** block.

- `label: statement`

  Labels the statement so that it can be the target of a **goto** statement.

- `goto label;`

  Switches control unconditionally to the statement that has the specified *label*, which must be in the same function.

- `continue;`

  Advances execution to the beginning of the next **while** or **for** loop iteration—continuing the next loop but advancing to the top of the next cycle. (But note: Within a **for** loop, *increment* is evaluated first.)

- `break;`

  Advances execution past the end of the innermost **if**, **for**, **switch**, or **while** statement, abruptly ending the loop.

- `return;`

  Returns control to the caller of the current function.

- `return expression;`

  Returns control to the caller of the function, passing back the value of the *expression*.

4.2 Null Statements (;) and Expression Statements

Null statements do nothing. Although rarely necessary, they are occasionally useful as placeholders—or in loops that don't need the body of the loop to do anything. A null statement consists only of:

```
;
```

Because null statements are permitted anywhere a statement is, C++ is forgiving when you enter multiple semicolons (;). Of course, entering unneeded semis is sloppy programming.

```
;;;;;;;
```

Expression statements are the most common kind of statements in C++. Such a statement is just an expression terminated with a semicolon (;). The action is simply to evaluate the expression, triggering any and all side effects. Assignments are typical examples of expression statements:

```
x = 0;
```

Such a statement evaluates the expression (in this case, x = 0) but does nothing more, because there is no enclosing expression. The expression x = 0 has a side effect, assigning 0 to x; afterward, it produces a reference to x. But because the expression is terminated with a semicolon, it results in no further action.

Expression statements are not useful unless they have side effects. The following all have side effects: assignments, incrementing, decrementing, and (often) function calls.

Note that only the final value is ignored. This next example is made up of several subexpressions, each of whose values are significant. In this case, the assignments in parentheses pass along values to the larger expression.

```
x = (y = 4 + 1) * (z = 2);
```

The effects are: x is assigned 10, y is assigned 5, and z is assigned 2.

The grouping of expressions into statements is not purely arbitrary: It guarantees order of evaluation. Most operators make no guarantee about the order in which subexpressions are evaluated; but placing them in separate statements does guarantee order.

For example:

```
++n;          // Increment n by 1.
j += 2;       // Increment j by 2.
n = j;        // Assign value of j to n.
```

This is predictable. But the following statement is difficult to predict, and different compilers can potentially generate code that causes different results. So beware of code like this!

```
n = ++j = ++n = ++j;
```

4.3 Compound Statements

A compound statement (also called a *statement block* or simply a *block*) consists of zero or more statements between two curly braces. For example:

```
{ int i = 5; ++i; cout << i; }
```

As with all C++ syntax (except for comments and preprocessor directives), the ends of lines (newlines) have little significance and are treated as whitespaces. Therefore, you can position the braces and statements anywhere you like, placing them on separate lines if you choose. The exact spacing is a matter of personal style.

```
{
    int i = 5;
    ++i;
    cout << i;
}
```

Compound statements are important in C++ for two major reasons. First, they are essential tools in writing control structures. Remember the fundamental rule: Anywhere a statement would be valid, a compound statement is also valid. Consider the **if** statement syntax:

```
if (condition) statement
```

The *statement* can be replaced by a compound statement:

```
if (condition)  {  statements }
```

All the statements inside the curly braces are executed or none of them are (assuming they are not interrupted). If *condition* is false, control is transferred past the end of the block.

Another significance of compound statements is that they define scope: Variables declared inside a block are visible in that block only. In this example (which repeats the previous one) the variable i is local to the three statements inside the braces.

```
{
     int i = 5;
     ++i;
     cout << i;
}
```

If the statements *outside* the braces declare a variable named i, that variable is unaffected by what happens to i inside the block.

```
int i = 10;

{
     int i = 5;
     ++i;
     cout << "inner i is " << i << endl;
}

cout << "outer i is still " << i << endl;
```

This code produces the following output.

```
inner i is 6
outer i is still 10
```

4.4 if and if-else Statements

The **if** statement (with its optional **else** variant) is the grammatically simplest way for a program to make a decision between alternative actions. The general syntax is:

```
if (condition)
      statement1
[ else
      statement2 ]
```

The brackets in this case are not intended literally but indicate that the **else** clause is optional.

The *condition* may be any valid C++ expression (except for a **void** expression, which has no value), but using a Boolean expression as the *condition* is strongly recommended.

```
if (a < b)
      cout << "a is less than b.";
```

A Boolean expression is one that is either **true** or **false**. The arithmetic comparison operators (<, >, <=, >=, ==, and !=) all produce Boolean expressions, as do the logical operators, && and ||.

If the *condition* expression is not Boolean, C++ accepts any valid expression unless it is **void**. In such a case, any nonzero value is treated as true. That fact makes certain programming shortcuts possible, but such practices result in less reliable code. Therefore—with a few exceptions, such as testing stream objects and pointers—I do not recommend them in this book. But the determined reader can discover them for him or herself.

It's both common and recommended practice to use compound-statement syntax with **if**:

```
if (a == b) {
      int i = 0;
      ++i;
      cout << i;
}
```

Many programmers use compound-statement syntax even when there is only one statement inside the braces. The advantage of this approach is that if you go back and add a statement to the body of the **if** statement later on, the syntax will continue to be correct.

```
if (a == b) {
      cout << "a is equal to b.";
}
```

You can also follow this practice when using an **if** statement with an **else** clause.

```
if (a == b){
     cout << "a is equal to b.";
} else {
     cout << "a is NOT equal to b.";
}
```

The examples in this section use the test-for-equality operator (==) in the *condition* expression rather than assignment (=). These two operators, == and =, do completely different things: The first is a Boolean operator that produces **true** or **false**; the second produces a reference to the left operand (and therefore will pass along the value that was assigned). Mistaking one of these operators for the other is one of the most common sources of errors, especially for people new to C and C++.

The recursive nature of **if-else** syntax makes it possible to in effect write as many "else if" clauses as you choose. Recall the syntax for **if-else**:

```
if (condition)
     statement1
else
     statement2
```

Now *statement2* can be any valid statement you want—including another **if** statement. Substituting an **if-else** statement for *statement2* produces the following:

```
if (condition1)
     statement1
else
     if (condition2) statement2 else statement3
```

which you can write as:

```
if (condition2)
     statement1
else if (condition2)
     statement2
else
     statement3
```

Consequently, you can write an unlimited number of "else if" clauses. An **else-if** clause, by default, applies to the nearest **if** statement. For more complex **if-else** logic, you need to use curly braces to clarify what's intended. But it's a good idea to use curly braces in any case.

```
if (i == 1) {
     if (j == 1) {
          cout << "i and j are each 1.";
     }
```

```
} else if (i == 2) {
     cout << "i equals 2";
}
```

Because of how the curly braces are used in this example, the condition "i == 2" is an alternative to the first use of **if**, not the second. Without the braces, the logic of this program would flow differently.

4.5 while and do-while Statements

The **while** statement is the simplest control structure for creating a loop—a group of statements executed repeatedly.

```
while (condition)  statement
```

Everything stated about the *condition* in Section 4.4 applies here. It's good programming practice to use a Boolean condition—such as the result of a comparison—but C++ accepts any expression in this context (unless it is **void**) and evaluates any nonzero value as true.

As with **if** statements, it's common for *statement* to be a compound statement, resulting in the following variation in which *statements* consists of zero or more statements:

```
while (condition) {
   statements
}
```

The action is to first test the *condition*. If true (nonzero), the *statement* (or statements) is executed. Control then returns to the top of the loop, and the condition is tested again. This process continues until *condition* is evaluated as false (zero), at which point the loop terminates.

For example, the following code prints the numbers from 1 to 5:

```
int i = 1;
while (i <= 5) {
     cout << i << " ";
     ++i;
}
```

By using the postfix increment (++), you can write this more succinctly, as:

```
int i = 1;
while (i <= 5) {
     cout << i++ << " ";
}
```

The **do-while** statement is similar to the **while** statement, but the statement in the body of the loop is guaranteed to be executed at least once.

```
do statement
while (condition);
```

The action is to execute *statement* and then evaluate the *condition*. If the condition is true (nonzero), the process is repeated; otherwise, the loop terminates. For instance, the previous example could be written as follows.

```
int i = 1;
do {
     cout << i << " ";
} while (i++ <= 5);
```

4.6 for Statements

The standard C++ **for** statement looks complicated when you first examine it, but it is flexible, versatile, and easy enough to use after you become familiar with it.

```
for (init; condition; increment)
    statement
```

The placeholders *init*, *condition*, and *increment* are all expressions. The action is first to evaluate *init* just one time, and then to set up a loop resembling a **while** loop: The *condition* is evaluated and, if true (nonzero), *statement* is then executed. In addition, *increment* is evaluated after each execution of *statement*.

Functionally, this is nearly identical to this construct:

```
init;
while (condition) {
     statement
     increment;
}
```

The only difference between this construct and **for** is that if a **continue** statement occurs within the body of a **for** loop, it evaluates *increment* before advancing the loop and retesting *condition*; but with a **while** loop, **continue** would cause *increment* to be skipped.

As with the **if** and **while** statements, it's common to use a compound statement—utilizing curly braces—in the body of a **for** loop. The following code prints the numbers from 1 to 5:

```
for (int i = 1; i <= 5; ++i) {
     cout << i << " ";
}
```

The *init* expression ("int i = 1") may declare one or more variables; in that case, the scope of the variable is local to the **for** loop. So in the following example, the inner loop variable, i, does not alter the value of i outside the loop:

```
int i = 100;
for (int i = 1; i <= 10; ++i) {
     cout << i << " ";
}
cout << endl;
cout << "The value of i is still " << i;
```

This example prints the numbers from 1 to 10 and then prints out a message saying the value of i is still 100. That's because the inner copy of i is local to the **for** loop, while the outer copy of i is unaffected by what happens inside the loop.

The *init* and *increment* expressions within a **for** loop are common places to use the join operator (,) to perform multiple actions. For example, the following code fragment prints the sequence 1, -1, 2, -2, 3, -3, 4, -4, 5, -5:

```
for (int i = 1, j = -1; i <= 5; ++i, --j) {
     cout << i << " ";
     cout << j << " ";
}
```

The following code fragment demonstrates a nested **for** loop—that is, a loop placed inside another. This code fragment prints out all the prime numbers between 2 and 100. The outer loop tests each number in turn for being a prime. The inner loop performs the actual test, by seeing if any number from 2 to the square root of the test number divides evenly into that test number.

When a number is found to be prime, it is output to the console followed by a tab (\t). Note that a program must include <cmath> to support the **sqrt** function.

```
#include <iostream>
#include <cmath>
using std::cout;

int main() {
     for(int i = 2; i <= 100; ++i) {
          bool is_prime = true;
          double x = sqrt(static_cast<double>(i));
```

```
            for (int j = 2; j <= x; ++j) {
                if (i % j == 0) {    // Number is not prime.
                    is_prime = false;
                    break;
                }
            } // End inner loop.
            if (is_prime) {
                cout << i << "\t";
            }
        } // End outer loop.
        cin.ignore();   // Wait for user to press ENTER.
        return 0;
}
```

4.7 Range-based for Statements (C++11)

This section presents a variation on the standard **for** statement; it is supported by C++11 compilers. This version of **for** can be used with a container such as an array or a Standard Template Library (STL) container. The great advantage of this syntax is that it frees you from worrying about boundary conditions. The compiler itself determines starting and ending conditions for any given container; consequently, out-of-range errors cannot happen. That eliminates an important source of errors.

I apologize in advance for having to make some forward references: Arrays are introduced in Chapter 6, "Pointers, Arrays, and References," but I assume some basic familiarity with arrays here. If you need to, consult Chapter 6 before reading the rest of this section.

The range-based **for** statement actually has two versions: one that uses a reference variable and one that does not. In the version that doesn't use a reference variable, you can access each element of a group but not change its value.

For each element in the *container*, *statement* is executed. If *variable* appears in the statement, it represents the value of the current element being accessed.

for (*type variable***:** *container***)** *statement*

In the reference-variable version—which uses an ampersand (&) to declare the loop variable as a reference type—changes to *variable* cause permanent changes to the elements themselves.

for (*type* **&***variable***:** *container***)** *statement*

The following example uses the first version: variable accessed by value. This code fragment prints out all the values of the array my_array:

```
int my_array[10] = {1, 2, 3, 4, 5, 6, 7, 8, 9, 10};

for (int i: my_array) {
     cout << i << " ";
}
```

The enclosed statement is executed once for each member of my_array. These iterations are performed in sequential order, starting with the first element and ending with the last, with i representing each element.

In the previous example, the variable i is declared by value (without an ampersand); therefore, any changes to i have no effect on the elements. In this next example, the code fails to initialize members of the array to 0, because changes to i do not affect the array:

```
for (int i: my_array) {
     i = 0;                  // THIS FAILS!
}
```

But this next version declares i to be a reference variable by using the ampersand (&). Because of the ampersand, this example succeeds in setting each element in my_array to 0:

```
for (int &i: my_array) {
     i = 0;                  // This works. Set elements to 0.
}
```

This construct, called "range-based for," can be used with the following kinds of containers: arrays, STL container classes (such as **vector**, **deque**, **list**, **map**, and so on), and any class that declares **begin()** and **end()** methods returning an iterator. See Chapter 15, "Introduction to STL (vector, deque)," for more information on iterators and containers.

The type of the *variable* must match the base type of the *container*. You can optionally use the **auto** keyword as the *type*, in which case the type of the *variable* automatically is given the base type of the *container*.

```
for (auto &i: my_array) {
     i = 0;
}
```

4.8 switch Statements

The **switch** statement provides a variation on **if-else** logic that is easier to read. It has the following syntax:

```
switch (value) { statements }
```

The action is to evaluate *value* and then jump to a statement within the block that has a matching case label. For example, if the value is 5, control switches to a statement with this label, if such a label exists:

```
case 5:
```

For example, suppose you want to print a message that depends on the value of err, an integer. One way to do this is to use an **if-else** statement:

```
if (err == 1) {
     cout << "Houston, we have a problem." << endl;
} else if (err == 2) {
     cout << "We are out of fuel." << endl;
} else if (err == 3) {
     cout << "Our computer broke down." << endl;
     cout << "We don't know what to do." << endl;
} else {
     cout << "The computer has taken over and is ";
     cout << "telling US what to do!" << endl;
}
```

The **switch-case** version has the virtues of being more readable and evaluating the switch test value (err, in this case) only once:

```
switch (err) {
case 1: cout << "Houston, we have a problem." << endl;
        break;
case 2: cout << "We are out of fuel." << endl;
        break;
case 3: cout << "Our computer broke down." << endl;
        cout << "We don't know what to do." << endl;
        break;
default:  cout << "The computer has taken over and is ";
          cout << "telling US what to do!" << endl;
}
```

The variable err is evaluated. The program then jumps to case 1, 2, or 3, depending on the value of err; if err has none of those values, the program jumps to the statement labeled **default**. If there is no **default** statement and no matching case, control passes to the end of the **switch** block.

Each case is terminated with a **break** statement. The effect of **break** is to exit the **switch** block, transferring control to the first statement after the end of the closing brace (}). This use of **break** is usually necessary because each instance of **case** is a label (and therefore the target of a jump), not the beginning of a separate block; consequently, control falls through to the next statement unless you use **break**. Omit it only if you want control to fall through to the next case.

Label syntax is recursive; you can label a statement that already has a label. The effect is to give the same statement multiple labels.

```
switch (c) {
     case 'a':
     case 'e':
     case 'i':
     case 'o':
     case 'u':
          cout << "Character is a vowel." << endl;
          break;
     default:
          cout << "Character is a consonant." << endl;
}
```

The **case** keyword does nothing but label a statement so that it can be the target of a jump; the action of **switch** is to jump to one of those labeled statements. Incidentally, C++ syntax rules imply that case labels do not have to appear on the same physical line, although placing them together that way makes the source code less readable (although compact) in my opinion.

```
     case 'a': case 'e': case 'i': case 'o': case 'u':
          cout << "Character is a vowel." << endl;
          break;
```

4.9 Jump Statements (break, continue, goto)

C++ provides several statements that perform direct transfer of control.

The **break** statement terminates the nearest enclosing **for**, **while**, or **switch** statement. The effect is to exit the control structure, transferring control just past the end of the current loop or switch block.

```
break;
```

In the case of **for** and **while** loops, **break** is useful when you want to terminate execution from the middle of the loop. For example, the following loop continues to perform an operation until the user enters a value of 0.

```
while (true) {
     cout << "Enter number (or 0 to terminate): ";
     cin >> n;
     if (n == 0)
          break;
     // Do some action based on value of n.
}
```

There's a flaw in this example, however: If the user enters a nondigit, the read fails and n continues to have its old value. A safer version of this code uses the following test:

```
     if (!cin || n == 0) {   // If read invalid OR is 0...
          break;
     }
```

The first exercise for Section 4.11, "Sample App: Guess-the-Number Game," discusses this test in more detail.

Like **break**, the **continue** statement is useful in a **for** or **while** statement. The action of **continue** is to advance to the next iteration of the loop.

```
continue;
```

In the following example, **continue** is used to go back to the top of the loop and reprompt the user rather than performing the bottom half of loop.

```
while (more_to_do) {
     cout << "Enter non-negative number: ";
     cin >> n;
     if (n < 0) }
          cout << "Re-enter." << endl;
          continue;
     }
     // Do some action based on value of n.
}
```

The action of **continue** within a **for** statement is different from its action within a **while** loop in one respect. In a **for** loop, execution advances to the next iteration of the loop—returning to the top—but first it causes execution of the *increment* expression.

Finally, C++ provides a **goto** statement to transfer execution to a labeled statement within the same function. As C++ is a structured language, the use of **goto** statements is intended to be infrequent. One of the few legitimate reasons for using a **goto** is when you need to jump out of a series of nested loops and a **break** statement would be inadequate.

A **goto** statement must always have a target label:

```
goto label;
```

The label, in turn, must be applied to a statement in the current function, or the **goto** is invalid. For example:

```
top_of_function:
    i = 0;
    // Do some stuff.

    goto top_of_function;
```

In this case, the name "top_of_function" labels the statement "i = 0;". When the **goto** is executed, it breaks out of enclosing loops, if any, and transfers control all the way back to top_of_function.

Programs that feature many **goto** statements are called "spaghetti code," which (no offense to Italian restaurants) is not intended as a compliment. The term harkens back to days when a computer was programmed by a set of cables or wires linking different locations on a switchboard. Computer languages soon took over, but some of the earliest programs—especially those written in machine code, primitive Fortran, or BASICA—often featured hundreds of jumps, or branches, back and forth through a program. Trying to read these programs was like looking at the tangled wires on a switchboard… or the tangled noodles on a plate of spaghetti.

So even if you like Italian food, you should minimize use of **goto** statements. The great majority of the time, you can achieve the desired results with other control structures.

4.10 Exception Handling (try, catch)

Exception handling provides a superior mechanism for dealing with runtime errors and other special events. When you write short C++ programs, exception handling may seem like a great deal of extra work for no obvious reason, and in fact it's difficult to demonstrate the usefulness of exception handling in small examples. If you never write programs longer than 200 or 300 lines, you probably don't need it.

But in the largest programs—particularly commercial software intended to be used by hundreds, thousands, or even millions of people—exception handling becomes not merely useful but necessary. For such programs, it's essential that errors and other exceptions are handled effectively, in a centralized location. That's what exception handling is about.

4.10.1 What Is an Exception?

Most exceptions are runtime errors such as arithmetic overflow; although in general an exception is just an event that happens at runtime and that the program must respond to immediately (*catching* the exception) or fail, terminating the program rudely and without warning.

You can optionally declare your own types of exceptions and generate them programmatically. This is called "throwing" an exception.

C++ provides an elegant, centralized mechanism for dealing with exceptions. Using the **try** and **catch** keywords, you can place your error-handling code in a single place, rather than having to propagate error signals up and down a chain of function calls.

C++ defines a series of standard exceptions, as listed in Table 4.1. There is a general exception class called **exception** that has two general subclasses. (See Chapter 7, "Classes and Objects," for more information on classes.)

All of these exceptions are defined when you include <stdexcept>, and they are part of the **std** namespace. (Remember that you can choose to omit the **std::** prefix with the help of a **using** statement.)

Classes in this second group, shown in Table 4.2, are all derived from **logic_error**. Admittedly, most of these look fairly obscure—until they happen.

Classes in the third group, shown in Table 4.3, are all derived from **runtime_error**.

Surprisingly, an attempt to divide an integer by zero does not throw an exception, although this situation does cause immediate program failure. Consequently, if your program does a lot of division by a number you aren't sure of in advance (such as in a Calculator program), you need to check for division by zero and handle the problem yourself—for example, by throwing an exception. Be careful when dividing.

TABLE 4.1 Basic Exception Classes Defined in the C++ Library

Exception	Description
std::exception	The base class for all C++ exceptions. You can call the **what()** method to retrieve a C-string describing the exception; that method is inherited by all subclasses.
std::logic_error	Derived from **exception**. Most of these are errors that library functions or operator functions may throw but are not caught by the compiler itself.
std::runtime_error	Derived from **exception**. This class includes common runtime errors.

TABLE 4.2 Logic-Error Exceptions

Exception	Description
std::bad_cast	Reports an invalid use of a **dynamic_cast** expression. (See Chapter 2 for more information on **dynamic_cast**.)
std::bad_typeid	Reports the use of the **typeid** operator on an object that turns out to have a **void** type (such as dereferencing a pointer with base type **void**).
std::domain_error	Reports violation of a precondition assumed by a function or other operation.
std::invalid_argument	A function may throw this exception to indicate an invalid argument. Normally, the compiler catches errors of this kind, but in special cases, they may not be caught until runtime.
std::length_error	Reports an attempt to create an object larger than the largest physical size supported for the type in question (such as attempting to create a larger array than the system will support).
std::out_of_range	Reports an attempt to use an argument that is outside the allowable range for that argument.

TABLE 4.3 Runtime-Error Exceptions

Exception	Description
std::bad_alloc	Reports failure to allocate requested memory—such as an attempt to use the **new** operator that requests a larger memory block than available.
std::overflow_error	Reports arithmetic overflow of a floating-point number.
std::range_error	Reports a result that falls outside of its allowable range. Some classes in the STL (such as **vector** and **deque**) throw this exception when the **at** member function is used with an out-of-range value.
std::underflow_error	Reports an arithmetic result with floating-point numbers that is too tiny to be stored in the supported range of the type.

4.10.2 try-catch Blocks: General Syntax

C++ uses **try-catch** blocks (with an optional **finally** clause) to handle exceptions. The syntax is a little complex, so I use brackets to indicate optional items. Ellipses (...) indicate that any number of **catch** blocks can be used.

```
try {
     statements
}
```

```
[ catch (exception_class object) { statements } ] ...
[ finally {statements }]
```

The action is to execute the statements following **try** unconditionally—bearing in mind, of course, that these statements can be interrupted at any time by an exception; but that's true for any block of statements.

If any exception is thrown during the execution of statements in the **try** block, the program attempts to match the exception against each of the **catch** blocks. (Note that exceptions having a derived class are matched as well, as explained in the next section.) The first **catch** block with a matching type is said to have "caught" the exception, and it gains control.

Exceptions can be caught no matter how deep they occur in the call stack. Assume one of the statements in the **try** block calls a function, which calls a function calling a function, and so on. If the innermost function throws an exception, that exception is propagated all the way up to the **catch** blocks—unless some intermediate **catch** block in the function hierarchy catches it first.

The words "try" and "catch" are apt. Program control is normally sequential or tightly controlled by a loop. But when an exception is thrown *anywhere* in the program, control is up for grabs until some block of code catches it and takes control. An exception may be caught in the function where it occurs or in a function above it on the call stack. The nearest applicable handler (that is, **catch** block) on the call stack is the one that catches the exception.

If no **catch** block matches the exception, the result is program failure.

The statements following the **finally** block are executed unconditionally, after the **try** block executes successfully or an exception is handled. The statements in a **finally** block are typically used to close any open resources.

4.10.3 catch Blocks and Exception Objects

Each **catch** block has the following syntax, in which the *object* is optional and may be omitted if you choose. The *statements* are zero or more statements.

```
catch (exception_class object)
    { statements }
```

At runtime, an exception matches *exception_class* if either (1) it has the same type or (2) the exception's type is an instance of a class derived from *exception_class*. In either case, the exception is caught and *statements* are executed.

Therefore, a **catch** block specifying the standard **exception** class catches all standard C++ exceptions (listed in the previous section). If *exception_class* is **runtime_error**, it catches exceptions of type **runtime_error** and any class derived from it.

A simple use of this syntax uses the **exception** class to catch all standard C++ exceptions. You can call the **what()** method to print out a description.

```
#include <stdexcept>
#include <iostream>
using namespace std;

try {
     // Do some stuff.
} catch (exception e) {
     cout << "Exception:  " << e.what() << endl;
}
```

As with all exception handling, the benefit in this example is that it enables the program to respond in a reasonable way and then continue (or not) as appropriate. In any case, control of what to do is handed to the programmer.

4.10.4 Throwing an Exception

The standard C++ exceptions listed in Section 4.10.1, "What Is an Exception?" do not cover every possible kind of runtime error you might want to deal with, such as divide-by-zero errors. For this reason, you may want to programmatically throw exceptions yourself. The syntax of the **throw** statement is:

```
throw exception_object;
```

There is one aspect of this syntax you may find counterintuitive: The type, rather than the value of the exception object, determines which block catches it.

The rest of this section presumes some understanding of classes and objects. You may want to consult Chapter 7 first, unless you already understand this subject.

To throw your own types of exceptions, you should first declare these types as classes. It is a good idea to derive them from **exception** or from **runtime_error**. For example:

```
#include <stdexcept>
#include <iostream>
#include <string>
using namespace std;

// Declare class DivError, with one constructor
class DivError : public runtime_error {
```

```
public:
     DivError(const string& msg) : runtime_error (msg) {}
};

// Later in the code...
if (divisor == 0)
     throw DivError("Variable divisor is zero.");
```

The last line in this example calls the DivError constructor to create a DivError object on the fly and then throw it as an exception. It will then be caught by a **catch** block, if any, at the same level or above it in the function-call hierarchy, looking for a DivError Exception.

```
catch (DivError e) {
      cout << e.what() << endl;
}
```

4.11 Sample App: Guess-the-Number Game

A classic child's game goes as follows: One person thinks of a number between 1 and 50 (or it could be between 1 and 20, or any agreed-upon range). The other player makes a guess and is told whether it is correct, too high, or too low. The process repeats until this player gets it right. Assuming the feedback given is correct—which it will be if everyone's telling the truth—the player should be able to deduce the answer in far fewer than 50 or even 25 tries.

The following program invites the user to play this game. First, the computer has to think of a secret number—at random. Randomness in a computer program is a tricky concept, which Chapter 19, "C++11 Randomization Library," discusses at length. But for the time being, we can make use of the **rand** function from the C standard library. Effective use of this function requires that you include the <cstdlib> and <ctime> headers and then include the following statement at the beginning of **main**:

```
srand(time(NULL));
```

This statement sets the random seed by using the system time. You can then use the **rand** function to get a random number in the **unsigned int** range. Applying the modulus operator (%) produces a random number from 0 to N-1:

```
int random_n = rand() % n;
```

There are some technical problems with this simple formulation as discussed in Chapter 19, but for this game, with its relatively low values of n, this approach to randomization is acceptable.

The rest of the program makes use of the **while**, **if**, and **break** control structures to (1) play the game until the user wants to quit, and (2) query the user during each game until he or she gets the right answer. If the user enters 0 at any time, the program quits.

```
#include <iostream>
#include <cstdlib>
#include <ctime>
using std::cin;
using std::cout;
using std::endl;

int main() {
      srand(time(NULL));        // Set random seed.
      bool play_more = true;
      int target = 0;
      int guess = 0;

      while (play_more) {       // While play_more is true...
            int target = 1 + rand() % 50;  // New target.
            while (true) {
                cout << "Guess the number, or 0 to quit: ";
                cin >> guess;
                if (guess == 0) {           // Time to quit.
                    play_more = false;
                    break;
                } else if (guess == target) {
                    cout << "CORRECT!!! Number is ";
                    cout << target << "! " << endl;
                    cout << "Let's play again!" << endl;
                    break;
                } else if (guess < target) {
                    cout << "Too low! Try again!" << endl;
                } else {
                    cout << "Too high! Try again!" << endl;
                }
            }  // End of inner while loop.
      }  // End of outer while loop.
      return 0;
}
```

This game can be amusing for a while—you see yourself gradually spiral into the answer, hunting down the secret number like a detective—until the correct strategy becomes crystal clear and the game becomes routine. But it's a good demo program; it only takes about a single page of C++ source code to create a playable game.

This program demonstrates control structures by featuring **if-else** blocks nested inside a **while** statement nested inside another **while** statement. The purpose of the outer loop is to keep playing the game until the user is tired of it. The purpose of the inner loop is to keep asking for guesses until the right guess is input.

The C++ code uses a convenient programming trick. When the user enters 0, the program uses **break** to exit the inner loop. But before it does, it sets the Boolean variable play_more to **false**; then, when control passes to the top of the outer loop, the test condition fails and that loop is terminated as well. The effect is to break out of both loops.

Another solution would have been to immediately exit by using the **return** statement, but that approach would have been less flexible.

Exercises

1. If the user fails to enter digits when prompted and instead enters nondigit text, the input statement "cin >> guess" fails. In that case, the end user may be left hanging with no way to even exit. Remedy this situation by having non-numeric text indicate a desire to exit. Hint: To test for input failure, you can test the stream operator (**cin**) itself, by making it part of the condition. If an input operation failed, **cin** evaluates to **false**. (Note: The error flags of **cin** can be cleared by calling **cin.clear()**.)
2. Revise the program so that when it begins, it prompts the user for any positive value of N and then uses 1 to N as the range rather than 1 to 50.
3. During any given game, track how many guesses were made and then print a message when the user finally gets the answer, such as, "It only took you *n* guesses," where *n* is the number of times the user guessed.
4. If you play the game even once or twice, the correct strategy should dawn on you. Given the range 1 to 50, what is the maximum number of guesses that should be required given a perfect strategy?
5. As an advanced challenge for math experts: Calculate the maximum number of guesses needed for *any* range 1 to N. Write a program that performs this calculation. Hint: Use the *log* function described in Chapter 12, "Math, Time, and Other Library Functions." You may find the following formula helpful: $\log_2(n) = \log(n)/\log(2)$.

4.12 Sample App: Computer Guesses the Number

If you've played the game featured in the preceding section, it should dawn on you pretty quickly (maybe before you've even played it) what the best strategy is. This strategy is at the heart of computer algorithms used later in the book. The implementations of **map** templates, discussed in Chapter 17, "STL Associated Containers," almost always use binary-tree search algorithms. Although Guess-the-Number involves no trees, thinking about this game should give you a good idea what binary searches are all about.

But how easy is it to make the computer adopt this same strategy and become the player of the game? I considered making this challenge an exercise for the last section but wanted the fun of presenting this program myself. It's a good demonstration of basic heuristics—computer strategy.

Each time the computer makes a guess, the end user must respond (honestly, it is hoped), with one of three answers, which can be offered in a simple menu:

```
Enter one of the three responses:
1=Correct!  2=Too low!  3=Too high!
```

The user must enter 1, 2, or 3 after each guess. The computer program, acting on this information, uses this feedback to logically infer what the secret number is.

Sound like magic? The strategy is simple, really.

1. At the beginning, set lower_bound to 1 and upper_bound to 50.
2. Average the two bounds together, rounding down to produce a number, n. Tell the user that this is the guess and get feedback.
3. If the guess is too low, set lower_bound to n + 1.
4. If the guess is too high, set upper_bound to n - 1.
5. If the guess is correct, exit; otherwise, loop back to step 2.

Here is the program that implements this simple, elegant strategy. You can run the program and now act as the other player: the one who thinks of the number and gives responses (too high, too low, or correct) to each computer guess. There's a caveat, though: If you give the program the wrong information, it will have severe problems.

```
#include <iostream>
#include <string>
using std::cout;
using std::cin;
using std::endl;

int main() {
     int lower_bound, upper_bound;   // Used in guessing.
     int n = 1;                      // This is the guess.
     int cmd = 1;                    // Menu command.
top_of_prog:
     lower_bound = 1;
```

```
        upper_bound = 50;
        cout << "Think of a number from 1 to 50." << endl;
        cout << "Then press ENTER.";
        cin.ignore();   // Wait for user to press ENTER.
        bool guess_again = true;
        do {
           n=static_cast<int>((lower_bound+upper_bound)/2.0);
           cout << "I guess " << n << "." << endl;
           cout << "Respond: 1=Correct!  2=Guess was too ";
           cout << "low!  3==Guess was too high! ENTER => ";
           cin >> cmd;
           if (cmd == 1) {
                cout << "Yay! I got it right!" << endl;
                guess_again = false;
           } else if (cmd == 3) {
                upper_bound = n - 1;
           } else {
                lower_bound = n + 1;
           }
        } while (guess_again);
        cout << "Play again? 1=Yes  2=No. ENTER: ";
        cin >> cmd;
        if (cmd == 1) goto top_of_prog;
        return 0;
}
```

Elegant though it is, there are several potential problems with this program. These are addressed in the exercises that follow.

Exercises

1. The most obvious flaw is that the program uses the dreaded **goto** statement, which is employed here to provide a quick-and-dirty way of implementing a "Play again?" loop. Revise the program to do the same thing but without **goto**.
2. Another problem is input handling. You should notice by now that using the stream-input operator, >>, makes for unreliable programs on the whole, although it is convenient in simple situations. If the user inputs a nondigit when the program attempts to read a number, the read fails and no input can be read again until the stream is cleared with the function call **cin.clear()**. Remember, also, that after an input operation fails, **cin** itself evaluates to **false** when tested in a condition. Given all of this, revise the program to do a better job of recovering from bad input.
3. Rewrite the series of **if-else** statements as a **switch** block. (Although this doesn't improve the performance of the program, it is a good exercise in using **switch-case** syntax.)

4. Finally, a major defect is that the program "goes off the rails" or degenerates if the user gives an incorrect answer as to whether the guess is too high or too low. Rewrite the program so that it detects when—as a result of a logically impossible situation—some untrue answer had to have been given by the user. When this problem is detected, the program should print, "You gave incorrect information at some point" and declare itself the winner.

CHAPTER 5

Functions

One of the key elements of most any programming language is that of *function*—which other languages sometimes refer to as "subroutine," "procedure," or "subprogram." It's a semiautonomous part of the program you can transfer control to and come back from.

Some languages have a different syntax for subroutines that return values as opposed to those that don't. But C++ considers them all functions whether they return a value or not.

```
read_in_file("readme.txt");    // Call read_in_file funct.
```

Traditionally, in C++ you must declare a function and give it a name before calling it. Most of this chapter describes that traditional approach.

The new C++11 specification also supports a new syntax called *lambda,* or anonymous, functions—functions with no name. The use of these is specialized, but they work well with specific parts of the Standard Template Library (STL). I explore this new feature near the end of the chapter.

5.1 Overview of Traditional (Named) Functions

Generally speaking, there are three steps in using a named function:

1. Prototype the function. This step is optional but usually a good idea.
2. Define the function. This tells what the function *does.*
3. Call the function. This can be repeated any number of times.

5.1.1 Function Prototypes versus Definitions

With the exception of **main**, you must declare a function before using it. There are two kinds of function declaration:

- A function prototype, which gives type information for a function but does not define it
- A function definition, which provides type information and also tells what the function does

Every definition is a declaration, but not all declarations are definitions.

One strategy (and I occasionally use it in this book purely for expediency) is to define a function and then call it without first prototyping it. This works fine as long as you can place the function definitions in the proper order—the reverse order of being called. Using this approach, you must define a function before calling it. For example:

```
void my_func() {
     cout << "This is my_func()";
}
int main() {
     my_func();      // Call my_func().
     return 0;
}
```

But what if two functions call each other? This is not necessarily wrong, and there are certain kinds of applications that rely on this technique.

```
int a_func(int n) {
     cout << "I'm in function a." << endl;
     if (n > 0)
          return b_func(--n);    // Call b_func()
     return n;
}
int b_func(int n) {
     cout << "I'm in function b." << endl;
     return a_func(--n);         // Call a_func()
}
```

But now, regardless of the order in which you place these definitions, there's a forward-reference problem: There's no way to avoid calling a function that hasn't been defined yet, because a_func and b_func call each other. As source code grows in complexity, it becomes difficult to anticipate what function might call what other function, and mutual self-references (such as this one) become more likely. It then becomes difficult to place all the definitions in the right order.

Because of these problems, the best policy for all but the simplest programs is to declare all your functions up front without defining them—prototyping the functions—except for **main**, which does not need to be declared. You can then place the definitions in any order that's convenient. For example:

```
// Function prototypes
int a_func(int n);
int b_func(int n);

// Now, a_func(), b_func(), and main() may be defined
//   in any order.
```

There are other situations in which prototypes are necessary. In a project with multiple modules linked together, a function must be defined in one and only one source file, but it must be declared in every module that calls it. In such projects, all the function prototypes are usually placed in a header file, which is then included in every module in the project:

```
#include "my_proj.h"  // my_proj.h contains all prototypes.
```

5.1.2 Prototyping a Function (Simplified Syntax)

Here is the simple function prototype syntax. (Section 5.3, "Complete Function Declaration Syntax," presents the more complete syntax.) Remember that a function prototype gives type information, describing a function's argument types and return type, but a prototype does not determine what the function *does.*

return_type name(*args*);

A *return_type* is necessary, but functions that do not return a value have a **void** return type. The *name* is a unique symbolic name, although overloading is permitted with certain restrictions. (See Section 5.4, "Function Overloading.")

The *args* consists of a list of arguments separated by commas if there is more than one. Each argument has to be declared separately with its own type. The basic syntax is:

type variable_name

The argument list may be empty, but an empty list does not, as in C, indicate an indeterminate argument list; instead, it indicates that the function takes no arguments at all.

Here is an example of a simple declaration (a prototype) for a function named imax. It takes two integer arguments and returns an integer.

```
int imax(int a, int b);
```

Note that the two integer arguments, a and b, cannot be declared together as they could be in a variable declaration. Each argument must be declared separately.

```
int a, b;  // This is valid in variable declarations ONLY.
```

Although it's good programming practice to include argument names (in part because you can copy and paste a prototype into the start of a definition), argument names are not strictly required. In a prototype, variable names may be omitted, listing only the types:

```
int imax(int, int);
```

5.1.3 Defining a Function

A function definition tells what a function does. It consists of a combination of local-variable declarations and/or executable statements. (Technically, you can have zero statements; that would be useful only in writing a "stub"—a function definition you intend to fill in later.)

All function definitions are also declarations; the difference is that a definition includes the body of the function—telling what it does—whereas a prototype does not include these statements.

```
return_type  name(args) {
     statements
}
```

This syntax is the same as for prototype declarations, except that it is not terminated by a semicolon (;). Instead, it is followed by curly braces enclosing zero or more *statements*.

Here is a simple function definition:

```
int imax(int a, int b) {
     if (a >= b) {
          return a;
     } else {
          return b;
     }
}
```

This function takes two arguments and returns the value of the largest one.

The **return** statement is used here to return a value and exit. Unless a function has **void** return type, it should always return some value. If the function does have **void** return type, it cannot return a value; but in that case, the **return** statement can still be used to exit early.

```
return;
```

By default, arguments in C++ are passed by value, meaning that a function gets its own copy of the data passed during the function call; the function can do anything to that data without affecting the rest of the program. Arrays (as explained in Chapter 6, "Pointers, Arrays, and References") are the exception.

To pass arguments by reference—in which case the function can make permanent changes to the variables passed during the call—you can use the & operator to declare an argument as a reference type, as described in Chapter 6. Alternatively, you can also pass a pointer to the value.

Variables declared within a function are local. For example, the following function declares a local variable, fahr, which has no effect on the value of fahr outside of this function:

```
double centigrade_to_fahrenheit(double cent) {
     double fahr = 0.0;

     fahr = cent * 1.8 + 32.0;
     return fahr;
}
```

This example is not the most efficient way to write this function, but it does illustrate the use of multiple statements and a local variable, fahr. A more compact version is:

```
double centigrade_to_fahrenheit(double cent) {
     double fahr = cent * 1.8 + 32.0;
     return fahr;
}
```

You could write an even more compact version.

```
double centigrade_to_fahrenheit(double cent) {
     return cent * 1.8 + 32.0;
}
```

5.1.4 Calling a Function

One of the chief benefits of writing a function is that the rest of the program can execute it—or rather, call it—any number of times. You can pass different values to the arguments each time.

You call a function by using the name in an expression, followed by parentheses. The parentheses enclose argument values, if any, to be passed. In C++, the parentheses must be used in a function call whether the argument list is empty or not.

```
init_program_files();
```

Note that the compiler will never confuse a function call with a function declaration because the former is not preceded by a type specifier.

Unless a function is declared with **void** return type, it must return a value. During a function call, that value is passed back to the caller and can be used as part of an enclosing expression. For example:

```
int a1 = 1, a2 = 2;
int b1 = 10, b2 = 20;
int c = 0;

c = imax(a1, a2) + imax(b1, b2);
```

The function call imax(a1, a2) returns the value 2, and the function call imax(b1, b2) returns the value 20. The result is that the statement assigns the value 22 to c.

Here's how the mechanics of the function calls work: The call imax(a1, a2) calls the imax function, passing the values of a1 and a2 to the arguments declared in imax. These arguments are equal to 1 and 2. This function returns the larger of these two values: in this case, 2.

The call imax(b1, b2) calls the imax function, passing the values b1 and b2 to the two arguments declared in imax. It returns the larger of these two values: in this case, 20.

5.2 Local and Global Variables

Within a function definition, you can declare one or more variables local to the function. In C++, you can declare variables local to any block, not just a function.

A local variable is visible only within a particular scope. The benefit is that each function (or block) can have its own copy of the variable, preventing interference with other functions.

For example, each function can have its own variable named i. When writing a function, this frees you from worrying about variable names used by other functions. In the following code, both funct1 and main have a variable named i. There is also a global variable with this name.

```
#include <iostream>
using std::cout;
using std::endl;
int i = 100;

int funct1(int n) {
     int i = n * 2;
```

```
        cout << "In funct1, i is " << i << endl;
        return i;
}

int main() {
        int i = 4;
        cout << "In main, i is " << i << endl;
        int j = funct1(i);
        cout << "In main, i is still " << i << endl;
}
```

This program prints out the following:

```
In main, i is 4
In funct1, i is 8
In main, i is still 4
```

The important point here is that both functions have their own copy of i, so changes to i in funct1() have no effect on changes to i within main(), and vice versa.

If this were *not* the case, name conflicts would introduce a major source of bugs into programs. Suppose two functions both had a variable named x... in that case, you could never have one function call another without potentially causing unintended side effects. That was the case in primitive versions of BASICA. (No offense to Bill Gates; he was working with less than 64K.)

The general rules for resolving name conflicts are as follows, in the order shown.

1. For a given data symbol (variable name) the compiler binds the symbol to a local variable if available—specifically, the matching name in the nearest enclosing level of scope.
2. In the case of class member functions (see Chapter 7, "Classes and Objects," for more information on classes), if there are no local variables matching the symbol, the compiler binds the symbol to a data member if available.
3. Finally, if no local or class variables match the name of the symbol, the compiler binds it to a matching global variable if available.

Local variables usually have automatic storage class, although the two concepts are not the same:

- *Scope* is a matter of visibility: Over what part of a program is a variable accessible?
- *Storage class* is a matter of how and where a variable is allocated in memory.

By default, local variables have automatic storage class, meaning that memory for the variable is allocated as the function is called. The variable is automatically removed from memory when the function terminates.

But if you choose, you can give a local variable static storage class—so that the variable persists throughout the life of the program—by using the **static** keyword:

```
int funct1(int n) {
     static int i = 2;   // Note: initialized only once!!
     n += i;
     return i;
}
```

A local variable with static storage class maintains its value in between calls to the function. Static locals observe another important rule: A static local is only initialized once, at the beginning of the program, no matter how many times the function is called.

Most local variables have automatic storage class and so are destroyed when they go out of scope. "Destroying" in this context means that the memory occupied by the variable is released and freed up for other uses.

5.3 Complete Function Declaration Syntax

Here is the more complete syntax for a function declaration. (It is followed by a semicolon, in the case of a prototype, or curly braces, in the case of a function definition.) The brackets in this case are not intended literally but indicate optional items.

[*modifers*] *return_type* *name*(*args*) [**override**] [**const**] [**final**]

If you include modifiers and there are more than one, they are separated by spaces, not commas. For example, the following code declares a function as both **static** and **inline**:

```
static inline int get_random_num();
```

Each of the arguments in *args*, the argument list, has this (more complete) syntax, in which brackets are not intended literally but indicate optional items:

type [*arg_name*] [=*init_value*]

The *arg_name* may be modified by the *, &, (), and [] operators as described in Chapter 6. (The function name may also be modified by these operators.) Optionally, *arg_name* may be omitted, in which case the *, &, (), and [] operators just follow the type name.

With function definitions, *arg_name* should not be omitted from an argument declaration, because then the statements within that definition would have no way to refer to the argument.

The *init_value* is used for default argument values as explained in Section 5.5, "Arguments with Default Values."

The following list describes each function modifier. Except for **const**, **final**, and **override**, these are placed in front of the function declaration when used.

- **`const`**

  Modifies member functions. The function cannot modify any of the class data members and it cannot call other member functions of the class, except those that are also declared **const**. Use of this keyword enables you to write member functions that are, in effect, "read-only" functions.

- **`constexpr`**

  C++11 specific. The compiler treats return values from the function as compile-time constants. The function must have exactly one **return** statement and no other executable statements. (It may, however, have any number of **using** and **typedef** statements.) See Section 5.8, "constexpr Functions (C++11)," for more information and examples.

- **`explicit`**

  Modifies member functions only (specifically, constructors, a concept explained in Chapter 7). When this keyword is applied, the constructor function is not used to supply an implicit conversion function.

- **`final`**

  C++11 specific. Modifies member functions only. This keyword, applied to a virtual function, prevents the function from being overridden by derived classes. (This keyword is normally applied to a virtual function within a derived class that may have its own derived classes; the point of **final** is to prevent any further overriding of the function.)

- **`inline`**

  Modifies any function. This keyword is an advisory to the compiler saying that it should implement the function as an inline function. The most up-to-date, modern compilers are optimizing compilers that make their own decisions as to what to inline, so this keyword—once considered important—is now just a suggestion to the compiler.

  When a function is inlined, it is not implemented as a call to a separate function—although it still looks like a normal function in the source code—but instead, the body of the function is expanded directly into the body of the calling function. It's usually efficient to inline short functions, removing function-call overhead. When a function is inlined, the compiler guarantees that the code produces exactly the same effects as it did before, just with a faster execution speed. The implementation of an inline function is seamless as far as the source code is concerned.

Recursive functions—functions that call themselves—cannot be inlined.

- **`override`**

  C++11 specific. Modifies member functions only. This keyword specifies that the function overrides a function declared in a base class. If there is no matching function name in a base class, the compiler flags it as an error. Use of this keyword helps catch function names that are misspelled.

- **`static`**

  When applied to global (nonmember) functions, causes the function to be visible within the current source file only. The function name is not given external linkage. By default, C++ function names have external linkage so that every module declaring a function by the same name must be referring to the same function (which must then be defined in one, and only one, module). If there is only one source file in the project, this usage has no effect.

  When applied to member functions, the function becomes a static member of the class so that it cannot access other class members except those that are also declared static. Such functions can be called through the syntax *class_name::function*.

- **`virtual`**

  Modifies member functions. The address of a virtual function is not resolved until runtime. Consequently, when an object's virtual function is accessed, the correct function is called, even if the object is accessed through a pointer with general type. See Chapter 7 for more information on virtual functions.

  Once a function is declared virtual in a base class, it is automatically virtual in all its descendant classes—that is, classes derived directly or indirectly. Member functions intended to be overridden should always be declared virtual.

5.4 Function Overloading

In most programming languages, function names must be unique. This makes sense: You can't have two different functions named "my_function", can you? But C++ lets you define multiple functions with the same name as long as they can be differentiated by their argument lists.

These functions are said to be *overloaded*. At compile time, the compiler checks the types and number of arguments passed to a function. It uses this information, along with the function name, to determine a unique function signature.

For example, consider a function called print_fillers. Suppose you define one version that prints a specified number of spaces, and another version that prints the specified number of characters, in which any character can be specified. Each version has its own declaration:

```
void print_fillers(int n);
void print_fillers(int n, char c);
```

Each overloaded function requires its own definition, as well.

```
void print_fillers(int n) {
     char c = ' ';
     for (int i = 0; i < n; i++)
          cout << c;
}

void print_fillers(int n, char c) {
     for (int i = 0; i < n; i++)
          cout << c;
}
```

These two functions have signatures print_fillers(int) and print_fillers(int, char), respectively. Even though they share the same name, the compiler has no trouble differentiating between these two functions, because each function has different type information.

The following example calls the second version of the function just shown, not the first:

```
print_fillers(10, ',');     // Print ten commas.
```

When overloaded functions are used, the C++ compiler is sometimes able to match a function call with more than one definition. For example, suppose that a program declares the following overloaded functions:

```
void display_number(int n);
void display_number(double x);
```

Either of these functions, by itself, could be matched to the following call, because the compiler promotes integer data to **double** when needed:

```
display_number(5);   // Call display_number() passing 5.
```

However, the compiler will make the best match it can, selecting the overloaded function with the closest match for the largest number of arguments. In this case, it would match the first version, which takes an **int** argument, because that is the better match. The compiler will do the fewest number of conversions it has to.

Each overloaded function can have a different return type. This type is not used to determine which version to call; the compiler must be able to determine which version to call from the argument list alone.

```
int invert_number(int n);
double invert_number(double x);
```

In contrast, the following declarations would be flagged by the compiler as a conflict, because they differ only in their return type and not in their argument lists:

```
int invert_number(int n);
double invert_number(int n);   // ERROR! Overloaded functs
                               //  not unique enough.
```

5.5 Arguments with Default Values

Default argument specifications utilize the following syntax:

```
type  variable_name = value
```

Consider the example of overloaded functions in Section 5.3.

```
void print_fillers(int n) {
     char c = ' ';
     for (int i = 0; i < n; i++)
          cout << c;
}

void print_fillers(int n, char c) {
     for (int i = 0; i < n; i++)
          cout << c;
}
```

In this case, these overloaded functions could be more efficiently written as just one function by using a default argument value.

```
void print_fillers(int n, char c = ' ') {
     for (int i = 0; i < n; i++)
          cout << c;
}
```

With this function definition, n is matched against the first argument in a call. If no second argument is given, a default value of a space (' ') is assumed for the second argument. For example:

```
print_fillers(12, '&');    // Print a dozen ampersands (&)
print_fillers(12);         // Print a dozen spaces.
```

You can specify any number of arguments with default values, but all such arguments must appear at the end of the argument list: That is to say, all arguments that do not have default values must appear before all arguments that do have default values.

If a function has multiple default arguments, and a function call only passes some of the arguments accepted, then the compiler attempts to match them in the order of the argument list. For example, consider a function declared with three default arguments:

```
silly_funct(int a = 0, int b = 10, int c = 20);
```

The following statements show how different function calls would be resolved:

```
silly_funct();              // a = 0, b = 10, c = 20.
silly_funct(100);           // a = 100, b = 10, c = 20.
silly_funct(100, 200);      // a = 100, b = 200, c = 20
```

Function signatures must be unique in terms of their nondefault argument values. You can mix overloaded functions with default argument values, but be sure that the compiler is always able to determine which function to call from the arguments that do not have default values.

5.6 Variable-Length Argument Lists

With C++, you can write functions that take any number of arguments. (An example is the **printf** function from the C standard library.) For example, you could write your own print_int function that prints any number of integers. The syntax for a function declaration taking a variable-length argument list is:

```
return_type  name(args ...);
```

In this case, the ellipses are intended literally. There must be at least one named argument, although you may have more than one. The ellipses follow the last named argument. In the following example, n is the only named argument.

```
void pr_ints(int n ...);
```

When the function is called, the first argument (which is passed as n in this case) can be followed by any number of other arguments. The first argument usually determines the number of arguments that follow it. For example:

```
print_ints(3, 10, 20, 30);
```

The rest of this section describes a series of macro functions that enable processing of the argument list. I then follow this with a complete example. To use these functions, first place the following **#include** directive in the source file:

```
#include <cstdarg>
```

Alternatively, you can also use the following **#include**, supported for backward compatibility:

```
#include <stdarg.h>
```

Descriptions of the argument-processing functions follow.

- **va_list(*list_name*);**

  Declares a list name, which is a unique symbolic name you choose. Basically, you can use any valid name for this list, as long as it isn't a keyword and doesn't conflict with another function or variable name you're using. For example:

  ```
  va_list(arglist);
  ```

- **va_start(*list_name*, *last_arg*);**

  Initializes the argument list. The *list_name* is a symbolic name declared with the **va_list** statement. The *last_arg* is the last named argument in the function's argument list.

  ```
  va_start(arglist, n);
  ```

- **va_arg(*list_name*, *type*)**

  Returns the next argument from the variable argument list; *type* is a type specifier, such as **int**, **double**, or a class name. The effect of the **va_arg** expression is to return the next argument and to advance one position in the argument list. If necessary, the compiler will convert the next argument in the function call to the specified *type*; but a conversion must be available. Reading of the argument list is sequential and goes in a forward direction only.

  This macro function, **va_arg**, is the one that you will likely call repeatedly. The others are usually called only once.

  ```
  int i = va_arg(arglist, int);
  ```

- **va_end(*list_name*)**

  Terminates reading of the argument list. You need to call this macro before returning from the function to make sure that the stack is correctly restored. It's not important to understand the technical reasons for doing this; you just need to do it to make sure your program works correctly.

  ```
  va_end(arglist);
  ```

The following example prints out all its integer arguments, assuming that the first argument, n, specifies the number of arguments that follow it.

```
#include <cstdarg>

void pr_ints(int n ...) {
     va_list(arglist);
```

```
        va_start(arglist, n);
        for (int i = 0; i < n; ++i) {
            cout << va_arg(arglist, int) << endl;
        }
        va_end(arglist);
}
```

The first two steps are to use the **va_list** and the **va_start** macros. These statements initialize reading of the variable-argument list, giving it the name arglist, although you can use any name you choose. Remember that the function must have at least one named argument; in this case that argument is n.

After the variable-argument list is initialized, each call to **va_arg** returns another argument value. In this case, each of those arguments has **int** type. You don't need to limit yourself to integers, but I've assumed an all-integer argument list in this case to keep the example simple.

An example that calls this function is:

```
int i = 400;
int j = 50;
pr_ints(4, 100, 200, i, i + j);
```

This example prints the values 100, 200, 400, 450, each on a separate line.

5.7 Lambda, or Anonymous, Functions (C++11)

One of the most anticipated new features in the C++11 specification is *lambda functions.* Simply put, these are functions without names.

Most of this chapter has been dedicated to extolling the virtues of named functions—how, once a function is defined, you can use its name to call it whenever you choose. What, then, is the benefit of a function with no name?

Most lambda use occurs in connection with STL containers and algorithms—described in Chapters 15 through 18. In general, a lambda may be useful anywhere you need to give a function as an argument but you'd prefer to give a brief, ad hoc function definition rather than a pointer to a definition provided somewhere else in the source file or even another module. A lambda can serve as a quick, convenient function given "on the fly" rather than formally defined. Because a lambda can be defined where it's used, it's easier to see what it does without searching through source code.

In Section 5.7.4, "Using Lambdas with the STL," I'll show some cases where this is useful. Lambdas are rarely if ever required to achieve a certain effect. In some situations, however, they are a definite convenience.

5.7.1 Basic Lambda Syntax

Here's the basic syntax of a lambda function. Note that brackets, [], are intended literally.

```
[closure] (args) {statements }
```

In this syntax, the compiler determines the return type implicitly (from the type of the **return** statement within the definition, if any). Optionally, the **return** type may be specified explicitly:

```
[closure] (args) -> return_type { statements }
```

Within the brackets (again, these are intended literally), the *closure*—which is an optional list of variables—may be empty. In this section, I'll assume closure is empty for the sake of simplicity. Section 5.7.2, "Lambda Closure Syntax," explains the use of *closure*.

The *args* is an argument list, just as in any other function. The *statements* comprise the body of the definition.

Here is an example of a simple lambda function.

```
[] (int a, int b) { return a + b; }
```

This function takes two integer arguments and returns their sum. It looks just like a simple traditional function, except that the brackets, [], appear in place of a function name. Otherwise, the syntax is almost the same except for return type: The return type may be specified explicitly, as just mentioned, but in this case, that return type is implicit. (That type is **int**.)

Here is a slightly more complex lambda—this one taking a single integer argument, n, and printing all the values from 1 to n.

```
[] (int n) {for (int i = 0; i < n; ++i) cout << i << endl;}
```

Remember that in C++, newlines are not significant and are treated just like spaces (with a few exceptions, such as comments). Therefore, you can use spacing that is easier to read, as in:

```
[] (int n) {
          for(int i = 0; i < n; ++i)
                 cout << i << endl;
}
```

The type of this function is **void**, because it returns no value. Again, you can always choose to make the return type explicit if you want. You can also use braces with **for** if you have the room.

```
[] (int n) -> void {
            for(int i = 0; i < n; ++i) {
                  cout << i << endl;
            }
}
```

In the following case, the return type, **double**, is significant, as it causes the compiler to convert the return value (10) to a **double**. Otherwise, it would return 10 as an integer. So here, the **double** type is made explicit.

```
[] () -> double { return 10; }
```

This does the same as:

```
[] (){ return 10.0; }
```

One of the simplest ways to use a lambda function is to store it in a variable and then use that variable as if it were a function name.

If your compiler is C++11 compliant, it supports not only lambda functions but the **auto** keyword as well; **auto** is needed here, because otherwise the declaration of f is complex and nonportable.

```
int i = 1;
int j = 2;
auto f = [] (int a, int b) { return a + b; };
cout << f(i, j) << endl;
```

This example involves a strange bit of syntax. Although the (nearly) ironclad rule in C++ says that a semicolon (;) does not follow the terminating brace of a function definition, in this case it does. A semicolon is required after the terminating brace because the statement is actually a data declaration for the variable f:

```
auto f = [] (int a, int b) {return a + b;};
```

Section 5.7.4 describes more useful ways of employing lambdas.

5.7.2 Lambda Closure Syntax

The syntax introduced in the preceding section included a *closure* placeholder but left it empty in all the examples. Here is that syntax again—and again, the brackets are intended literally.

```
[closure] (args) {statements }
```

The *closure* is an optional list of variables that are "captured" by the lambda function. To capture a variable is to allow the lambda function to refer to a variable declared in the surrounding code but outside the lambda itself.

This idea is easily clarified with an example. Suppose that a lambda appears within a block that also declares a variable named my_id. If my_id is "captured," then the lambda can refer to my_id internally without my_id having to be passed as an argument. For example:

```
[my_id] (int n) { return my_id + n; }
```

This lambda returns the total of my_id (a variable declared in the surrounding code) and n, an argument passed to the function.

Consider this example, which defines a lambda function, saves it, and then calls it twice.

```
int my_id = 5000;
auto fun = [my_id] (int n) { return my_id + n; };
cout << fun(5) << endl;    // Print 5005.
cout << fun(10) << endl;   // Print 5010.
```

In this case, just one argument is declared: n, to which is passed the value 5 in the third statement and 10 in the fourth. Because my_id is neither an argument nor a local declared inside the lambda, it must be "captured" to be accessed. (Global variables, of course, can always be accessed unless there's a conflict.) The implicit return type of this lambda, by the way, is **int**.

The previous example accesses, but does not change, the value of my_id. In order to enable the lambda to alter the value of my_id, it must be captured by reference, which is indicated by the ampersand prefix (&).

For example, the following lambda changes the value of my_id by adding n to my_id (n being the value of the argument passed to the function).

```
[&my_id] (int n) { my_id += n; return my_id; }
```

Using capture by reference, the example could be revised as follows:

```
int my_id = 5000;
auto fun = [&my_id] (int n) { my_id += n; return my_id; }
fun(5);
cout << "my_id is now " << my_id;    // Print 5005.
```

The following list summarizes the possible values of the *capture* placeholder. Again, the brackets are intended literally.

- `[]`

  No variables are captured. The lambda's definition can refer only to its own arguments, and to local variables (if any) and global variables. It cannot refer to local variables declared outside of the lambda's body. For example, the following lambda function returns **true** if the argument, n, is greater than zero. No outside variables are captured.

```
auto f =  [] (int n) { return n > 0; };
  if (f(x)) cout << "x is greater than 0.";
```

- **[=]**

  All the local variables declared in the surrounding code are accessible, but only by value. The lambda function can access these variables but cannot make changes to them. (Note, however, as explained in Section 5.7.3, that use of the **mutable** keyword enables the function to make temporary changes to variables captured by value.) For example, the following lambda returns the sum of a and b, which are declared in the surrounding level of scope.

```
int a = 1, b = 2;

auto f = [=] () { return a + b; };
cout << f() << endl;    // Print 3.
```

- **[&]**

  All the variables declared in the surrounding scope are captured by reference. The lambda's function definition can make changes to these variables, and such changes will be permanent—that is, they affect the value of those variables in the surrounding code.

```
int sum = 100;

auto f = [&] (int n) { sum += n; };
f(25);
cout << sum << endl;    // Print 125.
```

- **[*args*]**

  In this syntax, *args* is a list of variables (there are no type specifiers), in which each one may or may not have an ampersand prefix (&), specifying that it is accessible by reference. Variables listed in *args* without an ampersand are accessible by value: The lambda function can refer to them but not change their values.

  In the following example, the variables a and b are accessed by reference while x and y are accessed by value. Therefore, the lambda function can make changes to a and b but not to x or y. This lambda also uses an integer argument, n.

```
int a = 0, b = 0, x = 10, y = 20;
auto f = [&a, &b, x, y] (int n)
     { a = x; b = y + n; };
f(100);
cout << "a is now " << a << endl;    // Print 10.
cout << "b is now " << b << endl;    // Print 120.
```

- **[=, *args*]**

  All variables in the enclosing scope are captured by value, except for any *args*, which have the access specified.

  For example, the following closure specifies that all variables in the enclosing scope are accessible by value—the lambda function cannot make changes to them—except for sum, which is accessible by reference and therefore can be changed within the lambda.

```
int sum = 0;
int n = 7;

auto f = [=, &sum] () { sum += n; };
f();
cout << "sum is now " << sum << endl; // sum = 7.
```

- **[&, *args*]**

  All variables in the enclosing scope are captured by reference, except for any *args* that are specified, which have the access given in their declaration.

  For example, the following closure specifies that all variables in the enclosing scope are accessible by reference except for y, which is accessible by value and therefore cannot be changed. By default, the variable named sum is captured by reference (&).

```
int sum = 0;
int y = 5;

auto f = [&, y] () { sum += y; };
f();
cout << "sum is now " << sum << endl;   // sum = 5.
```

5.7.3 The mutable Keyword

The **mutable** keyword can be used with a lambda to indicate that variables captured by value can be changed, although only as temporary values within the lambda. Such changes have no effect on the value of the variable outside the lambda. Instead, the lambda function gets its own copy of such variables and may do with them as it chooses; but any changes are temporary.

The more complete syntax of a lambda function, including **mutable**, is:

```
[closure]  (args)    mutable   -> return_type    {statements }
```

The use of **mutable** is optional, as is the clause -> *return_type*; I've used extra spaces to help set these items apart.

For example, the lambda function in the following example prints out "Hi!" n times, where n is a variable captured by value. Because the **mutable** keyword is used to modify the lambda, changes to n are permitted; but because n is captured by value, the changes to n within the function definition are temporary and have no effect on the value of n outside the function.

```
int n = 5;
auto f = [n] () mutable {while (n-- > 0) cout << "Hi! ";};
f();    // Print "Hi!" five times.
cout << endl;
cout << "n is still " << n << endl;   // n is still 5.
```

Note that if a variable is captured by reference rather than by value, **mutable** is not necessary and has no effect, as changes to such a variable are always allowed.

5.7.4 Using Lambdas with the STL

You can use a lambda by storing it in a variable and then using that variable as a function name, as shown in previous examples. You can even call a lambda in the same statement that defines it, although the utility of such lambdas is dubious.

```
cout << [](int a, int b) { return a + b; } (x, y);
```

Not very useful, is it? Because I could have instead just written:

```
cout << x + y;
```

The most useful application of lambdas is with functions or templates that take a function pointer or object as an argument, and the largest source of these is the STL.

To show the usefulness of STL algorithms, I need to introduce arrays a little bit early. If you're already familiar with arrays, this is not a problem; otherwise, you might want to take a look at Chapter 6.

An array is a numbered collection of elements having the same base data type. For example, the integers 5, 10, 15, 20, and 25 can be placed into an array of base type **int**:

```
int arr[5] = {5, 10, 15, 20, 25};
```

One of the things you might want to do with an array is to print out all the elements. You can write a **for** loop that does this, but the **for_each** algorithm (enabled with the <algorithm> header) provides a more concise approach.

```
#include <algorithm>
#include <iostream>
using namespace std;
```

```
. . .
int arr[5] = {5, 10, 15, 20, 25};
for_each(arr, arr + 5, [] (int n) { cout << n << " "; } );
```

The first argument to **for_each** is the address of the first element of the array. The second argument is the address of the position one past the last element. The third argument is a function: in this case, a lambda. For each element in the array, **for_each** calls the lambda and passes the value of the element. The lambda receives that element as its one argument.

```
[] (int n) { cout << n << " "; }
```

The effect of the lambda is therefore to the print the element, followed by a space.

Another use of **for_each** is to total all the elements (although that can also be done with the **accumulate** algorithm; see Chapter 18, "STL Algorithms"). In this case, the lambda needs to capture the variable named sum by reference.

```
int arr[5] = {5, 10, 15, 20, 25};
int sum = 0;
for_each(arr, arr + 5, [&sum] (int n) { sum += n; } );
cout << "The sum of the elements is: " << sum << endl;
// This prints 75.
```

Here is the lambda itself:

```
[&sum] (int n) { sum += n; }
```

Remember that the action of **for_each** is to call the lambda once for each element, each time passing that element as the sole argument. The effect is therefore to add each element to sum; sum is captured by reference so that it can be modified.

5.7.5 Storing and Returning Lambdas

When storing and using lambdas, be aware that variables are captured *at the point of lambda definition*. For example:

```
int i = 10;
auto f = [i](int n) { return n > i; };
cout << "Is 5 > i? " << f(5) << endl;   // Print false (0).
i = 1;
cout << "Is 5 > i? " << f(5) << endl;   // Print false (0).
```

What's going on here? The first time the call f(5) is made, the lambda (a Boolean function in this case) tests whether 5 is greater than 10. That condition does not hold true, so the function returns **false**—printed on the console as 0.

But then i is set to 1, so you might think that when the lambda is used again to compare 5 to i, the result would now be **true** because i is equal to 1, and 5 is definitely greater than 1! But i was captured by value; and capture by value causes the lambda to use the value 5 for i each and every time it is called, because i contained the value 5 when the lambda was defined.

Look at what happens when i is instead captured by reference (&).

```
int i = 10;
auto f = [&i](int n) { return n > i; };
cout << "Is 5 > i? " << f(5) << endl;   // Print false (0).
i = 1;
cout << "Is 5 > i? " << f(5) << endl;   // Print TRUE (1).
```

Capture by reference does not capture a fixed value, but instead continually refers to the current value of i. So, in this example, as i changes, so does the effect of the lambda.

You can also write functions that return a lambda. The exact declaration required for a lambda function is complex and nonportable, but help is provided by the <functional> header, which enables you to declare return types for these situations. First, include <functional>: The name **std::function** is part of the **std** namespace, so either include a **using** statement or else remember to use the **std** prefix.

```
#include <functional>
using std::function;
```

Then, a function returning a lambda has this declaration:

function<*return_type*(*arg_type_list*)> *function_name*(*args*)

In this syntax, *return_type* is the return type of the lambda to be returned and *arg_type_list* is a description of the lambda's argument list: It consists only of the argument types, separated by commas if there is more than one.

For example, the following function returns a lambda that takes two integers and returns an **int**.

```
#include <functional>
using std::function;

function<int(int, int)> get_fun() {
     int n = 10;
     return [n] (int a, int b) {return a + b + n;};
}
```

The function get_fun returns a lambda function, which itself is a function that takes two integer arguments and returns another integer. You use get_fun by calling it to get the lambda and then storing the lambda in an **auto** variable. You can then use that variable as you would a function name:

```
#include <functional>
#include <iostream>
using namespace std;

function<int(int, int)> get_fun() {
     int n = 10;
     return [n] (int a, int b) {return a + b + n;};
}

int main() {
      auto f = get_fun();           // Get the lambda funct.
      cout << f(1, 2) << endl;      // Print 13.
}
```

The variable f gets assigned a lambda function, which in turn takes two integer arguments a and b; it then returns the total of a, b, and another variable, n.

At the time this lambda was defined, n was equal to 10. The effect was to permanently bind the value 10 to n inside the lambda's definition. So the action of the lambda is to add the two arguments passed to it, together with the value 10. f(1, 2) therefore produces 13.

But what if n were instead captured by reference? That's another matter. If n is captured by reference, then the lambda gets a reference to the variable n, and the value of this reference changes along with n itself.

Unfortunately, n is a local, nonstatic variable, and it goes out of scope and is destroyed after get_fun returns. The lambda then has what's called a *dangling reference*—a pointer to garbage.

```
function<int(int, int)> get_fun() {
     int n = 10;
     // n is captured by reference (&); BAD IDEA!
     return [&n] (int a, int b) {return a + b + n;};
}
```

You can call such a lambda function, but the value used for n in this case will be garbage—it will be a random, meaningless value. The lambda is still referring to a local variable n, even though n went out of scope and was destroyed.

So, in the case of a lambda that is returned to another function, you should only capture local variables by value, not by reference. An exception would be a local static variable, which goes out of scope but is not destroyed. It's okay to capture a static variable by reference.

You might well ask why a function would ever return a lambda to its caller. Admittedly, this is an advanced programming technique. But you might use it in a special situation in which you want to select from one of a number of different functions depending on the circumstances. A function like get_fun could be written to return any of several different lambdas.

5.8 constexpr Functions (C++11)

The **constexpr** keyword, when applied to a function, causes the compiler to treat calls to the function as runtime constants if possible.

Such a function may take one or more arguments: If it does, a call to the function is treated as a compile-time constant only if all the arguments passed are also compile-time constants. Otherwise, the function call is resolved at runtime. For example:

```
constexpr int sum_it(int x, int y) {
     return x + y;
}
. . .
const int n = sum_it(10, 20);
```

In this example, the compile-time constants 10 and 20 are passed to sum_it, so the expression "sum_it(10, 20)" is also treated as a compile-time constant.

Compile-time constants are significant because their values are computed entirely before the program ever runs. Whereas most calculations are performed at runtime, calculations of compile-time constants do not add to the execution time of the program at all.

Functions modified by the **constexpr** keyword have several restrictions.

- The function must have a non-**void** return type.
- The function can only have one executable statement, which must be a **return** statement.
- However, the function can have any number of optional **using**, **typedef**, and null statements (the last category being no-ops consisting of a semicolon only).

Despite these restrictions, it is sometimes possible to write sophisticated functions by making use of recursion, along with the conditional operator (?:). A **constexpr** version of a factorial function is:

```
constexpr int factorial(int n) {
     return (n <= 1) ? 1 : n * factorial(n-1);
}
```

When the program is run, calls to this factorial function—provided that it is passed a compile-time constant—do not take up any time at all during runtime. You can use factorial(10) in your program as if it were a constant, relying on the compiler to determine the value before program execution begins. (This usage, by the way, turns out to have the same effect as entering the numeric literal 3628800.)

```
std::cout << "factorial of 10 is " << factorial(10);
```

Functions modified by **constexpr** are treated as inline functions by the compiler and their definitions can (and should) be included in header files.

5.9 Sample App: Odds at Dice

This sample app demonstrates the basic programming technique of divide-and-conquer: using functions to break a complex task into several smaller tasks.

You've been hired as a consultant to the White Rabbit Tribe. They're building a casino, and the chief wants to know if he should invest in craps tables. He's been told this is a dice game that gives a slight edge to the casino, but he wants you to prove it. He's afraid that if the game doesn't truly favor the casino, then gamblers will show up, make a lot of bets, and take all the tribe's money.

The chief therefore wants you to write a computer program that mathematically and precisely determines the casino's chance of winning each bet.

Let's write such a program in C++. First, however, let's review the rules of the game. The player throws two 6-sided dice to get a total. The game proceeds as follows.

- If the player rolls a total of 7 or 11, the player is an instant winner, and the house pays up.
- If the player instead rolls a total of 2, 3, or 12, he or she is an instant loser.
- If the player rolls any other number, that number becomes the "point." The player then keeps rolling the dice until he or she either rolls the point or rolls a 7. If the point is rolled, the player wins the game. If a 7 is rolled, the player loses. For example, if the player (or "shooter") rolls a 6 on the first roll, he or she wants to roll a 6 again.

For the purposes of this game, how a player gets a certain total is irrelevant; only the total matters. There is no difference between 3-4 and 5-2, for example. They are both 7's.

The strategy of this program is to examine each of the potential first rolls—consisting of the numbers 2 through 12—and call a function to determine the probability of winning. This function, calc_roll, determines the probability of winning by means of that roll. So calc_roll(8) returns the probability that the player rolls an 8 on the first roll *and* goes on to win after rolling the 8.

Adding up the values returned by calc_roll for all the rolls produces the total probability of the player winning.

Payoffs are at even money, so the chief wants to know: Can you verify that a player's chance of winning is slightly less than 50%? We don't want the odds of a player winning to be too low, or no one will play the game. Ideally, the player's chances should be 49% or a tiny bit more.

Here is the program.

```
#include <iostream>
using std::cout;
using std::cin;

double calc_roll(int n);     // Function prototypes
double make_point(int n);

int dice_totals[11] = {1, 2, 3, 4, 5, 6, 5, 4, 3, 2, 1};

int main() {
     double prob_total = 0.0;  // Total probability of
                               //  player winning.
     for (int i = 2; i <= 12; ++i) {   // For each number,
          prob_total += calc_roll(i);  //   Find prob. of
     }                                 //   player winning.
     cout << "Total probability of winning: ";
     cout << prob_total;
     cin.ignore();  // Wait for user to press ENTER.
     return 0;
}

// Calc_roll: return the probability of rolling n AND
// going on to win the game. (In the case of 7 or 11,
// this is just the probability of rolling the number.)
//
double calc_roll(int n) {
     double d = dice_totals[n - 2];
     double prob_roll = d/36.0;

     switch(n) {
     case 2:
     case 3:
     case 12:                  // Instant loser.
          return 0;
          break;
```

```
        case 7:
        case 11:                    // Instant winner.
            return prob_roll;
            break;
        default:
            return prob_roll * make_point(n);
            break;
        }
}

// Make point function:
// Return probability of winning given a certain "point":
// This is equal to d/(d + 6), where d = number of ways to
// roll the point, and 6 = number of ways to roll 7.
double make_point(int n) {
    double d = dice_totals[n - 2];
    return d/(d + 6.0);
}
```

For this program, I've had to introduce the use of arrays one chapter early. (Chapter 6 explains the use of arrays in greater detail.) There is one way of rolling 2 (1-1), two ways of rolling 3 (1-2, 2-1), three ways of rolling 4 (1-3, 3-1, 2-2), and so on. This data—the number of ways of making each total—is stored in the array named dice_totals.

```
int dice_totals[11] = {1, 2, 3, 4, 5, 6, 5, 4, 3, 2, 1};
```

The number of ways of getting a certain total is therefore equal to dice_totals[n – 2], where n is the number in question. For example, the number of ways of rolling a total of 2 is stored in dice_totals[0], which is the first element of the array. The total number of possible rolls is 36. Consequently, the probability of rolling a number n is:

```
dice_totals[n - 2]/36.0
```

The number 36.0 is used here to force floating-point division.

When the program is run, it prints out this result:

```
Total probability of winning: 0.492929
```

In other words, the player has approximately a 49.2929% chance of winning. You can therefore reassure the chief that this game is a good one for the casino. For every dollar bet, the player should win back 49.2929 times two, or roughly 97.57 cents. Which means the casino will (in the long run) make 1.41 cents on every dollar bet.

Exercises

1. In this sample application, the function make_point is not really needed and adds unnecessarily to the size of the program. Revise it so that it does not call make_point but does the calculation it needs "in line" (that is, within the calc_roll function).
2. Most casinos permit a player to bet against the dice roller (also called the *shooter*). This betting option is called the "Don't Pass" bar. To ensure that they doesn't lose money on these bets, the casinos institute a special rule: If the shooter gets a total of 12 on his or her first roll, bets on the Don't Pass bar do not pay off; instead, a roll of 12 is considered a tie for the Don't Pass bettor and neither the bettor nor the house wins in that case. (However, the house still takes the shooter's money.) Write a program determining if the house or the bettors have the edge with Don't Pass bets. Which is the better gamble for the bettors: Pass (that is, shooter wins) or Don't Pass (shooter loses, but a tie is possible)?
3. Calculate the odds of a bettor winning when playing "the Field." Such bets pay off or lose immediately. A Field bet wins if the shooter rolls a total of 2, 3, 4, 9, 10, 11, or 12 on the very next roll; moreover, if the roll is 2 or 12, the Field bettor wins double the amount he or she put up. Playing the Field certainly *looks* like a good bet, but is it really?

CHAPTER 6

Pointers, Arrays, and References

C++ enables you to do a great deal by using simple variables. To write real programs, however, you need to learn how to create more complex data types, beginning with pointers, arrays, and references.

Arrays are important because they are the most basic kind of container in the language. By creating an array, you can have N of something, where N is any positive whole number. Pointers, a closely related topic, are important because they have a close relationship to arrays and are used to manipulate them.

I begin with the subject of references, however, because these are the easiest to start using in your own programs.

6.1 References

A reference is a variable that works as an alias for another variable. Reference types are most often used with function arguments—enabling a function to make permanent changes to a variable passed to it—but may be used in other places as well. You specify a reference by using the ampersand (&) within a declaration.

Note

What this chapter talks about as a "reference" is more correctly referred to as an *lvalue reference,* as explained in Appendix A, "A Painless Introduction to Rvalue References." For now, however, you can ignore the distinction.

6.1.1 Reference Arguments

By default, arguments are passed to C++ functions by value (the exception being array names, described later); this means that when a function is called, it gets its own copy of the data. In the case of the following example, the function gets its own copy of the argument n:

```
int triangle(int n) {
    int total = 0;
    while (n-- > 0)
         total += n;
    return total;
}
```

This function gets a copy of n and changes n during the course of function execution. But because the function has its own copy of the data, there is no permanent effect on the variable that was passed. For example:

```
int my_num = 6;
cout << triangle(my_num) << endl;
cout << "my_num is still " << my_num << endl;
```

Here, n is passed as an argument and used within that function, decrementing its copy of n all the way to 0—but after the function returns, the value of the caller's variable (my_num) is unchanged. Consequently, this example prints the following:

```
21
my_num is still 6
```

Sometimes, though, you *do* want to give a function the ability to alter the value of the variable passed to it. There are often good reasons for this. A function can return at most one value, but you might want the function to set a whole series of values. One way to do that is to declare all your variables as global variables, but that leads to global proliferation, which tends to lead to bugs. A better way is to let the function make changes to some or all of the variables passed to it.

To do that, the arguments need to be passed by reference. With pass by reference, the function gets access to the variable itself rather than a copy of it.

To declare a reference argument, use the ampersand prefix (&) in the argument's declaration. (Note: You can achieve the same effect by using pointers, as described in Section 6.3.2, "Pointers as Arguments," but the easiest way is to use reference arguments.)

The syntax for a reference argument is:

```
type  &variable_name
```

This syntax is equivalent to the following, which places the ampersand just after *type* but before the space. The difference between these two forms is a matter of style.

```
type&  variable_name
```

For example, in the following declaration, the first two arguments are passed by reference and the last three are passed by value. Consequently, any variables passed to the first two arguments, a and b, can be set to new values by my_func.

```
void my_func(int &a, int &b, int c, int d, double x);
```

This can be initially confusing, because the ampersand is also used as the unary address operator when it appears in an executable statement. (And it gets worse: As a binary operator, the ampersand is also used for logical and bitwise AND.)

But C++ has no problem distinguishing between these uses. The important thing to remember is that *when applied to a variable or argument being declared, the unary & operator indicates a reference type.*

Consider the following example, which uses the ampersand prefix (&) used to declare the argument n.

```
int double_it(int &n) {
     n *= 2;
     return n;
}
```

Now the function permanently changes the value of any variable passed to it:

```
int my_num = 3;
cout << "The value of my_num was " << my_num << endl;
double_it(my_num);
cout << "Now the value is " << my_num << endl;
```

This example prints:

```
The value of my_num was 3
Now the value is 6
```

Several guidelines apply to the use of reference types.

- Only lvalues can be passed to reference arguments. An lvalue, as explained in Chapter 3, “”Operators,” is an expression that would be valid on the left side of an assignment: This includes variables, but can also include array elements, class members, and fully dereferenced address expressions (pointers). You cannot pass a literal constant, such as “15.”
- Reference arguments do not result in a copy being made; instead, the function gains direct access to the variable that was passed. If the data passed to the argument is a very large item—such as a large array or object—this can be a significant advantage because it is more efficient at runtime, as no copying has to be performed.
- A reference argument, once bound to a variable, cannot be made to refer to something else—although each separate invocation of a function may result in the argument referring to a different variable.

- Remember that the unary ampersand operator (&) declares a reference only when applied to an item being declared. When the ampersand appears in an executable statement as a unary operator, it becomes the "address" operator, as explained in Section 6.3.1, "The Concept of Pointer." As a binary operator, it signifies bitwise AND.

You can use references with ordinary variables as well as arguments; this causes one variable to be an alias for another. Once a reference variable is bound in this way, it cannot be made to bind to something else. In C++, references to simple variables don't see much use, as they have little practical value; however, this does demonstrate a valid use of references.

```
int i = 0;
int &j = i;    // j is an alias for i.

++j;    // Changes to j do the same thing as changes to i.
++i;    // i has now been incremented by 2.
```

6.1.2 Returning a Reference from a Function

You can also write a function that has a return value with reference type. The function passes back direct access to an existing variable or other lvalue—which confers the ability to alter that variable.

Here's a simple example of a function returning a reference to an integer.

```
#include <iostream>
using namespace std;

int i = 5;

int& get_var() {
    return i:
}

int main() {
    ++get_var();
    cout << "The value of i is now " << i;
}
```

In this example, get_var does not return the value of i but a reference to i itself. (Note that precedence rules cause the function to be called before the prefix operator, ++, is applied.) Therefore, the global variable i gets incremented by the statement:

```
++get_var();
```

This example, though not especially practical, does demonstrate some important points. It works because i is a global variable. If a reference to a local variable were returned, the result would be undefined—that is, the example would produce a random bad result—because you can't refer to a variable that has been deleted from memory. (The memory occupied by a local variable is released from memory once the local variable goes out of scope unless the variable is declared static.) The function would return a reference to something that no longer exists.

```
int& get_var() {
   int local_var = 10;
   return local_var; // Danger! Variable goes out of scope!
}
```

Most compilers will not flag this as an error, but the value returned is unreliable; it's a reference to a memory address containing a random value—that is to say, garbage.

Chapter 7, "Classes and Objects," features a number of functions that return references to an object. This is actually the most common case of returning a reference.

6.1.3 References Modified by "const"

Upon occasion, you may want to declare a reference argument but modify it with the **const** keyword.

At first, such a declaration may seem odd. The purpose of a reference argument is to enable the function to change the argument's value; but the **const** keyword prevents such changes. How could this be useful?

Yet enabling changes to an argument is not the only consequence of using a reference argument. Equally important is that when a reference is used, no copying is performed.

Suppose you pass a large data structure. (Chapter 7 describes techniques for building larger data types out of smaller ones.) Making a copy every time you pass a large data structure would slow down the program. If the function doesn't need to make a copy, it is better to use a reference argument.

Yet you may also want to prevent the function from making changes to the data. A **const** reference argument fulfills this purpose. The argument refers to whatever was passed to it—so the laborious process of making a copy is avoided—but it protects the variable that was passed from being changed by the function. The syntax for such an argument declaration is:

const *type* **&***arg*

For example:

```
const double pi = 3.14159265;
void display_value(const double &x);
display_value(pi);    // This is okay.
```

One of the most important rules regarding the **const** keyword is that a non-**const** value can be passed as a **const** argument, but a **const** value cannot be passed as a non-**const** argument. This may seem convoluted at first, but it makes sense if you think about it.

The **const** keyword protects the value being passed from being changed. There is no penalty for extending this protection to an ordinary argument.

```
double x = 2.77;
void display_value(const double &x);
display_value(x);    // This is okay.
```

But the converse does not hold true. Passing a **const** value as a non-**const** argument would enable the function to change the value, thereby violating the "const contract."

```
const double pi = 3.14159265;
void display_value(double &x);
display_value(pi);    // ERROR! Not allowed.
```

When possible, then, declare reference arguments as **const**, unless you need to enable the function to make changes to the data.

6.2 Arrays

An array is a numbered collection of elements having the same type. Declaring an array of length N is a way of telling the compiler, "Create N of these things."

For example, if you need to store a thousand test scores, you can use a single declaration to put all of them into an array rather than declaring a thousand separate variables. That saves you, the programmer, from having to write 999 extra lines of source code just to declare your data!

In C++, arrays are zero-based, meaning the first element is indexed as 0, not 1. Figure 6.1 illustrates the concept of an array having five elements. In this case, the array is initialized to the values 80, 85, 82, 97, and 95, but they could be any five values of the base type (**int**).

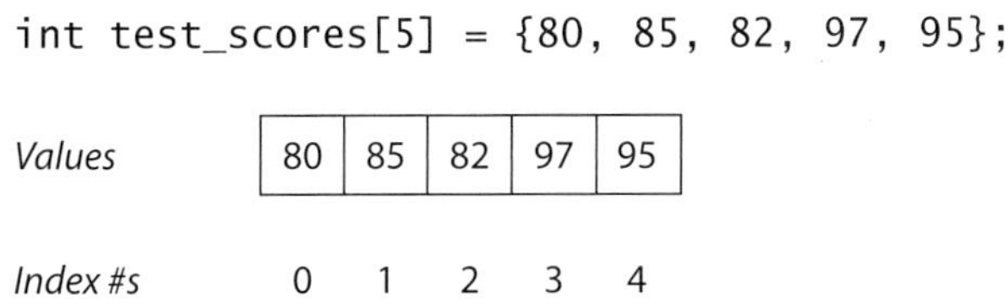

FIGURE 6.1 An array with five elements

6.2.1 Simple (One-Dimensional) Arrays

In C++, square brackets, [ ], are used to declare an array. The brackets here are intended literally.

```
type  array_name[length];
```

In this syntax, *array_name* is a symbolic name and *length* is a constant integer value. The *type* can be any primitive type or a user-defined type such as a class name. The *length* must be a compile-time constant, such as a numeric literal or **enum** constant—or an expression made up of these constants. (The bottom line is that the compiler must be able to determine the length before the program is run.)

The *length* is the number of elements to create.

The *length* can be omitted, if and only if the length can be determined from an initialization list. For example:

```
int test_scores[] = {80, 85, 82, 97, 95};
```

This creates an array of five integers. Even in this case, however, you can still choose to include the length specifier, which has the advantage of showing the array length at a glance.

```
int test_scores[5] = {80, 85, 82, 97, 95};
```

The initialization list is an *aggregate,* a comma-delimited list of values enclosed in braces ({}). If there are fewer values in the aggregate than there are places in the array, the front of the array is filled first, leaving the rest of the array initialized to zero or null values. For example:

```
int my_scores[10] = {10, 20, 30, 40, 50};   // Length = 10.
```

If the length specifier (10) were omitted a length of 5 would be assumed by the compiler.

```
int my_scores[] = {10, 20, 30, 40, 50};     // Length = 5.
```

Note that if a length specifier is given and there are *too many* initializers, the compiler reports an error.

Individual elements in an array are referred to by index number. Indexing in C++ is zero-based, so the first element is *array_name*[0], the second element is *array_name*[1], and so on.

```
int a[10];
a[0] = 10;     // Set first element to 10.
a[1] = 100;    // Set second element to 100.
a[2] = 64;     // Set third element to 64.
a[0] = a[4];   // Set first element to value of the fifth.
a[9] = a[0] + a[1]; // Tenth elem. = first + second
```

For an array of length n, the array elements run from 0 to n-1.

Note that the declarations in the next example, although they look similar, are not quite the same. The first initializes the array, implicitly setting all the values to zero. The second does not initialize values; but if the array is a global variable, its elements are initialized to zero anyway. These two declarations produce different results if the array is a local variable, because in that case, the second declaration causes elements to contain garbage. ("Garbage," remember, is a technical term for "random, meaningless values.")

```
int array1[10] = {};     // Initialize elements to 0.
int array2[10];          // If this is local, elements
                         //    contain garbage.
```

6.2.2 Array Processing with Loops

One of the chief advantages of arrays is that they can be processed efficiently with loops. The **for** keyword provides an efficient way of writing these loops. The following example sets all 100 elements of my_array to 50:

```
int my_array[100];
for(int i = 0; i < 100; ++i) {
     my_array[i] = 50;
}
```

This next example sets array elements to the values 0, 1, 2, 3...99.

```
int my_array[100];
for(int i = 0; i < 100; ++i) {
     my_array[i] = i;
}
```

Notice how boundary conditions are set in both of these cases. Remember that indexes in C++ are zero-based; therefore, the first element is indexed as my_array[0], and i should begin at 0.

The nth element of an array, remember, is indexed as array[n-1]. In an array of size 100, therefore, the index number of the last element is 99.

In these examples, the condition i < 100 enables the loop to run from 0 up to and including 99. It does not enable setting of my_array[100], which would be the 101st member and therefore out of range. In general, you should process an array by observing the following boundary conditions within a **for** loop:

- Set initial index to 0, as in i = 0.
- Test the index by using an expression such as i < n, where n is the length of the array.

If your compiler is C++11 compliant, you can in many cases use range-based **for**, which frees you from having to worry about boundary conditions altogether. For example, the following loop sets every member of the array named "arr" to 50.

```
for(auto &x : arr) {
     x = 50;
}
```

The limitation on range-based **for** is that it does not grant access to the loop variable (which is maintained internally and is hidden), so some kinds of loops are harder to write. For example, if you wanted to initialize an array to have the values 0, 1, 2, 3..., you'd need to artificially create a loop variable.

```
int i = 0;
for(auto &x : arr) {
     x = i++;
}
```

The declaration of an additional variable, i, was necessary here, although this is still fairly tight code.

6.2.3 Passing Arrays to Functions

When an array name appears in executable code in C++, it is translated into the address of the beginning of the array: that is, the address of the first element. That fact may not seem important in the preceding examples, but understanding it is vital when passing arrays to functions.

When you pass an array name to a function, you are in reality passing an address. You are not giving the function its own copy of the array. Instead, the function gets direct access to the original copy of the array—so array access, in effect, is by reference. The function can use that access to manipulate the array elements.

When you specify an array argument, you use brackets. Specifying the length is optional, but the length is usually left blank with one-dimensional array arguments.

```
type  array_arg[ ]
```

The standard programming tactic is to pass the length separately as an **int** argument; doing so gives the function flexibility to operate on arrays of different lengths. Here is an example of successful passing of an array, this time involving an array of floating-point values (**double**).

```
double my_data[100];    // Declare array of 100 doubles.
reset_flt_array(my_data, 100);
. . .
void reset_flt_array(double arr[], int n) {
     for (int i = 0; i < n; i++) {
          arr[i] = 0.0;
     }
}
```

Within this function definition, the argument, arr, is treated as a constant. Although you cannot assign values to arr itself, you can assign values to the array elements. C++ evaluates the expression arr[i] by taking the array address and adding the value of i after *scaling* it (multiplying by the size of the base type). The result of this operation is to obtain the address of the desired element, which is then dereferenced to get the data *at* that address.

Don't worry if this is confusing at first; this address manipulation is handled under the covers. A programmer new to C++ can treat it as magic, at least in the beginning. It becomes important to understand the details of this address manipulation when you start using pointers and pointer arithmetic to process arrays, as explained later in this chapter, in Section 6.3.4, "Pointer Arithmetic."

Range-based **for** (supported by compilers that implement the full C++11 specification) creates a problematic situation for arrays passed as arguments. Range-based **for** always works with global arrays—because their lengths are known—but not with arrays declared in other functions.

```
void reset_int_array(int arr[]) {
     for (int &i : arr ) {
          i = 0;     // ERROR! Boundaries of arr not known!
     }
}
```

6.2.4 Multidimensional Arrays

A two-dimensional array can be declared in C++ as follows (in which the brackets are intended literally):

```
type   array_name[rows][columns];
```

Likewise, a three-dimensional array can be declared as:

```
type   array_name[a][b][c];
```

where *a*, *b*, and *c* are the lengths of each of the three dimensions.

In both of these cases, the rightmost dimension changes most quickly and the leftmost dimension changes most slowly. For example, consider the following array declaration:

```
int matrix [3][2];
```

The elements are laid out in memory in this order:

```
matrix[0][0]
matrix[0][1]
matrix[1][0]
matrix[1][1]
matrix[2][0]
matrix[2][1]
```

Each dimension runs from 0 to n-1, where n is the length of that dimension. In this case, the row dimension (the first dimension) runs from 0 to 2, while the column dimension runs from 0 to 1.

The syntax of the declaration implies that a two-dimensional array is really an array of arrays, which it is.

```
base_type array_name[rows][columns];
```

An executable statement must use two pairs of brackets to access an individual member of a two-dimensional array, as you'd expect:

```
matrix[2][1] = 0;   // Set value of matrix[2][1] to 0.
```

In this case, the name "matrix" itself is an address. Moreover, so are the following:

```
matrix[0];    // Address of first row
matrix[1];    // Address of second row
matrix[2];    // Address of third row
```

Because these are addresses and not items in memory, you cannot directly assign values to them.

To initialize a multidimensional array, use a nested aggregate such as the following:

```
int matrix[3][2] = {{1,1}, {2,2}, {3,5}};
```

This declaration initializes the first row to {1, 1}, the second row to {2, 2}, and the third row to {3, 5}, so that the six values in the matrix are (in this order): 1, 1, 2, 2, 3, 5.

A nested **for** loop is the standard way to process a two-dimensional array. The following example sets each member of matrix to 0. In this case, NUMBER_OF_ROWS and NUMBER_OF_COLS are two predefined values.

```
#define NUMBER_OF_ROWS 3;
#define NUMBER_OF_COLS 2;
int matrix[NUMBER_OF_ROWS][NUMBER_OF_COLS];
for (int i = 0; i < NUMBER_OF_ROWS; i++) {
     for (int j = 0; j < NUMBER_OF_COLS; j ++) {
          matrix[i][j] = 0;
     }
}
```

The symbols NUMBER_OF_ROWS and NUMBER_OF_COLS are good candidates for the use of the **#define** preprocessor directive described in Chapter 8, "Preprocessor Directives." Alternatively, you can set the dimension lengths directly, but this makes for source code that is not as clear, reliable, or as self-documenting.

```
for (int i = 0; i < 3; i++) {
     for (int j = 0; j < 2; j ++) {
          matrix[i][j] = 0;
     }
}
```

When passing a multidimensional array as an argument (should you ever be inclined to do such a thing), remember that the compiler cannot make guesses about array dimensions at compile time—and to resolve indexes correctly, the compiler must be able to determine how long each row is. The function definition must always include enough information for the compiler to determine the base type of any address it handles.

In the case of multidimensional arrays, this means you need to include all array lengths except for the first one, which may be passed as a separate argument. In the following example, the number of columns (the last dimension) is assumed to be 100.

```
double my_matrix[50][100];

void reset_matrix(double a[][100], int nrows) {
     for (int i = 0; i < nrows; i++) {
          for (int j = 0; i < 100; j++) {
               a[i] = 0.0;
```

```
            }
        }
}
. . .
reset_matrix(my_matrix, 50);
```

In practice, it's usually easier to declare multidimensional arrays as global variables. Another approach I recommend is to use pointer access, as described in Section 6.3.3, "Pointers Used to Access Arrays," to process multidimensional arrays. Using that approach has some definite advantages, including potentially much better runtime performance.

6.3 Pointers

For programmers new to C and C++, the concept of pointers is usually the single biggest stumbling block. A pointer is just a variable that contains the address of another variable. The new programmer usually asks the following questions.

- Why would you want a variable to contain the address of another variable?
- How do you use this mechanism in C/C++ source code?

The sections that follow answer these questions. First, however, Section 6.3.1 elaborates some more on the general concept of pointer.

6.3.1 The Concept of Pointer

To declare a pointer variable, apply the "at" operator (*) as you declare it:

```
base_type  *pointer_name;
```

The variable, *pointer_name*, is declared to be a variable containing the address of another variable, which must have the same base type. For example, consider the following:

```
int i = 0;    // Integer.
int *p;       // Pointer to an integer.
p = &i;       // p now points to i.
```

The statement "p = &i;" uses the address operator (&) to initialize the pointer variable, p, to point to i—that is, to contain the address of i. The last two statements can be combined, as in:

```
int i = 0;
int *p = &i;   // Initialize p, a pointer p,to point to i.
```

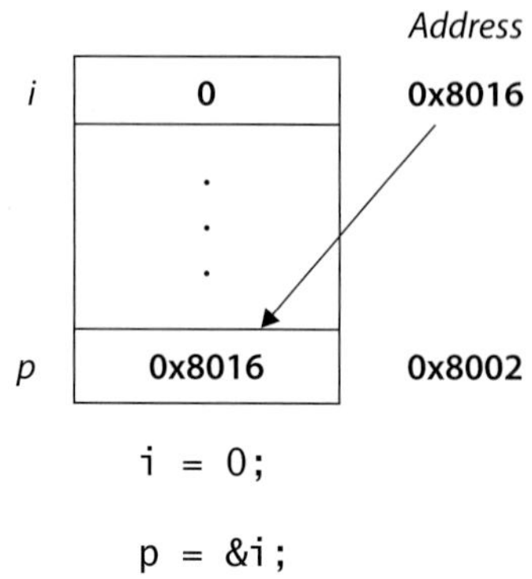

FIGURE 6.2 Memory layout of a pointer and integer

The resultant memory layout would look as depicted in Figure 6.2. For the memory addresses, I picked random locations.

Bear in mind that a numeric address is what the computer uses to refer to memory locations internally. When a program is translated into machine code, a CPU understands nothing but numbers. So a pointer is simply a variable that stores the location of another variable. In this case, p stores the location of i.

The pointer variable, p, contains the address of the variable i, and therefore "points" to it. Because it does, you can use p to alter the value of this variable by using the "at" operator (*), also called the indirection or dereferencing operator.

```
*p = 10;
```

What this says, literally, is, "Set the value of what is *at* the address contained in p to 10." Or, a bit more verbosely: "Find the memory location p points to and store 10 at that location." The memory will then have the layout shown in Figure 6.3.

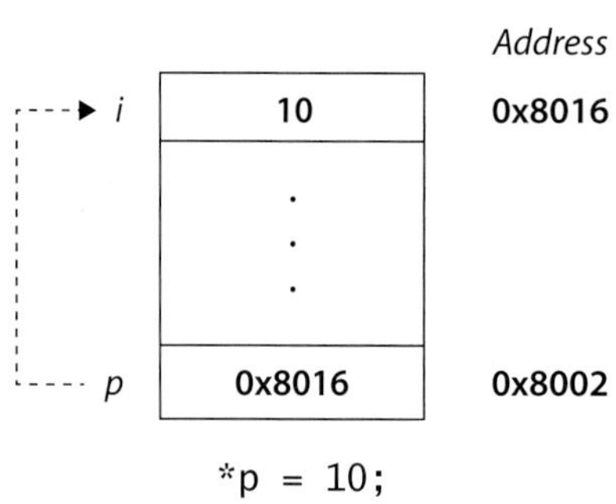

FIGURE 6.3 Memory layout after *p has been assigned 10

This operation is called *indirection,* because it uses a pointer, p, to indirectly change another variable (in this case, i). Likewise, you can use the increment operator (++) to change the value that p points to. The following statement dereferences p and then increments what it points to.

```
(*p)++;
```

In this case the parentheses are necessary. The expression "*p++" is equivalent to "*(p++)" and it increments p itself. (But as I will explain in the next section, you often *will* want to increment p.) Figure 6.4 shows the memory layout that results from "(*p)++;".

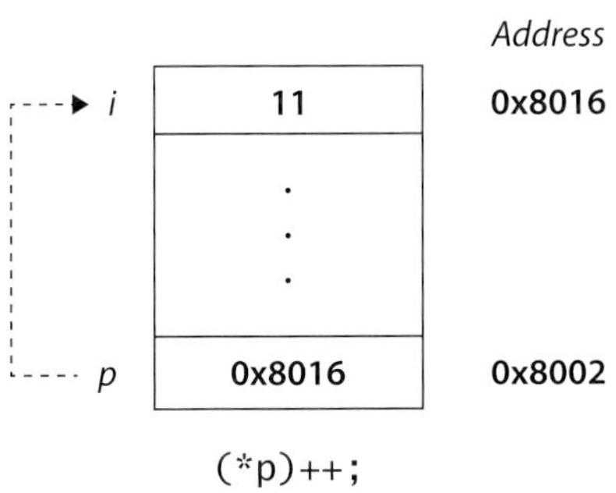

FIGURE 6.4 Memory layout after *p has been incremented

Beyond being able to make changes to *p, the C++ source code can make changes to p itself. Consider this statement:

```
++p;
```

The effect of this statement is to make p point to the next integer in memory. Normally, the increment operator (++) adds one to its operand; but where pointers are involved, the amount to be added is first scaled by the size of the base type—in this case, the size of an **int**. That result is then added to the address. (Section 6.3.4 explains this process in more detail.)

As a result, p points to the next item in memory. There is a caveat: Never make assumptions about how the compiler chooses to order things in memory except in the case of arrays.

The next few sections explain why it can be useful to change values through pointer indirection.

6.3.2 Pointers as Arguments

One of the most important uses for pointers is to achieve (or at least simulate) pass by reference. In the old C language, passing an address to a pointer argument was the only way to do this.

To use a pointer argument, you do the following: Instead of passing a variable to a function, you pass an address; the function then uses this address to manipulate the variable itself, indirectly. The effect is essentially the same as using a reference variable, although the syntax is different.

Here is the declaration of the double_it function using pointer syntax (*):

```
void double_it(int *p);
```

This declaration says that double_it expects a single argument, which is a pointer to an integer. The following code fragment demonstrates the process of calling this function.

```
int n = 5;
cout << "The value of n was " << n <<;
double_it(&n);
cout << "The value of n is now " << n <<;
...
void double_it(int *p) {
     *p = *p * 2;
}
```

The example prints the following:

```
The value of n was 5
The value of n is now 10
```

During the function call to double_it, the address operator (&) gets the address of n, which is then passed to the function. (This same symbol is used to declare references; but because it appears here in an executable statement, the ampersand, &, acts as the address operator.)

```
double_it(&n);
```

Within the function definition, the program uses the "at" operator (*), also called the indirection operator, to refer to the item at the address stored in p. (Remember, the variable n is at this address.)

```
     *p = *p * 2;
```

This could be more concisely written with the multiplication-assignment operator, *=. The asterisk (*) serves as the multiplication operator when it takes two operands and as the "at" operator when it takes one operand. C++ distinguishes these uses according to context.

```
*p *= 2;   // Multiply *p by 2.
```

To summarize:

- The "at" operator (*), used within a function declaration, indicates that an address is expected as the argument.

  type **ptr_name*

- Therefore, during a function call, an address must be passed to a pointer argument. The address operator (&) is used to get a variable's address.

  &*var_name*

- Within the function definition, use the "at" operator (*) again, to manipulate the thing pointed to. If p points to n, you can manipulate n by assigning values to *p.

6.3.3 Pointers Used to Access Arrays

In C++, there is a close relationship between pointers and arrays. As explained in Section 6.2.3, "Passing Arrays to Functions," when you give an array name as an argument to a function call, the address of the first element gets passed. This address can be passed to a pointer argument or array argument.

The following code uses the index operator, [ ], to set individual members of an array to zero.

```
void reset_dbl_array(double a[], int n) {
     for (int i = 0; i < n; ++i) {
          a[i] = 0.0;
     }
}
```

A pointer argument can receive this same address; consequently, this function could have been written the following way, which would have slightly better runtime performance:

```
void reset_dbl_array(double *p, int n) {
     for (int i = 0; i < n; ++i) {
          *p++ = 0.0;
     }
}
```

Precedence and associativity are important. Consider this statement:

```
*p++ = 0.0;
```

If you consult Table 3.1, you'll see that the postfix increment (++) has a higher precedence than the "at" operator (*). As a result, the statement is evaluated as if it were written this way:

```
*(p++) = 0.0;
```

Therefore, the statement does the following:

1. Gets the current address contained in p and passes this along.
2. Increments p *after* passing along this address.
3. Using the address that p pointed to—before being incremented—sets the element at this address to 0.0.

In summary, then, the statement assigns 0.0 to the element p points to and advances p to point to the next item in memory. Pointing to the next item in memory is a reasonable operation because an array is involved, and—as I stated earlier—the compiler guarantees that array elements are stored next to each other in the expected order.

The effect is the same as if the statement were broken down into the following:

```
*p = 0.0;   // Assign 0.0 to what p points to.
p++;        // Increment p itself, to point to
            //   the next item in memory.
```

This next example uses two pointer variables, to assign all the values in one array to another.

```
void copy_array(int *p1, int *p2, int n);   // Prototype
int arr1[10] = (0, 0, 0, 0, 0, 0, 0, 0, 0, 0);
int arr2[10] = {1, 2, 3, 4, 5, 6, 7, 8, 9, 10};

main() {
    copy_array(arr1, arr2, 10);
    . . .
}
void copy_array(int *p1, int *p2, int n) {
    for (int i = 0; i < n; i++) {
        *p1++ = *p2++;
    }
}
```

The statement inside the loop, "*p1++ = *p2++;", has the same effect as the following:

```
*p1 = *p2;      // Copy what is at p2 to what is at p1.
p1++;           // Advance p1 to point to the next item in memory.
p2++;           // Advance p2 to point to the next item in memory.
```

The same loop could have been written this way, using array indexes. This use of indexes is valid, because p1 and p2 store addresses, just as array names do.

```
for (int i = 0; i < n; ++i) {
     p1[i] = p2[i];
}
```

Considering that this operation can be performed with array indexes, what is the advantage of the pointer version?

The pointer version is more efficient because it avoids having to evaluate indexes and recalculate the position of elements over and over. It accesses an element directly and then moves to the next position. With one-dimensional arrays, this provides only a slight increase in efficiency—although this difference might be significant if, for example, you have a program that processes millions of elements.

With multidimensional arrays, the gain in efficiency is more significant, because calculation of positions within such an array is more complex. The pointer version bypasses those calculations. Here is the pointer version of a function that initializes a two-dimensional array to all-zero values:

```
void reset_2D_dbl_array(double **p, int nrows, int ncols) {
     int n = nrows * ncols;
     for (int i = 0; i < n; ++i) {
          **p++ = 0.0;
     }
}
```

Note that double indirection (**) is used to point to an element within a two-dimensional array. An example that calls this function is:

```
double  big_matrix[10][10];
reset_2D_dbl_array(big_matrix, 10, 10);
```

The pointer version could have been written a bit more concisely with a **while** loop:

```
void reset_2D_dbl_array(double **p, int nrows, int ncols) {
     int n = nrows * ncols;
     while (n-- > 0) {
          **p++ = 0.0;
     }
}
```

The gain in efficiency here is significant. Indexing an element of a two-dimensional array involves calculations based on two loop variables—which is perfectly fine for simple programs, but is considerably slower in a program that has to process thousands or even millions of elements. The pointer version eliminates most of the calculations that are necessary with the following, more traditional way of processing a two-dimensional array:

```
for (int i = 0; i < nrows; i++) {
     for (int j = 0; j < ncols; j++ {
          big_matrix[i][j] = 0.0;
     }
}
```

6.3.4 Pointer Arithmetic

The examples in the preceding section work because the following two expressions are interchangeable:

```
*(p + i)
p[i]
```

At compile time, these two expressions are handled the same way. The compiler evaluates p[i] by adding the number i to p, producing the address of the target element. Then it dereferences that address to get access to the array element itself.

When an integer (such as i) is added to a pointer or address expression, C++ observes the rules of pointer arithmetic. These rules permit integers to be added to addresses in meaningful ways.

- When an integer is added to an address, the integer is first multiplied by the size of the base type. Therefore, in the expression p + 2, 2 is automatically multiplied by the size of p's base type. If that type is **int** (and assuming that the **int** type is 4 bytes), then the final result is that eight bytes are added to p to produce a new address. This is all handled under the covers: that is, out of sight of the programmer.

  The upshot is that if arr is the name of an array, then arr is the address of the first element, arr+1 is the address of the second element, arr+2 is the address of the third element, and so on. This is why C++ and other C-like languages are zero-based.
- You can also subtract an integer value from an address expression. The integer is first multiplied by the address's base type. Again, this is all handled under the covers, so you don't have to worry about implementing it.
- Finally, you can subtract one address expression from another, assuming they share the same base type. The result is then divided by the size of their base type to produce a result that indicates how many positions apart two elements are within an array.

Remember that the concept of "X positions apart" only makes sense within an array. Outside of arrays, you should make no assumptions about the arrangement of items in memory.

6.3.5 Pointers versus Array Arguments

The following declarations look similar.

```
void reset_array(double arr[], int n);
void reset_array(double *p, int n);
```

Both of them support array indexing through the first argument. For example, the following code would be valid in both versions just shown, even though p is declared as a pointer argument:

```
for (int i = 0; i < n; ++i) {
     p[i] = 0.0;
}
```

Both arr and p are arguments to which an address is passed, so they can be used in similar ways. However, these two versions of reset_array are not entirely interchangeable. Declaring an argument as "double arr[]" causes the argument, arr, to be treated as an array name, not a pointer; consequently, arr is treated as a constant but p (declared as a pointer) is not.

Both p and arr in these examples contain the address of the first element. But you can modify p all you want. With the first version, which declares the first argument as "double arr[]", if you wanted to use the pointer-access technique you would need to first copy the array's address to a separate variable. You can't manipulate arr itself because it's treated as a constant.

```
void reset_array(double arr[], int n) {
     double *p = arr;     // Copy address to p.
     while (n-- > 0) {
          *p++ = 0.0;   // This is OK; p is not a constant.
     }
}
```

6.3.6 Pointers and Memory Allocation

Array declaration has a limitation: The declared length must be a compile-time constant; that is, the compiler must be able to determine what the exact length is at compile time, before the program is run. This means that you are limited to constants such as numeric literals, **enum** values, and constants created with the **#define** directive. As long as the compiler can determine a fixed value at compile time, the usage is permitted. For example:

```
#define NUMBER_OF_ROWS  100
int my_array[NUMBER_OF_ROWS + 1];
```

But sometimes you cannot determine how much memory is needed until runtime. For example, you might allocate memory in response to a user request. (The sample application in Section 6.7, "Sample App: Sieve of Eratosthenes," involves just such a situation.)

In these cases you need to allocate memory dynamically. C++ provides the **new** keyword for these situations. The **new** keyword has several versions, as explained in Chapter 3. To review, here are two versions of the syntax:

```
ptr = new type;
ptr = new type[num];
```

In the first version, **new** creates a single data object of the requested *type* and returns the address of the successfully allocated item in memory. That address should be saved by being assigned to a pointer of the appropriate base type.

For example, the following code allocates a single integer, stores its address in p, and finally assigns the value 0 to this new integer.

```
int *p;
p = new int;
*p = 0;
```

The second version of syntax for **new** likewise returns a pointer, but it allocates more than one item. What is returned is effectively an array address. The data items allocated are guaranteed to be next to each other in memory, so you can refer to items in this array with either pointer-dereference or array-indexing syntax.

For example:

```
int n = 10;
double *p_dbl;
p_dbl = new double[n];  // Allocate 10 floating points.
p_dbl[0] = 1.5;         // Assign 1.5 to first element.
p_dbl[4] = -33.3;       // Assign -33.3 to fifth element.
. . .
delete [] p;             // Done with the memory; free it!
```

Remember to use the **delete** keyword to release memory after you no longer need it. That frees up memory to be used by the rest of the program or by other processes. The second version below releases arrays created with **new** []; it doesn't matter what the length is.

```
delete ptr;
delete [] ptr;
```

If you use **new** to allocate data items at runtime and there is insufficient memory to allocate the item or items requested, the operator throws a **bad_alloc** exception. With today's sophisticated operating systems, it is not easy to produce such a situation. The maximum array size supported is no greater than the highest number in the **long** integer range; yet your system likely has gigabytes of memory to spare. Good luck in trying to get a **bad_alloc** exception.

Yet such exceptions are possible in some circumstances, such as when the end user is overtaxing his or her computer by having many applications open at the same time. So if you're writing professional software (especially commercial software intended to be used by thousands or millions of people), it's still a good idea to check for insufficient memory.

To use exception handling, see Chapter 4, "Control Structures." An alternative to exception handling is to check for a null pointer. If you use **std::nothrow** as shown in the next example (this requires the <new> header>), insufficient memory does not throw an exception but instead causes **new** to return a null pointer value. Here's how you would test for insufficient memory using this approach:

```
#include <new>
using std::nothrow;

int *p = new (nothrow) [big_number];
if (p == NULL) {
     std::cout << "Insufficient memory." << std::endl;
}
```

The **if** statement could also be written as:

```
if (!p) {
     std::cout << "Insufficient memory." << std::endl;
}
```

As a final note, this example used NULL as a value to test a pointer against. NULL is a symbolic constant defined by C++ header files. But if your compiler is compliant with the C++11 specification, it is better to use **nullptr** instead, because this recently supported keyword is directly supported within the language itself and does not rely on a symbolic-constant definition.

```
if (p == nullptr) {
     std::cout << "Insufficient memory." << std::endl;
}
```

6.3.7 Pointers to const Types

The **const** keyword is used frequently in C/C++ library functions. A **const** variable or argument is protected from change. For example, the following use of **const** causes the compiler to reject any subsequent statements that attempt to change the value of the variable pi:

```
const double pi = 3.141592;
```

So, given this declaration, the following statement is not allowed:

```
pi = 0.0;     // ERROR! pi is const.
```

The existence of pointers complicates the situation. You might think the following sneaky trick would get around the **const** restriction:

```
double *d_ptr;
d_ptr = &pi;    // ERROR! const -> non-const ptr not allowed.
*d_ptr = 0.0;   // This would've changed pi to 0.0!
```

But this is not allowed either; the compiler won't allow it, because the address of a **const** variable cannot be passed to a non-**const** pointer.

You can, however, pass such an address to a pointer of type **const double***. You can think of **const double** almost as a separate type. When a pointer points to a **const** type, you cannot change the value of the item pointed to.

```
const double *d_ptr;
d_ptr = &pi;        // This is okay, because d_ptr points to
                    //   const double.
*d_ptr = 0.0;       // ERROR: d_ptr is a const pointer, so
                    //   now this statement is not allowed.
```

The rules applying to **const** pointers are as follows.

- The address of a **const** variable can be assigned only to a pointer to a **const** type.
- The value of a pointer to a **const** type can be assigned only to another pointer to a **const** type.
- A dereferenced pointer to a **const** type (*p) cannot be the target of an assignment, increment, or decrement. It can, however, appear on the right side of an assignment.

These rules do not prevent the address of a non-**const** object being assigned to a **const** pointer. For example, given these declarations:

```
const int ci = 0, *ci_ptr;
int nci = 0, *nci_ptr;
```

the following statements are obviously legal:

```
ci_ptr = &ci;
nci_ptr = &nci;
```

And so are these:

```
ci_ptr = &nci;     // OK: non-const -> const ptr allowed.
ci_ptr = nci_ptr; // OK: non-const -> const ptr allowed.
```

But not these:

```
nci_ptr = &ci;     // ERROR! const -> non-const ptr illegal.
nci_ptr = ci_ptr; // ERROR! const -> non-const ptr illegal.
```

A little reflection shows why. When a variable or pointer's base type is **const**, the type gains special restrictions (specifically, the code cannot alter the variable). Assigning a non-**const** address to a **const** pointer causes the address usage to gain restrictions, not lose them, so that's not a problem. But going in the reverse direction—assigning a **const** address to a non-**const** pointer—would be an attempt to violate existing restrictions.

Consider what happens what you call a function with a **const** pointer argument:

```
void display_value(const int *p) { }
```

This declaration, in effect, creates a contract: It takes the address of an **int** and agrees to not change the thing pointed to. Given this declaration, you can pass both **const** and non-**const** addresses to it:

```
display_value(ci_ptr);
display_value(nci_ptr);
```

But the converse is not true. Suppose the function is declared this way:

```
void display_value(int *p) { }
```

Then the following function call is not allowed, because it would take away the **const** protection from a **const** address:

```
display_value(ci_ptr);    // ERROR! const pointer cannot
                          //  be passed to non-const arg.
```

Again, this is not allowed because it would enable the function to violate the **const** protection that *ci_ptr enjoys. The value pointed to is supposed to be protected from change, but passing its address to this function—which has no **const** protection—would enable the function to change the value. The compiler does not let that happen.

Similarly, the following code would also cause a compile-time error:

```
const int n = 100;
display_value(&n);    // ERROR! Cannot pass const address
                      //  to a non-const ptr.
```

This situation can create a problem by making it difficult to pass **const** addresses. For this reason, functions are sometimes overloaded:

```
const int display_value(const int *p) { . . .}
int display_value(int *p) { . . .}
```

This overloading is valid in C++. Which version is called depends on whether the address passed is a **const** or non-**const** address. Note that the return-value types may differ, as they do in this case.

But it's possible that upon occasion, you may really need to pass a **const** address to a non-**const** pointer argument. Obviously, this should be avoided the great majority of the time, because it defeats the purpose of the **const** keyword. You should only do it when you're clearly aware of the issues involved. Once a function gets a **const** address, it should not use that address to change the item pointed to. You can perform this transformation with a special cast, **const_cast**:

```
nci_ptr = const_cast<int *>(ci_ptr);
```

This cast removes the **const** attribute from the address expression so that it can be assigned to an ordinary (non-**const**) pointer. (The old C-language cast can also be used this way.) This example helps illustrate the principal reason for the new C++ cast operators: Casts like this are inherently dangerous, and the C++ cast operators force you to acknowledge the specific risks you're taking.

All the rules stated in this section apply to **const** reference arguments as well as pointers to **const** arguments. See Section 6.1.3, "References Modified by const," for examples.

6.3.8 Applying const to the Pointer Itself

The preceding section introduced the concept of pointers to **const** types. There are actually two ways in which a pointer can be declared **const**. The following pointer-declaration syntax uses brackets, not literally, but rather to indicate where the optional **const** attribute can be applied:

```
[const] type * [const] var_name
```

The first use of **const** in this syntax specifies that the base type is **const**; this means that *whatever is pointed to* is protected from change.

The second use of **const** in this syntax protects the pointer itself from change. For example, consider the following pointer definitions.

```
int n = 0, k = 1;
int *p1 = &n;
const int *p2 = &n;            // p2 points to const int
int * const p3 = &n;           // p3 itself is const
const int * const p4 = &n;     // p4 and *p4 are both const;
```

In this example, p4 and p2 are pointers to **const** types. This means that what is pointed to by each of these pointers cannot be changed. So the following would be illegal, because these next statements attempt to change what p2 and p4 point to:

```
*p2 = 5;       // ERROR! p2 points to a const int
*p4 = 5;       // ERROR! p4 points to a const int
```

The declaration of p3 involves a different use of **const**; there is no problem with making changes to what p3 points to, but changes to p3 itself are not allowed. You cannot, for example, assign a different address to p3:

```
p3 = &k;      // ERROR! p3 itself cannot change.
*p3 = k;      // But this is okay.
```

The pointer p4 is protected from both kinds of change; its declaration does not permit changes to either *p4 (what p4 points to) or p4 itself. As with p3, after it is initialized, it cannot be made to store a different address.

This kind of pointer declaration—preventing changes to the pointer itself—is much less used than the other use of **const**.

6.3.9 Void Pointers (void*)

Another special kind of pointer is the **void*** pointer, which is a *generic pointer*—a pointer with no base type. (This is not a "pointer to nothing," which is what a null pointer is.)

Generic pointers are mostly unnecessary in C++, because the role of generic types is usually implemented more effectively by templates and virtual functions. However, occasionally it's still necessary to use generic pointers: In particular, callback functions written for use with the C-library functions **qsort** and **bsearch** require them. (Note: The Standard Template Library [STL] supplies algorithm templates to do the same things more simply and reliably. See Chapter 18, "STL Algorithms," for more information.)

Here's an example of **void*** pointer use:

```
void* p;
int n = 0;
p = &n;   // OK; any addr may be assigned to void* ptr.
```

The rules applying to **void*** pointers are as follows.

- You can assign any address to a **void*** pointer or a **void*** pointer argument.
- However, you cannot go in the reverse direction; a **void*** pointer cannot be assigned to a pointer of more specific type (such as **int*** or **double***) without first being cast.
- You cannot dereference a **void*** pointer without first casting it to a more specific type.
- If pointer arithmetic is performed on a **void*** address, no scaling is performed.

The **qsort** and **bsearch** functions require you to write a callback function that takes pointers of type **const void*** and then use them to evaluate the elements they point to. This requires use of **reinterpret_cast**. (You can also use the old C-style cast, although use of that cast is frowned upon.)

Consider this function, which takes two pointers and returns an integer.

```
int compare_ints(const void *p1, const void *p2);
```

If you're supplying compare_ints as a callback function to **qsort**, you know what kind of data is actually being passed. Let's assume you're writing this function to work on data items of type **int**. In that case, you can dereference the pointers after casting them to **const int** type.

```
int i1 = *(reinterpret_cast<const int*>(p1));
int i2 = *(reinterpret_cast<const int*>(p2));
```

The declarations of p1 and p2 (whose **void*** type is mandated by **qsort**) pose a couple of challenges.

Because the arguments are **void*** pointers rather than **int*** pointers, they need to be cast to **int** base type before being dereferenced. You can't simply assign the pointer values to **int*** pointers without the appropriate kind of cast.

Another issue is that the arguments are **const** pointers. As explained in the preceding section, the **const** attribute prevents the values of such pointers (addresses) from being assigned to non-**const** pointers. (That *could* be done, but it would require a separate step, using **const_cast**.)

The first problem is solved by using **reinterpret_cast**, changing the base type from **const void*** to **const int***. This cast is used to reinterpret the base type of a pointer.

```
reinterpret_cast<const int*>(p1)
```

The second problem is solved because the recast pointers (now having type **const int***) are not assigned to non-**const** pointers. Instead, the pointers are dereferenced and the results are copied. All this does is copy data from the addresses pointed to; it does not attempt to change what's at those addresses. A *dereferenced* **const** pointer may be freely assigned to any compatible type.

```
int i1 = *(reinterpret_cast<const int*>(p1));
```

6.4 Complex Declarations Involving Pointers

The indirection (*), reference (&), and indexing ([ ]) operators can be used to create complex data types. In most cases, you can interpret complex declarations by asking: If the qualified item appeared in executable code and produced the type indicated, what would that imply about the symbol itself?

For example, consider this declaration:

```
int **ptr;
```

This declaration says that when indirection is used twice on ptr, the result is an **int** type. In other words, if:

```
**ptr
```

appears in executable code, the result is an integer—a variable of **int** type. Therefore, ptr is a pointer to a pointer; it must be dereferenced twice to produce an **int**. (Section 6.3.3 demonstrates the practical use of such a pointer in accessing a two-dimensional array.)

An even more challenging declaration is the following:

```
char *string_arr[4];
```

Is this a pointer to an array of **char**, four elements long, or is it an array of four pointers to **char**?

To answer this question, consider precedence (as explained in Chapter 3). The index operator ([]) has higher precedence than the "at" operator (*) and so is applied first. Therefore, the previous declaration is equivalent to:

```
char *(string_arr[4]);
```

This implies that when string_arr appears in executable code, it first takes an index ranging from 0 to 3 (so it has four elements) and is then dereferenced to get **char**. Each of these elements is therefore a pointer of type **char**.

Consequently, string_arr is an array of four C-strings (arrays of **char**) in which each of those strings is of indefinite length. Those lengths can be set through initialization, as in the following declaration:

```
char *string_arr[4] = {"John", "Paul", "George", "Ringo"};
```

Note: Some compilers complain with a warning or even refuse to compile if the **const char*** type is not used in this context, because in C++, string literals actually have **const char*** type rather than **char***. Therefore, to achieve more reliable, portable code, you'd write:

```
const char *string_arr[4] =
     {"John", "Paul", "George", "Ringo"};
```

Now consider the following declaration:

```
char (*string_ptr)[4];
```

This declaration says that string_ptr is a pointer to an array of four characters. It does not allocate any space in memory except for the pointer itself, which must be dereferenced to get a pointer to **char**. Once dereferenced, it is assumed to point to an array of four characters. Therefore, in this case, string_ptr is a pointer to an array—not an array of pointers. This is not a very useful declaration.

This analysis—what would the item imply if it were to appear in executable code?—also works with function pointers. A function pointer is a variable containing the address of a function. Like other pointer variables, it is wide enough to contain an address (four bytes on a 32-bit system), regardless of how long or short the function is that it points to. Also, like other pointer variables, a value of NULL indicates that it currently points nowhere. Before dereferencing it, you must first assign the address of a function.

For example:

```
int (*fp)(int, int);
```

This declaration implies that if the following appears in executable code, it produces an **int**, where i and j are integer arguments:

```
(*fp)(i, j)
```

C++ interprets this expression by doing the following: First get the thing fp points to, and then use that thing to execute a call passing two integer arguments. This implies that what fp points to must be a function. Therefore, fp is a pointer to a function taking two integer arguments and returning an integer. Here is an example using just such a function pointer.

```
int max(int a, int b) {
     if (a > b) return a;
     return b;
}
. . .
int (*fp)(int, int);
fp = max;                  // Assign addr of max funct. to fp.
std::cout << (*fp)(1, -2);    // Print maximum of 1 and -2;
```

Because fp is a function pointer and not a function, it must be assigned the address of a function before it is used in a call; not doing so results in program failure.

Function pointers are not common in short programs; but in certain advanced applications they are needed. In the old C language, tables of function pointers were the only way to implement virtual functions. In C++, such tables are automated for you.

Still, passing the address of a function is useful in many situations (for example, as shown in Chapter 18). Function pointers are needed in any situation, such as use of the C-library **qsort** function, requiring a callback function. A callback is a function address you pass to another function or another process, enabling that entity to call the function you wrote.

Now consider the other case.

```
int *fp(int, int);
```

The rules of precedence place the function-call operator, (), above the "at" operator. Therefore, the declaration just shown is equivalent to:

```
int *(fp(int, int));
```

This declaration implies that fp can be called directly and that it takes two integer arguments. The result produces a pointer to an integer. Therefore, fp is a function returning a pointer.

Such a declaration is valid as far as it goes. However, the function definition would need to be provided somewhere. (The declaration just shown is only a prototype.) And in this case, the name "fp" would be misleading. The following example provides a definition but with the more appropriate name, return_max_ptr. The function calculates the maximum of two integers, creates a new integer to hold the result, and then returns a pointer to this value.

```
// Return Max Ptr function.
// Takes two int's and returns a pointer to an int.
int *return_max_ptr(int a, int b) {
     int *p = new int;
     if (a > b)
           *p = a;
     else
           *p = b;
     return p;        // Return p, which points to max(a, b).
}
```

The **typedef** keyword first introduced in Chapter 2, “Data,” can be particularly helpful with complex declarations. For example, you can define IPTR as a pointer to an integer:

```
typedef int* IPTR;
```

If the **typedef** keyword were omitted, this declaration would have the effect of declaring IPTR as a pointer to an integer. Therefore, the effect of this **typedef** declaration is to make IPTR into a type that is equivalent to **int*** (a pointer to an integer). Likewise, the following use of **typedef** makes CSTR into a type that is equivalent to **const char*** (a pointer to a character value that cannot change).

```
typedef const char* CSTR;
```

With the CSTR type (**const char***) declared, you can then declare arrays of these pointers:

```
CSTR  array_of_strs[10];
```

Or you can declare a function taking such a type as an argument and then returning the same type: a pointer to a character.

```
CSTR  modify_name(CSTR name);
```

6.5 Passing and Returning Function Pointers

The preceding section introduced the concept of pointers to functions. Like any other kind of pointer, these entities hold an address (which, on a 32-bit system, is four bytes wide).

Function pointers have a great deal in common with lambda functions, which were introduced in Chapter 5, “Functions.” In particular, there are many parts of the STL that take a function as an argument; in these contexts you can supply either a lambda or the address of a named function. (There is even a third alternative. As described in

Chapter 7: You can pass an object that supports the function-call operator, (). Such an object is called a *function object.*)

One of the distinctive features of C++, for good or ill, is that there are often many ways of doing the same thing. Which you choose is often a matter of personal preference or convenience. The downside is that sometimes the range of choices is a little overwhelming.

Return values and function arguments can have function-pointer type. This results in some of the strangest syntax in C++. For example, the C-library **qsort** function (see Chapter 12, "Math, Time, and Other Library Functions") has the following declaration:

```
void qsort ( void * base, size_t num, size_t size,
       int ( * compare) ( const void *, const void * ) );
```

The fourth argument to **qsort** implies that you pass the address of a function having the following specifications: It must take two arguments of type **const void*** and it must return an integer. But the name of the function does not have to be "compare"; that name is just the name of the argument as it appears in this prototype.

A prototype may exclude argument names, giving only a function signature. When you do that, the **qsort** declaration looks even stranger:

```
void qsort ( void *, size_t, size_t,
       int (*) ( const void *, const void * ) );
```

Functions can also return the address of another function (!). Such declarations have some of the strangest syntax of all, echoing that shown for **qsort**.

You can reduce some of the strangeness by using a **typedef** statement to declare FPTR as a pointer to a function of the appropriate type. In fact, **typedef** is occasionally needed just to make sure the compiler can accept the declaration at all. (Some compilers may have a difficult time with very complex declarations, and simplifying declarations through the use of **typedef** can help.)

In the following code, the FPTR type is a pointer to a function taking a single **int** argument and returning an **int** value. get_function returns a pointer of type FPTR; it may therefore return a pointer to fun, an actual function.

```
// FPTR type is: pointer to a function taking an int arg
//    and having int return type.
typedef int (* FPTR)(int);

int fun(int n) {         // This is a FPTR-type function.
     return n * 2;
}
```

```
FPTR get_function() {   // This can return a FPTR funct.
     return fun;
}
```

Now, get_function can be used to get back a pointer, fp, which in turn can be used to call a function.

```
FPTR fp = get_function();
cout << (fp)(10) << endl;      // Print 20.
```

These statements end up calling fun, which returns twice the value of its argument.

6.6 Smart Pointers (C++11)

If you're familiar with the concepts in Section 6.3.6, "Pointers and Memory Allocation," you may want to utilize one of the new features in C++11: smart pointers, which aid in preventing memory leaks. A dynamically allocated item is deleted from memory whenever any and all smart pointers referring to it are deleted. (This happens automatically, by the way, when the pointers themselves go out of scope.) Some languages refer to this process as "garbage collection," suggesting something of its appeal: Emptying the garbage is something you'd prefer someone else do, so you can forget about it and focus on other tasks.

The smart-pointer types provided in the C++11 specification are **shared_ptr**, **unique_ptr**, and **weak_ptr**. To use these pointer types, first include the <memory> header:

```
#include <memory>
using namespace std;    // Or else use std::shared_ptr etc.
```

A small program is unlikely to cause the user any noticeable problem with memory leaks. At the termination of a C++ program, all memory objects are supposed to be returned to the system (assuming you're content to rely on compiler-implemented behavior).

But in a multitasking environment, a large program running in the background can cause problems if it allocates memory and does not release it. A common problem is to allocate memory, assign it to a pointer, and then forget to use delete before the pointer goes out of scope. The memory is never restored and becomes a "leak"; and after this happens many times, your users may find themselves wondering why they no longer have enough memory.

Therefore, it's good to get into the habit of programming defensively against leaks. Smart pointers take care of the issue for you. The C++11 specification provides them in the three forms shown in Table 6.1.

TABLE 6.1 Smart-Pointer Types in C++11

Type of Smart Pointer	Description
shared_ptr	Jointly owns a memory resource. An internal reference count is kept, and the resource is deleted only when the reference count goes to 0. Cannot be used to point to an array.
unique_ptr	Owns a memory resource that may not be shared with another pointer. The resource is deleted as soon as the pointer is. This pointer type can be used with a dynamically created array.
weak_ptr	Similar to shared_ptr, but it does not increase or decrease the reference count for the memory resource.

The use of **weak_ptr** is relatively obscure compared to **shared_ptr** and **unique_ptr**, so the next two sections focus only on the first two kinds of pointer.

Here's how automatic deletion (or "garbage collection") works: As soon as a smart pointer goes out of scope—assuming it is not declared **static**—it is deleted from memory. If such a pointer points to a valid memory object, the reference count decreases by one. In the case of shared pointers, if the value of the pointer is assigned to another pointer or passed to a function, the reference count is increased by one.

When the reference count of a dynamically allocated object goes to zero, it is automatically deleted and the memory it occupies is freed; this reference-count tracking is done internally for you, so you never have to track it directly... except maybe during debugging.

6.6.1 The shared_ptr Template

The **shared_ptr** and **unique_ptr** templates are not compatible with ordinary pointers and do not work interchangeably with them. Instead, you must use specific techniques to create and use smart pointers.

A shared pointer can point to a single memory object but not an array. (Use **unique_ptr** for that purpose.) To create a shared pointer attached to a new memory object, use the following syntax:

```
shared_ptr<type>  ptr_name(new type);
```

You can optionally initialize the memory object this way:

```
shared_ptr<type>  ptr_name(new type(init_value));
```

For example, the following statements all create shared pointers, each attached to a different object in memory.

```
#include <memory>   // Required for all smart pointers.
#include <string>   // String obj used in last line below.
using namespace std;

shared_ptr<int>  ip1(new int);     // Ptr to an int.
shared_ptr<int>  ip2(new int(5)); // Ptr to int eq. to 5.
shared_ptr<double>  dp(new double(0.0));
shared_ptr<string>  dp(new string("Hi!"));
```

You can also declare a shared pointer not attached to any memory object to begin with.

shared_ptr<*type*> *ptr_name*;

For example:

```
shared_ptr<int>  ip3;   // ip3 points nowhere.
```

One limitation of a smart pointer is that you can't use it with **new** in the same way you would an ordinary pointer. The compiler interprets any such action as an attempt to convert an ordinary pointer to a shared pointer, which it won't allow.

```
ip3 = new int(5);   // ERROR! Not allowed!
```

But because ip3 is a shared pointer, you can assign the value of another shared pointer to it. For example:

```
shared_ptr<int>  ip2(new int(5)); // Ptr to int eq. to 5.
shared_ptr<int>  ip3;

ip3 = ip2;
```

As a result of this last statement, ip3 points to the same item in memory that ip2 does: an integer containing the value 5. Moreover, since two pointers are now attached to this item, the internally tracked reference count is two. If ip2 or ip3 goes out of scope and consequently is deleted, the reference count is reduced by one. When the reference count goes to zero, the integer itself is deleted.

As a result, the integer created with **new** is automatically deleted, but only after both ip3 and ip2 are either deleted or detached from the integer.

If you want to attach a shared pointer to a new item after the pointer has been declared, you can do this by calling the **reset** member function. After this function is called, ip3 no longer is attached to the item it was attached to before (if any), and it becomes attached to the new item.

```
ip3.reset(new int(10));    // ip3 now points to a new int.
```

Once a shared pointer is attached to some item in memory, you can use the "at" operator (*) to perform indirection with it, just as you can with an ordinary pointer.

```
cout << *ip3 << endl;      // Print 10.
*ip3 = 20;
cout << *ip3 << endl;      // Print 20.
```

The following list summarizes the operations supported for a **shared_ptr** variable.

- *shared_ptr*.**reset()**

  Removes the association between *shared_ptr* and the memory object that it currently points to, if any. If there was such an object, its reference count is reduced by one. (Remember that an object is deleted when its reference count goes to zero.)

  ```
  shared_ptr<int> ip(new int);
  ip.reset();     // Release the integer.
  ```

- *shared_ptr*.**reset(***new_ptr***)**

  Performs the same action as the preceding version of **reset**—reducing the reference count of the currently attached memory object, if any—but then it associates *shared_ptr* with a new object in memory. The reference count of the new object starts at one.

  ```
  ip.reset(new int(500));    // ip now points to a new int
                             //    initialized to 500.
  ```

- *shared_ptr*

  Evaluates to **true** if *shared_ptr* currently points to a valid memory object. (That is to say, *shared_ptr* can be used by itself within a condition.)

  ```
  if (ip){
        cout << "ip points to " << *ip << endl;
        *ip = 500;
        cout << "Now the integer pointed to is 500.";
        cout << endl;
  }
  ```

- **shared_ptr*

  Dereferences the memory object pointed to. See preceding example.

- *shared_ptr*->*obj_member*

  Exactly equivalent to (**shared_ptr*).*obj*_member.

  ```
  shared_ptr<Point>  p(new Point(3, 4));
  cout << p->x;      // Print 3.
  ```

- *shared_ptr* op *shared_ptr2*

  Performs a comparison between two pointers of the same base type. The operators ==, !=, <, >, <=, >= are all supported in this context.

- *shared_ptr1* = *shared_ptr2*

  Causes *shared_ptr1* to point to the same object in memory as *shared_ptr2*. If *shared_ptr1* previously pointed to a valid memory object, the reference count for that object is reduced by one. At the same time, the reference count for the object pointed to by *shared_ptr2* is increased by one.

```
ip1 = ip2;    // Both pointers now point to
              //   what ip2 pointed to.
```

- *shared_ptr*.**get()**

  Returns the address of the memory object pointed to by *shared_ptr* (or **nullptr** if there is no such object); this address may then be assigned to an ordinary pointer. Be careful, however: This address should never be the target of **delete**. It cannot be directly assigned to a smart pointer. And this address becomes invalid if *shared_ptr* is deleted.

```
int *p = ip1.get();
```

- *shared_ptr*.**unique()**

  Returns **true** if the reference count for the object pointed to is exactly one.

- *shared_ptr*.**use_count()**

  Returns the reference count for the object pointed to, if any, or zero if there is none. This function is principally used for debugging purposes.

```
int the_count = ip.use_count();
```

6.6.2 The unique_ptr Template

The **unique_ptr** type (it's a template, actually) can be used in most of the ways that **shared_ptr** can, with two major differences.

- A unique pointer, unlike a shared pointer, owns a memory resource all to itself; that is, the reference count is always one. As soon as the unique pointer is deleted or breaks the attachment to the memory object, the memory object itself is deleted. You cannot assign the value of one unique pointer to another.
- Unique pointers are more flexible, however, in that a unique pointer can point to a dynamically allocated array, unlike a shared pointer.

Here is an example of a unique pointer initialized to point to a single integer:

```
unique_ptr<int>  up1(new int(-3));  // up1 points to -3.
```

By using brackets instead of parentheses, a unique pointer can point to the beginning of a dynamically allocated array. Then, as soon as the unique pointer is deleted or breaks the attachment, the entire array is deleted from memory.

For example, the following statement dynamically allocates 1,000 integers; the unique pointer, up2, points to the first element as a result.

```
unique_ptr<int>  up2(new int[1000]);
```

When a unique pointer points to an array in this manner, you can use indexing to refer to individual elements of that array, as usual.

```
up2[0] = 1;        // Init first element.
up2[1] = 555;      // Init second element.
// Init all remaining elements to 0.
for (int i = 2; i < 1000; ++i) {
     up2[i] = 0;
}
```

The **unique_ptr** template supports most of the operations supported by **shared_ptr**. These include the following. For examples, see the preceding section. Only brief descriptions are included here.

- *unique_ptr*.**reset()**

  Deletes memory object currently pointed to, if any.

- *unique_ptr*.**reset(***new_ptr***)**

  Deletes memory object currently pointed to, if any, and attaches *unique_ptr* to a new object in memory.

- *unique_ptr*

  Evaluates to **true** if *unique_ptr* currently points to a valid memory object. (That is to say, *unique_ptr* can be used by itself within a condition.)

- **unique_ptr*

  Dereferences object pointed to.

- *unique_ptr->obj_member*

  Exactly equivalent to (**unique_ptr*).*obj_member*.

- *unique_ptr* *op* *unique_ptr2*

  Performs a comparison between two pointers of the same base type. The operators ==, !=, <, >, <=, >= are all supported in this context.

- *unique_ptr*.**get()**

  Returns address of the memory object pointed to, if any, or **nullptr**. Note the concerns stated earlier, in regard to using the **get** function with shared pointers:

This address may be assigned to a standard pointer, but do not use **delete** with this pointer. Remember, also, that the address becomes invalid when the *unique_ptr* is destroyed.

6.7 Sample App: Sieve of Eratosthenes

The program in this section makes good use of a dynamically allocated array. The size of this array is determined at runtime, in response to the user. The program accesses elements by using the subscript operator, [], with a pointer.

This famous "Sieve" was invented around 250 B.C.E. by an ancient Greek scientist and mathematician named Eratosthenes. It turns out to be an excellent test for the performance of computers. The Sieve provides perhaps the fastest way possible to compile a large group of prime numbers. The technique is as follows.

1. Write out all the numbers from 2 to N, where N is the upper limit of numbers you want to examine.
2. Begin by assuming that all the numbers are prime; that is, they are not composite numbers (a composite number is a number that is the product of two other integers A and B, where neither is 1).
3. Beginning with 2, look at the current number. If this number is prime, cross out all the multiples of this number—except for the number itself. These crossed-out numbers are flagged as not being prime. For example, 2 is prime, so eliminate all the multiples of 2 beginning with 4, 6, 8, and so on.
4. Then advance to the next number and repeat step 3; continue until N is reached.
5. The numbers that are left—not crossed out—are prime. (This is why it is a "sieve": The primes are the numbers left over once the composite numbers—the non-primes—are eliminated. The numbers that "fall through," as if in a sieve, are the primes.)

The program in this section takes essentially the same approach, using a Boolean array and initializing all elements to **true**. Each element of the Boolean array corresponds to a number from 2 to N. If p[I] is **true**, that means I is a prime number. To keep the programming simple, the first two elements—representing 0 and 1—are included in the array but ignored.

Whenever a prime is found (that is, the corresponding element in the Boolean array is **true**), the process_prime function is called to do two things.

1. Print the number, followed by a tab.
2. Beginning with 2 times this number, flag all multiples by setting the corresponding elements in the Boolean array to **false**.

Here is the program listing.

```
#include <iostream>
using std::cout;
using std::cin;
using std::endl;

void process_prime(bool *p, int max_n, int n);

int main() {
     int max_n = 0;
     cout << "Calculate primes up to what number? ";
     cin >> max_n;
     bool *p = new bool[max_n + 1];      // Allocate array.
     for (int i = 2; i <= max_n; ++i) {      // Init array.
          p[i] = true;
     }
     for (int i = 2; i <= max_n; ++i) {      // Find primes.
          if (p[i]) {
               process_prime(p, max_n, i);
          }
     }
     cout << endl;
     delete [] p;          // Not absolutely necessary, but
                           //   a good idea.
     cin.ignore();         // Consume last carriage return.
     cin.ignore();         // Wait for user to press ENTER.
     return 0;
}

// Process Prime function.
// Print the number n passed to the function, then
//   flag all the elements in the Boolean array (p)
//   that correspond to a multiple of n as false.
//   So, p[i] <= false if i is a multiple of n.
void process_prime(bool *p, int max_n, int n) {
     cout << n << "\t";
     for (int i = n + n; i <= max_n; i += n) {
          p[i] = false;
     }
}
```

Exercises

1. Upon program termination, a C++ program is expected to release any memory resources still in use. Given this fact, why might it still be a good idea (or at least not a bad one) to include a **delete** statement?
2. Section 4.6, "for Statements," contained another program for calculating all the primes from 2 up to a given number. (This number was set to 100 in that example, but it could have been any positive integer.) Which program—the one in Section 4.6 or the Sieve program listed here—is likely to execute more quickly at runtime? Make an argument for one or the other having better runtime performance.
3. Some of the earliest C and C++ compilers had no **bool** type, as well as no **true** and **false** keywords. Instead, programmers had to use **int** variables to store Boolean values. Adapt the program so that it uses an array of integers rather than an array of **bool**. Instead of **true** and **false**, use 1 and 0. Although most of the time this is the last thing you'd want to do, it is still a useful programming exercise to demonstrate that you understand the variables and operators involved.
4. Revise the Sieve program to report the number of primes found.
5. Revise the Sieve program further to report only the primes in a given range, from N to M. (So you'll have to prompt the user for both a lower and upper bound.) Have the program print only primes in this range, and have it total the number of primes in this same range.
6. If your compiler is C++11 compliant, rewrite the application to use a smart pointer.
7. Add statements to handle the possibility of insufficient space for dynamic memory allocation (which tends to be rare on today's computers, but still possible). You can either write exception-handling code for a **bad_alloc** exception or use the **nothrow** keyword as described in Section 6.3.6, to get back a null pointer if and when **memory** allocation fails.

CHAPTER 7

Classes and Objects

One of the central features of C++ is that of *classes*, the single most important ability that C++ adds to C. There are many ways to think of a class. One of the best ways is this: A class is a user-defined type. Once you declare it, you can use it just as you would **int**, **char**, or **double**.

By declaring a class, you create a fundamental new data type, extending C++ itself. You can, if you choose, define how the type responds to operators (such as +, -, or <). You can also provide services in the form of member functions, effectively creating intelligent data types. An object "knows" how to respond to function calls and retains that knowledge even when it is accessed through a pointer of a more general type. (This is called *polymorphism*.)

Above all, classes provide a rational and flexible way to group together closely related functions and data. For larger projects, this is a superior way to design programs. Class-based architecture and design—known as object-oriented programming (OOP)—meshes well with the needs of event-driven, database, and graphical user interface applications.

7.1 Overview: Structures, Unions, and Classes

C++ extends the C concept of data structure (called a "data record" in some languages) to the wider concept of *class*. For example, here is a declaration of a simple class named Point:

```
class Point {
public:
     double x, y;
};
```

The Point class is now declared as a type. Given this declaration, the program can create any number of individual Point variables, called *objects*. All of these objects share the same structure: Each Point object contains its own x and y settings.

```
Point   my_point, your_point, pt1, pt2;
```

Each of these objects (my_point, your_point, pt1, and pt2) has its own x and y members. With each object, you can access its x and y values by using the *object.member* syntax.

```
my_point.x = 0.0;              // Access my_point members.
my_point.y = 0.0;
your_point.x = 1.5;            // Access your_point members.
your_point.y = -2.5;
pt1_point.x = 0.0;             // Access pt1 members.
pt1_point.y = 3.1415;
pt2_point.x = 100.0;           // Access pt2 members.
pt2_point.y = 250.7;
```

The **struct**, **class**, and **union** keywords all can be used to declare classes in a similar manner. The following list compares and contrasts the uses of these keywords.

- **struct**

  Creates a **struct** data type that is backward-compatible with how this keyword is used in C. Everything stated in this chapter about the **class** keyword applies equally to the **struct** keyword, with this difference: Members of a **struct** class are public by default. (They also use public inheritance by default; see Section 7.7.2, "Base-Class Access Specifiers.") Otherwise, the **struct** keyword can be used just like the **class** keyword.

  If you are porting code from C, you should expect classes created with **struct** to work in C++ just as they did in C. However, you have the option of adding member functions and operator support to existing structures, which you couldn't do in C.

- **class**

  Creates a class just as the **struct** keyword does, but member access is private by default. In C++, the **class** keyword is the preferred keyword for declaring new classes, but **struct** can be used as well. As with the **struct** keyword, the **class** keyword declares a type that can optionally provide services in the form of member functions and operators.

- **union**

  Creates a data type in which members have public access by default; but in a union, all the members share the same address in memory. As a result, the same location can be used to store different kinds of data at different times. A union can also be used to read data in one format and then read out the same bit pattern in a different format. Section 7.9, "Unions," covers unions.

7.2 Basic Class Declaration Syntax

Class syntax in C++ can become complex, so the sections that follow focus on the fundamentals of declaring and using an elementary class. Later sections introduce more advanced concepts such as constructors, operator functions, and deriving one class from another (subclassing).

7.2.1 Declaring and Using a Class

Here is the basic syntax for declaring a class. Although the **class** keyword is recommended for creating new data types, you can optionally use **struct** instead of **class**; the difference is that **struct** classes have members with public access by default.

```
class name {
     declarations
};
```

Again, remember that in C++, a **struct** declaration also creates a class, but its members are public by default:

```
struct name {
     declarations
};
```

A class declaration ends in a semicolon (;) following the closing brace (}). The semicolon is both required and essential, as it enables the C++ compiler to distinguish easily between class declarations and function definitions.

The *declarations* are a series of zero or more function and/or data declarations. Each such item—or "member"—has a name that becomes part of the class's namespace.

A class declaration can create one or more instances (objects), or it can terminate immediately. To declare objects at the end of a declaration, use this syntax:

```
class name {
     declarations
} obj_decl, obj_decl...;
```

Alternatively, after a class is declared, you can create objects in a separate statement by using the class name just as you would a primitive type name:

```
class_name  obj_decl, obj_decl...;
```

Each member *declaration* within the class follows the rules for a standard data or function declaration described in earlier chapters—although initialization is not supported, except in the C++11 spec. Otherwise, it's necessary to write a constructor to support initialization.

For example, here is a class declaration:

```
#include <string>

class EmpRec {
public:
     string name;
     string addr;
     int level;
     double salary;
};
```

The four data members—name, addr, level, and salary—are part of the EmpRec class's namespace. In this example, they are all made public, and as public members, they can be accessed once you instantiate objects.

Each data member, when public, can be accessed through the simple dot (.) syntax:

object.member

If you have a pointer to an object, you can refer to a member of that object with this syntax:

ptr->member

For example, the following statements create an EmpRec object named rec1—this is said to *instantiate* the class by creating an object of class type—and then use the *object.member* syntax to manipulate values within that object.

```
EmpRec my_record;            // Instantiate an object.
my_record.level = 5;         // Then access its members.
my_record.salary = 55000.89;
my_record.name = "Joe W. Rabbit";
my_record.addr = "123 Wonderland Street";
```

Member access through a pointer should not be confused with "pointer to member" operators, despite the similarity in names. Pointer-to-member operators are sufficiently rare and obtuse to be safely ignored by most programmers.

But getting a pointer to an object and then dereferencing it to access members is a very common and useful operation. For example:

```
EmpRec your_record;          // Instantiate an object.
EmpRec *p = &your_record;    // p points to this object.
p->level = 3;                // Use -> to access members.
p->salary = 28000;
```

This example uses a pointer to set the level and salary members of your_record to 3 and 28,000, respectively. This syntax:

pointer->member

is exactly equivalent to:

(**pointer*).*member*

7.2.2 Data-Member Access (Public, Private, Protected)

In the preceding section, the members name, addr, level, and salary could be accessed because the **public** keyword preceded their declarations. Consider a simple class that does not use the **public** keyword:

```
class Point {
     double x, y;
};
```

With the **class** keyword (unlike **struct**), members are private by default—which means that they cannot be referred to except within the class itself. So the following is illegal:

```
Point pt1;
pt1.x = 10.0;     // ERROR! x is private!
```

The problem is solved by use of the **public** keyword, combined with a colon (:) as a prefix to the data-member declarations. Public members can be freely accessed from outside the class.

```
class Point {
public:
     double x, y;
};

Point pt1;
pt1.x = 10.0;     // This is now ok; x is public.
```

In the next version of the Point class declaration, x is private but y is public:

```
class Point {
     double x;
public:
     double y;
};
```

Making some or all of the data members private is generally good programming practice, provided that they can all be accessed somehow (either directly or indirectly), as described in Section 7.2.3, "Defining Member Functions."

The three keywords determining member access—public, private, and protected—are described in the paragraphs that follow.

- `public`

  Public access (the default for data structures created with the **struct** keyword). Members that follow **public:** up to the next access-level keyword are public and therefore accessible by users of the class.

  But remember that members are part of the class namespace; you can refer to a member only through an object of the class or by clarifying the scope of a symbolic name (as in *class*::). There is one exception: Inside member functions of the class—covered in the next section—class members can be referred to directly.

- `private`

  Private access (the default for data structures created with the **class** keyword). Members that follow **private:** up to the next access-level keyword are private and therefore not visible except within the class's own member functions. There is an exception to this rule involving the **friend** keyword, described in Section 7.6.2, "Operator Functions as Friends." However, the **friend** keyword should be used sparingly.

  The private portion of a class is considered part of its internals (sometimes called its *implementation*) rather than part of its interface. The benefit of having such members, hidden from the rest of the code, is that programmers working on a class can revise its internals without unexpected effects to the rest of the project. Because outside code cannot "reach in" and access the internal portion of the class, there is far less tendency for updates to break the code outside the class due to unforeseen interdependencies.

- `protected`

  Protected access. Members that follow **protected:** up to the next access-level keyword are protected.

  Everything said about private member access applies equally to protected access, with one difference: A protected member is accessible in subclasses—either direct or indirect—of the class in which it is declared. This is only relevant to code that uses subclassing and inheritance, as described in Section 7.7, "Deriving Classes (Subclassing)."

7.2.3 Defining Member Functions

Member functions can be declared within a class just as data members can. Such functions define services, or operations, provided by all objects of the class.

Suppose you want to create a Point class but control how its values are set. The solution is to make the data members private and rely on member functions to provide indirect access.

```
class Point {
public:
     void set_x(double x);
     void set_y(double y);
     double get_x();
     double get_y();
private:
     double x, y;
};
```

The four member functions enable you to access data for a Point object by calling one of its functions. These function calls also use the dot-member (.) syntax.

In this version of the Point class, the functions are public and therefore can be accessed by users of the class. The data members are private and cannot be accessed—but that's what the member functions are for. Now the user can request that this or that data member be set, but as the author of the class, you control that access.

For example, in the following statements, the values stored in pointA and pointB are manipulated by calling their member functions, such as set_x and set_y.

```
Point pointA, pointB;    // Instantiate two Point objects.

pointA.set_x(1.5);     // Set the x member of pointA to 1.5.
pointA.set_y(2.2);     // Set the y member of pointA to 2.2.
pointB.set_x(0.1);     // Set the x member of pointB to 0.1.
pointB.set_y(0.7);     // Set the y member of pointB to 0.7.
```

The four member functions—set_x, set_y, get_x, and get_y—are all declared following standard declaration rules. But these functions also need to be defined somewhere. C++ provides two ways to provide definitions of member functions.

- A member function may be defined inline, by providing the definition within the class itself. The function prototype is immediately followed by curly braces ({}) containing the statements to be executed.
- A member function may be defined outside the class declaration. In that case, the function definition requires the scope operator (::) to clarify the scope of the function.

As with global functions modified by the **inline** keyword, calls to inline member functions are not implemented through regular function calls; instead, the body of such a function is expanded directly into the body of the calling function. This process is seamless and hidden from the C++ programmer.

You don't write or call inline functions differently from the way you'd call other functions. Implementation details are handled behind the scenes. The main thing you need to know as a programmer is what tradeoffs (space saving versus runtime efficiency) are involved. Inline functions tend to optimize runtime performance, although inlining large functions has the drawback of making the program occupy more space in memory. (Also, inline functions cannot be recursive; they cannot call themselves or be part of a group in which the functions mutually call each other.)

Inlining is the most efficient solution for short functions. The previous example featured four good candidates for inline function definitions. The inline definitions are shown here:

```
class Point {
public:
    void set_x(double newx)  { x = newx; }
    void set_y(double newy)  { x = newy; }
    double get_x()  { return x; }
    double get_y()  { return y; }
private:
    double x, y;
};
```

If you choose instead to provide a function definition outside of a class declaration, the definition can be placed anywhere in the source code after the class has been declared.

Member functions defined outside the class declaration involve the following syntax. Note the use of *class_name*:: syntax to qualify the function name.

```
return_type  class_name::function_name (args) {
    statements
}
```

In this next version of the Point class, the functions are prototyped within the declaration of Point and then defined using the "Point::" prefix to clarify scope.

```
class Point {
public:
    void set_x(double newx);
    void set_y(double newy);
    double get_x();
    double get_y();
```

```
private:
     double x, y;
};

void Point::set_x(double newx)  {
     x = newx;
}
void Point::set_y(double newy)  {
     y = newy;
}
double Point::get_x()  {
     return x;
}
double Point::get_y()  {
     return y;
}
```

Note the use of "Point::" to specify the scope of each of these function definitions. The use of "Point::" specifies that each of these function definitions has Point class scope (that is, it is a member function of the Point class). For the sake of illustration, the preceding example shows each of these qualified names in bold.

Although it involves a bit more work, defining a member function outside its class declaration enables you to write arbitrarily long functions without burdening the class declaration itself. For example, a longer version of set_x might be used to accept values only within a certain range. Again, for the sake of illustration, the qualified name, **Point::set_x**, is shown here in bold.

```
void Point::set_x(double newx)  {
    if (newx < 0.0) {
         x = -newx;
    } else {
         x = newx;
    }
}
```

The effect of this definition is to accept non-negative values for x but to turn negative values into positive ones. For example:

```
Point this_point;
this_point.set_x(99.0);        // Value 99.0 accepted.
this_point.set_x(-3.141592);   // x is set to +3.141592.
```

Again, each function definition gains class scope because it is modified by "Point::". The statements within the definition can refer directly to class members x and y without qualification because the entire function definition has class scope. Member functions can also call each other directly, without qualification.

Incidentally, this version of Point::set_x could be written more concisely by calling the **fabs** math function, which returns an absolute value. This function requires the use of the <cmath> header:

```
#include <cmath>

void Point::set_x(double newx)  {
    x = fabs(newx);
}
```

7.2.4 Calling Member Functions

Calling a member function uses syntax similar to the dot (.) notation used to access data members.

```
object.function(args)
```

You can also call a member function by dereferencing a pointer to an object:

```
pointer->function(args)
```

Here's an example of the dot (.) syntax, using the Point class declared in the previous section.

```
Point pt1, pt2, pt3;         // Create Point objects.
pt1.set_x(55.5);             // Set pt1.x.
pt1.set_y(77.7);             // Set pt1.y.
cout << "pt1.x is " << pt1.get_x() << endl; // Print pt1.x.
cout << "pt1.y is " << pt1.get_y() << endl; // Print pt1.y.
```

Given the definitions for these functions shown earlier, this code prints out the following:

```
pt1.x is 55.5
pt1.y is 77.7
```

Let's review the code. First, look at the statement creating the objects.

```
Point pt1, p2, pt3;
```

This statement declares three objects of class Point. Note that the class name can be used to create objects directly. In C, it was necessary to use the **struct** keyword not only to declare structures, but also to create them.

```
struct Point pt1, p2, pt3;
```

In C++ this usage is still supported for the sake of backward compatibility; but even if you choose to create a **struct** class (making member access public by default), it is not necessary to use the **class** or **struct** keyword when creating (instantiating) data items.

The three items (pt1, pt2, and pt3) are *objects*. The relationship of an object to its class is closely analogous to the relationship of individual integers to the **int** type.

In general, the procedure for creating and using an object is as follows.

1. First, declare a class (or include someone else's class declaration). In effect, this creates a new data type. A class can optionally have member functions—and if so, each member function must either be defined inline or be given a separate function definition that uses class_name:: to clarify scope.
2. Declare instances of the class: These are objects. There is a one-to-many relationship between a class and its objects; that is, you can create any number of objects for a given class. By analogy, there is one **int** type, but you can create any number of **int** variables. It's the same basic idea.
3. Manipulate each object by accessing its public data members or calling its member functions (but only the ones that are public).

For example, assume that pt1, pt2, and pt3 are declared as having Point type.

```
Point pt1, pt2, pt3;
```

Once created, each of these objects can be manipulated by calling Point member functions.

```
pt1.set_x(55.5);
pt1.set_y(77.7);
cout << "pt1.x = " << pt1.get_x() << endl;
```

These statements manipulate and access the state of pt1, a Point object. You can also use these function calls on pt2, another Point object, to manipulate the state of that object.

```
pt2.set_x(200.5);
pt2.set_y(-99.9);
cout << "pt2.x = " << pt2.get_x() << endl;
```

In fact, you can use these same operations on any object declared with the Point class. All Point objects share the same type and support the same operations, data format, and member functions.

Remember, also, that you can get a pointer to an object and then use the -> operator:

```
Point *ptr = &pt3;   // Pointer that can manipulate pt3.
ptr->set_x(200.5);
ptt->set_y(-99.9);
```

Functions and data have a different relationship to classes and objects.

- `Data members (state)`

  Each individual object has its own copy of the data members (except for static members, as described in Section 7.2.7, "Static Members"). This is because each individual object has its own state. By way of analogy, if you declare five **int** variables, each can be set to a different value independently of the other four. But they are all integers.

  Each individual object stores its own copy of each data member (except for static members, which are shared by all objects of a class). For example, pointA, pointB, and pointC, if they are all instances of the Point class, all have the same data format (x and y), but each has its own values for x and y. An object, therefore, is a unit of data.

- `Function members (code)`

  Although objects of the same class contain their own data settings, they share all the same function code. Another way to think of this code—made up of all the member functions of a class—is as *behavior* defined for all those objects. Of course, this behavior may be influenced by each object's internal state.

  The same function code applies to all objects of the class, so a class, in a sense, is a unit of source code. However (except for functions declared static), you call a member function through an individual object, not the class.

Programmers commonly think of data as associated with objects (because each object contains its own values) and function code as associated with classes (because all objects of the same class share function code).

7.2.5 Private Member Functions

A class can declare private member functions as well as private data members. Private functions can only be called by other functions within the same class (the exception being friend functions, described later).

A private member function is part of the class's implementation, hidden from outside. As with private data members, the advantage of a private member function is that the author of the class can add, modify, and delete such functions, knowing that users of the class cannot refer to them. This reduces the danger of other programmers making assumptions about the internals of the class, since they cannot "reach in" and manipulate these internals.

For example, a programmer might write a helper function, do_some_stuff, that supports internal operations of the class but is not intended to be accessed from outside:

```
class Point {
public:
    void set_x(double newx) { x = newx; do_some_stuff(); }
```

```
    void set_y(double newy);
    double get_x();
    double get_y();
private:
    double x, y;
    void do_some_stuff();
};
```

The set_x member function—which in this case is inlined—makes a call to do_some_stuff to offload some of the work. Because the do_some_stuff function is private, it can be revised, renamed, or even removed without affecting users of the class and thereby destabilizing the program.

A function member can also be made protected (by use of the **protected** keyword); in that case, the author of the class wishes programmers who write subclasses to be able to refer to or even modify (override) the function. The difference between private and protected is relevant only where subclassing is involved, as described in Section 7.7.

7.2.6 Classes Containing Classes

Member declarations within a class declaration can use any valid type—including other classes, with some restrictions.

The major rule is that, as always, a type must be declared before being used. Therefore, as long as you declare the Point class first, you can use that class as part of another class declaration:

```
class Point {
public:
    double x, y;
};

class Triplex {
public:
    Point pt1, pt2, pt3;
};
```

In this example, Triplex is a class containing three Point objects, each of which contains two **double** values. You can then declare a Triplex object and access a **double** value by making *two* uses of the dot (.) syntax:

```
Triplex my_triplex;
my_triplex.pt1.x = 1.5;
```

The following are some obvious restrictions.

- A class cannot contain an instance of itself.
- Classes cannot mutually contain each other. For example, if class A contains an instance of class B, then B cannot contain an instance of A.

However, although classes cannot contain instances of each other, they can contain links to each other in the form of pointers and references.

For example, you can create a linked-list structure in which there are two types of nodes—Data_node and String_node—that have pointers to each other… so a Data_node points to a String_node that points to a Data_node.

This is entirely possible in C++, but it opens up the problem of forward references: How do you refer to a class that has not yet been declared? Which do you define first? The solution is to partially declare a class with this syntax:

class *class_name*;

Here's an example that uses this syntax to create two classes referring to each other. This example uses partial class declarations to solve the forward-reference problem.

```
class Data_node;      // These are partial declarations,
class String_node;    //  solving the forward-ref problem.

class Data_node {
public:
     double x;
     String_node  *ptr_to_string_node;
};

class String_node {
public:
     char str[20];
     Data_node  *ptr_to_data_node;
};
```

A class declaration can also be placed inside another class declaration. Such a class is visible only within the scope in which it is declared. The effect is to create a hierarchy of members, which can be useful in organizing information, especially in larger classes. For example:

```
class A {
public:
     struct B {
          int i, j;
     } inner;
     double x;
};
```

Class B (declared here with the **struct** keyword, giving its members public access) is declared within class A and instantiated as the variable named inner. Class A has a data member named inner, and this member has class B as its type.

A also has one other member, x. Although I don't necessarily recommend this, A can have its own "outer" member named i, which does not conflict with the inner i variable because it has different scope. This reveals one of the purposes of hierarchical class-member relationships: to avoid name collisions.

```
class A {
public:
     struct B {
          int i, j;
     } inner;
     int i;    // Does not conflict with inner.i.
};
```

Here's an example of how you could instantiate and use such a class. Note how the dot (.) syntax is used to access the inner members i and j.

```
A an_object;
an_object.i = 0;          // "Outer" i set to 0.
an_object.inner.i = 1;  // inner.i set to 1.
```

7.2.7 Static Members

As stated in Section 7.2.4, "Calling Member Functions," data is usually owned by individual objects, not by the class. However, it is possible to declare one or more data members shared by all objects of the same class. Such a data member is static.

To declare a static data member, first precede its declaration with the **static** keyword.

```
     static int npoints;
```

The variable must then be defined once, and only once, *outside* the class in a separate declaration. (This is similar to the process of declaring and defining member functions.)

```
int Points::npoints = 0;
```

This statement—the one that defines the static variable outside of the class declaration—creates a global static variable within the Points namespace. For example, the following statements create a static member, npoints, declared within the Point class. Notice that npoints must be declared twice: once inside the class and once outside.

```
class Point {
public:
     static int npoints;  // Declares npoints as member.
     double x, y;
}
int Point::npoints = 0;  // This defines npoints.
```

In C++, there are two principal ways to refer to a static class member.

- You can refer to it through the class name, by using the scope operator. For example:

  ```
  Point::npoints++;
  ```

- You can also refer to a static member through any object of that class—although once again remember that this member is shared by all objects of the same class. In this case, apply the dot (.) syntax.

  ```
  pt1.npoints = 0;
  ```

Static data members can be given any access level desired: private, protected, or public.

There is one exception to the general procedure (declare within the class, and define the variable outside the class): A variable that is declared both **const** and **static** can be declared just once, within the class, and it can be initialized there. Remember that a **const** variable is protected from change.

```
class Point {
public:
     const static int npoints = 0;  // CANNOT CHANGE!
     double x, y;
};
```

Member functions can also be declared static. Static member functions are defined and declared just as other functions are, and, like other members, they can be public, private, or protected. But a static member function is restricted in its usage. It cannot refer to the **this** pointer (described in Section 7.5, "The Hidden "this" Pointer") and it cannot refer to any other members of the class except those that are also static.

The purpose of a static member function is usually to manipulate static data members. It is possible to write a class without any nonstatic members at all; such a class would function as a separate namespace.

One obvious use for npoints in the preceding examples is to keep track of the number of instances (that is, objects) of the Point class. You might use it this way:

```
Point pt1, pt2;
Point::npoints += 2;  // We created 2 new objects.
```

```
Point pt3;
++Point::npoints;      // We created 1 new object.
cout << "The number of points is " << Point::npoints;
```

Looking at this example, don't you think it would be convenient for the static member, npoints, to be automatically incremented each and every time a Point object was created? And for npoints to be automatically decremented whenever a Point object was destroyed?

That would be a highly useful feature—which it turns out C++ supports in the form of constructors and destructors. Section 7.3, "Constructors," and Section 7.4, "Destructors," describe the rules for constructors and destructors, respectively.

7.3 Constructors

A constructor is an initialization function, automatically called after an object is allocated in memory. Constructors have a unique syntax. They have the same name as the class itself and do not have a return type:

```
class_name(args)
```

You can create any number of different constructors as long as they are differentiated by the types in their argument lists. The arguments passed during object creation, if any, determine which constructor to call. For example:

```
Point point1(1.5, 3.1415);
```

This statement invokes the constructor that takes two floating-point arguments. (If no constructor exists that can be matched to the argument list, the compiler will flag the statement as an error.)

Unlike other functions, a constructor has no return value, not even **void**. The class name, in a sense, *is* the return value, because the action is to create an object of the class—although allocation of memory for the object happens implicitly. You only have to handle initialization.

Like other function members, constructors may be either inlined or defined outside the class. If you define a constructor outside the class, the scope operator (::) must be used, as usual.

```
class_name::class_name(args) {
    statements
}
```

As an example, the Point class, introduced earlier, can benefit from constructors that manage the npoints static member. These constructors can update the value of npoints automatically.

```
class Point {
public:
     static int npoints;
     double x, y;

     Point() {       // This is a Point constructor.
         x = y = 0.0;
         npoints++;
     }

};
int Point::npoints = 0;
```

In this example, the Point() constructor is inline, but it could have been defined separately, outside the class declaration, in which case it would have this definition:

```
Point::Point() {
    x = y = 0.0;
    npoints++;
}
```

This constructor initializes both x and y to 0.0 so that even if a Point object is declared locally, x and y will be properly initialized. It also increments npoints by one. Consequently, npoints, a static variable, will reflect the total number of Point objects, because the constructor is called each and every time a Point object is created. (Note, however, that for this to work consistently, you would also need to write a copy constructor, as described in Section 7.3.3, "Copy Constructor.")

7.3.1 The Default Constructor

The default constructor for a class is the constructor taking zero arguments. The preceding section featured an example of such a constructor.

The default constructor is called anytime an object of the class is created without being explicitly initialized. For example, the following statement causes the Point default constructor to be invoked three times:

```
Point pt1, pt2, pt3;  // Call def. constructor 3 times
```

A special rule applies to default constructors: If you do not write any constructors whatsoever, the compiler provides a default constructor that does nothing. But if you write at least one constructor of any kind, the compiler does not supply a default constructor—so it suddenly becomes impossible to create objects without explicitly initializing them.

If you want to prevent declaration of uninitialized objects, this behavior is desirable, but otherwise it can be a "gotcha." Suppose you add a constructor to a class (this one taking two floating-point arguments) but do not write a default constructor of your own. In that case, code that previously worked may break.

```
class Point {
public:
      double x, y;
      Point(double newx, double newy) {  // constructor
            x = newx;
            y = newy;
      }
};
```

This innocent-looking code now breaks the following statement—all because when the Point(double, double) constructor was added, the compiler took away the compiler-supplied default constructor.

```
Point pt1;   // ERROR! Default constructor not available!
```

There are a number of situations that invoke the default constructor: for example, when you use the **new** keyword to create an array of objects. Therefore, unless you want to force explicit initialization on the part of the users of the class, it is good defensive programming to include a default constructor for each new class you write, even if that default constructor does nothing.

```
class Point {
public:
      double x, y;

      Point() {}                         // Default constr

      Point(double newx, double newy) {  // Another constr
            x = newx;
            y = newy;
      }
};
```

These two constructors are defined inline, but (as usual) they could have been defined outside of the class declaration, as shown next. Note the use of the scope operator (::) in these definitions to clarify that the functions are members of the class.

```
class Point {
public:
      double x, y;
```

```
    Point();
    Point(double newx, double newy);
};

Point::Point() {}

Point::Point(double newx, double newy) {
    x = newx;
    y = newy;
}
```

As long as you take the time to write a default constructor, you should probably use it to set reasonable initial values. So a better version of the default constructor for this class is:

```
Point::Point() {
    x = 0.0;
    y = 0.0;
}
```

Constructors should be given public access, at least if you want to make them available to users of the class.

7.3.2 Overloaded Constructors and Conversion Functions

A class can have any number of overloaded constructors, each differentiated by the type information in its argument list.

For example, here is a class called Triplet that supports five constructors. For brevity's sake, I've defined them all inline, in the class declaration, although they could be defined separately.

```
class Triplet {
public:
    Triplet() {a = b = c = 0;}
    Triplet(int newa) {a = newa; b = c = 0; }
    Triplet(int newa, int newb){a = newa; b = newb; c = 0}
    Triplet(int newa, int newb, int newc )
       {a = newa; b = newb; c = newc; }
    Triplet(double x)
       {a = static_cast<int>(x); b = c = 0;}
private:
   int a, b, c;
};
```

The following statements create five Triplet objects, each invoking a different constructor.

```
Triplet tr1;
Triplet tr2(1);
Triplet tr3(0, 10);
Triplet tr4(100, 200, 300);
Triplet tr5(77.1);
```

In some cases, it's possible for the compiler to select more than one constructor, but it will always select the closest match. For example, if the only constructor supplied is the one taking a floating-point argument—Triplet(double)—the following statement will invoke that constructor:

```
Triplet my_object(5);
```

The integer argument would first be cast to floating-point type and then passed to the Triplet(double) constructor. However, because a constructor taking an integer happens to be available in this case—Triplet(int)—the compiler uses that constructor instead.

Constructors that take a single argument automatically define a conversion function. Consider the constructor Triplet(int), which takes a single integer:

```
    Triplet(int newa) {a = newa; b = c = 0; }
```

The existence of this constructor enables an integer to be used in any context requiring a Triplet object. Suppose that the following function is defined to print objects of this class.

```
void print_trip(Triplet t) {
    cout "a: " << t.a << end;
    cout "b: " << t.b << end;
    cout "c: " << t.c << end;
}
```

Because the constructor Triplet(int) takes a single integer argument, it implicitly defines a conversion function, enabling an integer to be used wherever a Triplet object is expected. So the following would be legal.

```
print_trip(100);   // Convert 100 to a Triplet and then print.
```

As a result, the program would print:

```
a: 100
b: 0
c: 0
```

Note that modifying a constructor with the **explicit** keyword prevents the constructor from working as a conversion function.

```
explicit Triplet(int newa) {a = newa; b = c = 0; }
```

7.3.3 Copy Constructor

Another special kind of constructor is the copy constructor, which takes an object of the same class as its only argument.

If the program does not provide a copy constructor explicitly, the compiler automatically supplies one: The action is to perform a simple member-by-member copy. In many cases, relying on this constructor is adequate, but it fails to make copies of resources, such as files and dynamically allocated memory. Such "deep copying" behavior is necessary for more complex objects that own resources. In such cases the compiler-supplied copy constructor may be inadequate and it becomes necessary to write one of your own.

A class's copy constructor is automatically invoked in several cases:

- When an object of the class is passed as an argument (unless it is passed by reference)
- When a function returns an object of the class (again, unless it is returned as a reference)
- When an object of the class is created and initialized from an existing object of the same class

The syntax of a copy-constructor declaration is specific and must use the reference operator (&) as follows:

```
class_name(const class_name &arg_name)
```

The first use of *class_name* is the name of the function—which in the case of all constructors is the same as the name of the class itself. The second use of *class_name* is the type of the argument, which is the same as the class, because that's what a copy constructor is: It tells how to create a new object from another object of the same class.

Note the use of the ampersand (&) to create a reference argument. If it were necessary to copy an object *before* making a copy of that object, the result would be an infinite regress! Infinite regress is avoided by passing the argument as a reference.

Because this argument is passed as a reference, the function gets direct access to the object itself rather than a copy. A constructor should not change the value of what's passed to it, which is why **const** is applied to the argument declaration.

If the copy constructor is defined outside the class declaration, it has the following syntax. The first occurrence of *class_name* clarifies the scope; it says that this definition is for a member function of this class. The second occurrence of *class_name* is the name of the function itself—which is the same as the class name because it's a constructor. The third occurrence of *class_name* is the argument type.

```
class_name::class_name(const class_name &arg_name) {
     statements
}
```

Here is a simple copy constructor for the Triplet class. It does nothing more than the compiler-generated copy constructor would do. This version—although it could have been inlined—is defined outside the class and therefore requires the use of the scope operator (::).

```
Triplet::Triplet(const Triplet &src) {
     a = src.a;
     b = src.b;
     c = src.c;
}
```

Within these statements, unqualified uses of a, b, and c refer to this object's copy of a, b, and c (that is, in the object being created) while src.a, src.b, and src.c all refer to a, b, and c in the source argument.

In another example, the Point copy constructor not only copies the value of x and y but also updates the value of npoints, a static member. This version is also defined outside its class declaration, so, once again, the scope operator (::) must be used.

```
Point::Point(const Point &source_point) {
     x = source_point.x;
     y = source_point.y;
     npoints++;
}
```

7.3.4 Constructor Initialization Lists

To make the work of writing constructors easier, C++ provides some time-saving techniques. This section presents one of those techniques—initialization lists—and the next two sections present features introduced in C++11.

Initialization lists are a convenient aid for writing constructors. In some cases, they provide the only way to initialize certain members. Here's a simple use of the technique:

```
Point {
public:
     double x, y;
     Point () : x(0.0), y(0.0) {}
};
```

Take another look at the constructor, which initializes x and y to 0.0 without using any assignment statements.

```
Point () : x(0.0), y(0.0) {}
```

This declaration introduces an alternative way of writing a constructor definition:

class_name **(***args***)** : *init_list* **{** *statements* **}**

In this syntax, *init_list* consists of one or more initializers, separated by commas if there is more than one. Each initializer has the following syntax:

*member***(***init_value***)**

The *init_value* can use the constructor's argument list. For example, the following constructor uses the arguments new_x and new_y to initialize data members x and y.

```
Point(double new_x, double new_y) : x(new_x), y(new_y) {}
```

Initialization lists are always used in a constructor definition, not a prototype. For example:

```
Point {
public:
     double x, y;
     Point ();
     Point (double nx, double ny);
};

Point::Point() : x(0.0), y(0.0) {}

Point::Point(double nx, double ny) : x(nx), y(ny) {}
```

In the case of **const** data members, an initialization list is the only way to initialize the member. Consider this example class:

```
#include <string>

class Dog {
public:
     const int gender;    // male = 1, female = 0
     int age;
     string name
```

```
    Dog(int m_f, int a, string nm) :
        gender(m_f), age(a), name(nm) { }
};
```

The data member "gender" is declared **const**. This makes a certain amount of sense; it says that even though a dog's age or name may change, its gender shouldn't. (I don't mean to be insensitive, but I have yet to meet any transsexual dogs.) But with gender declared **const**, how does it ever get a value? This can't be done inside a constructor:

```
Dog(int m_f)  {
    gender = m_f;   // ERROR! const member cannot be
}                   //   assigned a value.
```

The initializer "gender(m_f)", used in the preceding example, comes to the rescue. The effect is to initialize gender as if it had been declared as follows:

```
    const int gender = m_f;
```

Members with a reference type present a similar difficulty. A reference variable can't be made to refer to a new variable after being declared. But the following code gets around this problem.

```
class Funny_class {
public:
    int i;
    int &ref_i;
    Funny_class() : i(0), ref_i(i) { }
};
```

The result of this (somewhat peculiar) declaration is to make one member, ref_i, an alias for another, i. The effect is to initialize these members as if they'd been declared as follows:

```
int i = 0;
int &ref_i = i;
```

In the following declaration, the data member ref_i becomes an alias for the global variable nn so that nn can be manipulated from within Funny_class as if it were a member.

```
int nn;

class Funny_class {
public:
    int i;
    int &ref_i;
    Funny_class() : i(0), ref_i(nn) { }
};
```

Before leaving the topic, you should note that there are limitations to constructor initialization lists. A **string** member can be directly initialized with another **string** object, but initialization of a C-string (a traditional **char*** string) requires a function call.

```
#include <cstring>  // Support C-string library functions

class Dog {
public:
     const int gender;    // male = 1, female = 0
     int age;
     char name[21];
     Dog(int m_f, int a, char *nm) : gender(m_f), age(a)
          { strncpy(name, nm, 20); }
};
```

In this example, data members gender and age are initialized from the arguments m_f and a, but the data member called "name", a C-string, gets character data copied to it through the call to **strncpy**.

7.3.5 Delegated Constructors (C++11)

The task of writing constructors can become tedious after a while, although initialization lists help to reduce some of the work. Consider a simple class named EmpRec:

```
class EmpRec {
public:
     int level;
     long salary;
     string name;
     EmpRec(int n_level, int n_salary, string n_name) :
          level(n_level), salary(n_salary), name(n_name) {}
     EmpRec(int n_level, int n_salary) :
          level(n_level), salary(n_salary) {}
     EmpRec(string n_name) : level(0), salary(0), name(n_name) {}
     EmpRec() : level(0), salary(0) {}
};
```

Even this simple class involves four constructors that do largely the same thing: They initialize combinations of the three data members, level, salary, and name. (Note that name never needs to be initialized to an empty string, because the default constructor of the **string** class does that for you.)

Delegated constructors enable you to leverage some of the work. Within the EmpRec class, a constructor ideally ought to be able to delegate the task of initialization to another constructor.

C++11 enables you to do exactly that. Here are the last two constructors rewritten with delegators. Notice how this results in shorter lines of code.

```
EmpRec(string n_name) : EmpRec(0, 0, n_name) {}
EmpRec() : EmpRec(0, 0) {}
```

Each of these invokes an earlier constructor. For example, consider this declaration:

```
EmpRec() : EmpRec(0, 0) {}
```

This constructor—the default constructor—calls EmpRec(int, int), passing along the arguments 0 and 0. One constructor, in this case, is said to delegate to another.

Here is the general syntax of a constructor using a delegator:

```
class_name(arg_list1) : class_name(arg_list2) {
     statements
}
```

This syntax declares a constructor with *arg_list1*. When invoked, it calls the delegated constructor, optionally passing along some or all of its arguments to *arg_list2*. The delegated constructor is the constructor that appears after the colon (:). Afterward, the statements in the body of the function definition (if any) are executed.

7.3.6 Default Member Initialization (C++11)

When you look at the syntax for class declarations, you may wonder why C++ doesn't let you initialize data members just as you would other variables. The new C++11 specification finally allows you to do just that. (But note that you may need to check the documentation for your compiler to see exactly what is supported; not all new compilers are 100 percent compliant with C++11 as of this writing.)

```
Point {
public:
     double x = 0.0;
     double y = 0.0;
     // Point() constructor: x and y get 0.0
     Point () {}
     // Point(double, double) constructor: still works!
     Point (double new_x, double new_y)
         : x(new_x), y(new_y) { }
};
```

Within this class declaration, the default constructor, Point(), doesn't initialize x and y explicitly; instead, x and y assume the values 0.0 and 0.0, the values they were given when declared as class members.

```
double x = 0.0;
double y = 0.0;
```

Initializing x and y this way doesn't free you from the task of writing a default constructor—it just makes the task simpler.

The initial value for a data member can be overridden by any constructor. Therefore, the Point(double, double) constructor works just as it did before.

Initializing data members this way can be especially useful with classes that have many constructors. Each constructor can override a data member's default value; but if a constructor doesn't set or initialize a particular member, that member gets the value it had when declared.

7.4 Destructors

A destructor—despite the harshness of the name—has a benign purpose: to perform any cleanup of resources (or other relevant data) upon object termination.

There are several cases in which an object might be terminated, or otherwise removed from memory.

- When the object is declared as a (nonstatic) local variable. The object is destroyed as soon as it goes out of scope.
- When the **delete** keyword is applied to explicitly remove an object created dynamically with **new**.
- At the end of the program. In this case, the program usually performs cleanup of all remaining resources in the program.

You can have at most one destructor (it cannot be overloaded). It has the following syntax:

~*class_name* **( )**

A destructor might be used to release any resources currently owned by the object, such as dynamically requested memory and file handles.

Another case is the Point class example earlier in the chapter. To maintain an integer npoints tracking the number of such objects, each constructor should increment npoints (a static variable) by one; also, a destructor should be supplied to decrement this same variable.

Within the class declaration, the Point destructor has this prototype:

```
~Point();
```

Outside the class declaration, it would be defined as follows:

```
Point::~Point() {
    npoints--;
}
```

Or you can just inline the destructor by defining it inside the class declaration.

```
     ~Point() {npoints--;}
```

A destructor cannot be declared **const**, **volatile**, or **static**. It can, however, be declared **virtual**.

7.5 The Hidden "this" Pointer

One of the important ideas in this chapter is that when you call a function through an object, the function gets access to all that object's members. Consider a call to a member function through a Point object named a_point:

```
Point a_point;
a_point.set_x(99.0);    // Value 99.0 accepted.
```

The set_x function is called, which is defined as follows:

```
void Point::set_x(double newx)  {
    if (newx >= 0.0 && newx <= 100.0)
         x = newx;
    else
         x = 0.0;
}
```

This function manipulates a data member, x. But how does the function know whose copy of x to manipulate? In this case, the value that gets set is a_point.x. How does the function end up manipulating *this object's* copy of x and not some other object's copy of x?

Although the process is usually invisible to the source code, the function is passed a hidden pointer argument: That argument can be identified in the source code as **this**, which is a pointer to the object through which the function is called (see Figure 7.1). Within a function member, the **this** keyword is translated into the address of that object.

When you call a member function, you don't explicitly pass a pointer to the object; that's done for you automatically. But within the function definition, you can use the

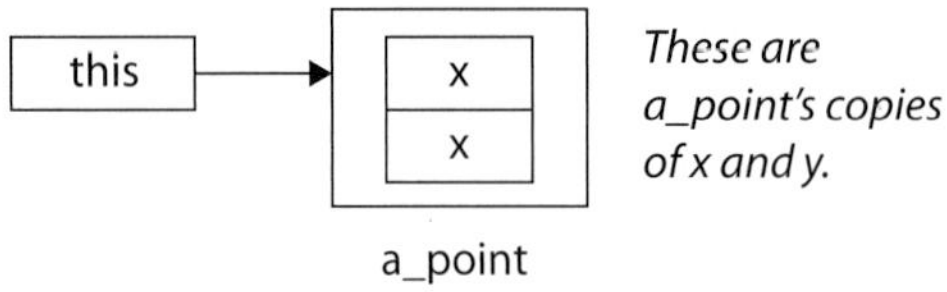

FIGURE 7.1 The this pointer

this keyword. For example, the previous function definition could have been written as follows (for clarity, I show its usage in bold).

```
void Point::set_x(double newx)  {
     if (newx >= 0.0 && newx <= 100.0) {
          this->x = newx;
     } else {
          this->x = 0.0;
     }
}
```

Normally, such usage is unnecessary, because by default, references to members are assumed to be references through the **this** pointer, making **this** unnecessary most of the time. There are several situations, however, where the keyword is needed.

- If there is a local variable with the same name as a member, the compiler matches symbols to local variables first. Use of **this**, in those situations, indicates that a member is being referred to, not the local variable.
- Occasionally, a member function may call another function and pass a pointer to the current object.
- Also—and this is probably the most common usage of **this**—certain operator functions return a reference to the object through which the function was called.

In the last case, it's necessary to return the object itself (not just a pointer to it), which is done through this statement:

```
return *this;
```

Section 7.6.3, "Assignment Operator (=)," presents function-definition code that uses such a statement.

7.6 Operator Functions (Op Overloading)

One of the notable features of C++ is that you can create new data types that are essentially extensions to the C++ language itself. C++ recognizes almost no difference between primitive types and classes—assuming, of course, that the class has been declared somewhere prior to use.

For the primitive data types, a number of operations are defined such as addition (+), subtraction (-), and multiplication (*). C++ enables you to define how these operators work with objects of your own classes: This is called *operator overloading*, because the same operator can perform different operations on different types.

A function that tells how your objects respond to a specific operator is called an operator function.

7.6.1 Operator Functions as Members

For a given operator—represented here as *op*—the syntax for declaring an operator function as a class member is:

```
return_type operator op ( )                  // Unary operator op
return_type operator op (right_arg)          // Binary operator op
```

Remember that *op* is a placeholder for a C++ operator symbol, such as +, -, *, and so on.

Such a function, once defined, is executed whenever the operator in question is applied to objects of the class.

A unary operator function, as a class member, takes no arguments. A binary operator takes one. For example, the following code defines how the unary negation (-) operator works when applied to an object of the Point class. Because the result is a new Point object, the function must allocate and return a new instance of the class.

```
Point Point::operator - () {
     Point new_point;       // Create new obj, to return
     new_point.x = -x;
     new_point.y = -y;
     return new_point;
}
```

If a Point(double, double) constructor is available, it's possible to write this function more concisely.

```
Point Point::operator - () {
     return Point(-x, -y);
}
```

This causes the expression "–pt1" to be evaluated by returning a new Point object copying the values x and y from pt1 but negating them. With these statements in place, the program can then apply unary negation (-) to objects of the Point class.

The following statement uses this operator (-) and then copies the resultant object to pt2.

```
Point pt2(-pt1);
```

A member function implementing a binary operator (that is, an operator taking two operands) has one argument. The left operand is associated with "this" object—that is, the object through which the operator function was called. The right operand is associated with the single argument.

This is easier to understand with an example. The following code implements binary addition (+) with another Point object:

```
Point Point::operator + (const Point &rh_arg) {
     Point new_point;
     new_point.x = x + rh_arg.x;
     new_point.y = y + rh_arg.y;
     return new_point;
}
```

In this code, the unqualified members "x" and "y" refer to the values in the left operand. The expressions "rh_arg.x" and "rh_arg.y" refer to the values in the right operand.

With this operator+ function defined, the following statements do what you'd expect:

```
Point pt1(100, 100);
point pt2(10, 20);
Point my_point(pt1 + p2);
```

The resultant object, my_point, has x and y values of 110.0 and 120.0, respectively.

The following rules apply to writing operator functions.

- Almost the entire set of C++ operators is available for use with operator functions. However, you are limited to just this set; you cannot make up new operators from characters outside the existing set of C++ operators.
- You cannot define a C++ operator as binary unless that syntax is supported, and you cannot define an operator as unary unless that syntax is supported. However, you can interpret the meaning of the operator (that is, what is does) however you choose. Of course, it is a good idea to try to preserve the original meaning as much as possible: For example, ideally an operator+ function ought to do something like addition.
- The rules of precedence and associativity described in Chapter 3, "Operators," are always observed, no matter how their functionality is implemented. For example, the binary * operator always has precedence over the binary + operator.
- Each assignment operator (=, +=, -=, *=, and so on) must be defined separately. By defining + and =, you don't get a free += function. Similarly with ++ and --.

- There is no free lunch in terms of commutivity, either: When mixing types, order is significant. For example, int+Point and Point+int are separate cases that must be implemented separately.

7.6.2 Operator Functions as Friends

You can also write operator functions as global functions (that is, functions that are not class members). For a given operator represented here as *op*, the syntax for declaring an operator function as a global function is:

```
return_type operator op (arg)                      // Unary operator op
return_type operator op (left_arg, right_arg)      // Binary operator op
```

Remember that *op* is a placeholder for a C++ operator symbol, such as +, -, *, and so on. For example, the binary + operator could be implemented for the Point class as follows:

```
Point operator + (const Point &left, const Point &right) {
     Point new_point;
     new_point.x = left.x + right.x;
     new_point.y = left.y + right.y;
     return new_point;
}
```

This function could have been written as a member function. There is one major reason for writing an operator function as a global (non-class-member) function: Sometimes it is the only way to provide the functionality. Use of a function member is valid when the left operand has class type. But you might want to support other expressions.

For example, if you're supporting multiplication, you'd want to define how multiplication works when applied to an integer and a Point object:

```
Point pt1(10, 20);
Point pt2 = 5 * pt1;
```

The problem is that in the expression "5 * pt1", the left operand is an **int** variable, not a Point object. But you cannot write member functions for the **int** type. Therefore, to define such operations, you must provide a global function.

```
Point operator * (int n, const Point &right_op);
```

But there's a further problem. Because this function is not a class member, it has no privileged access to the Point class: It cannot access private members. The solution is to declare the global function as a "friend" to the class by using the **friend** keyword. To do this, add a prototype of the function to the class and prefix it with **friend**:

```
class Point {
. . .
    friend Point operator *(int n, const Point &right_op);
}
```

A friend function has access to all the members of a class.

Here is a complete, albeit simple, example. The line that declares the operator function as a friend is shown in bold.

```
class Point {
private:
    double x, y;
public:
    Point () { x = y = 0; }
    Point (double newx, double newy) {x = newx; y = newy;}
    double getx() {return x;}
    double gety() {return y;}
    friend Point operator * (int n, Point pt);
};

Point operator * (int n, Point pt) {
    return Point(n * pt.x, n * pt.y);
}
```

With these declarations in place, you can then execute statements such as the following. (Note that so far, the operation int * Point is defined, but not Point * int, which requires a separate function.)

```
    Point pt1(1.5, 2.5);
    Point pt2(10 * pt1);
```

7.6.3 Assignment Operator (=)

The assignment operator function for a class, operator=, is a special function, just like the default constructor and copy constructor: If you do not supply this function, the compiler will supply its own version of it.

This function is invoked when an object is assigned to another object of the same type by use of the equal sign (=). Exception: When the equal sign is used during a declaration, the copy constructor is invoked, not the assignment operator.

```
Point pt1(1.5, 100.7);
Point pt2 = pt1;        // Invokes copy constructor
pt1 = pt2;              // Invokes operator= function
```

The compiler-supplied assignment operator function performs a simple member-by-member assignment. For some classes, this is sufficient. But this behavior is inadequate for more complex classes that require deep copying. Deep copying might be needed in a class that owns resources, such as memory, requiring each object to allocate its own copies of those resources.

To write your own assignment operator function, you need to use the proper declaration and to return a reference to the current object. The general syntax is:

```
class_name& operator=(const class_name &arg_name) {
    . . .
    return *this;
}
```

The **this** keyword, used here, is a pointer to the object itself—that is, the object on which the code operates (the left operand). The statement "return this;" (note the lack of the asterisk) would return a pointer to the object, which would be incorrect. But:

```
return *this;
```

essentially says, "Return myself!"

This is necessary because all assignment operations (including not only = but all the combined operators such as +=, -=, and so on) must return a reference to the left operand. That's exactly what "return *this;" does. It returns the object itself.

Assignment operators (and some other operators) return a reference to the left operand to enable statements such as the following. Ideally, this programming technique ought to work for any class that implements the assignment operator.

```
a = b = c = 0;
```

The return type should be a reference to the class, so a new copy does not need to be made.

Here's an example using the Triplet class introduced earlier. As with all function members, the operator= function can be defined inside the class (as an inline function) or outside the class. In the latter case, remember that the scope operator (::) must be used to prefix the function name, as always.

```
Triplet& Triplet::operator=(const Triplet &src) {
    a = src.a;
    b = src.b;
    c = src.c;
    return *this;
}
```

If you want to support the other assignment operators (+=, -=, *=, and so on) you must write individual operator functions for each of these separately. Each must return a reference to the left operand, and so each must use the "return *this" statement.

7.6.4 Function-Call Operator, ( )

In C++, parentheses, (), are used to call a function. That's a nearly universal syntax convention in higher-level programming languages; what's unusual is that in the C family of languages, parentheses are considered an operator. You can define this operator for your own classes.

The effect is to turn instances of the class into *function objects*. A function object can be given as an argument to any function or template expecting a callback function. You can also use a function object by calling it directly.

A member function defining the function-call operator has the following declaration:

return_type **operator () (***args***)**

This operator can be overloaded any number of times, provided that the overloaded versions have distinct argument-list signatures.

For example, the following statements declare a class named GetTwice along with an instance of that class named my_fun.

```
class GetTwice{
public:
     int operator () (int n) {return n * 2;}
} my_fun;
```

Because myfun is an instance of GetTwice, you can use my_fun just as you would a function: my_fun becomes a function object. The effect is to call a function that returns twice its argument.

```
cout << "my_fun(100) is ";
cout << my_fun(100) << endl;    // Print 200.
```

You may wonder why a class should be used this way at all, considering that it would be simpler just to write a function directly:

```
int get_twice(int n) {
     return n * 2;
}
```

The advantage of function objects is that they can have an internal state, enabling you to customize the effect of each function object. For example, the following code creates a class with a comparison function. Two instances of the class are created; and each of these instances, when called as a function, compares the argument n to its own internal state.

```
class Compare_Fun {
private:
     int my_dat;
public:
     Compare_Fun(int dat) {my_dat = dat;}
     bool operator() (int n) {return n < my_dat;}
};
Compare_Fun  less_than_5(5);     // This is a funct object.
Compare_Fun  less_than_10(10);   // So is this.
. . .
int i = 7;
cout << "i < 5? " << less_than_5(i) << endl;    // Print 0.
cout << "i < 10? " << less_than_10(i) << endl;  // Print 1.
```

These examples are simplistic, but they give some hint of how powerful this feature of C++ syntax is.

Note

The state of a function object should not change in the middle of executing an STL algorithm.

7.6.5 Subscript Operator, [ ]

One of the many things you can do with a class is to encapsulate an array. It's always possible, of course, to contain an array and make it a public member, permitting the class users to access elements of the array directly. And sometimes that's a perfectly good solution.

But with C++ classes, you also have the option of controlling access to an array. You might, for example, transform an index or reject attempts to use an out-of-bound index. You can do this by defining the indexing operator—or more formally, the *subscript operator* ([]).

A member function defining the subscript operator has the following declaration:

type& **operator[] (const int** *index***)**

in which *type* is the base type of the array, and *index* is the name of an argument passed an index number. The function returns a reference to the requested array element.

The following class supports an array of type **double**, 100 elements long. With this class, any attempt to use an index less than 0 or greater than 99 results in a reference to a data member named default_var. (Another approach, probably preferred by most experts, would be to throw an exception; but the following example still serves as a good illustration of how to implement the operator.)

```
class MyArrayClass {
private:
    double default_var;
    double arr[100];
public:
    double& operator[] (const int i) {
        if (i < 0 || i > 99) {
            return default_var;
        } else {
            return arr[i]; // Return ref. to array elem.
        }
    }
} my_array;
```

The virtue of this class is that its objects can be indexed without any possibility of bad memory access. This may not be, in all respects, a perfect solution, but it does prevent memory overwrites.

```
my_array[77] = 3.5;         // This is fine.
my_array[10] = 3.141592;    // So is this.
cout << my_array[10];       // Print 3.141592.
my_array[200] = 7;          // But this has effect of setting
                            //   my_array.default_var to 7.
```

Another possible use of overloading the subscript operator is to create a container that uses one-based indexing rather than zero-based indexing so that the first element is indexed as 1, the second is indexed as 2, and so on. I leave this as an exercise.

C++ permits you to write two versions of the subscript operator function: one that returns a **const** reference and one that does not. For example:

```
double& operator[] (const int i);
const double& operator[] (const int i) const;
```

The implementation of these functions will usually be similar. Although it may seem like extra work to provide both a **const** and non-**const** version of the subscript function, it is good programming practice if you intend to create a robust class. If an object of the class is declared **const**, the **const** version of the subscript operator function will be called, returning a **const** reference.

7.6.6 Increment and Decrement (++, --)

The increment and decrement operators are not free: A class does not automatically support these operators just because it supports addition and subtraction; instead, each operator—both postfix and prefix—must be defined separately.

This section considers increment operators (++). The same principles apply to decrement operators (--); so, to get examples that demonstrate decrementing, just substitute -- for ++ in the syntax and examples that follow.

The syntax for increment operator functions—assuming you are going to support both prefix and postfix versions—is:

```
class_name& operator++ ()              // Prefix version
class_name operator++(int)             // Postfix version
```

The postfix version includes a dummy argument to distinguish it from prefix. Otherwise, this dummy argument has no use. For example, here are declarations for a simple Point class that responds to the increment operator by incrementing its two data members, x and y:

```
class Point {
public:
     double x, y;

     Point& operator++ () {       // Prefix version: ++point
          ++x; ++y;
          return *this;
     }

     Point operator++ (int) {  // Postfix version: point++
          Point temp_pt = *this;
          ++x; ++y;
          return temp_pt;
     }
};
```

Each function returns either a reference to a base-class object or an object of the base class, passed back by value. In the case of prefix increment or decrement, the task of the function is straightforward: Increment the data members and then return a reference to the current object by using “return *this;”.

The postfix version has more work to do. It can’t just return the current object, because the current object (“this” object) necessarily will have different values from what gets returned. Instead, values must be copied to a temporary object, which then gets returned after incrementing has been performed on the current object’s copies of x and y.

This example demonstrates why the postfix versions of increment and decrement are now frowned upon whenever there is a choice. The implementations of postfix increment and decrement require the creation of an extra copy of the object, which the prefix versions do not. When complex objects are involved, this extra copying could have an impact on performance (although the impact when operating on simple integers is negligible).

7.6.7 Incoming and Outgoing Conversion Functions

C++ supports two ways for a class to provide conversion functions, enabling data conversions between instances of the class and another type.

A constructor with a single argument serves as an incoming conversion function unless the **explicit** keyword is applied. (You can also use an operator= function to enable incoming assignments, although that approach is less versatile.)

An operator function with the following syntax defines an outgoing conversion:

operator *type* ()

For example, you might define incoming and outgoing conversions for a Point class in which you do the following.

- You convert from a single floating-point number (**double**) to a Point object by setting x to the floating-point value and y to 0. A constructor supplies this incoming conversion.
- You convert from a Point object to a floating-point number by writing an **operator double** () function. (There are different ways to handle this, but one obvious strategy is to return the distance from the origin to the point.) This is an outgoing conversion.

Here is a simple version of the class, in which—for ease of illustration—all members are public.

```
#include <cmath>    // To support sqrt function.
class Point {
public:
     double x, y;
     Point() {x = y = 0;}
     Point(double newx, double newy) : x(newx), y(newy) {}

     // Incoming conversion (from double)
     Point(double newx) : x(newx), y(0) {}
     // Outgoing conversion (to double)
     operator double () {
```

```
        return sqrt(x * x + y * y);
    }
};
```

Given this declaration, conversions can be applied in either direction, and they can be explicit or implicit. A Point object can be used in any context in which a **double** would be valid and vice versa—as long as the code is unambiguous in terms of what conversion is called for.

```
Point point1, point2;
// Conversions from double to Point (incoming):
point1 = 7.5;                                 // Implicit.
point2 = Point(100.0);                        // Explicit.
// Conversions from Point to double (outgoing):
double x = point1;
std::cout << 1.5 + point2 << std::endl;  // Implicit.
std::cout << double(point1);                  // Explicit.
```

7.7 Deriving Classes (Subclassing)

Subclassing, also called class *derivation* or *inheritance*, is a major part of object-oriented languages such as C++, because it allows you to create class hierarchies. A hierarchy can feature a general class—such as a window, control, or container—to which another programmer can then implement a more specific class containing new, more customized functionality.

That may not sound exciting until you consider that all graphical user interfaces (such as Windows and Macintosh) require this kind of functionality. So does any kind of component architecture. Either the language itself must provide such functionality or it must be simulated.

Another way to think of a class hierarchy is as a means to create a general protocol or interface. Derived classes can implement the protocol by providing a given set of services, but each is free to implement the services in its own way. This provides a structured and rational way for component objects to interact smoothly within a complex system.

7.7.1 Subclass Syntax

To write a class derived from another class—that is, a subclass—the basic syntax is:

```
class class_name : public base_class {
    declarations
};
```

The effect of this declaration is to declare *class_name* as a subclass of *base_class*; the subclass automatically inherits all the members of its base, except for constructors.

Because constructors are not inherited, the *declarations* must include any and all constructors needed in the new class. (Exception: C++11 enables you to inherit base-class constructors, as described in Section 7.7.3, "Inherited Constructors (C++11).")

The **public** keyword in this context is a base-class specifier; it can be replaced by **private** or **protected** as described in the next section, but you will almost always want to use **public**.

Inheritance is cumulative. If class A is a subclass of B, and B is a subclass of C, then A inherits all of C's members along with B's, except of course for constructors. C in this case would be an indirect base class of A.

C++ supports multiple inheritance. So the more complete syntax permits any number of base classes, separated by commas if there is more than one.

```
class class_name : public base_class, public base_class... {
    declarations
};
```

Here is an example of single inheritance, in which class Dog is derived from a base class, Mammal:

```
#include <string>

class Dog : public Mammal {
public:
    Dog() {breed = ""; }
    Dog(string new_breed) {breed = new_breed; }
    void bark();
private:
    string breed;
};
```

The Dog class is derived from Mammal, so it automatically contains all the members that Mammal does—both data members and member functions—except for constructors. In addition, Dog declares a new function, bark, and a new data member, breed; consequently, every Dog object has all the members of a Mammal object *plus* these two other members: bark and breed.

The Dog class also provides two constructors, both of which are (in this case) inline. The bark function is only prototyped here, so a definition of bark must be provided separately.

There is a caveat that should go without saying: The base class declaration must already be provided somewhere (either directly in the source code or by an include file). This is a consequence of the general rule in C++ that you cannot refer to a type until it has been declared.

Here is a simple example of a base class and a subclass:

```
class C1 {
public:
     int a, b, c;
};

class C2 : public C1 {
public:
     int d, e, f;
};
```

C2 is a subclass (or derived class) of C1 and therefore inherits all C1 members other than constructors. An instance of C2 therefore has six data members: a, b, c, d, e, and f.

```
C2  an_obj;
an_obj.a = 10;      // This is legal (inherited member).
an_obj.f = -5;      // So is this.
```

7.7.2 Base-Class Access Specifiers

As stated in the preceding section, you will almost always want to use the **public** keyword as a base-class specifier, as in:

```
class Dog : public Mammal { . . . };
```

However, the C++ language provides three levels of base-class access—public, private, and protected—but giving them special meaning in this context.

- **public**

  All members of the base class (except, of course, for constructors) are inherited as they are, with their level of member access preserved. So private members are inherited as private members, public members are inherited as public members, and so on. It may seem that this level of base-class access should be the default, but it is not the default when the derived class is declared with the **class** keyword. (However, it is the default for classes declared with **struct**.) Therefore, it's important to remember to use **public** as the base-class access specifier unless you really want to use one of the other specifiers

- **private**

  This is the default for data structures created with the **class** keyword. Members of the base class are inherited, but all of them—whether public, private, or protected—become private in the subclass. This means that the subclass functions can refer to these members, but users of the subclass will not be able to refer to any of them.

- **`protected`**

  With this access level, private and protected members of the base class are inherited as is, but public members become protected in the subclass.

7.7.3 Inherited Constructors (C++11)

When deriving classes, one of the most important rules to remember is that all member functions, as a general rule, are inherited except for constructors. Each subclass has to supply its own constructors.

But the C++11 specification enables a derived class to inherit all the constructors of its base class. The syntax that enables this feature is:

`using` *`base_class::base_class;`*

Within a derived class, this declaration causes the class to inherit all the constructors from *base_class*. The derived class can still add additional constructors of its own and override inherited ones.

As a simple example, consider a Dog class derived from a Mammal class.

```
#include <string>

enum sex {male, female};

class Mammal {
public:
      string name;
      double avg_life_span;
      sex gender;
      Mammal() : name(""), avg_life_span(0.0),
             gender(female) { }
      Mammal(string nm, double lf, sex gn) : name(nm),
             avg_life_span(lf), gender(gn) { }
};

class Dog : public Mammal{
public:
      string breed;
      using Mammal::Mammal;
};
```

As a result of the "using Mammal::Mammal" statement, the Dog class inherits the two Mammal constructors as if they were Dog constructors.

7.7.4 Up-casting: Child Objects and Base-Class Pointers

C++ has a rule with major implications for class hierarchies and the role of virtual functions:

> You can assign the address of a subclass object to a pointer of base-class type (you can cast *upward* through the hierarchy) but not vice versa.

Here's another way to look at this principle: A pointer to something general can be replaced with something more specific. Consider a class hierarchy with Animal at the root.

```
class Animal {
public:
     void eat();
     void drink();
} objAnimal;

class Rabbit : public Animal {
public:
     void hop();
} objRabbit;
```

Suppose you declare a pointer of base type Animal:

```
Animal *ptrAnimal;
```

Such a pointer has to be able to support function calls to the eat and drink functions, which it can do if it points to a Rabbit object:

```
ptrAnimal = &objRabbit;
ptrAnimal->eat();
ptrAnimal->drink();
```

This works because a rabbit, being an animal, can do everything an animal can do. Therefore, a pointer of a general type can point to an instance of a derived type. But the converse is not true. Every rabbit is an animal, but not every animal is a rabbit. Likewise, not every function supported by the more specific class (Rabbit) is supported by the general class (Animal):

```
Rabbit *ptrRabbit;
. . .
ptrRabbit->hop();   // This only works if ptrRabbit
                    //  points to a Rabbit object.
```

Therefore, a pointer to a derived type cannot point to an object of the base type.

```
ptrRabbit = &objAnimal;        // ERROR! Not allowed.
```

The principle applies to descendant classes. Suppose that Rabbit itself has a derived class.

```
class WhiteRabbit : public Rabbit {
public:
     void look_at_watch();
} objWhiteRabbit;
```

Because of how inheritance works, an instance of the WhiteRabbit class supports all the functions declared by the Rabbit class as well as functions of the Animal class. Therefore, the following is valid:

```
ptrAnimal = &objWhiteRabbit;  // Assign upward to ptrAnimal
ptrAnimal->eat();
```

But the converse is not:

```
ptrWhiteRabbit = &objAnimal;   // ERROR! Not allowed.
```

The problem is that an instance of Animal does not support look_at_watch, a function of the WhiteRabbit class. Remember that the following statement needs to work correctly:

```
ptrWhiteRabbit->look_at_watch();
```

Therefore, a pointer to the more general class (ptrAnimal) can point to instances of that class or any of its derived classes (Animal, Rabbit, WhiteRabbit); but a pointer to a specific class (ptrWhiteRabbit) cannot point to instances of one of its base classes.

Figure 7.2 summarizes the relationships for this class hierarchy.

This rule—that a pointer to a base class can be made to point to an object of a derived class—has an important consequence: When you are handed a pointer from another process, you cannot know whether it points to an object of that type… or to an object of a derived class. But you do know, for example, that ptrRabbit (unless it points to null) will always point to an object that supports all of the member functions of the Rabbit class.

As you'll see in the next section, even though member function calls through ptrRabbit are always valid, objects may come with their own implementations of some of the functions.

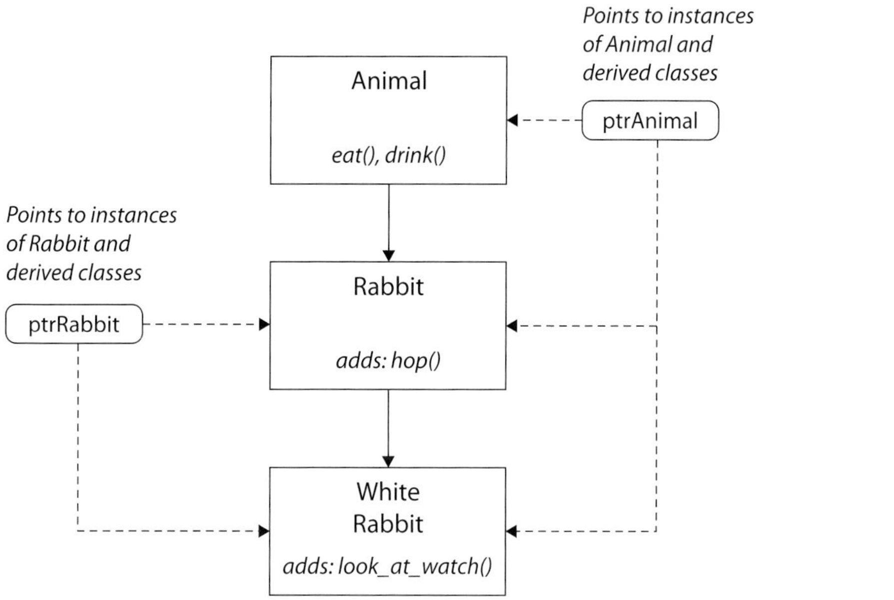

FIGURE 7.2 Pointers within a class hierarchy

7.7.5 Virtual Functions and Overriding

Let's review the basic syntax for declaring a subclass.

```
class class_name : public base_class {
    declarations
};
```

The class being created (*class_name*) contains all the members of *base_class*—other than constructors—along with any new members created in the *declarations*.

These declarations may also declare members that are already members of the base class. In this case, they are said to *override* the old declarations. As a general rule, you should not override data members. In contrast, overriding member functions is not only valid, but also useful.

Yet that raises an issue: Which version of an overridden function gets called at runtime? To solve this problem, C++ provides the **virtual** keyword.

Declaring a function virtual ensures that no matter how you access an object at runtime, the version that gets called is the one implemented for the actual class of the object—in other words, the function that gets called is the "right" one for the object.

Consider another class hierarchy.

```
#include <iostream>
using namespace std;

class Mammal () {
public:
     virtual void sound();
};

class Dog: public Mammal () {
public:
     void sound();  // OVERRIDE!
};

class Cat : public Mammal () {
public:
     void sound();  // OVERRIDE!
};
```

Each version of the sound function has a different implementation.

```
void Mammal::sound() { }
void Dog::sound() {cout << "Ruff! "; }
void Cat::sound() { cout << "Meow... "; }
```

Given all these declarations and definitions, what does the following do?

```
Mammal *ptr_to_mammal;
. . .
ptr_to_mammal->sound();
```

The answer is that it depends on what object ptr_to_mammal actually points to at runtime. At compile time, this cannot reliably be known. Remember that the pointer can be assigned to point to an object of type Mammal or any of its derived classes.

```
Mammal m_obj;
Dog d_obj;
Cat c_obj;
ptr_to_mammal = &d_obj;
ptr_to_mammal->sound();    // Call Dog::sound()
ptr_to_mammal = &c_obj;
ptr_to_mammal->sound();    // Call Cat::sound()
```

In the fifth and seventh lines of this example, the same line of code calls Dog::sound and Cat::sound, respectively. So the exact same line of code can result in a call to a different function.

This example is simplistic, but the uses of virtual functions are both interesting and helpful. Suppose the Mammal class is made available to other programmers. Suppose, also, that someone has implemented his or her own derived class—call it Aardvark—and that at runtime, some outside process or network location hands the program a pointer to an Aardvark object.

```
ptr_to_mammal = get_foreign_object();
```

The program doesn't know exactly what the pointer points to, except that it must be an instance of Mammal or some class derived from Mammal. It may get back a pointer to an Aardvark object even though at the time you wrote the code, *you never heard of the Aardvark class!*

And yet, because the function is virtual, Aardvark's implementation of the sound function will be correctly called at runtime.

This is why virtual functions supply the flexibility required for truly object-oriented programming and design: They enable new classes, and with them, new function code, to be plugged into existing frameworks. The same result can be achieved with callback functions, but callback functions are not type-safe: Their argument lists are not checked by the compiler.

To declare a function virtual, precede its declaration in the base class by the **virtual** modifier:

virtual *function_declaration*;

Several rules and guidelines apply to virtual functions.

- In general, any function that might be overridden should be declared virtual.
- When you override a function, the type information must match the type information in the **overridden** function (in terms of return value and argument types) exactly.
- The **virtual** keyword needs to be applied to a function only once—in the base class in which it is initially declared. Thereafter, in all subclasses, direct or indirect, every overridden version of that same function is automatically virtual as well.
- You should generally avoid making a virtual function inline. Technically, virtual functions can be inline, but they are problematic. The compiler must be able to determine the exact class of the object to resolve such a function call correctly. This defeats much of the purpose of virtual functions.
- Constructors cannot be virtual, although destructors can be.

7.7.6 Pure Virtual Functions

In the preceding section, the Mammal class provided its own implementation of the sound() function, but it was an implementation that did nothing. Alternatively, you can declare Mammal to have no implementation of sound() at all.

```
class Mammal () {
public:
     virtual void sound() = 0;
};
```

The syntax used here creates a *pure virtual function.*

```
virtual function_declaration = 0;
```

The result is that the function is not defined in the base class; it may, however, be defined (or rather implemented) by any of its subclasses.

A class with at least one pure virtual function is an *abstract class*. Such a class cannot be instantiated, meaning that you cannot use it to declare objects, at least not directly. You can, however, declare a pointer to the class.

```
Mammal *ptr_to_mammal;
```

Classes that provide implementations for all their functions can be instantiated.

```
Dog my_dog;    // Legal as long as Dog implements sound().
```

Some languages, such as Java, provide something called *interfaces,* which are restricted base classes that only declare a set of methods, or services, to be implemented by subclasses. In C++, you can do the same thing by using abstract classes—that is, classes with pure virtual functions.

7.7.7 Override Keyword (C++11)

Overriding member functions has a potential gotcha: You can make mistakes due to typos and spelling errors. For example, suppose you are trying to override the sound function:

```
class Dog: public Mammal () {
public:
     void ssound();   // OOPS!
};
```

This misspelling of "sound" does not have the desired effect. The C++ compiler goes ahead and creates a new member called "ssound" and neglects to override sound. The compiler does not flag this typo as an error. Errors may result, but the error messages will be confusing because the compiler did something different from what you expected.

C++11 provides the **override** keyword, which is self-documenting and helps to prevent such confusing errors.

```
function_declaration override;
```

For example:

```
class Dog: public Mammal () {
public:
     void ssound() override;   // FLAGGED AS ERROR.
};
```

Essentially, the override keyword says, "Allow this declaration only if it overrides some declaration in a base class; otherwise, flag it as an error."

7.7.8 Resolving Name Conflicts within Hierarchies

One of the many uses of the scope operator (::) is to clarify function use within a class hierarchy. By default, a reference to a member function is interpreted as meaning the class's own version of that function: For example, the function call "myfunction()" within the class C is interpreted as C::myfunction(). Sometimes, however, you may want to refer to an implementation of a function from the base class.

For example, suppose that sound is a function declared in Mammal (the base class) and in Dog (the subclass). The subclass code can call the implementation in the base class.

```
void Dog::sound() {
     Mammal::sound();
     std::cout << "Ruff! ";
}
```

This implementation, in effect, says, "Perform the version of sound() implemented for the base class, Mammal, and then perform another action."

In some cases, explicit reference to the base-class implementation might be the only way to achieve a desired effect. That could be the case if Mammal::sound accessed private members.

Use of the scope operator can be important with multiple inheritance. Suppose that class Dog is derived from two classes:

```
class Dog: public Mammal, public Pet {
. . .
};
```

What happens if Mammal and Pet both provide a function called feed_me()? The Dog class inherits both of them, and calls to feed_me need to be clarified when used within Dog member functions.

```
Mammal::feed_me();
```

7.8 Bit Fields

Bit fields have been around since the early days of the C language, primarily as a way to tightly pack information into a single byte. (You can achieve the same results with bitwise operations, but that involves more programming.) Where space is at a premium—for example, you have to store many records of tightly packed information on a disk—bit fields can still be useful.

Note

Bit fields are also useful to programmers who need to manipulate individual bits because (for example) they are working with hardware registers. But unless you're writing device-driver or operating-system code, you want to avoid doing that because such code is extremely nonportable.

A bit field is a class member (meaning it can also be a member of a **struct** class, of course) that occupies less than a byte. Such a member has the following declaration:

unsigned *field_name* : *integer*;

The type may be any integer or enumerated type, yet **unsigned** is recommended because the meaning of negative values in a bit field is undefined. But as long as the enumerated values are never less than 0—which is true by default—you can use an enumerated type. (Note: The **bool** type *ought* to work in this context, but I've found that it causes the class to take up an additional four bytes rather than one bit! So, stick to enumerated and **unsigned** bit fields.)

Here is an example using a 2-bit field to represent an enumerated field (suit) and an unsigned 4-bit field to represent one of the values 1 through 13. The card may also be either marked or unmarked, and you can have up to 63 copies of the card.

```
enum card_suit {clubs, diamonds, hearts, spades };

class CardClass {
public:
     card_suit suit   : 2;     // Stores four possible vals.
     unsigned rank    : 4;     // Stores values 0 to 15.
```

```
    unsigned marked : 1;     // 1 = true, 0 = false
    unsigned copies : 6;     // Stores values 0 to 63
} a_card;
```

Given these declarations, members named suit, rank, and marked are packed into seven bits. The fourth field, copies, will be aligned on the next byte, leaving an intervening bit unused (see Figure 7.3).

The suit, rank, marked, and copies fields can be treated like unsigned integer members, except that you should not exceed the limit of what can be stored in each field.

```
a_card.suit = hearts;     // This stores the 10 of hearts.
a_card.rank = 10;
a_card.marked = false;
a_card.copies = 1;
```

To determine how wide a given bit field needs to be, use powers of two, as shown in Table 7.1. Acceptable values range from 0 to 2 to the Nth power minus 1, where N is the width of the field. For example, if the width of a bit field is 5, it can store a value no higher than 31.

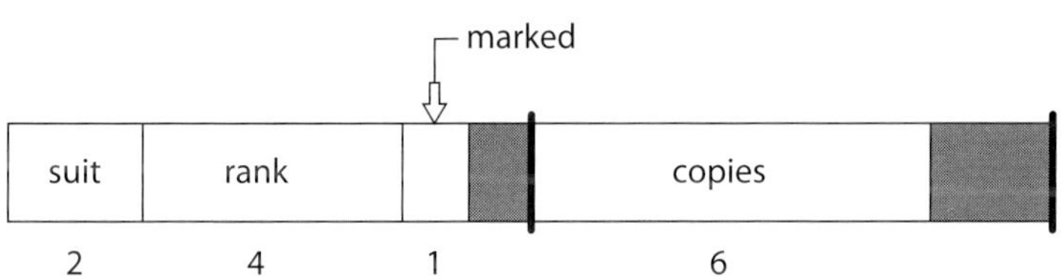

FIGURE 7.3 Sample bit fields

TABLE 7.1 Width and Range of Bit Fields

Bit-Field Width	Maximum Range of Values Supported
1	0–1
2	0–3
3	0–7
4	0–15
5	0–31
6	0–63
7	0–127

Note

The platform can influence bit-field results due to "endian-ness." Suppose you store 1000 as a two-byte integer. A big-endian system (such as Mac OS running a Motorola processor or PowerPC) stores this value, 03E8 hex, in the order 03 E8. A little-endian system (such as Windows running on Intel hardware) stores this value in the order E8 03.

The issue of endian-ness becomes a factor when you serialize bit-field data—that is, read or write it to a file—and the data is shared among multiple platforms; in that case, it may be necessary to convert from one byte order to another. You should also bear endian-ness in mind when using bit fields to analyze a number initialized as an integer.

The terminology is due to Jonathan Swift's *Gulliver's Travels,* in which the Lilliputians and their neighbors waged a hundred-year war over whether a boiled egg should be cracked at the little end or the big end. It didn't matter which approach was used, as long as everyone could just agree and thereby stop fighting. Thus, "Little Endians" and "Big Endians."

7.9 Unions

A union, unlike a **class** or **struct** declaration, creates a data type in which the members share the same address in memory. For example, a union can define a type that contains either integer or floating-point data, but not both at the same time.

By far the most common application (though not the only one) is to create a variant data type, which can store a single data item in any of several formats, each time using the same starting address. Where memory is at a premium, such variant types can sometimes be useful.

C++ provides two kinds of unions: named unions and anonymous unions.

7.9.1 Named Unions

A named union has the same syntax that **class** and **struct** declarations do, and it can optionally contain member functions (although in practice such functions are rare). Union members are public by default. An example of a named union is:

```
union Var_data {
     int n;
     double x;
     char *name[20];
};
```

In the resultant data type, members n, x, and name all share the same address in memory.

Now the object of the enclosing class—Variant—can store data in any of three formats (**int**, **double**, and **char***). Two of these formats are used in the following example.

```
Var_data  v1;
v1.n = 5;
std::cout << v1.n << endl;
v1.x = 3.141592;
std::cout << v1.x << endl;
```

In this example, the object v1 contains integer data some of the time and floating-point data at other times. But—and this is the critical difference between unions and other classes—only one value is contained in the union at any given time. The members (n, x, and name) are not at separate addresses as they would be in a **class** or **struct** type.

You *could* store a value in one format and then attempt to read it out in another, but the effect would be to reinterpret the same pattern of bits in a new data format. This is usually not a good idea. For example, consider:

```
v1.n = 100;
std::cout << v1.x << endl;    // Prints ????
```

These statements are valid as far as C++ syntax goes, but the effect is to take an integer value (100) and print out what the bit pattern would represent *if interpreted in floating-point format*. The **reinterpret_cast** operator (see Chapter 3) can be used to similar effect. A **class** or **struct** declaration, in contrast, creates objects that can store any number of different values side by side. That is not the case with a union, which stores all its data at the same starting address.

It is common to nest a union declaration inside a **class** or **struct** declaration. For example:

```
enum type_list {INTEGER, FLOAT, STRING };

class Variant {
public:
     type_list t;
     union Var_data {
          int n;
          double x;
          char *name[20];
     } v;
};
```

Given this declaration, the Variant class can be used to instantiate objects, such as my_data in the example that follows. Note that the union members are nested and therefore have to be accessed through *two* uses of the dot (.) notation.

```
Variant my_data;
my_data.t = INTEGER;
my_data.v.n = 64;
my_data.t = FLOAT;
my_data.v.x = 3.141592;
```

Anonymous unions, described in the next section, make it possible to write this same code without the need for nested-member access.

In this example, constructors can be used to automatically set the t field to indicate the data format during object creation. (Note that function prototypes for these constructors would also need to be added to the class declaration.)

```
Variant::Variant(int new_n) {
      t = INTEGER;
      v.n = new_n;
}

Variant::Variant(double new_x) {
      t = FLOAT;
      v.x = new_x;
}
```

Given these constructor definitions, the class becomes more useful.

```
Variant v1(5);              // v1 stores 5 as an integer.
Variant v2(3.141592)        // v2 stores 3.141592 as fl. pt.
if (v1.t == INTEGER) {
      std::cout << v1.v.n;
} else if (v1.t == FLOAT) {
      std::cout << v1.v.x;
}
```

7.9.2 Anonymous Unions

An anonymous union is not given a name but instead creates members that have the same scope as the surrounding code.

```
union {
      data_declarations
};
```

An anonymous union has some restrictions: It cannot declare member functions and it cannot instantiate objects.

A common way to use an anonymous union is to nest it inside a class. For example:

```
class Variant {
public:
     type_list t;
     union {
          int n;
          double x;
          char *s[20];
     };
};
```

This use of an anonymous function makes some of the coding simpler than the Variant class in the preceding section. The union members—n, x, and s—can now be referred to directly.

```
Variant my_obj, your_obj;
my_obj.t = INTEGER;
my_obj.n = 15;
your_obj.t = FLOAT;
your_obj.x = 1.1616;
```

The union members—n, x, and s—become part of the namespace of the enclosing class (Variant) and so must not conflict with the names of other Variant members.

7.10 Sample App: Packed Boolean

The program in this section declares a dynamic container of Boolean values, in which each Boolean is stored in just one bit. Much of this functionality is duplicated by the **bitset** template described in Chapter 15, "Introduction to STL (vector, deque)"—although that template does not permit dynamic sizing; it works only with fixed lengths known at compile time. It is therefore much less flexible than the class built in this example.

Another part of the STL that provides direct-bit access is the **vector<bool>** specialization, also mentioned in Chapter 15. However, that type has been officially deprecated by the C++ standards committee and therefore may not always be supported. It's better, then, to know how to create your own packed-Boolean class.

The Sieve of Eratosthenes example at the end of Chapter 6, "Pointers, Arrays, and References," used a dynamic array of **bool** values. Although the C++ specification gives compilers some leeway, what most every compiler does is to allocate at least one byte per Boolean element, even though in theory it takes only one bit to store a Boolean: A bit is either true (1) or false (0).

Therefore, you should be able to pack eight Boolean values into a single byte. Where space is at a premium and you have to store many Booleans, such a container could prove useful.

What follows is a class declaration for a Pack_bool type. It is a container of size N in which the user of the class accesses a bit value ranging from 0 to N-1. The size, N, is set when the object is created, by a Pack_bool(int) constructor.

```
// Packed Boolean class: creates a virtual Boolean array
// of dynamic length, storing each Boolean in one bit.
//
class Pack_bool {
private:
     int max_n;                  // Number of bits.
     int nbytes;                 // Number of bytes required.
     unsigned char *ptr;         // Pointer to the bit data.
public:
     Pack_bool(int max);         // Constructor — sets # bits.
     void set_bit(int n);
     void clear_bit(int n);
     bool get_bit(int n);
     void set_all_true() {
         for(int i = 0; i < nbytes; ++i) {ptr[i]=0xFF;}
     }
     void set_all_false() {
          for(int i = 0; i < nbytes; ++i) {ptr[i]=0x00;}
     }
};

// Constructor: divide max by 8 and round up
// to get number of byes to allocate.
//
Pack_bool::Pack_bool(int max) {
     max_n = max;
     nbytes = (max_n + 7) / 8;
     ptr = new unsigned char[nbytes];
}

// Set Bit member funct:
// Find the target bit and use bitwise OR to turn it on.
//
void Pack_bool::set_bit(int n) {
     int i = n / 8;
```

```
     int j = n % 8;
     ptr[i] = ptr[i] | (0x01 << j);    // Turn it on!
}

// Clear Bit member funct:
// Find the target bit and use combination of bitwise
// negation and bitwise AND to set it to zero.
//
void Pack_bool::clear_bit(int n) {
     int i = n / 8;
     int j = n % 8;
     ptr[i] = ptr[i] & ~(0x01 << j);
}

// Get Bit member funct:
// Find the target bit and use bitwise AND to get its value.
//
bool Pack_bool::get_bit(int n) {
     int i = n / 8;
     int j = n % 8;
     return (ptr[i] & (0x01 << j)) != 0;
}
```

The code just shown provides the Pack_bool class declaration along with associated member-function definitions. The following test program puts this class through its paces by allocating a Pack_bool object containing 64 bits. Then it sets all the bits to 0 (false), sets every other bit to 1, and prints the contents.

```
#include <iostream>
using namespace std::cout;
using namespace std::cin;
using namespace std::endl;

// INSERT Pack_bool DECLARATIONS HERE!

int main() {
     Pack_bool pb(64);
     pb.set_all_false();
     for (int i = 1; i < 64; i += 2) {  // Set odd bits.
          pb.set_bit(i);
     }
     for (int i = 0; i < 64; ++i) {     // Print results.
           cout << pb.get_bit(i) << "\t";
     }
     cout << endl;
     cin.ignore();      // Wait for user to press ENTER.
     return 0;
}
```

Exercises

1. Combine the Pack_bool class with the Sieve of Eratosthenes example from the end of Chapter 6.
2. Ideally, the class should include a destructor to free the memory allocated when a Pack_bool object is deleted. Write this destructor.
3. Two of the statements in the source code use operations of the form lvalue = lvalue op value. Revise these so that they use assignment operators having the form op=.
4. Add range checking to the set_bit, clear_bit, and get_bit member functions so that bad index values such as n < 0 or a value of n that is too high is handled without overwriting memory. At minimum, these functions should perform a no-op or return false (in the case of get_bit); however, other responses are possible. For example, you could throw an exception for invalid index numbers.
5. Add a resize member function that preserves as much data as possible. For example, if a Pack_bool object of size 1000 is resized to size 500, preserve the first 500 bits of data. If an existing object is increased in size, then extend existing data and insert zero (false) values at the end.
6. If you are extremely bold, you might try the following, but it is quite difficult: Enable the subscript operator, [], for this class. Because C++ does not allow a reference to a bit field, you have to do some very tricky programming. This involves creating an additional member for the Pack_bool class, the purpose of which is to act as a "wrapper." This new member must have a pointer back to the array data. The subscript-operator function returns a reference to this member. This extra member—for which you must write its own class—evaluates incoming and outgoing assignments to **int** type by getting or setting bits. (Refer to Section 7.6.7, "Incoming and Outgoing Conversion Functions.") If you can get to this work, you can consider yourself an accomplished C++ programmer indeed.

CHAPTER 8

Preprocessor Directives

A directive—unlike a declaration or executable statement—is a general command to the compiler carried out by the preprocessor. The preprocessor decides which lines to compile; it also carries out search-and-replace on the source code before the rest of compilation takes place. Although the compiler never alters the original copies of the source files, the effect is as if the files were changed just prior to being compiled.

Probably the most essential directive is **#include**, which brings in a set of declarations from another file, saving the considerable work you'd do if you had to declare everything yourself.

Another use for directives is conditional compilation, which is a way to maintain different versions of the same program. Consider what happens if you write a 50,000-line program and want to maintain a different version for platforms such as Windows, Macintosh, 32-bit, 64-bit, and so on. Writing complete, separate versions would require tens of thousands of extra lines of code. Conditional compilation enables you to maintain just one set of source files, isolating specific lines of the program to be either compiled or skipped depending on the target platform.

Directives also enable you to define symbolic constants and macro functions.

8.1 General Syntax of Preprocessor Directives

Unlike C++ declarations and executable statements, preprocessor directives are not terminated by semicolons. Instead, the compiler uses context to determine where directives begin and end. However, they are generally one per line. Two guidelines should be followed.

- A directive should begin in column 1, the left edge of the source file.
- You should place each directive on its own line. If you need to continue past the end of a line, you should use a backslash (\) as a line-continuation character, which creates a "virtual line" extending to the next physical line.

Some compilers are more forgiving than others, which is why I call these guidelines rather than rules. Many of the older C and C++ compilers strictly require that a directive begin in column 1, while newer compilers are more tolerant and require only that the directive (beginning with the pound sign, #) be the first non-whitespace character on the line. However, for the most consistent results, it is wise to follow these guidelines.

Directives differ from statements in that most of them involve text manipulation during preprocessing. The preprocessor has no concept of types or other attributes. It is mostly a search-and-replace text engine that the compiler runs prior to doing anything else.

The preprocessor skips quoted strings and comments when doing text replacement. For example, consider this code, which uses the **#define** directive to replace "rows" with "10" throughout the program.

```
#define rows 10

char *msg = "Too many rows.";
char *msg2[rows];
```

If the preprocessor replaced text within quoted strings, it would change the first declaration to:

```
char *msg = "Too many 10.";
```

But it does not do that. Instead, it just replaces the text "rows" with "10" when found *outside* comments and quoted strings.

```
char *msg2[10];
```

This text replacement is not visible within the source code itself (the compiler will not alter your own files); instead, the result is written to a temporary file on which subsequent passes of the compiler operate. Some compilers enable you to view that temporary file; see your compiler documentation for information on that option.

8.2 Summary of Preprocessor Directives

This section summarizes the use of the standard C++ processor directives. Subsequent sections explain more about the **#define** directive (for defining symbols and macro functions) and conditional compilation.

As with most lists in this book, the directives are presented here in alphabetical order.

▸ **`#define`** *`symbol`*

Creates a symbolic name and assigns an empty string to it (so that each subsequent occurrence of *symbol* is replaced by an empty string). Simply defining a symbol can affect the action of subsequent **#ifdef** directives. For example, a header file may contain the following directive, which can affect subsequent directives that check for the symbolic name "WINDOWS":

```
#define WINDOWS
```

- **#define** *symbol value*

Creates a symbolic name and assigns replacement text to it. The effect is that during preprocessing, each occurrence of the *symbol* (outside of comments and quoted strings) is replaced by *value*. The compiler executes a simple search-and-replace-text operation. This use of **#define** is helpful for replacing "magic numbers" (that is, arbitrary-looking digits) with meaningful names. For example:

```
#define N_ROWS  250
#define N_COLS  10
```

- **#define** *symbol(args) value*

Creates a macro function. During preprocessing, the compiler looks for occurrences of *symbol* in the program (outside of comments and quoted strings) and replaces each such occurrence with *value*, expanding *symbol*(*args*) by placing the actual arguments used into the *value* string as indicated. For example, suppose the following **#define** directive appears at the beginning of the program:

```
#define MIN(A,B) ((A)<(B)?(A):(B))
```

Given this definition, a call to MIN(x+1,y) would be expanded into MIN((x+1)<(y)?(x+1):(y)).

- **#elif** *condition*

Starts an alternative conditional compilation block; such a directive should follow a previous block started with the **#if** or **#ifdef** directive. The use of **#elif** is analogous to **else if** but involves conditional compilation (governing what version of the program gets built) rather than executable statements.

- **#endif**

Ends a conditional compilation block.

- **#error** *message_text*

Ends compilation immediately; the build fails, and the *message_text* is printed. The end user of the program does not see this text; rather, it is a compile-time message sent to the programmer attempting to build the program. This directive is almost always used in conjunction with conditional compilation, when some erroneous situation is detected. For example:

```
#ifndef VERSION
#error VERSION symbol not defined.
#endif
```

- **#if** *condition*

Begins a conditional compilation block. The *condition* is a true/false value returned by the **defined** function or is a C++ expression made up only of operators and compile-time constants (including symbols created by the **#define** directive). Conditional compilation enables the compiler to skip entire blocks of code, depending on the circumstances. If the condition following **#if** evaluates to true (nonzero), the lines of code following the **#if** directive, up to and including the next **#elif** or **#endif** directive, are compiled. Otherwise, they are skipped.

The following example compiles code if the symbol named “flag” has been defined.

```
#if defined(flag)
// If flag is defined, this compiles
#endif
```

This next example compiles a block of code if flag is set to 3.

```
#define flag 3
. . .
#if flag==3
// This code compiles
#endif
```

- **#ifdef** *symbol*

Begins a conditional compilation block, just as the **#if** directive does. The directive checks to see if the specified symbol is defined, ignoring its value, if any: All that matters is whether the symbol was defined at all (even if it was defined as an empty string). If the symbol is defined, the lines of code following **#ifdef**, up to the next **#elif** or **#endif** directive, are compiled. Otherwise, they are skipped. For example:

```
#ifdef flag
// If flag is defined, this compiles
#endif
```

- **#ifndef** *symbol*

Begins a conditional compilation block, just as the **#if** and **#ifdef** directives do. The lines of code following **#ifndef**, up to the next **#elif** or **#endif** directive, are compiled if the symbol is *not* defined. For example:

```
#ifndef flag
// If flag is NOT defined, this compiles
#endif
```

- **#include** <*file_name*>

Temporarily suspends compilation of the current source file and reads in the contents of *file_name*, which are then compiled as source code; afterward, compilation of the current source file resumes as normal. It is typical for such “include files” to contain declarations and type information needed by the program.

With this syntax, *file_name* may be the name of an actual file, or it may be a precompiled header. The compiler looks for the file in the standard LIB directory (set with the computer's environment variables). For example:

```
#include <iostream>
```

- **#include** "*file_name*"

Similar to the other use of **#include** but intended to be used with a project's own header files. Note that this version uses quote marks ("") rather than brackets. Unlike the previous version of #include—which uses brackets—this version not only looks in the directories indicated by LIB, but also looks in the project file itself. For example:

```
#include "myproject.h"
```

- **#line** *line_number*

Sets the next line of code to the number indicated (for "current line" purposes). Doing so affects the reporting of messages when compilation fails or generates warnings. Line numbering continues sequentially until another **#line** directive is read. For example, the line of code following this directive is numbered as 55 for message reporting:

```
#line 55
```

- **#line** *line_number* *file_name*

Sets the current file name and line number to the values indicated—affecting the reporting of errors and warning messages—starting with the line of code following this directive. Action is similar to the other use of the **#line** directive, except that in addition to resetting line numbering, the current file (for message-reporting purposes) is set to *file_name* until another use of the **#line** directive changes it. This is useful when an error occurs in one file but you want it to be reported as if it were appearing in another file (such as an include file).

For example:

```
#line 55 "project1.cpp"
```

- **#pragma** *command_text*

Responds to a compiler-vendor-specific directive. Each compiler vendor has its own list of pragmas that it supports. See your compiler documentation for more information.

- **#undef** *symbol*

Removes a symbol definition. The result is that when *symbol* appears in the program, it will not be replaced but left as is.

8.3 Using Directives to Solve Specific Problems

The next three sections discuss the use of **#define**, **#ifdef**, and other directives to solve some of the most common programming problems:

- Creating meaning symbols with **#define**
- Creating macros with **#define**
- Conditional compilation (**#if**, **#endif**, and so on)

The most important directive is probably **#include**; however, its usage is straightforward and is described fully in the preceding section, so I don't describe it here

8.3.1 Creating Meaningful Symbols with #define

The **#define** directive has a number of uses; one of these is to reduce the use of "magic numbers" from most of the source code: By "magic numbers," I mean numbers that appear in a program without any obvious meaning. A common example is array bounds.

```
for (int i = 0; i < 253; i++) {
     my_array[i] = 0;
}
```

Why does the **for** loop check for i less than 253 rather than any other number? There is no explanation for this, unless you use a comment to describe why 253 was chosen. Use of a **#define** directive provides a way to make the code more readable:

```
#define ARR_SIZE 253
. . .
for (int i = 0; i < ARR_SIZE; i++) {
     my_array[i] = 0;
}
```

The directive causes the preprocessor to replace "ARR_SIZE" with "253" throughout the program before regular compilation takes place. In effect, then, ARR_SIZE becomes a compile-time constant that means 253; to a programmer reading the code, the purpose of ARR_SIZE is much more obvious than the number 253 appearing over and over.

The preprocessor will not replace text inside a comment or quoted string. Consider this example.

```
#define ARR_SIZE 253
. . .
std::cout << "ARR_SIZE set to" << ARR_SIZE;
```

Because the first occurrence of "ARR_SIZE" is in a quoted string, it is not replaced. But the second usage is replaced, causing the program to print:

```
ARR_SIZE set to 253
```

This use of **#define** confers another benefit, even more important than readability: It controls the setting of a commonly used number in a single line and therefore improves consistency and reliability.

For example, you may need to declare arrays many times in a program. If they all need to be ARR_SIZE long, that quantity can be set in just one line. If ARR_SIZE needs to be set to a different number later on, only this one line needs to change. You don't have to hunt down all the lines of code that depend on this value. This approach reduces a potentially huge source of errors.

```
// The next line is the only line that needs to be changed
//   if you need to adopt a larger array size.
#define ARR_SIZE 253
. . .
int my_array[ARR_SIZE];
. . .
int another_array[ARR_SIZE];
. . .
for (int i = 0; i < ARR_SIZE; i++) {
     my_array[i] = 0;
}
```

Remember that the preprocessor carries out search and replacement of source-code text. The effect is the same as if you had typed "253" every place that "ARR_SIZE" appears.

Another use for **#define** is to create a set of flag values to be used with **case** or **if-else** statements. These are arbitrary values used to indicate some condition. Use of symbols is much more meaningful than simple numbers unattached to names.

```
#define DOG 0
#define CAT 1
#define RABBIT 2
```

The program can now use the symbolic names "DOG", "CAT", and "RABBIT" to represent different cases, rather than using the numbers 0, 1, and 2, to represent dogs, cats, and rabbits, respectively.

But note that most of the time, the **enum** keyword (described in Chapter 2, "Data") provides an easier way to achieve the same effect Also, with some development environments, **enum** constants are recognized by the debugger while **#define** constants are not.

```
enum (DOG, CAT, RABBIT);
```

8.3.2 Creating Macros with #define

A macro function executes a search-and-replace operation but takes arguments that are expanded into the replacement string. This expansion is what gives macros their name. Use of a macro looks like a function call, although technically it is not the same thing.

Macros can be a convenience, but they do have some drawbacks. Remember that they carry out search and replace during preprocessing (though not, of course, altering the original copies of your source files). You can alternatively use inline functions and templates to achieve similar effects more reliably. Yet it's often quicker and easier to write macros.

Here is a simple macro, a first attempt at writing a primitive MAX function:

```
#define MAX(A, B)  (A>B?A:B)
```

The effect is to replace each subsequent occurrence of MAX in the source code by looking for two arguments, which must be present (or the compiler flags the usage as an error). These argument values are then expanded into the replacement string. For example, given the **#define** directive just shown, consider what happens with this line of code:

```
std::cout << MAX(i, j);
```

There exists a definition for MAX, so during preprocessing, i and j are expanded into the MAX replacement string, producing the following:

```
std::cout << (i>j?i:j);
```

The effect is to print the maximum of i and j by applying a greater-than comparison (>) and the conditional operator (?:). (Recall from Chapter 3, "Operators," that the conditional operator evaluates the expression before the question mark (?); if this expression is true, the conditional operator evaluates and returns the "A" expression—that is, the first expression after the colon. Otherwise, it returns the "B" expression.)

Things get more complicated if different arguments are used. Consider the following.

```
MAX(i+j, *p)
```

During preprocessing, this is expanded into:

```
(i+j>*p?i+j:*p)
```

Already you should see a problem: There is no control over the precedence of operators inside the arguments relative to the operators around them. For this reason, it is wise to make generous use of parentheses when writing a macro, to prevent things from being evaluated in a different order from what you expected.

```
#define MAX(A, B)   ((A)>(B)?(A):(B))
```

Another issue remains. Using macros with expressions that have side effects can produce unwanted results. Consider:

```
MAX(++i, ++j)
```

What does this do? It ought to increment i and j and then return the maximum of the two, right? Instead, it ends up incrementing each one of these variables not once but twice!

```
((++i)>(++j)?(++i):(++j))
```

The moral is clear. Macros are convenient, but when using them, proceed with caution—especially when using arguments that may have side effects.

8.3.3 Conditional Compilation (#if, #endif, and so on)

Conditional compilation (realized principally with **#if**, variations on **#if**, and **#endif**) has a number of uses. For large software projects, it enables the maintenance of multiple versions without having to keep entire copies of all the source files. Changes necessary for a specific version can be isolated to specialized blocks of code which can then be switched on or off by setting the appropriate symbol definition.

For example, suppose that VERSION is a compile-time symbol set by a **#define** directive.

```
#define VERSION 3.0
```

That symbol definition can then control the effects of subsequent #if directives. In the following example, "VERSION > 2.50" can be evaluated because both "VERSION" and "2.50" are constants that can be determined at compile time.

```
#if VERSION > 2.50
// Place statements here that are appropriate
//  to Version 2.5 and higher.
#endif
```

This example is entirely different from the use of the C++ **if** keyword. In the case of the **#if** directive, the compiler determines whether to compile the statements between **#if** and **#endif** at all, not whether to execute them at runtime. This is not a matter of runtime behavior but of which version of the program to build.

You can use either **#if defined()** or **#ifdef**, to check to see whether a symbol has been defined at all.

```
#ifdef XENIX
// Place statements here that are appropriate
//  to targeting the XENIX platform.
#endif
```

Another use for conditional compilation is for efficiently "commenting out" entire blocks of code that you do not want to include in the current version of the program but do not want to delete, because you may want to include these lines at some future time.

In C, a common way to comment out blocks of code was to use the C-language comment symbols (still supported in C++ for backward compatibility): Everything between /* and */ is considered a comment and is therefore skipped by the compiler.

```
/*
void silly_function(int n) {
    int i = 0;
    return 5;
}
*/
```

This approach works fine unless you have embedded comments; if you do have embedded comments, strange, unexpected errors arise!

```
/*
void silly_function(int n) {
/*    int i = 0; */
    return 5;
}
*/
```

The problem here is that the compiler interprets everything between the opening /* *and the very next* */ as comments, so (in this case) the compiler attempts to compile the bottom half of the function.

Use of the **#if** and **#endif** directives solves this problem. Using **#if 0** begins a block that is not compiled. You can nest these noncompiled blocks to any level.

```
#if 0
void silly_function(int n) {
#if 0
    int i = 0;
#endif
    return 5;
}
```

```
#endif
// After second #endif, compilation is turned back on.
```

Yet another use for conditional compilation is to avoid including a file more than once. This can be an issue if you include multiple files, and they include other files, and so on. In such a situation, you can lose track of what file included what other file... and if a file is included more than once, fatal errors are certain to result.

The solution is to use the **#ifndef** directive, which compiles a line of code if and only if the symbol in question is *not* defined.

```
#ifndef PROJ_INCLUDED
#define PROJ_INCLUDED
#include "proj.h"
#endif
```

This example first checks to see if the symbol PROJ_INCLUDED is defined. If not, the compiler defines the symbol itself and then includes the file proj.h, but if the symbol is defined, the compiler skips the next two lines.

The symbol PROJ_INCLUDED is used as a simple on/off flag, which, once set, prevents further inclusion of proj.h during this compilation. No matter how many places these four lines occur, the file proj.h is not included more than once. In effect, the compiler looks for a free ladder (metaphorically speaking). If it finds one, it then climbs up and pulls the ladder behind it.

8.4 Preprocessor Operators

C++ provides several operators that are sometimes useful in conjunction with preprocessor directives, especially with **#if**, **#elif**, and **#define**.

- *#macro_arg*

  "Stringizing" operator, used within the expansion string of a **#define** directive that takes arguments (that is, a macro). Action is to expand the macro argument by placing double quotation marks around it and then placing it into the rest of the replacement string, as usual. For example:

  ```
  #define print_it(X) (cout<<#X)
  ```

  As a result, this macro call:

  ```
  print_it(Output some text.);
  ```

  is expanded into this:

  ```
  (cout << "Output some text.");
  ```

- *token1##token2*

  Token-compression operator, used within **#define** macro definitions. Action is to concatenate the values of the two tokens together. Each *token* may be either a simple string of text (with no internal spaces) or the name of a macro argument. For example:

```
#define incfile(X) X##.h
```

  Given this definition, consider the following macro use:

```
incfile(myfile)
```

  This is expanded into:

```
myfile.h
```

- **defined(***args***)**

  Evaluates to a true/false value depending on whether the symbol has been defined. Note that what value the symbol has is irrelevant (it may be an empty string); all that matters is that it has been defined. This preprocessor operator is an alternative to the use of **#ifdef**. It is also useful with **#elif**. The following example assumes that the symbols XENIX and WINDOWS have been defined or not defined in order to control which blocks of code get skipped or compiled.

```
#if defined(XENIX)
// Compile XENIX-specific code
#elf defined(WINDOWS)
// Compile WINDOWS-specific code
#endif
```

8.5 Predefined Macros

The C++ preprocessor provides a series of predefined macros that are useful mainly for printing diagnostics at runtime; they can potentially be an aid in debugging, although it's not required that you ever use them. Relying on the development environment (such as Microsoft Visual Studio) usually provides sufficient debugging tools. However, the predefined macros in this section can sometimes be used as an aid for users who experience runtime errors; those users can note errors reported by the program and pass them on to the development team.

For example, a problematic portion of the program might print the following message.

```
using namespace std;
. . .
cout << "This problem occurred at line " << __LINE__;
```

```
cout << " in file " << __FILE__ << endl;
cout << "Date of compilation is: " << __DATE__;
```

The rest of this section summarizes the standard list of predefined macros supported in C++. Note that some compiler vendors may support others as well.

- **assert(*statement*)**

  Causes immediate program termination and prints a diagnostic if the *statement* is not true. When the development team, or the programmer, learns of an assert error, he or she has a good clue as to what went wrong with the program because the assert error states directly that a particular condition was not true at runtime. (Generally such a condition is something that must be assumed to be true for the program to work correctly. See the example that follows.)

  The <cassert> header must be included.

  ```
  #include <cassert>
  . . .
  assert(divisor != 0);  // Terminate if divisor is zero.
  ```

- **static_assert(*statement*, *fail_message*)**

  C++11 specific. This statement is similar to **assert**, but it requires no header file, and it reports an error at compile time, not runtime. The *statement* can refer only to compile-time constants. If *statement* is not true, compilation fails and *fail_message* is printed.

  ```
  #define NUMBER 5
  static_assert(NUMBER < 6, "Number too large.");
  ```

  static_assert can be especially helpful within templates, because **assert** cannot detect an error until after a template is instantiated.

- **NDEBUG**

  Turns off debugging behavior, thereby disabling the use of **assert** macros. **assert** is a special macro-function call that causes immediate program termination if it is not true; it is supported by the <cassert> header. For example:

  ```
  #include <cassert>
  . . .
  assert(divisor != 0);  // Terminate if divisor is zero.
  ```

  To disable such statements, define **NDEBUG** just prior to including <cassert>:

  ```
  #define NDEBUG
  #include <cassert>
  ```

- **__DATE__**

  Produces an 11-character quoted string containing the date of the compilation in the format "*Mmm dd yyyy*". *Mmm* is a three-letter abbreviation of the month (usually the first three letters), and *dd* is the day of the month, containing a leading blank space if the day is less than 10. For example:

```
cout<<__DATE__;
```

causes the program to print out a string such as:

```
Apr  1, 2012
```

- **__FILE__**

  Produces a quoted string containing the name of the current file being compiled. For example:

```
cout << "File being compiled is : "
cout << __FILE__;
```

- **__LINE__**

  Produces text containing the current line number. For example:

```
cout << "Line being compiled is : "
cout << __LINE__;
```

- **__STDC__**

  Defined if the compiler is supporting standard C only.

- **__TIME__**

  Produces an eight-character quoted string containing the current time (of compilation) in the format *hh:mm:ss*, in which hours run from 00 to 23 (military time). For example, if the compilation is run a few seconds after 8:30 p.m., then:

```
std::cout << __TIME__;
```

causes the program to print out a string such as:

```
20:30:04
```

- **__cplusplus**

  Produces a digit string; this symbol is defined if the C++ language is supported by the compiler (as opposed to running C language only). The number is a version number that should be equal to at least 199711 if the compiler supports ANSI 1998 C++ or later. For example:

```
#ifndef(__cplusplus)
#error Compiler does not support full C++
#endif
```

8.6 Creating Project Header Files

In this section, I assume you're working with a development environment (such as Microsoft Visual Studio, just to name one) that gives you the option of splitting development work into several source files to be compiled and then linked together to produce a single application.

A project's header file is intended to be included by each and every individual source file, or module, in your project. For example, if your project is named "my_proj," you might include the following directive in each of your source-file modules:

```
#define "my_proj.h"
```

The file my_proj.h, in turn, should include any or all of the following.

- A prototype of each and every function intended to be shared by all the modules.
- **extern** declarations for all global data intended to be shared by the modules.
- Class declarations for the project. (These should include no executable code except for inline function definitions.)
- **enum** and **typedef** declarations.
- **#define** directives (symbolic constants and macro functions).

Except in the case of inline function definitions inside a class declaration, a header file should, as a general rule, never contain executable code. The reason for this rests on the all-important distinction in C++ between declarations and definitions.

- A *declaration* provides type information only—unless it is also a definition. One of the most important rules in C++ is that within any given source file, all variables, functions, and user-defined types (such as classes) must be declared before being referred to. This includes variables and functions defined in other modules.

  In the case of functions, this means prototyping every function intended to be shared. In the case of variables, this means including an **extern** declaration for every global variable intended to be shared. (Note: A local variable cannot be declared **extern**.)
- A *definition* actually creates a function or variable. (Note that every definition is also a declaration, but the converse is not true.) Because a definition creates a function or variable, each must be defined once, in exactly one module.

To take a simple example, suppose you have a project made up of three source files. The global functions shared by all modules in the project consist of the following functions: drink_me, open_alice_files, process_rabbit_files, and fight_jabberwocky. The global variables shared by all modules in the project are time_remaining, alice_size, and rabbit_time. The project header should include declarations—but no definitions—of all seven of these items.

```
// wonderland.h
// This file contains external declarations for
//   WONDERLAND project.

// Prototypes (of functions to be shared):
void  drink_me();
int   open_alice_files();
int   process_rabbit_files();
bool  fight_jabberwocky();

// External variables;
// These are declarations only, and do not create
//  the variables.
extern double time_remaining;
extern double alice_size;
extern double rabbit_time;
```

Assuming this file is named "wonderland.h", each source file in the project should include it by using the **#include** directive. Doing so places all these declarations at the beginning of each source file.

```
#include "wonderland.h"  // Include project-header file.
```

In addition to being declared this way, each of these seven items—the four functions and the three external variables—must also be defined in *exactly one* of the source files linked into the project.

Note that a variable declaration is a variable definition if it is not an **extern** declaration or if it initializes the variable.

For example, the following declaration defines the variable named rabbit_time. In this context, "defining" a variable means to cause the compiler to actually create the variable by allocating memory for it and then (optionally) initializing it.

```
double rabbit_time = 3.14;  // Place this in EXACTLY ONE of
                            //  the C++ source files.
```

As mentioned in Chapter 2, the same source file may contain both an **extern** declaration of a variable and a definition of that variable, which is why there is no conflict putting **extern** declarations in a header file and including that file in *all* modules, including a module that defines some of the **extern** variables.

CHAPTER 9

Creating and Using Templates

Once a programming problem has been solved, you shouldn't have to solve it again. One way to reuse code with different types is to write preprocessor macros, but that technique has drawbacks. It is not *type-safe,* meaning that there is no enforcement of correct type usage at compile time. A superior alternative is to use templates: generalized classes and functions that can be reused with different base types.

The best source of ready-made templates is the Standard Template Library (STL). Although not all of the earliest C++ compilers came with the STL, support for this template library is now standard.

This chapter is primarily about how to create your own templates. But even if you don't create new templates, the chapter is helpful as background for using and applying templates in general.

9.1 Templates: Syntax and Overview

The basic syntax for creating a template is:

```
template<template_params>  declaration
```

The *declaration* is a function or class declaration (which may use **class**, **struct**, or **union**). The *template_params* is a list of template parameters, separated by commas if there is more than one. Each parameter has one of the following forms:

```
typename type_arg
int numeric_arg
```

In the first case, *type_arg* is a name that stands in for a type name to be supplied later.

Note

The **class** keyword can be used instead of **typename**, but I don't recommend it. C++ compilers more than five or ten years old did not recognize **typename**, and so **class** was required to be used in this context; but such usage was confusing because in any other context, **class** has a more specific meaning. Therefore, I am adopting the more modern practice of using **typename** to declare parameterized types.

In the second case, *numeric_arg* is a name that stands in for a numeric value to be supplied later. In addition to the **int** type, you can use other integer types in this context.

In the simplest cases, there is just one template argument, a parameterized type:

template<typename *type_arg*> *declaration*

When the template is used, it is said to be *instantiated*. In this case, instantiation is not exactly the process of creating an object, but rather applying a template to a specific type.

An example should help clarify. Here is the declaration of a simple template class named Vec2D:

```
template<typename T>
class Vec2D {
public:
     T x, y;
};
```

Let's deconstruct this. The first part of this template declaration is:

```
template<typename T>
```

This says: "What immediately follows is a template declaration; within this declaration, each occurrence of T is a type to be supplied later." The class declaration then follows. This declaration (for the sake of illustration shown here without the "template<typename T>" prefix) is:

```
class Vec2D {
public:
     T x, y;
};
```

This looks like an ordinary class declaration; the only difference is that T is a type that is yet to be named. You supply an actual value for T when instantiating the template.

```
Vec2D<int>     vec_of_ints;    // Contains 2 ints.
Vec2D<double>  vec_of_dbl;     // Contains 2 doubles.
Vec2D<char*>   vec_of_cstr;    // Contains 2 char* strings.
Vec2D<Point>   vec_of_pnts;    // Contains 2 Point objects;
                               //    Point is assumed to be
                               //    already declared.
```

9.2 Function Templates

Function templates are the easiest to declare and use, because they are easy to instantiate: You just call them. The compiler instantiates a function template by using the type information in the argument list of the function call. Some examples will make this process clear.

9.2.1 Function Templates with One Parameter

The simplest function templates are built around one generalized (or *parameterized*) type.

```
template<typename type_arg >   function_declaration
```

The *function_declaration* that follows **template<typename** *type_arg*> has the same syntax as any other function definition. (It may even use modifiers such as the **inline** keyword.) A complete function syntax looks like this:

```
template<typename type_arg>  return_type name (args) {
     statements
}
```

You can also prototype the function (as usual) before defining it.

```
template<typename type_arg>   return_type name (args);
```

The function declaration is normal in every respect, except that it may refer to the *type_arg*, the parameterized type. The *args* of the function should use *type_arg* to declare at least one argument, but there may be other arguments as well.

Consider a template function that swaps two variables having the same type. You could do the same thing with a preprocessor macro (using **#define**), but such a macro would not be type-safe. It would not check to see if the arguments were compatible. This is why templates are superior.

Here's how you could write this as a template function. The reference operator (&) is used to declare that the arguments to the function are passed by reference, not by value. For ease of understanding, I have placed "template<class T>" on its own line, but remember that C++ does not consider newlines significant for the most part (treating them as white spaces), so you could place "template<class T>" on the same line as the function name, t_swap, if you chose.

```
template<typename T>
void t_swap(T &x, T &y) {
     T z = x;
```

```
        x = y;
        y = z;
}
```

Remember that T (the parameter inside the angle brackets, <>) is a name representing a type to be supplied later.

To instantiate a template function, simply call it. The compiler determines how to replace T from the type or types in the argument list. For example:

```
int a = 1, b = 2;
unsigned int i = 10, j = 20;
double phi = 1.616, pi = 3.14159;

t_swap(a, b);         // Call with int arguments.
t_swap(i, j);         // Call with unsigned int arguments.
t_swap(phi, pi);      // Call with double arguments.
```

The first function call, t_swap(a, b), applies the t_swap template to integers. (The first time this happens, the template is instantiated for integers.) The function is executed as if it were written this way:

```
void t_swap(int &x, int &y) {
        int z = x;
        x = y;
        y = z;
}
```

Note

Sometimes you may need to specify the template parameter, T, explicitly, as described in the next section. Most of the time, however, you instantiate a template function by just calling it directly.

The third call to t_swap checks the types of pi and phi, and interprets the template as if **double** were substituted for T in the function definition.

```
void t_swap(double &x, double &y) {
        double z = x;
        x = y;
        y = z;
}
```

Moving on to another example, these next lines of code produce a version of the MAX function that's more reliable than the macro function presented in Chapter 8, "Preprocessor Directives." Again, for ease of understanding, I've placed the first part of the template declaration on its own physical line, although it doesn't have to be.

```
template<typename T>
T t_max(T a, T b) {
      if (a > b)
           return a;
      else
           return b;
}
```

As in the earlier examples, the prefix “template<class T>” declares the name “T” as the parameterized type. The code following it is a function definition that treats T as if it were a type already declared. When the template is instantiated, T is replaced with a specific type.

Again, to instantiate a template function, just call it.

```
int a = 20, b = -21;

int c = t_max(a, b);
```

The two arguments have type **int**. The effect is to interpret the function as though T were replaced in the template declaration with **int**:

```
int t_max(int a, int b) {
      if (a > b)
           return a;
      else
           return b;
}
```

9.2.2 Dealing with Type Ambiguities

When a parameterized type (such as T) is repeated in the function's argument list as in the previous examples, the compiler requires that argument types match exactly during instantiation. For example, the following call to t_max involves both an integer and a floating-point argument. How does the compiler instantiate the types… as **int** or **double**?

```
double x = t_max(10, -3.5);  // Error: compiler cannot resolved
```

This is a fatal error, because the ambiguity cannot be resolved as the statement stands. One solution in such cases is to use the **static_cast** operator to force the two types to match.

```
double x = t_max(static_cast<double>(10), -3.5);
```

Another solution is to declare the function template's parameter (or parameters) explicitly. When there is no template argument, the compiler must attempt to determine t_max's type information from context; but since the template argument *is* given in this case (specified by "<double>"), the compiler doesn't have to make a guess as to whether to use **int** or **double** as the parameterized type.

```
double x = t_max<double>(10, -3.5);
```

This statement causes the template parameter T to be explicitly given type **double** during instantiation of t_max. The arguments 10 and -3.5 are therefore passed to a function taking two **double** arguments. The integer, 10, is promoted as it would be in any situation taking two such arguments.

9.2.3 A Function Template with Two Parameters

The preceding section illustrated the use of templates with a single parameterized type:

```
template<typename T>
```

The name "T", of course, could have been any available symbolic name. (This name is local to the template and temporarily overrides the name of other variables if they conflict.) For example:

```
template<typename MyType>
```

This section illustrates a case involving two parameterized types.

```
template<typename T1, typename T2>
```

Testing the t_swap function from the preceding section involves writing some repetitive lines of output. For example:

```
using std::cout;
using std::endl;
. . .
int a = 1, b = 100;
cout << "a is: " << a << endl;
cout << "b is: " << b << endl;
t_swap(a, b);
cout << "a is: " << a << endl;
cout << "b is: " << b << endl;
```

If you perform several tests on the t_swap function, you are going to write out nearly the same lines of code again and again. It would be nice to automate the printing of these values with a function.

```
int a = 1, b = 100;
pr_items(a, b);
t_swap(a, b);
pr_items(a, b);
```

The problem is that to make pr_items work on different types, it's necessary to create something more flexible than an ordinary function. One approach is to use a preprocessor macro, but a more reliable technique is to write another template function.

The following template function does what is needed for any type, provided that type supports stream output with <<.

```
using std::cout;
using std::endl;

template<typename T1, typename T2>
void pr_items(const T1 &item1, const T2 &item2) {
     cout << "first item is:  " << item1 << endl;
     cout << "second item is: " << item2 << endl;
}
```

The first part of this declaration says that *two* types are parameterized—to be filled in when the class is instantiated.

```
template<typename T1, typename T2>
```

The rest of the declaration treats T1 and T2 as valid type names, although (of course) they are actually types to be filled in later. Note that these are passed as **const** references for the sake of efficiency. The function does not need to make its own copies of these arguments or change them, so a reference that is made to **const** is the best way to declare these arguments.

```
void pr_items(const T1 &item1, const T2 &item2) {
     cout << "first item is:  " << item1 << endl;
     cout << "second item is: " << item2 << endl;
}
```

This function template, while useful, can be improved. It would be even better to be able to call a function with four arguments:

- The name of the first variable, a character string (**const char***)
- The value of the first variable, an instance of a parameterized type
- The name of the second variable, a character string (**const char***)
- The value of the second variable, an instance of a parameterized type

What's needed is a function template taking four arguments, only two of which are parameterized types.

Here's the solution. This version of the function template, pr_items, declares two arguments of type **const char*** in addition to the arguments of type T1 and T2. (Because there is no reason to alter the value of the strings, they are declared not just **char*** but **const char***; this enables you to pass string literals without risking a compile error.)

```
template<typename T1, typename T2>
void pr_items(const char *s1, const T1 &item1,
              const char *s2, const T2 &item2) {
     std::cout << s1 << " is:  " << item1 << std::endl;
     std::cout << s2 << " is:  " << item2 << std::endl;
}
```

Now it's easy to write code that tests the t_swap function and outputs results.

```
int a = 1, b = 100;
double x = 0.0, pi = 3.14159;
pr_items("a", a, "b", b);
t_swap(a, b);
pr_items("a", a, "b", b);
pr_items("x", x, "pi", pi);
t_swap(x, pi);
pr_items("x", x, "pi", pi);
```

Could the pr_items template have been written to require the two values to be of the same type? Yes, although that would make the template less flexible. Such a function template would involve only a single parameterized type. During instantiation of this template, the compiler would require that the types of the third and fourth arguments match precisely.

```
template<typename T>
void pr_items(const char *s1, const T &item1,
              const char *s2, const T &item2) {
     std::cout << s1 << " is:  " << item1 << std::endl;
     std::cout << s2 << " is:  " << item2 << std::endl;
}
```

9.3 Class Templates

A class template creates a generalized class that can be built on top of most any data type. The STL provides a number of such generalized classes: Most of these are container classes such as **list**, **stack**, or **vector**. Such a container holds any number of the desired kind of object and also provides services in the form of member functions.

This section describes how to create simple template classes. Section 9.5, "Using Integer Template Parameters," explains how to add member function definitions to template classes.

The simplest way to create a class template is to use a single parameterized type:

```
template<typename type_arg>
class class_name {
     declarations
}
```

As always, you can declare a class with **struct** or **union** as well as with the **class** keyword.

9.3.1 Simple Class Templates

The following code declares a class template named Multi as a container of three objects. Immediately following "template<typename T>" is a class declaration.

```
template<typename T>
class Multi {
public:
     T a, b, c;
};
```

You can, of course, write this so that it is more compact if you choose, placing the **template** keyword on the same line as the class declaration.

```
template<typename T>  class Multi {
public:
     T a, b, c;
};
```

This next example declares a container type with four members, using the name "MyType" for the parameterized type rather than "T".

```
template<typename MyType>
class Multi4 {
public:
     MyType a, b, c, d;
};
```

Alternatively, you can use the **struct** keyword, resulting in a template class whose members are public by default.

```
template<typename MyType>
struct Multi4 {
     MyType a, b, c, d;
};
```

Finally, here is a class template that makes more extensive use of the parameterized type (again using T in this case) by containing an array as well as two pointers to the base type.

```
template<typename T>
class thing_container {
public:
     T arr_of_things[10];
     T *a_ptr;               // Ptr to base type.
     T *another_ptr;         // Another ptr to base type.
};
```

Remember that you don't have to use T; it's just a symbolic name like any other. You could, for example, write the same template using another type symbol such as MyType:

```
template<typename MyType>
class thing_container {
public:
     MyType arr_of_things[10];
     MyType *a_ptr;          // Ptr to base type.
     MyType *another_ptr;    // Another ptr to base type.
};
```

9.3.2 Instantiating Class Templates

Instantiating a template class is more complex than instantiating a function template, because you can't simply call it. You have to use the "template_name<type>" syntax.

By instantiating a template, you cause the compiler to apply the template to a specific type or types. To instantiate a template class, use this syntax:

```
template_name<template_arguments>
```

In the case of simple templates, this means instantiating a template by supplying a single type specification:

```
template_name<type>
```

You can therefore use a template to declare an object as follows:

```
template_name<type>  obj_declaration;
```

Consider the simple class template, Multi, introduced at the beginning of the preceding section. This creates a container of three objects of the same type.

```
template<typename T>
class Multi {
public:
     T  a, b, c;
};
```

With this template declared, you can create container classes around any types you like, including primitive types, classes, and more complex types such as pointers, arrays, and so on. The following example assumes that Point is a class that's already been declared.

```
Multi<int>       my_ints;       // Create three ints.
Multi<double>    some_dbls;     // Create three flt. point.
Multi<Point>     my_pnts;       // Create three Point objs.
Multi<int*>      ptrs_to_ints; // Create three ptrs to ints.
```

The first line of code in the example just shown instantiates the Multi template as a class containing three **int** members. The class is interpreted as if written this way:

```
class Multi<int> {
public:
     int  a, b, c;
};
```

The most obvious reason for instantiating a class template is to declare an object. But you can also refer to an instantiated class anywhere by using the syntax "template_name<type>".

For example, the following code creates both a Multi<int> object and a pointer to it:

```
Multi<int>  my_ints;
Multi<int>  *ptr;  // Ptr to a Multi<int> object.
ptr = &my_ints;
```

You can also declare an array of Multi<int> objects. The effect of the following declaration is to create 30 integers. Each element of big_array is a Multi<int> object containing three integers.

```
Multi<int>  big_array[10];
```

Here are some statements that manipulate the items created in the previous examples.

```
my_ints.a = 5;
ptr = &my_ints;
cout << ptr->a;      // Print "5".
big_array[2].b = 255;
```

9.4 Class Templates with Member Functions

Class templates, although interesting in themselves, are far more useful when you add member functions to them. As with any other class, there are two ways to define these functions.

- As an inline function.
- As a function prototyped within the class but defined outside it. In the case of templates, this requires a not-so-obvious syntax, explained in Section 9.4.2, "Class Templates with Separate Function Definitions."

9.4.1 Class Templates with Inline Member Functions

Defining inline functions for a template class is easy. Just add the function definitions to the class as you normally would. For example, here is a version of the Vec2D class that controls access to private members through a series of inline functions.

```
template<typename T>  class Vec2D {
private:
     T x, y;
public:
     Vec2D() { };
     Vec2D(T newx, T newy) {x = newx; y = newy; }
     void set(T newx, T newy) {x = newx; y = newy; }
     T get_x() {return x;}
     T get_y() {return y;}
};
```

As with all class templates, the key to understanding this example is to bear in mind that T is not the name of the class, but rather the base class (the type to be supplied later). For example, the class can be instantiated and used with base-type **double**:

```
Vec2D<double>   coords;
coords.set(0.1, 3.14159);
double xx =  coords.get_x();
```

9.4.2 Class Templates with Separate Function Definitions

Defining a member function outside a class template is more complex. In the case of a single parameterized type, the definition of a member function—outside the class declaration itself—has the following general syntax:

```
template<typename type_arg>
return_type  class_name<type_arg>::function_name(args) {
     statements
}
```

Let's deconstruct this. The first part is a template declaration, using *type_arg* (which can be a name such as "T") as a parameterized type. We've seen this before.

```
template<typename type_arg>
```

The next part is the return type, as usual. Every function, unless it's a constructor, has a return type.

```
return_type
```

The qualified function name follows next. Here's the tricky part. The function name must have the scope of the appropriate class: In this case, that scope is class_name<type_arg>. When the class template is instantiated, the scope of this function will be instantiated along with it.

```
class_name<type_arg>::function_name
```

This clarifies the scope as being that of the class template. The rest of the function syntax follows as usual. For example, assume that the get_y() function was not defined within the class template but only prototyped:

```
template<typename T>  class Vec2D {
private:
     T x, y;
public:
     Vec2D() { };
     Vec2D(T newx, T newy) {x = newx; y = newy; }
     void set(T newx, T newy) {x = newx; y = newy; }
     T get_x() {return x;}
     T get_y();              // NOT DEFINED HERE
};
```

Here is the definition of get_y, defined outside the class, shown with the qualified function name in bold:

```
template<typename T>
T  Vec2D<T>::get_y() {
     return y;
}
```

Take another look at the qualified function name. The scope here is **Vec2D<T>**.

```
Vec2D<T>::get_y()
```

Similarly, if the set() member function were defined outside the class, its definition would be:

```
template<typename T>
void  Vec2D<T>::set(T newx, T newy) {
     x = newx; y = newy;
}
```

Again, the prefix "Vec2D<T>::" qualifies the name. The same rules apply to constructors. Here's how the default constructor would be defined outside of the class:

```
template<typename T>
Vec2D<T>::Vec2D() {
}
```

This may look strange at first. With the first occurrence of "Vec2D," the class name uses the "name<type>" syntax, producing "Vec2D<T>", but the second occurrence of "Vec2D" does not use this syntax.

But that's how it works. You just need to remember that the parameterized type list (<T> in this case) is part of the scope prefix but not the function name.

9.5 Using Integer Template Parameters

Once again, here is the basic syntax for defining template classes and functions:

```
template<template_params>   declaration
```

Throughout this chapter, I've used examples with parameterized types; these are declared with the **typename** keyword, and they stand in for a type to be supplied later. But you can also use template parameters that are integers.

A common use for these nontype parameters is to set a size or limit of some kind. For example, you can create a template class that contains an array of the requested size. This is a typical use.

```
template<typename T, int size_n >
class my_array {
private:
     T data[size_n];
public:
     T get_elem(int i) { return data[i]; }
     void set_elem(int i, T new_val)
          { data[i] = new_val; }
};
```

This template, my_array, has two parameters.

- The first template parameter is T, a parameterized type (as we've seen many times before in this chapter).
- The second parameter is size_n, an integer, which is used here as a size specifier. This is a stand-in for a constant integer value that must be provided later, during instantiation.

Note that now there are two template parameters. Here is a declaration that instantiates this class. It must supply two arguments: a type and a numeric constant.

```
my_array<double, 10>  arr_of_flts;
```

The compiler instantiates arr_of_flts as an object containing an array of ten values of type **double**. Because the array data is contained in a private member, it cannot be accessed directly. Access is provided through member functions get_elem and set_elem:

```
arr_of_flts.set_elem(0, 3.14159);  // Set first element.
cout << arr_of_flts.get_elem(0);   // Print first element.
```

If these member functions are defined outside of the class declaration, you need to define those functions using "my_array<T, size_n>" to clarify the scope. For example:

```
template<typename T, int size_n >
T my_array<T, size_n>::get_elem(int i) {
     return data[i];
}
template<typename T, int size_n >
void my_array<T, size_n>::set_elem(int i, T new_val) {
     data[i] = new_val;
}
```

9.6 Template Specialization

In most cases, when you write a template, you want every possible base type (or types) handled in the same way. Sometimes, however, you might want to handle a certain type in a different way. This is what template specialization is for.

Let's examine a simple case. Here is a template for a "get minimum" function, t_min.

```
template<typename T>
T t_min(T a, T b) {
      if (a < b)
            return a;
      return b;
}
```

This works fine for any types that support the less-than operator (<). But an optimization is possible in the case of **bool** arguments. To return the minimum of two **bool** arguments, we could write the function this way:

```
bool t_min(bool a, bool b) {
     return a && b;     // Return result of logical AND
}
```

This is a nice optimization, but now there's a name conflict. What we'd really like to do is incorporate this special handling of **bool** into the existing template. Here's how to do that:

```
template<>
bool t_min(bool a, bool b) {
     cout << "Using specialized version:  ";
     return a && b;
}
```

In general, the following syntax is used for template specialization. The template's parameter list is blank. The *declaration* contains a template name but uses specific types.

```
template<>  declaration
```

The following example, when executed, prints diagnostics showing which version of the template function is being used.

```
#include <iostream>
using std::cout;
using std::cin;
using std::endl;

template<typename T>
T t_min(T a, T b) {
     cout << "Using generic version:  ";
     if (a < b)
          return a;
     return b;
}

template<>
bool t_min(bool a, bool b) {
     cout << "Using specialized version:  ";
     return a && b;
}
```

```
int main() {
     cout << "t_min(10, 15) = " << t_min(10, 15) << endl;
     cout << "t_min(true, true) = " << t_min(true, true);
     cout << endl;
     cin.ignore();    // Wait for user to press ENTER.
     return 0;
}
```

9.7 Variadic Templates (C++11)

Variadic templates are one of the most exciting new features in C++11. Section 9.2, "Function Templates," concluded with an example hard-wired to require exactly four arguments. But how would you like to be able to write a function template that took an argument list of any size?

The variadic feature enables you to do just that. The key to understanding it is to recognize that the general pattern involves three basic steps.

1. Write a terminal version of the function, usually taking just one argument.
2. Write a variadic-template version of the function. This is instantiated when the first version (the terminal case) cannot be, usually because there is more than one argument.
3. From within the variadic template, expand the multiple-argument list, causing the template to call itself with one fewer argument.

Consider the following example. This template prints every argument you give it by sending it to **cout**. After all the arguments are printed, it appends a newline. For example:

```
int i = 10, j = 20;
printv("i = ", i, ", j = ", j, ".");
```

This prints the following:

```
i = 10, j = 20.
```

The beauty of this function template is that it imposes no practical limits on the size of the argument list. Here's the template itself. I'll go through each part of it carefully.

```
// Terminal version: called when there is one arg.
template<typename T>
void printv(T val) {
     std::cout << val << std::endl;
}
```

```
// Variadic version: called when there is more than one arg.
template<typename T, typename... TArgs>
void printv(T val, TArgs... args) {
     std::cout << val;  // Print first arg (val).
     printv(args...);   // Pass along the rest.
}
```

There are two versions of printv. The first is a simple template function that takes one argument and prints it. If printv is called with one argument, this is the version used.

```
printv("Sing the Barney song.");  // Inst. simple template.
```

This is simple. But what happens when there are two or more arguments?

```
printv("i = ", i, ".");
```

This statement causes instantiation of the second version of printv. The first argument is passed to "val". The remaining arguments are packed into an argument list, which is passed to "args".

Take another look at the template-function header. The first parameter to the template has a parameterized type, T, while the second is a variadic parameter given the name TArgs. Within the function declaration, the arguments after val—that is, all the arguments after the first—are packed into a list having type "TArgs...".

```
template<typename T, typename... TArgs>
void printv(T val, TArgs... args) { // Definition follows.
```

The variadic-template version of the function has to do two jobs. To begin with, it must print the first argument (val), which is easy to do.

```
std::cout << val;
```

Now comes the interesting part. The following function call unpacks args; printv calls itself, and in doing so passes along every argument except the first (the first argument, remember, being stored in val). So printv is called with one less argument.

```
printv(args...);
```

Eventually, printv is instantiated with one argument remaining. At that point, the terminal version of printv is invoked. This terminal version—unlike the other, variable-length version—prints and appends a newline. Therefore, a newline is appended after the last argument is printed.

```
std::cout << val << std::endl;
```

For example:

```
std::string s1("He loves you. ");
std::string s2("You love he. ");
std::string s3("You are Barney's family.");
printv(s1, s2, s3);
```

This prints:

```
He loves you. You love he. You are Barney's family.
```

Although the recursive calls to printv do not occur in the source code, you can rest assured they happen. Table 9.1 summarizes the process.

Figure 9.1 illustrates the process of calling printv(s1, s2, s3) graphically, showing how it results in a call with one less argument: s2 and s3 are packed into the list called "args" while s1 is passed to val. A recursive call to printv then unpacks "args" back into the list s2, s3.

Note that only a small change or two are necessary to make printv print out the arguments in reverse order. I leave that as an exercise for the reader.

TABLE 9.1 Example of Recursive Calls to Variadic Function (printv)

Function Call	Action
printv(s1, s2, s3);	Instantiated as variadic version. Print s1 and then call printv(s2, s3).
printv(s2, s3)	Instantiated as variadic version. Print s2 and then call printv(s3).
printv(s3)	Terminal version. Print s3 followed by **endl**.

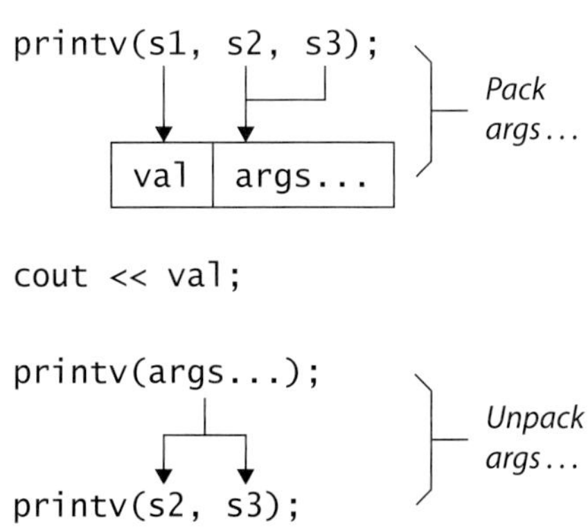

FIGURE 9.1 Recursive call to printv

9.7.1 A More Sophisticated Variadic Template

The following example shows a more sophisticated use of a variadic template by using the first argument as a format string, as in the C-library **printf** function—except that it uses no formatting characters other than a simple percent sign (%):

```
int i = 100;
int j = 200;
printvf("i = %, j = %.", i, j);  // i and j are the value
                                 //   arguments
```

This prints:

```
i = 100, j = 200.
```

The code for this more function—printvf—follows. As with printv, it has both a terminal and a variable-length version. In this case, the first version is not templated.

This function proceeds by working its way through the format string (s), one character at a time, printing a value argument when an ampersand (%) is encountered in that string; then it prints the value argument near the front of the list—just after the format string—and calls itself recursively, dropping that argument in the process. Eventually, there will be just one argument left: the format string, s. At that point the function prints the remaining characters in this string, if any, and is done.

```
void printvf(const char* s){       // Terminal version.
     std::cout << s;
}

// Variadic version of the function follows:
// If "%" is encountered in the format string,
//  print the first value argument and then call the
//  function recursively, dropping that argument;
//  the next value argument goes to head of the list.

template<typename T, typename... TArgs>
void printvf(const char* s, T val, TArgs... argList) {
     while (*s) {
          if (*s == '%' && *(++s) != '%') {
               std::cout << val;
               printvf(s, argList...);
               return;
          }
          // If the char is not "%", just print it.
          std::cout << *s++;
     }
}
```

9.7.2 Summary of Rules for Variadic Templates

There's even more to variadic templates than I've shown in the two examples so far. In this section, I summarize the more general rules.

You can declare parameter packs for class templates as well as function templates—although class templates (mainly used to create tuples) are more difficult to write correctly. In either case, the use of three dots (...) following **typename** creates a parameter pack. Here the dots are intended literally.

```
template<parms, typename... pack_name>  class_declaration;
template<parms, typename... pack_name>  function_declaration
```

In both cases, *parms* consists of one or more ordinary template parameters (such as "typename T").

Within a function declaration, a parameter pack can be used to declare a packed argument list, which must come at the end of the list of function arguments. During instantiation, arguments not passed to one of the named *args* will be packed into the *arg_list* at the end.

The argument-list name can be qualified with **const** and/or reference operators. (See Appendix A, "A Painless Introduction to Rvalue References (C++11)," for use of &&.)

```
return_type  function_name(args, pack_name... arg_list) {}
return_type  function_name(args, const pack_name&... arg_list) {}
return_type  function_name(args, pack_name&&... arg_list) {}
```

Later, when the argument list is expanded, it will be expanded with the same **const** and reference-type attributes, if any, used in the declaration.

For example, the template heading and function declaration in the preceding section are:

```
template<typename T, typename... TArgs>
void printvf(const char* s, T val, TArgs... argList) {
```

The argument list (argList) contains zero or more items. When printvf is called, all arguments after the first two are packed into the argument list. If only two arguments are passed to printvf, argList will be empty (but still valid).

Note that you cannot use a parameter pack or argument list to instantiate an object.

```
Targs    x;          // ERROR!
auto x = argList;    // ERROR!
```

You can only use packed parameter and argument lists in one of two ways. You can determine number of elements through a specialized use of the **sizeof** operator. You can also expand the list. Both of these uses involve the dot syntax (...).

```
size_t  n = sizeof...(TArgs);

f1(argList...);
f2(x, argList..., y);
```

This last line of code in this example is instructive because it shows that unpacking an argument list is a more intelligent operation than simple text replacement. If argList is empty, the call to f2 will still be syntactically correct. (In effect, C++ will ignore one of the commas in that case.) Again, note that **const** and reference-type attributes, if any, are preserved in the expansion of arguments. But otherwise, unpacking an argument list is not so different from macro expansion.

9.7.3 Tuples

It's perfectly possible to create variadic class templates, but these are difficult to write correctly. The most common use for such a template by far is to create tuples—arbitrary collections of different types. But C++11 provides this functionality by adding **tuple** to the STL, so there's usually not much reason to write this template yourself.

A *tuple* is a collection of elements of any types and of any length. (This makes the template flexible indeed!) C++11 supports not only this generalized template, but also several helper functions and classes.

To begin with, include the <tuple> header. As usual, all templates declared in this header are part of the **std** namespace.

```
#include <tuple>
using std::tuple;
using std::make_tuple;
```

You can then create a tuple by using either a tuple constructor or the **make_tuple** function.

```
tuple<int, string, double>  my_tup(1, "hello", 3.14);
auto my_tup2 = make_tuple(2, string("goodbye"), 2.5);
```

Both of these examples create a tuple that combines the types **int**, **string**, and **double**, in that order. But you can combine any types you want.

```
auto my_big_tup = make_tuple("hello goodbye", 0, 1, 3.14);
```

The single most useful helper function for dealing with tuples is the **get** function. It has the following syntax, in which *n* is a zero-based position number. Because it is a template argument, *n* must be a compile-time constant.

get<*n*>**(***tuple***)**

Here's an example that uses this template function. (Remember that **get** is part of the **std** namespace and that positions are zero-based.)

```
using std::get;
std::cout << "Here is 4th tuple element: ";
std::cout << get<3>(my_big_tup) << std::endl;
```

This prints:

```
Here is 4th tuple element: 3.14
```

To get the number of elements of an arbitrary tuple, use the **tuple_size** template class. It has just one member, value. You can use it with the following syntax:

tuple_size<decltype(*tuple***)>::value**

For example:

```
using std::tuple_size;
using std::cout;
using std::endl;

cout << "Num. of elements of my_big_tup is: ";
cout << tuple_size<decltype(my_big_tup)>::value << endl;
```

This prints:

```
Num. of elements of my_big_tup is 4
```

Remember that **tuple_size** returns the number of tuple elements, not the total size of these elements in bytes.

Similarly, you can use the **tuple_element** template class to get the type of an element. This class has one member, **type**, which can be used to declare variables or be given as an operand to **typeid**.

tuple_element<*n***, decltype(***tuple***)>::type**

9.8 Sample App: Type Promotion, v 2

The following program revises the type-promotion application from the end of Chapter 2, so you can determine the type that results when any two expressions are added together—provided that this type is **int**, **unsigned**, **double**, **float**, or **char**. (If the expression has none of these types, the program prints the word "other".) The type comparison is delegated to a function. Without the template feature of C++, it would be impossible to write this function.

```
#include <iostream>
#include <string>

using std::cout;
using std::cin;
using std::endl;
using std::string;

template<typename T1, typename T2>
string return_type(T1 a, T2 b) {
     if (typeid(a + b) == typeid(int))
          return "int";
     if (typeid(a + b) == typeid(unsigned))
          return "unsigned";
     if (typeid(a + b) == typeid(float))
          return "float";
     if (typeid(a + b) == typeid(double))
          return "double";
     if (typeid(a + b) == typeid(char))
          return "char";
     return "other";
}

int main() {
     char ch = 'a';
     int si = 0;
     unsigned ui= 0;
     double x = 0.0;
     float flt = 0.0F;

     cout << "ch + si => " << return_type(ch, si) << endl;
     cout << "si + si => " << return_type(si, si) << endl;
     cout << "si + ui => " << return_type(si, ui) << endl;
     cout << "si + x  => " << return_type(si, x) << endl;
     cout << "x + flt => " << return_type(x, flt) << endl;
     cin.ignore();    // Wait for user to press ENTER.
     return 0;
}
```

Exercises

1. Include support for **unsigned** and **unsigned long** in the template function, and perform a test within **main**. Are **int** and **long** utterly interchangeable or are they separate types in some sense?
2. If your compiler supports the **long long** integer type, add support for this type in the template function, along with **unsigned long long**. Perform tests for these types within **main**.

CHAPTER 10

C-String Library Functions

C++ provides two formats for text strings. One is the old C-string type from the C language, supported for backward compatibility; the other is the Standard Template Library (STL) **string** class, which is safer, more convenient, and easier to use. (See Chapter 14, "The C++ STL String Class.")

This chapter presents the C-string library functions, because sometimes it is necessary to support old code. Moreover, the individual-character functions, also presented in this chapter, are useful with all kinds of strings.

This chapter covers

- C-strings and functions that manipulate them
- Individual-character functions (testing and converting)
- Block memory operations
- Wide-character strings, which support two bytes per character inside of only one

10.1 Overview of the C-String Format

A C-string, having type **char**[], is an array of bytes. Each byte is a numeric value that represents a character according to the ASCII coding system. A terminating null byte (value 0) indicates the current end of the string. This convention enables a string to grow until it exhausts its initial storage capacity. There are two distinct pieces of information about a string.

- Its total storage capacity, including room for the terminating null.
- The number of characters that appear before the null. This is the string's current length.

The first measure (total storage capacity) never changes for a C-string once it's allocated, but the current length can change many times. For example, the following string can store up to ten bytes: a maximum of nine characters plus a terminating null.

```
char a_string[10] = "Kit";
```

This declaration causes the compiler to set aside ten bytes of storage for a_string. The initial data consists of the ASCII character codes for 'K', 'i', and 't', plus a terminating null. [Although during initialization, the remainder of the array is set to zero (null) values anyway; see Section 6.2.1, "Simple (One-Dimensional) Arrays."]

C-string functions assume there is sufficient storage space and that a terminating null is present. These assumptions should never be violated. If you initialized the individual characters as shown, neglecting the terminating null, it would be dangerous to attempt printing the string.

```
#include <iostream>
char a_string[3] = {'K', 'i', 't'};
std::cout << a_string;   // ERROR! There's no terminator!
```

Fortunately, when a string literal involving double quotation marks appears in C++ code, the compiler allocates enough room for the terminating null. Again consider this declaration:

```
char a_name[10] = "Kit";
```

The compiler allocates ten bytes and initializes them as shown in Figure 10.1.

Because the string a_name was declared with size 10, it has more bytes than needed initially. If a_name needs to expand, it can grow to have no more than nine characters, leaving space for the null, for a total of ten bytes. The **strcat** function adds another string onto the end of the first.

```
#include <cstring>
char a_name[10] = "Kit";
strcat(a_name, "Kat");
```

The result is to concatenate the string "Kat" onto "Kit"; the characters 'K', 'a', and 't' are copied to the end of "Kit", as shown in Figure 10.2.

The result is that a_name now contains the six characters "KitKat," along with a terminating null, for a total of seven bytes. Its current length is now six. a_name can

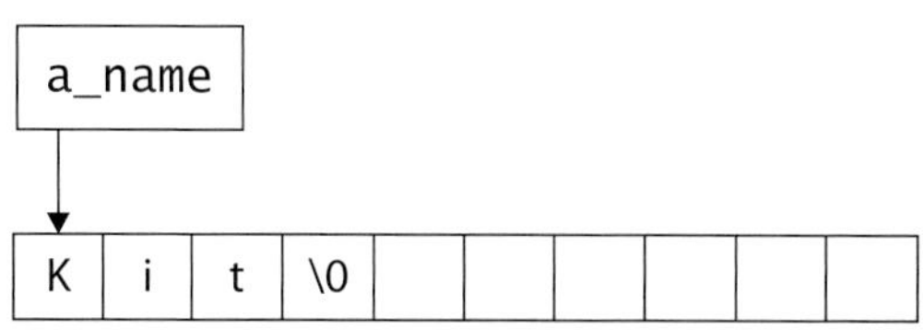

FIGURE 10.1 String initialization

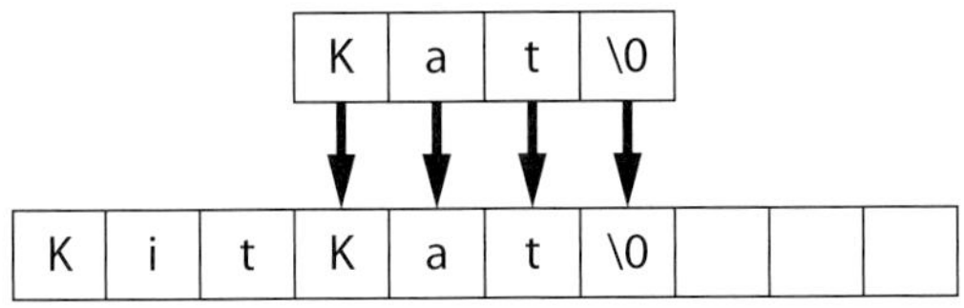

FIGURE 10.2 String concatenation

grow at most three more bytes. Any expansion beyond that causes memory to be overwritten.

```
strcat(a_name, "Kar");    // a_name is now at its limit.
```

This limitation—a_name must not grow beyond nine characters, plus one position for the terminating null—demonstrates a drawback of C-strings. If you're going to manipulate strings with functions such as **strcat**, you need to ensure that lengths will not be exceeded.

The **strcat** and **strcpy** functions are dangerous except when used in elementary programs. There's no guarantee they won't cause overwriting of memory. Because length and capacity are issues, the standard library supports several "n" functions, such as **strncat**, which copies no more characters than indicated by the third argument—and then adds a terminating null. For example, the following code will cause only two more characters to be written onto the end of a_name in this situation:

```
#define MAX_CHARS 10
char a_name[MAX_CHARS+1] = "KittyKat";
strncat(a_name, "Kar", MAX_CHARS – strlen(a_name));
```

C-strings are implemented as arrays of **char**, so you can always access individual characters by using the subscript operator ([]).

```
s[1] = 'a';    // Place 'a' into second position of s.
```

10.2 Input and Output with C-Strings

C-strings work with the overloaded stream-output operator, <<, so you can print them.

```
#include <iostream>
using namespace std;
char a_name[] = "John W. Rabbit";
cout << "The string is: " << a_name << endl;
```

The stream-input operator (>>) also works with C-strings. The following statement reads a string from the input stream (**cin**, console input) up until the first whitespace character, and copies the characters—not including the whitespace itself—into a_name; then it adds a terminating null. But an error occurs if the string-data read exceeds the space allocated.

```
cin >> a_name;
```

If the user enters the following data, only the first substring ("John") is read into the string. The subsequent strings "Q" and "Public" require separate read operations.

```
John Q Public
```

A more flexible way to read strings is to read an entire line of input at a time by using the **cin.getline** member function. Input is read from the console up to the first newline. The resultant string can then be analyzed after being read (using string functions such as **strtok**).

```
cin.getline(a_name, 80);    // Read in the entire line of input.
```

For best results, the string involved should be declared to take the largest number of characters possible in a line of input. If the physical screen width is 80, it would make sense to allocate 81 characters (leaving one extra byte for the terminating null).

```
using namespace std;
#define SCREENWIDTH 80
. . .
char input_line[SCREENWIDTH + 1]
cin.getline(input_line, SCREENWIDTH);
```

The **getline** function is safer than other C-string operations because the second argument specifies a maximum number of characters to read; this argument should be one less than the array size (storage capacity) of the strings.

10.3 C-String Functions

Before using any of the functions in this section, include the <cstring> header.

```
#include <cstring>
```

For backward compatibility, the following **#include** is also supported.

```
#include <string.h>
```

The examples in this section often refer to **cout**. The following lines are also needed to make the examples work:

```
#include <iostream>
using std::cout;
using std::endl;
```

In the syntax descriptions for the functions in this section, *s* is a **char*** pointer (or address) pointing to a null-terminated string of characters, as are *s1* and *s2*.

A string literal causes the compiler to allocate space for the data and produce its address. String literals have type **const char**[] (which is essentially the same as **const char***). You refer to strings, in effect, by passing their addresses. So the following does what you'd expect:

```
strcat(str, "suffix");  // Put "suffix" onto end of string.
```

Most of these functions return either a position or the address of the string that was operated on so that you can pass along strings to larger expressions.

```
strcat(strcat(s1, s2), s3);
```

ch is an individual character. Remember that C++ represents individual characters (as opposed to arrays) by using single quotation marks:

```
int ch = 'a';     // ch = ASCII value of 'a'.
```

Descriptions of the C-library string handling functions follow.

- **strcat(*s1*, *s2*)**

  Concatenates string *s2* onto the end of *s1*. Returns *s1*. This function can easily overwrite memory, so you should take care that *s1* has enough space allocated to contain both its current data and the string, *s2*. (See **strncat** for a safer version of this function.) For example, the following code appends the string ".com" onto the string company_name. Then it prints that name: "trucks.com".

  ```
  char company_name[20] = "trucks";
  strcat(company_name, ".com");
  cout << company_name;         // Print "trucks.com"
  ```

- **strchr(*s*, *ch*)**

  Returns a pointer to the first character within the string matching *ch*; returns a null pointer if the character is not found. The substring returned will contain the target character forward to the end of string *s*. For example, the following code finds the substring starting just after the first blank space.

  ```
  char name[] = "White Rabbit";
  char *substr = strchr(name, ' ');
  if (substr) {
     cout << "Last name is " << substr + 1;
  }
  ```

These statements print:

```
Last name is Rabbit.
```

- **strcmp(*s1*, *s2*)**

  String compare. Returns an integer less than, equal to, or greater than 0, depending on the result of a comparison between strings *s1* and *s2*. The string contents are compared, not the numeric addresses. If *s1* comes before *s2* in alphabetical order, the function returns a negative integer; if *s1* comes after *s2* in alphabetical order, the function returns a positive integer. If *s1* and *s2* contain the same string, the function returns 0. For example, the following code tests to see if two strings contain identical contents:

```
if (strcmp(string1, string2) == 0) {
     cout << "the strings contain same data.";
}
```

- **strcoll(*s1*, *s2*)**

  Performs the same action as **strcmp**, but carries out the comparison according to the localization setting in LC_COLLATE. For example:

```
if (strcoll(string1, string2) == 0) {
     cout << "the strings contain same data.";
}
```

- **strcpy(*s1*, *s2*)**

  String copy. Copies the contents of *s2* into *s1*, replacing the old contents. Returns *s1*. Care should be taken to ensure that the destination string *s1* was allocated with enough space to contain the string data copied from *s2*; otherwise, memory will be overwritten. (See **strncpy** for a safer version of this function.) For example, the following code copies new string data ("John W. Rabbit") into my_name, replacing "Joe Bloe".

```
char my_name[30] = "Joe Bloe";
strcpy(my_name, "John W. Rabbit");
```

- **strcspn(*s1*, *s_reject*)**

  Get-span-until-character function. Returns the length of the span of the substring in *s1* (from beginning of string) that consists only of characters *not* matching any in *s_reject*. The effect is to return the zero-based position of the first character matching any character in *s_reject*—or the length of *s1* if none are found. For example, in the following code, *n* is set to the position of the first digit in the string named lic, which is 3:

```
char lic[] = "KAR123";
char digit_str[] = "0123456789";
int n = strcspn(lic, digit_str);
cout << "Position of first digit is: "<<n<< endl;
```

This next code example copies the nondigits into another string, nondigit_str, using **strncpy**.

```
char nondigit_str[20]= "";
strncpy(nondigit_str, lic, n);
cout << nondigit_str << endl;
```

- **strerror(*errno*)**

  Returns the system's text string for the specified error number.

```
cout << "Error message: " << stderror(err)<<endl;
```

- **strlen(*s*)**

  String length function. Returns the length of string *s*: This length is the number of bytes up to but not including the terminating null. For example, the following code prints out the length of str, which is 3:

```
char str[100] = "NYC";
int n = strlen(str);
cout << "Length of str is " << n;    // Print 3.
```

- **strncat(*s1, s2, n*)**

  Performs the same action as **strcat** (string concatenation) but concatenates only the first *n* characters from *s2*, plus a terminating null, onto the end of *s1*. If used correctly, this function enables you to prevent memory from being overwritten. For example:

```
char str[10] = "TuxRUs";
strncat(str, ".com", 9 - strlen(str));
cout << str;      // This prints "TuxRUs.co"
```

  The number 9 is used in the third line of this example, rather than 10, to leave room for the terminating null; it allows only three characters to be added onto str.

- **strncmp(*s1, s2, n*)**

  Compares at most *n* characters in *s1* to *s2*. If *n* is greater than the length of s1, the function compares the entire string contents. Otherwise, the action of the function is the same as **strcmp**.

- **strncpy(*s1, s2, n*)**

  Performs the same action as **strcpy**, copying string data into *s1*, but copies at most *n* characters plus a terminating null. For example, if a string has 20 bytes allocated for maximum storage, at most 19 text characters should be copied (leaving one byte for the terminating null).

```
char a_name[20];
strncpy(a_name, new_string, 19);
```

- **strpbrk(*s1*, *s2*)**

  String pointer-to-break function. Returns a pointer to the first character within *s1* that matches any of the characters in *s2*; returns a null pointer if none are found. The value returned is a pointer to the substring beginning with the character found, forward to the end of the string *s1*. For example, the following code finds the substring starting with the first space, comma, or tab in name:

```
char name[] = "White Rabbit";
char *substr = strpbrk(name, " ,\t");
if (substr) {
    cout << "Last name is " << substr + 1;
}
```

- **strrchr(*s*, *ch*)**

  String-reverse-character function. Searching from the end (that is, in reverse order), this function returns a pointer to the first character within string *s* matching *ch*; returns a null pointer if *ch* is not found. The return value is in effect a pointer to the substring beginning with the target character, forward to the end of the string. For example, the following code finds the substring starting just after the last blank space.

```
char name[] = "Alice Liddel Hargreaves";
char *substr = strrchr(name, ' ');
if (substr) {
    cout << "Last name is " << substr+1; << endl;
}
```

  These statements, when executed, print:

```
Last name is Hargreaves
```

- **strspn(*s1*, *s_accept*)**

  String-span function. Returns the length of the span of the substring in *s1* (from the beginning of the string) that consists only of characters in *s_accept*. The effect is to return the zero-based position of the first character in *s1* not matching any character in *s_accept*—or the length of *s1* if none are found. For example, in the following code, *n* is set to the (zero-based) position of the first nondigit in the string s, which is 8:

```
char s[] = "44400022a0"
char digit_str[] = "0123456789";
int n = strspn(s, digit_str);
cout << "Pos. of first non-digit is: " << n;
```

- **strstr(*s1*, *s2*)**

  String-within-string (substring function). Searches for first occurrence of substring *s2* within *s1*: If *s2* is found, the function returns a pointer to that substring (but note, this is a pointer to that substring *within* s1, not a separate string); if not found, function returns a null pointer.

The following example counts the number of occurrences of the word "Bat" within a string pointed to by p. Each successful call to **strstr** causes n, the counter, to increment. In addition, the pointer p is advanced exactly one character position—so each call to **strstr** will look for the *next* occurrence of "Bat". The overall effect is to find "Bat" repeatedly, advancing continually through the string, until a null pointer is returned.

```
char target[] = "Bat";
char *p = "Batmen run for Bat pole and "
          "Bat-mobile, Batman!";
int n = 0;
while(p = strstr(p, target)) {
     ++n; p += 3;
}
cout << "Bat occurred " << n << " times." <<endl;
```

- **strtok(*source*, *delims*)**

String-tokenizing function. See Section 10.4, "String Tokenizing with strtok," for a longer description and examples. In brief, the action is: If string argument *source* is not a null pointer, the function returns a pointer to a string containing the first token found, using all the characters in string argument *delims* as delimiters separating tokens in *source*. (Delimiters might include spaces and commas, for example.) The string returned is a new string that contains only a copy of the token itself. If string argument *source* is a null pointer, then the call to **strtok** uses the same source string as in the previous call to **strtok**, but it looks for the *next* token within the source string. In either case, the function returns a null pointer if it can find no more tokens.

For example, the following code prints out all the tokens in the string source_str, one to a line—in which tokens are considered to be substrings in source_str separated by commas and/or spaces.

```
char *tok;
tok = strtok(source_str, " ,");
while (tok) {
     cout << tok << endl;
     tok = strtok(NULL, " ,");
}
```

- **strxfrm(*s1*, *s2*, *n*)**

Transforms *s2* so that in comparisons with **strcmp** it will reflect the setting of LC_COLLATE. Transformed string is copied into *s1*, but at most n characters are copied.

10.4 String Tokenizing with strtok

The string functions in the preceding section enable you to analyze and search strings. Using these functions, you can (for example) analyze a string that was read in with the **getline** function for its component parts.

Such operations are called lexical analysis or *tokenizing*, the process of extracting individual words (tokens) from a string. To tokenize a string, first decide what separator characters are going to be used: These are called delimiters. It's common to use blank spaces as delimiters. For example, assume blank spaces are delimiters for the following string:

```
John Q. Public
```

The process of tokenization would then break this one string into three tokens: "John", "Q.", and "Public".

You can carry out such operations yourself, but in simple cases, the use of just one function—**strtok**—performs all the lexical analysis you need, saving a lot of programming headaches. Here's how this function works.

- If you call **strtok** and specify a source string as the first argument, the function returns a pointer to the first token in the string. (The string returned is a new string, containing just the token itself.)
- If you call **strtok** and specify a null pointer in the first argument (NULL), the function uses the source string from the previous call and returns the *next* token within that same string.

So, if you make repeated calls with a null pointer in the first argument, **strtok** remembers where it is in the current source string, so it can retrieve one token after another rather than starting over.

```
p = strtok(NULL, " ");   // Get the NEXT token in current string.
```

But if you specify any non-null string for the first argument, tokenizing is reset. This sets a new source string and also resets the tokenizing process to the beginning of this string.

```
p = strtok(source_string, " ");   // Get the first token.
```

The second argument to **strtok** is a string containing one or more delimiters. (Each delimiter is a single character, but you can specify any number of them.) You can, if you choose, specify a different set of delimiters each time, but generally you ought to use a consistent set.

The following example reads a line of input, using the **cin.getline** function, and then prints each token from that string, one to a line. Delimiters in this case include blank spaces and commas—so we are looking for words separated by spaces and/or commas.

The **strtok** function returns a null pointer if no tokens are read. In the case of repeated tokenizing (as performed in this example), a null result means that the end of the string has been reached.

```
#include <cstring>
#define SCRN_WIDTH 80   // Usually this is wide enough.
using namspace std;

char  *token, input_ln[SCRN_WIDTH+1];
cout << "Enter line of input: ";
cin.getline(input_ln, SCRN_WIDTH);
token = strtok(input_ln, " ,");  // Try to read a token.
while (token) {                  // While there's a token,
     cout << token << endl;          // Print this token.
     token = strtok(NULL, " ,");     // Read the next one.
}
```

Note

One of the drawbacks of the **strtok** function is that it reuses hidden global data, so the function fails if there is more than one thread in the project using **strtok**; the function is therefore not safe for multithreaded applications. Recent versions of C++ provide the **strtok_r** function, which does essentially the same thing as **strtok** except that it is thread-safe. It requires a third argument, ***saveptr*, which is a pointer to a char* variable. This extra pointer argument must be supplied so that **strtork_r** can save its context between function calls. For example:

```
char *ptr;   // Extra ptr var; pass to strtok_r.
token = strtok_r(input_ln, " ,", &ptr);
```

10.5 Individual-Character Functions

The C library contains a series of functions for testing and transforming individual characters. Before using any of the functions in this section, include the <ctype> header.

```
#include <cctype>
```

For backward compatibility, the following **#include** is also supported:

```
#include <ctype.h>
```

Each of these functions accepts and returns character values as integer types (**int**). This integer may contain an ASCII character with the upper two bytes set to 0. The functions beginning with “is” return a **bool** value (**true** or **false**). For example:

```
#include <cctype>
#include <iostream>      // To support cout.
using std::cout;
using std::endl;

if (isalpha(s[2])) {
     cout << "Third elem in s is an alpha character.";
}
```

- **isalnum(*ch*)**

  Returns **true** if the character, *ch*, is any uppercase or lowercase letter or a digit.

  ```
  if (isalnum(c)) {
       cout << "Character c is alphanumeric.";
  }
  ```

- **isalpha(*ch*)**

  Returns **true** if the character, *ch*, is any uppercase or lowercase letter.

  ```
  if (isalpha(c)) {
       cout << "Char. c is alphabetic (a letter).";
  }
  ```

- **iscntrl(*ch*)**

  Returns **true** if the character, *ch*, is a “control character”: These include ASCII values 0 through 15 as well as ASCII value 255. These character codes perform special functions, such as inserting a tab or making a beeping sound, and do not correspond to a printable character.

  ```
  if (iscntrl(c)) {
       cout << "Character c is a cntrl character.";
  }
  ```

- **isdigit(*ch*)**

  Returns **true** if the character, *ch*, is any of the decimal digits 0 through 9.

  ```
  if (isdigit(c)) {
       cout << "Character c is a digit." << endl;
  }
  ```

- **isgraph(*ch*)**

  Returns **true** if the character, *ch*, is a printable character but not a space. (' ').

  ```
  if (isdigit(c)) {
       cout << "Character c is graphical." << endl;
  }
  ```

- **islower(*ch*)**

  Returns **true** if the character, *ch*, is any lowercase letter.

```
if (islower(c)) {
     cout << "Character c is a lowercase letter.";
     cout << endl;
}
```

- **isprint(*ch*)**

  Returns **true** if the character, *ch*, is any printable character. This function is the logical converse of **iscntrl**. ASCII characters are considered printable except for control characters such as tab, newline, form feed, and so on.

```
if (isprint(c)) {
     cout << "Character c is printable." << endl;
}
```

- **ispunct(*ch*)**

  Returns **true** if the character, *ch*, is a punctuation character such as "," or "?".

```
if (ispunct(c)) {
     cout << "Character c is a punctuation ";
     cout << "character." << endl;
}
```

- **isspace(*ch*)**

  Returns **true** if the character, *ch*, is a blank space or another whitespace character such as a newline, form feed, or tab.

```
if (isspace(c)) {
     cout << "Character c is a space." << endl;
}
```

- **isupper(*ch*)**

  Returns **true** if the character, *ch*, is any uppercase letter.

```
if (isupper(c)) {
     cout << "Character c is an uppercase ";
     cout << "letter." << endl;
}
```

- **isxdigit(*ch*)**

  Returns **true** if the character, *ch*, is one of the digits 0 through 9 or an uppercase or lowercase letter A through F.

```
if (isxdigit(c)) {
     cout << "Character c is a hexadecimal ";
     cout << "digit." << endl;
}
```

▸ **tolower(*ch*)**

If *ch* is an uppercase letter, returns the lowercase version of the letter as an **int**; otherwise, returns *c* as is. (Note that because the return value is **int**, not **char**, the value may need to be cast back to **char** form before being printed.)

The following example uses a less-than-or-equal-to comparison (<=), rather than less than (<), in order to copy the terminating null.

```
char str1[] = "Hello World";
char str2[12];
for (int i = 0; i <= strlen(str1); i++) {
     str2[i] = tolower(str1[i]);
}
cout << str2 << endl;    // Print "hello world"
```

▸ **toupper(*ch*)**

If *ch* is a lowercase letter, returns the uppercase version of the letter as an **int**; otherwise, returns *c* as is. Note that because the return value is **int**, not **char**, the value may need to be cast back to **char** form before being printed.

```
char str1[] = "Hello World";
char str2[12];
for (int i = 0; i <= strlen(str1); i++) {
     str2[i] = toupper(str1[i]);
}
cout << str2 << endl;    // Print "HELLO WORLD"
```

10.6 Memory-Block Functions (memcpy, and so on)

The <cstring> also supports a series of "mem" functions that are optimized to efficiently copy or set large blocks of memory.

```
#include <cstring>
```

The arguments to the "mem" functions—*dest*, *src*, and *buf*—are **void*** pointers, which means that they can receive any addresses or pointer values. The arguments *ch* and *n* take integer values (n is actually **size_t**, an unsigned integer large enough to hold the size of any object in memory).

▸ **memccpy(*dest*, *src*, *ch*, *n*)**

Copies *n* bytes from address *src* to address *dest*, until the byte value *ch* is encountered. (Copying stops when *ch* is read or when *n* bytes have been copied, whichever happens first.) Like **memcpy**, this function can produce erroneous results if the memory blocks overlap. (See **memmove**.) Returns a **void*** pointer to *dest*.

For example, the following statement copies bytes—no more than the length of arr1—unless a null value is encountered, at which point copying stops.

```
memcpy(arr1, arr2, '\0', sizeof(arr1));
```

- **memchr(*buf, ch, n*)**

  Scans buffer (starting address *buf*), searching for byte value *ch* but terminating the search after *n* bytes have been scanned. Returns a **void** pointer to the matching byte if found; otherwise, a null pointer is returned. For example, the following code looks for the byte value 0 and returns its position if found.

```
void *p = memcpy(arr1, '\0', sizeof(arr1));
if (p) {
    std::cout << "Offset of character found is ";
    std::cout << p – arr1;
} else {
    std::cout << "Character not found.";
}
```

- **memcmp(*buf1, buf2, n*)**

  Performs a byte-by-byte comparison between memory areas with starting addresses *buf1* and *buf2*. Bytes are compared beginning with the first byte in each block; the comparison continues until a byte in *buf1* is found that differs from the corresponding byte in *buf2*, or until *n* pairs of corresponding bytes have been compared. If the result of the comparison is that *buf1* has a byte with a lower value than the corresponding byte in *buf2*, the function returns a negative integer; if *buf1* has a byte with a higher value, the function returns a positive integer. If the two blocks have identical contents, the function returns 0.

```
int n = memcmp(arr1, arr2, sizeof(arr1));
if (n == 0) {
     std::cout << "The two blocks have thc ";
     std::cout << "same contents.";
}
```

- **memcpy(*dest, src, n*)**

  Copies *n* bytes from *src* to *dest*. This function can produce erroneous results if the two memory blocks overlap: for example, the block size is 1,000 but the starting addresses are only 500 bytes apart. (See **memmove** for handling overlapping blocks of memory.) Returns a **void*** pointer to *dest*.

  For example, the following statement copies bytes from arr2 to arr1. The number of bytes copied, in this case, is determined by the length of arr1.

```
memcpy(arr1, arr2, sizeof(arr1));
```

- **memmove(***dest, src, n***)**

  Copies *n* bytes from address *src* to address *dest*. Unlike **memcpy**, this function correctly handles overlapping blocks of memory (for example, they are 500 bytes apart, but the block size is 1,000). The function first copies the contents of *dest* to a temporary buffer in order to achieve this solution. Returns a **void*** pointer to *dest*.

  For example, the following statement copies bytes from *buffer2* to *bufferl*.

  ```
  memcpy(bufferl, buffer2, sizeof(bufferl));
  ```

- **memset(***dest, ch, n***)**

  Sets each and every one of the n bytes at starting address *dest*, to the byte value *ch*. Returns a **void*** pointer to *dest*. For example, the following statement sets all the bytes in arrl to null values (\0).

  ```
  memset (arrl, '\0', sizeof(arrl));
  ```

10.7 Wide-Character Functions (wstrcpy, and so on)

The standard C/C++ library supports a series of functions for handling wide-character strings. These strings are the same as standard C-strings (**char***), except that they use two bytes to represent each character. The advantage of the wide-character format is that it supports character sets (such as Russian, Chinese, and Japanese) that are not supported by the more limited ASCII character set.

To include type information for wide-character functions, include <cwchar>:

```
#include <cwchar>
```

This directive is also supported for backward compatibility:

```
#include <wchar.h>
```

Each **wcs***xxx* function ("wide-character string") works almost identically to its **str***xxx* counterpart except for a few differences. Most importantly, such strings have type **wchar_t*** instead of **char***. To initialize such strings, use the wide (long) character format, which prefixes a string literal with L:

```
wchar_t  wname[] = L"John Q Public";
```

This initialization works because wide-character sets are almost always supersets of the ASCII character set. Therefore, you can use ASCII characters along with extended characters coded by using escape sequences. (See Chapter 2, "Data," for information on coding escape sequences.)

Where wide-character functions take a string argument, remember to pass a string of type **wchar_t*** (such as wname, discussed earlier); where they take a character argument, pass a character of type **wchar_t**. Single-character literals also use the L prefix.

```
wchar_t  wch = L'a';
```

Stings of type **wchar_t*** are null-terminated and have the same drawbacks as C-strings; they cannot grow without limit.

Note that **wchar_t*** strings cannot be printed successfully to **cout**. Instead, use **wcout**. But note that **endl** still works as a newline indicator. (In the following code, the #include <iostream> directive brings in declarations for **wcout** as well as **cout** and **endl**.)

```
#include <cwchar>
#include <iostream>
using namepsace std;
wcout << L"This is a message." << endl;
```

The wide-character string functions are nearly identical to the string functions described in Section 10.3, "C-String Functions," except that the prefix "str" in the name of the function should be replaced by "wcs", and these functions take arguments of type **wchar_t*** and **wchar_t** rather than **char*** and **char**. Remember, also, that you should pass string literals and character literals with an "L" prefix as just shown.

◆ ◆ ◆ CHAPTER 11

C I/O Library Functions

The old-style C I/O functions (**printf**, **fprintf**, and so on) comprise another area of the library supported for backward compatibility. If you have a choice, you should use the C++ I/O stream classes and objects such as **cin** and **cout** to perform input and output. The advantages of the latter are that they have greater flexibility and ease of use; in particular, you can extend your own classes to work with them. They also work more smoothly with the C++ Standard Template Library (STL) **string** class.

printf, **scanf**, **fprintf**, and other old-style C I/O functions support a fixed set of format specifiers that cannot be extended to work with classes and do not work directly with the **string** class.

For these reasons, I definitely recommend using the C++ I/O stream classes, described in Chapter 13, "C++ I/O Stream Classes," whenever possible. You should really only use the functions in this chapter to support C legacy code.

11.1 Overview of C Library I/O

Here is a summary of the mechanics of old (C language) input/output.

- You can read and write directly to the console or to a file with **printf**, **scanf**, and other functions. The console I/O functions automatically write to **stdout** or read from **stdin**, which are predefined file pointers.
- To read or write to a file, first use **fopen** to get a file pointer of type **FILE***. This pointer can then be given as an argument to file-oriented I/O functions such as **fprintf** and **fputs**.
- Format specifiers, such as "%i" (integer) and "%s" (C-string), determine the format of I/O operations with **printf**, **scanf**, and related functions.

For example, you can write a string directly to the console by using **puts**, which prints a C-string to the console and appends a newline.

```
puts("Hello, White Rabbit.");
```

However, you cannot use the C++ STL **string** class with **puts** without first converting the **string** object by calling the **c_str** member function.

```
#include <cstdio>
#include <string>

string a_message = "Hello, White Rabbit.";
puts(a_message.c_str());
```

Probably the most common I/O function is **printf**, which takes a format string. You can print a string without format specifiers:

```
printf(str);
```

But the preferred way to use **printf** is to print formatted data:

```
char *error_msg = "Out of bounds";
printf("The error is %i: %s.\n", 10, error_msg);
```

This code prints the following:

```
The error is 10: Out of bounds.
```

The substrings "%i" and "%s" are format specifiers—specifying decimal integer and string, respectively—as described in Section 11.3.1, "printf Format Specifiers (%)."

11.2 Console I/O Functions

Before using any of the functions in this section, include the <cstdio> header.

```
#include <cstdio>
```

For backward compatibility, the following **#include** is also supported.

```
#include <stdio.h>
```

Descriptions of the C-library console I/O functions follow, along with examples.

- **getchar()**

  Returns the next character from the console's input buffer (**stdin**); returns EOF if there was an error reading the character or the end-of-file condition has been reached (although that shouldn't happen unless input is being redirected from a file). The character is returned as type **int**, but unless EOF is returned, this character is an ASCII value.

  ```
  int c = getchar();
  ```

▸ **gets(*input_str*)**

Reads an entire line of input from the console into *input_str*, a C-string (type **char***), and returns a pointer to this same string. The function reads all the characters, up until the next newline or end-of-file character, from the input buffer. The newline itself is not read, but the function appends a terminating null. You must take care to make sure the input string has enough room to take a full line of console input.

```
#define SCRN_WIDTH 80
char input_line[SCRN_WIDTH+1]
printf("Enter input: ");
gets(input_line);    // Get a line of input
```

A safer alternative to the use of gets is to use the **fgets** function, specifying **stdin** as the file pointer. With **fgets**, you specify a maximum number of characters to read. For information on **fgets**, see Section 11.5.3, "Reading and Writing Text Files."

▸ **putchar(*ch*)**

Prints a single character to the console (**stdout**). For example:

```
putchar('A');
```

▸ **puts(*str*)**

Prints a C-string to the console (**stdout**), and appends a newline.

```
puts("This is a warning.");    // Print warning,
                               //  (plus newline);
```

▸ **printf(*format_str* [, *args...*])**

Prints formatted output to the console. The *format_str* is a C-string (of type **char***) that is printed as is, except where a format specifier is encountered: These are substrings beginning with the % symbol and ending with one of the format characters such as "s" or "d". The formats can also specify other characteristics such as print-field width and precision. For each specifier, the function prints out the value of the corresponding argument. For example:

```
int i = 10, j = 20, k = 50;
printf("i: %d, j: %d, k: %d\n", i, j, k);
```

This example prints the following output, replacing each occurrence of "%d" in the format string with one of the values i, j, or k.

```
First: 10, second: 20, third: 50.
```

If the first argument, *format_str*, contains no format specifiers, **printf** just prints the string to the console.

See Section 11.3, "Print/Scan Formats," for a description of print formats.

▸ **scanf(*format_str* [, *args*...])**

Reads formatted input from the console. Each **scanf** argument is an address at which to store the data read. The *format_str* contains specifiers beginning with % just as a **printf** format string does. The other characters in *format_str* are literal characters that **scanf** attempts to match, character by character. The function fails and stops reading when a character does not match. Exception: A whitespace in a **scanf** format string will match any number of consecutive whitespaces in the input buffer.

For example, the following code reads the next three items input as integers and stores them in a, b, and c. Note that the *addresses* of a, b, and c are arguments to **scanf**.

```
int a = 0, b = 0, c = 0;
printf("Enter three numbers: ");
scanf("%i %i %i", &a, &b, &c);
```

This next example reads a single number—in this case, a floating point, so the function will successfully read input such as "3", "3.0", or "3.141592".

```
double x = 0.0;
printf("Enter a floating pt number: ");
scanf("%f", &x);
```

See Section 11.3.3, "Using Format Specifiers with scanf," for more information on **scanf** format specifiers.

▸ **unget(*ch*, *file_stream*)**

Places the specified character back onto the input buffer for the indicated stream (**stdin** in the case of console input), as if it were never read. This is a convenient feature that enables the program to look ahead before reading a character.

```
int c = getchar();
if (c == target) {
     // Do some stuff.
} else {
     unget(c, stdin);     // Put the char. back.
}
```

▸ **wscanf(*format_str* [, *args*...])**

Performs the same action as **scanf**, but takes a format string that is a wide-character (**wchar_t***) string. Wide-character string literals use an "L" prefix.

▸ **wprintf(*format_str* [, *args*...])**

Prints formatted output to the console as **printf** does, but the first argument is a wide-character string (type **wchar_t***). (String literals become wide-character strings when the "L" prefix is used, as in the example that follows.) Otherwise, the arguments are handled the same way as in **printf**. Note that to print a **wchar_t*** string rather than a **char*** string, use the "l" (long) size specifier, as in "%ls". For example:

```
#include <cwchar>
#include <cstdio>

char_t w_msg[] = L"Hello!";
int i = 10;
wprintf(L"Number: %i, message: %ls", i, w_msg);
```

This code prints the following:

```
Number: 10, message: Hello!
```

11.3 Print/Scan Formats

printf and related functions (such as **sprintf** and **fprintf**) recognize a common set of format indicators: for example, %d and %s. The format specifiers may be modified as described in Section 11.3.2, "Advanced printf Format Syntax." Section 11.3.3 summarizes **scanf** formats.

11.3.1 printf Format Specifiers (%)

An occurrence of the percent sign (%) within a format string is interpreted as having special meaning as described in the list that follows. (To represent a literal %, use two in a row: %%.)

When one of the following character combinations occurs in a format string (the first argument to **printf**), it represents a value to be supplied by the argument list.

- **%c**

  A single character. This is an ASCII value output in its character representation.

- **%d**

  A signed decimal integer. This format specifier prints out a numeric value in its decimal form. Examples: "10", "-15".

- **%i**

  A signed decimal integer (identical to the %d format).

- **%e**

  A floating-point number in scientific notation, using lowercase "e" to separate mantissa and exponent. Example: "1257e+2".

- **%E**

  A floating-point number in scientific notation, using uppercase "E" to separate mantissa and exponent. (This is the same as the %e format, except for its use of uppercase "E".) Example: "1257E+2".

- **%f**

  A floating-point number in ordinary decimal format (not scientific notation). Example: "125.7".

- **%g**

  A floating-point value, using either the %e or %f format, whichever would generate fewer characters. For example, 125.7 is printed as "125.7", but 105000000 is printed as "105e+6".

- **%G**

  A floating-point value, using either the %E or %f format, whichever would generate fewer characters. For example, 125.7 is printed as "125.7", but 105000000 is printed as "105E+6". (This is the same as the %g format, except for the use of uppercase "E".)

- **%o**

  An unsigned octal number. For example, the decimal value 16 is printed as "20". Note that the **printf** family of functions do not output any format prefixes unless you provide them yourself or use the # flag, as in "%#o". See Section 11.3.2 for more information on flags.

- **%s**

  A C-string. The characters pointed to are printed until a terminating null is encountered. Remember that objects of the STL **string** class are not accepted unless explicitly converted with the **c_str** member function.

- **%u**

  An unsigned decimal integer. Negative values are interpreted as unsigned.

- **%x**

  An unsigned hexadecimal number, using lowercase letters for the six highest digits ("a" through "f"). For example, the decimal value 127 is printed as "ff", and 62 is printed as "3e". Note that **printf** does not output format prefixes unless you provide them yourself or use the # flag, as in "%#x".

- **%X**

  The same as %x, except that it uses uppercase letters as digits. For example, the decimal value 127 is printed as "FF", and 62 is printed as "3E".

- **%p**

  A pointer (or address) value. By convention, addresses are written in hexadecimal. Given a 32-bit architecture, %p almost certainly renders an address as an eight-digit hexadecimal number, printed with leading zeroes if needed to fill out eight digits. Example: &a might be printed as "022C0BC4".

- **%%**

  Writes a literal "%".

As an example of the use of printf format specifiers, consider the following call to **printf**.

```
#include <cstdio>
int n = 29;
double x = 3.14159;
printf("There were %d amounts equal to %f.\n", n, x);
```

This prints the following output on the console, interpreting the n and x arguments in the %d (decimal integer) and %f (floating-point) formats, respectively.

```
There were 29 amounts equal to 3.14159.
```

If you want to print out octal or hexadecimal numbers with prefixes you need to put those prefixes in the format string yourself, or else use the # flag as described in the next section.

```
printf("The value of n in hex is 0x%X.\n", n);
```

This prints out the hexadecimal value of n (decimal 29):

```
The value of n in hex is 0x1D.
```

11.3.2 Advanced printf Format Syntax

The full syntax for a **printf** format specifier is as follows, in which the brackets ([]) are not intended literally but indicate optional items:

```
% [flags] [width] [.precision] [length_char] specifier
```

The *flags* indicate general information about how the data is to be printed. Any number of these may be used, and they are not separated by spaces or commas.

- +

  Causes a + or – sign to be printed for signed values, even if the value is positive.

- `-`

  Left-justifies the output if it has a smaller width than the print-field width.

- `#`

  Causes an octal prefix (0) or hexadecimal prefix (0x) to be printed for o, x, and X formats, as appropriate. For floating-point formats, this flag forces a decimal point (.) to be written, even when there are no nonzero digits to the right of the decimal point.

- `(space)`

  Causes a single blank space to be printed if no + or – sign is going to be printed. (In this case, a blank space is not a separator, but a flag.) The purpose of this flag is to help positive and negative numbers line up correctly when you print them in columns.

- `0`

  If the field is going to be padded with spaces (because the width of the output is smaller than the print-field width), causes the result to be padded with 0's instead of spaces.

The *width* is a decimal number indicating the minimum print-field width. If this is larger than the number of characters that would otherwise be printed, the output is right-justified by default, although that can be changed to left justification with the minus-sign flag (-). The print field is padded with spaces by default, although the 0 flag specifies padding with leading zeroes. (Exception: Left-justified print fields for integers are never padded with trailing zeroes.)

Note

If the characters to be printed exceed the *width*, they are not truncated.

With floating-point formats, *precision* is the number of digits to be printed after the decimal point if scientific notation is used (specified by the "e" and "E" formats); the result is rounded or printed with trailing zeroes if necessary. If the format is integer, *precision* is the minimum number of digits to be printed; if fewer digits would be printed than the *precision* number, the digits are padded with leading zeroes.

The *length_char* modifies the type of the format as follows.

- `h`

  Short integer format. %hi means **short int**, and %hu means **short unsigned int**.

- `l`

  Long. Modifies integer formats to mean **long int** or **long unsigned int**, as appropriate. Character (%lc) and string (%ls) formats are modified to mean **wchar_t** and **wchar_t*** strings, respectively. Use "%ls" to print a wide-character string.

▸ L

Long double. Applies to floating-point fields.

To take a simple example, you can use %ls to print a wide-character string:

```
#include <cwchar>
#include <cstdio>

wchar_t wstr[] = L"This is a wide character string.";
printf("%ls", wstr);
```

The *width* and *precision* specifiers are useful in formatting output numbers so that they align when you print them in columns. For example, the following statement prints a floating-point number in a ten-character print field and displays three digits after the decimal point:

```
double temperature = 98.7777;
printf("Temperature is %10.3f", temperature);
```

Because the precision of temperature in this case is four digits, but the print format specifies only three digits of precision, rounding occurs. Because the number's print-field width is 10, the print field is padded with four spaces.

```
Temperature is     98.778
```

If a zero is inserted in front of "10.3", it is interpreted as a flag; the "0" flag specifies that zeroes are to be used for padding instead of spaces.

```
printf("Temperature is %010.3f", temperature);
```

This produces the output:

```
Temperature is 000098.778
```

11.3.3 Using Format Specifiers with scanf

The **scanf** family of functions use format specifiers similar to those for **printf**, but this set is more limited; **scanf** is flexible in accepting user input. For example, with floating-point fields (%f), **scanf** accepts floating-point numbers in both standard decimal and scientific notations.

When reading a string (%s), **scanf** stops reading as soon as it encounters a whitespace. An alternative approach to reading strings from a file or console is to read in an entire line of text, separate it into individual tokens if needed, and then use the **atoi** and **atof** functions (described in Chapter 12, "Math, Time, and Other Library Functions") to convert digit strings into numbers.

A **scanf** format string typically consists of format specifiers separated by spaces. A whitespace in the format string matches any number of whitespaces in the input.

You can place other characters—which are neither format specifiers nor spaces—into a **scanf** format string, but I wouldn't usually recommend it. **scanf** attempts to match the format string to the input buffer, character by character. If it cannot match every character, the read operation fails, and **scanf** returns its failure code, EOF. No more text can be read until error flags are cleared.

After the format-string argument, the arguments to **scanf** are addresses to which to write the data.

Here are the **scanf** formats. The complete syntax, given later in this section, can modify these.

- %c

  Reads a character and copies it to the address in the corresponding argument, which must have type **char***. By default, only one character is read, but if width specification (explained later) is greater than 1, subsequent characters are read to the address contained in the argument, treating it as an array.

- %d

  Reads a digit string as a decimal integer, optionally preceded by a + or – sign, and writes the numeric value to the address in the corresponding argument, which must have type **int***. For example, reading "25" causes the value 25 to be stored in the **int** that was pointed to.

  When **scanf** uses this format, it will not read a floating-point expression. So if "1.5" appears in the input buffer, only the digit "1" is read. The next field, if it is floating point (%f), will read ".5" as a valid floating-point number equal to 0.5.

- `%f, %e, %E, %g, %G`

  Reads a floating-point expression and writes the value to the address in the corresponding argument, which should have type **double***. (If the format is modified, as in "%hf", these formats write to an address of type **float*** instead.) The input may use standard decimal notation or use scientific notation. Examples: "2", "3.1415", "-7.8e+15".

- %o

  Reads an integer digit string in octal format and writes the numeric value to the address in the corresponding argument, an **int*** address. For example: Reading "100" from the input buffer causes the value 64 to be written to the indicated address.

- **%s**

  Reads characters from the input buffer until a whitespace or newline is encountered. The characters are written to the address in the corresponding argument. For example:

  ```
  char my_name[1000];      // Reserve lots of room!
  scanf("%s", my_name);    // Write to my_name.
  ```

  You need to ensure that the address is large enough to contain any data written to it. This is why I recommend using **fgets** to receive string input instead.

- **%u**

  Reads a digit string as an unsigned decimal integer and writes the numeric value to the address in the corresponding argument, which should have type **unsigned int***.

- **%x, %X**

  Reads a digit string in hexadecimal format and writes the numeric value to the address in the corresponding argument, which has type **int***. The input can include the hexadecimal digits "a" through "f" and "A" through "F". The input can include the hexadecimal prefix "0x" or "0X", but such a prefix does not have to be present. For example, "10", "1E", and "0x1f" are all accepted—interpreted as 16, 30, and 31, respectively.

The following example combines the use of several of these **scanf** formats.:

```
#include <cstdio>

char name[SCRN_WIDTH+1];
int i = 0;
double x = 0.0;
printf("Enter a name, integer, and flt pt: ");
scanf("%s %i %x", name, &i, &x);
```

The call to **scanf** expects from the console input such as the following:

```
Rabbit  15  3.1415965
```

What happens if the input is not in the expected format? Then **scanf** will read it and interpret it as best it can, returning EOF if it fails. For example, suppose the input is:

```
Rabbit   Dodgson  15  3.14159265
```

In this case, because %s reads a string up to the first whitespace or newline, only the name "Rabbit" is read into the string variable, name. The function then attempts to read "Dodgson" as an integer and fails.

But this is not the only thing that can go wrong. Suppose the input buffer contains:

```
Alice   7.5  3.14
```

The string "Alice" is correctly read. Then the function reads "7" as an integer but stops at the decimal point (.) because it expects an integer for this data field, not floating point. The next two characters, ".5", are then read into the floating-point field, and "3.14" is not read.

Here is the complete syntax for **scanf** formats. The brackets ([]) are not intended literally but indicate optional items.

%[*][*width*][*length_char*]*specifier*

The asterisk (*), if present, indicates that the data is to be read but ignored.

The *width* specifies the maximum number of characters to be read for this input field.

The *length_char* modifies the size of the data type involved. It can have the following values.

- **h**

  Short. Applies to integer formats: "%hi" specifies **short int**, and "%hu" specifies **short unsigned int**.

- **l**

  Long. Modifies integer formats to mean **long int** or **long unsigned int**, as appropriate. Character (%lc) and string (%ls) formats are modified to mean **wchar_t** and **wchar_t*** strings, respectively. Use "%ls" to read a wide-character string.

- **L**

  Long double. Applies to floating-point fields.

For example, the following statements read a **short** and **long** integer:

```
short  s_int;
long   l_int;
printf("Enter two integers: ");
int n = scanf("%hd %ld", &s_int, &l_int);
if (n != EOF) {
     puts("Scanf successful.");
}
```

11.4 Input and Output to Strings

In addition to reading and writing to the console (as described in earlier sections) and to files (as described in Section 11.5, "File I/O"), you can read and write to strings.

Although writing to a C-string is risky—unless you are careful to make sure the C-string is not overwritten—string-based I/O can be a powerful tool. It's possible to analyze strings yourself, but reading and writing strings as if they were input/output devices enables you to use all the convenient formatting tools of **printf** and **scanf**. (C++ I/O stream classes support a similar technique through the use of "string streams," as described in Chapter 13.)

For example, you can build a formatted string by calling **sprintf**:

```
#include <cstdio>
#define STR_MAX 255
char my_str[STR_MAX + 1]
int n = 5;
int x = 3.141592
sprintf(my_str, "This string contains %d and %.3f." n, x);
```

After this code is executed, the string my_str contains the following characters:

```
This string contains 5 and 3.142.
```

Descriptions of the string-based I/O functions follow.

- **sprintf(*dest_str*, *format_str* [, *args*])**

  Performs the same actions as **printf**, except that the output is written to *dest_str*, a C-string (type **char***), instead of to the console. This function does not guarantee that *dest_str* will not be overwritten, so take care to make sure it is large enough to hold the data written to it.

- **sscanf(*source_str*, *format_str* [, *args*])**

  Performs the same action as **scanf**, except that the input is read from *source_str*, a C-string (type **char***), instead of from the console.

11.5 File I/O

C library functions include support for reading and writing to disk files. (But note that C++ I/O streams, described in Chapter 13, support file operations as well.)

Including <cstdio> supports C-style file I/O, as well as all the console functions introduced earlier.

```
#include <cstdio>
```

The following included directive is also supported for backward compatibility:

```
#include <stdio.h>
```

There are four basic steps in reading and writing to a disk file using old-style C library functions.

1. Declare a pointer of type **FILE***. The **FILE** type is defined in the header file, <cstdio>.

   ```
   FILE *fp;
   ```

2. Get a file pointer by calling **fopen**, specifying file name and mode. If it is successful, **fopen** returns a pointer of type **FILE***. If it fails, the function returns a null pointer.

   ```
   fp = fopen(filename, "r");
   ```

3. Use this file pointer (assuming it is not null) to read and write to the file by passing it to text-oriented functions such as **fopen**, **fputs**, and **fscanf**, or by passing it to the binary functions **read** and **write**.

   ```
   fputs("Hello, here I am.", fp);
   ```

4. Finally, use the file pointer to close the file.

   ```
   fclose(fp);
   ```

11.5.1 Opening a File

To open a file for reading and writing, call the **fopen** function, which has this syntax:

fopen(*filename_str*, *mode_str***)**

If the file is successfully opened, **fopen** returns a usable pointer of type **FILE***; otherwise, it returns a null pointer.

The *filename_str* is a C-string containing the file specification. At minimum, this is a file name. However, depending on the platform, this string may contain a path name. Note: If the pathname involves a backslash, you must use two backslashes within a literal string.

```
"readme.txt"
"Looking Glass.docx"
"C:\\bin\\my_binary_fil.bin"
```

The *filename_str* argument does not have to be a string literal; it can (for example) be a string supplied by the user.

The *mode_str* is a C-string that contains one or more mode specifiers, described next. Although the first six (r, w, a, r+, w+, a+) are mutually exclusive, they may be combined with either t (text) or b (binary).

- **r**

  Read-only mode. The file must already exist, or file open fails.

- **w**

  Creates a new file for writing. If the file specified already exists, its current contents are erased and the file is treated as new.

- **a**

  Append mode. The file is opened for writing, but all writing begins at the end of the file, protecting existing contents.

- **r+**

  Read/write mode (existing file). The file is opened for both reading and writing. It must already exist, or the file open fails.

- **w+**

  Read/write mode (new file). The file is opened for both reading and writing. If it already exists, its contents are erased and the file is treated as new.

- **a+**

  Append read/write mode. Previous contents are protected: New information to be written is appended to the end of the old contents. The file pointer may be moved back to read the old contents, but those contents cannot be overwritten; writing operations move the file pointer to the new section of the file.

- **t**

  Text mode (the default). Text mode is intended to be used with text-oriented I/O such as **fprintf** and **fputs**. The effect of specifying text mode is that newlines are translated into carriage-return/form-feed pairs during output; conversely for input.

- **b**

  Binary mode. The "b" for binary can be combined with the earlier mode specifiers, as in "rb", "wb", "ab", "rb+", "wb+", and so on. In binary mode, intended to be used with the low-level I/O functions **read** and **write**, no translation of newlines is performed.

For example, the following statement attempts to open a file named "my_stuff.txt" in read-only text mode (text mode being the default). Such a file must already exist in the current directory—because no path was given—or **fopen** returns a null pointer to indicate failure.

```
FILE *fp;
fp = fopen("my_stuff.txt", "r");
```

Because there is no guarantee that the file exists, you should always test the file pointer. If **fopen** failed to open the file, fp is set to a null pointer.

```
if (!fp) {          // If file-open failed,
     return -1;     // return from function
}
```

C programmers traditionally like to combine these operations. Note that the equal sign (=) is an assignment here, not a test for equality. The return value of **fopen** is assigned to fp, which is then tested to see if it is a null value.

```
if (! (fp = fopen("my_stuff.txt", "r")) {
     return -1;     // Open failed; return from function
}
```

The following statement attempts to open the file for binary reading and writing. As with "r" mode, the file must already exist, or the attempt to open the file fails.

```
fp = fopen(file_spec, "rb+");
```

Again, the value returned by **fopen** should be tested before attempting any operations on the file.

11.5.2 Closing a File

It's a good idea to close a file when you are done reading and writing to it, especially in a multiprocessor or multithreaded environment. Depending on the file system and the platform, keeping a file open may potentially lock the file and prevent other processes from gaining access.

Closing a file when done is important for another reason. Changes to a file may not always be written out immediately. Depending on the details of a file system, the output buffer may not always be "flushed" (it's scary to think of your data as going through a toilet, but still…). Closing a file forces the output buffer to be flushed and changes to or from the physical file to be immediately realized.

To close a file, just use the following simple syntax.

fclose(*file_ptr*);

The *file_ptr* is a file pointer previously returned by a successful **fopen** call.

The return value of **fclose** is 0 if successful, or EOF if not.

11.5.3 Reading and Writing Text Files

The functions for reading and writing text files are similar to the I/O console functions, but sometimes there are important differences. For example, the **puts** console function prints a string and appends a newline:

```
puts("This is a message.");    // Newline appended.
```

But the **fputs** function, which writes a string to a text file, does not append a newline.

```
fputs("This is a message.", fp);
```

You can use the file I/O functions to perform console I/O by using **stdin** or **stdout** as the file pointer. For example, to print a string to the console without appending a newline, use:

```
fputs("This is a message.", stdout);
```

Of course, an important difference between console functions and file I/O functions is that the latter are most always used with a file pointer. For example:

```
#include <cstdio>
. . .
FILE *fp;
fp = fopen("readme.txt", "w");
if (! fp) {
     puts("File could not be opened);
     return -1;
}
fputs("Here is some text.", fp);
fclose(fp);
```

Remember that all functions in this chapter (except the wide-character functions) assume that you have included <cstdio>:

```
#include <cstdio>
```

Descriptions of the C-library text-file I/O functions follow.

- **fgetc(*file_ptr*)**

  Returns the next character from the specified input stream (*file_ptr*).

  ```
  char c = fgetc(fp);
  ```

- **fgets(*str*, *n*, *file_ptr*)**

  Reads characters from the specified input stream (file_ptr) until a newline or end-of-file is encountered. Those characters, not including the newline, are read into *str*, a C-string, along with a null terminator. The function returns *str*. The *n* argument specifies the maximum number of characters to read, including the terminating null.

```
char line_of_input[256];
fgets(line_of_input, 256, fp);
```

Note that **fgets** takes a maximum number of characters to read while **gets** does not. You can adapt this function to read from the console by using the predefined file pointer **stdin**:

```
char line_of_input[256];
fgets(line_of_input, 256, stdin);
```

- **fprintf(*file_ptr*, *format_str* [,*args*])**

Writes formatted output to the specified output stream (*file_ptr*). Aside from the fact that **fprintf** writes to a text file, it is in every way similar to **printf**. See Section 11.3.

```
double pi = 3.14159;
fprintf(fp, "Here's the value of pi: %f \n", pi);
```

This operation writes the following string to the file corresponding to fp, appending a newline (because of the "\n" character):

```
Here is the value of pi: 3.141592
```

- **fputc(*ch*, *file_ptr*)**

Writes an individual character to the specified file. For example, the following statement appends a newline to the output.

```
fputc('\n', fp);
```

- **fputs(*str*, *file_ptr*)**

Writes a C-string, *str*, to the specified output stream (*file_ptr*). Unlike **puts**, **fputs** writes a string without appending a newline to it.

```
fputs("Here is text to put into a file", fp);
```

- **fscanf(*file_ptr*, *format_str* [,*args*])**

Reads text from the specified input stream (*file_ptr*) and interprets it according to the format specifier, if any, in *format_str*. Aside from the fact that **fscanf** reads from a text file, it works the same way as **scanf**. See Section 11.3.3 for more information.

For example, the following statements read two consecutive digit strings (separated by any number of whitespaces) from the file pointed to by fp. The first string of digits is read as an integer and the second as a floating-point number.

```
int i = 0;
double x = 0.0
fscanf(fp, "%d %x", &i, &x);
```

- **getc(*file_ptr*)**

  Returns the next character from the specified input stream (*file_ptr*). This performs essentially the same action as **fgetc** but is implemented as a macro.

- **putc(*ch*, *file_ptr*)**

  Writes an individual character *ch* to the specified file. This performs essentially the same action as **fputc** but is implemented as a macro.

- **ungetc(*ch*, *file_ptr*)**

  Places character *ch* into the front of the input buffer, and rewinds the file-position indicator by one. This has the effect of "ungetting" a character that was just read by placing it back. For example, the following code ungets a character if it is a newline:

  ```
  char c = get(fp);
  if (c == '\n') {
       ungetc(c, fp);
  }
  ```

11.5.4 Reading and Writing Binary Files

Although all files ultimately store data numerically, a binary file is one in which values are written directly without first being translated into text representation. So, for example, the unsigned value 254 is directly written as binary value 1111 1110 rather than as the ASCII codes for the characters "2", "5", and "4".

When reading or writing binary files, you need to understand how to interpret the data, because you cannot rely on newlines, null terminators, and spaces as you can with a text file. Coming up with a file data format, and then implementing it, are important tasks for software designers and programmers. The C++ compiler itself does no formatting of a binary data file.

The binary I/O functions take a **char*** pointer, even though you may need to deal with data in other formats. Therefore, you must use the **reinterpret_cast** operator introduced in Chapter 3, "Operators," to read or write values other than characters. For example:

```
int n = 25;
char *p = reinterpret_cast<char*>(&n);
```

The pointer, p, now points to an integer containing the value 25. But it has been cast to **char*** type so that p can be passed as an argument to the **fwrite** function.

Descriptions of the binary I/O functions follow.

▸ **fread(*p_data*, *size*, *count*, *file_ptr*)**

Reads data from the specified stream (*file_ptr*) and stores it at the address specified by *p_data*, a pointer of type **char***. The number of bytes to read is *size * count*; the number actually read is returned by the function. The *size* and *count* arguments are integers of type **size_t**; *count* should be 1 unless you are reading into an array.

For example, the following code reads an **int** (four bytes wide on a 32-bit system) directly from a file and stores that value in the variable n.

```
int n = 0;
char *p = reinterpret_cast<char*>(&n);
int bytes_read = fread(p, sizeof(int), 1, fp);
if (bytes_read != sizeof(int)) {
     puts("Read error.");
     return -1;
}
```

▸ **fwrite(*p_data*, *size*, *count*, *file_ptr*)**

Writes data from the address specified by *p_data*, a pointer of type **char***, to the specified stream (*file_ptr*). The number of bytes to write is *size * count*. The number of bytes actually written is returned by the function. If these two amounts differ, there was an error. The *size* and *count* arguments are integers of type **size_t**; count should be 1 unless you are writing data from an array.

For example, the following lines of code write the value of n to the specified file (fp), writing the two bytes of data contained in n directly into the file. This value is 127, which is written as the two-byte pattern 00000000 01111111.

```
short n = 127;
char *p = reinterpret_cast<char*>(&n);
int bytes_read = fwrite(p, sizeof(short), 1, fp);
```

11.5.5 Random-Access Functions

Random-access functions move the file-position indicator. By default, this position moves sequentially so that (for example) if you read four bytes, the file position is moved ahead by four.

The random-access functions are typically used with a binary file containing fixed-length records. For such a file, the position of the Nth record is:

```
position = (N - 1) * size of record
```

▸ **fgetpos(*file_ptr*, *fpos_ptr*)**

Saves the current file position of the specified stream (*file_ptr*) into an object of type **fpos_t** pointed to the second argument (so the argument has type **fpos_t***). This object holds a position that can then be restored with the **fsetpos** function.

```
fpos_t  this_position;
fgetpos(fp, &this_position);
```

▸ **fsetpos(*file_ptr*, *fpos_ptr*)**

Restores a saved file position for the specified stream (*file_ptr*). The second argument is a pointer to an **fpos_t** object previously saved with **fgetpos**.

```
fpos_t  this_position;
fgetpos(fp, &this_position); // Save position.
. . .
fsetpos(fp, &this_position); // Restore it.
```

▸ **fseek(*file_ptr*, *offset*, *origin*)**

Sets the file-position indicator for the specified stream (*file_ptr*) to an offset from a specified point of origin. The *offset* is an integer of type **long int**. The *origin* argument is an integer with one of several values.

- SEEK_SET indicates the beginning of the file.
- SEEK_CUR indicates the current position.
- SEEK_END indicates the end of the file.

For example, the following statements read the sixth record from a file consisting of fixed-length records of type MyRec—a class assumed to be previously declared.

```
RecClass MyRec;
char *pRec = reinterpret_cast<char*>(&MyRec);
size_t rec_size = sizeof(MyRec);

int recno = 5;                // Get sixth record.
fseek(fp, recno * rec_size, SEEK_SET);
fread(pRec, sizeof(myRec), 1, fp);
```

▸ **ftell(*file ptr*)**

Returns the file-position indicator for the specified stream (*file_ptr*). This value is returned as a **long int**. If **ftell** fails (if, for example, it was used with an invalid file-stream pointer), it returns -1 and sets the value of the global variable errno.

The following function returns the length of the named file, or returns -1 if the file cannot be opened.

```
long get_file_size(char *file_name);
     FILE *fp;
     fp = fopen(file_name, "rb");
     if (fp) {
          fseek(fp, 0, SEEK_END); // Seek to end.
          return ftell(fp);       // Get pos.
     } else {
          return -1L;       // Return -1 on error.
     }
}
```

11.5.6 Other File-Management Functions

Other C I/O functions enable you to interact with or get the status of files.

- **clearerr(***file_ptr***)**

  Clears the error status of the specified stream. There is no return value. For example, the following statement clears the error flags for standard input (**stdin**).

```
clearerr(stdin);
```

- **ferror(***file_ptr***)**

  Returns a nonzero (true) value if there is an error condition associated with *file_ptr*.

- **fflush(***file_ptr***)**

  Flushes the input or output buffer for the stream if specified (*file_ptr*). If the second argument is a null pointer, the function flushes all I/O buffers associated with the program. The effect of flushing is to immediately read or write all data in the buffer.

```
fflush(NULL);    // Flush all buffers. Whoosh!!
```

- **freopen(***filename_str, mode_str, file_ptr***)**

  Attempts to close the specified stream (*file_ptr*). It then reassigns the stream to the named file (*filename_str*) in the specified mode so that input and output to and from *file_ptr* go to the file. (The first and second arguments are both C-strings having type **char***.) One of the principal uses of this function is to redirect standard output to a text file:

```
FILE* fp = freopen("readme.txt", "w", stdout);
puts("Here is some redirected text.");
fclose(fp);
```

  When the **fclose** statement is executed normal printing of text to standard output resumes. After these lines are executed, the file readme.txt contains the sentence:

```
Here is some redirected text.
```

- **remove(***filename_str***)**

  Deletes the named file from the disk or other medium; *filename_str* is a C-string (type **char***) that can be an ordinary file name or a path name if the file system recognizes such names. The conventions used for naming files and paths are system-dependent.

- **rename(***oldname_str, newname_str***)**

  Renames the specified *oldname* to a *newname*. Both arguments are C-strings (type **char***).

- **rewind(*file_ptr*)**

  Resets the position indicator to the beginning for the specified stream (*file_ptr*). The function also clears the error settings, and for files opened in update (read/write) mode, calling this function enables the program to safely switch from reading to writing operations.

- **tempfile()**

  Returns a file-stream pointer (type **FILE***) that can be used as a temporary file; it is guaranteed to have a name that does not conflict with an existing file. The file is opened in "wb+" mode (binary read/write).

- **tempname(*str*)**

  Returns an available temporary-file name as a C-string (type **char***). This name is guaranteed not to conflict with the name of any existing file. You can use this function—as opposed to tempfile—to get a temporary file name and then open that file in any mode you choose.

◆ ◆ ◆ CHAPTER 12

Math, Time, and Other Library Functions

C++ inherits all the functions of the old C-language library, improving on some of them by providing overloaded versions of the functions.

In some cases, C++ provides a better way to do something than was available in C: For example, the **bsearch** and **qsort** functions are largely superseded by Standard Template Library (STL) algorithms (see Chapter 18, "STL Algorithms"); but many of the functions in this chapter are still quite useful. This chapter covers the remainder of the C-language library, broken down into the following functional areas.

- Trigonometric math functions
- Other math functions, primarily used to operate on floating-point values (these are overloaded for **float**, **double**, and **long double** types).
- Date and time functions. These enable you to get and display the current time, calculate elapsed time, and even determine the day of the week for any date.
- String-to-number conversion functions such as **atof** and **atoi**.
- Memory-allocation functions. These are generally superseded by the **new** and **delete** operators but are supported for backward compatibility (although **realloc** provides useful functionality that **new** and **delete** do not).
- Searching and sorting functions, namely **bsearch** and **qsort**.
- Other standard C library functions. These include some integer-based math (abs) functions, along with functions that interact with the system generally.

The trig and math functions require the <cmath> header; the date and time functions require <ctime>, and the rest require <cstdlib>.

12.1 Trigonometric Functions

To use the math function in this section, include <cmath>:

```
#include <cmath>
```

The following include is also supported for backward compatibility:

```
#include <math.h>
```

The trigonometric functions (**sin**, **tan**, **cos**, and so on) work with the radian measure rather than degrees. To convert degrees to radians, use this conversion:

```
radians = degrees * pi/180
```

To convert radians to degrees, use the reverse conversion:

```
degrees = radians * 180/pi
```

For example, suppose the base of a building is 1,000 feet away from a surveyor. The following function calculates the height of the building based on the angle of elevation observed. (Note that the surveyor is a white rabbit, so he can take measurements from right at ground level, rather than five or six feet up!) Figure 12.1 is a graphical depiction of the problem. This scenario calculates the height based on the tangent of the angle, which gives the ratio of height to base.

The following function determines the tangent of the angle and then multiplies by 1,000 to get the height of the building.

```
#include <cmath>

double find_height(double angle) {
     double pi = 3.14159265;
     double angle_in_radians = angle * pi / 180;
     return tan(angle_in_radians) * 1000.0;
}
```

For example, if the angle of elevation is 21.78 degrees, the building is about 400 feet tall.

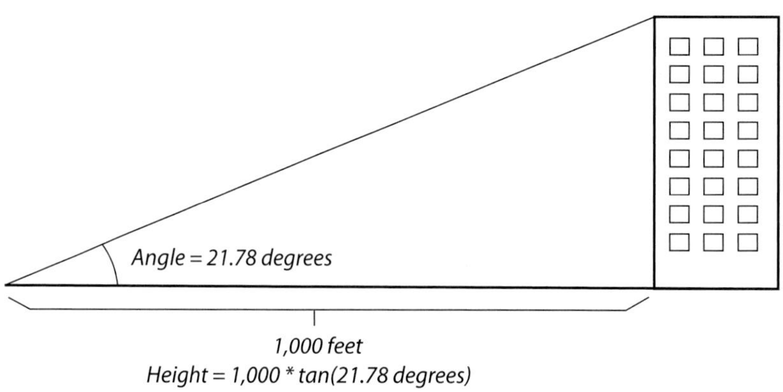

FIGURE 12.1 Using a tangent function to calculate height

You can calculate pi using the **atan** (inverse tangent) function, because the inverse tangent ("arc tangent") of 1 is pi/4:

```
double pi = atan(1.0) * 4;
```

In the descriptions of functions that follow, *x* is a floating-point number. In C, *x* is always type **double**, but in C++, overloaded versions of the functions are provided so that if *x* has type **float**, the function returns a **float** result; if *x* is **double**, the function returns a **double** result; and if *x* has type **long double**, the function returns a **long double** result.

As a consequence, you cannot use an argument of type **int** without casting it, because if you do, the compiler cannot determine which of several overloaded versions to use. **static_cast** solves the problem, as does the use of floating-point literals (for instance, "3.0"). For example:

```
double x = sqrt(3.0);    // Okay: 3.0 has type double.
```

Descriptions of the trig and hyperbolic functions follow.

- **acos(*x*)**

  Returns the inverse cosine of *x*; this return value is an angle expressed in radians.

- **asin(*x*)**

  Returns the inverse sine of *x*; this return value is an angle expressed in radians.

- **atan(*x*)**

  Returns the inverse tangent of *x*; this return value is an angle expressed in radians.

- **atan2(*x*, *y*)**

  Calculates the ratio *y* divided by *x* and then returns the inverse tangent of that ratio, expressed in radians.

- **cos(*x*)**

  Returns the cosine of *x*, an angle expressed in radians. The cosine is the ratio of the adjacent angle over the hypotenuse.

- **cosh(*x*)**

  Returns the hyperbolic cosine of *x*.

- **sin(*x*)**

  Returns the sine of *x*, an angle expressed in radians. The sine is the ratio of the opposite side over the hypotenuse.

- **sinh(*x*)**

  Returns the hyperbolic sine of *x*.

- **tan(*x*)**

  Returns the tangent of *x*, an angle expressed in radians. The tangent is the ratio of the opposite side over the adjacent side. (See Figure 12.1 for an illustration.)

- **tanh(*x*)**

  Returns the hyperbolic tangent of *x*.

12.2 Other Math Functions

As with the trig functions in the preceding section, the functions in this section require the <cmath> header:

```
#include <cmath>
```

Except where otherwise stated, the functions in this section take a floating-point number and return a result of the same type. In C++ these functions are all overloaded so that an argument of type **float** produces a **float** return value, a **double** argument produces a **double** return value, and so on. Therefore, if you need to use an **int** argument, use **static_cast** to cast the argument to one of the floating-point types; otherwise, the function call is ambiguous.

- **abs(*x*)**

  Returns the absolute value of *x*. If *x* is less than 0, the function returns -*x* (producing a positive number); otherwise, it returns *x*.

- **ceil(*x*)**

  Rounds upward to the next-highest integer. Note that the return value has floating-point type and must be cast if you want to assign it to an **int** variable.

  ```
  // Round x upward to -1 and place in integer i.

  double x = -1.998;
  int i = static_cast<int>(ceil(x));   // Now i = -1.
  ```

- **exp(*x*)**

  Returns the value of e (the mathematical constant) raised to the power of *x*. For example, to get e itself:

  ```
  double e = exp(1.0);
  std::cout << e << endl;     // Prints 2.7182818...
  ```

  The input to **exp** must be 1.0, not 1, because otherwise the compiler would not know which of several overloaded functions to use.

▸ **fabs(*x*)**

Produces the same result as the **abs** function.

▸ **floor(*x*)**

Rounds downward to the next-lowest integer value (or produces *x* itself if *x* has no fractional portion). The return value is of floating-point type and should be cast if you want to assign it to an integer.

```
// Round x downward to -2 and place in integer i.

double x = -1.998;
int i = static_cast<int>(floor(x));    // Now i = -2.
```

▸ **fmod(*num*, *den*)**

Performs modular division: This is the floating-point remainder after *num* (numerator) is divided by *den* (denominator). This function is similar to integer-remainder division, performed by the %, but is not exactly the same. The mathematical relationship is:

```
num = n * den + remainder
```

in which n is the highest integer value yielding a non-negative remainder. One of the most common uses for this function is to efficiently extract the fractional portion of a number. See also **modf**.

```
double remainder = fmod(7.677, 1.0);
cout << remainder << endl;   // Print 0.677
```

▸ **frexp(*x*, *ptr_n_exp*)**

"Free exponent." Takes a floating-point value, *x*, and breaks it down into mantissa and exponent portions. The function returns the mantissa and stores the exponent in the integer pointed to by *ptr_n_exp* (which should have type **int***).

The mantissa/exponent fields are representations of binary storage, not decimal. Even though the results may be displayed in decimal format (as in the following example), they reflect how the computer stores floating-point numbers internally.

```
int n = 0;
double x = 7;
double man = frexp(x, &n);
// Print 0.875 and 3:
std::cout << "mantissa is " << man << std::endl;
std::cout << "exponent is " << n << std::endl;
```

▸ **ldexp(*mantissa*, *n_exp*)**

"Load exponent." Assembles a floating-point number from *mantissa*, a floating-point argument, and *n_exp*, an integer (type **int**); the function returns the resultant floating-point number. The effect is essentially that of multiplying *mantissa* by 2 raised to the power of *exp*.

```
double x = ldexp(0.875, 3);    // x <= 7.
```

- **log(*x*)**

  Returns the natural logarithm of *x*, which uses base e. The logarithm is the exponent that e is raised by to produce *x*. (Note: e, an irrational number, is approximately 2.7182818 and can be produced by the **exp** function.)

- **log10(*x*)**

  Returns the logarithm of *x* using base 10 (decimal). The logarithm is the exponent that 10 is raised by to produce *x*. For example, the log of 1,000 is 3:

```
// Print 3:
std::cout << log10(1000.0) << std::endl;
```

- **modf(*x*, *ptr_x_integer*)**

  Returns the fractional portion of *x* and assigns the integer portion to the floating-point variable (or lvalue) pointed to by *ptr_x_integer*. The values returned always have the same sign as *x*. For example, the following statements print -5 and -0.3:

```
double i_part;
double x = -5.3;
double y = modf(x, &i_part);
std::cout << "Integer portion is: "<< i_part;
std::cout << std::endl;
std::cout << "Fractional portion is: " << y;
std::cout << std::endl;
```

- **pow(*base*, *exponent*)**

  Returns the *base* raised to the power of *exponent*. The two arguments may be of type **float**, **double**, or **long double**, but the types need to match. Note that you cannot use two **int** values without casting at least one of them, because the compiler needs to resolve which of several overloaded versions to use. But using floating-point literals (such as “2.0”) solves the problem.

```
double x = exp(2.0, 5.0);  // x = 2 to the 5th.
```

- **sqrt(*x*)**

  Returns the square root of its floating-point argument. This function is affectionately referred to as the “squirt” function. As with the other math functions, you cannot use this function with an **int** argument without casting it, because in C++ the compiler must choose between several overloaded versions (**float**, **double**, **long double**). However, the following statement is fine because the literal 2.0 has type **double**.

```
std::cout << "Square root of 2 is " << sqrt(2.0);
std::cout << std::endl;
```

Remember that you can always use a cast when working with integers.

```
int n = 2;
std::cout << sqrt(static_cast<double>(n));
```

12.3 The C Date and Time Library

The C-language date and time library enables you to do a number of useful things: get a date/time stamp, display time information, calculate elapsed time between events, and determine the day of the week for a date in the past or in the future.

To use the functions and macros provided, include the <ctime> header:

```
#include <ctime>
```

The following include is also supported for backward compatibility:

```
#include <time.h>
```

Although there are a number of ways to use the functions provided in the date and time library, the typical procedure is as follows.

1. First, you'll often want to call the **time** function to get the current time and store it in a **time_t** value, which is implemented as an integer type (usually **unsigned long**).

   ```
   time_t  right_now = time(NULL);
   ```

2. Typically, the next action is to pass a **time_t** pointer to the **localtime** function, which returns a pointer to a **tm** structure; this structure breaks the time value into component parts including year, month, day, hours, minutes, and seconds.

   ```
   tm *pTM = localtime(&right_now);
   ```

3. To display a formatted date/time string, you can pass a pointer to the **tm** structure to **strftime**.
4. Alternatively, you can display a standard timestamp by just passing a pointer to the **time_t** value (obtained in step 1) to the **ctime** function.

   ```
   cout << ctime(&right_now) << endl;
   ```

Important data types include **time_t** and **tm**. Here are some typical declarations:

```
time_t right_now;      // Holds a time value returned by time().
tm     *pTM;           // Points to a tm structure, returned
                       //   by localtime() or gmtime().
```

12.3.1 Date and Time Functions

Remember to include the <ctime> or <time.h> header:

```
#include <ctime>
```

In the function descriptions that follow, *time_t_ptr* is the address of a **time_t** value, *tm_ptr* is the address of a **tm** structure, and *n* is an integer.

- **asctime(*tm_ptr*)**

  Takes a pointer to a **tm** structure and returns a C-string in the format "*Ddd Mmm dd hh:mm:ss yyyy*" in which *Ddd* is an initial-uppercase day of the week (three-letter abbreviation), *Mmm* is an initial-uppercase month name (three-letter abbreviation), *dd* is the day of the month, *hh:mm:ss* contains hour, minutes, and seconds in military (24-hour) time, and *yyyy* contains the year. Note: A pointer to a **tm** structure can be produced by a call to **gmtime** or **localtime**.

  For example:

```
tm *pTM;
time_t right_now = time(NULL);
pTM = localtime(&right_now);
std::cout << "Date/time stamp: ";
std::cout << asctime(pTM) << "." << std::endl;
```

  A typical output for this code is:

```
Date/time stamp: Wed Aug 15 22:30:15 2012.
```

- **clock()**

  Returns the number of internal clock ticks—a clock tick being about 1/1000th of a second—since the program began. This number can be converted to seconds by dividing by the constant CLOCKS_PER_SEC (which is predefined by the <ctime> include).

```
double time_passed =
  clock()/static_cast<double>(CLOCKS_PER_SEC);
std::cout << "Program has been running for ";
std::cout << time_passed << " seconds."
```

  If you want the most precise possible measurement of runtime performance, use of clock ticks is much more accurate than the **time** function. The following code is useful for measuring the performance of a loop:

```
long x1 = clock();       // Get time now.

long big_array[10000000];
for(int i = 0; i < 10000000; i++) {
     big_array[i];
}
long x2 = clock();       // Get time again.
```

```
std::cout << "Time passed in microsecs: "
std::cout << x2 - x1;
```

- **`ctime(`*`time_t_ptr`*`)`**

  Returns a C-string displaying a timestamp, taking a pointer to a **time_t** value as its argument. (You can get a **time_t** value by calling the **time** function.) The format is "*Ddd Mmm dd hh:mm:ss yyyy*", the same used by **asctime**.

  ```
  time_t right_now = time(NULL);
  std::cout << "Date/time stamp: ";
  std::cout << ctime(&right_now) << std::endl;
  ```

  A typical output for this code is:

  ```
  Date/time stamp: Wed Aug 15 22:30:15 2012.
  ```

- **`difftime(`*`time_t_2`*`, `*`time_t_1`*`)`**

  Returns the number of seconds that have elapsed between *time_t_1* and *time_t_2*, in which each of the arguments has type **time_t**. This is *time_t_2 - time_t_1*, rounded to the nearest second. For example, the following code records the time of two different events and then reports how many seconds have elapsed between them.

  ```
  time_t time1 = time(NULL);    // During event 1
  . . .
  time_t time2 = time(NULL);    // During event 2
  std::cout <<
    "Number of seconds between the events is: ";
  std::cout << difftime(time2, time1) << std::endl;
  ```

- **`gmtime(`*`time_t_ptr`*`)`**

  Uses the **time_t** value pointed to by *time_t_ptr* to create and fill out a **tm** structure; the function returns a pointer to this structure. To use this function, get a **time_t** value (often done by calling the **time** function) and then pass the address of that value.

  The **gmtime** function produces Greenwich mean time by checking the system's time zone and then adjusting settings accordingly.

  ```
  time_t right_now = time(NULL);
  tm *pTM = gmtime(&right_now);
  ```

- **`localtime(`*`time_t_ptr`*`)`**

  Uses the **time_t** value pointed to by *time_t_ptr* to create and fill out a **tm** structure; the function returns a pointer to this structure. This function performs an action similar to **gmtime** but uses local time settings, ignoring time-zone considerations.

  ```
  time_t right_now = time(NULL);
  tm *pTM = localtime(&right_now);
  ```

- **mktime(*tm_ptr*)**

  Returns a **time_t** value corresponding to the **tm** structure pointed to by *tm_ptr*.

  This function also adjusts settings in the structure pointed to by the *tm_ptr* argument. It ignores tm_wday and tm_yday and sets these members based on the rest of the data. Therefore, one of the uses of **mktime** is to determine the day of the week for any day in the future or recent past.

  ```
  time_t my_time = mktime(pTM);
  ```

- **strftime(*dest_str*, *n*, *fmt_str*, *tm_ptr*)**

  Writes a formatted date/time string to *dest_str*, a C-string. The function uses the date/time information in the **tm** structure pointed to by *tm_ptr*. The action is to copy characters from *fmt_str* but to write out date/time information as text wherever it encounters a format specifier; these are substrings beginning with "%" and followed by a format character. For example, "%a" means day of the week, abbreviated, so where the format string contains an occurrence of %a, **strftime** would write "Wed" (if the day stored in the **tm** structure was Wednesday) to the destination string.

  The *n* argument specifies the maximum number of characters to write, including the terminating null. The function returns the number of characters written as long as *n* is not exceeded; otherwise, it returns zero, indicating there was insufficient room.

  See Section 12.3.3, "Date/Time Format Specifiers (strftime)," for a description of the date/time format specifiers and extended examples of using **strftime**.

- **time(*time_t_ptr*)**

  Returns the current time as a **time_t** value (this type is usually equivalent to **unsigned long**). The argument has type **time_t***; if this argument is not a null pointer, then the value pointed to is set to the same value returned by the function. For example:

  ```
  time_t right_now;
  time(&right_now);
  ```

  This next line of code produces the same effect as the preceding two.

  ```
  time_t right_now = time(NULL);
  ```

12.3.2 The TM ("Time") Data Structure

Along with the date and time functions, the <ctime> header defines a **tm** (time) structure that contains date/time information broken down into components including month, day, year, hour, and so on. You can generate such a structure by calling **localtime** or **gmtime**.

One of the more interesting uses of a **tm** structure is to initialize all the members except for tm_wday and tm_yday, and let the **mktime** function fill these out, thereby informing you what the correct day of the week and day of the year are for that date. For example, the following code determines what the day of the week will be on January 1, 2100.

```
#include <ctime>
#include <iostream>
using std::cout;
using std::endl;
. . .
tm theday;
theday.tm_mday = 1;       // 1 = first of month.
theday.tm_mon = 0;        // 0 = January
theday.tm_year = 200;     // 2100 = 200 years since 1900
theday.tm_hour = 12;      // Let's just go with noon.
theday.tm_min = 0;
theday.tm_sec = 0;

mktime(&theday);          // Fill out rest of TM structure.

char date_str[256];
strftime(date_str, 256, "Day of the week is %A.", &theday);
cout << date_str << endl;
```

If you run this code, you'll discover that January 1, 2100 falls on a Friday. So that's it… start preparing for the first New Year's Eve party of the next century. It will be on a Friday!

Descriptions of the members of a **tm** structure follow. All of these members have **int** type.

- **tm_sec**

  Seconds, ranging from 0 to 59.

- **tm_min**

  Minutes, ranging from 0 to 59.

- **tm_hour**

  Hours, ranging from 0 to 23. (So 10 p.m. would produce a tm_hour value of 22.)

- **tm_mday**

  Day of the month, ranging from 1 to 31.

- **tm_mon**

  Month, ranging from 0 to 11. January is represented as 0 and December as 11.

- **tm_year**

  Number of years since 1900. The year 2001 is therefore represented by a **tm_year** value of 101.

- **tm_wday**

  Day of the week, ranging from 0 to 6. This is essentially the number of days past Sunday, so Sunday is 0, Monday is 1, Tuesday is 2, and so on.

- **tm_yday**

  Day of the year, ranging from 0 to 365. This is the number of days past January 1 of the same year. New Year's Day is 0.

- **tm_isdst**

  Indicates whether daylight saving time (DST) is in effect. A positive integer value specifies that DST is in effect; a value of 0 specifies that it is not in effect; and a negative value indicates that the DST setting is unknown.

12.3.3 Date/Time Format Specifiers (strftime)

The C-library format specifiers, used with the **strftime** function, provide a convenient way to display date and time information according to a customized format string. For example, instead of giving the month before the day, as in the American style, you can use the European style of giving the day first. The following statements illustrate how.

```
#include <ctime>
#include <iostream>
using std::cout;
using std::endl;

char str[256];
tm *pTM;
time_t right_now = time(NULL);  // Get current time.
pTM = localtime(&right_now);    // Convert to tm structure.
strftime(str, 256, "Today's date is %d %B, %Y.", pTM);
cout << str << endl;
```

Typical output for this example is:

```
Today's date is 15 August, 2012.
```

In this example, substrings %d, %B, and %Y specify day, month, and year, respectively. Unlike **printf**, the **strftime** function does not expect a separate argument for each specifier. All the date/time information is extracted from one source: the **tm** structure pointed to by pTM.

To take another example, suppose the day is Monday. %A specifies day of the week.

```
strftime(str, 256, "%A, %A...", pTM);
cout << str << endl;
```

This prints out (with apologies to the singing group The Mamas & the Papas):

```
Monday, Monday...
```

Descriptions of **strftime** formats follow. Note that case is significant.

- **%a**

  Day of the week, as a three-letter abbreviation. For example: "Mon", "Tue", "Wed". (In all cases, the abbreviation is the first three letters, at least in English.)

- **%A**

  Day of the week spelled out. For example: "Monday", "Tuesday", "Wednesday".

- **%b**

  Name of the month as a three-letter abbreviation. For example: "Jan", "Feb", "Mar", "Apr", "May", and so on. (In all cases the abbreviation is the first three letters.)

- **%B**

  Name of the month spelled out. For example: "January".

- **%c**

  Complete date and time in the format *mm/dd/yy hh:mm:ss*. For example: "08/15/12 12:31:00" means August 15, 2012 at exactly 12:31.

- **%d**

  Day of the month as a two-digit number ranging from "01" to "31".

- **%H**

  Hour as a two-digit number ranging from "00" to "23" (based on a 24-hour clock).

- **%I**

  Hour as a two-digit number ranging from "00" to "11". This is based on a 12-hour clock cycle and should generally be used in conjunction with the %p specifier, which prints an "AM" or "PM" designation.

- **%j**

  Day of the year, output as a three-digit string ranging from "001" to "365".

- **%m**

  Month as a two-digit decimal number ranging from "01" to "12".

- **%M**

  Minutes as a two-digit decimal number ranging from "00" to "59".

- **%p**

  A two-character a.m./p.m. designation: "AM" or "PM".

- **%S**

  Seconds as a two-digit decimal number ranging from "00" to "59".

- **%U**

  Week number as a two-digit number ranging from "00" to "53". With this format, the first Sunday is considered the beginning of week 1; therefore, if New Year's Day falls on another day of the week (for example, Friday) it will be a part of week 0.

- **%w**

  Weekday as a decimal digit ranging from "0" to "6", with Sunday considered to be "0".

- **%W**

  Week number as a two-digit number ranging from "00" to "53". This is the same as %U except that the first Monday, not Sunday, is considered to start week 1.

- **%x**

  Locale-dependent representation of the date. For example: "08/15/12". Country settings could affect the order of the month and day in this case.

- **%X**

  Locale-dependent representation of the time of day. For example: "12:30:00".

- **%y**

  Two-digit string containing the last-two digits of the year. For example: "12".

- **%Y**

  Four-digit string containing the year. For example: "2021".

- **%Z**

  Time zone. For example: "Pacific Daylight Time". This is determined by the computer's internal time-zone setting.

- **%%**

  Prints a literal percent sign (%).

12.4 String-to-Number Conversions

C++ provides a number of ways to convert a string of digits into a numeric value. You can, for example, use **sscanf** as described in Chapter 11, "C I/O Library Functions." But the most direct way is to use the string conversion functions in the C library. To use these functions, include the <cstdlib> header:

```
#include <cstdlib>
```

The following include is also supported for backward compatibility:

```
#include <stdlib.h>
```

In the following summaries, *s* is a C-string and *ptr_to_s* is a pointer of type **char****, a pointer to a pointer. (The examples should clarify.)

- **atof(*s*)**

  Reads a digit string and returns a value of type **double**. The function ignores any number of leading whitespace characters and starts reading at the first digit or + or – sign it sees. Characters continue to be read as long as they are part of a floating-point expression: This may include an exponent portion, consisting of "e" or "E" followed by a number. Returns 0.0 if no valid floating-point number is read.

  The following are all valid inputs: "3", "0.87e12", "-303.107". Here is a simple example:

  ```
  char str[] = "    3.14159265";
  double pi = atof(str);         // pi = 3.14159265
  ```

- **atoi(*s*)**

  Reads a digit string and returns a value of type **int**. The function ignores any number of leading whitespace characters and then starts reading the first digit or + or – sign it sees. Characters continue to be read as long as they are part of a well-formed integer. Returns 0 if no valid integer is read.

  ```
  char str[] = "  -2001";
  int num = atoi(str);               // num = -2,001
  ```

- **atol(*s*)**

  The action is the same as **atoi**, except that the value returned has type **long**. (But note that on 32-bit systems, the **int** and **long** types are both four-byte integers.)

- **strtod(*s*, *ptr_to_s*)**

  Performs the same action as **atof**, but if *ptr_to_s* (which should be the address of a **char*** pointer) is not null, the function sets *ptr_to_s* to the first character not successfully read. This is a useful result when you are reading multiple numbers from the same string, because it marks the position at which to begin the next read.

```
char str[] = "25.37  3.141596";
char *p;
double x = strtod(str, &p);        // x = 25.37
double y = strtod(p, NULL);        // y = 3.1415927
```

- **`strtol(`*`s`*`, `*`ptr_to_s`*`)`**

  Performs the same action as **atol**, but if *ptr_to_s* (which should be the address of a **char*** pointer) is not null, then the function sets *ptr_to_s* to the first character not successfully read. This is a useful result when you are reading multiple numbers from the same string, because it marks the position at which to begin the next read.

```
char str[] = "7  -50";
char *p;
long i = strtol(str, &p);        // x = 7
long j = strtol(p, NULL);        // y = -50
```

- **`stroul(`*`s`*`, `*`ptr_to_s`*`)`**

  Performs the same action as **strol**, but reads only unsigned digit strings and returns an unsigned long result. Consequently, negative signs are not accepted.

```
char str[] = "7  550";
char *p;
long i = strtoul(str, &p);        // x = 7
long j = strtoul(p, NULL);        // y = 550
```

12.5 Memory-Allocation Functions

The C++ **new** and **delete** operators are usually preferable to the C memory-allocation functions. The latter are supported in C++ primarily for the sake of backward compatibility.

A drawback of the C functions in this section is that they require the use of the **reinterpret_cast** operator to access memory, because they return a **void*** pointer that must be cast to a specific type before being used. The **new** operator, in contrast, returns a pointer of the specified type and therefore is both easier to use and more reliable.

An advantage of the C functions is that they include **realloc**, which resizes an array while preserving its contents. (You could do that with **new**, but you must copy the old contents yourself.)

The functions in this section all require the <cstdlib> header:

```
#include <cstdlib>
```

The following include is also supported for backward compatibility:

```
#include <stdlib.h>
```

▸ **calloc(*size*, *count*)**

Attempts to allocate a memory block *size* * *count* bytes large, with each argument being an integer (**size_t**). If the allocation succeeds, the function returns a **void*** pointer to the beginning of the new block. If it fails, the function returns a null pointer.

The **void*** pointer returned must be cast before being used. For example, the following statements allocate room for a floating-point array; in this case, the array contains 1,000 elements, but the array can be of any size determined at runtime as long as physical limits are not exhausted. The example then assigns numbers to some of the elements of this dynamically allocated array.

```
int n = 1000;
void *p = calloc(sizeof(double), 1000);
double *d_ptr = reinterpret_cast<double*>(p);
d_ptr[0] = 1.5;
d_ptr[2] = 2.5;
```

▸ **free(*ptr*)**

Releases memory previously allocated with **calloc** or **malloc**. The *ptr* argument is a pointer of type **void*** (although any type of pointer can be passed to a **void*** argument, so *ptr* is essentially any pointer); if this is a null pointer, no action is taken.

```
free(p);
```

▸ **malloc(*size*)**

Attempts to allocate a memory block *size* bytes large, where this argument has integer type (**size_t**). This function performs the same action as **calloc**, but the size and count arguments are combined into one argument, *size*. **malloc** attempts to create a block *size* bytes in length.

```
int n = 1000;
void *p = malloc(sizeof(double) * 1000);
double *d_ptr = reinterpret_cast<double*>(p);
d_ptr[0] = 1.5;
d_ptr[2] = 2.5;
```

▸ **realloc(*ptr*, *new_size*)**

Reallocates the memory block pointed to by *ptr*, adjusting the memory block to have *new_size*. If the memory allocation fails, **realloc** returns a null pointer.

If *new_size* is greater than the current size of the block pointed to by *ptr*, the function may move the block to a new area of memory; if it does, the contents of the old memory block are copied to the new one. Upon success, the function returns a **void*** pointer to the new memory block.

As with **calloc** and **malloc**, the pointer returned must be cast before being used.

The following example allocates a block of 1,000 floating-point numbers, assigns some values, and then reallocates the memory block.

```
using std::cout;
using std::endl;

int n = 1000;
void *p = malloc(sizeof(double) * 1000);
double *d_ptr = reinterpret_cast<double*>(p);
d_ptr[0] = 1.5;
d_ptr[2] = 2.5;
// Reallocate.
p = realloc(p, sizeof(double) * 2000);

// Verify that values were preserved.
d_ptr = reinterpret_cast<double*>(p);
cout << d_ptr[0] << endl;
cout << d_ptr[2] << endl;
```

12.6 Standard C Randomization Functions

The standard C randomization functions—**rand** and **srand**—are no longer the best randomization tools available. See Chapter 19, "C++11 Randomization Library," for a discussion of the limitations of the C randomization functions.

Still, the C randomization functions work perfectly well for simple programs, and they may be the only randomization tools available if your compiler is not C++11 compliant.

The **rand** function returns a number in the **unsigned int** range. The easiest way to convert this to an integer from 0 to N-1 is to use remainder division (%), even though this results in a bias toward lower values. But for low values of N, this bias is so tiny as to be virtually undetectable.

```
int r = rand() % n;    // r = random 0 to n-1.
```

The **rand** function returns the next number from a series of pseudorandom numbers. The series must be started with a properly chosen seed; otherwise, calls to **rand** produce the same results every time the program is run.

The best—or at least most convenient—way to choose the seed is to call the **time** function. This requires the program to include <ctime> as well as <cstdlib>, which declares **rand** and **srand**:

```
#include <cstdlib>
#include <ctime>
```

- **rand()**

  Returns the next number in the pseudorandom number series. The program should almost always call **srand** on startup, before any calls are made to **rand**.

  The largest possible value result is MAX_RAND. **rand** returns a number in the range 0 to MAX_RAND with an even probability distribution throughout this range.

  The following example function returns a random number from 0 to N-1. If you add one to this result, you get a random number from 1 to N.

```
long rand_0_n1(int n) {
     return rand() % n;
}
```

- **srand()**

  Sets a seed for random-number generation. Programs that are going to call **rand** at any point should call **srand** once at the beginning of the program.

```
srand(time(NULL));
```

12.7 Searching and Sorting Functions

The **bsearch** and **qsort** functions were often highly useful to C programmers, but they are now superseded by the **binary_search** and **sort** algorithms presented in Chapter 18. **bsearch** and **qsort** are still supported for backward compatibility; otherwise, there is not much reason to use them.

These functions require the use of callback functions; moreover, they also require the use of **void*** pointers, which must be cast to more specific types with the **reinterpret_cast** operator (itself an inherently dangerous weapon). The use of STL algorithms is both safer and more convenient, as they remove the need for **reinterpret_cast**.

These functions require the <cstdlib> header (or <stdlib.h>):

```
#include <cstdlib>
```

12.7.1 The bsearch Function (Binary Search)

The **bsearch** function searches an array for a target value, returning a pointer to the found element or a null pointer if no matching element is found. The array must be presorted, arranging elements in ascending order. This function can efficiently search a large array quickly, as it uses a binary-search technique. Here is the declaration of **bsearch**:

```
void* bsearch(
      void* key_elem_ptr,
      void* base_elem_ptr,
      int n,
      int size,
      comparison_funct
)
```

key_elem_ptr is a pointer to an element to match. This argument is a **void*** pointer, so you can pass an address of any type to it.

base_elem_ptr is a pointer to the beginning of the array to be searched. It also has type **void***, and you can pass an address of any type to it.

n and *size* are integer arguments; *n* specifies the number of elements in the array to be searched and *size* specifies the size of each element.

Finally, *comparison_funct* is the address of a callback function (which you supply) having the following prototype:

```
int comparison_funct (const void* ptr1, const void* ptr2)
```

This callback function takes two **const void*** pointers as arguments. It should return -1, 0, or 1 as follows: If the object pointed to by *ptr1* is less than the object pointed to by *ptr2*, return -1; if they are equal, return 0; if the object pointed to by *ptr1* is greater than the object pointed to by *ptr2*, return 1.

The following example searches an integer array to determine whether a specified value (entered by the end user) is present.

```
#include <cstdlib>
#include <iostream>
using std::cout;
using std::cin;
using std::endl;

int arr[] = {-5, -1, 10, 35, 78, 79, 82, 99, 101, 103 };
int key = 0;
```

```
int icomp(const void* p1, const void* p2) {
     int i1 = *(reinterpret_cast<const int*>(p1));
     int i2 = *(reinterpret_cast<const int*>(p2));
     if (i1 < i2) {
          return -1;
     } else if (i1 == i2) {
          return 0;
     } else {
          return 1;
     }
}

main() {
     cout << "Enter value to search for: ";
     cin >> key;
     void *p;
     p = bsearch(&key, arr, 10, sizeof(int), icomp);
     if (p) {
          cout << key << " was found." << endl;
     } else {
          cout << key << "was not found." << endl;
     }
}
```

The icomp function demonstrates the challenge of using **void*** pointers in even a trivial example. Although addresses of any type can be passed to p1 and p2, these arguments must be recast with **reinterpret_cast** and then dereferenced before being used.

```
int i1 = *(reinterpret_cast<const int*>(p1));
int i2 = *(reinterpret_cast<const int*>(p2));
```

The value returned by **bsearch** is a pointer of type **void***. Although it points to the integer found, you must nonetheless recast this pointer from **void*** to **int*** if you want to dereference it:

```
void *p;
p = bsearch(&key, arr, 10, sizeof(int), icomp);
int *ip = reinterpret_cast<int*>(p);
cout << "The element is " << *ip << endl;
```

12.7.2 The qsort Function (Quick Sort)

The **qsort** function sorts all the values of an array, leaving it in ascending order. It uses the quick-sort algorithm, which—especially for large arrays—is more efficient than the relatively more "brute force" bubble-sort algorithm.

qsort has no return value (it has **void** return type).

The function has the following declaration:

```
qsort(
      void* base_elem_ptr,
      int n,
      int size,
      comparison_funct
)
```

base_elem_ptr is a pointer to the beginning of the array to be sorted. It has type **void***, so you can pass an address of any type to it.

n and *size* are integer arguments; *n* specifies the number of elements in the array to be searched and *size* specifies the size of each element.

Finally, *comparison_funct* is the address of a callback function (which you supply) having the following prototype:

```
int comparison_funct (const void* ptr1, const void* ptr2)
```

This callback is a comparison function that should return -1, 0, or 1, depending on whether the object pointed to by *ptr1* is less than, equal to, or greater than the object pointed to by *ptr2*. Because this function is a callback, it's one you usually have to write yourself.

Everything said about the callback function for **bsearch** applies here, so see the previous section for more information on this comparison function.

The following example sorts an array of integers and prints out the elements. It uses the same callback function, icomp, used in the **bsearch** example.

```
#include <cstdlib>
#include <iostream>
using std::cout;
using std::cin;
using std::endl;

int arr[] = {99, -107, 103, -5, 10, -1, 35, 78, 366, 82,};

int icomp(const void* p1, const void* p2) {
     int i1 = *(reinterpret_cast<const int*>(p1));
     int i2 = *(reinterpret_cast<const int*>(p2));
     if (i1 < i2) {
          return -1;
     } else if (i1 == i2) {
          return 0;
```

```
        } else {
            return 1;
        }
}

main() {
        qsort(arr, 10, sizeof(int), icomp);
        for (int i = 0; i < 10; i++) {
            cout << arr[i] << "    ";
        }
        cout << endl;
}
```

12.7.3 Comparison Functions Using C-Strings

When working with the **bsearch** and **qsort** functions, the recasting of **void*** pointers is fairly straightforward. But searching and sorting arrays of C-strings is more complicated because it involves pointers to pointers.

If you have an array of C-strings such as the following, each member of the array is an address of type **char***.

```
char *group[4] = {"John", "Paul", "George", "Ringo"};
```

Because each element has type **char***, a pointer to such an element has type **char****. Here is a comparison function for C-strings.

```
#include <cstdio>
#include <cstring>

int strcomp(const void* p1, const void* p2) {
        char *s1 = *(reinterpret_cast<const char**>(p1));
        char *s2 = *(reinterpret_cast<const char**>(p2));
        return strcmp(s1, s2);
}
```

The action of the first two lines of this function is to cast the **void*** pointer to type **char**** and then dereference it one time, producing **char***.

12.8 Other Standard C Library Functions

The remainder of the C library consists of functions requiring the <cstdlib> header. (<stdlib.h> is always supported, for backward compatibility.)

```
#include <cstdlib>
```

The functions in this section fall into two categories.

- Integer math functions: **abs**, **div**, **labs**, and **ldiv**. These supplement the floating-point math functions in <cmath>.
- System-oriented functions: **abort**, **atexit**, **exit**, **getenv**, and **system**. These all interact with the operating system.

Several of these functions take a function address as an argument. This is a callback function; see the example under **atexit**.

▸ **abort()**

Causes immediate termination of the program; the **atexit** function is not called and no object destructors are called. This function has no return value.

```
abort();
```

▸ **abs(*n*)**

Returns the absolute value of its integer argument. This is the same as *n* unless *n* is less than zero, in which case –*n* is returned.

```
int n = -5;
int m = abs(n);    // m = 5
```

▸ **atexit(*funct*)**

Registers an exit function to be called on termination. The argument *funct* contains the address of the function to register; this exit function has the following declaration:

void *funct***()**

If the function is successfully registered, **atexit** returns zero to indicate success; otherwise, it returns a nonzero value. You can register more than one such function; if you do, then upon program termination, these functions are called in the reverse order in which they were registered. C++ compilers are guaranteed to support at least 32 such functions.

```
#include <cstdlib>
#include <iostream>
using std::cout;
using std::endl;

void my_exit_function() {
    cout << "Program terminating! Bye!" << endl;
}

main() {
    atexit(my_exit_function);  // Register funct.
    exit(0);                   // Then terminate.
}
```

▸ **div(*n_numerator*, *n_denominator*)**

Divides the integer *n_numerator* by the integer *n_denominator* and returns a **div_t** structure consisting of two public **int** members: quot (quotient) and rem (remainder).

```
#include <cstdlib>
#include <iostream>
using std::cout;
using std::endl;

div_t divdata;
divdata = div(53, 10);
cout << divdata.quot << endl;    // Print 5.
cout << divdata.rem << endl;     // Print 3.
```

▸ **exit(*n_status*)**

Causes the program to end normally, returning the status code (*n_status*, an integer) to the system. Unlike the **abort** function, this function causes all exit functions, registered with **atexit**, to be executed.

A status code of EXIT_SUCCESS, or 0, indicates that the program was successful. A return code of EXIT_FAILURE, or any nonzero status, indicates an error of some kind. The exit function itself has no return value.

```
exit(0);
```

▸ **getenv(*env_var_str*)**

Returns the specified environment variable as a C-string (type **char***). The argument, *env_var_str*, is also a C-string. For example, the following prints the setting of the environment variable named PATH:

```
using std::cout;
using std::endl;
cout << "PATH = " << getenv("PATH") << endl;
```

▸ **labs(*n*)**

Performs the same action as **abs**—returns the absolute value of an integer—but takes and returns an argument of type **long** (long integer). But note that on a 32-bit system, **int** is usually equivalent to **long** anyway.

```
long n = -5;
long m = labs(n);    // m = 5
```

▸ **ldiv(*n_numerator*, *n_denominator*)**

Performs the same action as **div**, except that it takes arguments of long integer (**long**) type and returns results in an **ldiv_t** structure rather than a **div_t** structure. But note that on a 32-bit system, **int** is usually equivalent to **long** anyway.

```
using std::cout;
using std::endl;

ldiv_t divdata;
divdata = ldiv(53, 10);
cout << divdata.quot << endl;    // Print 5.
cout << divdata.rem << endl;     // Print 3.
```

- **system(***command_str***)**

  Sends the command string, a C-string, to the system to be executed. The meaning and interpretation of the command string is system-dependent. Console applications on DOS/Windows systems support the "pause" command, which is useful because it delays execution while waiting for the end user to press a key, thus keeping a DOS box from immediately disappearing at the end of the program.

```
system("PAUSE")';
```

12.9 Sample App: Idiot Savant

In the movie *Rain Man,* Dustin Hoffman's character is an *idiot savant,* one of those people who can recall astounding bits of information without the aid of a computer or other device. If you give them a date such as January 1, 3000, they can inform you that this date will fall on a Wednesday. (Good to know: Get ready for the next millennium now!) This is exactly the kind of mental feat we'd like to give to a computer.

The sample program in this section builds on the example in Section 12.3.2, "The TM ("Time") Data Structure." But this application prompts the user for the target date.

I have found that the **mktime** function doesn't seem to accept dates much earlier than 1970 or so, which seems to be a limitation of the system.

```
#include <iostream>
#include <string>
#include <ctime>
using std::cout;
using std::cin;
using std::endl;
using std::string;

string input_str;   // Use for "Y or N?" input.

int main() {
  int a_year = 0, a_month = 0, a_day = 1;
```

```
    do {
        cout << "Enter a year from 1900 onward: ";
        cin >> a_year;
        cout << "Enter a month from 1 to 12: ";
        cin >> a_month;
        cout << "Enter a day of the month, from 1 to 31: ";
        cin >> a_day;

        tm theday;                // Fill out tm structure.
        theday.tm_mday = a_day;
        theday.tm_mon = a_month - 1;
        theday.tm_year = a_year - 1900;
        theday.tm_hour = 12;      // Let's just go with noon.
        theday.tm_min = 0;
        theday.tm_sec = 0;

        time_t this_time = mktime(&theday);  // Get data.
        if (this_time != -1) {               // If date valid,
            char date_str[256];
            char format_str[] = "The day is %A, %d %B, %Y.";
            strftime(date_str, 256, format_str, &theday);
            cout << date_str << endl;
        }  else {
             cout << "Sorry. Invalid date." << endl;
        }
        cout << "I'm an excellent driver... ";
        cout << "Do again? (Enter Y or N.)";
        cin >> input_str;
        if (input_str[0] != 'Y' && input_str[0] != 'y') {
              break;
        }
    } while(true);
    return 0;
}
```

Exercises

1. Right now, the sample app accepts specification of the target month in the form of a number from 1 to 12. Revise the application so that it instead accepts input in the form of a string: "January", "February", and so on. You'll need to build an array of strings and test the string entered by the user, comparing the user input against elements of the array to find a matching string.

2. Expand on the preceding exercise by accepting input in either the full name of the month or a three-letter abbreviation such as "Jan" or "Feb". You should also accept the numbers 1 through 12 to represent months. If the input is not in the acceptable range, reprompt the user. You may find it convenient to hand off the inputting of the month to a separate function.

CHAPTER 13

C++ I/O Stream Classes

One of the first innovations introduced in C++ was the use of stream classes and objects to perform input and output. These classes replace the old C-language functions **printf**, **scanf**, and so on. The latter are still supported for backward compatibility, but the more objected-oriented approach—using **cin**, **cout**, and the stream classes—offers many advantages.

Not only are the stream classes easier to use than C I/O functions, but they are also more extensible. By overloading the stream I/O operators, for example, you can make stream objects work smoothly with any types.

Another advantage is that all the operations and functions used for console input/output work exactly the same way with file objects and strings: You just read (or write) to a file object rather than a console object. This means that console and file I/O techniques are more consistent with each other. In short, anytime you have a choice, you should use the I/O techniques in this chapter rather than the old C-language way of doing things.

13.1 The Basics of C++ I/O Streams

The classes and objects discussed in this chapter require the <iostream> header. (Depending on the situation, some other headers are required as well, as mentioned later in this chapter, including <fstream>, <iomanip>, and <sstream>.)

```
#include <iostream>
using namespace std;
```

All the standard-library class and object names in this chapter are part of the **std** namespace, so either include the **using** statement, or refer to these names with their **std::** prefix. You can choose to apply **using** more selectively.

```
using namespace std::cout;
using namespace std::cin;
using namespace std::endl;
```

In order to make all the examples fit without requiring extra space, the rest of the chapter assumes these statements are in place at the beginning of the program.

13.1.1 Writing Output with <<

When **cout** is the leftmost operand, you can use the left-shift operator (<<) to print any number of objects. This works because the operator returns a reference to the stream itself (**cout**). The statement:

```
cout << "The value of n is " << n << "." << endl;
```

is resolved as if it were written this way, due to left-to-right associativity:

```
((((cout << "The value of n is ") << n) << ".") << endl;
```

And this has the same effect as:

```
cout << "The value of n is ";
cout << n;
cout << " .";
cout << endl;    // Append a newline.
```

If n holds the value 25, this example prints out the following and appends a newline:

```
The value of n is 25.
```

If you want to print a series of numbers, **cout** does not add spaces or commas, so you must explicitly insert any that are needed. For example:

```
cout << i << ",  " << j << ",  " << k << endl;
```

If i, j, and k are equal to 1, 2, and 3, this example prints out the following text and appends a newline:

```
1, 2, 3
```

Some objects can be "sent" to the console not to print anything but to modify the way other things are printed. Consider this statement:

```
cout << hex << 255;
```

This prints the value 255 in its hexadecimal representation: "ff". **hex** is another predefined object—in this case, a stream manipulator. The effect of **hex** is to change the format.

13.1.2 Reading Input with >>

The following statement accepts two integers and a floating-point number from the console.

```
int i = 0; j = 0;
double x = 0;
cout << "Enter two ints and a floating pt: ";
cin >> i >> j >> x;
```

Because the overloaded >> operator returns a reference to the stream object itself (and because associativity is left to right), the preceding statement has the same effect as:

```
cin >> i;
cin >> j;
cin >> x;
```

Data is therefore read into the variables in this order: i, j, k. The objects receiving input from **cin** must be lvalues—except in the case of a C-string, in which case you pass an address: that is, the name of the string or a pointer to the first character.

```
char cstr[256];
cin >> cstr;
```

This statement reads text input, up to but not including the first whitespace, into str.

Despite the ease of use offered by the stream input operator (>>), it has some limitations. As a stream operator, >> behaves much like the **scanf** function.

- In the case of **cin** (console input), no input appears in the buffer until the end user presses ENTER. At that point, characters can be read. But if there is no readable data, the program pauses. If the user just keeps pressing ENTER, nothing happens.
- Leading whitespaces are ignored.
- When a nonwhitespace character is read, the program attempts to interpret the data. If the character is not part of a digit string, attempts to read data into a numeric variable fail. No further reads are possible until the error flags are cleared.
- If the character is accepted, additional characters are read as long as possible. Floating-point reads accept exponent expressions such as "3e22", but integer reads do not. In the case of reading an integer, "3" would be read successfully and "e" would be left in the input buffer as the next character to be read.

Consider an attempt to read two integers followed by a floating-point number.

```
cin >> i >> j >> x;
```

If the end user types the following text and then presses ENTER, everything is fine.

```
12     -3    1.345
```

But consider this input:

```
m2     -3     3.14159
```

The problem is that the first character read—an "m"—cannot be read successfully as numeric data. The read fails, and the input stream (**cin**) is in an error state until it is cleared.

```
cin.clear();
```

Even reading a string with >> can produce unsatisfactory results, because the process stops at the first whitespace. What if you try to read a name, and the user enters the following?

```
Elvis Aaron Presley
```

This input would have to be read as three separate strings.

Because of all these problems, I don't usually recommend using the overloaded right-shift operator (>>) except for the simplest cases. It's often better to read an entire line of input at once and then analyze it yourself, as described in the next section.

13.2 Reading a Line of Input with getline

C++ provides two major versions of the **getline** function for reading a line of input from the console (or, in the case of text files, reading character data until a newline is encountered).

As a member function, **getline** reads input into a C-string and requires specification of a maximum number of characters to write to the string. The use of this argument prevents the function from overwriting memory.

```
#define STR_SZ 256
char input_cstring[STR_SZ];
cin.getline(input_cstring, STR_SZ);
```

The **getline** function is also a global function: This version of **getline** reads data into a **string** object.

```
#include <string>
using std:string;
string my_str;
getline(cin, my_str);
```

Detailed descriptions follow. Both versions of this function return a reference to the input stream (*istream_obj*) so that the stream can be reused within a larger expression if you choose.

▸ *istream_obj*.**getline(***cstr*, *n* [, *delim_ch* = '\n'])

Reads a line of input into a C-string (*cstr*). The brackets indicate that the third argument is optional; if this is omitted, the delimiter character is a newline. The function reads input into the specified C-string up to but not including the delimiter or until an end of file is detected. The delimiter is not copied, but a terminating null is appended. *n* is the maximum number of characters to write, including the null.

```
char cstr[255];
cin.getline(cstr, 255);
```

If a delimiter character is specified (*delim_ch*), the function stops reading input when it encounters this character instead of a newline.

```
char cstr[255];
cin.getline(cstr, 255, '#');   // Use # delimiter.
```

▸ **getline(***istream_obj*, *str_obj* [, *delim_ch* = '\n'])

Reads a line of input into a **string** object. The brackets indicate that the third argument is optional; if omitted, the delimiter character is a newline. The action is to read input into the specified **string** object (*str_obj*) up to but not including the first newline, or until an end of file is detected. The delimiter itself is not copied.

```
#include <string>
string aString;
getline(cin, aString);
```

If a delimiter character is specified (*delim_ch*) the function stops reading input when it encounters this character instead of a newline.

```
#include <string>
string aString;
getline(cin, aString, '#');   // Use # delimiter.
```

In summary: Use the **getline** member function to read a line of input into a C-string; use the **getline** global function to read a line of input into a **string** object. After you read a line of input, you can process that line in any of several ways. For example, when reading a number, you can convert the text by calling **atof** or **atoi** to convert the line of input to a single numeric value. (See Chapter 12, "Math, Time, and Other Library Functions," for more information.)

```
#include <iostream>
#include <cstdlib>   // Supports atoi & atof.
#include <string>
using namespace std;
```

```
double get_floating_pt() {
     string s_input;
     cout << "Enter a number and press ENTER: ";
     getline(cin, s_input);
     return atof(s_input.c_str());
}
```

After prompting the user, the function waits for text input. If the user presses ENTER, the **getline** returns an empty string. The **atof** function then returns 0.0. A virtue of this example is that it returns 0.0 as a default value instead of waiting for the user to enter some digits.

To interpret complex lines of input, you can tokenize it by converting it to C-string form and then call **strtok** (string tokenize) as explained in Chapter 10, “C-String Library Functions.” Or you can tokenize it yourself, using functions described in Chapter 14, “The C++ STL String Class.”

13.3 The C++ Stream-Class Hierarchy

The stream-class hierarchy involves a number of important relationships. The **cout** object is an instance of the **ostream** class, which is derived from its base class, **ios** (see Figure 13.1).

Stream output objects are instances of **ostream** or, in the case of file output objects, a class derived from it. The **ofstream** class supports all the **ostream** member functions but also adds other functions more specific to file operations.

There is a similar hierarchy for input classes (see Figure 13.2).

The predefined object **cin** is an instance of **istream**. The **ifstream** class supports all the **istream** member functions but also adds other functions more specific to file operations.

Descriptions of the predefined stream objects follow.

- **cout**

  Console output. Instance of **ostream**. Programs can write to the console by using the stream output operator (<<).

  As with all output streams, the type of an object—the right operand—determines how it is written. For example, integers are written as digit strings, and **char** arrays are written as a series of characters until a null is encountered.

  ```
  cout << a_message;
  ```

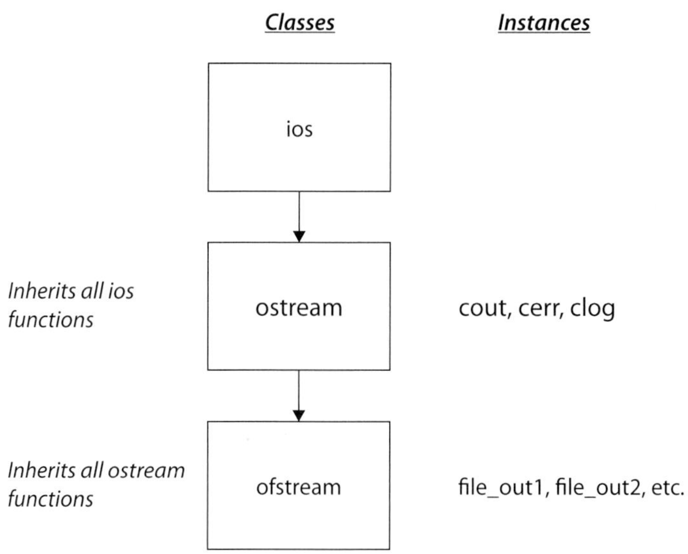

FIGURE 13.1 Simplified hierarchy of stream output classes

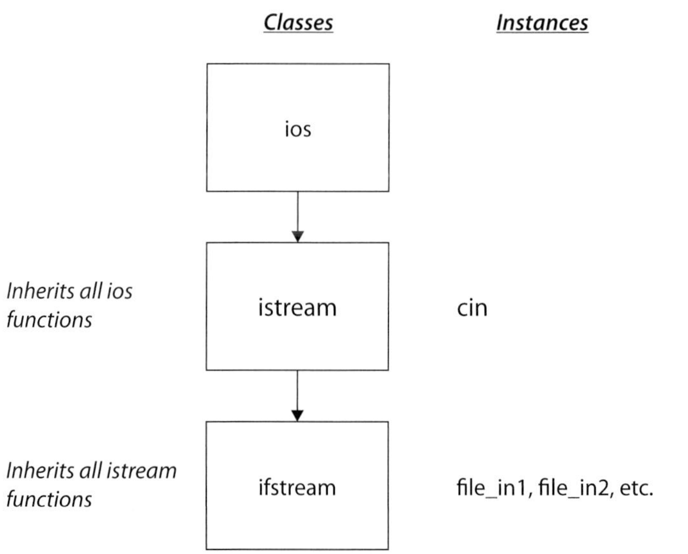

FIGURE 13.2 Simplified hierarchy of stream input classes

▸ `cin`

Console input. Instance of **istream**. With console input, no data is available in the input buffer until the user presses ENTER. Characters are then read in the proper format for the receiving field, which is an lvalue or the address of a **char** array.

```
int n = 0;
cin >> n;
```

The stream input operator (>>) first skips over leading spaces in the input buffer. Then it attempts to read and interpret the characters. If the text does not express a value that can be read into the right operand, the read fails and an error flag is thrown for the stream.

Note that you can test a stream for error conditions by testing the stream itself, within an **if** or **while** condition.

▸ `cerr`

Console error output. Instance of **ostream**. By default, writing to **cerr** sends output to the console just as writing to **cout** does. However, **cerr** is a separate stream that can be redirected to a file without redirecting **cout**.

```
cerr << "Run time error detected.";
```

▸ `clog`

Console log output. Instance of **ofstream**. Like **cerr**, **clog** is a separate stream that (by default) writes to the console but can be redirected without affecting **cout** or **cerr**.

13.4 Stream Objects: Manipulators and Flags

The C++ stream classes and predefined objects provide many ways to control the format of input and output.

Including the <iostream> header gives you access to most of the predefined objects and flags in this chapter, because this header contains declarations from <ios> and <iosbase>. However, some of the stream manipulators—those with a "set" or "reset" name—require <iomanip>.

Therefore, if you're going to work with I/O flags and manipulators, I recommend including both <iostream> and <iomanip>:

```
#include <iostream>
#include <iomanip>
```

All the manipulators and I/O flags are part of the **std** namespace; therefore, for expediency, I assume the following:

```
using namespace::std;
```

As mentioned before, there are good reasons to avoid **using namespace** generally—when you have more room than I do in this book. I use it in this chapter only to conserve space. Alternatively, you can include a **using** statement for each and every individual symbol that you use—or adopt the practice of referring to each symbol with its **std::** prefix. For example:

```
using std::cout;
using std::cin;
using std::endl;
using std::hex;
using std::dec;
```

And so on.

13.4.1 Stream Manipulators

The **istream** and **ostream** classes support a series of predefined objects called *manipulators*. "Sending" such a manipulator to **cout** or "reading" it from **cin** modifies the stream's format in some way. All input and output streams—including file streams—work with these same objects.

Manipulators change the format of subsequent operations on the stream until the format is reset. For example, the following code prints i and j in decimal format and prints h in hexadecimal:

```
int i = 100, j = 200;
int h = 0x1fff;
// Next statement uses dec. format by default.
cout << "i is: " << i << endl;
// Change to hex format.
cout << "h is: " << hex << h << endl;
// Finally, change back to decimal.
cout << "j is: " << dec << j << endl;
```

Let's deconstruct the sixth line in this example. Because of left-to-right associativity, and because the stream output operator (<<) returns a reference to the stream itself, the sixth line in the example just shown has the same effect as the following:

```
cout << "h is: ";
cout << hex;
cout << h;
cout << endl;
```

First, the string "h is:" is printed to the console. Then **cout** "prints" the predefined object **hex**. The effect of this operation is not to print anything but to change the output format of **cout** to hexadecimal. The variable h is therefore printed in its hex form (1fff) rather than in decimal form (8191). The next statement changes the format back to decimal before printing j:

```
cout << "j is: " << dec << j << endl;
```

Although **hex** and **dec** change output format for integers, the **hex** manipulator does not cause the "0x" prefix to be displayed for hexadecimal numbers unless **showbase**, another manipulator, is "sent" to **cout**.

```
int h = 0x1fff;
cout << h << endl;                    // Print 8191.
cout << hex << h << endl;             // Print 1fff.
cout << showbase << h << endl;        // Print 0x1fff.
cout << h << endl;                    // Print 0x1fff.
```

The last statement in this example prints output in the same format as the one before it; that's because the format of a stream is maintained until the format is reset or changed again.

Some of the manipulators affect input format as well as output. For example, **hex** causes the input stream to read "0xff" or "ff" as a hexadecimal integer.

```
int n = 0;
cin >> hex;
cin >> n;    // Accepts "0xff" or "ff" as the value 255.
```

The stream manipulators fall into a number of categories. Except where otherwise stated, these affect output streams but have no effect on input. The manipulators consist of the following.

- Manipulators that set the base in which to display integers: **dec**, **hex**, and **oct**. These affect both input and output streams.
- Manipulators that affect how floating-point numbers are displayed: **fixed** and **scientific**.
- Manipulators that control how print fields are justified when the print field is larger than the number of characters to print: **left**, **right**, and **internal**.
- The **endl** and **ends** manipulators, which print a newline and null terminator, respectively.
- The **ws** manipulator, which skips over leading spaces. This affects input streams only.
- Manipulators that set a specific flag: **boolalpha**, **showbase**, **showpoint**, **showpos**, **skipws**, **unitbuf**, and **uppercase**. Along with these are a matching set of manipulators that turn off those same flags: **noboolalpha**, **noshowbase**, **noshowpoint**, **noshowpos**, **noskipws**, **nounitbuf**, and **nouppercase**.

- Manipulators that set width, fill character, precision, and other flags: **setfill**, **setprecision**, **setw**, **setiosflags**, and **resetiosflags**. These are parameterized manipulators, meaning they each take an argument. All of these require <iomanip> to be included in addition to <iostream>.

Detailed descriptions of the stream manipulators follow, in alphabetical order.

▸ boolalpha

Causes **true** and **false** to be printed as "true" and "false" rather than as 1 and 0 (the default behavior).

```
bool is_less_than = (10 < 20);
cout << is_less_than << endl;     // Print "1".
cout << boolalpha;
cout << is_less_than << endl;     // Print "true".
```

▸ dec

Specifies decimal format for integers (the default). Affects both **ostream** and **istream**.

```
cout << dec << i;    // Reset to decimal, print i.
```

▸ endl

Prints a newline character when sent to an output stream.

```
cout << endl;
```

▸ ends

Prints a null character (ASCII value 0.)

▸ fixed

Specifies fixed-point format for floating-point numbers: No exponent is displayed. The number of digits to the right of the decimal point is determined by the precision (set by the **setprecision** manipulator). In some cases, this may cause a tiny value to be rounded to 0.

```
double x = 1e-10;
cout << "x is " << x << endl;
cout << fixed;
cout << "x is " << x << endl;  // Rounded to 0.
cout << 3.0 << endl;
```

This code outputs:

```
x is 1e-010
x is 0.000000
3.000000
```

The default behavior (with neither fixed nor scientific format in force) is to print a floating-point number in as few characters needed to display it as accurately as possible. The default behavior can be restored by using the **resetiosflags** manipulator.

- `flush`

  Flushes the buffer associated with the stream so that all input or output in the buffer is immediately written to its destination.

```
file_out << flush;    // Flush the stream! Whoosh!
```

- `hex`

  Specifies hexadecimal format for integers. This affects input streams as well as output. Note that for output streams, **uppercase** and **nouppercase** determine whether hex digits are displayed as uppercase or lowercase letters.

```
cout << hex << 255;    // Print "ff".
int n = 0;
cin >> hex >> n;     // Read n as hex; For example,
                     //  "10" read as 16 decimal.
```

- `internal`

  Sets print-field justification to internal, rather than left or right: If the number of characters to print is less than the print-field width (set with **setw**), then the extra space is filled by padding fill characters in between the plus or negative sign or the base prefix (such as 0x) on the left, and the rest of the number on the right. The fill character is a space by default. If there is no sign or base prefix, or if the value to be printed is not numeric, the **internal** setting has the same effect as **right**. For example:

```
#include <iostream>
#include <iomanip>
. . .
cout << setw(6) << internal;
cout << -2;
```

  This code displays a number by padding four spaces between the negative sign (-) and 2:

```
-    2
```

- `left`

  Causes print fields to be left-justified; this only affects output streams and only when the number of characters to be printed is smaller than the print-field width.

- `noboolalpha`

  Turns off the **boolalpha** setting so that **bool** values are not printed as "true" and "false" but by their numeric value (1 or 0). This is the default behavior.

- **noshowbase**

Turns off the **showbase** setting so that octal and hexadecimal prefixes are not automatically printed for those bases. This is the default behavior.

```
// Print ff, not 0xff.
cout << noshowbase << hex << 255;
```

- **noshowpoint**

Turns off the **showpoint** flag so that floating-point numbers are not forced to be printed with a decimal point. This is the default behavior.

```
double x = 3.0;
cout << noshowpoint;   // Turns off showpoint.
cout << x;             // Prints "3"
```

- **noshowpos**

Turns off the **showpos** flag so that positive signed numbers are not displayed with a leading plus sign (+). This is the default behavior.

- **noskipws**

Turns off the **skipws** flag so that leading spaces are not skipped in the reading of individual **char** values. This affects input streams only. When individual **char** data is read, this setting causes the next character to be read even if it is a space. When strings are read, this setting causes a strange result: An empty string is read, because a leading space both begins and terminates the string! Therefore, I don't recommend using **noskipws** except when you are reading characters from the input stream one at a time.

```
char a1, a2, a3;
cin >> noskipws;
cin >> a1 >> a2 >> a3; // Read three chars as is.
cin >> skipws;         // Turn skipws back on.
```

- **nounitbuf**

Turns off the **unitbuf** flag, which causes the stream's buffer to be flushed after every read or write operation. **nounitbuf** restores the default behavior, which, for files, is to flush the buffer only when full. (Console output usually flushes the buffer anyway.)

```
file_out << nounitbuf;  // Turn off unitbuf flag.
```

- **nouppercase**

Turns off the **uppercase** flag, which causes hexadecimal digits, hexadecimal prefixes (0x), and exponent expressions to be printed in uppercase letters. Use of lowercase letters is restored. This is the default setting; the **uppercase** manipulator (see the listing later in this section) can be used to specify uppercase letters for these situations rather than lowercase.

```
cout << showbase << hex;
cout << nouppercase;    // Use lowercase letters.
cout << 255 << endl;    // Print "0xff".
```

- **`oct`**

  Specifies octal as the integer format. This affects both input and output streams. If **showbase** is on, a leading zero is printed to indicate the number is octal.

```
cout << oct << 16 << endl;    // Print "20".
cout << showbase;
cout << 16 << endl;           // Print "020".
```

- **`resetiosflags(`*`bitmask`*`)`**

  Clears the format flags indicated by the *bitmask* argument. For each bit set to 1 in *bitmask*, this manipulator turns off the corresponding flag. The next section lists these flags. You can use bitwise OR (|) to combine multiple flags.

  This manipulator requires <iomanip> to be included. For example, the following code restores default handling of floating-point numbers for the **cout** stream by turning off the **scientific**, **fixed**, and **showpoint** flags.

```
#include <iostream>
#include <iomanip>
. . .
cout << resetiosflags(ios_base::scientific |
                      ios_base::fixed |
                      ios_base:showpoint);
```

- **`right`**

  Causes print fields to be right-justified; this only affects output streams and only when the number of characters to be printed is smaller than the print-field width. This is the default behavior.

- **`scientific`**

  Specifies scientific format for floating-point numbers so that an exponent portion is always displayed separately from the rest of the number. For example:

```
double x = 3.0;
cout << "x is " << x << endl;
cout << scientific;
cout << "x is " << x << endl;
```

  This code outputs:

```
x is 3
x is 3.000000e+000
```

  The default behavior (with neither fixed nor scientific format in force) is to print a floating-point number in as few characters needed to display it accurately as possible. That behavior can be restored by using the **resetiosflags** manipulator.

- **`setfill(`*`ch`*`)`**

  Sets the fill character to *ch*; this character is used when the number of characters to be printed is smaller than the print-field width. For example:

```
#include <iostream>
#include <iomanip>
. . .
cout << setw(6) << setfill('0');
cout << -2 << endl;
```

  This code prints:

```
0000-2
```

- **`setiosflags(`*`bitmask`*`)`**

  Sets the format flags indicated by the *bitmask* argument. (The next section lists these flags.) For each bit set to 1 in *bitmask*, this manipulator turns on the corresponding flag for the stream. You can use bitwise OR (|) to combine multiple flags.

  This manipulator requires <iomanip> to be included. For example, the following code switches on the **fixed** and **showpoint** flags:

```
#include <iostream>
#include <iomanip>
. . .
cout << setiosflags(
     ios_base::fixed | ios_base:showpoint
);
```

- **`setprecision(`*`n`*`)`**

  Sets precision for printing floating-point numbers to *n*: If **showpoint** is in effect, precision is the total number of digits to be printed (to the left and right of the decimal point); if **fixed** or **scientific** is in effect, precision is the number of digits to be printed to the right of the decimal point. This manipulator requires the <iomanip> header.

```
#include <iostream>
#include <iomanip>
. . .
double x = 33.0;
cout << showpoint << setprecision(5);
cout << x << endl;     // Print "33.000"
cout << fixed;
cout << x << endl;     // Print "33.00000"
cout << scientific;
cout << x << endl;     // Print "3.30000e+001"
```

- **setw(*n*)**

  Sets minimum print-field width to *n*. If the number of characters to be printed is less than this number, the text is left-, right-, or internal-justified (it is right-justified by default) by being padded with the fill character. This character is a space unless set to a different character with **setfill**. Both **setw** and **setfill** require <iomanip> to be included.

  ```
  #include <iostream>
  #include <iomanip>
  . . .
  cout << "Number:";
  cout << setw(6);
  cout << -2 << endl;
  ```

  This code prints:

  ```
  Number:    -2
  ```

- **showbase**

  Turns on the **showbase** flag so that hexadecimal and octal numbers are printed with a "0x" (hex) or leading zero (octal) prefix.

  ```
  cout << showbase << hex << 255; // Print "0xff".
  ```

- **showpoint**

  Turns on the **showpoint** flag so that floating-point numbers are printed with a decimal point even when they are whole numbers. Note: When this setting is on but neither **fixed** nor **scientific** is on, precision determines the total number of digits to be printed.

  ```
  double x = 333.0;
  cout << showpoint;
  cout << setprecision(5);
  cout << x;              // Prints "333.00"
  ```

- **showpos**

  Turns on the **showpos** flag so that positive numbers are printed with a leading plus sign (+).

- **skipws**

  Turns on the **skipws** flag, causing leading whitespaces to be skipped during stream input operations (affects stream input only). This is the default behavior. Turning this flag off (with **noskipws**) may be useful when reading individual characters as **char** values, but otherwise leads to strange results. Usually, this flag should be left on.

- **unitbuf**

  Causes the output buffer to be flushed after each write operation.

▸ **uppercase**

Turns on the **uppercase** flag, which causes hexadecimal digits, hexadecimal prefixes (0x), and exponent expressions to be printed in uppercase letters. **noupper-case**, the default setting, causes these items to be printed in lowercase letters.

```
cout << showbase << hex;
cout << uppercase;     // Use uppercase letters.
cout << 255 << endl;   // Print "0XFF".
```

▸ **ws**

Reads and ignores as many whitespaces as it finds until a nonwhitespace character is found; that character is then left in the buffer as the next character to be read. This affects input streams only. Note that the **skipws** flag, which is on by default, causes leading whitespaces to be skipped anyway, so the **ws** manipulator is only rarely useful.

13.4.2 Stream Format Flags

This section summarizes the flags that can be used with the **setiosflags** and **resetios-flags** manipulators described in the previous section. The bitwise OR operator (|) can be used to combine flags. For example:

```
cout << setiosflags(ios_base::fixed | ios_base:showpoint);
```

This has the same effect as:

```
cout << setiosflags(ios_base::fixed);
cout << setiosflags(ios_base:showpoint);
```

The formatting flags can be grouped into several categories:

- Flags that determine number base: **dec**, **hex**, **oct**
- Flags that determine how a field is justified: **left**, **right**, **internal**
- Flags that determine floating-point display: **fixed**, **scientific**, **showpoint**
- Other flags: boolalpha, showbase, showpos, skipws, unitbuf, uppercase

The following descriptions state how behavior is affected when the corresponding flag is on.

▸ **ios_base::boolalpha**

Displays **true** and **false** Boolean values as "true" and "false" rather than 1 and 0.

▸ **ios_base::dec**

Displays and reads integers in decimal format (the default).

- **`ios_base::fixed`**

  Displays floating-point numbers in fixed-point format.

- **`ios_base::hex`**

  Displays and reads integers in hexadecimal format.

- **`ios_base::internal`**

  Uses internal-justifying in print fields so that padding occurs between the plus/minus sign or base prefix on the left, and the rest of the number on the right. For non-numeric fields, this is the same as right-justifying.

- **`ios_base::left`**

  Uses left-justifying in print fields.

- **`ios_base::oct`**

  Displays and reads integers in octal format.

- **`ios_base::right`**

  Uses right-justifying in print fields.

- **`ios_base::scientific`**

  Displays floating-point numbers in scientific format.

- **`ios_base::showbase`**

  Displays a base prefix for hexadecimal and octal numbers.

- **`ios_base::showpoint`**

  Specifies that a floating-point number is always to be printed with a decimal point. How many digits are printed to the right of the decimal point depends on the precision setting.

- **`ios_base::showpos`**

  Displays a positive-number sign (+) for positive numbers.

- **`ios_base::skipws`**

  Prevents an input stream from skipping leading whitespaces. (Note: Except in the case of individual character reads, this can lead to unexpected behavior.)

- **`ios_base::unitbuf`**

  Causes the input buffer is to be flushed after each read and write operation.

- **`ios_base::uppercase`**

  Displays hexadecimal prefix, hexadecimal digits (A through F), and floating-point exponent indicator (E) as uppercase letters. The default is to use lowercase letters.

13.5 Stream Member Functions (General Purpose)

Because of the class hierarchy, the task of documenting the member functions for streams poses a challenge. The next three sections list the functions useful for I/O streams regardless of the class in which they are defined. In Section 13.6, "File Stream Operations," I describe functions useful for file stream operations.

Here, and throughout this chapter, I assume that the following **using** statement has been included near the beginning of the source file (even though it's advisable to make more selective use of **using** when you have the space to support longer examples than I can in this book).

```
using namespace std:
```

The next three sections cover, in this order:

- Input stream functions (**cin** and other input streams)
- Output stream functions (**cout** and other output streams)
- Flag-setting functions, which are supported by both kinds of streams

13.5.1 Input Stream Functions

Except where otherwise stated, each of these functions returns a reference to the input stream itself. *ch* is a single character, and *n* is an integer.

▸ *istream_obj*.**gcount()**

Returns the number of characters read by the last call to the **getline** or **get** function.

```
int n = gcount();    // n = number of chars read by
                     //  last get or getline.
```

▸ *istream_obj*.**get()**

Gets the next character from the input buffer and returns it as an integer (type *int*). The value returned can be compared to EOF, which indicates an end-of-file condition.

```
int c;
c = cin.get();
if (c == EOF) {
    cout << "End of file encountered.";
}
```

- *istream_obj*.**get(*ch*)**

Gets the next character from the input buffer and places it in *ch*, a reference to a **char** lvalue. The end-of-file condition has to be tested separately (with the **eof** function).

```
char c;
cin.get(c);
```

- *istream_obj*.**get(*cstr*,*n* [, *delim_ch* = '\n'])**

Gets up to *n* characters, stopping at the delimiter character, which by default is the newline ('\n'). The brackets indicate that specifying this argument is optional.

This function performs the same action as **getline**, except that the delimiter character is not removed from the input buffer: It remains there for the next read operation. As with **getline**, up to n-1 characters are copied to the address *cstr* and then appended with a null.

The delimiter character can be read separately or skipped with the **ignore** function.

```
#define SCRN_WIDTH 81;
char input_str[SCRN_WIDTH];

// Read up to next newline
cin.get(input_str, SCRN_WIDTH);
cin.ignore();           // Skip newline char before
                        //   next read.
```

- *istream_obj*.**getline(*cstr*, *n* [, *delim_ch* = '\n'])**

Reads a line of input as described in Section 13.2, "Reading a Line of Input with getline." In this syntax, brackets indicate that the third argument is optional; if it's omitted, the delimiter character is the newline ('\n').

This version of the **getline** function retrieves text from an input stream and places it in a null-terminated C-string. (To instead read text into a **string** object, use the global **getline** function as explained in Section 13.2.)

```
#define SCRN_WIDTH 81;
char input_str[SCRN_WIDTH];
cin.getline(input_str, SCRN_WIDTH);
```

- *istream_obj*.**ignore([*n* = 1] [, *delim_ch* = EOF])**

Reads up to *n* characters or until the delimiter character is read, whichever comes first, and ignores them. The current-position indicator for the stream, however, is advanced.

The brackets indicate that both arguments are optional. If only one argument is given during a call, it is interpreted as *n*, the number of characters to read and ignore. If no arguments are given, then *n* takes the default value of 1, and the delimiter character is EOF (end of file).

```
cin.ignore(2);    // Read and ignore next 2 chars.
```

- *istream_obj*.**peek()**

  Returns the next character in the input buffer without removing it from the buffer. This enables "look ahead" functionality. Although most of the time this function returns a character that can be held in a **char** variable, the return type is **int**, enabling the function to return the special value EOF.

```
int c;
c = cin.peek();
```

- *istream_obj*.**putback(*ch*)**

  Puts a character (a variable of type **char**) back into the input buffer so that the position indicator is decremented by 1 and the character *ch* is the next to be read.

```
putback(c);    // Push c back onto input stream.
```

13.5.2 Output Stream Functions

The following functions all return a reference to the output stream itself, so the output stream may be reused as part of a larger expression. In these descriptions, *ch* is a single character and *n* is an integer.

- *ostream_obj*.**put(*ch*)**

  Puts a character *ch* into the output stream. For example, the following statement outputs a newline.

```
cout.put('\n');
```

- *ostream_obj*.**fill(*ch*)**

  Changes the fill character to the specified character, *ch*. This character is used for padding when the number of characters to print is less than the print-field width.

```
cout.fill('0');       // Set '0' as fill character.
```

- *ostream_obj*.**flush()**

  Flushes the output buffer for the stream so that data in the buffer is immediately written to the file. Normally, with file operations, data remains in the buffer until the buffer is filled, reducing the number of write-to-disk operations.

```
file_out.flush();     // Flush the buffer! Whoosh!
```

- *ostream_obj*.**precision(*n*)**

  Sets the precision for outputting floating-point numbers. If the **fixed** or **scientific** flag is set for the specified stream, precision determines how many digits are printed to the right of the decimal point; otherwise, precision determines the total number of digits to print.

```
cout.precision(5);  // Set precision to 5 digits.
```

▸ *ostream_obj*.**width(*n*)**

Specifies the minimum print-field width for the next output operation. If the number of characters to print is smaller than this width, the field is padded with the fill character.

```
cout.width(10);    // Set print-field width to 10.
```

13.5.3 Flag-Setting Stream Functions

The functions in this section provide yet another way to set format flags. They are somewhat redundant with the **setiosflags** and **resetiosflags** manipulators, but they provide a way to save the previous format-flag settings.

In the descriptions that follow, the *bitmask* argument is an integer value (of type **ios_base::fmtflag**) formed from flag values presented in Section 13.4.2, "Stream Format Flags."

This section also includes the **sync_with_stdio** function, which is useful if you want to support both C++ I/O stream classes and C-library I/O in the same program.

▸ *stream_obj*.**bad()**

Returns **true** if the "bad" bit is set for the stream, indicating an error condition; returns **false** otherwise. The "bad" bit indicates there is a problem with the stream itself, whereas "fail" indicates a problem with the last I/O operation. If the "bad" bit is set, the stream object may not have a valid stream associated with it.

```
bool is_bad_set = file_in.bad();
```

▸ *stream_obj*.**clear()**

Clears the error flags for the stream. This function has no return value.

```
cin.clear();
```

▸ *stream_obj*.**copyfmt(*stream*)**

Copies the format-flag settings from another stream. For example, the following statement causes the stream output object file_out to use the settings for **cout**.

```
file_out.copyfmt(cout);
```

▸ *stream_obj*.**fail()**

Returns **true** if the "fail" bit or "bad" bit is set for the file stream, indicating an error condition; returns **false** otherwise.

```
int n;
cin >> n;           // Attempt to read an integer.
if (cin.fail()) {   // If it fails,
```

```
    n = 0;            // Assume a value of 0.
    cin.clear();      // Start over w/ next read.
}
```

- *stream_obj*.**flags()**

  Returns the current state of format flags as an integer of type **ios_base::fmtflags**. You can test this value by applying the bitwise "and" operator (&) to see if a specific value was set. For example:

```
ios_base::fmtflag fmt = cout.flags();
bool is_boolaplha =
     ((fmt & ios_base::boolalpha) != 0);
```

  Another way to use this function is to save the format flags so that they can be restored later by using the other, overloaded version of **flags**. That version is described next.

- *stream_obj*.**flags(***bitmask***)**

  Sets the flag values according to the values in *bitmask*, an integer of type **ios_base::fmtflags**. All those flags whose corresponding bit is set to 1 in *bitmask* are turned on; all those flags whose corresponding bit is set to 0 are turned off. The function returns the previous flag settings, which can be restored by calling the function again.

  For example, the following statements switch on **hex** and **showbase** flags and turn all others off. After printing a value, it restores the previous flag values.

```
ios_base::fmtflag fmt;
fmt =
  cout.flags(ios_base::hex | ios_base::showbase);
cout << 255 << endl;    // Print 0xff.
cout.flags(fmt);
```

- *stream_obj*.**good()**

  Returns **true** if the "good" bit is set for the file stream, indicating a lack of error conditions; returns **false** otherwise. When this bit is set, the file stream is valid, and there was no error in the last I/O operation.

```
if (cin.good()) {
     cout << "No read errors. Proceed." << endl;
}
```

- *stream_obj*.**setf(***bitmask***)**

  This version of **setf**—note that there are two overloaded versions—turns on the flags indicated by *bitmask*; other flags are unchanged. A flag is switched on if the corresponding bit in *bitmask* is 1. No flags are switched off.

  This function returns an integer of type **ios_base::fmtflag** containing the previous flag settings; these can be restored later by a call to the **flags** function.

For example, the following statements use the **setf** function to switch on the **hex** flag for **cin** and the **hex** and **showbase** flags for **cout**. Later, the previous flag settings are restored.

```
ios_base::fmtflag cin_prev, cout_prev;
cin_prev = cin.setf(ios_base::hex);
cout_prev =
   cout.setf(ios_base::hex | ios_base::showbase);
. . .
cin.flags(cin_prev);    // Restore previous flags.
cout.flags(cout_prev);
```

- *stream_obj*.**setf(***bitmask1*, *bitmask2***)**

  This is the second overloaded version of **setf**. Only the flags specified by *bitmask2* are changed. (The bit masks are both integers of type **ios_base::fmtflag**.) Here are the specifics.

  - If a bit is 1 in *bitmask2* and 1 in *bitmask1*, the corresponding flag is switched on.
  - If a bit is 1 in *bitmask2* and 0 in *bitmask1*, the corresponding flag is switched off.
  - If a bit is 0 in *bitmask2*, the corresponding flag is not changed.

  The *bitmask2* argument can be a setting made up of several bits.

  ios_base::floatfield combines **ios_base::scientific** and **ios_base::fixed**.

  ios_base::basefield combines **ios_base::hex**, **ios_base::dec**, and **ios_base::oct**.

  ios_base::adjustfield combines **ios_base::left**, **ios_base::right**, and **ios_base::internal**.

  So, for example, the following statement turns off both ios_base::scientific and ios_base::fixed in cout, restoring the default behavior for displaying floating-point numbers in that output stream. Other flags are unaffected.

  ```
  cout.setf(0, ios_base::floatfield);
  ```

  This function returns the previous format flag settings for the stream, which can be restored by calling the **flags** function.

- *stream_obj*.**unsetf(***bitmask***)**

  Switches off the flags indicated by *bitmask*; other flags are unchanged. That is, a flag is switched off if its corresponding bit in *bitmask* is 1. No flags are switched on by this version of the function.

  This function returns an integer of type **ios_base::fmtflag** containing the previous flag settings. These can be restored by calling the **flags** function.

For example, the following statement turns off both **ios_base::scientific** and **ios_base::fixed** in **cout**, restoring the default behavior for displaying floating-point numbers in that output stream.

```
cout.setf(ios_base::scientific|ios_base::fixed);
```

- *stream_obj*.**sync_with_stdio([***on/off* = **true)**

  Turns on synchronization between stream classes and the C standard I/O functions presented in Chapter 11, "C I/O Library Functions." The *on/off* argument, if given, turns synchronization on or off, depending on whether the value of the argument is **true** or **false**; but by default, this value is **true**.

  This function is a static function, so it can be called through any object of class **ios_base** or a class derived from **ios_base**. For example:

  ```
  cout.sync_with_stdio();
  ```

  The function returns a **bool** value; if **true**, this indicates that synchronization is to be turned on.

13.6 File Stream Operations

The C++ stream classes support both text-file and binary-file input and output. With text files, you read or write to a file object using exactly the same operations and functions you would use with **cin** or **cout**. Here's a typical statement used to print output:

```
cout << "The value of n is: " << n << endl;
```

You can use a similar statement to write to a text-file object (file_out in this case). The operations and functions supported for file objects are identical to those for **cin** and **cout**.

```
file_out << "The value of n is: " << n << endl;
```

13.6.1 Overview: Text versus Binary File I/O

Although all data in a computer is ultimately numeric, a text file can be thought of as a series of characters. Each character is actually an ASCII code number.

When numeric values are written to a text file, each such value is formatted into a series of text characters. For example, consider this output statement:

```
int a = 5, b = -1, c = 100;
text_file_out << a << ", " << b << ", " << c;
```

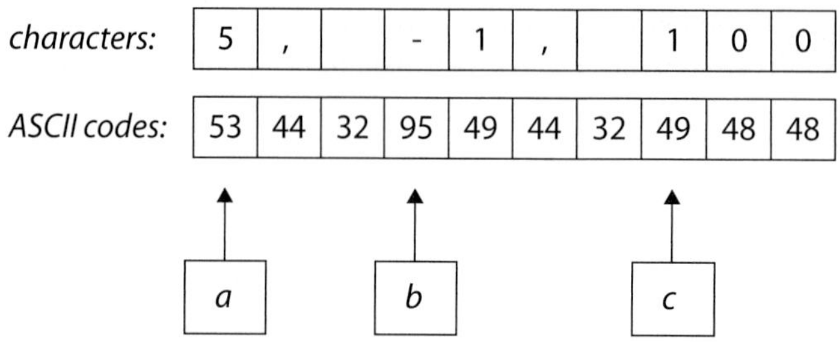

FIGURE 13.3 Writing to a text file

Figure 13.3 shows how a, b, and c are formatted as digit strings "5", "-1", and "100".

Binary file I/O, in contrast, reads and writes numeric values directly (see Figure 13.4). For example:

```
short a = 5, b = -1, c = 100;
bin_file.write(reinterpret_cast<char*>(&a), sizeof(short));
bin_file.write(reinterpret_cast<char*>(&b), sizeof(short));
bin_file.write(reinterpret_cast<char*>(&c), sizeof(short));
```

Each write operation outputs exactly two bytes to the file—no more, no less—regardless of the value, because the size of **short** is two bytes on virtually all C++ platforms.

Binary input/output uses space more efficiently. It has a limitation, however: Because binary I/O does no formatting of any kind, a program cannot successfully read a binary file unless it knows in advance exactly how to interpret the data.

But binary files also have a couple of advantages over text files. Because no formatting is performed, reading and writing numeric values is potentially much faster. For example, instead of reading and translating a digit string such as "1.005e+001"—which is a complex operation—a floating-point value is simply copied directly into a variable, which is very fast.

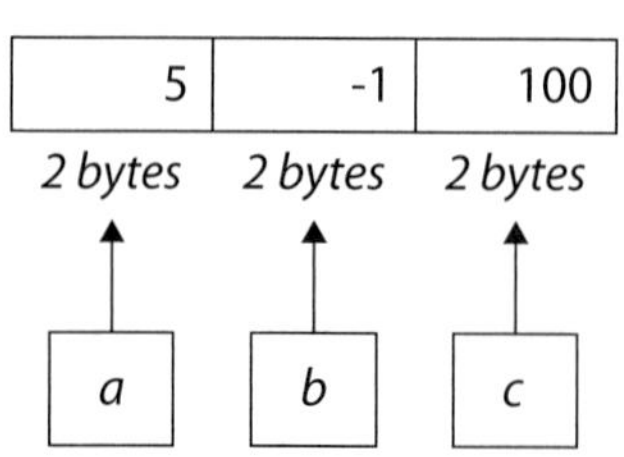

FIGURE 13.4 Writing to a binary file

13.6.2 Creating a File Object

Before you can read or write a file, you must create a file-stream object and associate it with a file. First, however, include the <fstream> header, required by the file operations in this chapter.

```
#include <fstream>
#include <iostream>
using namespace std;
```

If you want to be able to read and write to the console (**cin**, **cout**) in addition to reading and writing to files, you need to include both <fstream> and <iostream>.

To open a text file for reading or writing, you can create an **ifstream** or **ofstream** object and give the name of the file to be opened. For example:

```
ifstream file_in("text1.txt");
ofstream file_out("readme.txt");
```

These statements open the files text1.txt and readme.txt for text input and text output, respectively. In this case, the files are in the current directory; however, as with the C I/O functions, you can give a complete file specification including path name.

The file-name argument is a C-string; it does not need to be a string literal but can be a string supplied by another source such as the end user. Most newer compilers overload the file-stream constructors to support **string** objects, but some older compilers insist on C-strings. If necessary, convert a string object to a C-string by calling the **c_str** function:

```
string filename;
// Initialize filename somehow. . .
ifstream file_in(filename.c_str());    // Necessary with
                                       //   older compilers.
```

The file-stream constructors take an optional second argument specifying file mode; if omitted, default settings are used. Text-file mode is always the default setting. Input mode is the default for the **ifstream** class, and output mode is the default for the **ofstream** class.

If you do choose to specify mode flags, use the following values. These are bit-flag values, so they can be combined using bitwise OR (|).

- **`ios_base::app`**

  Append mode. If the file already exists, it is opened in append mode; new data can only be written to the end of the file. Before every write operation, the file's position indicator is moved to the end of the file. If the file does not already exist, it is created.

- **`ios_base::ate`**

  At-end mode ("AT End"). The file's position indicator is moved to the end of the file when it is opened. This mode needs to be combined with **in**, **out**, or **app**.

- **`ios_base::binary`**

  Binary mode. No translation of newlines is performed. This mode is intended to be used with the **read** and **write** functions as explained in Section 13.6.4, "Reading and Writing in Binary Mode."

- **`ios_base::in`**

  Input mode. This is the default for the **ifstream** class. The file must already exist, or the attempt to open fails.

- **`ios_base::out`**

  Output mode. This is the default for the **ofstream** class. If the file does not yet exist, it is created. If the file already exists, it is overwritten.

- **`ios_base::trunc`**

  Truncate. If an existing file is opened in this mode, its current contents are erased and the new file length is zero.

For example, the following statement attempts to open the file data.bin for binary output:

```
ofstream bin_file(
     "data.bin", ios_base::binary | ios_base::out
);
```

In my view, the file modes are confusing and not well documented. I have combined the best advice into the following guidelines.

- To write data to a new file or replace an existing one, use **ios_base::out**. If you open an existing file, its current contents are replaced. This is the default for **ofstream** objects.
- To read an existing file, use **ios_base::in** mode. The file must already exist, or the attempt to open it fails. This is the default for **ifstream** objects.
- To read to and write to an existing file, use a combination of in and out modes (**ios_base::in | ios_base::out**). This is the default for **fstream** objects. As with **ios_base::in** mode, the file must already exist or the attempt to open it fails.
- But sometimes you might want to do the following: Try to open a file for input and output—if it already exists, then use that file; if not, then create it as a new file.

This last option—create a file if it doesn't exist but otherwise use the existing one—is not directly supported by any mode. Instead, you must do the following: First, attempt to open the file in the combined in/out mode. If that fails, then open the file for writing and close it immediately, in order to create a file of length 0; then reopen it again for input and output.

```
fstream file_io("test.txt");
if (!file_io) {
     cout << "Creating file text.txt." << endl;
     file_io.open("text.txt", ios_base::out);
     file_io.close();
     file_io.open("text.txt");
}
```

Before proceeding to use any file object, you should test it to make sure the file was successfully opened.

```
if (!bin_file) {
     cout <<
     return -1; // Indicate failure.
}
```

Instead of opening a file when you create the object, you can open the file in a separate statement, although this isn't necessary except in cases in which you're going to open, close, and reopen a file. The **open** member function has the same arguments as the file-object constructor.

```
ofstream file_out;
file_out.open("readme.txt", ios_base::out);
```

Once a file is open in text mode (the default), you can read or write to it using the stream operations described for **cin** and **cout**.

```
file_out << "Here is some text." << endl;
file_out << "Here is the hex equivalent of 31: ";
file_out << showbase << hex << 31 << endl;
```

Again, I recommend using the **getline** function for reading input from a text file. The following function displays the first two lines of text from a specified file.

```
#include <fstream>
#include <iostream>
#include <string>
using namespace std;

void display_2_lines(string filename) {
     string input_str;
```

```
        ifstream file_in (filename.c_str());
        if (!file_in) {
            cout << "File could not be opened." << endl;
            return;
        }
        getline(file_in, input_str);    // Read and display line #1
        cout << input_str << endl;
        getline(file_in, input_str);    // Read and display line #2
        cout << input_str << endl;
        file_out.close():
}
```

This example assumes that the file has two lines of text to be read. Usually, when reading a file, you'll want to test for the end-of-file condition to determine whether to read more text. For example, the following statements print out all the contents of a text file, one line at a time.

```
while (!file_in.eof()) {
        getline(file_in, input_str);
        cout << input_str << endl;
}
```

As soon as you are done reading or writing a file, you should close it. Calling the **close** function unlocks the file and frees it up so that other programs and other processes can access it.

```
file_out.close();
```

13.6.3 File-Specific Member Functions

The **ifstream** and **ofstream** classes (as well as **fstream**, which can be used for both reading and writing operations) support the following member functions, as well as all the member functions presented earlier in the chapter.

- *fstream_obj*.**close()**

  Closes the file associated with the stream object, if any. If no file is associated with the object, this function has no effect. This function has no return value.

  ```
  file_out.close();
  ```

- *fstream_obj*.**eof()**

  Returns **true** if the end-of-file condition is detected for the stream; returns **false** otherwise.

  ```
  #include <fstream>
  #include <iostream>
  ```

```
#include <string>
using std::string;
. . .
string input_str;

while (!file_in.eof()) {
     getline(file_in, input_str);
     cout << input_str;
}
```

- *fstream_obj*.**is_open()**

  Returns **true** if the stream object has a file associated with it open for reading or writing.

  ```
  bool is_open = file_in.is_open();
  ```

- *fstream_obj*.**open(***filename* [, *mode*]**)**

  Opens a file, using the arguments described in Section 13.6.2, "Creating a File Object." This function takes the same arguments as an **ifstream**, **ofstream**, or **fstream** constructor when it is used to open a file. The function returns a reference to the stream itself.

  ```
  ofstream file_out;
  file_out.open(
     "readme.txt", ios_base::out | ios_base::append
  );
  ```

13.6.4 Reading and Writing in Binary Mode

With binary input and output, there is no formatting, as there would be in a text file in the form of commas, spaces, or newlines. Another issue with binary I/O is that the functions take a **char*** pointer, even though you may need to deal with data in other formats. This requires use of the **reinterpret_cast** operator to use types larger than one byte.

Detailed descriptions of the binary I/O functions follow.

- *istream*.**read(***p_data*, *size***)**

  Reads *size* bytes directly from the stream and stores it at the address specified by *p_data*, a pointer of type **char***; *n* is an integer of type **streamsize**. The function returns a reference to the stream itself. You can determine how many bytes were actually read by calling the stream's **gcount** member function.

  The following example reads a long integer directly from a file and stores that value in n.

```
long n = 0;
char *p = reinterpret_cast<char*>(&n);
file_in.read(p, sizeof(long));
if (file_in.gcount() != sizeof(long)) {
     cout << "Read error." << endl;
     return -1;
}
```

This next example reads data into an array of ten **double** values.

```
double arr[10];
char *p = reinterpret_cast<char*>(arr);
file_in.read(p, sizeof(arr));
if (file_in.gcount() != sizeof(arr)) {
     cout << "Read error." << endl;
     return -1;
}
```

- *ostream*.**write(***p_data*, *size***)**

  Writes *size* bytes from the address specified by *p_data*, a pointer of type **char***, directly to the stream; *size* is an integer of type **streamsize**. The function returns a reference to the stream itself. You can determine whether an error occurred by calling the stream's **fail** or **bad** member functions.

  For example, the following lines of code write the value of n to a stream object by writing the two bytes of data contained in n directly to the file. The value 127 is directly written (not, as in a text file, as the ASCII character codes for '1', '2', and '7').

```
short n = 127;
char *p = reinterpret_cast<char*>(&n);
file_out.write(p, sizeof(short));
```

In reading and writing binary values, it's critical to understand precisely how many bytes to read or write during each given operation. The **int** type is the most likely to change from platform to platform. It's safer to stick to **short** and **long** as types with which to perform binary I/O.

13.6.5 Random-Access Operations

One of the easier ways to use a binary file is to decide on a fixed-length record format. For example, assume the following structure has been declared:

```
struct EmpRec {
     char name[30];
     char addr[40];
     short salary;
     short level;
};
```

Then, to write a record, use statements like the following:

```
EmpRec my_rec;
// Fill out record, and then...
char *p = reinterpret_cast<char*>(&my_rec);
file_out.write(p, sizeof(my_rec));
```

The code is reliable as long as all the programs that read or write this data agree as to the format of EmpRec. An easy way to do that, in turn, is to place the declaration of EmpRec in a header file and have it included by all files that read or write these records.

```
#include "emprec.h"
```

One of the advantages of this approach is that it facilitates random access. For a file made up completely of fixed-length records, the formula for determining the offset of the Nth record is:

```
offset = (N-1) * sizeof(record)
```

If you consider the first record to be record #0, the formula is even simpler:

```
offset = N * sizeof(record)
```

To go to a desired offset, use the **seekg** or **seekp** member function. These do essentially the same thing, except that **seekg** ("seek get") is supported for input streams, and **seekp** ("seek put") is supported for output streams.

For example, the following statements prompt the end user for a record number, seek to the desired record (assuming that the first record is considered #1, not #0), and then read that record into a variable named my_rec.

```
EmpRec my_rec;
cout << "Enter record number: ";
cin >> n;
file_obj.seekg((n – 1) * sizeof(my_rec);
char *p = reinterpret_cast<char*>(&my_rec);
file_obj.read(p, sizeof(my_rec));
```

What happens if you attempt to seek past the end of the file? It depends on what kind of operation is attempted next. If an attempt is made to write output to the file, the file length is extended as needed. But if you attempt to read from a file position that does not yet exist, zero values will be read and the "fail" bit will be set.

Descriptions of the "seek" and "tell" functions follow.

▸ *istream*.**seekg(***n* [, *ref_point*]**)**

Moves the stream's position indicator to *n*, where *n* is an offset from the beginning of the file (the default) or from the specified reference point.

If *ref_point* is specified, it can have the value **ios_base::beg** (beginning of file), **ios_base::cur** (current position), or **ios_base::end** (end of file). In all cases, *n* specifies the number of bytes to move forward from this point. If you want to work backward from the end of the file, then *n* should be negative, and *ref_point* should be **ios_base::end**.

Seeking past the end of the file causes no immediate error. But a subsequent read operation will cause the "fail" bit to be set and the position indicator to be set to -1.

For example, for a file made up of fixed-length records, the following statement moves the position indicator to the tenth record, if it exists.

```
io_file.seekg(9 * sizeof(EmpRec));
```

▸ *ostream*.**seekp(***n* [, *ref_point*]**)**

Performs the same operation as **seekg** but is supported by output streams. Streams opened for both input and output can use either. If you seek past the end of the file and then write data, the file is extended in length.

▸ *istream*.**tellg()**

Returns an integer of type **streamoff** containing the current position indicator: This represents an offset from the beginning of the file to the indicator. For example, the following statements calculate the length of the file by seeking to the end of the file and returning the offset. These statements produce correct results because when the position indicator is moved to the end of the file, it is one position past the last readable character.

```
io_file.seekg(0, ios_base::end);
cout << io_file.tellg(); // Print exact length of file in bytes.
```

But if there is an attempt to read data at this point, the "fail" bit is set and the file pointer is reset to -1. Note that type **streamoff** (an **std** namespace symbol) is an integer large enough to contain the offset of any position in a file. It's usually equivalent to **unsigned long**.

```
streamoff off = io_file.tellg();
```

▸ *ostream*.**tellp()**

Performs the same operation as **tellg** but is supported by output streams. Streams opened for both input and output can use either.

13.7 Reading and Writing String Streams

Creating a string stream lets you leverage all the tools of formatted I/O to strings. Although there are often other ways of achieving the same results, this ability is a great convenience.

For example, consider the problem of representing a number in hexadecimal format and storing the digits in a string. Although you could output hexadecimal digits one at a time yourself, it's much easier to write formatted output to a **stringstream** object.

```
#include <string>
#include <sstream>
using namespace std;
. . .
stringstream string_output;
int n = 255;
string_output << "The value of the number in hex is ";
string_output << hex << showbase << n << ".";
```

After these statements are executed, the string stream contains the following text:

```
The value of the number in hex is 0xff.
```

The text is not yet in string format, but to get this data you need only call the **str** function.

```
string s = string_output.str();
```

If you then need the string data in C-string form, you can get that by calling the string object's **c_str** function.

```
char *cstring = s.c_str();
```

There are several members of the **stringstream** class in addition to those inherited from **istream** and **ostream**: two constructors, and another function, **str**, which provides access to the string data. These functions require inclusion of the <sstream> header as well as the <string> header.

```
#include <sstream>
#include <string>
```

Descriptions of the two constructors follow. The brackets in each case indicate that *mode* is an optional argument.

- **`stringstream`** *`name`*`( [`*`mode`*` ] )`

  stringstream constructor: creates a **stringstream** object initialized with an empty string. (The data will remain empty until written to.) The mode, if included, can have values as described in Section 13.6.2. If *mode* is omitted, then by default the mode is **ios_base::in | ios_base:out**, opening the stream for both reading and writing.

You can write to such a stream as you would write to **cout**. You can also (depending on the mode) read its contents.

For example, the following statements open my_str as a **stringstream** object and write the text representations of 64 and 16 in octal format ("0100" and "020"), separated by a space and a comma.

```
stringstream my_str;
my_sstr << "Octal values of 64 and 16 are: ";
my_sstr << oct << showbase << 64 << ", " << 16;
```

When writing to a string stream, you can truncate the string data, if you need to, by writing **eos**. This might be necessary if you were overwriting an existing string.

```
my_sstr << eos;
```

You can also write embedded newlines; these can be significant if the string data is eventually going to be printed or if the newlines are used as delimiters.

```
my_sstr << endl;
```

▸ **stringstream** *name*(*str_obj* [, *mode*])

stringstream constructor: creates a **stringstream** object initialized with string data from *str_obj*, an object of class **string**. This constructor is necessary if you are going to successfully read from the stream without first writing to it. You can read from such a stream just as you would from **cin**.

The *mode*, if included, can have the values described in Section 13.6.2. If mode is omitted, then by default the mode is **ios_base::in | ios_base:out**, opening the stream for both reading and writing.

The following example reads the hexadecimal number ff into an integer variable n.

```
string s("ff");
stringstream my_str(s);
int n = 0;
my_str >> hex >> n;
```

Descriptions of member functions follow. These are versions of the **str** function.

▸ *streamstream_obj*.**str()**

Returns a **string** object containing the current text data stored in the stream. The string contains a snapshot of the stream contents. If subsequent writing is done to the stream, another call to **str** will be necessary to get the updated results.

```
stringstream my_sstr;
my_sstr << "Octal values of 64 and 16 are: ";
```

```
my_sstr << oct << showbase << 64 << ", " << 16;
string s = my_sstr.str(); // Put contents into s.
```

- *streamstring_obj*.**str**(*str_obj*)

  Performs the same action as the other version of **str**, except that it takes *str_obj* as an argument: This is a reference to a **string** object. The action of the function is to place the string data into this object. There is no return value.

```
string s;
my_sstr.str(s);             // Put contents into s.
```

There are many situations in which string streams are useful. Consider the problem of letting the end user enter a number with commas (,) or other thousands-place separators used in international formats. The following function strips a string of nondigit characters and reads it into a number.

```
#include <string>
#include <sstream>
#include <iostream>
#include <cctype>
using namespace std;

int get_number() {
     string s;
     int n;
     stringstream ss;
     cout << "Enter number: ";
     getline(cin, s);
     for (int i = 0; i < s.size(); i++) {
          if (isdigit(s[i]) || s[i] == '-') {
               ss << s[i];
          }
     }
     ss >> n;
     return n;
}
```

This function works by first prompting and storing a line of input in **string** object s. That string is then analyzed one character at a time. If a character is a digit or negative sign, it gets written to the string stream, ss; otherwise, it's ignored. Given this function, the program can correctly interpret user input such as:

```
1,200,305
```

The get_number function (just shown) responds to this input by stripping this input of commas (,), and then reading it as "1200305" and finally converting it to its numeric value.

13.8 Overloading Shift Operators for Your Classes

One of the biggest advantages of the C++ stream classes is that you can extend them to work smoothly with your own classes.

If you understand operator functions (see Chapter 7, "Classes and Objects," for a review), along with the basics of stream-class input and output, writing the necessary operator functions for formatted I/O should be an easy task. This is especially true for formatted output (<<). Formatted input can be a little trickier because you may need to parse a string.

As an example, assume you have declared a simple fraction class, fract, as follows:

```
class fract {
public:
     int num;    // Numerator
     int den;    // Denominator
     fract() { num = 0; den = 1; }
     fract(int new_n, int new_d)
          { num = new_n; den = new_d; }
};
```

For a fraction class, it would be desirable to be able to automatically read and write fractions in the format *num/den* so that a fraction value of num=3 and den=4 would be printed as:

```
3/4
```

It's easy to write an operator function that implements this.

```
ostream& operator<< (ostream &os, const fract &fr) {
     os << fr.num << "/" << fr.den;
     return os;
}
```

It's that simple!

The function takes two reference arguments and returns a reference to the output stream, os. Arguments are passed by reference, to let the function work directly on the stream itself and on the right-hand operand rather than with copies. The second argument should be declared **const**.

Given this function, the following code does what you'd expect:

```
fract my_fract(3, 4);
cin << "The fraction is " << my_frac << ". " << endl;
```

This prints:

```
The fraction is 3/4.
```

Implementing formatted input is trickier, because input such as "33/100" needs to be parsed. The strategy of this function definition is: Input a string, read an integer from the digits preceding the first slash (/), and then read another integer. Use a default value of 1 for the denominator.

```
#include <iostream>
#include <string>
#include <cstdlib>    // To get support for atoi().
using std::string;
. . .
istream& operator>> (istream &is, fract &fr) {
     string s;
     is >> s;      // Input a string up to first whitespace.
     fr.num = atoi(s.c_str());    // Read digits before '/'.
     int pos = s.find('/');
     if (pos >= 0) {              // Read digits after '/'.
          fr.den = atoi(s.c_str() + pos + 1);
          if (fr.den == 0) {
               fr.den = 1;    // Don't permit 0 denominator.
          }
     } else {
          fr.den = 1;         // Den. of 1 is the default.
     }
     return is;
}
```

Sometimes stream operator functions may need to access private data of the class. If that's the case, make the operator functions friends to the class, as shown here:

```
class fract {
public:
     int num;    // Numerator
     int den;    // Denominator
     fract() { num = 0; den = 1; }
     fract(int new_n, int new_d)
          { num = new_n; den = new_d; }
     friend ostream& operator<< (ostream &os,
       const fract &fr);
     friend istream& operator>> (istream &is, fract &fr);
};
```

13.9 Sample App: Text File Reader

Reading and displaying a text file is fairly easy and straightforward, as it mostly comes down to just a few lines of code:

```
while(!file_in.eof()) {
     getline(file_in, input_str);
     cout << input_str << endl;
}
```

The application in this section adds some sophistication. It only displays enough of a text file to fit on one typical console (approximately 25 lines), and then prompts the user before displaying more text. That makes this application useful for reading both large text files and small.

```
#include <string>
#include <iostream>
#include <fstream>

using std::cout;          // Alternatively, you can use
using std::cin;           //   using namespace std;
using std::endl;
using std::string;
using std::ifstream;

#define VERT_LINES  25    // # of vertical lines per screen.

bool ask_more();          // Function used for pausing.

int main() {
     string fname;        // File name.
     string input_str;    // String used to hold file input.
     int n = 0;
     cout << "Enter file name: ";
     getline(cin, fname);
     ifstream file_in(fname);
     if (!file_in) {
          cout << "Could not open file." << endl;
     } else {
          while(!file_in.eof()) {
               getline(file_in, input_str);
               cout << input_str << endl;
               ++n;
               if (n % (VERT_LINES - 2) == 0) {
                    if (!ask_more()) {
                         break;
                    }
               }
```

```
        } // End while
    } // End else clause
    cout << "Press ENTER to quit program.";
    cin.ignore();  // Wait for user to press ENTER.
    return 0;
}

// Ask More function:
// Pause and prompt the user as to whether to continue;
// Return true unless user wants to quit.
bool ask_more() {
    string input_str;
    cout << endl << "[PRESS ENTER for more, Q to quit]: ";
    getline(cin, input_str);
    if (input_str.size() > 0) {
        char c = input_str[0];
        if (c == 'Q' || c == 'q') {
            return false;
        }
    }
    return true;
}
```

Exercises

1. Revise the application so that it keeps prompting the user at the beginning until (a) the name of a valid file is entered or (b) the user presses ENTER without typing input, at which point it quits.
2. Display the text of the file as all-uppercase letters. (Nonletters should be displayed as they are.)
3. After displaying a file, the application should prompt the user for another file name, but again, allowing the user to quit by just pressing ENTER. Revise the application to do that.

CHAPTER 14

The C++ STL String Class

Once upon a time there was the C language, developed to allow you to program close to the metal, writing efficient code while taking responsibility for all risks.

C's handling of text strings is typical of this close-to-the-metal approach; the old C-language string type is a simple array of **char**. C and C++ don't stop you from reserving ten bytes for a string and then trying to write 11 characters to it.

But for a number of years now, C++ compilers have supported the new **string** class as part of the Standard Template Library (STL). Although the old C-string type is still supported, and it's sometimes necessary to convert to or from that type, the new **string** class is an improvement in almost every way. Such a string can grow without limit, freeing you from having to constantly check for potential memory violations.

```
#include <string>
using std::string;
. . .
string breed = "mutt";
breed = "Great Dane";   // No problem! String can grow!
```

Unless your compiler is so out of date that it does not include the STL, you can assume it supports the **string** class.

14.1 Overview of the String Class

To use the **string** class, include the <string> header.

```
#include <string>
```

Both the <string> and <cstring> headers are potentially useful. Although they differ by just one character (!), they have different—though related—purposes:

```
#include <string>          // Support STL string class.
#include <cstring>         // Support C-string functs.
```

The <cstring> header is equivalent to the <string.h> header, so you can also use:

```
#include <string>          // Support STL string class.
#include <string.h>        // Support C-string functs.
```

The <string> header supports the **string** class, which is the new class. The <cstring> header (or alternatively, <string.h>) supports old C-language functions that work on C-strings. Although you will usually want to stick to one type or the other, there are situations in which you may want to have both parts of the library available. String literals are C-strings.

The name **string** is part of the **std** namespace, so include the following statement, or refer to **string** by using its **std::** prefix.

```
using namespace std;
```

Remember that you can also employ the **using** statement more selectively, which is what many C++ gurus strongly recommend; this approach reduces the chance of name conflicts in complex programs (although it's usually less of an issue in shorter programs):

```
using std::cout;
using std::cin;
using std::endl;
using std::string;
```

(Note that most of this chapter assumes that these statements are already in force, so I did not reenter the **std::** prefix for each and every example.)

You can use **string** to declare any number of objects:

```
#include <string>
using std::string;

string  s1, s2, s3;
```

Unlike C-strings, objects of this class are declared without sizes. Each **string** object manages its own length. If the string grows in size, internal housekeeping functions reallocate the data to a new area of memory as needed. The process is mostly invisible to the user of the string.

Operations are straightforward and intuitive. The following statements do what you'd expect, including concatenation (+).

```
string first_name = "Jack";
string last_name = "Jones";
string full_name = first_name + " " + last_name;
cout << full_name << endl;
```

14.2 String Class Constructors

There are several ways to create **string** objects—that is, to use string class constructors. Remember, as always, to include the <string> header if you want to create string objects. Also remember that the name **string** is part of the **std** namespace.

```
#include <string>
using std::string;
```

Descriptions of the string class constructors follow, in which *cstr* is a C-string (a **char*** pointer) and *string_obj2* is another **string** object.

- **string** *name*

  Default constructor. The object is initialized as an empty string.

  ```
  string s1;
  ```

- **string** *name(cstr)*

  Initializes content from *cstr*, a C-string. This is a frequently used constructor for this class, as it enables you to use string literals to initialize an object.

  The first, second, and fourth lines of the following code invoke this constructor.

  ```
  string name1("John Q. Public");
  string name2 = "Mary Mary";
  char group[] = "beetles";
  string group_str(group);
  ```

  This constructor creates a conversion function. Consequently, a C-string can be used as an argument anywhere a **string** object would be accepted, as long as the compiler can unambiguously determine that the conversion is called for.

- **string** *name(cstr, n)*

  Initializes content from the first *n* bytes of *cstr*, a C-string argument.

  ```
  string s1("I did it... not really!", 9);
  cout << s1 << endl;
  ```

  This example prints:

  ```
  I did it.
  ```

- **string** *name(string2_obj)*

  Copy constructor. Initializes a new object from the data in the existing **string** object, *string2_obj*.

  ```
  string s2("A B C.");
  string s1(s2);        // Use copy constructor.
  ```

▸ **string** *name(string2_obj, pos [, n])*

Initializes the new object with a substring of *string2*. The *pos* argument is an integer specifying the starting position of this substring using a zero-based index; *n* specifies the maximum number of characters to copy. If *n* is omitted or greater than the number of the remaining characters, the data copied consists of characters from position *pos* forward to the end of the string.

```
string quip1("No Way!!")
string quip2(quip1, 3);
string quip3(quip1, 3, 4);
cout << quip2 << endl << quip3 << endl;
```

This example prints:

```
Way!!
Way!
```

▸ **string** *name(n, ch)*

Initializes the new **string** object with character *ch* repeated *n* times. For example, the following statement initializes blankies with 20 blank spaces.

```
string blankies(20, ' ');
```

14.3 String Class Operators

The **string** class overloads a number of useful operators, including assignment (=), addition (+), the comparison operators (==, as well as <, >, <=, and >=), and indexing, [ ].

14.3.1 Assigning Strings (=)

If the assignment operator (=) is used within a declaration, it invokes a constructor; but outside a declaration it invokes assignment, which copies data to an existing string.

```
using std::string;
string s1, s2;
s1 = "Hello, world.";     // Assign "Hello, world." to s1.
s2 = s1;                  // Assign contents of s1 to s2.
char cstr1[10] = "Hello!";
s1 = cstr1;               // Assign "Hello!" to s1.
```

Note that if you need to copy data from a **string** object into C-string format use the **c_str** member function, as described in Section 14.4, “Concise Summary of Member Functions.”

14.3.2 Joining Strings (+)

One of the advantages of the **string** class is the ease with which you can concatenate strings using the addition operator (+) as a "join" or concatenation operator. The result of this operation is a new **string** object, which can in turn be assigned to yet another object.

You can join two string objects together, or join a combination of **string** objects and C-strings, as long as at least one is a **string** object. For example:

```
string first_name = "Elvis";
string last_name = "Presley";
string name = first_name + " " + last_name;
```

This last statement works because it combines **string** objects and a C-string (the literal, " ") in the same expression. The binary addition operator (+) associates left to right, so the statement is evaluated as if written this way:

```
string name = (first_name + " ") + last_name;
```

This use of the addition operator (+) creates readable, concise code, but it results in temporary **string** objects being created. Depending on the optimizing capabilities of your compiler, this may be less efficient at runtime than use of the **append** member function.

As long as there is at least one **string** operand, you can place a C-string on either side of the concatenation.

```
string full_name = "Rock Star " + name;
```

But you can't concatenate two string literals together, because they are C-strings. The compiler would interpret this as an attempt to add two addresses.

```
string name = "Rock " + "Star";  // ERROR! Attempt to add
                                 //   2 char* addresses.
```

If you need to join two string literals, however, you can just place them next to each other. The C++ compiler interprets two adjacent string literals as if they were one continuous string.

```
string name = "Rock " "Star";
```

The string class also supports addition assignment (+=). For example:

```
string name;
name += first_name;
name += " ";
name += last_name;
```

14.3.3 Comparing Strings

The comparison operators (==, <, >, <=, >=), when applied to **string** objects, compare the contents of the strings.

```
using namespace std;
string dog1 = "Great Dane";
string dog2 = "Great Dane";
if (dog1 == dog2) {
     cout << "strings contain same text." << endl;
}
```

You can also compare a **string** object to a C-string.

```
if (dog1 == "Great Dane") {
     cout << "strings contain same text." << endl;
}
```

All of the comparison operators return a **bool** result. One string is "less than" another (so < returns **true**), if it comes earlier in alphabetical order than another.

Case is significant. In the ASCII coding system, all lowercase letters are later in alphabetical order than all uppercase letters and are therefore "greater." These relationships are demonstrated by the following comparisons, both of which produce **true**:

```
if(string("xyz") > string("abc")) {
     cout << "xyz is 'greater' than abc" << endl;
}
if (string("abc") > string ("XYZ")) {
     cout << "abc is 'greater' than XYZ" << endl;
}
```

Unfortunately, it's not immediately obvious how to carry out a case-insensitive comparison, in which "a" and "A" are treated the same way. Some compilers provide their own library functions to do that (check your compiler documentation), but otherwise, the easiest way is to write a function that builds temporary strings that are all uppercase or all lowercase and then compares these temporary strings. The next section shows how to do that.

14.3.4 Indexing Strings ([ ])

The subscript operator, [ ], indexes a **string** object to provide access to individual characters.

string_obj[*pos*]

As with array indexing, there is always the danger of using out-of-bound indexes unless you are careful. Alternatives include

- Use of iterators to access individual characters, as described in Section 14.6, "String Class Iterators" (basic_string)"
- Range-based **for** (if your compiler is C++11 compliant)
- The **at** member function, which does the same thing the subscript operator does but throws a **range_error** exception for out-of-bound indexes

You can use the subscript operator to perform case-insensitive alphabetical comparisons between two strings.

```
#include <string>
#include <cctype>   // Need this to support toupper.
using std::string;
...
int compare_no_case(const string &s1, const string &s2) {
     string temp1 = s1;
     string temp2 = s2;
     for (int i = 0; i < temp1.size(); i++) {
           temp1[i] = toupper(temp1[i]);
     }
     for (int i = 0; i < temp2.size(); i++) {
           temp2[i] = toupper(temp2[i]);
     }
     return temp1.compare(temp2);
}
```

The strategy is to copy string data into temporary strings, convert each temporary string to all uppercase, and then perform a comparison on the temporary strings. Indexing a **string** object returns a reference to an individual character so that it can be the target of an assignment:

```
           temp1[i] = toupper(temp1[i]);
```

Each **for** loop in the example compares the index to the size of the string. This prevents out-of-bound index numbers.

Given this function definition, you could perform case-insensitive comparisons, such as the following code, which does what you'd expect.

```
string s1 = "abc";
string s2 = "Xyz";
if (compare_no_case(s1, s2) < 0) {
     cout << "abc < Xyz!" << endl;
}
```

```
if (compare_no_case(a1, "ABC") == 0) {
     cout << "abc == ABC" << endl;
}
```

14.4 Concise Summary of Member Functions

Section 14.5, "Member Functions in Detail," describes the remaining member functions in detail, including examples and complete syntax. Table 14.1 summarizes the most commonly used **string** member functions.

14.5 Member Functions in Detail

In the descriptions that follow, brackets are not intended literally but indicate an optional argument. *string_obj* is an object of string type, *pos* is a zero-based index number, and *n* is an integer.

TABLE 14.1 Summary of string Class Member Functions

Member Function(s)	Description
append	Appends another string onto existing string contents.
assign	Replaces existing string contents with another string or substring.
compare	Compares string with another string or substring.
copy, **c_str**	Gets string contents in C-string form.
erase	Removes some or all of existing contents.
find	Returns position of target substring.
find_first_not_of, **find_first_of**, **find_last_not_of**, **find_last_of**	Returns position of first or last character to match criterion (such as whether it belongs to a certain group of characters).
insert	Inserts new string data into existing string.
length, **size**	Returns length of string data.
replace	Replaces part of the string with text from another string or substring.
substr	Returns a new string consisting of a substring within existing string—specified by position and length.
swap	Swaps contents with another **string** object.

Remember that you must include the <string> header, and that the name **string** is part of the **std** namespace, as are **cout**, **cin**, and **endl**:

```
#include <string>
using std::cout;
using std::endl;
using std::string;
```

The examples in the remainder of the chapter assume these declarations.

Except where otherwise stated, each of these functions returns a reference to *string_obj*—the object through which the function was called.

- *string_obj*.**append(***string2_obj***)**

  Appends the contents of *string2_obj* onto the end of the contents of *string_obj*. The effect is to concatenate contents directly without having to create a temporary object (which the + operator does). This function performs the same action as the += operator.

  ```
  string file_name("readme"), ext_name(".txt");
  file_name.append(ext_name);
  cout << file_name;    // Prints "readme.txt"
  ```

- *string_obj*.**append(***string2_obj*, *pos*, *n***)**

  Appends the specified substring onto the end of *string_obj*; the substring starts at zero-based position *pos* within *string2_obj* and contains no more than *n* characters.

- *string_obj*.**append(***cstr* [, *n*]**)**

  Appends characters from *cstr*, a C-string, onto the end of *string_obj*. The optional *n* argument, if specified, is the maximum number of characters to append. If *n* is omitted, the function appends all the data from *cstr* (which in that case must be null-terminated).

  ```
  string file_name("readme");
  file_name.append(".txt");
  cout << file_name;    // Prints "readme.txt"
  ```

- *string_obj*.**append(***n*, *ch***)**

  Appends *n* copies of character *ch* onto the end of *string_obj*.

- *string_obj*.**assign(***string2_obj***)**

  Replaces the contents of *string_obj* with those of *string2_obj*. The effect of this function is the same as the assignment operator (=). To replace only some of the current string, see the **replace** function.

  ```
  string my_pet("dog");
  string your_pet("cat");
  ```

```
// After next stmt, my_pet will contain "cat".
my_pet.assign(your_pet);
```

- *string_obj*.**assign(***cstr* [,*n*]**)**

  Replaces the contents of *string_obj* with those of *cstr,* a C-string. *n*, if specified, is the maximum number of characters to copy. If *n* is omitted the function copies all of *cstr.*

- *string_obj*.**assign(***string2_obj*, *pos*, *n***)**

  Replaces the contents of *string_obj* with the substring formed from *string2_obj* starting in position *pos* and containing no more than *n* characters. If *n* would extend beyond the length of the string or has a negative value the function uses all of *string2_obj* starting with position *pos.*

- *string_obj*.**assign(***n*, *ch***)**

  Replaces existing contents with a string made up of character *ch* repeated *n* times.

- *string_obj*.**at(***pos***)**

  Returns a reference to the character at zero-based position *pos.* This function performs the same action as the subscript operator, [ ], except that the **at** member function throws an **out_of_range** exception if *pos* is out of range.

  This example is adapted from the example in Section 14.3.4, "Indexing Strings ([])," which assumes that both <string> and <cctype> have been included.

```
for (int i = 0; i < templ.size(); ++i) {
        templ.at(i) = toupper(templ.at(i));
}
```

- *string_obj*.**capacity()**

  Returns an integer containing the current capacity of *string_obj.* This is neither the current length of the string nor its ultimate physical capacity. The current length is found by the **size** or **length** function. The ultimate capacity is found by calling **max_size**.

  Capacity is the number of bytes currently reserved for the string. When the string needs to grow larger than this number, new memory is allocated and the data is moved. This function is of interest only to code that—for efficiency reasons—reserves a certain number of characters for a series of complex operations. See the **reserve** function.

```
string s("Hello!");
cout << "Length is: " << s.size() << endl;
cout << "Capacity is: " << s.capacity() << endl;
```

▸ *string_obj*.**clear()**

Sets the contents of *string_obj* to an empty string. This function has no return value.

```
s.clear();
```

▸ *string_obj*.**compare(***string2_obj***)**

Compares the contents of *string_obj* to those of *string2_obj*. The function returns a negative integer, zero, or a positive integer, depending on whether the contents are "less than," identical to, or "greater than" the contents of *string2_obj*.

In this context, "less than" means that a string is earlier in alphabetical order. Comparisons are case-sensitive, and all lowercase letters are later in alphabetical order (therefore "greater") than uppercase letters. See Section 14.3.3, "Comparing Strings," for sample code that performs case-insensitive comparisons.

```
string str1("cat"), str2("dog");
if (str1.compare(str2) < 0) {
     cout << "cat is less than dog.";
}
```

▸ *string_obj*.**compare(***cstr***)**

Performs a comparison between the contents of *string_obj* with the specified C-string *cstr*. See the previous listing for the **compare** member function.

▸ *string_obj*.**compare(***pos*, *n*, *string2_obj***)**

Performs a comparison between two strings: a substring of *string_obj* beginning in position *pos* and consisting of at most *n* characters; and *string2_obj*, another **string** object.

▸ *string_obj*.**compare(***pos1*, *n1*, *string2_obj*, *pos2*, *n2***)**

Performs a comparison between two strings: a substring of *string_obj* beginning in position *pos1* and consisting of at most *n1* characters; and a substring of *string2_obj*, another **string** object, beginning in position *pos2* and consisting of at most *n2* characters.

```
string s1 = "I am the cat."
string s2 = "Thou art the kat."
if (s1.compare(9, 3, s2, 13, 3) < 0) {
     cout << "'cat' is before 'kat'." << endl;
}
```

▸ *string_obj*.**compare(***pos*, *n*, *cstr* [, *n2*]**)**

Performs a comparison between two strings: a substring of *string_obj* beginning in position *pos* and consisting of at most *n* characters; and *cstr*, a C-string. The optional *n2* argument, if specified, is the maximum number of characters of *cstr* to use. (Only the first *n2* characters will be used.)

▸ *string_obj*.**copy**(*cstr*, *n* [, *pos*])

Copies raw character data from *string_obj* into *cstr*, a **char** array, but does not append a terminating null. *n* is the maximum number of characters to copy. *pos*, if included, is the zero-based position within string at which to begin copying; by default, this is 0. The function returns the number of characters copied.

See also **c_str** and **data**.

```
#define MAX_SIZE 255  // Hopefully 255 is enough.
char array[MAX_SIZE+1];
getline(cin, s);      // Get input from user.
int n = s.copy(array, MAX_SIZE);
array[n] = '\0';      // Append null.
```

▸ *string_obj*.**c_str**()

Returns the address of string data as a C-string, guaranteeing that it is null-terminated.

The function returns a **const char*** pointer. Although **const_cast** can be used to "cast away" the **const** attribute, doing so would facilitate risky behavior. If you need to manipulate or save the data returned, you should make a copy of this string.

The address returned is of an internal area of memory that should not be changed by the program. Subsequent changes to *string_obj* may invalidate the data at this address.

The following example uses this function to convert the data into C-string format; it can then be passed to **strtok**, one of the more useful C-string functions, to tokenize the input.

```
#include <string>
#include <cstring>    // Supports strtok declaration.
#include <iostream>

using std::cout;
using std::cin;
using std::endl;
using std::string;

#define SCRN_WIDTH 80

main() {
    string s;
    char input_line[SCRN_WIDTH+1], *ptr;
    cout << "Enter some input: ";
    getline(cin, s);
    strncpy(input_line, s.c_str(), SCRN_WIDTH);
    ptr = strtok(input_line, " ,");
    while (ptr) {
```

```
            cout << ptr << endl;
            ptr = strtok(NULL, " ,");
        }
        return 0;
}
```

▸ *string_obj*.**data()**

Performs the same action as the **c_str** member function—copying data to a **char** array and then returning the address—but does not add a terminating null.

This example uses the **new** operator to allocate a large enough **char** array to hold the data from string s, plus a terminating null (which must be added "manually").

```
string s;
char *input_line, *ptr;
cout << "Enter some input: ";
getline(cin, s);
input_line = new [s.size()+1];  // Allocate cstr.
strcpy(input_line, s.data());
input_line[s.size()] = '\0';    // Add null.
```

▸ *string_obj*.**empty()**

Returns **true** if string's contents consist of an empty string; returns **false** otherwise.

```
if (s.empty()) {
     cout << "The string is empty." << endl;
}
```

▸ *string_obj*.**erase(**[*pos*] [, *n*]**)**

Removes characters from string, beginning with zero-based position *pos* and removing at most *n* characters.

If one argument is given during a function call, that argument is passed to *pos*. If no arguments are given, *pos* takes the default value of 0, and the function has the same effect as **clear**.

The following example removes spaces and commas from an input string, s, by removing one character at a time.

```
getline(cin, s);
for (int i = 0; i < s.size(); i++) {
     if (s[i] == ' ' || s[i] == ',') {
          s.erase(i, 1);
     }
}
```

▸ *string_obj*.**find(***string2_obj* [, *pos*]**)**

Returns (zero-based) position of target substring *string2_obj* within *string_obj*. If the substring is not found, the function returns **string::npos**. The optional *pos* argument, if specified, is the zero-based position within *string_obj* at which to begin searching; otherwise, the entire contents of *string_obj* are searched.

With this function and the other versions of **find**, all the characters in the substring must match, and in the order specified. Matching is case-sensitive.

For example, the following statements count the number of occurrences of "Bat":

```
string s;
s = "Batman uses the Batpole to get to the "
    " Batmobile in the Batcave.";
string sub = "Bat";
int n = 0;
int pos = 0;
pos = s.find(sub);              // Find first token.
while (pos != string::npos) {
      ++n;
      pos = s.find(sub, pos + 1);  // Find next.
}
cout << "Number of occurrences: " << n << endl;
```

- *string_obj*.**find(***cstr* [, *pos*] [, *n*]**)**

  Performs the same action as the previous version of **find**, except that it searches for a substring specified by *cstr*, a C-string.

- *string_obj*.**find(***ch* [, *pos*]**)**

  Performs the same action as the previous versions of **find**, except that it searches for a specific character, *ch*.

- *string_obj*.**find_first_not_of(***string2_obj* [, *pos*]**)**

  Returns the position of the first character in *string_obj* that does not match any character in *string2_obj*. If no such character is found, the function returns **string::npos**. *pos*, if specified, is the zero-based position within *string_obj* to start searching; if *pos* is omitted, the whole string is searched beginning with the first character.

  The following example strips leading spaces (if any) from an input string and prints the results.

```
string input_str, wspaces(" \t\f\v\n");
cout << "Enter string: ";
getline(cin, input_str);
cout << "Stripping leading spaces..." << endl;
int pos = input_str.find_first_not_of(wspaces);
input_str.erase(0, pos);
cout << "->" << input_str << "<-" << endl;
```

- *string_obj*.**find_first_not_of(***cstr* [, *pos*] [, *n*]**)**

  Performs the same action as the previous version of **find_first_not_of**, except that it searches for the first character not matching any in *cstr*, a C-string. *pos*, if specified, is the position within *string_obj* to start searching; *n*, if specified, is the maximum number of characters from *cstr* to use, starting from the beginning of the string. (This is useful if *cstr* is not null-terminated.) If only two arguments are specified, the second argument is taken as a value for *pos*, not *n*.

- *string_obj*.**find_first_not_of(***ch* [, *pos*]**)**

  Performs the same action as the previous versions of **find_first_not_of**, except that it searches for the first character not matching character *ch*.

- *string_obj*.**find_first_of(***string2_obj* [, *pos*]**)**

  Returns the position of the first character in *string_obj* that matches any character in *string2_obj*. If no such character is found, the function returns **string::npos**. *pos*, if specified, is a zero-based position within *string_obj* to start searching; if *pos* is omitted, the whole string is searched beginning with the first character.

  The following example finds the first name from an input string by stripping leading spaces and then erasing all text after the first whitespace found. So, for example, if the user enters "Elvis Aaron Presley," this code prints "Elvis."

```
string input_str, wspaces(" \t\f\v\n");
cout << "Enter a name: ";
getline(cin, input_str);
int pos = input_str.find_first_not_of(wspaces);
input_str.erase(0, pos); // Strip leading spaces.
// Erase all text after first white space found.
pos = input_str.find_first_of(wspaces);
input_str.erase(pos);
cout << "First name is: " << input_str << endl;
```

- *string_obj*.**find_first_of(***cstr* [, *pos*] [, *n*]**)**

  Performs the same action as the previous version of **find_first_of**, except that it searches for the first character matching any in *cstr*, a C-string. *pos*, if specified, is the zero-based position within *string_obj* to start searching; *n*, if specified, is the maximum number of characters from *cstr* to use, starting from the beginning of the string. (This is useful if *cstr* is not null-terminated.) If only two arguments are given during a function call, the second argument is passed to *pos*, not *n*.

- *string_obj*.**find_first_of(***ch* [, *pos*]**)**

  Performs the same action as the previous versions of **find_first_of**, except that it searches for the first character matching character *ch*.

- *string_obj*.**find_last_not_of(***string2_obj* [, *pos*]**)**

  Returns the position of the last character in *string_obj* that does not match any character in *string2_obj*. If no such character is found, the function returns **string::npos**. *pos*, if specified, is a zero-based position within *string_obj*; the string is searched up to this position. (You can think of the search as starting in this position and moving backward.) If *pos* is omitted or greater than the length, the whole string is searched.

The following example removes trailing spaces by finding the last nonspace character in the string and then erasing all contents to the right of that position.

```
string s;
string wspaces(" \t\f\v\n");
cout << "Enter a string: ";
getline(cin, s);
int p = s.find_last_not_of(wspaces);
if (p != string::npos) {
     s.erase(p + 1); // Erase text to right of p.
} else {
     s.clear();      // Erase entire string.
}
cout << "I'm going to strip trailing spaces...";
cout << "->" << s << "<-" << endl;
```

- *string_obj*.**find_last_not_of(***cstr* [, *pos*] [, *n*]**)**

  Performs the same action as the previous version of **find_last_not_of**, returning the position of the first character not matching any character in the string argument—except that the string, *cstr*, is a C-string. (See that description for more information.) *n*, if specified, is the maximum number of characters from *cstr* to use, starting from the beginning of the string. This is useful if *cstr* is not null-terminated. If only two arguments are specified, the second argument is passed to *pos*, not *n*.

- *string_obj*.**find_last_not_of(***ch* **[,** *pos***])**

  Performs an action similar to the previous versions of **find_last_not_of**, returning the position of the first character not matching character *ch*.

- *string_obj*.**find_last_of(***string2_obj* [, *pos*]**)**

  Returns the position of the last character in *string_obj* that matches any character in *string2_obj*. If no such character is found, the function returns **string::npos**. *pos*, if specified, is a zero-based position within *string_obj*; the string is searched up to this position. (You can think of the search as starting in this position and moving backward.) If *pos* is omitted or greater than the length, the whole string is searched.

  The following example extracts a last name by finding the last whitespace in the string and copying characters beginning with one position to the right of that space, if found. If no space is found, the code copies the entire string. (Note that the example assumes no trailing spaces.) So, for example, if the user enters "Elvis Aaron Presley," this example prints "Presley".

```
string s;
string last_name;
string wspaces(" \t\f\v\n");
```

```
cout << "Enter name: ";
getline(cin, s);
int p = s.find_last_of(wspaces);
if (p == string::npos) {
     last_name.assign(s);
} else {
     last_name.assign(s, p + 1, s.size());
}
cout << "Last name is: " << last_name << endl;
```

▸ `string_obj.find_last_of(cstr [, pos] [, n])`

Performs the same action as the previous version of **find_last_of**, returning the position of the first character matching any character in the string argument—except that the string, *cstr*, is a C-string. (See that description for more information.) *n*, if specified, is the maximum number of characters from *cstr* to use, starting from the beginning of the string. This is useful if *cstr* is not null-terminated. If only two arguments are specified, the second argument is passed to *pos*, not *n*.

▸ `string_obj.find_last_of(ch [, pos])`

Performs an action similar to the previous versions of **find_last_of**, returning the position of the first character matching character *ch*.

▸ `string_obj.insert(pos, string2_obj)`

Copies and inserts the contents of *string2_obj* into the contents of *string_obj*, beginning at *pos* (so that the beginning of *string2_obj* is now in that position). For example, the following statements print "Mac the Knife." As always, *pos* is zero-based.

```
string name = "Mac Knife";
string mid = "the ";
name.insert(4, mid);
cout << name << endl;   // Print "Mac the Knife".
```

▸ `string_obj.insert(pos1, string2_obj, pos2, n)`

Performs the same action as the previous version of **insert**—copying and inserting data at position *pos1*—except that the data to be inserted consists of that portion of *string2_obj* beginning in position *pos2* and consisting of no more than *n* characters.

▸ `string_obj.insert(pos, cstr [, n])`

Performs the same action as the previous versions of **insert**—copying and inserting data at position *pos*—except that the string data to be inserted consists of no more than the first *n* characters of *cstr*, a C-string. (If *n* is greater than the length of *cstr*, then all of *cstr* is inserted.) For example:

```
string name = "Mac Knife";
name.insert(4, "the ");
cout << name << endl;   // Print "Mac the Knife".
```

▶ *string_obj*.**insert**(*pos*, *n*, *ch*)

Inserts *n* copies of character *ch* into string, beginning at position *pos*.

▶ *string_obj*.**length**()

Returns the length of *string_obj* contents as an integer. This number should not be confused with either current capacity (which is temporary) or ultimate physical capacity. This function performs the same action as **size**.

The following example transforms each character in string temp1 by converting it to all uppercase (nonletters are not affected):

```
#include <string>
#include <cctype>
. . .
for (int i = 0; i < temp1.length(); i++) {
      temp1[i] = toupper(temp1[i]);
}
```

▶ *string_obj*.**max_size**()

Returns the ultimate physical capacity of strings supported by the compiler and the platform: This is usually an extremely high number, although you should use this function to check if you have any doubts.

```
cout << "Max. size is: " << s.max_size() << endl;
```

▶ *string_obj*.**push_back**(*ch*)

Appends a single character, *ch*, onto the end of the contents of *string_obj*. To append a string rather than a single character, see **append**.

```
string s;
s.push_back('a');
s.push_back('b');
s.push_back('c');
```

▶ *string_obj*.**replace**(*pos*, *n*, *string2_obj*)

Selects text within *string_obj* for replacement beginning in position *pos* and consisting of *n* characters. If *n* is negative (such as the value **string::npos**) or would extend beyond the rest of the string, the function uses the remainder of the string.

The text selected for replacement is then replaced with the contents of *string2_obj*. For example, the following statements replace the first occurrence of "Bat" within string super with "Cat."

```
string msg = "It's Batwoman!";
int pos = msg.find("Bat");
msg.replace(pos, 3, "Cat");
cout << msg << endl;  // Print "It's Catwoman!"
```

Combining this ability with the search algorithm I gave in the example for **find**, you can write a loop that replaces *all* occurrences of "Bat" with "Cat":

```
string msg = "Batwoman ran to the Batmobile!";
int pos = msg.find("Bat");          // Find "Bat".
while (pos != string::npos) {
     msg.replace(pos, 3, "Cat");    // Replace.
     pos = msg.find("Bat", pos + 1); // Find next.
}
cout << msg << endl;
```

These statements print out:

```
Catwoman ran to the Catmobile!
```

- *string_obj*.**replace** (*pos*, *n*, *string2_obj*, *pos2*, *n2*)

  Performs the same action as the previous version of **replace**, except that the selected text is replaced by the specified text within *string2_obj*—consisting of text beginning in *pos2* and up to *n2* characters in length (following rules parallel to those for *pos* and *n*).

- *string_obj*.**replace** (*pos*, *n*, *cstr* [, *n2*])

  Performs the same action as the previous versions of **replace**, except that the selected text is replaced by *cstr*, a C-string. The optional *n2* argument, if included, is the maximum number of characters from *cstr* to use.

- *string_obj*.**replace** (*pos*, *n*, *ch*)

  Performs the same action as the previous versions of **replace**, except that the selected text is replaced by a single character, *ch*.

- *string_obj*.**replace** (*pos*, *n*, *n2*, *ch*)

  Performs the same action as the previous versions of **replace**, except that the selected text is replaced by *n2* copies of the character *ch*.

- *string_obj*.**reserve**(*n*)

  Sets the capacity of the string to *n* characters. Normally, management of reserve capacity is invisible to the user of a **string** object. But if you know in advance that you are going to be performing many operations writing to the string, you can marginally improve runtime performance by reserving the needed capacity in advance. For example, the following code reserves enough capacity ahead of time to read in the contents of a text file. (For space reasons, most of that program is not included here.)

  ```
  string s;
  string input_line;
  . . .
  s.reserve(file_length);  // Prepare for reads.
  ```

```
while(!file_in.eof()) {
     getline(file_in, input_line);
     s.append(input_line);
     s.push_back('\n');
}
cout << "File contents:" << endl << s << endl;
```

- *string_obj*.**resize(***n* [,*ch*]**)**

  Resizes string contents to *n* characters. If *n* is smaller than the current length of the string, the string is truncated. If *n* is larger than the current length of the string, the string is padded with the character *ch* at the end. If the optional *ch* argument is omitted and the string needs to be expanded, it is padded with nulls.

```
string quip("You are so right... NOT.");
int n = quip.find('.');
quip.resize(n + 1);
cout << quip << endl;    // "You are so right."
```

- *string_obj*.**rfind(***string2_obj* [, *pos*]**)**

  Reverse find: returns the position of the last instance of substring string2 in *string_obj*. The function returns **string::npos** if the substring is not found.

  The optional *pos* argument, if specified, is the last character in the string to examine, so the area of the string to search consists of bytes 0 to *pos*. (Conceptually, you can think of *pos* as being the first byte position to search when scanning from the end of the string.) If this argument is omitted, the entire string is searched.

  The following example counts the number of occurrences of the word "Bat"; it achieves the same result as the example for **find**, but *pos* is adjusted to the left each time, moving from high values (at the end of the string) to lower ones. A statement is included here to demonstrate that action by printing the positions.

```
string s;
s = "Holy Batwing, Batman! Someone stole the "
    "Batmobile and the Bat-computer is missing "
    "from the Batcave.";
string sub = "Bat";
int n = 0;     // Number of occurrences.
int pos;
pos = s.rfind(sub);
while (pos != string::npos) {
      ++n;
      cout << "pos is " << pos << endl;
      pos = s.rfind(sub, pos - 1);
}
cout << "Number of occurrences: " << n << endl;
```

▸ *string_obj*.**rfind(***cstr* [, *pos*] [, *n*])

Reverse find: performs the same action as the previous version of **rfind**, except that the search string is specified in *cstr*, a C-string, and there are two arguments, *pos* and *n*. If only two arguments are specified during the call, then the second argument is assigned to *pos* and no value is passed to *n*.

▸ *string_obj*.**rfind(***ch* [, *pos*])

Performs the same action as the previous versions of **rfind** (reverse find), but searches for a single character *ch*.

▸ *string_obj*.**size()**

Returns the length of *string_obj* contents as an integer. This number should not be confused with either current capacity (which is temporary and usually not of interest to programs) or ultimate physical capacity. This function performs the same action as **length**. See **length** for an example.

▸ *string_obj*.**substr(***pos* [,*n*])

Returns a **string** object containing a substring of *string_obj*. The optional *n* argument, if specified, is the number of characters to copy starting in zero-based position *pos*. If *n* is omitted—or if *n* is less than 0 or greater than the number of remaining characters—the string returned contains all the characters in *string_obj* starting with *pos*.

The **find** family of functions, when they fail to find a match, return **string::npos** (-1), which, if given as the *n* argument to **substr**, causes the remainder of the string to be extracted starting with *pos*. This is helpful in the following example.

This example extracts the first name from "Elvis Aaron Presley", but will work on the string "Elvis" as well. The values pos1 and pos2 are determined by finding the first nonspace and then finding the first space after that position.

```
string name = "Elvis  Aaron Presley";
int pos1 = name.find_first_not_of(" \t");
int pos2 = name.find_first_of(" \t", pos1 + 1);
// Get the substring:
string first = name.substr(pos1, pos2 - pos1);
cout << "First name is ->" << first << "<-";
cout << endl;
```

▸ *string_obj*.**swap(***string2_obj*)

Exchanges the contents between *string_obj* and *string2_obj*—both of which must be **string** objects. For example, after a call to **swap**, the strings side1 and side2 contain what the other string contained at the beginning.

```
string side1 = "heads";
string side2 = "tails";
```

```
cout << side1 << " I win, " << side2;
cout << " you lose." << endl;
side1.swap(side2);
cout << "No... " << endl;
cout << side1 << " I win, " << side2;
cout << " you lose." << endl;
```

14.6 String Class Iterators

As an STL class, the **string** class supports a convenient feature called an *iterator.* An iterator is essentially a wrapper around a pointer; you can do many of the same things with iterators that you can with pointers, although they are not interchangeable.

Chapter 15, "Introduction to STL (vector, deque)," discusses iterators further. The next few sections introduce the use of iterators with regard to the **string** class.

14.6.1 Standard (Forward) Iterators

To declare a **string** class iterator, use this syntax:

string::iterator *iterator_name*;

If you have not previously included a **using** statement to get direct access to the **string**, then you must use the **std::** prefix, of course.

std::string::iterator *iterator_name*;

For example:

```
string::iterator it;
```

or alternatively:

```
std::string::iterator it;
```

Until it is initialized, an iterator does not point to anything. Two **string** class member functions are especially useful for doing that: **begin** and **end.**

- *string_obj*.**begin()**

  Returns an iterator that refers to the first character in a string. For example:

  ```
  string my_str = "Hello";
  string::iterator it = my_str.begin();
  cout << *my_str;    // Print 'H'.
  ```

- *string_obj*.**end()**

  Returns an iterator referring to the end of the string: This is not the last character in the string, but rather one position *past* the last character. The **end** iterator is in effect an "off the edge" pointer. It should never be dereferenced.

  ```
  string my_str = "Hello";
  string::iterator it = my_str.end();
  ```

Iterators for the **string** class support most of the operations that pointers do. For example, you can get a reference to an individual character by using the "at" operator (*).

```
it = my_str.begin();
cout << *it;              // Print first character.
*it = 'A';                // Replace first character with 'A'.
```

You can also increment an iterator, causing it to point to the next character.

```
++it;
```

The following loop combines these abilities to print out every character in the string.

```
string my_str = "Hello";
string::iterator it;
for (it = my_str.begin(); it != my_str.end(); ++it) {
     cout << *it;
}
```

All this example does is print a string. The following example is more interesting. It prints a string in all-uppercase letters. (Note the use of **static_cast** to ensure that the value returned by **toupper** is printed as a character, not an integer.)

```
#include <string>
#include <cctype>    // Needed to support toupper()
using std::string;
using std::cout;
. . .
string a_msg = "I'm trying to use the phone!";
string::iterator it;
for (it = a_msg.begin(); it != a_msg.end(); ++it) {
     cout << static_cast<char>(toupper(*it));
}
```

This prints:

```
I'M TRYING TO USE THE PHONE!
```

The most interesting expression in this last example is the following:

```
it != a_msg.end()
```

```
string s("John Doe");
```

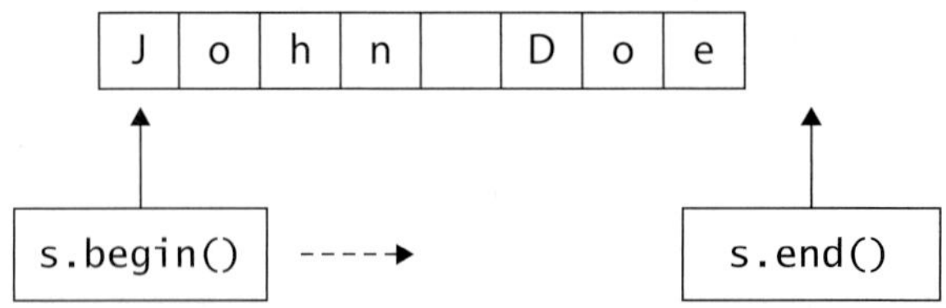

FIGURE 14.1 Forward iterators in a string object

Remember that the iterator returned by the **end** member function does not point to the last character, but one position *past* that character. That fact makes this loop work correctly.

The beauty of this approach is that you never have to worry about how many characters are in the string or how the upper bound should be set. You just compare the loop's iterator to the value returned by the **end** function. Figure 14.1 illustrates how the **begin** and **end** functions work.

Remember that the **end** function returns an "off the edge" iterator that does not point to an actual character. The value returned by **end** should only be used for comparisons.

14.6.2 Reverse Iterators

The iterators in the preceding section are designed to traverse a string from beginning to end. To scan a string in the opposite direction (starting with the last character and moving toward the beginning), you need to use a reverse iterator.

string::reverse_iterator *iterator_name*;

For example:

```
string::reverse_iterator rv_it;
```

To work with a reverse iterator, use the **rbegin** and **rend** functions.

- *string_obj*.**rbegin()**

  Returns an iterator that refers to the last character in a string. This is intended to initialize a reverse iteration through a string.

```
string my_str = "Hello";
string::reverse_iterator rv_it = my_str.rbegin();
cout << *my_str;   // Print 'o'.
```

- *string_obj*.**rend()**

  Returns an iterator referring to the "reverse end" of the string. This is one position *before* the first character.

  ```
  string my_str = "Hello";
  string::reverse_iterator rv_it = my_str.rend();
  ```

Figure 14.2 illustrates the iterators returned by **rbegin** and **rend**. These are not simply the converse of **begin** and **end**, but point to different positions altogether.

Another difference between the two kinds of iterators is that when incremented, a forward iterator moves forward through the string, but a reverse iterator moves backward. This may be a little counterintuitive at first, but it makes sense if you think about it.

```
++rv_it;     // Move one place to the LEFT!
```

A loop using a reverse iterator looks similar to the loops shown earlier for forward iterators.

```
string s = "god live no tips";
string::iterator rv_it;
for (rv_it = s.rbegin(); rv_it != s.rend(); ++rv_it) {
     cout << *rv_it;
}
```

This example prints:

```
spit on evil dog
```

14.6.3 Iterator Arithmetic

Although iterators are not exactly the same as pointers, they support many of the same operations. Iterators for the string class support adding and subtracting

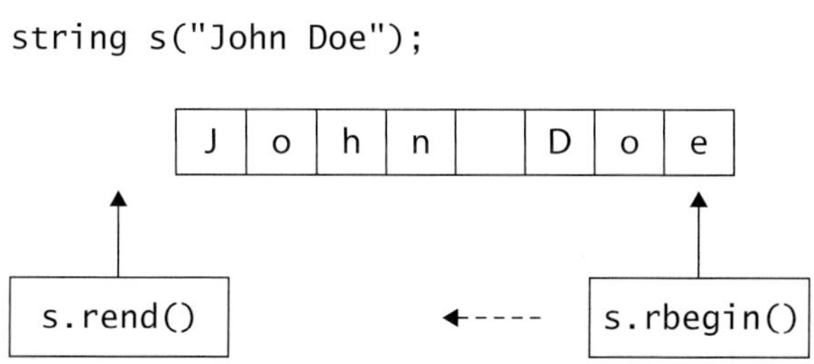

FIGURE 14.2 Reverse iterators in a string object

integers, although you should be careful about not going out of range. For example, consider the following string:

```
Elvis Aaron Presley
```

Suppose you want to print the substring starting with the seventh character, up to and including the ninth character from the end. You could do that as follows:

```
string name = "Elvis Aaron Presley";
string::iterator it;
for(it = name.begin() + 6; it < name.end() - 8; it++) {
     cout << *it;
}
```

These statements print:

```
Aaron
```

The seventh character is accessed by adding 6, not 7, because (as always in C++) positions are zero-based.

```
name.begin() + 6
```

Reverse iterators work in a similar fashion but with one critical difference: They reverse the direction, so adding a positive integer moves the iterator to the left and subtracting a positive integer moves it to the right.

14.6.4 Member Functions Using Iterators

A number of member functions have a version that employs two iterator arguments—a beginning character position and an "end" position. Remember that this end position is an "off the edge" pointer that refers to one position after the last character. The functions use text *up to but not including* the position pointed to by this iterator. For example:

```
string name = "Elvis Aaron Presley";
string s;
s.assign(name.begin() + 6, name.end());
```

These statements assign the text "Aaron Presley" to the string object s.

The following statement assigns the text "Aaron":

```
s.assign(name.begin() + 6, name.begin() + 11);
```

Brief descriptions of the member functions using iterators follow.

- *string_obj*.**append**(*begin_iter*, *end_iter*)

  Appends the contents of *string_obj* with text from *begin_iter* up to but not including the character pointed to by *end_iter*. (These iterators refer to characters in another string.)

- *string_obj*.**assign**(*begin_iter*, *end_iter*)

  Replaces the existing contents of string, if any, with text from *begin_iter* up to but not including the character pointed to by *end_iter*.

- *string_obj*.**erase**(*iter*)

  Erases the contents of *string_obj*, beginning with *iter* forward to the end of the string; *iter* is an iterator that must refer to a character within *string_obj*.

- *string_obj*.**insert**(*iter*, *ch*)

  Inserts a character *ch* at the position pointed to by *iter*; *iter* must refer to a character within *string_obj*.

- *string_obj*.**insert**(*iter*, *n*, *ch*)

  Inserts n copies of character *ch* at the position pointed to by *iter*; *iter* must refer to a character within *string_obj*.

- *string_obj*.**insert**(*iter*, *begin_iter*, *end_iter*)

  Inserts a substring at the character position pointed to by *iter* (which must refer to a character within *string_obj*). The text to be inserted consists of text from *begin_iter* up to but not including the character referred to by *end_iter*.

- *string_obj*.**replace**(*begin_iter*, *end_iter*, *string2_obj*)

  Marks text within *string_obj* for replacement: These characters consist of those from *begin_iter* up to but not including *end_iter* (these two arguments must refer to characters within *string_obj*). Those characters are replaced with the contents of *string2_obj*.

- *string_obj*.**replace** (*begin_iter*, *end_iter*, *cstr* [, *n*])

  Performs the same action as the previous version of **replace**, except that the indicated text is replaced by *cstr*, a C-string. The optional *n* argument, if included, is the maximum number of characters from *cstr* to use.

- *string_obj*.**replace** (*begin_iter*, *end_iter*, *n*, *ch*)

  Performs the same action as the previous versions of **replace**, except that the indicated text is replaced by *n* copies of character *ch*.

- *string_obj*.**replace** (*begin_iter1*, *end_iter1*, *begin_iter2*, *end_iter2*)

  Performs the same action as the previous versions of **replace**, except that the indicated text is replaced by text specified by the last two arguments: The replacement text, which may be provided by another string, consists of all characters beginning with *begin_iter2* up to but not including *end_iter2*.

14.7 Wide-Character String Class (basic_string)

The **string** class is actually a predefined adapted class that builds on the **basic_string** template of the STL (which, like string, is declared in the <string> header). The following declarations are equivalent:

```
std::string str1;
std::basic_string<char> str1;
```

To develop applications that use wide-character strings instead of 8-bit strings, you can use the **basic_string** template on the **wchar_t** type rather than **char**. For example:

```
#include <string>
#include <iostream>
using std::basic_string;
using std::wcout;

basic_string<wchar_t> wstr = L"To be or not to be.";
wcout << wstr << std::endl;
wcout << L"Position of 'be' is at: ";
wcout << wstr.find(L"be") << std::endl;
```

The preceding example demonstrates several important aspects of working with the **basic_string<wchar_t>** type. Note the following similarities and differences.

- A wide-character string declared with the **basic_string** template supports all the member functions and operators described in this chapter for the **string** type. This is because these functions are actually defined in the **basic_string** template, so they are supported no matter what type you use as the base type for **basic_string**.
- When using string literals with wide-character strings, use the "L" prefix with the literals. Otherwise, the literals will have a character width that is incompatible with **basic_string<wchar_t>**.
- When printing a wide-character string to the console, send the output to **wcout** rather than to **cin**.
- Similarly, use **wcin** to get input to be stored and operated on as a wide-character string.

CHAPTER 15

Introduction to STL (vector, deque)

When the template-creation facility was introduced into C++, it promised to save programmers a great deal of work.

Someone, of course, had to write the templates. But since the first generation or two of C++, compiler vendors have provided a Standard Template Library (STL) that takes care of many of the most common programming tasks: searching, sorting, inserting, and deleting.

Much of the STL consists of *containers,* which are collections built around a type you specify. Each of the containers—there are different kinds and each has its pros and cons—comes with many built-in capabilities.

This chapter begins with a guided tour of the container templates, providing an overview of what kinds are best used to solve what kinds of problems. It then presents the random-access containers, which can be efficiently accessed by index number.

- **vector**
- **deque** (double-ended queue)
- **bitset**

15.1 A Tour of the Container Templates

The STL is divided into two major parts: container templates and algorithm templates.

Containers are built around most any type of data you want to use—including classes and structures you write yourself—with a few restrictions. The requirements are as follows.

- Types used as base types for STL containers must support assignment and copy operations. This includes all C++ primitive types. Classes usually support these operations unless they've been disabled.

- Some STL containers—those that keep elements in a sorted order—require that the base type support the less-than comparison operator (<) according to strict weak ordering [a concept explained in Section 16.1, "Sorting Elements (Strict Weak Ordering)"].

The STL also provides generic *algorithms,* which work on containers of many types to solve a great variety of problems: For example, **find_if** finds the first element in a container fulfilling some specified condition.

The container classes can be broken down into sequence containers and associated containers, as shown in Table 15.1.

Sequence containers: The sequence containers (also called "sequential containers") provide access to elements according to position. Elements are accessed either through an index number—in the case of **vector** or **deque** objects—or sequentially. List objects can be accessed sequentially only. Order is significant: {10, 15, 20} is not the same as {20, 10, 15}.

Associated containers: The associated (or mapped) containers provide access to elements according to each element's unique *key value*—such as name or Social Security number (SSN). These containers involve more overhead than sequence containers, but given a key value, they provide fast access without having to search through the entire collection. Order is determined by key value, so the order of insertion usually makes no difference. (However, in the case of the new unordered map and set containers—supported in C++11—the internal ordering is not meaningful at all, except that items with identical keys are next to each other.)

For example, let's say you have an application that enables an end user to enter a name—such as "Brian Overland"—and get back a data record. A sequence container could be used for such a purpose and might be acceptable for tiny databases. But if

TABLE 15.1 Summary of STL Container Templates

Sequence Containers: Access by Position	Associated (Mapped) Containers: Access by Key
vector (random access)	**map**
deque (random access)	**set**
bitset (random access)	**multimap**
list	**multiset**
stack (adapted)	Unordered (hash-table) versions of the above. C++11 only.
queue (adapted)	
priority_queue (adapted)	

TABLE 15.2 Descriptions of the Major Container Templates

Container	Category	Description
vector	Sequence, random access	An array that can grow without limit. Access sequentially or by index number.
deque	Sequence, random access	Double-ended queue, which can grow efficiently at either end. Access sequentially or by index number. (Similar to vector, but you cannot assume that a deque occupies a single contiguous block of memory.)
bitset	Sequence, random access	A container of individual bit fields. Access each bit by index number.
list	Sequence	Doubly linked list. Indexing is not supported, but elements can be efficiently added and deleted in the middle of the list. This container must be accessed sequentially.
map	Associated	Access elements directly by key value, such as name or SSN. Key values must be unique.
set	Associated	Similar to **map**, but each element is its own key value. Elements must be unique.

there are thousands or millions of elements, the performance penalty is significant; the program would have to search, on average, half the list, maybe millions of records! An associated container, by contrast, provides virtual one-step access to an element by key value.

Table 15.2 summarizes the major types of containers, both sequence and associated.

15.2 Introduction to Iterators

Most of the container classes are designed to be used with *iterators*. An iterator is essentially a wrapper around a pointer. You can use an iterator to step through a collection, one element at a time. This is called *iterating* through the collection. Although there are many similarities between iterators and pointers, there are important differences.

- Iterators are a distinct type and cannot be used interchangeably with pointers.
- Each container type (such as **vector<int>**) defines its own distinct set of iterators.
- Depending on the container, some but not all pointer operations are supported for iterators. All iterators support increment, decrement, and indirection. However, only the random-access containers (such as vector) support iterator arithmetic and subscripting.

- Iterators are more sophisticated than pointers because incrementing an iterator may involve traversing a tree or linked list. All of this is handled under the covers.

Here's an example of an iterator used to step through a list container for integers, printing out each integer as it cycles from beginning to end.

```
#include <list>
#include <iostream>
using namspace std;
. . .
list<int> ilist;
// Assume ilist has been assigned values.
list<int>::iterator   iter;
for(iter = ilist.begin(); iter != ilist.end(); ++iter) {
     cout << *iter << endl;
}
```

There's another important thing to know about iterators: The **end** function returns an iterator that points one position *past* the last element, not the last element itself. This enables you to write clean, simple loop conditions such as:

```
iter != ilist.end()
```

The **end** function returns an "off the edge" position. This is easier to code than having to iterate to the last element and then perform an additional look-ahead operation on top of that. This makes for very clean for-loop code.

15.3 The vector Template

A vector is an array that can grow virtually without limit. Elements in a vector can be accessed by index number, and (unlike other containers) a vector guarantees that all the members are always next to each other in memory. Figure 15.1 illustrates the layout of a vector.

Note

The **vector** template has long supported a specialization, **vector<bool>**, which packs Boolean values into single bits, as does the Pack_bool example at the end of Chapter 7, "Classes and Objects." However, this specialized use of **vector<bool>** has been deprecated by C++ standards committees in recent years, so use it at your own risk.

Vectors hide certain details of memory management: When needed, a vector will request a new memory block and move its data there. You can use ordinary pointers with a vector, but any operation that changes the size of a vector potentially invalidates such pointers.

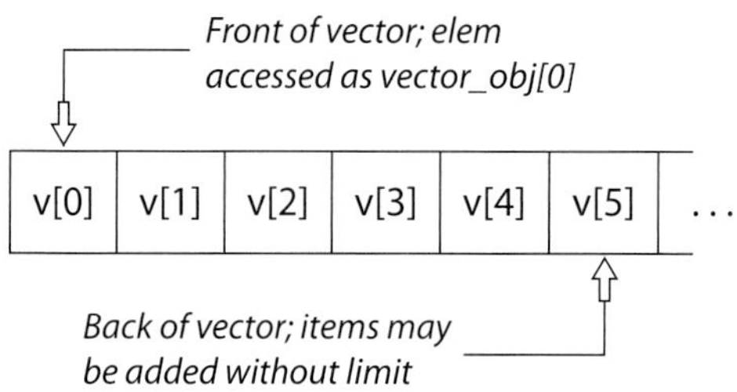

FIGURE 15.1 The vector template

Vector member functions support insertion and deletion, with the **insert** and **erase** functions, respectively. The vector responds by adjusting the elements so that they always remain in contiguous order in memory. For example, suppose a vector contains the values 10, 20, 30, 40, and 50; and a new element, -5, is inserted into the second position. As Figure 15.2 illustrates, the last four elements are moved over by one position and then the value -5 is copied.

Such operations, while convenient (remember that the vector handles all the details for you), do impact performance in the case of very large vectors.

Once you create a vector, you'll want to add elements to it. One way to do that is to use the **push_back** member function, which adds elements to the end (that is, the "back").

```
#include <vector>
using std::vector;
. . .
vector<int>  iVec;
iVec.push_back(10);
iVec.push_back(20);
iVec.push_back(30);
iVec.push_back(40);
```

These statements create a vector containing 10, 20, 30, and 40, in that order.

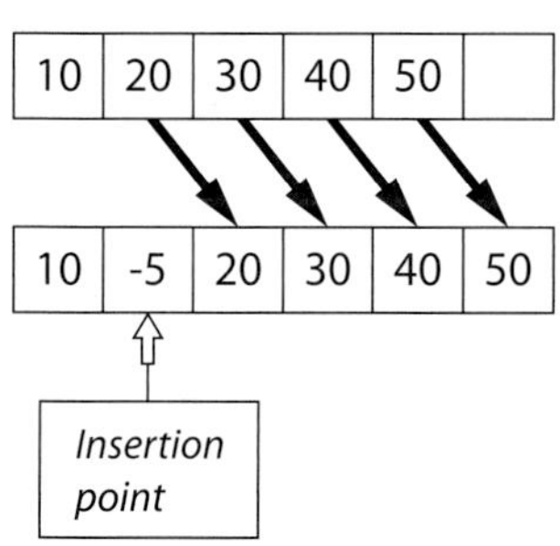

FIGURE 15.2 Inserting an element into a vector

The C++11 specification enables you to initialize vectors much more efficiently, as described in Section 15.3.3, "List Initialization (C++11)." But if your compiler lacks this support, you can initialize a vector most efficiently from an array:

```
int arr[4] = {10, 20, 30, 40}
vector<int> vec(arr, arr + 4);
```

15.3.1 Vector Iterators

The syntax for declaring an iterator for a vector of the desired base type is:

vector<*type*>::iterator *var_name*;

As with most of the containers supported by the STL (except for adapted containers), vector iterators can be used with **begin** and **end** to step through the container. For example, the following statements print out the contents of iVec, a vector created earlier:

```
vector<int>::iterator  iter;

for(iter = iVec.begin(); iter != iVec.end(); ++iter) {
     cout << *iter << " ";
}
```

You can increment (++) and decrement (--) iterators for a vector. You can also add and subtract integer values, performing *iterator arithmetic*. For example, the following expression points to the element three positions past the first element (in other words, it points to the fourth element):

```
iVec.begin() + 3
```

The comparison operators <, >, <=, and >= also work on iterators for vectors, something you cannot do with the iterators of most other containers.

```
if (iter1 < iter2) {
     cout << "iter1 refers to a position lower in ";
     cout << "memory than iter2's position." >> endl;
}
```

Figure 15.3 shows how iterators work within a vector. This is also how they work within other container classes, although the underlying implementation of the container may differ.

The **vector** template also supports reverse iterators. Reverse iterators have a symmetrical relationship to ordinary iterators. The **rbegin** function returns an iterator

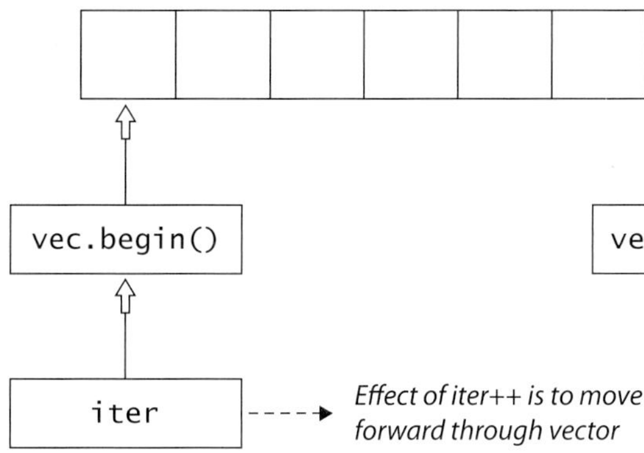

FIGURE 15.3 Iterators within a vector

pointing to the last element, and **rend** returns an iterator pointing to one position *before* the first element. (Figure 15.4 illustrates this behavior, which may seem peculiar.)

When you increment (++) a reverse iterator, it moves backward through the list rather than forward. The meaning of the decrement operator (--) is also reversed.

The following statements print out the contents of an integer vector in reverse order:

```
vector<int>::reverse_iterator  ri;

for(ri = vec.rbegin(); ri != vec.rend(); ++ri) {
     cout << *ri << " ";
}
```

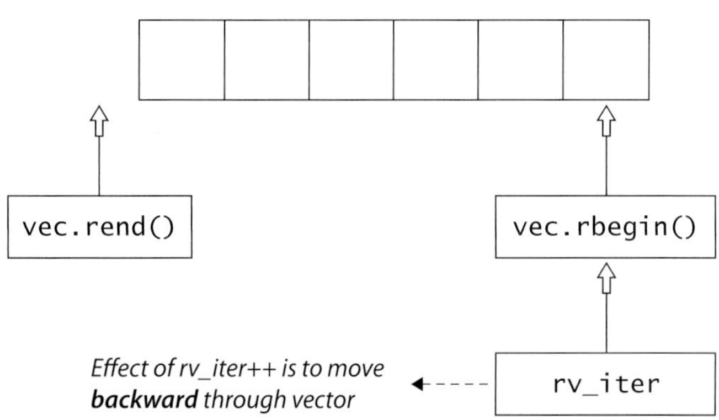

FIGURE 15.4 Reverse iterators within a vector

Insertions and deletions—as illustrated earlier in Figure 15.2—have a destabilizing effect on a vector, even though the result is guaranteed to keep all elements next to each other in memory and in the same order they were before. But after an insertion or deletion, iterators, pointers to elements, and references to elements may become invalidated.

The vector template, along with most containers, also supports the **const_iterator** and **const_reverse_iterator** types. These iterators can be used to get element values but not modify them. One of the advantages of these types is that they can be used by **const** member functions.

```
vector<int>::const_iterator c_it;
for(c_it = ilist.begin(); c_it != ilist.end(); ++c_it) {
     cout << *c_it << endl;
}
```

Note that you can't do the following:

```
*c_it = 0;    // ERROR! Iterator is const.
```

15.3.2 Vector Constructors

To create a vector, remember to first include the <vector> header; also include the **using** statement unless you're willing to refer to the name **vector** as **std::vector**.

```
#include <vector>
using std::vector;
```

Descriptions of the vector constructors follow.

- **vector**<*type*> *name*

  Creates a vector with the specified *name*, for the specified base *type*. The vector is initially empty. For example, the following statements create a vector of string objects and a vector of short integers, both of which are empty.

  ```
  vector<string>  my_strings;  // Create a string vector.
  vector<short>   my_shorts;   // Create a short vector.
  ```

- **vector**<*type*> *name*(*n*, *value*)

  Creates a vector with the specified *name* and base *type*, initializing it with n copies of the *value* (in which *n* is a non-negative integer); *value* is a data item that is compatible with the base type, either matching it or having a type that can be converted.

  ```
  vector<double>  xvec(5, 1.5); // Init with 5 copies of 1.5
  vector<string>  sv(3, "Hi");  // Init with 3 copies of "Hi"
  ```

- **vector**<*type*> *name*(*first_iter*, *last_iter*)

  Creates a vector with the specified *name* and base *type*, initializing from a range identified by *first_iter* and *last_iter*. The *first_iter* argument is an iterator (or pointer) pointing to the first item to copy, and *last_iter* points to one position past the last element to copy.

  This makes possible efficient initialization from any container—including a standard C++ array, because you can use pointers like iterators in this case. If your compiler is not C++11 compliant, this is often the most convenient way to initialize a container:

  ```
  string arr[4] = ("John", "Paul", "George", "Ringo" };
  vector<string> beatVec(arr, arr + 4);
  ```

15.3.3 List Initialization (C++11)

The C++11 specification provides a superior way to initialize elements of a container. (Note: As of this writing, not all new compilers implement this feature yet.) During its declaration, you can use an aggregate to initialize a vector or other container. An aggregate is a list of values enclosed in curly braces ({}), separated by commas if there is more than one:

```
{ init_value [, init_value]… }
```

With C++11, you can initialize a vector as easily as you can a standard array:

```
vector<int>  my_ints = { 5, 3, -83, 101, -1, 20 };
```

Assuming a Point class has been declared, and that this class has a Point(double, double) constructor, you could initialize a Point vector as follows:

```
vector<Point>  pt_vec = {
     Point(1.0, 3.5), Point(1, 0), Point(1, 3.141592)
};
```

15.3.4 Concise Summary of Vector Functions

The vector template provides a fairly large collection of member functions. Table 15.3 summarizes the most essential, commonly used functions. Section 15.3.5, "Vector Member Functions in Detail," describes these along with the remaining member functions.

All of these functions maintain the ordering within the vector. If elements are inserted or removed from the middle, adjustments are made so that the rest of the content is unchanged.

TABLE 15.3 Commonly Used Functions of the vector Template

Member Function	Description
push_back	Adds a new element to the end of the vector.
size	Returns the number of elements currently in the vector.
begin, end	Return starting and ending iterators for standard, forward iteration.
rbegin, rend	Return starting and ending iterators for reverse iteration.
at	Performs same operation as [ ], but throws an out_of_range exception if the index is bad.
erase	Removes one or more elements from any position in the vector.
insert	Inserts one or more new elements at any position in the vector.
resize	Truncates or extends the vector.

15.3.5 Vector Member Functions in Detail

Before using the **vector** template or its member functions, remember to include the <vector> header. The name **vector** is part of the **std** namespace, so either employ a **using** statement or refer to vector by its **std::** prefix.

```
#include <vector>
using std::vector;
```

The examples in this section also assume direct access to the names **cout**, **endl**, and **string**:

```
#include <string>
using std::cout;
using std::endl;
using std::string;
```

Descriptions of the member functions for the template follow.

- *vector_obj*.**assign(***n*, *value***)**

  Replaces existing contents, if any, with *n* copies of *value*, a data item that has the same base type as *vector_obj* or can be converted to that type. This function is similar to the constructor that takes *n* and *elem* as arguments. The function has no return value.

```
vector<string>  strVec(1, "hi");
strVec.assign(10, "is");  // Assign 10 copies of
                          //   "is", replacing old
                          //    contents.
```

- *vector_obj*.**assign(***first_iter*, *last_iter***)**

  Replaces existing contents, if any, with content copied from another container. The arguments *first_iter* and *last_iter* are iterators or (in the case of standard arrays) pointers. Elements are copied beginning with the element pointed to by *first_iter*, up to but not including the element pointed to by *last_iter*. The function returns no value.

```
string clowns[3] = { "Moe", "Larry", "Curly" };
vector<string>  clownVec;
clownVec.assign(clowns, clowns + 3);
```

- *vector_obj*.**at(***pos***)**

  Performs essentially the same function as the subscript operator, [], returning a reference to the element at index number *pos* (in which this index is zero-based). The difference is that this function throws an **out_of_range** exception if *pos* is not a valid index.

```
string clowns[] = { "Moe", "Larry", "Curly" };
vector<string>  clownVec(clowns, clowns+3);
// Print out all elements.
for (unsigned i = 0; i < clownVec.size(); ++i) {
     cout << clownVec.at(i) << " " << endl;
}
```

- *vector_obj*.**back()**

  Returns the value of the last element.

```
string clowns[] = { "Moe", "Larry", "Curly" };
vector<string>  clownVec(clowns, clowns + 3);

cout << clownVec.back();  // Print "Curly".
```

- *vector_obj*.**begin()**

  Returns an iterator pointing to the first element in the vector.

```
vector<string>::iterator  it;
for(it = clownVec.begin; it != clownVec.end();
 ++it) {
     cout << *it << endl;  // Print all elements.
}
```

- *vector_obj*.**capacity()**

  Returns the current capacity of the vector in number of elements: This number should not be confused with the ultimate physical capacity of the vector, which is many times larger. (Most applications can regard physical capacity as unlimited.) Nor should capacity be confused with size, which is the number of elements the vector currently holds.

When current capacity is exceeded, new memory is allocated. However, because such operations do take some time, you may want to reserve a large block of memory if you are going to be doing many operations that add an element. See the **reserve** function.

```
cout << "Current capacity for iVec is: ";
cout << iVec.capacity();
```

- *`vector_obj`*`.`**`clear()`**

Removes all the contents of the vector, leaving it empty (and therefore with a size of 0).

```
xVec.clear();
```

- *`vector_obj`*`.`**`empty()`**

Returns **true** if the vector currently holds no elements; returns **false** otherwise.

```
if (xVec.empty()) {
     cout << "xVec is empty." << endl;
}
```

- *`vector_obj`*`.`**`end()`**

Returns an iterator pointing one position past the last element in the vector. See the **begin** function for an example.

- *`vector_obj`*`.`**`erase(`***`pos_iter`***`)`**

Removes the element at the position pointed to by *pos_iter*, an iterator, and adjusts the vector accordingly. This function returns an iterator pointing to the element that would have been next (after *pos_iter*). For example:

```
string clowns[] = { "Moe", "Larry", "Curly" };
vector<string>  clownVec(clowns, clowns + 3);
// Get rid of Curly!
clownVec.erase(clownVec.begin() + 2);
```

This next example demonstrates a loop that removes *all* negative elements in the integer vector my_int. In this case, the value returned by **erase** is used to keep iterating to the next element. For clarity, I have put the call to **erase** in bold.

```
int arr[5] = {10, -104, 20, -555, 30 };
vector<int> my_ints(arr, arr + 5);
vector<int>::iterator it;
for (it = my_ints.begin(); it != my_ints.end();){
     if (*iter < 0) {               // If item < 0,
         it = my_ints.erase(it);   // Erase it.
     } else {
         ++it;
     }
}
```

- *vector_obj*.**erase(*first_iter*, *last_iter*)**

  Removes the elements in the indicated range and adjusts the vector accordingly. Elements are erased beginning with the element pointed to by *first_iter*, up to but not including the element one position past *last_iter*.

```
string clowns[] = { "Moe", "Larry", "Curly" };
vector<string>  clownVec(clowns, clowns + 3);
vector<string>::iterator itiot=clownVec.begin();
// Get rid of Moe and Larry!
clownVec.erase(itiot, itiot + 2);
```

- *vector_obj*.**front()**

  Returns the value of the first element.

```
string clowns[] = { "Moe", "Larry", "Curly" };
vector<string>  clownVec(clowns, clowns + 3);
cout << "Hey ";
cout << clownVec.front() << "!" << endl;
```

  This prints:

```
Hey Moe!
```

- *vector_obj*.**insert(*pos_iter*, *value*)**

  Inserts the specified value just in front of the element pointed to by *pos_iter* and returns an iterator pointing to the new item.

```
int dat[] = {10, 20, 30, 40, 50};
vector<int>  iVec(dat, dat + 5);
iVec.insert(iVec.begin() + 2, -1);
```

  This example initializes a vector with the values 10, 20, 30, 40, 50 and then inserts the value -1 at the third position, (iVec.begin() + 2). If the vector is then printed out, the values are:

```
10 20 -1 30 40 50
```

- *vector_obj*.**insert(*pos_iter*, *n*, *value*)**

  Inserts *n* copies of the specified value at *pos_iter*, an iterator pointing to a position within *vector_obj*. For example, the following statements insert the three values -1, -1, -1 beginning at the third position, iVec.begin() + 2.

```
int dat[] = {10, 20, 30, 40, 50};
vector<int>  iVec(dat, dat + 5);
iVec.insert(iVec.begin() + 2, 3, -1);
```

  If the vector is printed out, the values are (in this order):

```
10 20 -1 -1 -1 30 40 50
```

- *vector_obj*.**insert(*pos_iter*, *first_iter*, *last_iter*)**

  Inserts the specified range of elements just before the item pointed to by *pos_iter*, an iterator of *vector_obj*. Values are copied beginning with the element pointed to by *first_iter*, up to but not including the element pointed to by *last_iter*.

```
string rockers[3] = {"Mick", "Keith", "Hendrix"};
string beats[4] =
     {"John", "Paul", "George", "Ringo"};
vector<string>  beatVec(beats, beats + 4);
beatVec.insert(
   beatVec.begin() + 1, rockers, rockers + 3)
);
for (unsigned i = 0; i < beatVec.size(); ++i) {
     cout << beatVec[i] << endl;
}
```

  This example inserts the contents of the array rockers into beatVec, starting at the vector's second position, beatVec.begin() + 1, and then prints the updated contents:

```
John
Mick
Keith
Hendrix
Paul
George
Ringo
```

  If the *pos_iter* argument is *vector_obj*.**end**(), the new elements are added to the end of the vector; this concatenates the contents of one vector onto another.

- *vector_obj*.**max_size()**

  Returns the largest number of elements the vector can physically grow to. With modern computers, this number typically runs in the thousands of millions. (Note: If you need an even larger container, you may need to use a deque instead.)

- *vector_obj*.**pop_back()**

  Removes the last element of the vector.

```
string clowns[3] = { "Moe", "Larry", "Curly" };
vector<string>  clownVec(clowns, clowns + 3);
// Get rid of Curly!
clownVec.pop_back();
```

- *vector_obj*.**push_back(*elem*)**

  Adds the specified element value (*elem*) onto the end of the vector (so the new element is in the last position). For example, the following code adds John, Paul, George, and Ringo to a vector, beatVec, built on the **string** class:

```
vector<string>  beatVec;
beatVec.push_back("John");
beatVec.push_back("Paul");
beatVec.push_back("George");
beatVec.push_back("Ringo");
```

- *vector_obj*.**rbegin()**

  Returns an iterator pointing to the last element in the vector. This function is used in conjunction with the **rend** function, to iterate backward. Note that incrementing an iterator declared as **reverse_iterator** moves it one position backward, not forward. The following loop prints the strings in beatVec (initialized in the preceding example) but in reverse order:

```
vector<string>::reverse_iterator  r;
for(r = beat_vec.rbegin(); r != beat_vec.rend();
 ++r) {
     cout << *ri << endl;
}
```

  This prints out:

```
Ringo
George
Paul
John
```

- *vector_obj*.**rend()**

  Returns a reverse iterator pointing one position *before* the first element in the vector. See **rbegin** for an example.

- *vector_obj*.**reserve(*n*)**

  Reserves enough capacity to hold *n* elements. Although vectors can grow almost without limit (see **max_size**), only a certain amount of capacity is reserved for the vector at any given time. When the vector grows beyond this capacity, new memory is allocated and the contents may be moved to a new address. This process is automatic.

  The only problem is that if you're going to do a large number of operations that grow the array, the process of allocating memory may have to be done many times, which can impact performance. In those cases, you might consider reserving capacity ahead of time.

  The following statements create a vector containing ten million (!) integers. To increase program performance, enough space is reserved for all the elements before any are added.

```
#include <vector>
#include <ctime>
using namespace std;
#define BIG_NUM 10000000
```

```
. . .
long x1 = clock();          // Get time now.
vector<int>  big_vector;
big_vector.reserve(BIG_NUM);
for(int i = 0; i < BIG_NUM; i++) {
     big_vector.push_back(i);
}
long x2 = clock();          // Get time again.

cout << "Time passed in clocks: " << x2 – x1;
cout << endl;
```

As explained in Section 12.3.1, "Date and Time Functions," the **clock** function returns the number of system clock ticks since the program began running; there are usually about 1,000 clock ticks per second.

If you run this code you should find, as I have, that the use of the **reserve** function improves runtime performance, though only marginally.

- *vector_obj*.**resize(***n* [, *value*]**)**

Truncates or extends the vector so that it ends up having *n* elements. If *n* is less than the current size of the vector, elements are removed from the end. If *n* is greater than the current size of the vector, elements are added to the end.

The optional *value* argument, if included, specifies the value to add to the end of the array if *n* is larger than the current size. If *value* is omitted and the array needs to grow, then (if the base type is a class) the type's default constructor is called to initialize each element.

The following example creates a vector containing floating-point values 7.5, 2.5, and 3.5, and then grows the array by adding two instances of -12.1 to the end of the array.

```
vector<double>  xvec;
xvec.push_back(7.5);
xvec.push_back(2.5);
xvec.push_back(3.5);
xvec.resize(5, -12.1);
```

- *vector_obj*.**size()**

Returns the number of elements currently contained in the vector. The following example employs the **size** member function to determine how many elements to print.

```
for (unsigned i = 0; i < iVec.size(); ++i) {
     cout << iVec[i] << " ";
}
```

▸ *vector_obj*.**swap(***vector_obj2***)**

Exchanges the contents of two vector objects sharing the same base type.

```
#include <vector>
#include <string>
using namespace std;
. . .
string rockers[4] =
     {"Mick", "Keith", "Dylan", "Cobain"};
vector<string>  rockersVec(rockers, rockers + 4);
string beats[4] =
     {"John", "Paul", "George", "Ringo"};
vector<string>  beatVec(beats, beats + 4);

beatVec.swap(rockersVec);
```

After the call to swap, beatVec will contain Mick, Keith, Dylan, and Cobain, while rockersVec will contain John, Paul, George, and Ringo.

15.4 The deque Template

After vectors, a deque (pronounced "deck") is the container type most similar to a standard array. Like a vector, a deque provides random access and therefore supports indexing.

A deque, or double-ended queue, has one obvious advantage over a vector. Elements can be efficiently added to the front of a deque *or* to the back, whereas adding a new element to the end of a vector is efficient but insertion at the front is not. Also—depending on the platform—the ultimate physical size of a deque is sometimes much larger than a vector.

But when using a deque, you cannot assume the elements are next to each other in physical memory. A deque is stored internally as a series of memory blocks. This is an implementation detail invisible to the user of the deque and you can mostly ignore it. But it means that it's a serious mistake to use pointer operations that treat the deque as a single block.

For example, the first loop shown in the following example is safe while the second loop will blow up any program foolish enough to try it.

```
#include <deque>
using std::deque;
. . .
deque<int> dq(10, 0);   // Init with 10 copies of 0.
```

```
for (int i = 0; i < dq.size(); ++i) {
     dq[i] = 1;    // This is the right way!
}
int *addr = &(dq[0]);
int *p = addr;
while(p < addr + dq.size()) {
    *p++ = 1;     // ERROR! NEVER perform this on a deque!
}                 // (This is OK with a vector, tho.)
```

Conceptually, you can think of a deque as having the logical structure illustrated in Figure 15.5.

This logical structure is not so different from that of a vector, except that it implies that insertions can be made to the front of the container more efficiently. Otherwise—aside from issues relating to internal structure and performance—a deque is functionally similar to a vector, differing in having two extra member functions (**push_front**, **pop_front**) and lacking two functions (**reserve**, **capacity**) specific to vectors.

As with a vector or array, a deque maintains index numbers with 0 always referring to the first element, no matter how many insertions and deletions are made or where they are made.

Figure 15.6 illustrates the internal (physical) structure of a deque. This particular deque extends across three memory blocks; but as it grows larger, more memory blocks are automatically allocated for it.

This internal organization makes iteration through a deque slightly slower. On the other hand, some systems accommodate a larger ultimate size for deques than for vectors, because they impose a limitation—usually many megabytes—on the size of a single block of data; but a deque can be made up of multiple blocks. Therefore, the ultimate physical limit on the size of a deque may be many times larger.

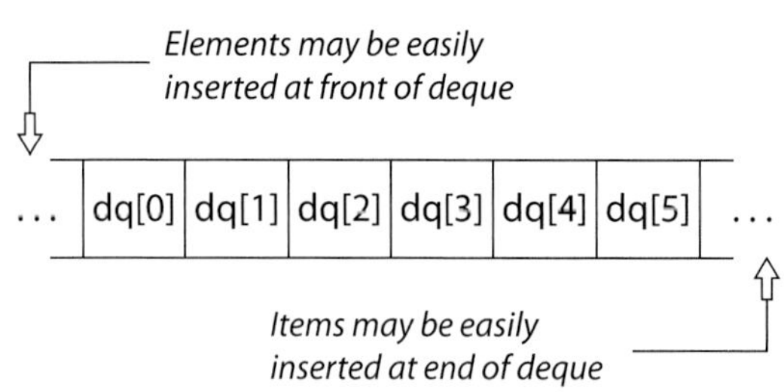

FIGURE 15.5 The deque (double-ended queue) template

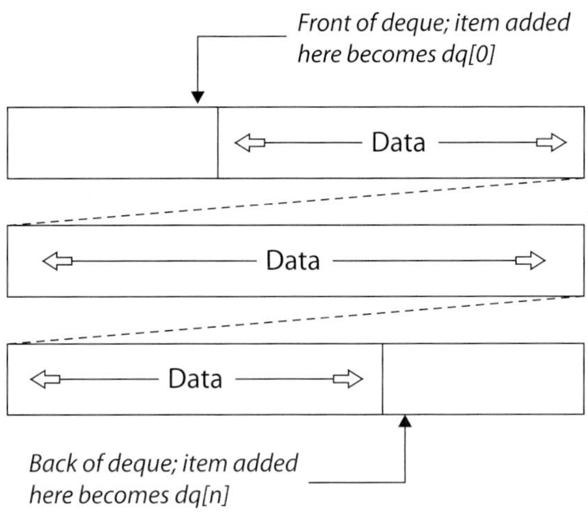

FIGURE 15.6 Physical structure of a deque

Because of this internal structure, insertions and deletions at the front and back are particularly efficient, but insertions and deletions in the middle are inefficient even in comparison to vectors.

15.4.1 Deque Iterators

Whereas iterators for vectors are little more than wrappers around pointers, iterators for deques are smarter. They navigate a deque's internal storage, hiding the details. At the same time, deque iterators support all the operations that vector iterators do, including iterator arithmetic and comparisons. It's safe to add an integer to a deque iterator (as long as you stay within range), though not to a raw pointer containing the address of a deque element.

The syntax for declaring a deque iterator is:

deque<*type*>**::iterator** *name*;

As with other containers, you can iterate through the deque by using the **begin** and **end** functions.

```
#include <deque>
#include <iostream>
using std::deque;
. . .
int arr[5] = {1, 100, 20, 50, 25 };
deque<int> dq(arr, arr + 5);     // Init from array.
deque<int>::iterator it;
```

```
for (it = dq.begin(); it != dq.end(); ++it) {
     cout << *iter << " ";        // Print elements.
}
```

You can use iterator arithmetic on deque iterators just as you can with iterators in a vector. For example, the following iterator, it, points four positions to the right of the beginning—in this case, to the fifth element:

```
deque<int>::iterator it = dq.begin() + 4;
```

This iterator can be used to initialize a second container. For example, the following declaration initializes the container another_dq from the first four members of dq.

```
deque<int>  another_dq(dq.begin(), it);
```

Like most containers, deques support **reverse_iterator**, **const_iterator**, and **const_reverse_iterator** as well as **iterator**.

15.4.2 Deque Constructors

To declare a deque, remember to first include the <deque> header. The name **deque** is part of the **std** namespace, so either employ a **using** statement or refer to deque with its **std::** prefix.

```
#include <deque>
using std::deque;
```

The C++11 specification lets you initialize a deque container (and other kinds of containers) by using an aggregate. This is by far the most convenient technique. For example:

```
deque<int>  iDeq = {10, 20, 30, -25, -50, 17 };
```

If your compiler is not C++11 compliant, you can use one of the constructors described in this section. These constructors are similar to the ones supported for vectors.

- **deque**<*type*> *name*

  Creates a deque container with the specified *name*, for the specified base *type*. The deque is initially empty. For example, the following statements create a deque container for string objects and another for short integers, both of which are empty.

  ```
  deque<string>  strDeq;     // Make a string deque.
  deque<short>   shortDeq;   // Make a short deque.
  ```

  You can then add values using the **push_back** member function. For example:

  ```
  strDeq.push_back("hi");       // Add "hi".
  strDeq.push_back("there");    // Add "there".
  ```

- **deque<*type*>** *name*(*n*, *value*)

  Creates a deque container with the specified *name* and base *type*, initializing it with *n* copies of *value* (in which *n* is a non-negative integer); *value* is a data item that is compatible with the base type, either matching it or having a type that can be converted.

```
deque<double> xDeq(5, 1.5);    // 5 copies of 1.5
deque<string> sDeq(3, "Hi");   // 3 copies of "Hi"
```

- **deque<*type*>** *name*(*first_iter*, *last_iter*)

  Creates a deque container with the specified *name* and base *type*, initializing it from another container. Values are copied beginning with the element pointed to by *first_iter*, up to but not including the element pointed to by *last_iter*.

  This makes possible efficient initialization from any container—including a standard C++ array. If your compiler is not compliant with the C++11 specification, this is often the most convenient way to initialize a container:

```
string a[4] =("John", "Paul", "George", "Ringo");
deque<string> beatDeq(a, a + 4);
```

15.4.3 Concise Summary of Deque Functions

As shown in Table 15.4, the deque template supports nearly the same set of functions that the vector template does, with some differences. Deque containers do not support the **capacity** or **reserve** functions, because they do not place all data into a single memory block. (Memory management for a deque is invisible to the user.)

TABLE 15.4 Commonly Used Functions of the deque Template

Member Function	Description
push_back, **pop_back**	Insert and remove elements from the back of the deque.
push_front, **pop_front**	Insert and remove elements from the front of the deque.
size	Returns the number of elements currently in the deque.
begin, **end**	Return starting and ending iterators for standard, forward iteration.
rbegin, **rend**	Return starting and ending iterators for reverse iteration.
at	Performs the same operation as [ ], but throws an **out_of_range** exception if the index is bad.
erase	Removes one or more elements from any position in the deque.
insert	Inserts one or more new elements at any position in the deque. This function can also be used to concatenate the contents of another container onto the end of the deque.
resize	Truncates or extends the deque.

However, deque containers contain functions for accessing and removing both ends of the data, front and back.

All of these functions—notably **erase** and **insert**—maintain the integrity of ordering within the deque. If elements are inserted or removed from the middle, these functions make adjustments so that the rest of the content is unchanged, and the elements are maintained in contiguous order: That is to say, they are next to each other in memory.

15.4.4 Deque Functions in Detail

Before using the **deque** template or its member functions, remember to include the <deque> header. The name **deque** is part of the **std** namespace, so either employ a **using** statement or refer to deque with its **std::** prefix.

```
#include <deque>
using std::deque;
```

The examples in this section also assume direct access to the names **cout**, **endl**, and **string**:

```
#include <string>
using std::cout;
using std::endl;
using std::string;
```

Descriptions of the member functions for the template follow.

- *deque_obj*.**assign**(*n*, *value*)

  Replaces existing contents, if any, with *n* copies of *value*, a data item that has the same base type as *deque_obj* or can be converted to that type.

  ```
  deque<string>  strDeq(1, "hi");
  // Assign 10 copies of "is", replace old contents
  strDeq.assign(10, "is");
  ```

- *deque_obj*.**assign**(*first_iter*, *last_iter*)

  Replaces existing contents, if any, with the specified range. Elements are copied beginning with the element pointed to by *first_iter*, up to but not including the element pointed to by *last_iter*.

  ```
  string clowns[] = { "Moe", "Larry", "Curly" };
  deque<string>  clownDeq;
  clownDeq.assign(clowns, clowns + 3);
  ```

- *deque_obj*.**at**(*pos*)

  Performs essentially the same function as the subscript operator, [], returning a reference to the element at zero-based index *pos*. The difference is that this function throws an **out_of_range** exception if *pos* is not a valid index.

```
string clowns[] = { "Moe", "Larry", "Curly" };
deque<string>  clownDeq(clowns, clowns + 3);
// Print all clowns.
for (unsigned i = 0; i < clownDeq.size(); ++i) {
     cout << clownDeq.at(i) << endl;
}
```

- *deque_obj*.**back**()

  Returns the value of the last element in the deque.

```
string clowns[] = { "Moe", "Larry", "Curly" };
deque<string>  clownDeq(clowns, clowns + 3);
cout << clownDeq.back();  // Print "Curly".
```

- *deque_obj*.**begin**()

  Returns an iterator pointing to the first element in the deque. The following example calls this function as part of a for loop that prints out all the elements.

```
string clowns[] = { "Moe", "Larry", "Curly" };
deque<string>  clownDeq(clowns, clowns + 3);
deque<string>::iterator  it;
for(it = clownDeq.begin; it != clownDeq.end();
  ++it) {
     cout << *it << endl;
}
```

- *deque_obj*.**clear**()

  Removes all elements from the deque, leaving it empty.

```
aDeque.clear();
```

- *deque_obj*.**empty**()

  Returns **true** if the deque is empty; returns **false** otherwise. See **pop_back** for an example.

- *deque_obj*.**end**()

  Returns an iterator pointing *one position past* the last element in the deque. This function is frequently used with the **begin** function, to iterate forward through the list. See **begin**.

- *deque_obj*.**erase**(*pos_iter*)

  Removes the element pointed to by *pos_iter*. Returns an iterator pointing to the element that would have been next (after *pos_iter*).

```
string clowns[] = { "Moe", "Larry", "Curly" };
deque<string>  clownDeq(clowns, clowns + 3);
// Get rid of Moe!
clownDeq.erase(clownDeq.begin());
```

You can use the return value of **erase** to help process an entire deque. For example, the following loop removes all elements whose string length is greater than 3.

```
deque<string>::iterator it = clownDeq.begin();
while(it != clownDeq.end()){
     if((*it).size() > 3) {
          it = clownDeq.erase(it);
     } else {
          ++it;
     }
}
```

- *deque_obj*.**erase(***first_iter*, *last_iter***)**

  Removes the elements in the indicated interval, returning an iterator pointing to the element that would have been next (after the last element within this interval). The interval to be erased begins with the element pointed to by *first_iter*, up to but not including the element pointed to by *last_iter*.

```
string clowns[] = { "Moe", "Larry", "Curly" };
deque<string>  clownDeq(clowns, clowns + 3);
deque<string>::iterator itiot = clownDeq.begin();
// Get rid of Moe and Larry!
clownDeq.erase(itiot, itiot + 2);
```

- *deque_obj*.**front()**

  Returns the value of the first element.

```
string clowns[] = { "Moe", "Larry", "Curly" };
deque<string>  clownDeq(clowns, clowns + 3);
cout << "Hey ";
cout << clownDeq.front() << "!" << endl;
```

This prints:

```
Hey Moe!
```

- *deque_obj*.**insert(***pos_iter*, *value***)**

  Inserts the specified value just before the element pointed to by *pos_iter*.

```
int dat[] = {10, 20, 30, 40, 50};
deque<int>  my_ints(dat, dat + 5);
my_ints.insert(my_ints.begin() + 2, -1);
```

This example initializes a deque with the values 10, 20, 30, 40, 50 and then inserts the value -1 at the third position. If the deque is printed out, the values are:

```
10 20 -1 30 40 50
```

- *deque_obj*.**insert**(*pos_iter*, *n*, *value*)

  Inserts *n* copies of *value* just before the position pointed to by *pos_iter*. For example, the following statements insert the three values -1, -1, -1 beginning at the third position.

```
int dat[] = {10, 20, 30, 40, 50};
deque<int>  my_ints(dat, dat+5);
my_ints.insert(my_ints.begin() + 2, 3, -1);
```

  If the deque is printed out, the values are (in this order):

```
10 20 -1 -1 -1 30 40 50
```

- *deque_obj*.**insert**(*pos_iter*, *first_iter*, *last_iter*)

  Inserts the specified range of elements just before the position pointed to by *pos_iter*. Elements are copied beginning with the element pointed to by *first_iter*, up to but not including the element pointed to by *last_iter*. In the following example, the call to the **insert** function is shown in bold.

```
#include <deque>
#include <string>
using namespace std;
. . .
string rockers[3] = {"Mick", "Keith", "Hendrix"};
string beats[4] =
     {"John", "Paul", "George", "Ringo"};
deque<string>  beatDeq(beats, beats + 4);
beatDeq.insert(
     beatDeq.begin() + 1, rockers, rockers + 3
);
for (unsigned i = 0; i < beatDeq.size(); ++i) {
     cout << beatDeq[i] << endl;
}
```

  This example inserts the contents of the string array, rockers, into beatDeq, starting at the deque's second position, (beatDeq.begin() + 1). The example then prints:

```
John
Mick
Keith
Hendrix
Paul
George
Ringo
```

  Note that if the *pos_iter* argument is *deque_obj*.**end**(), the new elements are added to the end; this concatenates one container onto the end of another. For example:

```
beat_dq.insert(beat_dq.end(), rockers, rockers + 3);
```

- *deque_obj*.**max_size()**

  Returns the largest possible physical size the deque can grow to. With modern computers, this number typically runs in the thousands of millions.

- *deque_obj*.**pop_front()**

  Removes the first element (index position 0) from the deque.

- *deque_obj*.**pop_back()**

  Removes the last element of the deque. For example, the following statements print the elements of clownDeq, one at a time, while also emptying the deque. (This prints them in reverse order, as they would be from a stack data structure.)

```
string clowns[4] =
     { "Moe", "Larry", "Curly", "Shemp"};
deque<string>  clownDeq(clowns, clowns + 4);
while (!clownDeq.empty()) {
     cout << clownDeq.back() << endl;
     clownDeq.pop_back();
}
```

- *deque_obj*.**push_front(*elem*)**

  Inserts a new element to the front of the deque. For example, the following statement inserts a new member, Pete Best, at the first position of beatDeq:

```
beatDeq.push_front("Pete Best");
```

- *deque_obj*.**push_back(*elem*)**

  Inserts a new element at the end (last position) of the deque. For example, the following code adds John, Paul, George, and Ringo to a deque, in that order.

```
deque<string>  beatDeq;
beatDeq.push_back("John");
beatDeq.push_back("Paul");
beatDeq.push_back("George");
beatDeq.push_back("Ringo");
```

- *deque_obj*.**rbegin()**

  Returns an iterator pointing to the last element in the deque. This function is used in conjunction with the **rend** function, to iterate backward through the container. Note that incrementing an iterator declared as **reverse_iterator** moves it one position backward, not forward, through the deque. The following loop prints the strings in beatDeq (initialized in the preceding example), but in reverse order:

```
deque<string>::reverse_iterator  ri;
for(ri = beatDeq.rbegin(); ri != beatDeq.rend();
  ++ri) {
     cout << *ri << endl;
}
```

This prints out:

```
Ringo
George
Paul
John
```

- *deque_obj*.**rend()**

  Returns a reverse iterator pointing one position *before* the first element in the deque. See **rbegin** for an example.

- *deque_obj*.**resize(***n* [, *value*]**)**

  Truncates or extends the deque to *n* elements. If *n* is less than the current size of the deque, elements are removed from the end. If *n* is greater than the current size of the deque, elements are added to the end.

  The optional *value* argument, if included, specifies the value to add if *n* is larger than the current size. If *value* is omitted and the deque needs to grow, then (if the base type is a class) the class's default constructor is called to initialize each element.

  The following example creates a deque containing the integers 1, 2, 3, and then grows the array by adding two instances of -1 to the end of the array.

```
deque<int>  my_ints;
my_ints.push_back(1);
my_ints.push_back(2);
my_ints.push_back(3);
my_ints.resize(5, -1);
// Deque now contains 1 2 3 -1 -1.
```

- *deque_obj*.**size()**

  Returns the current number of elements.

```
for (unsigned i = 0; i < my_ints.size(); ++i) {
     cout << my_ints[i] << " ";
}
```

- *deque_obj*.**swap(***deque_obj2***)**

  Exchanges the contents of two deque objects sharing the same base type.

```
#include <deque>
#include <string>
using namespace std;
. . .
string rockers[3] = {"Mick", "Keith", "Hendrix"};
deque<string>  rockersDeq(rockers, rockers + 3);
```

```
string beats[] =
     {"John", "Paul", "George", "Ringo"};
deque<string>  beatDeq(beats, beats + 4);

beatDeq.swap(rockersDeq);
```

After the call to swap, beatDeq will contain Mick, Keith, and Hendrix, while rockersDeq will contain John, Paul, George, and Ringo.

15.5 The bitset Template

The **bitset** template is a specialized container with one purpose: to store and access individual bits. You can use this template to do most of what the sample application does at the end of Chapter 3, "Operators." (Note, however, that **bitset** doesn't do absolutely everything that example does; it does not format output by putting in a space between each group of four bits.)

This template enables you to print and accept input in binary form, as well as efficiently store Boolean values as individual bits. However, unlike the sample applications in Chapter 3 and Chapter 6, "Pointers, Arrays, and References," the **bitset** template cannot be sized dynamically in response to runtime conditions.

To use this template, first include the <bitset> header. As with other STL names, **bitset** is part of the **std** namespace.

```
#include <bitset>
using std::bitset;
```

The examples in this section also assume direct access to **cout**, **endl**, and **string**:

```
using std::cout;
using std::endl;
using std::string;
```

To instantiate the **bitset** template, you must specify an integer, which must be a compile-time constant. This parameter determines the length of the object to instantiate: that is, how many bits wide it is. You can optionally supply an initial value for a **bitset** container at the time of construction.

```
bitset<10>  name(ival);    // Create a bitset 10 bits wide.
```

One way to use **bitset** is to display the binary pattern of a number. In the following example the container size, 8, is a constant, but n—the initial value—can be determined at runtime. The **to_string** member function produces a **string** object displaying the bit pattern.

```
n = 15;
bitset<8>  mybits(n);
cout << mybits.to_string() << endl;  // Print "00001111"
```

In C++11, the **bitset** template supports a string constructor. This makes it possible to go in the reverse direction, specifying a string made up of "0" and "1" digit characters and getting the corresponding integer value by calling the **ulong** function. For example:

```
bitset<8>  mybits("00000110");
cout << mybits.to_ulong() << endl;        // Print 6.
```

The **bitset** template enables you to use the subscript operator, [], to access individual bits. For example:

```
bitset<4>  some_bits(0);      // Initial value is all 0's.
some_bits[0] = 1;
cout << some_bits.to_string() << endl;    // Print "0001"
some_bits[1] = 1;
cout << some_bits.to_string() << endl;    // Print "0011"
```

15.5.1 bitset Constructors

Descriptions of **bitset** constructors follow, in which brackets are not intended literally but indicate an optional argument.

- **`bitset`**`<`*`size`*`>` *`name`*

  Creates an uninitialized bitset.

  ```
  bitset<10>  my_bits;
  ```

- **`bitset`**`<`*`size`*`>` *`name`***`(`***`ival`***`)`**

  Creates a bitset and initializes it to the integer value *ival*.

  ```
  bitset<4>  my_bits(13);     // Init to 1101.
  ```

- **`bitset`**`<`*`size`*`>` *`name`***`(`***`str_obj`* `[, `*`pos`*`] [, `*`n`*`]`**`)`**

  C++11 only. Initializes a bitset from a string object *str_obj*. The optional *pos* and *n* arguments specify the starting position of the string and the number of characters to use.

  ```
  bitset<8>  some_bits("00001111");
  cout << "Value of 00001111 is ";

  // This next statement prints 15:
  cout << some_bits.to_ulong() << endl;
  ```

15.5.2 bitset Member Functions

Descriptions of the **bitset** member functions follow. In these descriptions, brackets ([ ]) are not intended literally but indicate an optional argument.

- *bitset_obj*.**any()**

  Returns **true** if any of the bits in *bitset_obj* are set to 1.

- *bitset_obj*.**count()**

  Returns the number of bits in *bitset_obj* that are set to 1. For example, the following statements report that four bits are set to 1 in the binary representation of 15.

```
bitset<8>  my_bits(15);
cout << "Number of bits switched on is ";
cout << my_bits.count() << endl;     // Print 4.
```

- *bitset_obj*.**flip()**

  Reverses the setting of all the bits in *bitset_obj.*

```
bitset<8>  my_bits(-1);        // Init to all 1's.
my_bits.flip();                // Reverse bits.
cout << "my_bits now contains ";
cout << my_bits.to_ulong() << endl;  // Print 0.
```

- *bitset_obj*.**none()**

  Returns **true** if none of the bits in *bitset_obj* are set to 1.

- *bitset_obj*.**reset(** [*pos*] **)**

  Sets the indicated bit position to 0; or, if *pos* is omitted, sets all bits to 0.

```
my_bits.reset();                     // Clear bits.
cout << "my_bits now contains ";
cout << my_bits.to_ulong() << endl;    // Print 0.
```

- *bitset_obj*.**set(** [*pos*] [, *val*] **)**

  Sets the bit at the specified position. If position argument *pos* is omitted, the function sets all the bits. The *val* argument is the value (1 or 0) to set the bit to; if this argument is omitted, then it is 1 by default. (If only one argument is specified, it is passed to *pos*.)

```
bitset<4>  some_bits(0);  // Init. value all 0's.
some_bits.set(0);
cout << some_bits.to_string() << endl;  // "0001"
some_bits.set(1);
cout << some_bits.to_string() << endl;  // "0011"
some_bits.set(3);
cout << some_bits.to_string() << endl;  // "1011"
```

- *bitset_obj*.**size()**

  Returns the number of bits in *bitset_obj*.

- *bitset_obj*.**test(*pos*)**

  Returns the value of the bit at position *pos*; throws an **out_of_range** exception if this position is not valid.

- *bitset_obj*.**to_string()**

  Returns a **string** object containing a representation of the bits. The length of the string is equal to the number of bits supported by this particular bitset. See the **set** function for examples.

- *bitset_obj*.**to_ulong()**

  Returns the value of *bitset_obj* as an **unsigned long**. If the bitset is wider than 32 bits, calling this function may cause problems by exceeding the range of the data type.

- *bitset_obj*.**to_ullong()**

  C++11 only. Returns the value of *bitset_obj* as an **unsigned long long**. If the bitset is wider than 64 bits, calling this function is likely to cause problems by exceeding the range of the data type. (Although this is a large range.)

15.6 Sample App: Alpha File Organizer

The sample application in this section has great practical value: In past projects, I have used similar applications to help create long, alphabetized lists, similar to an index.

When writing this application, I benefited from the **vector** template in two ways: A vector grows without limit, so I was freed from worrying about size issues, and the **vector** template comes with a built-in **insert** function, which simplified some of the programming.

The application opens an input file and an output file, checking to see if the streams are valid. It then reads from the input file one line of text at a time, placing that text string into string_vec by calling the insert_string function. This function iterates through the vector until it finds a string that it is not, alphabetically speaking, greater than (or until the end of the vector is reached). At that point, the string is inserted. The effect is to keep the strings sorted in alphabetical order.

```
#include <iostream>
#include <fstream>
#include <string>
```

```
#include <vector>

using std::cout;              // Alternatively, you can use
using std::cin;               //  "using namespace std;"
using std::endl;
using std::fstream;
using std::string;
using std::vector;

vector<string> str_vec;          // Holds lines of text.
vector<string>::iterator it;     // Iterator into str_vec.
void insert_string(string s);    // Inserts strings in alpha
                                 //   order.
int main() {
     string ifname;
     string ofname;
     string input_str;
     cout << "Enter name of input file: ";
     getline(cin, ifname);
     ifstream file_in(ifname);
     if (!file_in) {
          cout << "File could not be opened." << endl;
          system("PAUSE");
          return -1;
     }
     cout << "Enter name of output file: ";
     getline(cin, ofname);
     ofstream file_out(ofname);
     if (!file_out) {
          cout << "File could not be opened." << endl;
          system("PAUSE");
          return -1;
     }
     // Read in lines of text and insert into str_vec.
     while(!file_in.eof()) {
          getline(file_in, input_str);
          insert_string(input_str);
     }
     // Write out contents of str_vec to file_out.
     for(it = str_vec.begin(); it != str_vec.end(); ++it) {
          file_out << *it << endl;
     }
     cout << "Alphabetizing complete." << endl;
     cout << "Press ENTER to exit.";
     cin.ignore();  // Wait for user to press ENTER.
     return 0;
}
```

```
// Insert String function.
// Search for proper insertion spot according to alpha
//   order; then insert the string.
void insert_string(string s) {
       it = str_vec.begin();
       while(it != str_vec.end() && s > *it)
            ++it;
       str_vec.insert(it, s);
}
```

Exercises

1. Revise the application so that it writes output to the console as well as to an output file. As it writes to the console, have it place a ">" sign at the beginning of each line of text.
2. Revise the application so that it performs case-insensitive comparisons so that (for example) the letters "a" and "A" are treated the same for sorting purposes.
3. Write an application that does the same thing but hands off most of the work to several functions. Use the **main** function to set up **try-catch** blocks that handle failure to open files. The function that opens the files should throw an exception if the files cannot be successfully opened.
4. Rewrite the application using the **list** template. Everything should be the same after you substitute **list** for **vector**. If you need to, consult Chapter 16, "STL Sequence Containers (List)." The other change to make is to use **push_back** to add a string to the list and then (after all the lines of text have been added to the list) call the **sort** function to sort the collection:
   `str_list.sort();`

CHAPTER 16

STL Sequence Containers (List)

For many years, computer programming students have been writing linked-list code, useful in accessing a collection sequentially. The advantage of a linked list is that you can insert and delete elements from the middle of the collection while not disturbing the rest of it in any way.

How would you like to have all these list operations automated for you… and more?

The Standard Template Library (STL) automates linked-list programming, providing all the standard capabilities of a container, plus several built-in, special capabilities unique to lists, including removal, merging, and splicing.

One of the most useful of these extra functions is **sort**. This chapter therefore begins by discussing the requirements for sorting. It then describes the **list** template and several adapted containers (**stack**, **queue**, and **priority_queue**) that are special-purpose and—like lists—must be accessed sequentially.

- **list**
- **stack**
- **queue**
- **priority_queue**

16.1 Sorting Elements (Strict Weak Ordering)

Sorting a list, as well as many of the STL algorithms and the **priority_queue** template, requires that the base type support the < operator or that a less-than comparison function is provided. Such a function returns **true** when the first of two arguments passed to it is less than the second.

The comparison operation must obey certain rules. Computer scientists call these rules *strict weak ordering.*

- Transitivity. If A < B and B < C, then A < C.
- Asymmetry. If A < B, then it cannot be true that B < A.
- A < A is never true. (This follows from the first two rules.)

These rules are usually met easily. If strict weak ordering holds, then for a group of elements, there will always be an unambiguous way of ordering them from lowest to highest: All the items on the left of an item will be less than the item, and all the items on the right will be greater than the item (although if items are equal, they will be adjacent).

For example, for the following group of animals, strict weak ordering holds for size because we can arrange these in a strict sequence from smallest to largest, such that an animal is bigger than everything on its left and smaller than everything on its right.

```
cell  butterfly  mouse  dog  zebra  elephant  whale
```

If you add other animals to this list, the comparison might not always be clear: for example, comparing dog to wolf. (A Great Dane is bigger than a wolf, but a Dachshund is not.) But if you instead treat these items as words to be alphabetized, the ordering is always unambiguous. Alphabetical order produces:

```
butterfly  cell  dog  elephant  mouse  whale  zebra
```

These rules are "weak" only in the sense that just one operator need be defined: less-than (<). It's obvious how greater-than comparisons are achieved from less-than (you simply reverse the operands), but equality can be deduced as well. If A is not less than B and B is not less than A, strict weak ordering implies that A and B are equal. Many functions and containers in the STL use this logic and therefore require only that less-than (<) be defined. Equality is inferred.

16.2 The list Template

A list container is implemented as a doubly linked list, as shown in Figure 16.1. Each element has a link to the element before it and after it.

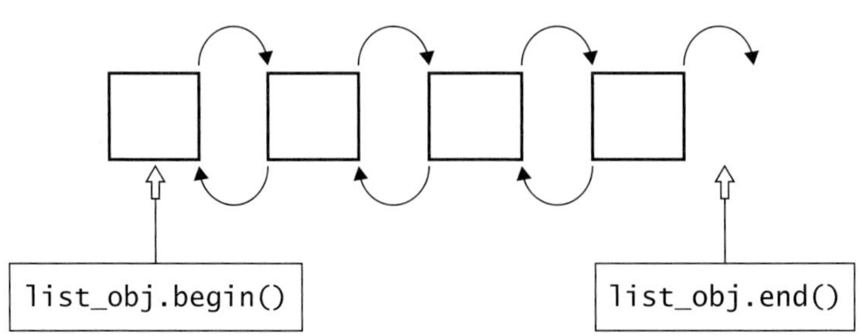

FIGURE 16.1 The list template

Because of this structure, list containers are ideal for sequential processing, in which you step through one element at a time.

To use the **list** template, include the <list> header. Like all templates in the C++ standard library, the name **list** is part of the **std** namespace.

```
#include <list>
using std::list;
```

You can then declare list objects and initialize them. For example, to create a list of integers:

```
list<int>  iList;
iList.push_back(30);
iList.push_back(20);
iList.push_back(10);
```

As with vector and deque containers, you can initialize a list container more efficiently by using an aggregate if your compiler is fully C++11 compliant and supports this behavior.

```
list<int>  iList = {30, 20, 10};
```

If your compiler does not fulfill the C++11 specification, you can most efficiently initialize from an array:

```
int arr[3] = {30, 20, 10};
list<int>  iList(arr, arr + 3);
```

Unlike other container types, such as vector and deque, list containers provide no indexing of any kind.

On the other hand, list containers provide some unique advantages. Member functions provide support for sorting, merging, and splicing.

16.2.1 List Iterators

List containers must be accessed sequentially through the use of iterators. List iterators are smarter than ordinary pointers, because they know how to traverse the links while hiding the details. But these iterators are more limited in some respects.

- List iterators support increment (++) and decrement (--) but no other arithmetic.
- List iterators can be tested for equality (==) or inequality (!=). But less-than (<) and greater-than (>) comparisons are not supported.

The **begin** and **end** member functions provide direct access to iterators pointing to the front and back of the list, respectively, so you can efficiently start processing at either end. But elements in the middle have to be reached by sequential processing from one end or another.

You can declare a list iterator as follows:

list<*type*>**::iterator** *name*;

For example, the following statements create a list of strings called beats and use an iterator to print out the strings, one at a time:

```
#include <list>
#include <iostream>

using std::list;        // Alternatively, you can use
using std::string;      //  using namespace std;
using std::cout;
using std::endl;

string str_arr[4] = {"John", "Paul", "George", "Ringo"};
list<string> beats(str_arr, str_arr[4]);
list<string>::iterator  it;
for(it = beats.begin(); it != beats.end(); ++it) {
     cout << *it << endl;
}
```

If you need to get the Nth member, you have to step through the list N times, a potentially expensive operation for large values of N. For example, to print the fourth member of beats:

```
for(int i = 0, it != beats.begin(); i < 4; ++i) {
     ++it;
}
cout << "The fourth member is " << *it << endl;
```

This prints out:

```
The fourth member is Ringo.
```

On the positive side, insertions and deletions (as mentioned) are particularly clean and efficient. For example, the following statements delete the second element in the list. (Sorry, Paul!)

```
it = beats.begin();
++it;   // Step to the 2nd element.
it = beats.erase(it);
```

Figure 16.2 illustrates how this deletion is carried out, leaving another iterator (it2) unaffected. Links of the immediately surrounding elements (John, George) are reassigned.

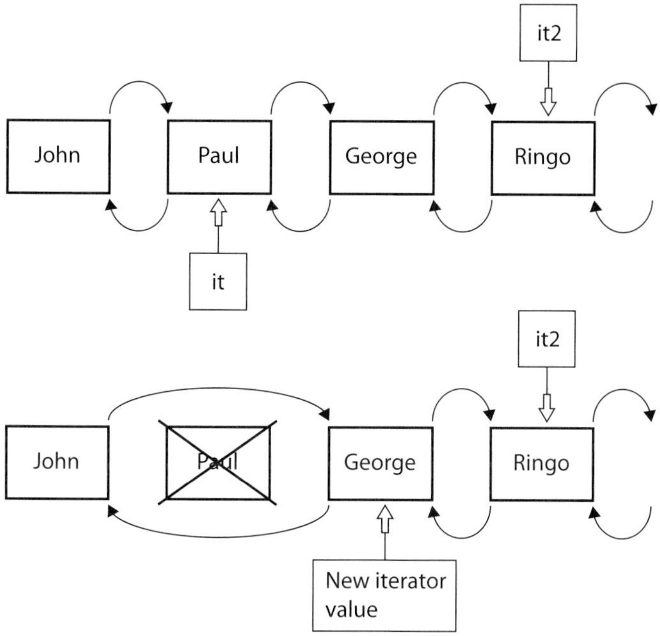

FIGURE 16.2 Deletion of a list element

The **erase** function returns an iterator to the element that would have been next—in this case, George. (Refer to Figure 16.2.) Therefore, the following statement restores Paul to the group, placing him back in his original position:

```
beats.insert(it, "Paul");   // Bring back Paul!
```

In addition to **iterator**, list containers support **reverse_iterator**, **const_iterator**, and **const_reverse_iterator**. The reverse iterators—intended to be used with the **rbegin** and **rend** member functions—reverse the meaning of incrementing and decrementing, so applying ++ to a reverse iterator moves backward through the list instead of forward.

16.2.2 List Constructors

You can always populate an empty list by calling the **push_back** member function. But the **list** template supports several constructors that initialize a list with one or more elements. Remember to include the <list> header and that the name **list** is part of the **std** namesapce.

```
#include <list>
using std::list;
```

▸ `list<`*`type`*`>` *`name`*

Creates a list with the specified *name*, for the specified base *type*. The list is initially empty. For example, the following statement creates a list of short integers.

```
list<short>  short_list;
```

You can then add values using the **push_back** member function or the **assign** function. For example:

```
short_list.push_back(100);  // 100 is first elem.
short_list.push_back(-5);   // -5 is second elem.
```

▸ `list<`*`type`*`>` *`name`*`(`*`n`*`,` *`value`*`)`

Creates a list with the specified *name* and base *type*, initializing it with *n* copies of *value* (in which *n* is a non-negative integer); *value* is a data item compatible with the base type, either matching it or having a type that can be converted to it.

```
// Initialize with 5 copies of 3.7.
list<double>  aList(5, 3.7);
// Initialize with 2 copies of "Hi".
list<string>  aList2(2, "Hi");
```

▸ `list<`*`type`*`>` *`name`*`(`*`first_iter`*`,` *`last_iter`*`)`

Creates and initializes a list from a range of values in another container. The *first_iter* and *last_iter* arguments are iterators or pointers to elements in this other container. Values are copied into the new list, starting with the element pointed to by *first_iter*, up to but not including the position pointed to by *last_iter*.

If you lack C++11 support for direct initialization of containers (by the use of aggregates enclosed in curly braces), the most convenient way to initialize a list is usually to use an array, as follows:

```
string  beats[4] =
     {"John", "Paul", "George", "Ringo"};
list<string>  beatList(arr, arr + 4);
```

▸ `list<`*`type`*`>` *`name`*`(`*`list2`*`)`

Creates and initializes a list by copying all the values of another list of the same base type. For example, the effect of the following statements is to create two lists—IntList1 and IntList2—having identical contents initially. Subsequent operations, of course, may cause the lists to have different contents.

```
int  a[6] = {100, 15, -3, 202, 27, 87 };
list<int>  iList1(a, a + 6);  // Init from array.
list<int>  iList2(iList1);  // Init from iList1.
```

16.2.3 Concise Summary of list Functions

The **list** template supports a group of member functions similar to that for **vector**, but it lacks support for direct access; it therefore provides no **at** function and no support for the [ ] operator. One of the most convenient features of the list template, however, is that it provides a **sort** function; the **merge** and **splice** functions also provide distinct list capabilities.

Table 16.1 summarizes the most common member functions for this template, roughly in order of how often they're used. Table 16.2 summarizes the powerful list-manipulation functions.

The **list** template includes several unique list-manipulation capabilities not provided by most of the other container classes.

TABLE 16.1 Commonly Used Functions of the list Template

List Member Function	Description
begin, end	Return starting and ending iterators for forward iteration.
rbegin, rend	Return starting and ending iterators for reverse iteration.
insert	Inserts one or more new elements at any position in the list.
erase	Removes one or more elements from any position in the list.
push_back, push_front	Add a new element to the end or front of the list.
size	Returns the number of elements currently in the list.

TABLE 16.2 List Manipulation Functions

List Member Function	Description
remove, remove_if	Remove all elements from the list that meet a specified condition.
sort	Sorts all the elements in the list according to value; this works most easily if the < operator is defined for the base type. Otherwise, you need to provide a comparison function.
reverse	Reverses the order of all elements in the list, so what was the first element becomes the last and vice versa.
merge	Moves all the elements from another list and empties that list; each element is moved into the first ordered position, so the effect of a merge is to place elements in order.
splice	Moves all or some elements from another list and removes them from that list. Elements are inserted directly, without sorting.

16.2.4 List Member Functions in Detail

When calling **list** member functions, remember to include the <list> header and that the name **list** is part of the **std** namespace.

```
#include <list>
using std::list;
```

The examples in this section also assume the following:

```
#include <iostream>
#include <string>
using std::string;
using std::cout;
using std::endl;
```

Descriptions of **list** member functions follow.

- *list_obj*.**assign(***n*, *value***)**

  Similar to the **list**<*type*>(*n*, *pos*) constructor, except that values are copied to an existing list; previous contents, if any, are erased. Effect is to assign n copies of *value*.

  ```
  // Initialize with two copies of "a".
  list<string>  strList(2, "a");
  // Assign 10 copies of "abc"; erase old contents.
  strList(10, "abc");
  ```

- *list_obj*.**assign(***first_iter*, *last_iter***)**

  Similar to the **list**<*type*>(*first_iter*, *last_iter*) constructor. The previous contents of *list_obj* are erased. Effect is to copy values from another container, beginning with the element pointed to by *first_iter* (an iterator or pointer), up to but not including *last_iter*.

  ```
  int arr[8] = {10, 20, 30, 40, 50, 60, 70, 80 };
  shortList.assign(arr, arr+8);
  ```

- *list_obj*.**back()**

  Returns the value of the last element in the list.

  ```
  string beats[4] =
     {"John", "Paul", "George", "Ringo" };
  list<string> beatList(beats, beats + 4);
  cout << "The last member to join was ";
  cout << beatList.back();
  ```

  These statements print out:

  ```
  The last member to join was Ringo.
  ```

▸ *list_obj*.**begin()**

Returns an iterator pointing to the first element in the list. This is often used in conjunction with the **end** function, to iterate the list. For example, the following statements print out the contents of a list called beat_l:

```
list<string>::iterator  it;
for (beat_l.begin(); it != beat_l.end(); ++it) {
     cout << *it << endl;
}
```

▸ *list_obj*.**clear()**

Removes all the elements in the list.

```
beat_l.clear();
```

▸ *list_obj*.**empty()**

Returns **true** if the list has no elements; returns **false** if it does have elements. For example, the following statements print out all the elements in beat_list from beginning to end, while simultaneously emptying the list.

```
while (! beat_list.empty()) {
     cout << beat_list.front() << endl;
     beat_list.pop_front();
}
```

▸ *list_obj*.**end()**

Returns an iterator pointing to *one position past* the last element in the list. This is typically used in conjunction with the **begin** function to iterate the list. See **begin**.

▸ *list_obj*.**erase(*pos_iter*)**

Removes the element at the position pointed to by *pos_iter*, an iterator, and returns an iterator to the item that would have been the next after *pos_iter*.

For example, the following statements remove the first item of iList that is equal to 0:

```
int arr[6] = {1, -2, 3, -4, 5, -6 };
list<int>  iList(arr, arr + 6);
list<int>::iterator it;
for(it = iList.begin(); it != iList.end(); ++it){
     if (*it == 0) {
          iList.erase(it);
          break;
     }
}
```

After executing these statements, the list contains the values 1, 3, -4, 5, -6. This next example removes *all* elements less than 0 (reducing the list to 1, 3, 5). This example takes advantage of the value returned by **erase**. Assume iList and it have already been created.

```
for (it = iList.begin(); it != iList.end(); ) {
     if (*cur < 0) {
          it = iList.erase(cur);
     } else {
          ++it;
     }
}
```

Note, however, that this same functionality is also provided—in a one-statement form—by the **remove** function.

- *list_obj*.**erase**(*first_iter*, *last_iter*)

Removes elements in the list beginning with the one pointed to by *first_iter*, up to but not including the element pointed to by *last_iter*. For example, one way to remove the first three elements is to use the following code:

```
int arr[6] = {1, -2, 3, -4, 5, -6 };
list<int>  iList(arr, arr + 6);
list<int>::iterator  it1, it2;
it1 = it2 = iList.begin();
++it2;
++it2;
++it2;
iList.erase(it1, it2);
// List now contains -4, 5, -6.
```

- *list_obj*.**front**()

Returns the value of the first element in the list (that is, at the head of the list). To get an iterator pointing to this element, see **begin**.

```
string beats[4] =
     {"John", "Paul", "George", "Ringo"};
list<string> beatList(beats, beats+4);
cout << "The first member to join was ";
cout << beatList.front();
```

These statements print out:

```
The first member to join was John.
```

- *list_obj*.**insert**(*pos_iter*, *value*)

Inserts the specified *value* at the position pointed to by *pos_iter*, an iterator. The new element is inserted just before the one pointed to by *pos_iter*. The function returns an iterator pointing to the new item.

The following example function inserts a number into iList, a list of integers (which this example assumes has already been declared and initialized), after first skipping past smaller values. Consistent use of this function keeps a list continually sorted.

```
void insert_item(int new_val) {
     list<int>::iterator it = iList.begin();
     while (it != iList.end() && *it < new_val) {
          ++it;
     }
     iList.insert(it, new_val);
}
```

- *list_obj*.**insert(***pos_iter*, *n*, *value***)**

  Performs the same action as the previous version of **insert**, except that it inserts *n* copies of *value* rather than just one copy. For example, the following statements insert two copies of the value 3.141592 at the front of xList, a floating-point list.

  ```
  // Init with one copy of 0.5
  list<double> xList(1, 0.5);
  xList.insert(xList.begin(), 2, 3.141592);
  ```

  Printing out the contents of this list would now produce this output:

  ```
  3.141592  3.141592  0.5
  ```

- *list_obj*.**insert(***pos_iter*, *first_iter*, *last_iter***)**

  Performs the same action as the previous version of **insert**, except that the elements inserted are copied from another container: These elements begin with the one pointed to by *first_iter*, up to but not including the element pointed to by *last_iter*.

  For example, the following statements create a list, beat_list, from the array beats; they then insert the contents of the rockers array into the front of beat_list.

  ```
  string rockers[4] =
       {"Mick", "Keith", "Dylan", "Cobain"};
  string beats[4] =
       {"John", "Paul", "George", "Ringo"};
  list<string>  beatList(beats, beats + 4);
  beatList.insert(beatList.begin(), rockers,
       rockers + 4);
  ```

  After this operation, Mick, Keith, Dylan, and Cobain are now at the front of the list.

- *list_obj*.**max_size()**

  Returns the ultimate number of elements that the system will support for lists. On modern computers, this number tends to run into the thousands of millions, at least.

- *list_obj*.**merge(***list2_obj***)**

  Copies all the elements from another list, *list2_obj*, into *list_obj*; the elements copied are each added in sorted order, so as **merge** adds a new element, it skips over the elements in the target range that are smaller in value. Merging is most appropriate when dealing with lists that are already sorted. See also **insert**, **sort**, and **splice**.

```
int arr1[] = {10, 20, 30, 40};
int arr2[] = {15, 25, 35};
list<int> iList1(arr1, arr1 + 4);
list<int> iList2(arr2, arr2 + 3);
iList.merge(iList2);

list<int>::iterator it;
for(it = iList.begin(); it != iList.end(); ++it){
     cout << *it << " ";
} cout << endl;
```

These statements print out:

```
10 15 20 25 30 35 40
```

- *list_obj*.**merge(***list2_obj*, *compf***)**

Performs the same action as the previous version of **merge**, except that comparisons are based on *compf*, a function you supply: This function takes reference to two arguments of the list's base type and returns **true** if the first element is less than the second. See the **sort** function for an example of a comparison function.

- *list_obj*.**pop_back()**

Removes the last element from the list. For example, the following statements print out the elements of beatList *in reverse order*, while simultaneously emptying the list. (This is the behavior of a stack.)

```
string beats[] =
     {"John", "Paul", "George", "Ringo" };
list<string> beatList(beats, beats + 4);
while (!beatList.empty()) {
     cout << beatList.back() << endl;
     beatList.pop_back;
}
```

- *list_obj*.**pop_front()**

Removes the first element from the list. For example, the following statements print out the elements of beatList *in order*, while simultaneously emptying the list. (This is the behavior of a queue.)

```
string beats[] =
     {"John", "Paul", "George", "Ringo"};
list<string> beatList(beats, beats + 4);
while (!beatList.empty()) {
     cout << beatList.front() << endl;
     beatList.pop_front;
}
```

- *list_obj*.**push_back(***value***)**

  Inserts an element with the specified *value* at the end of the list. This function (as well as **push_front**) is, unlike some functions, completely safe to use with empty lists, and so is an alternative technique for initializing a list—although there are more convenient techniques available. The following statements initialize beatList to contain elements in this order: "John", "Paul", "George", and "Ringo".

```
list<string>  beatList;
beatList.push_back("John");
beatList.push_back("Paul");
beatList.push_back("George");
beatList.push_back("Ringo");
```

- *list_obj*.**push_front(***value***)**

  Inserts the specified *value* at the front of the list. For example, the following statement inserts the string "Pete Best" at the front of the beatList container from previous examples.

```
beatList.push_front("Pete Best");
```

- *list_obj*.**rbegin()**

  Returns a reverse iterator pointing to the last element in the list. This function is intended to be used along with **rend**, to iterate backward through a list. For example:

```
string beats[4] =
     {"John", "Paul", "George", "Ringo"};
list<string>  beatList(beats, beats + 4);
list<string>::reverse_iterator ri;
ri = beatList.rbegin();
while (it != beatList.rend()) {
     cout << *it++ << endl;
}
```

  These statements print out:

```
Ringo
George
Paul
John
```

- *list_obj*.**remove(***value***)**

  Removes all elements from the list that match the specified element value. For example, the following statement removes all values from iList that are equal to zero:

```
iList.remove(0);    // Remove all zero elements.
```

- *list_obj*.**remove_if(*condf*)**

  Removes all elements from the list that meet a condition specified by *condf*, a function object, function address, or lambda function. This function takes one argument having the same type as the base type of *list_obj*. The function is passed each element's value in turn, and it returns **true** if the element is to be removed.

  For example, the following code removes all integers from iList that are even numbers.

```
bool is_even(const int &val) {
     return (val % 2 == 0);
}
. . .
iList.remove_if(is_even);
```

- *list_obj*.**rend()**

  Returns an iterator pointing to one position *before* the first element in the list. This function is typically used with **rbegin**, to iterate backward through a list. See **rbegin**.

- *list_obj*.**resize(*n* [, *value*])**

  Truncates or adds elements to the list until its size is *n* elements. If the current size is greater than *n*, elements are removed from the end of the list. If the current size is less than *n*, elements are added to the end. The optional *value* argument specifies the value of each element to add; if this argument is omitted, and the base type is a class, then the class's default constructor is called to initialize each element added.

  For example, the following statement adds two elements to the end of the beatList container (which starts out as four elements long) shown in previous examples. Each of these two new strings has the value "Pete Best".

```
beatList.resize(6, "Pete Best");
```

  The next statement resizes beatList back to a length of 4, in the process removing both instances of "Pete Best." (Sorry, Pete!)

```
beatList.resize(4);
```

- *list_obj*.**reverse()**

  Reverses the order of all the elements in the list. For example:

```
beatList.reverse();
```

  Assuming that beatList started out in the order John, Paul, George, and Ringo, the new order is now Ringo, George, Paul, and John.

- *list_obj*.**size()**

  Returns the number of elements in the list. One common way to use this function is to evaluate whether it is greater than zero; this produces the same result as calling the **empty** function and logically negating it. For example:

```
while (beatList.size() > 0) {
     cout << beatList.back() << endl;
     beat_list.pop_back;
}
```

- *`list_obj`*`.`**`sort(`**`[`*`compf`*`]`**`)`**

  Sorts all the elements into ascending order. This function uses an optional compare function, *compf*, if supplied; otherwise, it relies on the less_than operator (<) of the base type. For example, the following code sorts an array of unsorted integers:

  ```
  int arr[6] = {10, -5, -101, -30, 66, -27 };
  list<int> iList(arr, arr + 6);
  iList.sort();
  for(it = iList.begin(); it != iList.end(); ++it){
       cout << *it << " ";
  }
  ```

  This code prints out the values in this order: -101, -30, -27, -5, 10, 66. This next version uses a comparison function to arrange this same list of integers according to their absolute values. In this example, I have placed the call to **sort** in bold for the sake of emphasis.

  ```
  #include <cstdlib>
  bool comp_ints(int &a, int &b) {
       int temp_a = abs(a);
       int temp_b = abs(b);
       return temp_a < temp_b;
  }
  . . .
  iList.sort(comp_ints);
  for(it = iList.begin(); it != iList.end(); ++it){
       cout << *it << " ";
  }
  ```

  This version of the code prints out the integers in the order -5, 10, -27, -30, 66, -101. If your compiler is C++11 compliant, you can save some space by using a lambda function instead of writing a named function.

  ```
  #include <cstdlib>
  . . .
  iList.sort( [] (int a, int b) -> int {
       int tempa = abs(a), int tempb = abs(b);
       return tempa < tempb;
  } );
  ```

- *`list_obj`*`.`**`splice(`***`pos_iter`*`, `*`list2_obj`***`)`**

  Splices the elements of *list2_obj* into *list_obj*. The effect is twofold: Empty the contents of *list2_obj*, and insert those elements at the position pointed to by *pos_iter*, an iterator of *list_obj*. (An insertion places the new elements just before this position.)

For example, the following statements splice the contents of new_ints, an integer array, onto the end of old (another integer array), emptying list2 in the process.

```
int a1[4] = {10, 20, 30, 40};
list<int>  old(a1, a1 + 4);       // Init from a1.
int a2[3] = {-100, -200, -300};
list<int>  new_ints(a2, a2 + 3); // Init from a2.

old.splice(old.end(), new_ints);
```

After this last statement is executed, the array named "old" contains the values 10, 20, 30, 40, -100, -200, -300; and new_ints is emptied. (The number of elements in new_ints before the splice was three; afterward it is zero.)

- *list_obj*.**splice**(*pos_iter*, *list2_obj*, *iter2*)

Performs the same action as the previous version of **splice**, except that it splices elements from *list2_obj* beginning with the element pointed to by iterator *iter2,* forward to the end of that list. (The elements are inserted in list_obj and removed from list2_obj.)

For example, the following call to old.splice copies the members -200, -300 (which start in the second position of new_ints) onto the end of the list named "old", while simultaneously removing these elements from new_ints.

```
int a1[] = {10, 20, 30, 40};
list<int>  old(a1, a1 + 4);       // Init from a1.
int a2[] = {-100, -200, -300};
list<int>  new_ints(a2, a2 + 3); // Init from a2.
list<int>::iterator it = new_ints.begin();
++it;    // Increment to 2nd position of new_ints.

// Splice from second position in new_ints onto
//    end of old.
old.splice(old.end(), new_ints, it);
```

After these statements are executed, the list named "old" contains all its initial data, as well as the first two elements that new_ints was initialized to, resulting in these values: 10, 20, 30, 40, -200, -300. The new_ints list, meanwhile, is shortened to only contain -100.

- *list_obj*.**splice**(*pos_iter*, *list2_obj*, *first_iter*, *last_iter*)

Performs the same action as previous versions of **splice**, except that it only splices elements from the specified range. This range consists of elements beginning with the one pointed to by *first_iter,* up to but not including the element pointed to by *last_iter,* in which these two arguments are iterators of *list2_obj.*

The following code splices the first two elements in new_ints onto the front of the list named "old." (See the previous example for how these lists are initialized.)

```
list<int>::iterator it = new_ints.begin(), it2;
it2 = it;
++it2;
++it2;   // Increment twice.

old.splice(old.begin(), new_ints, it, it2);
```

After the call to old.splice, the list named "old" contains -100, -200, 10, 20, 30, 40, while new_ints is shortened to only contain -300.

- *list_obj*.**swap(***list2_obj***)**

  Swaps the contents of *list_obj* with *list_obj2*. For example, the following statement swaps the contents of two lists. After the call to **swap**, lst1 will contain five copies of "bye" and lst2 will contain two copies of "hi".

```
int<string> lst1(2, "hi");    // 2 copies of "hi"
int<string> lst2(5, "bye");   // 5 copies of "bye"

lst1.swap(lst2);   // Switch them!
```

16.3 The stack Template

A stack container is a last-in-first-out (LIFO) storage device that has many uses in computer programming and design. You can think of a stack as similar to a stack of plates, in which the plate most recently placed ("pushed") onto the stack must be taken off before other plates are removed.

The **stack** template is an adapter container; by default, stacks are built on top of the **deque** (double-ended queue) template, which is almost always the best choice to support the stack mechanism.

To use the stack template, include the <stack> header. As with all templates in the C++ standard library, the name **stack** is part of the **std** namespace.

```
#include <stack>
using std::stack;
```

You can then create a stack using the stack template. Elements can be added to the stack by using the **push** member function:

```
stack<int>  st;
st.push(1);
st.push(2);
st.push(3);
```

Figure 16.3 illustrates the result of these three calls to **push**. Note that the last element to be pushed onto the stack is always on top.

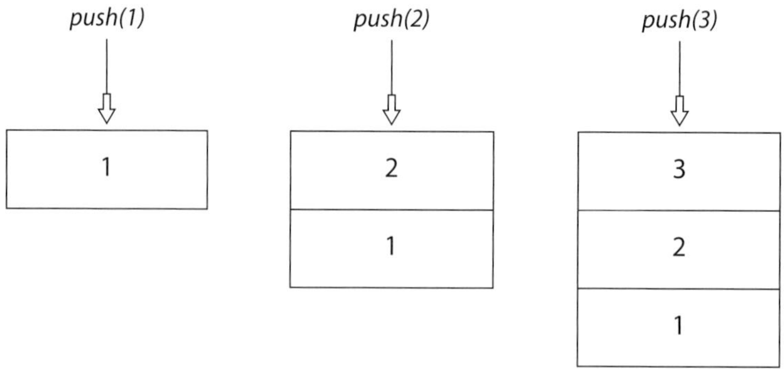

FIGURE 16.3 Pushing elements onto a stack

After the three **push** operations, the stack contains the numbers {3, 2, 1}, in that order. If you then start using this data, the element on the top of the stack—in this case, 3—is available to be read. If the program has used this value and is done with it, the element should be popped off the stack.

The next few statements use the top two elements in the order {3, 2}, removing each element after it has been used. Unlike most stack mechanisms, STL stacks require both **top** and **pop** to be called to achieve this effect.

```
std::cout << st.top() << std::endl;      // Print 3.
st.pop();
std::cout << st.top() << std:: endl;     // Print 2.
st.pop();
```

Figure 16.4 illustrates the effect of these two top-and-pop operations. A call to the **top** function is necessary to get the top element; a call to **pop** then removes that element, letting the next one rise to the top.

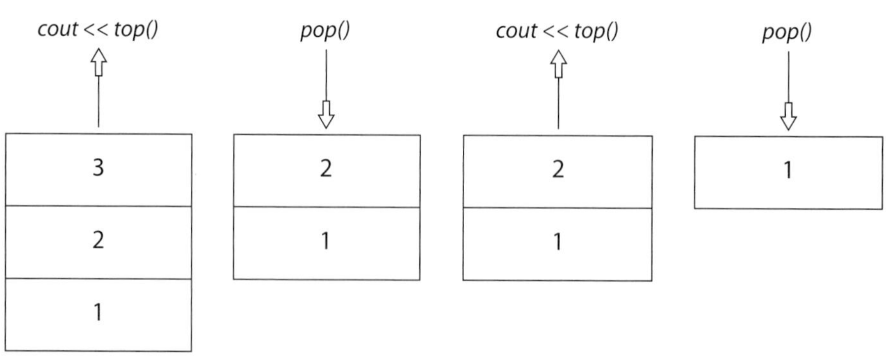

FIGURE 16.4 Popping elements from a stack

The following simple program, utilizing the **stack** template and the **string** class, prints out the contents of a string array in reverse order.

```
#include <stack>
#include <string>
#include <iostream>

using std::stack;
using std::string;
using std::cout;
using std::endl;

string beats[4] = {"John", "Paul", "George", "Ringo"};
stack<string>  beatStack;

int main() {
     unsigned int i = 0;
     for(i = 0; i < 4; ++i) {
          beatStack.push(beats[i]);
     }
     while(!beatStack.empty()) {
          cout << beatStack.top() << endl;
          beatStack.pop();
     }
}
```

This program prints out the strings in the reverse order in which they were placed on the stack:

```
Ringo
George
Paul
John
```

Descriptions of the **stack** template member functions follow. Because stacks are special-purpose, only five functions are provided. Remember to include the <stack> header and that **stack** and **cout** are symbols in the **std** namespace.

```
#include <stack>
using std::stack;
using std::cout;
using std::endl;
```

- *stack_obj*.**empty()**

  Returns **true** if the vector has no elements; returns **false** otherwise.

  ```
  while (!mystack.empty())  {
       cout << mystack.top() << endl;
  ```

```
        mystack.pop();
}
```

- *stack_obj*.**pop()**

  Removes the top element from the stack. This function, by itself, does not return a value. Typically, use of the stack involves getting the top value and popping it, so the **top** and **pop** functions are typically used together. Remember to "top and pop"—in that order!

  ```
  cout << beat_stack.top() << endl;
  beat_stack.pop();
  ```

- *stack_obj*.**push(*value*)**

  Pushes a new element onto the top of the stack. This element becomes the new top, thereby pushing any existing elements "down." As the top element, it is the only element accessible through stack member functions, and it remains so until it is popped off.

  ```
  stack<double>  xStack;
  xStack.push(3.14159265); // Push onto xStack.
  ```

- *stack_obj*.**size()**

  Returns the number of elements currently in the stack. This value is returned as an unsigned integer.

  ```
  while (mystack.size() > 0) {
       cout << mystack.top() << endl;
       mystack.pop();
  }
  ```

- *stack_obj*.**top()**

  Returns the value of the element on the top of the stack. This element is always the last element that was pushed onto the stack. The **top** function is often called along with **pop**; otherwise, the same element remains at the top of the stack and nothing else can be accessed.

  ```
  cout << "The top element on the stack is: ";
  cout << mystack.top() << endl;  // Get top value.
  mystack.pop();                  // Pop it off.
  ```

16.4 The queue Template

Like the stack template, the queue template is a special-purpose container. But unlike a stack, a queue is a first-in-first-out mechanism (FIFO) rather than last-in-first-out (LIFO). The **queue** template is an adapter container; by default, queues are built on top of the **deque** (double-ended queue) template.

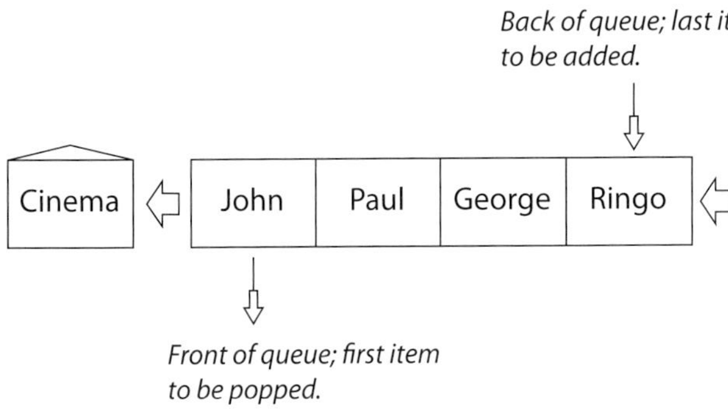

FIGURE 16.5 Using a queue template

To use the queue template, include the <queue> header. Like all templates in the C++ standard library, the name **queue** is part of the **std** namespace.

```
#include <queue>
using std::queue;
```

Queues are easily understood with a simple analogy. Suppose John, Paul, George, and Ringo go to see their favorite new film, *Help, Part III in 3-D*. They line up in that order—John, Paul, George, Ringo. Because this line is a queue, John gets his ticket first when the box office opens. If this line worked like a stack, Ringo would instead be the first to get a ticket. Figure 16.5 illustrates this queue.

A queue provides access to both the front and the back. However—and this is the important part—elements are pushed onto one end of the queue (the back), and the **pop** function removes elements from the other end (the front).

For example, the following program prints out the members of the array in order after first placing them inside a queue.

```
#include <queue>
#include <string>
#include <iostream>

using std::queue;
using std::string;
using std::cout;
using std::endl;

string beats[] = {"John", "Paul", "George", "Ringo" };
queue<string>  beat_q;
```

```
int main() {
     unsigned int i = 0;
     for(i = 0; i < 4; i++) {
          beat_q.push(beats[i]);
     }
     while(!beat_q.empty()) {
          cout << beat_q.front();
          cout << " gets a ticket." << endl;
          beat_q.pop();
     }
}
```

This code prints out the following:

```
John gets a ticket.
Paul gets a ticket.
George gets a ticket.
Ringo gets a ticket.
```

Descriptions of the **queue** template member functions follow. Because stacks are special-purpose, only five functions are provided. Remember to include the <queue> header and that the **queue** and **cout** symbols are both part of the **std** namespace.

```
#include <queue>
using std::queue;
using std::cout;
using std::endl;
```

- *queue_obj*.**back()**

  Returns the last element to be added—that is, the newest one. If all the elements are popped, this element would be the last to be removed.

  ```
  beat_q.push("Ringo");   // Add Ringo.
  cout << "The last member to join was ";
  cout << beat_q.back() << endl;
  ```

  This prints:

  ```
  The last member to join was Ringo.
  ```

- *queue_obj*.**empty()**

  Returns **true** if the queue has no elements; returns **false** otherwise.

  ```
  while(!beat_q.empty()) {
       cout << beat_q.front();
       cout << " gets a ticket." << endl;
       beat_q.pop();
  }
  ```

- *queue_obj*.**front()**

  Returns the value of the element at the front of the queue. The front element is the oldest element—that is, the first of all the remaining elements to be added. The **front** function is often called along with **pop**; otherwise, the same element always remains at the front.

```
cout <<
   "The element at the front of the queue is: ";
cout << my_q.front() << endl;  // Get front.
my_q.pop();                    // Remove it.
```

- *queue_obj*.**push(*value*)**

  Pushes the specified value onto the back of the queue. This element does not reach the front until all elements in front of it (the older elements) have been removed by being popped.

```
stack<double>  xQueue;
xQueue.push(3.141592); // Push onto back of q.
```

- *queue_obj*.**pop()**

  Removes the front element from the queue. This function, by itself, does not return a value. Typically, the **front** function is used together with **pop**, to get access to an element and then remove it so that the next element can be accessed in its turn.

```
cout << beat_q.front() << endl;
beat_q.pop();
```

- *queue_obj*.**size()**

  Returns the number of elements currently in the queue (returning that value as a long integer). In the following statements, this function is used to help print out—while emptying out—the queue.

```
while (my_q.size() > 0) {
     cout << my_q.front() << endl;
     my_q.pop();
}
```

16.5 The priority_queue Template

The **priority_queue** template creates a queue in which the element with the highest value is always first. When you instantiate a priority queue, either the base type must support the less-than operator (<) or you must provide a comparison function. In either case, the rules stated in Section 16.1, "Sorting Elements (Strict Weak Ordering)," apply.

To support this template, include the <queue> header. Also, the **priority_queue** is part of the **std** namespace, so either include a using statement or refer to **priority_queue** with its **std::** prefix.

```
#include <queue>
using std::priority_queue;
```

As an example, imagine an executive dining hall. If this were an ordinary lunchroom, employees would get served in the order they showed up. But in this place, higher-ranked employees automatically go to the front of the line. When the CEO arrives, he or she is served first.

But to make the comparisons simpler, let's return to boring old integers. A priority queue can be initialized upon declaration, much like a vector, deque, or list:

```
int arr[5] = {10, 4, -30, 100, 75};
priority_queue <int>  pq(arr, arr+5);
```

Within pq, the elements are arranged so that the highest element is always at the front of the list, as shown in Figure 16.6.

Like the **stack** and **queue** templates, the **priority_queue** template is an adapted container; but it is built on a vector rather than a deque.

Note

A priority queue only guarantees that the front member (the first to be "popped") is the one with the highest value. The rest of the priority queue is organized internally as a "heap," as defined in Section 18.6.4, "Heap Algorithms." After the front item is popped, the queue will be reorganized so that the new highest member goes to the front. The advantage of this special "heap" organization is that it enables items to be added and deleted from very large queues (even millions of elements in size) in just a few steps.

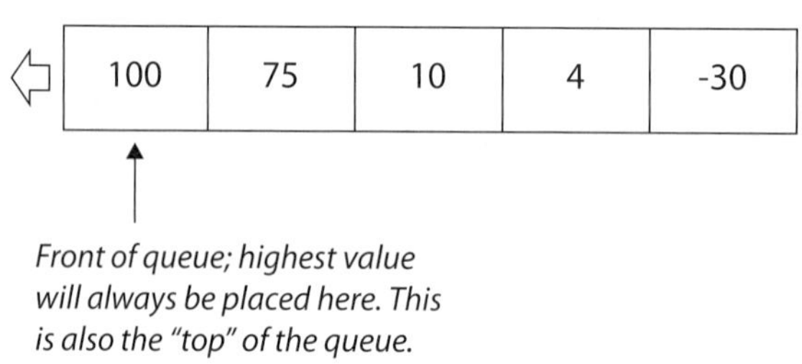

FIGURE 16.6 The priority_queue template

Here is a simple application using a priority queue. The effect is to print out the numbers from the array {10, 4, -30, 100, 75}, arranged in order from highest to lowest.

```
#include <iostream>
#include <queue>
using std::priority_queue;
using std::cout;
using std::endl;

int main() {
    int arr[5] = {10, 4, -30, 100, 75};
    priority_queue<int> pq(arr, arr + 5);
    while(!pq.empty()) {
        cout << pq.top() << " ";
        pq.pop();
    };
    cout << endl;
    return 0;
}
```

The output of this program is:

```
100 75 10 4 -30
```

16.5.1 Priority Queue Constructors

When using this template, remember to include the <queue> header and that **priority_queue** is part of the **std** namespace, as are **cout** and **endl**.

```
#include <queue>
using std::priority_queue;
using std::cout;
using std::endl;
```

Descriptions follow.

- **priority_queue**<*type*> *name*

  Creates a priority queue that is initially empty. The base type must support the less-than operator (<).

  ```
  priority_queue<int>  pqInt;
  ```

  You can add values using the **push** member function.

  ```
  pqInt.push(100);  // Add 100 as first elem.
  pqInt.push(200);  // Add 200, goes to front of q.
  ```

- **priority_queue**<*type*> *name*(*less_than_f*)

  Creates a priority queue that is initially empty and uses the comparison function *less_than_f*. The function returns **true** if the first of two arguments passed to it is less than the second.

  For example, the following code creates a priority queue in which elements are sorted according to absolute value (negatives are sorted as if they were positive):

```
#include <queue>
#include <cstdlib>
using std::priority_queue;

bool comp_ints(int &a, int &b) {
     return abs(a) < abs(b);
}
priority_queue<int>  pqInt(comp_ints);
```

- **priority_queue**<*type*> *name*(*first_iter*, *last_iter* [, *less_than_f*])

  Creates a priority queue and initializes it from another container. The optional *less_than_f* argument, if included, specifies a function to use for comparisons. The constructor copies values beginning with the element pointed to by *first_iter*, up to but not including the element pointed to by *last_iter*.

  This enables efficient initialization from arrays.

```
double arr[5] = {10, 4, -30, 100, 75};
priority_queue<double> pq(arr, arr + 5);
```

16.5.2 Priority Queue Member Functions

Again, when using this template, remember to include the <queue> header. The examples in this section assume that this header is included, along with **using** statements.

```
#include <queue>
#include <iostream>
using std::priority_queue;
using std::cout;
using std::endl;
```

Descriptions of the **priority_queue** member functions follow.

- *pr_queue_obj*.**empty()**

  Returns **true** if the vector has no elements; returns **false** otherwise.

```
while (!pq.empty())  {
     cout << pq.top() << endl;
     pq.pop();
}
```

- *pr_queue_obj*.**pop()**

  Removes the front element from the priority queue. This function parallels the use of the **pop** function with the **stack** template, but the element removed is from the front; with a priority queue, this element is necessarily the largest in value.

  The **pop** function does not return a value. The **top** and **pop** functions are typically used together. Remember to "top and pop"—in that order.

```
cout << pq.top() << endl;
pq.pop();
```

- *pr_queue_obj*.**push(*value*)**

  Adds the specified value to the priority queue. It is automatically placed in its proper position according to the rules of a "heap." (See Section 18.6.4 for more information on this special data structure.)

```
priority_queue<double>  pqNums;
pqNums.push(3.141592); // Place into pqNums.
```

- *pr_queue_obj*.**size()**

  Returns the number of elements currently in the priority queue. This value is returned as an unsigned integer.

```
while (pq.size() > 0) {
     cout << pq.top() << endl;
     pq.pop();
}
```

- *pr_queue_obj*.**top()**

  Returns the value at the front of the priority queue—which necessarily is also the highest in value. The **top** function is often called along with **pop**; otherwise, the same element remains at the top of the queue and nothing else can be accessed.

```
cout << pq.top() << endl;  // Get first element.
pq.pop();                  // Pop it.
```

16.6 Sample App: Find the Median

The median of a group—as opposed to the *mean,* or average—is a value N such that the number of elements greater than N is the same as the number of elements less than N. So the median of {0, 1, 2, 3, 4, 95} is not 25 (the average), but 3.

The sample program in this section reads a series of numbers from the console and inserts them into a list container. Then the program sorts the numbers and finds the average of the N1th and N2th numbers, where N1 and N2 are the middle two positions of the list.

If there is an odd number of numbers in the list, N1 and N2 are the same. For example, if there are three items, then N1 and N2 are both 1, which indexes the second position.

In either case, averaging N1 and N2 together produces the median, which is the desired value.

```
#include <iostream>
#include <string>
#include <sstream>
#include <list>

using std::string;         // Alternatively, you can use
using std::stringstream;   //  using namespace std.
using std::list;
using std::cout;
using std::cin;
using std::endl;

list<double> numList;

double get_nth_item(int n);

int main() {
     string input_str;
     cout << "Enter a series of numbers: ";
     getline(cin, input_str);
     stringstream ss(input_str);
     double x = 0.0;
     while (ss >> x) {
          numList.push_back(x);
     }
     numList.sort();
     int n1 = numList.size()/2;
     int n2 = (numList.size() - 1)/2;
     cout << "Median value is: ";
     cout <<  (get_nth_item(n1) + get_nth_item(n2)) / 2;
     cout << endl;
     cout << "Press ENTER to exit.";
     cin.ignore();
     return 0;
}

double get_nth_item(int n) {
     list<double>::iterator it = numList.begin();
     while(n-- > 0) {
          ++it;
     }
     return *it;
}
```

Exercises

1. Revise the application so that rather than iterating through a list, the program initializes a vector from numList after initializing this list and sorting it. The vector can then be indexed directly with the numbers n1 and n2 rather than calling get_nth_item. Do you think this is more efficient, or not?
2. Extend the application so that it reports average, minimum, and maximum as well as the median.
3. What happens if the list is empty (if the end user enters no numbers at all)? Write appropriate error-handling code to prevent a runtime error.
4. Write an application to calculate standard deviation. The standard deviation is defined as follows, in which S is the sum of $(\text{elem} - \text{avg})^2$ for each element, and N is the number of elements. For example, for {1, 2, 3}, subtract each element from the average, 2, and square the results, to get {1, 0, 1}; then sum these to get 2. The standard deviation would then be the square root of 2/3, or approximately 0.82.

   ```
   S = Σ(elem – avg)²
   Standard Deviation = Square-root(S/N)
   ```

CHAPTER 17

STL Associated Containers (map, set)

The most sophisticated STL containers are the associated containers, which are effectively rudimentary databases.

Although associated containers lack several database features, such as a query language and a user interface, they do support the basic storage and lookup operations of a database engine. In fact, maps are sometimes referred to as "data dictionaries," and they can be used for many tasks related to database operations, such as data translation.

The need for associated containers became evident when programmers had to store large amounts of data and realized that constantly searching an array was inefficient. An associated container, by contrast, offers virtual one-step access to an element according to its key value. (In reality, such access is not instantaneous, of course; this chapter discusses the underlying implementation.)

This chapter briefly describes the **pair** template, which is used to associate two objects with each other, and then covers each of the associated container classes:

- **pair**
- **map**
- **set**
- **multimap**
- **multiset**
- Unordered (hash-table) versions of **map**, **set**, **multimap**, and **multiset** (C++11 only)

17.1 The pair Template

Using the **map** template requires use of the **pair** template. The latter is necessary because it enables you to pair a key value with its associated value, which maps require. Fortunately, use of the **pair** template is easy.

The **pair** template is provided when you include the <map> header. The name **pair** is part of the **std** namespace, so either include the **using** statement or use the **std::** prefix.

```
#include <map>
using std::pair;
```

A pair can be created with either of the following constructors:

```
pair<type1, type2>  name
pair<type1, type2>  name(arg1, arg2)
```

The following statements create some sample pairs.

```
pair<int, double>       nums(5, 3.141592);
pair<int, const char*>  i_str(1, "cat");
```

The most important thing to know about this template is that it defines two members, which—logically enough—are named **first** and **second**.

```
pair_obj.first                    // First member
pair_obj.second                  // Second member
```

For example:

```
#include <string>

using std::string;
using std::pair;
using std::cout;
using std::endl;

pair<string, string>  my_name("White", "Rabbit");
cout << "My name is " << my_name.first << " ";
cout << my_name.second << "." << endl;
```

Or, as another example:

```
pair<string, double>  height_data1("Tom", 6.1);
cout << "The height of " << height_data1.first;
cout << "is " << height_data1.second << endl;
```

This prints:

```
The height of Tom is 6.1
```

C++ provides a simple, useful function for making pairs, named **make_pair**, which determines the types from the arguments provided.

For example, the following statement creates a pair of type pair<int, int> and then assigns it to a previously created, but empty, pair.

```
pair<int, int> pair_o_ints;
pair_o_ints = make_pair(9, 7);
```

17.2 The map Template

This is the most sophisticated of the STL container classes. To use the **map** template, first include the <map> header. The name **map** is part of the **std** namespace, so remember to include a **using** statement unless you're willing to refer to the template name as **std::map**.

```
#include <map>
using std::map;
```

You can then use the following syntax to create an empty map object:

```
map<key_type, val_type>  name;
```

in which *key_type* can be any type that supports the less-than operator, <, according to the rules of strict weak ordering described in Section 16.1, "Sorting Elements (Strict Weak Ordering)." (Alternatively, you can supply a comparison function, as described in Section 17.2.6, "Map Constructors.")

For example, the following declarations create several map objects, each of them using a **string** object as a key field. It's not required that you use a string as a key value, but it's common.

```
map<string, int>     map1;
map<string, double>  map2;
map<string, string>  empMap;
```

The first map object, map1, is a container in which each element has a string as its key and an integer as its associated value. Similarly, map2 is a container using a string key value for an element that contains an associated value of type **double**. One way to use such a container is to look up special values such as pi:

```
#include <map>
using std::map;
map<string, double>  wordNums;
wordNums["pi"] = 3.141592;
wordNums["e"] = 2.7182818;
wordNums["phi"] = 1.6083399;
```

This container, wordNums, could be used to efficiently translate names into numeric values. For example, a program might read words from a file and translate special words, as appropriate. In this case, the value of pi could be printed this way:

```
std::cout << wordNums["pi"];
```

The preceding statement prints:

```
3.141592
```

This syntax introduces a new way of using the subscript operator. Up until now, all the other container types that supported indexing—arrays, vectors, and deques—required that an index be an integer. But a map container uses a value of *key_type* as an index. Or, in terms, of syntax:

map_name[*key_val*]

in which *key_val* is a data item having type *key_type*. This produces a reference to the value associated with its key. Because this is a reference, you can use it to either get or set the associated value. The behavior differs depending on whether an element identified by the *key_arg* value already exists.

- If the element identified by *key_val* already exists, the use of *map_name*[*arg*] finds that element and returns a reference to the associated value.
- If the element identified by *key_val* does not exist, it's added to the map.

The next section shows how to use this syntax to populate a simple database.

This **string** type is ideal, in part because of its meaningful support for <. You could, of course, use a C-string. But to use a C-string (declared as type **const char** *) for the key value, it's necessary to supply a comparison function that calls **strcmp**. Otherwise, the map would resolve comparisons according to numeric addresses of the pointers involved (which are arbitrary) rather than by alphabetical order of strings. See Section 17.2.6 for more information.

17.2.1 Populating a Map

A good way to think of a map is as a rudimentary database. Suppose the MicroSlop Corporation commissions you to create an employee database, with the following specification.

- The first member of each record is the employee ID (an email alias such as "BrianO").
- The second member of each record is the job title.

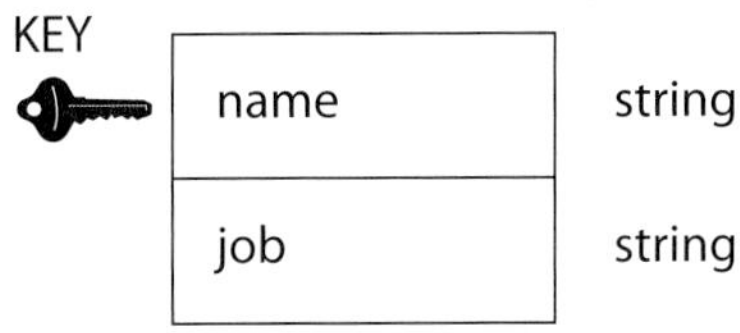

FIGURE 17.1 Design of a simple database

The company wants its human resources personnel to be able to enter an employee name and get back the job title. The employee name is therefore the key field. We can conceive of this simple database design as it is shown in Figure 17.1.

The following statements implement this database by creating a map object consisting of records made up of the two string members, representing employee name and job title.

```
#include <map>
#include <string>
using std::map;
using std::string;
. . .
map<string, string>  empMap;
empMap["BillG"] = "CEO";
empMap["BrianO"] = "Programmer";
empMap["SteveB"] = "Executive VP";
empMap["SamIAM"] = "Product Manager";
empMap["Drone"] = "Director of Bureaucratic Proliferation";
```

Each time the index operator is used on a key value (such as "BillG"), the container searches for this key in the database. If no matching element is found, a new element is inserted. Because all these entries are new, each statement has the effect of adding an element.

For example, the following statement did not find an element whose key value was "BillG"—because the database was empty at that point—so it inserted a new element with the pair "BillG" and "CEO".

```
empMap["BillG"] = "CEO";
```

Once a map is populated with elements, you can use the same syntax to retrieve values.

```
std::cout << "Bill's job title is: " << empMap["BillG"];
```

Assuming that the BillG record is already in the database, the effect of the statement is to find that record and get a reference to the associated value. So the statement prints:

```
Bill's job title is CEO
```

You can also use the indexing syntax to change Bill's title or to promote Steve.

```
empMap["BillG"] = "Chairman";
empMap["SteveB"] = "President";
```

Assuming the records identified with key values "BillG" and "SteveB" already exist, the effect of these statements is not to add new elements but to change their associated values (job titles).

This syntax is powerful and versatile. However, it doesn't do everything you might want. A common operation with databases is to first inquire as to whether a certain element (as identified by key value) is in the container; and then, depending on whether it is there, take different actions. The **find** member function, described in the next section, enables this process.

Figure 17.2 illustrates the database resulting from the statements shown earlier. (Note: Here I've adopted abbreviations of some of the job titles, such as "D.B.P." for "Director of Bureaucratic Proliferation.") Elements are ordered by key value, not by associated value.

This is the logical structure of the database as seen from the standpoint of a user. It's like a magic box in which you hand a slip of paper saying "BillG" and you get back another slip of paper saying "CEO". These lookups are fast, but they do have a cost, even though it is small. Section 17.2.5, "Map Implementation: Binary Trees," discusses performance and implementation issues.

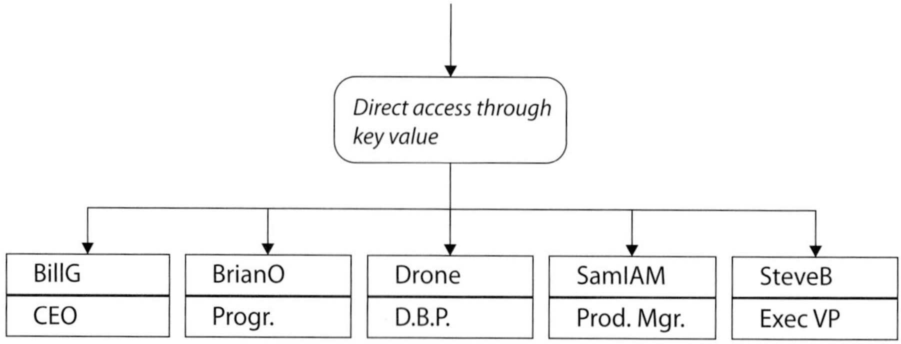

FIGURE 17.2 Contents of a simple database

17.2.2 Finding an Existing Map Element

When working with a database, it is common to do the following.

- Get a target key value.
- Search for this key value within the container, and if an element with that key is found, report back the associated value of the element.
- If the key value is not found, report that there is no such element.

The subscript operator, [], fails to meet this need, because if the key value is not found, the container goes ahead and adds a new element without telling you.

The **map** template's **find** function meets the desired need in this case. It takes a key value as its argument:

```
map_object.find(key_value)
```

If the search is successful, the **find** function returns an iterator pointing to the element found. If unsuccessful, the function returns *map_object*.**end**().

A map iterator, in turn, points to a **pair** object. The first member of this pair is its key value; the second is its associated value.

```
map_iterator->first            //  Key value
map_iterator->second           // Associated value
```

The following example function uses the **find** member function to search the MicroSlop employee database, identified as empMap in the code. The function takes an employee name as its first argument. If this name is found, the function returns **true** and places the associated value in the second argument to the function (job). Otherwise, it returns **false**.

```
bool find_rec(string name, string& job) {
     map<string, string>::iterator it;
     it = empMap.find(name);      // Try to find record.
     if (it != empMap.end()) {    // Record was found.
          job = it->second;
          return true;
     }
     return false;      // Record not found; return false.
}
```

This example introduces the use of an iterator for the **map** template. Like iterators for the other templates, it's a sophisticated pointer that can be used to step through the container. It's also used in this context, to hold the return value of the **find** member function.

```
     map<string, string>::iterator it;
```

The example then gets the second member in the pair pointed to by the iterator. This produces a reference to the associated value, which the function then places in the argument named "job."

```
     job = it->second;
```

Having written the find_rec function, you can now respond to database inquiries. For example:

```
string empName = "BillG";    // Person to find.
string empJob;
if find_rec(empName, empJob) {
     cout << "Job title is: " << empJob << endl;
} else {
     cout << "Employee not found." << endl;
}
```

17.2.3 A More Sophisticated Record Type

A more realistic scenario is a database that stores several values in each record. For example, assume the database design record shown in Figure 17.3.

Given this design, the key value (name) is still a string, but the associated values (that is, the nonkey values) are all placed into a class.

```
class empRec {
public:
     string job;
     int salary_level;
     int year_hired;
     empRec() {}
     empRec(string nJob, int nSal, int nYear) :
       job(nJob), salary_level(nSal), year_hired(nYear)
       {}
};
```

This class includes a couple of constructors. The second constructor can be used to efficiently declare and initialize elements. For example:

```
map<string, empRec> empMap;
empMap["BillG"]  = empRec("CEO", 10, 1979);
empMap["SteveB"] = empRec("Executive VP", 9, 1980);
empMap["BrianO"] = empRec("Programmer", 3, 1986);
empMap["SamIAM"] = empRec("Product Manager", 5, 1990);
empMap["Drone"]  = empRec(
     "Director of Bureaucratic Proliferation", 8, 1999);
```

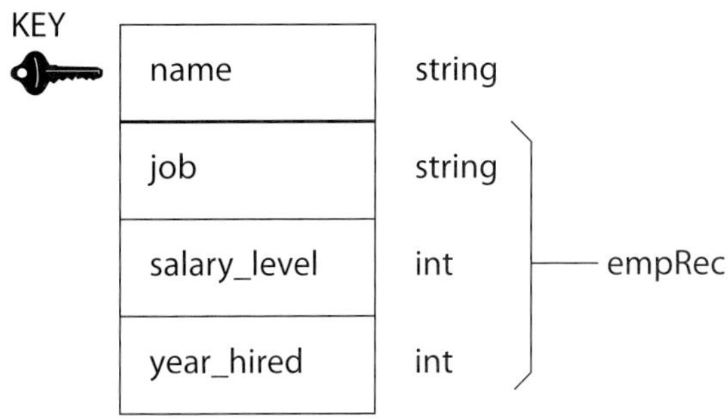

FIGURE 17.3 Design for a more complete database

Assuming the database starts out as empty, these uses of the subscript operator cause insertion of new elements, creating the database shown in Figure 17.4. Logically, the structure is the same as the earlier example, except that each associated value (empRec) holds more data.

Both the subscript operator, [], and the **find** member function can be used to retrieve data, but they can result in different levels of efficiency at runtime.

For example, one obvious way to change Bill's salary level from 10 to 11 is to look up his record, modify the pay level, and then store the new object.

```
empRec my_rec = empMap["BillG"];  // Get current settings
                                  //  for BillG.
++my_rec.salary_level;            // Change salary.
empMap["BillG"] = my_rec;         // Store updated record.
```

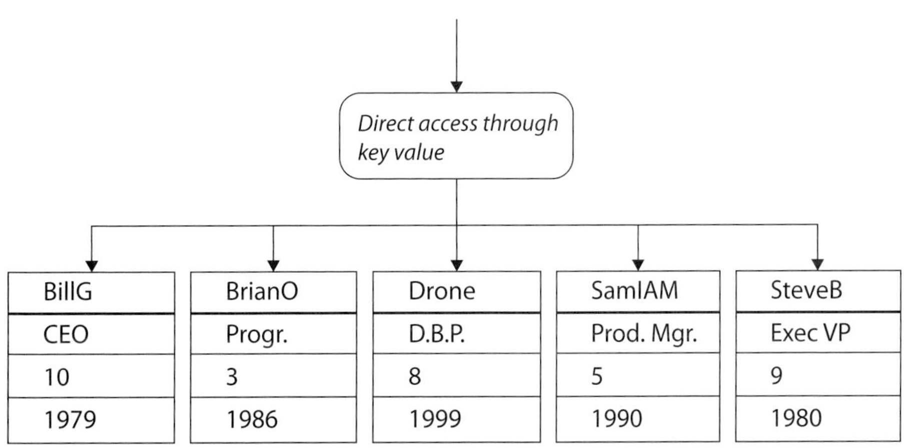

FIGURE 17.4 A more complete employee database

Although this code succeeds in raising BillG's pay, it's not the most efficient technique. The program will have better runtime performance when you reduce the number of lookups, as in:

```
map<string, empRec>::iterator it;
it = empMap.find("BillG");
if (it != empMap.end()) {
     ++(it->second).salary_level;
}
```

This approach eliminates a second lookup operation and reduces the amount of copying. In this case, **find** returns an iterator, which is used to increase Bill's earnings.

To be safe, the previous example made sure that the record existed before updating it. Another approach is the following, which—unlike the previous example—goes ahead and adds a record if it's not there already. This is the most concise approach, but it assumes you want to add the record if it's missing, which might not always be the case.

```
++empMap["BillG"].salary_level;
```

This statement first looks up the BillG record. If BillG can't be found, the map adds the record whether you want it to or not. But, unless salary_level is initialized to a reasonable value, salary_level won't be meaningful for a newly added element in this case.

Given the new declarations, the tools for inserting and finding records are almost the same as they were for the simpler database. One difference, of course, is that the associated value is now an object of type empRec rather than a single string. Therefore, the find_rec function needs to be revised as follows (with the changes shown here in bold for illustration):

```
bool find_rec(string name, empRec& my_rec) {
     map<string, string>::iterator it;
     it = empMap.find(name);
     if (it != empMap.end()) {  // Record found.
          my_rec = it->second;
          return true;
     }                          // Record not found.
     return false;
}
```

You can now write a sample application that builds a database and enables the user to query the database as many times as desired. The program does the following.

- It populates the map with a series of records.
- It sets up a loop to query the end user. If the user presses ENTER with no input, the program quits. If the user enters an employee name, the program searches for

the record having that name as key, and, if that record exists, the program prints all the values in the record. If the name is not found, the program reports that fact.

- It continues querying the user until it quits.

Here is the complete program.

```
#include <map>
#include <string>
#include <iostream>

using std::map;              // Alternatively, you can use
using std::string;           //  using namespace std;
using std::cout;
using std::cin;
using std::endl;

class empRec {
public:
     string job;
     int salary_level;
     int year_hired;
     empRec() {}
     empRec(string nJob, int nSal, int nYear) :
      job(nJob), salary_level(nSal), year_hired(nYear)
      {}
};

map<string, empRec> empMap;

bool find_rec(string name, empRec& my_rec) {
     map<string, empRec>::iterator it;
     it = empMap.find(name);       // Try to find record.
     if (it != empMap.end()) {     // Record was found.
          my_rec = it->second;
          return true;
     }
     return false;     // Record not found; return false.
}

int main() {
     string strInput, strTitle;
     empRec my_rec;
     // Populate the database with five records.
     empMap["BillG"]  = empRec("CEO", 10, 1979);
     empMap["SteveB"] = empRec("Executive VP", 9, 1980);
     empMap["BrianO"] = empRec("Programmer", 3, 1986);
```

```
    empMap["SamIAM"] = empRec("Product Mgr.", 5, 1990);
    empMap["Drone"]  = empRec(
       "Director of Bureaucratic Proliferation", 8, 1999);
    while(true) {
         cout << "Enter name (or press ENTER to exit): ";
         getline(cin, strInput);
         if (strInput.size() == 0) {
              break;
         }
         if (find_rec(strInput, my_rec)) {
              cout << "job: ";
              cout << my_rec.job << endl;
              cout << "year hired: ";
              cout << my_rec.year_hired << endl;
              cout << "salary level: ";
              cout << my_rec.salary_level << endl << endl;
         } else {
              cout << "Employee not found." << endl;
         }
    }
    return 0;
}
```

17.2.4 Iterating through a Map

When declaring an iterator, remember that two types need to be matched in declarations, not just one:

map<*key_type*, *val_type*>**::iterator** *name*

For example, here are the declarations for empMap along with an iterator for that map. Assume that the empRec class has already been declared.

```
#include <map>
#include <string>
using std::map;
using std::string;

map<string, empRec>  empMap;
map<string, empRec>::iterator  it;  // Matching iterator.
```

Remember, also, that with a map container, an iterator points to a pair that has a **first** member (the key value) and a **second** member (the associated value). For example, the following statements iterate through the entire database from beginning to end, printing out each record:

```
map<string, empRec>::iterator  it;
empRec my_rec;
for (it = empMap.begin(); it != empMap.end(); ++it) {
     cout << "Employee ID (name): " << it->first;
     my_rec = it->second;
     cout << "Job: " << my_rec.job << endl;
     cout << "Level: " << my_rec.salary_level << endl;
     cout << "Year hired: " << my_rec.year_hired << endl;
}
```

Although map containers support the subscript operator directly, this is a specialized usage; maps are not truly random-access containers, and map iterators do not support the subscript operator or iterator arithmetic—aside from increment (++) and decrement (--). Dereferencing an iterator produces a pair in which the first member is the key value and the second is the associated value.

17.2.5 Map Implementation: Binary Trees

The object-oriented paradigm encourages magical thinking to a degree. An object's users are encouraged to think of an object as a black box that takes an input (in this case, a key value) and gives back a result. But performance considerations still matter. It helps to understand how STL containers are implemented. The **map** template is usually implemented as a binary tree.

Starting with the small database in this chapter (five employees), assume two more are added: "Clod", a marketing exec, and "ElenA", a software tester. This brings the total to seven elements. In alpha order from first to last, the key values are:

```
BillG   BrianO   Clod   Drone   ElenA   SamIAM   SteveB
```

Figure 17.5 illustrates a binary-tree representation of the database. Each left child in the tree has a less-than relationship to its parent and each right child has a greater-than relationship to its parent.

As the number of elements increases, the length of time needed for a lookup increases logarithmically. If you're a math major, you know what this means. If not, consider the following.

- It takes roughly ten comparisons, on average, to find a target key value out of one thousand elements (or failing that, to verify that the element does not yet exist).
- It takes roughly 20 comparisons to find a target key value out of one million elements.
- It takes roughly 30 comparisons to find a target key value out of one *billion* (thousand million) elements.

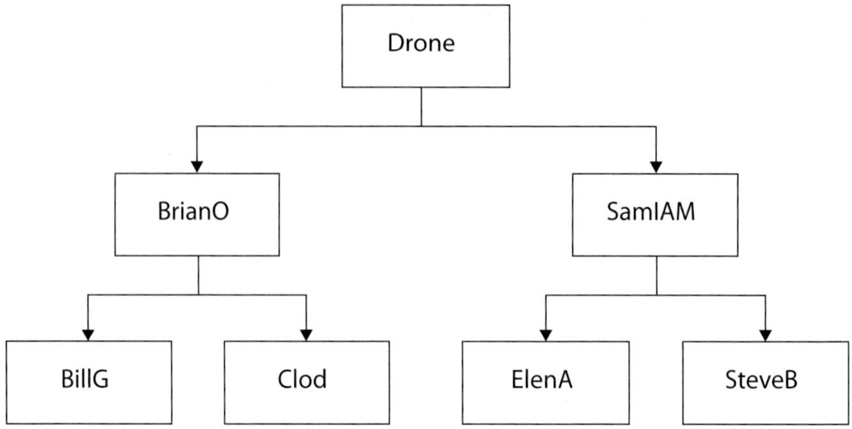

FIGURE 17.5 Binary tree implementation

Admittedly, 30 comparisons take longer than ten—although for modern computers, the difference between them can be measured in a tiny fraction of a second.

Now imagine a database built on top of an array or linked list. Even if such a list is maintained in continually sorted order, you still have to search, on average, half the list. In the case of one billion records that would mean doing *five hundred million* comparisons rather than 30!

Yet there is a tradeoff. Lookup operations are potentially many times faster with a binary tree. Against that, binary trees require greater overhead, as extra work has to be done each time an element is inserted or deleted.

Consider this problem.

- You want to write all the map contents out to a data file at the end of a session.
- The obvious way to do this is to write out elements one record at a time. You start at the beginning with *map_obj*.**begin()** and iterate through the container. Elements are written to the file in order of their key values.
- The next day, someone opens the file, and the program loads the contents into a map. The records are read in sequential order, with each key value less than the one it precedes, because they were written out that way.

Because the elements are read in this order, it looks like the tree will be one-sided: All the elements are added as the right child of the previous element, causing the tree to degenerate into a one-dimensional linked list.

Fortunately, binary trees for wide commercial use (including STL **map** templates) use techniques to keep the tree well balanced after each and every insertion and deletion. The most popular solution is the red-black-tree algorithm. It's not necessary to go into details here, except to note that the red-black-tree algorithms guarantee that the path from the root to the farthest leaf is no longer than twice the path from the root to the shortest leaf.

But—and this is the important point—there is some overhead for tree-balancing algorithms. The potential delay is proportional to the depth of the tree, not to its size; so again, the maximum performance penalty possible increases logarithmically. But still, such operations are not entirely cost-free.

17.2.6 Map Constructors

In using any of the **map** template member functions, remember to include the <map> header. The name **map** is part of the **std** namespace, so either include a **using** statement or refer to the map template with its **std::** prefix.

```
#include <map>
#include <string>
using std::map;
using std::string;
```

The map template constructors provide several ways to create and initialize a **map** class. The key type must provide a meaningful less-than operator (<), or a comparison function must be provided that returns **true** if the first argument is less than the second.

- **map**<*key_type*, *val_type*> *name*

  Creates a map object with specified *key_type* and *val_type*, initially empty.

  ```
  map<string, double>  wordx;
  ```

- **map**<*key_type*, *val_type*, *less_than_class*> *name*

  Creates a map object and provides a comparison function in the form of a function-object class (see example). This function takes two arguments of the *key_type* and returns **true** if the first argument is less than the second.

  For example, the following statements create a map with a C-string key and a floating-point (**double**) associated value. The C-string type is implemented as **const char ***, enabling string literals to be used. A comparison function is necessary to produce meaningful comparisons between C-strings; otherwise, the comparison would compare which of two addresses was lower in memory.

  ```
  #include <cstring>
  typedef const char* CSTR;
  ```

```
class compstr_class {
public:
   bool operator() (CSTR s1, CSTR s2) const{
      return strcmp(s1, s2) < 0;
   }
};

map<CSTR, double, compstr_class>  wordx;
map<CSTR, double, compstr_class>::iterator it;
```

▸ **map**<*key_type*, *val_type*, *less_than_type*> *name*(*less_than_f*)

Similar to the previous constructor, except that the comparison function is provided as a function pointer, *less_than_f*. In addition, the function-pointer type must be provided as a third template argument, as shown in the following example:

```
#include <cstring>
typedef const char* CSTR;

bool compstr(CSTR s1, CSTR s2) {
     return strcmp(s1, s2) < 0;
}

map<CSTR, double, bool(*)(CSTR, CSTR)>
  wordx(compstr);
map<CSTR, double, bool(*)(CSTR, CSTR)>::iterator
  it;
```

▸ **map**<*key_type*, *val_type*> *name*(*first_iter*, *last_iter*)

Creates a map object and initializes it from elements in another container. Each such element should be a **pair** container, in which the types are compatible with *key_type* and *val_type*. For example:

```
typedef  pair<string, double>  rec_type;
rec_type arr[4] = { {"pi", 3.141592},
                    {"e", 2.7182818},
                    {"phi", 1.6083399},
                    {"sqrt2", 2.414214}
};
map<string, double>  wordx(arr, arr + 4);
```

This constructor can also specify a comparison-function class or a comparison function as shown with previous constructors. If a comparison function is used, it is the constructor's third argument.

▸ **map**<*key_type*, *val_type*> *name*(*map_obj2*)

Creates a map and initializes its contents from an existing map object with compatible types. For example, the following statements create a map, empMap1, and then use it to initialize a second map, empMap2. They will initially have identical contents.

```
std::pair<string, string> empArr[3] =
     { {"BillG", "CEO"}, {"SteveB", "Exec VP"},
       {"BrianO", "Programmer"} };
map<string, string>  empMap1(empArr, empArr + 3);

map<string, string>  empMap2(empMap1);
```

This constructor can also specify a comparison-function class or a comparison function as shown with previous constructors. If a comparison function is used, it is the constructor's second argument.

17.2.7 Concise Summary of Map Functions

Table 17.1 summarizes the most essential commonly used functions for map containers. Section 17.2.8, "Map Member Functions in Detail," describes these in detail, along with the remaining member functions.

In addition to the member functions, the map template supports the subscript and assignment operators. The subscript operator, [], described earlier, can be used to insert, find, or update a record associated with a specified key.

For example, the following statement retrieves the employee record for BillG (assuming that the associated value has empRec type):

```
empRec my_rec = empMap["BillG"];
```

TABLE 17.1 Commonly Used Functions of the map Template

Member Function	Description
find	Searches for an element according to its key value and returns an iterator pointing to the element if found; returns *map_obj*.**end**() otherwise.
insert	Inserts one or more elements. The version that inserts one element returns a pair containing a true/false flag indicating whether the element is new.
erase	Removes one or more elements, specified by key value, iterator, or a range of elements.
begin, **end**	Return starting and ending iterators for standard, forward iteration.
rbegin, **rend**	Return starting and ending iterators for reverse iteration.
size	Returns the number of elements in the map.
lower_bound, **upper_bound**	Return iterators bounding a specified range (for example, all records with keys between "A" and "B").

The **map** template also supports an assignment operator (=) for copying the contents of one map container to another.

```
map<string, empRec>  empMap1;
map<string, empRec>  empMap2;
// Add some records to empMap1...
. . .
empMap2 = empMap1;   // Now copy the map.
```

17.2.8 Map Member Functions in Detail

In using any of the **map** template member functions, remember to include the <map> header. The name **map** is part of the **std** namespace, so either include a **using** statement or refer to the map template with its **std::** prefix.

```
#include <map>
using std::map;
using std::pair;   // Include if referring to "pair"
```

Examples in this section also assume the following:

```
#include <iostream>
#include <string>
using std::cout;
using std::endl;
using std::string;
```

Descriptions of the **map** member functions follow.

- *map_obj*.**begin()**

  Returns an iterator pointing to the first element in the map. This is always the element that has the lowest key value, not necessarily the first element to be inserted. For example, the following statements print out the contents of a map in order of key values.

```
map<string, string>  empMap;
map<string, string>::iterator  it;
empMap["ElenA"] = "Tester";
empMap["SteveB"] = "Executive VP";
empMap["BillG"] = "CEO";
empMap["BrianO"] = "Programmer";
for (it = empMap.begin(); it != empMap.end();
  ++it) {
     cout << it->first << " \t";
     cout << it->second << end;
}
```

This prints out:

```
BillG     CEO
BrianO    Programmer
ElenA     Tester
SteveB    Executive VP
```

▸ *map_obj*.**clear()**

Removes all elements from the map object, reducing its size to zero. For example:

```
empMap.clear();    // Fire everyone!
```

▸ *map_obj*.**count(***key_val***)**

Returns an integer containing the number of elements that have the specified key value. With map containers (as opposed to **multimap** template classes), the value returned is either 1 or 0. This is an alternative to the **find** function.

```
if (empMap.count("BillG") == 0) {
     cout << "BillG was not found." << endl;
     cout << "(Perhaps he retired.)" << endl;
}
```

▸ *map_obj*.**empty()**

Returns **true** if there are no elements in the map container; returns **false** otherwise.

▸ *map_obj*.**end()**

Returns an iterator pointing *one position past* the last element. This function is most often used in conjunction with **begin** to iterate through the container, and with **find** as a return value that indicates an element was not found. See **begin** and **find** for examples.

▸ *map_obj*.**erase(***key_val***)**

Erases the element identified by the key value, if any, and returns either 1 or 0 (the number of elements erased). If 0 is returned, no element with the key value was found.

For example, the following statement removes BrianO from the employee database, but advises the user in case the record identified by the "BrianO" key value did not exist.

```
if(empMap.erase("BrianO") > 0) {
     cout << "Removal successful." << endl;
} else {
     cout << "BrianO not found." << endl;
}
```

- *map_obj*.**erase**(*pos_iter*)

  Erases the element pointed to by *pos_iter*, an iterator.

```
map<string, string>  empMap;
map<string, string>::iterator  it;
empMap["BillG"] = "CEO";
empMap["Drone"] =
  "Director of Bureaucratic Proliferation";
. . .
it = empMap.find("Drone");
if (it != empMap.end()) {
     erase(it);                    // Fire Drone!
}
```

- *map_obj*.**erase**(*first_iter*, *last_iter*)

  Erases a range beginning with the element pointed to by *first_iter*, up to but not including the element pointed to by *last_iter*. For example, the following statements remove all records from the database whose key values lie between "A" and "C". This has the effect of removing every element with a key that starts with the letter "A" or "B".

```
map<string, string>  empMap;
map<string, string>::iterator  it1, it2;
. . .
it1 = empMap.lower_bound("A");
it2 = empMap.upper_bound("C");
empMap.erase(it1, it2);
```

- *map_obj*.**find**(*key_val*)

  Searches for an element with a matching key value and returns an iterator to that element. If none was found, the iterator returned has the value *map_obj*.**end**(). For example, the following statements search for the value "theta".

```
map<string, double>  wordx;
map<string, double>::iterator  it;
wordx["pi"] = 3.14159265;
wordx["e"] = 2.7182818;
wordx["phi"] = 1.618034;
. . .
it = wordx.find("theta");     // Look for theta.
if (it == wordx.end()) {
     cout << "Theta not found." << endl;
} else {
     cout << "Value is " << it->second << endl;
}
```

- *map_obj*.**insert**(*elem_value*)

  Inserts an element passed as a pair of type **pair**<*T1*, *T2*>, where *T1* is the map's key-value type and *T2* is the map's associated-value type. If an element with the specified key value already exists, the function makes no change.

  The value returned is another pair: The **first** member of this return-value pair is an iterator to the element that was inserted, so it has type **map**<*T1*, *T2*>**::iterator**. The **second** member of the pair is a **bool** value that is **true** if the insertion created a new element. For example, the following statements attempt to add an element with key value "BillG" and associated value "CEO".

```
map<string, string>  empMap;

map<string, string>::iterator  it;
typedef  map<string, string>::iterator  it_type;
pair<it_type, bool>  rv;
. . .
// Add some values...
. . .
rv =   empMap.insert(make_pair("BillG", "CEO"));
if (rv->second) {
   it = rv->first;         // Insertion succeeded;
                           // Save iterator.
   cout << "BillG added to database." << endl;
} else {
   cout << "BillG already in database." << endl;
}
```

- *map_obj*.**insert**(*pos_iter*, *elem*)

  Inserts an element passed as a pair of type **pair**<*T1*, *T2*>, where *T1* is the map's key-value type and *T2* is the map's associated-value type. If an element with the specified key value already exists, the function makes no change.

  This version of **insert** is similar to the previous version but uses *pos_iter*, an iterator, as a hint as to where to insert an element. The value returned is an iterator to the element that was inserted. If an element already existed with the same key value, then the function returns an iterator pointing to that element.

  The *pos_iter* is a suggestion of where to look for an insertion point: If *pos_iter* points to the position just before the position where the element should be inserted, the insertion is done with maximum efficiency, reducing lookup time. This can enable a series of efficient insertions of elements at consecutive positions in the map. For example:

```
map<string, string>  empMap;
map<string, string>::iterator  it;
it = empMap.insert(empMap.end(),
       make_pair("BarbaraAnn", "VP"));
```

```
it = empMap.insert(it, make_pair("BillG","CEO"));
it = empMap.insert(it, make_pair("BonniE",
   "Tester"));
it = empMap.insert(it, make_pair("Bore",
   "Director of Bureaucratic Proliferation."));
it = empMap.insert(it, make_pair("BrianO",
   "Programmer"));
```

▸ *map_obj*.**insert(***first_iter*, *last_iter***)**

Inserts a series of elements from another container, beginning with the element pointed to by *first_iter*, up to but not including the element pointed to by *last_iter*. Each of these elements must have type **pair**<*T1*, *T2*>, where *T1* is the map's key-value type and *T2* is the map's associated-value type. For each item inserted, the insertion only succeeds if there does not yet exist an element in map_obj with a matching key value.

```
map<string, double> wordx;
typedef  pair<string, double>  rec_type;
rec_type arr[3] = { {"pi", 3.141592},
                    {"e", 2.7182818},
                    {"phi", 1.60834}
};
empMap.insert(arr, arr + 3);
```

▸ *map_obj*.**lower_bound(***key_value***)**

Returns an iterator pointing to the first element whose key is greater than or equal to the specified *key_value* argument. For example:

```
map<string, double> wordx;
map<string, double>::iterator it;
wordx["pi"] = 3.141592;
wordx["e"] = 2.7182818;
wordx["phi"] = 1.60834;
it = wordx.lower_bound("p");
cout << "The first element starting with p is: ";
cout << it->first << "." << endl;
```

This prints:

```
The first element starting with p is phi.
```

▸ *map_obj*.**rbegin()**

Returns an iterator pointing to the last element in the map. This is always the element that has the greatest key value (not necessarily the last to be inserted).

This function can be used in conjunction with the **rend** function to iterate backward through the map. Note that incrementing a reverse iterator moves backward through the elements, not forward. For example, the following statements print out a database in reverse order of key values:

```
map<string, string>  empMap;
map<string, string>::reverse_iterator  rit;
empMap["ElenA"] = "Tester";
empMap["SteveB"] = "Executive VP";
empMap["Clod"] =
    "Director of Bureaucratic Proliferation";
empMap["BillG"] = "CEO";
empMap["BrianO"] = "Programmer";
for (rit = empMap.rbegin(); rit != empMap.rend();
++rit) {
     cout << rit->first << " \t";
     cout << rit->second << end;
}
```

This prints out:

```
SteveB     Executive VP
ElenA      Tester
Clod       Director of Bureaucratic Proliferation
BrianO     Programmer
BillG      CEO
```

- *map_obj*.**rend()**

  Returns an iterator pointing *one position before* the first element in the map. See **rbegin** for an example.

- *map_obj*.**size()**

  Returns the number of elements in the map object.

```
cout << "The database has " << empMap.size();
cout << " records." << endl;
```

- *map obj*.**swap(***map_obj2***)**

  Exchanges the contents of *map_obj* with those of *map_obj2*. The two maps must have the same structure.

```
map<string, double>  wordx1;
map<string, double>  wordx2;
. . .
wordx1.swap(wordx2);    // Swap!
```

- *map_obj*.**upper_bound(***key_value***)**

  Returns an iterator pointing to the first element whose key is greater than the specified *key_value*. For example, the following statements use the **lower_bound** and **upper_bound** functions to print all names in the database beginning with a capital "B".

```
map<string, string>  empMap;
map<string, string>::iterator  it, it1, it2;
empMap["ElenA"] = "Tester";
```

```
empMap["SteveB"] = "Executive VP";
empMap["BillG"] = "CEO";
empMap["BrianO"] = "Programmer";
empMap["Clod"] =
     "Director of Bureaucratic Proliferation";
empMap["BonniE"] = "Product Manager";
it1 = empMap.lower_bound("B");
it2 = empMap.upper_bound("C");
for(it = i1; it != it2; ++it) {
     cout << it->first << " \t";
     cout << it->second << endl;
}
```

These statements print:

```
BillG     CEO
BonniE    Product Manager
BrianO    Programmer
```

17.3 The set Template

The **set** template is similar to the **map** template, except that its elements have no associated value. Each element has just one value, which is also its key. Each element in a set must be unique.

Sets are usually implemented as binary trees, so the container can quickly look up an element directly, according to its value. (See Section 17.2.5 for more information on binary trees.)

To use the **set** template, include the <set> header. Also include a **using** statement unless you're willing to refer to the template name with its **std::** prefix.

```
#include <set>
using std::set;
```

You can then use the template to create a set. For example, the following declarations create a set of integers and a set of floating-point numbers (type **double**):

```
set<int>     intSet;
set<double>  fltSet;
```

Note that the base type (**int** and **double** in these cases) must support the less-than operator (<), or a comparison function must be provided.

The **set** template corresponds closely to the mathematical notion of a set. An element of a set has no associated value: An item either is in the set or is not in the set.

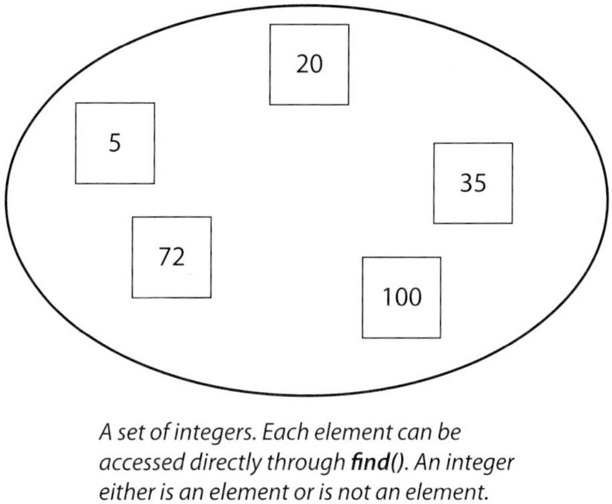

FIGURE 17.6 A set of integers

Consider a set containing the integers 5, 20, 35, 72, and 100, as shown in Figure 17.6. You can think of these numbers as independent elements to which the STL container provides direct, (virtual) one-step access.

You might object that in a mathematical set, order does not matter: {5, 20, 35, 72, 100} is equivalent to {72, 35, 100, 5, 20}.

But STL sets are ordered only for the purposes of searching and iteration. You can initialize one set from the array {5, 20, 35, 72, 100} and another from the array {72, 35, 100, 5, 20}, and the sets that result will be identical. It's possible that they may have binary trees that differ in some respects, but that detail is hidden; the two sets will be functionally the same.

17.3.1 Populating a Set

The **set** template does not support the subscript operator, [], as the **map** template does, but there are a couple of ways of inserting elements. You can, for example, insert elements during initialization.

If your compiler is fully compliant with the C++11 specification, elements can be added to sets more concisely and efficiently:

```
set<int>  my_num_set = {1, 2, 3, 10, 50, 74};
```

If your compiler is not C++11 compliant, you can still initialize from an array.

```
int arr[6] = {1, 2, 3, 10, 50, 74};
set<int>  my_num_set(arr, arr + 6);
```

You can also insert new elements at any time by calling the **insert** member function.

For example, the following statements create a set called most_wanted and then add the names of criminals.

```
#include <string>
using std::string;

set<string>  most_wanted;
most_wanted.insert("Al Capone");
most_wanted.insert("Professor Moriarty");
most_wanted.insert("John Dillinger");
most_wanted.insert("Barney");   // He loves u, u love he.
```

Note that attempting to insert Al Capone into the list a second time has no effect. (The return value, in that case, indicates that no insertion was made; see the **insert** function description in Section 17.3.5, "Set Member Functions in Detail.")

```
most_wanted.insert("Al Capone");
```

17.3.2 Finding an Element in a Set

The **find** member function searches for an element in the set and returns a valid iterator if the element was found. If the element was not found, the function returns *set_obj*.**end**().

So, using the example in the previous section, you can find whether an individual is in the most_wanted set by these statements:

```
set<string>::iterator  it;
it = most_wanted.find("Al Capone");
if (it != most_wanted.end()) {
     cout << "Al Capone is on the list." << endl;
} else {
     cout << "Capone is not on the list." << endl;
}
```

This example introduces the use of a set iterator. To declare an iterator for a set, use this syntax:

set<*base_type*>**::iterator** *name*

Once an iterator is declared, you can use it to step through the entire set, in order of the values of the elements.

```
string names[4] = {"Al Capone, "Professor Moriarty",
   "John Dillinger", "Clyde Barrow", "Bonnie Parker"};

set<string>  most_wanted(names, names + 4);
set<string>::iterator  it;

for (it = most_wanted.begin(); it != most_wanted.end();
++it) {
     cout << *it << endl;
}
```

These statements print out:

```
Al Capone
Bonnie Parker
Clyde Barrow
John Dillinger
Professor Moriarty
```

17.3.3 Set Constructors

The constructors for the **set** template parallel the constructors for the **map** template; the difference being that there is only one base type, rather than two. Remember to include the <set> header and that **set** is part of the **std** namespace.

```
#include <set>
using std::set;
```

Descriptions of the set constructors follow.

- **set**< *type*>   *name*

  Creates a map object containing an object of the specified *type*. This container is initially empty.

  ```
  set<double>  set_of_x;
  ```

- **set**<*type*, *less_than_class*>   *name*

  Creates a set object and provides a comparison function in the form of a function-object class (see example). This function takes two arguments of the base *type* and returns **true** if the first argument is less than the second.

  For example, the following statements create a set with C-string base type. The C-string type is implemented as **const char** *, enabling string literals to be used.

A comparison function is necessary to produce meaningful comparisons between C-strings; otherwise, the comparison would simply compare which of two addresses was lower in memory.

```
typedef const char* CSTR;

class compstr_class {
public:
     bool operator() (CSTR s1, CSTR s2) const {
          return strcmp(s1, s2) < 0;
     }
};

set<CSTR, compstr_class>  most_wanted;
set<CSTR, compstr_class>::iterator it;
```

- **set**< *type*, *less_than_type*> *name*(*less_than_f*)

Similar to the previous constructor, except that the comparison function is provided as a function pointer, *less_than_f*. In addition, the function-pointer type must be provided as a second template argument, as shown in the following example:

```
#include <set>
#include <cstring>
using namespace std;
typedef const char* CSTR;

bool compstrs(CSTR s1, CSTR s2) {
     return strcmp(s1, s2) < 0;
}

set<CSTR, bool(*)(CSTR, CSTR)>  wanted(compstrs);
set<CSTR, bool(*)(CSTR, CSTR)>::iterator it;
```

- **set**<*type*> *name*(*first_iter*, *last_iter*)

Creates a set object and initializes it from elements in another container. For example:

```
double arr[3] = {3.141592, 1.1618034, 2.7182818};

set<double>  set_of_x(arr, arr + 3);
```

This constructor can also specify a comparison object or comparison function as shown with previous constructors. If a pointer to a comparison function is used, the function address is passed as the constructor's third argument.

▸ **set**<*type*> *name*(*set_obj2*)

Creates a set and initializes its contents from an existing set object with compatible types. For example, the following statements create a set, setx1, and then use it to initialize setx2. They will initially have identical contents.

```
double arr[3] = {3.141592, 1.1618034, 2.7182818};
set<double>  setx1(arr, arr + 3);

set<double>  setx2(setx1);
```

This constructor can also specify a comparison object or comparison function as shown with previous constructors. If a pointer to a comparison function is used, the function address is passed as the constructor's second argument.

17.3.4 Concise Summary of Set Functions

Table 17.2 summarizes the most essential commonly used functions for set containers. Section 17.3.5 describes these in detail, along with the remaining member functions.

In addition to the member functions, the **set** template supports an assignment operator (=) for copying the contents of one map container to another.

```
set<string>  most_wanted;
set<string>  set_of_perps;
// Add some records to most_wanted...
. . .
set_of_perps = most_wanted;    // Now copy the first set.
```

TABLE 17.2 Commonly Used Functions of the set Template

Member Function	Description
find	Searches for an element and returns an iterator pointing to the element if found; returns *set_obj*.**end**() otherwise.
insert	Inserts one or more elements. The version that inserts one element returns a pair containing a true/false flag indicating whether the element is new.
erase	Removes one or more elements, specified by key value, iterator, or a range of elements.
begin, **end**	Return starting and ending iterators for standard, forward iteration.
rbegin, **rend**	Return starting and ending iterators for reverse iteration.
size	Returns the number of elements in the set.
lower_bound, **upper_bound**	Return iterators bounding a specified range (for example, all elements between "A" and "B").

17.3.5 Set Member Functions in Detail

When using any of the **set** template member functions, remember to include the <set> header. The name **set** is part of the **std** namespace, so either include a **using** statement or refer to the **set** template with its **std::** prefix.

```
#include <set>
using std::set;
```

Examples in this section also assume the following:

```
#include <iostream>
#include <string>
using std::cout;
using std::endl;
using std::string;
```

Descriptions of the member functions follow.

- *set_obj*.**begin()**

  Returns an iterator pointing to the first element in the set. This is always the element with the lowest value. For example, the following statements print out the contents of a set in alphabetical order. The order in which they were inserted does not matter.

```
string names[7] = { "Clyde Barrow",
     "Bonnie Parker",  "Al Capone",
     "Professor Moriarty", "Joker",
     "John Dillinger", "Barney" };
set<string>  most_wanted(names, names + 7);
set<string>::iterator  it;

it = most_wanted.begin();
while(it != most_wanted.end()) {
     cout << *it++ << endl;
}
```

  This prints out:

```
Al Capone
Barney
Bonnie Parker
Clyde Barrow
John Dillinger
Joker
Professor Moriarty
```

- *set_obj*.**clear()**

  Removes all elements from the set, reducing its size to zero.

```
most_wanted.clear();     // Remove everyone!
```

- *set_obj*.**count(*value*)**

  Returns the number of elements that have the specified value. With set containers (as opposed to **multiset** template objects), the value returned is either 1 or 0.

```
if (most_wanted.count("Knave of Hearts") == 0) {
     cout << "The knave is not on list." << endl;
     cout << "(Perhaps he is innocent.)" << endl;
}
```

- *set_obj*.**empty()**

  Returns **true** if there are no elements in the set; returns **false** otherwise.

- *set_obj*.**end()**

  Returns an iterator that points *one position past* the last element. This function is most often used in conjunction with **begin** to iterate through the container, and with **find** as a return value that indicates an element was not found. See **begin** and **find** for examples.

- *set_obj*.**erase(*value*)**

  Erases the element with the specified value, if any, and returns either 1 or 0: This is the number of elements removed, so if 0 was returned, the element was not found.

  For example, the following statement removes "Dr. Richard Kimble" from the most_wanted set but advises the user in case that name was not found.

```
if (most_wanted.erase("Dr. Richard Kimble") > 0){
     cout << "Removal successful." << endl;
} else {
     cout << "Dr. Kimble not on list." << endl;
}
```

- *set_obj*.**erase(*pos_iter*)**

  Erases the element pointed to by *pos_iter*, an iterator.

```
set<string> empMap;
set<string>::iterator  it;
. . .
it = most_wanted.find("Dr. Richard Kimble");
if (it != most_wanted.end()) {
     erase(it);                 // Free Dr. Kimble!
}
```

▸ *set_obj*.**erase(***first_iter*, *last_iter***)**

Erases a range beginning with the element pointed to by *first_iter*, up to but not including the element pointed to by *last_iter*. For example, the following statements remove numbers beginning with 10, up to but not including 20.

```
int arr[5] = {5, 10, 15, 20, 25};
set<int>  set_of_ints(arr, arr + 5);
set<int>::iterator  it1, it2;
. . .
it1 = set_of_ints.find(10);
it2 = set_of_ints.find(20);
set_of_ints.erase(it1, it2);
```

After these statements are executed, the contents of the set are 5, 20, 25.

Note that if 20 was not found, it2 would have been assigned the value set_of_ints.end(), which would have caused the **erase** function to delete all elements from the one pointed to by it1 forward to the end of the set.

See also **lower_bound** and **upper_bound** for ways to select a subrange of a container.

▸ *set_obj*.**find(***value***)**

Searches for an element with a matching value and returns an iterator to that element. If value is not found, the function returns an iterator equal to *set_obj*.**end()**.

```
set<string>  most_wanted;
set<string>::iterator  it;
// Add some names to most_wanted.
. . .
it = most_wanted.find("Dr. Richard Kimble");
if (it == most_wanted.end()) {
     cout << "Dr. Kimble not on list." << endl;
} else {
     cout << "Dr. Kimble still wanted." << endl;
}
```

▸ *set_obj*.**insert(***value***)**

Inserts an element with the specified value. If an element with that value already exists, the function makes no change.

The value returned is a pair. The **first** member of this return-value pair is an iterator to the element that was inserted. The **second** member of the pair is a **bool** value that is **true** if the insertion created a new element and **false** if it did not.

For example, the following statements attempt to add the White Rabbit to a set.

```
set<string>  most_wanted;
set<string>::iterator  it;
```

```
// Add some names...
pair<set<string>::iterator, bool>  return_val;

return_val = most_wanted.insert("White Rabbit");
if (return_val->second) {
     it = return_val->first;   // Success;
                               // Save iterator.
     cout << "Rabbit added to list." << endl;
} else {
     cout << "The White Rabbit was already on ";
     cout << "the list." << endl;
}
```

- *set_obj*.**insert(***pos_iter*, *value***)**

  This version of **insert** is similar to the previous version but uses *pos_iter*, an iterator, as a hint as to where to insert an element. The value returned is an iterator to the element that was inserted; if an element already existed with the same value, the function returns an iterator pointing to that element.

  The *pos_iter* is a suggestion of where to look for an insertion point: If *post_iter* points to the position just before the position where the element should be inserted, the insertion is done with maximum efficiency, reducing lookup time. This can enable a series of efficient insertions of elements at consecutive positions in the set. For example:

```
set<string>  most_wanted;
set<string>::iterator  it = most_wanted.end();

it=most_wanted.insert(it, "Barney");
it=most_wanted.insert(it, "Barzini");
it=most_wanted.insert(it, "Billy the Kid");
it=most_wanted.insert(it, "Billy the Kidder");
it=most_wanted.insert(it, "Billy the Kidnapper");
it=most_wanted.insert(it, "Bonnie Parker");
```

- *set_obj*.**insert(***first_iter*, *last_iter***)**

  Inserts a series of elements from another container, beginning with the element pointed to by *first_iter*, up to but not including the element pointed to by *last_iter*. Inserting values that are already in the set has no effect; the other insertions are still valid, however.

```
// Order before insertion doesn't matter.
arr int[5] = {10, 66, 50, 27, 100};
set<int>  set_of_ints;
set_of_ints.insert(arr, arr + 5);
```

▸ *set_obj*.**lower_bound(*value*)**

Returns an iterator pointing to the first element whose value is greater than or equal to the specified value. For example:

```
string names[8] = { "Clyde Barrow",
     "Barney, "Bonnie Parker", "Knave of Hearts",
     "Al Capone", "Billy the Kid",
     "Professor Moriarty", "John Dillinger"};
set<string>  most_wanted(names, names + 8);
set<string>::iterator  it;

it = most_wanted.lower_bound("B");
cout << "The first name with a B ";
cout << "(or greater) is " << *it << endl;
```

This prints:

```
The first name with a B (or greater) is Barney
```

▸ *set_obj*.**rbegin()**

Returns an iterator pointing to the last element in the set. This function can be used in conjunction with the **rend** function to iterate backward. Note that incrementing a reverse iterator moves backward through the elements, not forward. For example:

```
int arr[6] = {100, 10, 20, 30, 40, 50};
set<int>  setInts(arr, arr + 6);

set<int>::reverse_iterator rit;

rit = setInts.rbegin();
while(rit != setInts.rend()) {
     cout << *rit++ << "  ";
}
```

This prints out:

```
100, 50, 40, 30, 20, 10
```

▸ *set_obj*.**rend()**

Returns an iterator pointing *one position before* the first element in the set. See **rbegin** for an example.

▸ *set_obj*.**size()**

Returns the number of elements in the set.

```
cout << "The most wanted list has ";
cout << most_wanted.size();
cout << " names on it." << endl;
```

- *set_obj*.**swap(***set_obj2***)**

  Exchanges the contents of *set_obj* with those of *set_obj2*. The two sets must have the same base type.

```
set<int>  set_of_ints1;
set<int>  set_of_ints2;
// Insert some elements into the sets.
. . .
set_of_ints1.swap(set_of_ints2);    // Swap!
```

- *set_obj*.**upper_bound(***key_value***)**

  Returns an iterator pointing to the first element whose value is greater than the specified value. For example, the following statements use the **lower_bound** and **upper_bound** functions to print all names on the most wanted list beginning with a capital "B".

```
string names[9] = { "Barney", "White Rabbit",
     "Professor Moriarty", "Clyde Barrow",
     "Barzini", "Billy the Kid", "Al Capone",
     "Bonnie Parker", "John Dillinger"};
set<string>  most_wanted(names, names + 9 );
set<string>::iterator  it, it1, it2;
it1 = most_wanted.lower_bound("B");
it2 = most_wanted.upper_bound("C");
for (it = it1; it != it2; ++it) {
     cout << *it << endl;
}
```

  These statements print:

```
Barney
Barzini
Billy the Kid
Bonnie Parker
```

17.4 The multimap Template

The **multimap** template is similar to the **map** template and supports nearly all the same functions and operations. There are a couple of important differences, however.

- A multimap does not require key values to be unique; moreover, it does not require the combined key-associated-value pair to be unique, either.
- The **multimap** template does not support the subscript operator, [].

A few of the functions behave differently: For example, calling the **count** member function with a map returns 1 or 0. But calling **count** with a multimap may return a value higher than 1.

To use the template, include the <map> header. Remember, also, that **multimap** is part of the **std** namespace.

```
#include <map>
using std::multimap;
```

The syntax for declaring a multimap is:

```
multimap<key_type, val_type>  name
```

Note that the **multimap** template supports all the constructors that **map** does. The syntax for declaring a multimap iterator is:

```
multimap<key_type, val_type>::iterator  iterator_name
```

One possible use for a multimap is as a database that keeps track of student test scores. For each student, you need to be able to store any number of scores. The following example creates a database called test_scores and enters four test results.

```
#include <map>
using std::multimap;
using std::make_pair;

multimap<string, int>  test_scores;
test_scores.insert(make_pair("Nina", 100));
test_scores.insert(make_pair("Nina", 100));
test_scares.insert(make_pair("Nina", 95));
test_scores.insert(make_pair("Aaron", 89));
```

There are now three elements with the key value of "Nina". Two of these elements are entirely duplicates. Nina scored 100 twice, and on the third test her score fell to 95.

This database has one limitation: There's no way to know if one of the scores was accidentally entered more than once. Presumably, Nina scored 100 twice, and the second instance was not an error.

A multimap might seem to be a good solution for an author database. For example, you might want to store multiple records that have "Dickens" as their key while having different associated values: "A Tale of Two Cities", "Oliver Twist", "Great Expectations", and so on. In that scenario there would be three entries with a key value of "Dickens."

The problem is that a multimap enables the same pair—for example, "Dickens"/ "Oliver Twist"—to be entered any number of times. A better solution would be to create a map or set built on a key-value class made up of author name *and* book title (a double key, in effect). Such a class would need to provide a less-than operator function (<), comparing author name and title.

But the test_score database seems to be a good use for a multimap. The next issue is: What is the best way to retrieve information?

When you want information on a student, you usually want to get a list of *all* that student's scores. One way to do that is to specify upper and lower bounds for an iterator.

- Calling **lower_bound** on a key value gets the first element in the container with a key equal to or greater than the specified key.
- Calling **upper_bound** on a key value gets the first element whose key is strictly greater than the specified key.

Consequently, the following statements produce a range that includes all elements with a key value of "Nina":

```
multimap<string, int>::iterator it, it1, it2;
it1 = test_scores.lower_bound("Nina");
it2 = test_scores.upper_bound("Nina"):
```

The call to **lower_bound** gets an iterator to the first element with a key value of "Nina". The call to **upper_bound** gets an iterator to the first element having a key value greater than "Nina" (greater in the sense of coming later in alphabetical order).

Consequently, the following statements get all the information on Nina's scores:

```
multimap<string, int>::iterator it, it1, it2;
it1 = test_scores.lower_bound("Nina");
it2 = test_scores.upper_bound("Nina"):
double sum = 0.0;   // Force flt-pt division later.
for (it = it1; it != it2; ++it) {
     std::cout << it->second << " ";   // Print score
     test_sum += it->second;
}
std::cout << std::endl;
if (test scores.size() > 0) {    // Avoid dividing by zero!
     std::cout << "Average score: ";
     std::cout << test_sum/test scores.size() << std::endl;
}
```

The basic idea of this code is: Iterate from the lower bound up to (but not including) the upper bound. These bounds select the range of elements all having a key of "Nina". (Incidentally, if the upper bound is test_scores.end(), the code still works fine.) The sum is accumulated in the variable test_sum. I declared this variable as type **double** so that later, when test_sum is divided by the container's size, the code will force floating-point division rather than integer division.

The statements output all of Nina's scores, followed by the average.

```
100 100 95
Average score:  98.3333333
```

Another way to achieve the same results is to call the **equal_range** function, which gets lower and upper bounds for a particular key value (just as was done for Nina in the preceding example). The **equal_range** function returns a pair object, in which the **first** element is an iterator to the lower bound and the **second** element is an iterator to the upper bound.

So, instead of using these statements:

```
it1 = test_scores.lower_bound("Nina");
it2 = test_scores.upper_bound("Nina"):
```

I could have used the following, although it involves slightly more lines of code:

```
typedef  multimap<string, int>::iterator  it_type;
std::pair<it_type, it_type>  ret_val;
ret_val = test_scores.equal_range("Nina");
it1 = ret_val.first;
it2 = ret_val.second;
```

17.5 The multiset Template

The **multiset** template provides functionality nearly identical to that of the **set** template, with the important difference that multisets permit any number of duplicate values.

To use the **multiset** template, include the <set> header. The name **multiset** is part of the **std** namespace.

```
#include <set>
using std::multiset;
```

The syntax for declaring a multiset is:

```
multiset<type>  name
```

Note that the **multiset** template supports all the constructors that **set** does. The syntax for declaring a multiset iterator is:

```
multiset<type>::iterator  iterator_name
```

A good use for a multiset is a database that holds test scores without recording who received which score: It's just a set of numbers, in which each number can appear multiple times.

For example, the following multiset contains the numeric scores for a class, recording only the scores themselves. Such a multiset might be used to store a set of numbers so that they can be analyzed statistically. Obviously, duplicate values need to be permitted for this container.

```
int  arr[10] = {70, 89, 85, 90, 90, 70, 70, 75, 89, 67 };
multiset<int>  scores(arr, arr + 10);
```

The scores, when printed out, will be arranged in order of their values.

```
multiset<int>::iterator it;
for (it = scores.begin(); it != scores.end(); ++ i) {
     std::cout << *it << "  ";
}
```

These statements print:

```
67 70 70 70 75 85 89 89 90 90
```

Additional scores can be added at any time, of course, by calling the **insert** function:

```
scores.insert(95);
scores.insert(73);
```

One way to use the information in a multiset is to call the **count** function to determine how many times a particular score appears.

```
std::cout << "A score of 70 appears ";
std::cout << scores.count(70) << " times." << std::endl;
```

These statements print:

```
A score of 70 appears 3 times.
```

When dealing with multisets, the **lower_bound** and **upper_bound** functions are often useful for accessing a range of values. Here is a quick review.

- A call to **lower_bound**(*value*) returns an iterator to the first element that is equal to or greater than the specified value.
- A call to **upper_bound**(*value*) returns an iterator to the first element that is strictly greater than the specified value.

To count the number of elements in the range of values from 70 to 79, inclusive, you could use the following statements:

```
multiset<int>::iterator it, it1, it2;
it1 = scores.lower_bound(70);
it2 = scores.upper_bound(79);
int n = 0;
for (it = it1; it != it2; ++i) {
     ++n;
}
std::cout << "The number of scores between 70 and ";
std::cout << "79, inclusive, is " << n << "." << std;:endl;
```

Another use that multisets are suited for is determining median value. To determine the median for this set—the value N for which the number of values less than N is equal to the number of values greater than N—you can use code similar to that for the sample application at the end of Chapter 16, "STL Sequence Containers (List)." I leave that as an exercise for the reader.

17.6 Unordered Containers (C++11)

C++11 adds four new containers—the unordered, or hash-table, containers—that are exciting additions to the STL because they can significantly speed up applications. These containers are not right for every situation, but they add nicely to the choices the STL offers.

Each of these containers is an unordered version of one of the four containers introduced earlier: **map**, **set**, **multimap**, and **multiset**. Table 17.3 shows the correspondence and the header required for each container.

TABLE 17.3 Unordered Containers and Header Files

New C++11 Container	Corresponds to	Header
unordered_map	map	<unordered_map>
unordered_multimap	multimap	<unordered_map>
unordered_set	set	<unordered_set>
unordered_multiset	multiset	<unordered_set>

17.6.1 Unordered Containers: Basic Concepts

Unordered containers use an internally maintained hash table to look up elements, rather than a binary tree. Consequently, the following rules apply to these containers.

- Unordered containers provide significantly faster lookups than ordered containers.
- But unordered containers also take up more space.
- An unordered container does not order elements by key value, nor does it organize elements according to order of insertion. The order is effectively random as far as the user of the container is concerned.
- However, in unordered multimaps and multisets, elements with identical key values are guaranteed to be next to each other, so iteration is still a useful way to access all the elements having the same key (or the same value, in the case of a set).
- Unordered containers support forward iterators only, not reverse or bidirectional iterators.
- For a type to serve as the key for an unordered container, a hash function must be provided for that type. C++11 provides hash functions for the following: built-in types, pointers, smart pointers, and standard string types (**const char***, **string**, and their wide-character versions). If you want to use a key-value type that is not one of these standard types, you'll have to do some extra programming.

Unordered containers support almost all the same member functions as their ordered counterpart, with a few differences.

- Unordered containers do not support the **upper_bound** and **lower_bound** functions or functions that return a reverse iterator.
- Unordered containers provide some additional member functions that enable you to analyze and fine-tune performance.

But otherwise, most of the code that manipulates an ordered container can be reused with the unordered version of that container.

The following examples use a map and an unordered map. Aside from how the templates are declared, the code looks almost the same. However, when the two containers are printed out, one observes order according to key value and the other does not.

Assume the following directives are in place:

```
#include <string>
#include <iostream>
using namespace std;       // Used here for convenience.
```

Here is the code that creates and iterates through an ordered map. If you've read the earlier sections in the chapter, this code should look familiar by now.

```
#include <map>              // Supports map and multimap
map<string, string> o_map;

o_map["John"] = "Harmony Guitar";
o_map["Paul"] = "Bass Guitar";
o_map["George"] = "Lead Guitar";
o_map["Ringo"] = "Drums";
o_map["Brian"] = "Manager";
cout << "Ordered version:" << endl;
for (auto x: o_map) {
          cout << x.first << "\t";
          cout << x.second << endl;
}
```

This code, when executed, prints the following. As you'd expect, order is maintained alphabetically by key value, regardless of the order in which the elements were inserted.

```
Ordered version:
Brian   Manager
George  Lead Guitar
John    Harmony Guitar
Paul    Bass Guitar
Ringo   Drums
```

Now here is the code that uses **unordered_map**. Except for the include file (<unordered_map>) and the template name, the source code is essentially the same.

```
#include <unordered_map>  // Supports unordered_map and
                          //   unordered_multimap.
unordered_map<string, string> u_map;
u_map["John"] = "Harmony Guitar";
u_map["Paul"] = "Bass Guitar";
u_map["George"] = "Lead Guitar";
u_map["Ringo"] = "Drums";
u_map["Brian"] = "Manager";
cout << "Unordered version:" << endl;
for (auto x: u_map) {
     cout << x.first << "\t";
     cout << x.second << endl;
}
```

This source code, when executed, prints the following. The results may vary depending on the platform and implementation.

```
Unordered version:
Ringo   Drums
John    Harmony Guitar
Brian   Manager
Paul    Bass Guitar
George  Lead Guitar
```

There is an underlying order, but it arises from the implementation of the hash-table technique. (It is not an order that is in any way helpful to the user of the container.) The rest of this section discusses this technology.

To determine the position at which to store an element, the container first converts a key value (or element value, in the case of unordered sets) into an integer. This integer is then used to select a memory slot—called a *bucket*—within the data area.

Converting the key is called *hashing*, and the integer is the *hash value*. The goal of a good hash function is to convert even similar-looking keys (such as "John" and "Johnny") into widely different integers so that the elements do not end up in the same bucket. Ideally, the function should produce uniform distribution throughout the **size_t** range (usually defined as an unsigned long integer).

Yet even with a good hash function, some items will (more or less at random) end up in the same bucket. A linked list is used to connect items in the same bucket.

Figure 17.7 illustrates the hashing-and-lookup process.

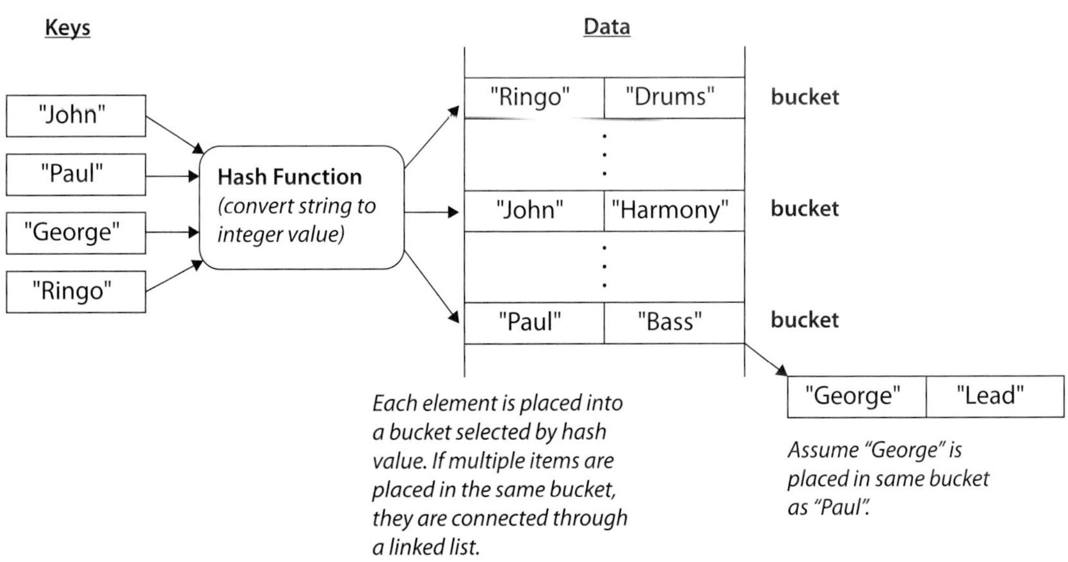

FIGURE 17.7 Hash table example

As long as individual buckets do not accumulate too many items, lookups are fast. A lookup is usually a two-step process: (1) convert key to hash value, (2) use hash value to select a bucket. At that point, it might also be necessary to step through a list, but only if the bucket has multiple items.

Various techniques can be used in producing hash values. One approach widely used on strings is to use an algorithm similar to the following, in which P is a prime number (such as 31). Hash functions return a value of type **size_t** (usually an unsigned long integer).

```
size_t accum = 0;    // Accumulated hash value.
char *s = str;
while (s < str + length) {
      accum = (accum * P) + *s++;
}
```

The hash value that results is then used to select a bucket. A typical method for converting a hash value to a bucket number is to use *hash_value* **mod** *N*. If N (the number of buckets) is a power of two, then bucket selection is fast indeed.

Remember that the goal of hashing is to widely distribute keys among different buckets (ideally one per bucket), no matter what patterns might arise in the keys themselves. The effect is not so different from a cryptology program. You should be able to insert a hundred elements having key values beginning with "B", for example, and they should be distributed more or less equally among different buckets. The result will be an apparently random order. Yet the goal is not to achieve a meaningful order, but to assign each item its own bucket.

The ultimate goal, of course, is to provide fast access to individual elements. But precisely for that reason, the hash-table technique needs to distribute elements among different buckets as much as possible.

17.6.2 Fine-Tuning Hash-Table Performance

You can fine-tune performance by managing the number of buckets. In the most degenerate case—every element in the same bucket—lookups would be no faster than searching through a linked list, which would be unacceptably slow for large N.

Increasing the number of buckets can reduce the number of collisions and therefore increase speed. But it also increases the amount of memory occupied by the container.

The *load factor* is the number of elements divided by the number of buckets:

```
Load Factor  =  Num. of elements  /  Num. of buckets
```

Each unordered container maintains a maximum load factor. As entries are added, the load factor increases. When the container's maximum load factor is exceeded, the container automatically increases the number of buckets and *rehashes,* reassigning elements to buckets.

By default, the maximum load factor for a container is 1.0. Lowering this number potentially increases performance by forcing an increase in buckets. Usually, however, a load factor of 0.6 or 0.7 comes close to producing optimal speed. Making the load factor smaller than that tends to yield little benefit. Remember, also, that as you increase the number of buckets, the container occupies more memory, so load factors below 0.6 tend to be wasteful of space.

One way to increase the number of buckets is to call the **rehash** function, specifying a new number of buckets. As soon as another element is inserted, the number of buckets is adjusted upward.

```
cout << "# of buckets: " << u_map.bucket_count() << endl;
u_map.rehash(16);   // Increase to at least 16 buckets.
u_map["George M"] = "Producer";
cout << "# of buckets: " << u_map.bucket_count() << endl;
```

Or you can adjust the container's maximum load factor. Reducing this setting from 1.0 to 0.7 is likely to improve lookup speed but also increase memory usage.

```
u_map.max_load_factor(0.7F);
```

The rest of this section summarizes the functions for analyzing and fine-tuning hash-table performance. In each case, *cont_obj* is a container object created with one of the **unordered** templates.

- *cont_obj*.**begin(***n***)**

  Returns an iterator pointing to the first element in the bucket specified by *n*, a zero-based number. This iterator can be used to step through the elements in the bucket. For example, the following code prints the keys of all the elements in each bucket.

  ```
  for (int i = 0; i < u_map.bucket_count(); ++i) {
        cout << i << ": ";
        auto it = u_map.begin(i);
        while (it != u_map.end(i)) {
              cout << it->first << ", ";
              ++it;
        }
        cout << endl;
  }
  ```

  You can run code like this during debugging and development to verify the quality of the hash technique. For large N, collisions should be infrequent—elements should rarely be in the same bucket—although for small samples especially, don't expect perfect distribution.

- *cont_obj*.**bucket(***key_value***)**

  Returns the bucket in which the *key_value* is located. Bucket numbers are zero-based, as they are essentially index numbers. At least in my implementation (Microsoft Visual C++), the *key_value* does not necessarily have to correspond to an existing item. The value returned is the bucket number that would be selected if the element did exist.

```
cout << "John is in bucket #";
cout << u_map.bucket("John") << cout;
```

- *cont_obj*.**bucket_count()**

  Returns the number of buckets currently used by the container.

```
cout << "# of buckets: " << u_map.bucket_count();
```

- *cont_obj*.**end(***n***)**

  Returns an iterator serving as the one-past-the-end indicator for the bucket specified by *n*. See the description of **begin(***n***)** for an example.

- *cont_obj*.**load_factor()**

  Returns the current load factor, which is the number of elements divided by the current number of buckets.

```
cout << "Current L.F.: " << u_map.load_factor();
```

- *cont_obj*.**max_load_factor()**

  Returns the container's maximum-load-factor setting (which by default is 1.0). When the load factor exceeds this number—due to new elements being inserted—the container automatically increases the number of buckets and rehashes.

```
cout << "maximum load factor: "
cout << u_map.max_load_factor();
```

- *cont_obj*.**max_load_factor(***new_lf***)**

  Sets the maximum load factor for the container to *new_lf*, a floating-point number having type **float**. Calling this function potentially forces an increase in the number of buckets.

```
// Lower max. load factor from 1.0 to 0.65.
u_map.max_load_factor(0.65F);
```

- *cont_obj*.**rehash(***n_buckets***)**

  Increases the number of buckets to at least the specified number as soon as any elements are inserted. This causes a rehash, which reassigns each element to a new bucket.

```
u_map.rehash(300); // Reserve at least 300 buckets.
```

▸ *cont_obj*.**reserve**(*n_elems*)

Reserves space for the specified number of elements. The number of buckets is increased accordingly so that the maximum load factor will not be exceeded.

If you're about to insert a large number of elements, you can improve runtime performance by calling this function before making the insertions. Doing so results in only one rehash rather than several.

```
u_map.reserve(200); // Reserve space for 200 elements.
```

17.6.3 Writing Your Own Hash and Equals Functions

To use an unordered container with a complex key-value type (not a built-in type or a string), you need to provide a customized hash function and also provide a test-for-equality function.

Testing for equality is straightforward. It's less obvious how to write a good hash function.

C++11 provides a **hash** template that returns a hash function for the specified built-in type, pointer type, or string type. You can apply this template to each component of the key and then add the values returned by the functions to produce one hash value. This does not produce an especially strong hashing function, and some experts would consider it weak. But it may be good enough to be practical. (Better results may be possible by purchasing specialized libraries developed by experts.)

hash<*type*>**()**

The following example employs a key value consisting of two separate strings: author and title.

```
class BookID {
public:
     string  author, title;
};
```

To build an unordered map with this class as its key-value type, you need to provide a hash function and a test-for-equality function for BookID objects. You can build a wrapper class around each of these functions.

```
// Wrapper class for the hashing function for BookID.
class BookHashf {
public:
     size_t operator () (const BookID& arg) {
          return hash<string>()(arg.author) +
                 hash<string>()(arg.title);
     }
};
```

```
// Wrapper class for the test-for-eq. function for BookID.
class BookEqf {
public:
     bool operator()(const BookID& lhs, const BookID &rhs){
          return lhs.author == rhs.author &&
                 lhs.title == rhs.title;
     }
};
```

This approach (using wrapper classes) is not the only way to specify these functions, but it's convenient because it keeps the syntax for unordered-map declaration relatively simple.

```
#include <unordered_map>

unordered_map<BookID, int, BookHashf, BookEqf>  books;
```

With this declaration in place, you can proceed to insert elements into this map just as you would an ordered map. The purpose is to store a page count for each book. (You could just as easily store other kinds of information, such as word count or ISBN number.)

```
books[BookID("Homer", "Odyssey")] = 180;
books[BookID("Homer", "Iliad")] = 185;
books[BookID("Tolkien", "The Hobbit")] = 300;
books[BookID("Tolkien", "LOTR")] = 1500;
books[BookID("Austen", "Emma")] = 240;
books[BookID("Austen", "Pride and Prejudice")] = 250;
```

If you print out the contents, you will probably not see elements grouped together by author. This is by design. Within this database, each combination of author and title is a unique key, and the purpose of a hashing function is to reduce the chance of any two elements ending up in the same bucket—as long as the keys differ by so much as a single character.

If you create an unordered multimap (permitting multiple listings of the same book), there's the possibility of adding more than one item with an identical key. Identically keyed items are placed in the same bucket, but only if they match exactly, by both author *and* title.

What if you wanted a book database that grouped books by the same author together, so you could iterate through all the books by Jane Austen? In that case, the only good choice would be to use an ordered map rather than an unordered one.

Here is sample code for printing out the contents:

```
for (auto x: books) {
     cout << x.first.author << "\t";
```

```
        cout << x.first.title << "\t";
        cout << x.second << endl;
}
```

It might seem unreasonable that an unordered map would not group elements in a meaningful way—ordering all the books by the same author together—but that's not the purpose of an unordered container. Unordered containers are intended for direct access of individual elements. If used only for this purpose, they tend to be several times faster than their ordered counterparts.

17.7 Sample App: Guess-the-Word Game

The program in this section is a variation on the Guess-the-Number game from Chapter 4, "Control Structures," but this version of the game is (in my opinion) a hundred times more interesting. I have played it and sometimes found it a great challenge, almost frustrating at times.

The Guess-the-Number game quickly becomes routine after you play it a few times, because adopting a binary-search technique enables you to deduce the answer relatively quickly.

Guessing a random *word* is far more challenging, because the range of words is not 1 to 50 but many thousands. If a word is randomly selected from the English language, the use of letters is not equally distributed; moreover, there is no maximum word length, making matters even more challenging for the player. But the more you know about letter combinations, the better you should do. In theory, a human guesser ought to be able to get the answer faster than a computer program unless that program has considerable linguistic knowledge.

But how do you get a random word from the English (or any other) natural language?

That problem is solved with help from the **set** template and file I/O operations. It's only necessary to read in all the words from some text file, such as readme.txt. (With Microsoft Visual Studio, a readme.txt file is automatically created for you and placed in the current folder; isn't that convenient?) Because the container is a set, no individual word will be stored more than once, so an unusual word is as likely to be chosen as a common word such as "the". The program then randomly generates a number from 0 to N-1, where N is the size of the set, and uses that number to select a word.

```
#include <set>
#include <string>
#include <cctype>     // is_alpha() needed for purging.
#include <iostream>
#include <fstream>
```

```
#include <cstdlib>    // Include these 2 headers to support
#include <ctime>      //   srand, rand, time functs.

using std::set;       // Alternatively, you can use
using std::string;    //  using namespace std;
using std::ifstream;
using std::cout;
using std::cin;
using std::endl;

set<string> word_set;              // Word database.

string select_nth_word(int n);     // Iterate thru the set.
void purge_word(string &s);        // Get rid of non-letters.
void play_the_game(const string &target);

int main() {
     string fname;                 // Name of text file.
     string a_word;                // Word to guess.

     cout << "Input name of a file to pick a word from: ";
     getline(cin, fname);
     ifstream file_in(fname);
     if (! file_in) {
          cout << "Could not open file." << endl;
          system("PAUSE");
          return 1;
     }

     // The next 3 lines populate the set. It's this easy!
     // Note that file_in returns FALSE when the read fails
     //  because it has reached EOF.
     while(file_in >> a_word) {
          word_set.insert(a_word);
     }

     // Now select a random word from the set, and "purge"
     //  it, removing non-alphabetic characters.
     srand(static_cast<unsigned>(time(NULL)));
     int n = rand() % word_set.size();
     a_word = select_nth_word(n);
     purge_word(a_word);
     play_the_game(a_word);
     cout << endl;
     cin.ignore();   // Wait for user to press ENTER.
     return 0;
}
```

```
string select_nth_word(int n) {
     set<string>::iterator it;
     it = word_set.begin();
     while (n-- > 0) {
          ++it;
     }
     return *it;
}

void purge_word(string &s) {
     for (unsigned i = 0; i < s.size(); ++i) {
          if (!isalpha(s[i])) {
               s.erase(i);
          }
     }
     if (s.size() == 0) {
          s = "unknown";
     }
}

void play_the_game(const string &target) {
     string my_guess;
     while(true) {
          cout << "Enter your guess or press ENTER to exit: ";
          getline(cin, my_guess);
          if (my_guess.size() == 0) {
               return;
          } else if (my_guess < target) {
               cout << "Secret word is later in alpha order.";
          } else if (my_guess > target) {
               cout<<"Secret word is earlier in alpha order.";
          } else {
               cout << "That's it exactly! YOU WIN!" << endl;
               return;
          }
          cout << " Guess again." << endl;
     }
}
```

Exercises

1. Revise the application to perform case-insensitive comparisons so that the player can ignore the difference between uppercase and lowercase letters.
2. Revise the application to play the game repeatedly, but don't forget to give the player a way to terminate. One technique is to print the message "Play again?

(Enter Y or N)" and then play again unless the user enters a string that starts with "N" or "n".

3. If the game is going to be played repeatedly, it makes sense to create the word database just one time and pick a new word from that database for each game; but in that case, it's more efficient to use a vector, because vectors are easy to get the Nth member of. Rewrite the application so that after the set is created, the contents are copied to a vector. Then, at the beginning of each game, pick a random word from this vector. Note: Doing so should reduce the overall amount of source code rather than increase it.

4. The user may get frustrated and want to end a game early, but not without learning the answer that eluded him or her. Give the user an out by providing some way to exit the current game; but print the answer before quitting. (You can, if you choose, print a taunting comment such as, "I'm surprised you couldn't get that!")

CHAPTER 18

STL Algorithms

Much of computer programming comes down to standard tasks such as sorting, searching, counting, and selecting items from a collection. The STL algorithms are function templates that perform these general functions on nearly any kind of data and most any kind of collection: standard C++ arrays as well as any of the collection classes.

After presenting some general concepts, this chapter summarizes the STL algorithm templates by category—there are quite a number of them! Then it describes all of the templates in detail, in alphabetical order.

18.1 STL Algorithms: General Concepts

Most of the STL algorithm templates require the <algorithm> header. A few of them, called "numeric" algorithms, require the use of the <numeric> header. Both kinds of algorithms are part of the **std** namespace, so once again, either include the **using** statement, or else refer to each algorithm name with its **std::** prefix.

Despite the potential disadvantages of **using namespace std**, I assume its use in this chapter because otherwise the examples would take up too much space for this book.

```
#include <algorithm>    // For most algorithms
#include <numeric>      // For the numeric algorithms only.
using namespace std;
```

Each STL algorithm is a template function. As you may recall from Chapter 9, "Creating and Using Templates," template functions can be instantiated directly. The template generates the correct source code for the argument types (although normally you never see that generated code).

The arguments to an STL algorithm usually include iterators that point to beginning and ending positions within the container (or subrange), referred to as *beg* and *end*, respectively. There may be other arguments as well.

Each container must provide its own iterator, but standard C++ arrays provide this support in the form of pointers. So, for example, the **sort** algorithm has this syntax:

sort(*beg*, *end***)**

This says that you provide two iterators: *beg* points to the first element in a range; *end* points to one position past the last element in the range. That's the rule for all STL algorithms, containers, and functions: *end* always points to one position past the last element to be included.

This rule makes code easy to write, as you can supply arguments such as *container.* **end**(), which always points to the position just past the last element; or you can use array_name + n, where n is the size of the array. For example:

```
#include <algorithm>
#include <iostream>
using namespace std;
. . .
int arr[8] = {100, 1, 40 , 50, 72, 76, -5, 27};
sort(arr, arr + 8);
```

Having sorted the array, it would be useful to print out its contents. You can do that with a traditional **for** loop, but you can also use the **for_each** algorithm.

for_each(*beg*, *end*, *fnct***)**

for_each is a good example of an algorithm taking a function as argument. There are several ways to specify a function. The most obvious way is to write a traditional function and pass its address.

```
void output_f(int n) {cout << n << "  "; }
. . .
for_each(arr, arr + 8, output_f);
```

These statements, when executed, print this output:

```
-5  1  27  40  50  72  76  100
```

With all the algorithms, you can provide a function in any of the following forms:

- The address of a traditional function (as just demonstrated in the example)
- A function object
- A lambda function—if your compiler is C++11 compliant

The next section gives examples that use lambda functions.

You can also use the second approach: supplying a function object. As explained in Chapter 7, "Classes and Objects," a function object is an instance of a class that defines the function-call operator, (). For example:

```
class output_int_class {
public:
     void operator() (int n) {cout << n << " ";}
} output_int_obj;

for_each(arr, arr + 8, output_int_obj);
```

Occasionally there are advantages to using a function object, but in this case, the code is starting to get a little verbose. If your compiler is C++11 compliant, the most concise way to print out elements is to use range-based **for**.

```
for (int i : arr) {
     cout << i << "  ";
}
```

But this **for** loop can be correctly compiled only if the bounds of arr are known to the compiler. If you pass the address of arr to another function, it cannot use range-based **for**.

In contrast, one of the advantages of STL containers is that their upper and lower bounds can always be determined. The following statement should always work for a container.

```
for_each(container.begin(), container.end(), my_func);
```

Admittedly, this only saves a moderate amount of effort, but it's still helpful. A **for** loop that does essentially the same thing can be written as:

```
container_type<base_type>::iterator it;
for(it = container.begin(); it != container.end(); ++it) {
     my_func(*it);
}
```

For ease of illustration, this chapter sticks mostly to simple arrays for examples. Yet one of the most important features of algorithms is that you can use them with most any STL container; subject only to some restrictions on what kinds of iterators can be accepted by certain algorithms (as explained in more detail in Section 18.3, "Algorithms and Iterators").

For example, you can just as easily sort and print a vector:

```
#include <algorithm>
#include <iostream>
```

```
#include <vector>
using namespace std;

void output_f(int n) {cout << n << "  ";}
. . .
int arr[8] = { 100, 1, 40 , 50, 72, 76, -5, 27 };
vector<int>  iVec(arr, arr + 8);                 // Init iVec.
sort(iVec.begin(), iVec.end());                  // Sort it.
for_each(iVec.begin(), iVec.end(), output_f); // Print it.
```

18.2 Using Lambda Functions (C++11)

If your compiler is C++11 compliant, you can use lambda functions. These are also called "anonymous functions." Lambdas are convenient because they are more compact than standard (named) functions, and they can be defined in the place they are used.

Chapter 5, "Functions," presents the complete syntax for writing lambda functions. To review, here is a simple version of lambda syntax. Note that the brackets are intended literally.

```
[ ] (args) {statements}
```

So the **for_each** example in the previous section could be written as:

```
for_each(iVec.begin(), iVec.end(),
    [] (int n) {cout << n << " ";}
);
```

This example iterates through the vector iVec from beginning to end, each time passing the value of the current element to a function taking a single argument—an integer in this case, because the container has integer base type. The lambda function itself is:

```
    [] (int n) {cout << n << " ";}
```

Another useful feature of lambda functions is the ability to capture variables. "Capturing" a variable means that you give the lambda function access to a variable declared in the surrounding code.

Suppose you try to use **for_each** to sum all the values in a vector of integers.

```
int sum = 0;
for_each(iVec.begin(), iVec.end(),
    [] (int n) {sum += n;}     // ERROR! sum not accessible.
);
```

The problem is that a lambda defines its own level of scope just as any function does, so there is no access to local variables outside the lambda's definition. Fortunately, there's an easy solution. The lambda can be written this way:

```
    [&sum] (int n) {sum += n;}
```

Placing "&sum" inside the brackets "captures" the variable sum—in plain wording, it makes this variable accessible inside the lambda's definition even though the variable was declared outside the lambda. Within the brackets, [ ], the variable name "sum" is preceded by the reference operator (&) so that the variable is captured by reference: Doing so enables the lambda function to make changes to the variable.

The revised example is:

```
int sum = 0;
for_each(iVec.begin(), iVec.end(),
    [&sum] (int n) {sum += n;}     // This works.
);
```

This case demonstrates what a great convenience the variable-capture feature is. Without this ability, the only way to make this example work with **for_each** would be to make sum a global variable. But as a general rule, it's good programming practice to reduce the number of globals.

The return-value type of a lambda function (in this case, **void**) is determined by context; but sometimes the compiler is unable to determine that type. In such cases, you can use additional syntax to clarify the type of what is returned:

[ ] (args) -> *return_type* {*statements*}

For example:

```
    [] (int n) ->void {cout << n << " ";}
```

18.3 Algorithms and Iterators

Each algorithm works with specific kinds of iterators. Some are more restrictive than others. The most flexible kind of iterator—random access—supports all the capabilities required for every algorithm. Pointers into an array are random-access iterators.

Bidirectional iterators are a subset of random-access iterators. Nearly all containers provide bidirectional iterators, and these are sufficient for most (but not all) algorithms.

Table 18.1 summarizes the characteristics of the different kinds of iterators required.

TABLE 18.1 Categories of Iterators

Type of Iterator	Description
Random-access	Supports all capabilities of iterators, including addition and subtraction, comparisons with other iterators (>, <, and so on), incrementing, decrementing, getting and setting element values, and indirection through the index operator, [ ]. You can do almost anything with a random-access iterator that you can do with a pointer. (Note that pointers are, in effect, random-access iterators.) Vectors, deques, and arrays provide these iterators.
Bidirectional	Supports a subset of features that random-access iterators provide, including incrementing, decrementing, and getting or setting element values from dereferencing. Almost all container types support bidirectional iterators as long as the iterators are not **const**.
Forward	Same as bidirectional, but such iterators are not required to support decrementing (--).
Input	Supports a subset of forward-iterator features. Element may be dereferenced and used as the source of an assignment. **const_iterator** is allowed. Simply put, an input iterator is an iterator you can use to get input from a container, so you are copying values from, not to, the container.
Output	Supports a subset of forward-iterator features. Element may be dereferenced and used as the target of an assignment (lvalue). Simply put, an output iterator is an iterator you can use to send output to a container.

The two most important principles to keep in mind about iterators are the following.

- If the algorithm requires random-access iterators, it works only with arrays, vectors, and deques (or with a user-created template class that provides random-access iterators).
- If the algorithm requires an input iterator, then it is safe to use an iterator declared as **const_iterator**; otherwise, such an iterator may not work.

All iterators, except for output iterators, must support comparison with one another by way of the == and != operators. This requirement is easily met by arrays as well as all the STL containers. Only random-access iterators need to support less-than and greater-than comparisons.

18.4 Insert Iterators

In addition to the iterators presented in the previous section, the STL provides a group of template functions called *insert iterators,* the purpose of which is not to iterate through a container (as an ordinary iterator would), but rather to insert new elements.

The insert iterators are used primarily with STL algorithms, which is why I am presenting them in this chapter. Note that they work only with STL containers, not C++ arrays.

To use insert-iterator functions, include the <iterator> header. The names are part of the **std** namespace.

```
#include <iterator>
using namespace std;
```

The syntax for the insert-iterator functions is:

```
back_inserter(container)    // Insert new item(s) at end
front_inserter(container)   // Insert new item(s) at beginning
inserter(container, it)        // Insert new item(s) before iterator it
```

A simple way to use one of these functions is to call it directly to insert an item. For example:

```
#include <iterator>
#include <vector>
using namespace std;
. . .
vector<int>  my_ints;    // Create an empty vector
back_inserter(my_ints) = 10;
```

This last statement has the same effect as the following, which inserts the value 10 to the end of the vector.

```
my_ints.push_back(10);
```

The **back_inserter** function is more useful when used with one of the "copy" algorithms. Normally, such algorithms copy data to a destination range by overwriting existing elements. But **back_inserter** causes a new item to be inserted just before it is written to, so that no old elements are overwritten. Consider this example, which does not use an inserter:

```
#include <iterator>
#include <algorithm>
#include <vector>
using namespace std;
```

```
. . .
int arr[5] = {10, 20, 30, 40, 50};
vector<int>  iVec(5, 0);   // Init with 5 copies of 0.
copy(arr, arr + 5, iVec.begin());   // Overwrite iVec.
```

In this example, there are five elements in iVec, all of which are overwritten. But you could instead start with iVec being empty and then cause new items to be inserted:

```
vector<int>  iVec;
copy(arr, arr + 5, back_inserter(iVec));
```

The last statement just shown is translated into a series of calls to the vector's **push_back** function. This example works because vectors support a **push_back** member function.

If the example instead used **front_inserter**, it would make a series of calls to **push_front**. Because vectors do not support a **push_front** member function, they cannot be used with **front_inserter**. But list and deque containers (as well as most other STL containers) do support **push_front** and so therefore can be used with this inserter.

For example:

```
#include <iterator>
#include <algorithm>
#include <list>
using namespace std;
. . .
int arr[5] = {10, 20, 30, 40, 50};
list<int>  iList;
copy(arr, arr + 5, front_inserter(iList));
```

The elements copied from the array, arr, are—in this order—10, 20, 30, 40, and 50. Using **front_inserter** causes **push_front** to be called repeatedly so that iList ends up containing:

```
50 40 30 20 10
```

Table 18.2 summarizes the action of the three iterators, in which *con* is an STL container and *it* is an iterator of that container.

TABLE 18.2 Insert-Iterator Functions

Iterator Function	Calls	Supported By
back_inserter(*con***)**	*con***.push_back(***val***)**	Most STL containers (but not arrays).
front_insert(*con***)**	*con***.push_front(***val***)**	Most STL containers other than vectors.
inserter(*con, it***)**	*con***.insert(***it, val***)**	Most STL containers.

18.5 Sample App: Finding the Median

This section presents a complete program that takes advantage of one of the STL algorithm templates: **sort**. This is a simple but powerful algorithm useful in many applications.

The following program is a variation on the program at the end of Chapter 15, "Introduction to STL (vector, deque)." It prompts the end user for a series of numbers and then reports the median value. This is not necessarily the same as arithmetic mean (average): Instead, it is the middle value, which has as many greater elements as lesser elements. If there is an even number of elements, the middle two values are averaged to produce the median value.

The median value is easy to calculate after the elements have been arranged in order. That's why the key line in this program makes use of the **sort** algorithm to place the elements of xVec—a vector containing floating-point numbers—in order from lowest to highest:

```
sort(xVec.begin(), xVec.end());
```

The program takes advantage of the **vector** template, creating an array for which there is no practical limit on size. Likewise, use of the **string** object, instead of a C-string, frees you from having to worry about limits on input-string size.

Here is the complete program. For ease of illustration, the use of **sort** is placed in bold. (Note that the condition in the **while** loop, "ss >> n", returns the value of the stream object, ss, which is set to **false** if a read fails. Therefore, the condition "ss >> n" reads the next number and fails when there is no more data to read, causing the loop to terminate.)

```
#include <iostream>
#include <string>
#include <sstream>
#include <algorithm>
#include <vector>
using namespace std;

int main() {
     int n = 0;
     string inStr;              // Input string.
     vector<double>  xVec;      // Vector to contain numbers.
     cout << "Enter nums: ";
     getline(cin, inStr);       // Get line of input.
     stringstream ss(inStr);
     while (ss >> n {             // While there's another
           xVec.push_back(n);     //    num to read, add it
     }                            //    to the vector.
```

```
    sort(xVec.begin(), xVec.end());
    n = xVec.size();
    int n1 = xVec[n/2];           // Get middle 2 values.
    int n2 = xVec[(n - 1)/2];
    cout << "Median val. is: " << (n1 + n2)/2 << endl;
    cin.ignore();          // Wait for user to press ENTER.
    return 0;
}
```

18.6 Concise Summaries of Algorithms

The STL supports so many algorithms that a concise summary needs to group them into categories. The next few sections group them into the following areas:

- Read-only algorithms
- Modifying algorithms (which change the value of elements)
- Sorting and reordering algorithms (which change the order)
- Heap algorithms (these are specialized, and they are provided mainly to support implementations of the **priority_queue** template)
- Numeric algorithms (which apply a mathematical operation to the elements)

18.6.1 Read-Only Algorithms

The algorithms summarized in this section process a container without directly modifying it. This group also includes a couple of algorithms that can be applied to any two values of matching base type (**max**, **min**); these do not necessarily need to be part of a container.

To use any of these algorithms, include the <algorithm> header. All the algorithm names are part of the **std** namespace.

```
#include <algorithm>
using namespace std;
```

Table 18.3 summarizes the read-only algorithms.

18.6.2 Modifying Algorithms

Modifying algorithms are those that modify the contents of one or more containers. This group also includes the **swap** algorithm, which exchanges any two values having the same base type.

TABLE 18.3 Summary of Read-Only Algorithms

Algorithms	Description
adjacent_find	Finds the first occurrence of two consecutive elements having the same value.
all_of, any_of, none_of (C++11)	Test a container or subrange to determine if all, any, or none of the elements fulfill a specified condition.
binary_search	Searches an ordered container for a specified value.
count, count_if	Return the number of elements matching a specified value or condition.
equal	Compares two containers or subranges for equality: Each corresponding element must be equal for the two ranges to be considered equal.
for_each	Performs a specified action for each element.
find, find_if	Find the first element matching a specified value or condition.
find_if_not (C++11)	Finds the first element not fulfilling a specified condition.
find_end	Finds the last occurrence of a complete subrange within a larger range.
find_first_of	Finds the first element matching any element that is also an element of a specified range.
includes	Determines whether *every* element in a range matches some element in another container or subrange.
lower_bound, upper_bound, equal_range	Return the iterators representing lower and upper bounds for a range specified according to value(s).
max	Returns the larger of two values (not necessarily part of a container).
min	Returns the smaller of two values (not necessarily part of a container).
max_element, min_element	Find the position of the maximum or minimum element.
minmax_element (C++11)	Returns positions of minimum and maximum elements as a pair.
mismatch	Compares two ranges and reports first mismatch between them.
search_n	Searches for a series of consecutive elements all meeting some specified condition.
search	Finds the first occurrence of a complete subrange within another range, much like looking for a substring within a string.

To use any of these algorithms, include the <algorithm> header. All the algorithms are part of the **std** namespace.

```
#include <algorithm>
using namespace std;
```

Table 18.4 summarizes the modifying algorithms.

TABLE 18.4 Summary of Modifying Algorithms

Algorithms	Description
copy, **copy_backward**	Copy elements in a range into a destination range (in the same container or another container).
copy_n, **copy_if** (C++11)	Variations on copy.
fill, **fill_n**	Set all the elements in a specified range to a particular value.
generate, **generate_n**	Set the elements in a specified range by calling a generator function.
iter_swap	Swaps two elements.
merge, **inplace_merge**	Merge two sorted ranges together into a single sorted range, copying the results to a specified destination.
move, **move_backward** (C++11)	Move all the elements of one range into another: This is not a copy action, but a potentially destructive (though potentially much more efficient) data transfer.
remove, **remove_if**, **remove_copy**, **remove_copy_if**	Remove one or more elements that meet a specified condition.
replace, **replace_if**, **replace_copy**	Replace the value of one or more elements that meet a specified condition.
swap	Exchanges any two values having the same base type (not necessarily part of a container).
swap_ranges	Swaps two ranges of elements.
transform	Performs an operation on a range of elements (or two ranges), and places the results in a destination.

18.6.3 Sorting and Reordering Algorithms

Sorting and reordering algorithms sort or reorder the contents of a container or a subrange of that container.

To use any of these algorithms, include the <algorithm> header. All the algorithms are part of the **std** namespace.

```
#include <algorithm>
using namespace std;
```

Table 18.5 summarizes the sorting and reordering algorithms, including those that may not actually perform sorting but have a closely related purpose (such as determining if the container is already sorted).

TABLE 18.5 Summary of Sorting Algorithms

Algorithms	Description
is_permutation (C++11)	Compares two ranges to see if they are permutations (rearrangements) of the same set of values.
is_sorted, **is_sorted_until** (C++11)	Return **true** if the range is already sorted—or return the position of the first element breaking the sorted order.
partial_sort, **partial_sort_copy**	Sort part of a range so that the first portion contains the smallest elements of the whole range, in order, and the second portion contains the remaining elements, unsorted.
is_partitioned (C++11)	Returns true if the range is ordered as a partition, in which all the elements that satisfy a specified condition precede all those that do not.
partition_point (C++11)	Finds the element that divides the container into a partition, as just described. (See **is_partitioned**.)
prev_permutation, **next_permutation**	Rearrange elements so that they form the previous or next permutation (unique arrangement of elements).
random_shuffle	Randomly shuffles the contents of a container or subrange.
reverse, **reverse_copy**	Rearrange a series of elements so that their order is the exact reverse of their previous order.
rotate, **rotate_copy**	Move element values forward or backward in the container through "rotation," causing elements at the end to move back to the beginning, or vice versa.
set_difference	Finds the "difference" between two ordered ranges: This difference consists of the elements that exist in the first range but not the second. Copy the result to a destination range.
set_intersection	Creates an intersection between two ordered ranges, copying the result to a destination range.
set_symmetric_difference	Finds the symmetric difference between two ordered ranges: This consists of the elements that exist in either range but not both. Copies the result to a destination range.
set_union	Creates a union between two ordered ranges, copying the result to a destination range.
sort	Sorts a container or subrange.
stable_sort	Sorts a container, preserving the relative position of elements with equal values.
unique, **unique_copy**	Remove consecutive elements having the same value.

18.6.4 Heap Algorithms

The STL algorithms use the term "heap" in a highly specialized way. The principal use for heap algorithms is to create an underlying implementation for a **priority_ queue** template. [See Chapter 16, "STL Sequence Containers (List)."] Essentially, these algorithms reorder a random-access container (array, vector, or deque) to treat it as a virtual, top-down binary tree.

In this context, a *heap* is an arrangement of elements in a random-access container that reflects the layout of a binary tree in which the following statements are true.

- The highest element (or element not less than the highest) is the root of the tree.
- Each child of a node is less than or equal to the node itself.

When an array, vector, or deque is arranged into a heap, it is not a real binary tree, of course, because there are no internal pointers. However, the heap arrangement reflects the structure of such a hypothetical tree. For example, consider this collection:

```
#include <algorithm>
#include <vector>
using namespace std;
int arr[10] = {1, 1, 2, 3, 3, 4, 4, 4, 5, 6};
vector<int>  my_heap(arr, arr+10);
```

A binary tree fulfilling the criteria just given has the structure shown in Figure 18.1. This tree, you'll note, has another special feature: It is balanced, with each level filled from left to right before any nodes appear on the level below it.

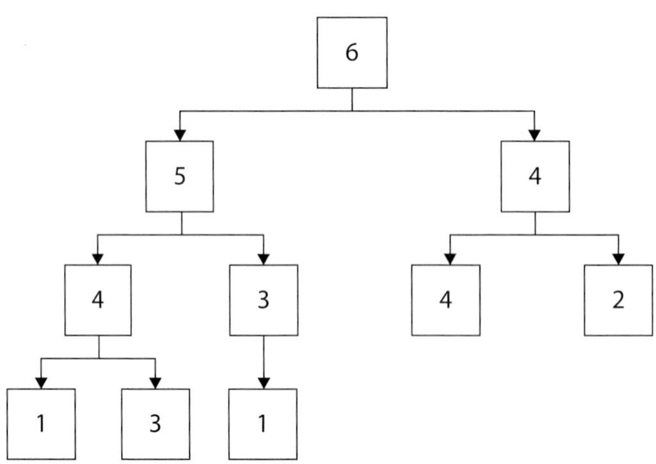

FIGURE 18.1 Binary-tree organization of a heap

A vector or array does not have a nodal structure, obviously, but once it is ordered into a heap, its arrangement reflects the structure of this hypothetical tree, beginning with the root node. Using the **make_heap** algorithm produces the following order:

```
6 5 4 4 3 4 2 1 3 1
```

After I add spaces for clarification, compare these numbers to the four levels of the tree in Figure 18.1. The correspondence should become easy to see.

```
6   5 4   4 3 4 2   1 3 1
```

Because the vector is a random-access container, an algorithm can move to the next level of the hypothetical tree by adding a power of 2 (1, 2, 4, 8, and so on) to an iterator. It's therefore possible to treat the container as if it were a binary tree.

As a consequence, elements in heap can be inserted more quickly into large collections than they can with linear searches. The heap search time grows logarithmically: Searching a container with a million elements takes only twice as long as searching a container with a thousand elements. The advantages are similar to those for a binary tree implemented for **map** containers, as described in Chapter 17, "STL Associated Containers (map, set)."

The heap-related algorithms are summarized in Table 18.6.

TABLE 18.6 Summary of Heap Algorithms

Algorithms	Description
make_heap	Reorders a range within a random-access container so that it fulfills the conditions of a heap.
is_heap (C++11)	Returns **true** if the specified range is arranged as a heap.
is_heap_until (C++11)	Returns the first position in the container that breaks the requirements of a heap.
pop_heap	Removes the front element of the heap and rearranges the remaining elements so that they fulfill the conditions of a heap.
push_heap	Inserts a new element into a heap so that a heap of size N becomes a heap of size N+1.
sort_heap	Sorts a range ordered as a heap into the traditional sorted order from lowest to highest.

18.6.5 Numeric Algorithms

The numeric algorithms are special in a couple of ways. First, to use these algorithms, include the <numeric> header. (All the algorithms are part of the **std** namespace.)

```
#include <numeric>
using namespace std;
```

Second, the numeric algorithms involve mathematical manipulation or calculation, unlike the algorithms presented earlier. Table 18.7 summarizes these.

18.6.6 Predefined Function Objects

The numeric algorithms work with functions and with function objects. For convenience, the C++ library provides a series of templates that return function objects performing addition, subtraction, and so on, freeing you from having to write these functions yourself. All of these templates require the <functional> header, and they are all part of the **std** namespace.

```
#include <functional>
using namespace std;
```

For example, **multiplies<int>()** returns a function object that multiplies two integers. You can use this function object directly:

```
cout << "The product 100 * 100 is ";
cout << multiplies<int>()(100, 100) << endl;
```

This isn't very useful, as you could have more simply typed "100 * 100"; however, the usefulness of this object is evident when you need to supply an operation to the

TABLE 18.7 Summary of Sorting and Reordering Algorithms

Algorithms	Description of Default Behavior
accumulate	Adds up the contents of a range and returns the result.
adjacent_difference	Finds the difference between each element and the one next to it, copying the results to a destination range.
inner_product	Accumulates the "inner product," obtained by multiplying corresponding elements in two ranges.
iota (C++11)	Sets the first element in a range to a specified value and then sets each other element to 1 plus the value of the previous element.
partial_sum	For each element, finds the partial sum formed by adding it to all preceding elements; copies the results to a destination range.

accumulate algorithm. The following statement multiplies together all the elements in arr and assigns the results to n:

```
double arr[5] = {10, 20, 0.5, 3, 27.1};
double n = accumulate(arr, arr + 5, 1.0,
   multiplies<double>()
);
```

Brief descriptions of the function-object templates follow.

- **plus**<*type*>**()**

  Returns a function object that adds together its two arguments.

- **minus**<*type*>**()**

  Returns a function object that subtracts the second argument from the first.

- **negate**<*type*>**()**

  Returns a function object that produces the arithmetic negation (reversing the sign) of its unary argument.

- **multiplies**<*type*>**()**

  Returns a function object that multiplies its two arguments.

- **divides**<*type*>**()**

  Returns a function object that produces the quotient when the first argument is divided by the second.

- **modulus**<*type*>**()**

  Returns a function object that performs modulus, or remainder division (%).

- **equal_to**<*type*>**()**

  Returns a function object that tests its two arguments for equality (==).

- **less**<*type*>**()**

  Returns a function object that performs a < b.

- **greater**<*type*>**()**

  Returns a function object that performs a > b.

- **less_equal**<*type*>**()**

  Returns a function object that performs a <= b.

- **greater_equal**<*type*>**()**

  Returns a function object that performs a >= b.

- **logical_not**<*type*>**()**

  Returns a function object that produces the logical negation of its unary argument.

- **`logical_and`**`<`*`type`*`>()`

  Returns a function object that performs logical AND on its two arguments.

- **`logical_or`**`<`*`type`*`>()`

  Returns a function object that performs logical OR on its two arguments.

- **`bit_and`**`<`*`type`*`>()`

  Returns a function object that performs bitwise AND on its two arguments.

- **`bit_or`**`<`*`type`*`>()`

  Returns a function object that performs bitwise OR on its two arguments.

- **`bit_xor`**`<`*`type`*`>()`

  Returns a function object that performs bitwise exclusive-OR on its two arguments.

18.7 Detailed Descriptions of Algorithms

This section describes algorithms in straight alphabetical order. In order to save space, I have adopted several conventions.

- Unless otherwise stated, use of these algorithms requires you to include the <algorithm> header.
- Every algorithm name is part of the **std** namespace, so either include the **using** statement or use the **std::** prefix with algorithm names.
- The arguments *beg* and *end* indicate a range within a container as follows: *beg* is an iterator that points to the first element in the range; *end* points to the position one past the last element in the range. Remember that *end* is always an "off the edge" iterator.
- In the case of arrays, pointers serve as random-access iterators.
- *less_than_f* is a comparison function that returns **true** if the first of two arguments passed to it—both having the base type of the container—is less than the second. If this argument is part of the algorithm syntax but is not specified during a call, then the base type must support the less-than operator (<), and this operator is used for comparisons. (However, even if the base type does support the < operator, a *less_than_f* argument can be used to override it.) In either case, the principles that apply are those in Section 16.1, "Sorting Elements (Strict Weak Ordering)." These principles are used to infer numerical relationships including greater-than and equality.
- Similar considerations apply to *eq_f*; this is a comparison function that returns **true** if the two arguments passed to it are equal. If omitted, the container's base type must support the test-for-equality operator (==), and this operator is used

for comparisons. Yet even if the base type does support the == operator, an *eq_f* argument can be used to override it.

Brackets in syntax are not intended literally in this chapter but indicate that the *less_than_f* and *eq_f* arguments are optional. Remember that the < and == operators of the base type normally implement comparisons, but if they don't, these arguments become required.

Note carefully that—purely for space reasons—the examples that follow assume **using namespace std**, although this is not something I recommend generally. The problem with this statement is that it increases the possibility of name conflicts.

```
using namespace std;     // Use this with caution.
```

Detailed descriptions follow.

▸ **accumulate(***beg*, *end*, *init_val* [, *op*]**)**

Requires the <numeric> header rather than <algorithm>.

Default behavior is to sum elements in the range (*beg*, *end*), adding it to *init_val*. The first two arguments are input operators. The *op* argument may specify an operation other than addition: either a function taking two operands or one of the functional objects listed in Section 18.6.6, "Predefined Function Objects." The following example totals an array, printing the resultant value, 15:

```
#include <numeric>
. . .
int arr[5] = {1, 2, 3, 4, 5};
cout << accumulate(arr, arr + 5, 0); // Print 15.
```

The next examples use subtraction and multiplication. They print 35 and 120.

```
#include <numeric>
#include <functional>
int my_f(int a, int b) {return a * b;}
. . .
int arr[5] = {1, 2, 3, 4, 5};
cout << accumulate(arr, arr + 5, 50,
     minus<int>()); //  35.
cout << endl;
cout << accumulate(arr, arr + 5, 1,
     my_f);         // 120.
```

▸ **adjacent_difference(***beg*, *end*, *dest* [, *op*]**)**

Requires the <numeric> header rather than <algorithm>.

Default behavior is to find the difference between each element in the range (*beg*, *end*) and the element preceding it—except for the first, which is just copied—copying the results to a destination range beginning with *dest*. The first two arguments are input operators; *dest* is an output iterator.

So, for example, the Nth element in the destination range is set to the Nth element in the source range minus the N - 1 element in that range. The *op* argument may specify an operation other than subtraction; *op* is an argument that contains a function address, lamdba, or function object.

The following example finds the difference between each pair of adjacent Fibonacci numbers, for the first seven numbers, and copies the results to the arr_dest array.

```
#include <numeric>
. . .
int arr[7] = {1, 2, 3, 5, 8, 13, 21};
int arr_dest[7];
adjacent_difference(arr, arr + 7, arr_dest);
```

After these statements are executed, the array arr_dest contains—surprise!—the Fibonacci sequence itself, adjusted by one position.

```
1 1 2 3 5 8 13
```

- **adjacent_find(*beg*, *end* [, *eq_f*])**

Searches the specified range and returns an iterator pointing to the first occurrence of two consecutive elements having the same value. If no such occurrence is found, the function returns *end*. The first two arguments are forward iterators. (For *eq_f*, see the beginning of this section.)

```
int arr[5] = {10, 50, 30, 30, 40};
int *p = adjacent_find(arr, arr + 5);
if (p != arr + 5) {
     cout << "Dups occur starting in position ";
     cout << p - arr << " (zero-based)." << endl;
}
```

This prints:

```
Dups occur starting in position 2 (zero-based).
```

- **all_of(*beg*, *end*, *cond_f*)**

C++11 specific. Returns **true** if all the elements in the range (*beg*, *end*) fulfill a specified condition or if the range has no elements. The *cond_f* argument is a function that takes a single argument of the base type and returns **true** if the condition is fulfilled.

For example, the following statements test each of two arrays (arrA, arrB) to see if all the values in the array are positive. (Only the second statement is printed in this case.)

```
bool is_pos(int n) { return n > 0;}
. . .
int arrA[5] = {10, 15, 77, -10, 3};
int arrB[4] = {1, 5, 2, 100};
if (all_of(arrA, arrA + 5, is_pos)) {
     cout << "All of arrA is positive." << endl;
}
```

```
if (all_of(arrB, arrB + 4, is_pos)) {
     cout << "All of arrB is positive." << endl;
}
```

- **any_of(*beg*, *end*, *cond_f*)**

C++11 specific. Returns **true** if any of the elements in the range (*beg*, *end*) fulfill a specified condition; returns **false** otherwise. A value of **false** is returned for a range of zero elements. The *cond_f* argument is a function that takes an argument of the base type and returns **true** if the condition is fulfilled. For example, the following statements combine **any_of** with the conditional operator (?:) to print "has" or "does not have":

```
bool is_neg(int n) { return n < 0;}
. . .
int arrA[5] = {10, 15, 77, -10, 3};
cout << "Arr ";
cout << (any_of(arrA, arrA + 5, is_neg)?
         "has " : "does not have");
cout << "at least one negative." << endl;
```

This prints:

```
Arr has at least one negative.
```

- **binary_search(*beg*, *end*, *value* [, *less_than_f*])**

Searches the sorted range (*beg*, *end*) for an occurrence of *value* and returns **true** if it is found. The range must be presorted from low to high. Although this function will work with forward iterators, it is much more efficient when used with random-access iterators—supported by arrays, vectors, and deques. (For *less_than_f*, see the beginning of this section.)

```
vector<int> v;
for (int i = 0; i < 1777000; ++i) {
     v.push_back(i);
}
if (binary_search(v.begin(), v.end(), 555000)) {
     cout << "555000 was found." << endl;
}
```

- **copy(*beg*, *end*, *dest*)**

Copies elements in the range (*beg*, *end*) to a destination range of equal length beginning with *dest*. The first two arguments are input iterators and the last is an output iterator.

```
int arr[5] = {10, 20, 30, 40, 50};
vector<int>  iVec(5, 0);
copy(arr, arr + 5, iVec.begin());
```

After these statements are executed, iVec is overwritten, so it contains:

```
10 20 30 40 50
```

Alternatively, you can use one of the insert-iterator functions for the destination; in that case, no data is overwritten.

```
#include <inserter>
. . .
copy(arr, arr + 5, back_inserter(iVec));
```

- **copy_backward(*beg*, *end*, *end2*)**

  Performs the same action as **copy** but executes the copying in reverse order, starting by copying *(--*last*) to *(--*end2*) and working backward. All three arguments are bidirectional iterators. Use this version of the template to copy in a backward direction when the ranges overlap.

- **copy_if(*beg*, *end*, *beg2*, *condf*)**

  Copies elements in the range (*beg*, *end*) to a destination range beginning with *dest*, copying only those elements that fulfill a specified condition. The first two arguments are input iterators; the third, *beg2*, is an output iterator. The *condf* argument is a function that returns **true** if the argument passed to it meets the condition.

  The following example copies only odd numbers from arr to iVec, which initially holds seven instances of 0.

```
bool is_odd(int n) { return n % 2 != 0; }
. . .
int arr[7] = {1, 2, 3, 4, 5, 6, 7};
vector<int>  iVec(7, 0);
copy_if(arr, arr + 7, iVec.begin(), is_odd);
```

  After these statements are executed, iVec contains:

```
1 3 5 7 0 0 0
```

  Alternatively, you can use one of the insert-iterator functions for the destination; in that case, no data is overwritten. In this example, iVec starts out empty.

```
#include <inserter>
. . .
int arr[7] = {1, 2, 3, 4, 5, 6, 7};
vector<int>  iVec;
copy_if(arr, arr + 7, back_inserter(iVec),
     is_odd);
```

  After this last statement is executed, iVec contains:

```
1 3 5 7
```

- **copy_n(*beg*, *n*, *beg2*)**

  Performs the same action as **copy** but copies *n* elements beginning with the element pointed to by *beg*; *beg2* points to the beginning of the destination range. The first argument is an input iterator and the third argument is an output iterator.

```
int arr[5] = {10, 20, 30, 40, 50};
vector<int>  iVec(5, 0);
copy_n(arr, 4, iVec.begin());
```

After these statements are executed, iVec contains:

```
10 20 30 40 0
```

Alternatively, you can start out with an empty container and use one of the insert operators to insert new data rather than overwriting existing values.

```
#include <iterator>
. . .
int arr[5] = {10, 20, 30, 40, 50};
vector<int>  iVec;
copy_n(arr, 5, back_inserter(iVec));
```

- **count(***beg***,** *end***,** *value***)**

  Returns the number of times the specified *value* is found in the range (*beg*, *end*). The first two arguments are input iterators. For example, the following statements find three copies of 100.

  ```
  int a[8] = {5, 50, 100, 3, 17, 100, 0, 100};
  cout << "100 was found " << count(a, a + 8, 100);
  cout << " times." << endl;
  ```

- **count_if(***beg***,** *end***,** *condf***)**

  Returns the number of times an element is found that fulfills a specified condition, as determined by *condf*: This is a function that takes an element of the base type and returns **true** if the condition is met. The first two arguments, *beg* and *end*, are input iterators. For example, the following statements count the number of elements less than zero.

  ```
  bool is_neg(int n) { return n < 0;}
  . . .
  int arr[8] = {10, 20, 30, -15, -100, 0, 67, -2};
  cout << count_if(arr, arr + 8, is_neg);
  cout << " negative elements found." << endl;
  ```

  This code prints:

  ```
  3 negative elements found.
  ```

- **equal(***beg***,** *end***,** *beg2* **[,** *eq_f***])**

  Compares values in the range (*beg*, *end*) to those in a range of equal length beginning with *beg2*; returns **true** if each value in the first range is equal to the corresponding value in the second range. All three iterators are input iterators. (For *eq_f*, see the beginning of this section.)

  ```
  int arr[6] = {10, 20, 30, 40, 50, 60 };
  vector<int>  iVec(arr, arr + 6);
  ```

```
if (equal(arr, arr + 6, iVec.begin())) {
     cout << "The two ranges are equal." << endl;
}
```

▶ **`equal_range(`*`beg`*`, `*`end`*`, `*`value`*` [, `*`less_than_f`*`])`**

Searches the range (*beg*, *end*) and returns a **pair** with lower and upper bounds of the subrange containing *value*. The first two arguments are forward iterators. (For *less_than_f*, see the beginning of this section.) If *value* does not occur at all, *end* is returned as both lower and upper bounds.

The **first** member of the pair returned is the lower bound; the **second** member is the upper bound. The lower bound is an iterator pointing to first element greater than or equal to the specified value; the upper bound is an iterator pointing to the first element greater than this value.

For example, the following statements find the subrange consisting of values of 20; the pair returned consists of a pointer to the first occurrence of 20 (lower bound) and a pointer to the first occurrence of a value greater than 20 (upper bound).

```
typedef pair<int*, int*> return_type;
int arr[6] = {10, 20, 20, 20, 30, 50 };
return_type ret = equal_range(arr, arr + 6, 20);
for (int *p = ret.first; p != ret.second; ++p) {
     cout << *p << " ";
}
```

These statements print the range of values found, made up of three copies of 20:

```
20 20 20
```

▶ **`fill(`*`beg`*`, `*`end`*`, `*`value`*`)`**

Sets each element in the range (*beg*, *end*) to the specified *value*. The two iterators are forward iterators.

```
int arr[8] = {10, 20, 30, 40, 50, 60, 70, 80 };
fill(arr + 4, arr + 8, 0);
```

After these statements are executed, the array contains these values:

```
10 20 30 40 0 0 0 0
```

▶ **`fill_n(`*`beg`*`, `*`n`*`, `*`value`*`)`**

Sets each element in the specified range to *value*. The range consists of elements beginning with *beg*, *n* elements long. *beg* is a forward iterator.

```
int arr[8] = {10, 20, 30, 40, 50, 60, 70, 80 };
fill_n(arr + 2, 3, 0);
```

After these statements are executed, the array contains these values:

```
10 20 0 0 0 60 70 80
```

- **find(*beg*, *end*, *value*)**

  Returns an iterator pointing to the first element in the range (*beg*, *end*) that contains the specified *value*. Returns *end* if the value is not found. The first two arguments are input iterators. In the following example, 70 is found in position 6 (using zero-based positions).

```
int arr[8] = {10, 20, 30, 40, 50, 60, 70, 80 };
int *p = find(arr, arr + 8, 70);   // Look for 70.
if (p == arr + 8) {
   cout << "70 not found." << endl;
} else {
   cout << "70 found @ pos. " << p — arr << endl;
}
```

- **find_end(*beg*, *end*, *beg2*, *end2* [, *eq_f*])**

  Searches for a complete occurrence of the subrange (*beg2*, *end2*) in its entirety and in order, within the larger range (*beg*, *end*). Returns an iterator pointing to the beginning of the subrange found, or *end* if it is not found. This algorithm is similar to the **search** algorithm, except that it searches for the last occurrence of the subrange. The first four arguments are forward iterators. (For *eq_f*, see the beginning of this section.)

```
int arr1[8] = {10, 20, 30, 40, 10, 20, 30, 40};
int arr2[3] = {20, 30, 40};
int *p= find_end(arr1, arr1 + 8, arr2, arr2 + 3);
if (p == arr1 + 8) {
     cout << "Sub-range not found." << endl;
} else {
     cout << "Sub-range last found @ position ";
     cout << p-arr1 << endl;
}
```

- **find_first_of(*beg*, *end*, *beg2*, *end2* [, *eq_f*])**

  Returns an iterator pointing to the first element in the range (*beg*, *end*) that matches any element in the range (*beg2*, *end2*). If no such element is found, *end* is returned. The first four arguments are forward iterators. (For *eq_f*, see the beginning of this section.)

  For example, the following code finds the first element in arr1 matching 30, 33, or 39. The element is found at position 3.

```
int a1[6] = {-30, 10, 20, 30, 40, 50};
int a2[3] = {30, 33, 39};
int *p = find_first_of(a1, a1 + 6, a2, a2 + 3);
cout << "First element in a1 equal to 30, 33,";
cout << " or 39 is in position " << p — arr1;
```

The following version of the code finds the first matching element if the negative sign is ignored (which results in a match in position 0 in this case):

```
#include <cstdlib>
bool f(int a, int b) {return abs(a) < abs(b);}
. . .
int *p= find_first_of(a1, a1 + 6, a2, a2 + 3, f);
```

▶ **find_if(*beg*, *end*, *condf*)**

Returns an iterator pointing to the first element in the range (*beg*, *end*) that fulfills a specified condition. Returns *end* if no such element is found. Both iterators are input iterators. The *condf* argument is a Boolean function that takes one argument of the base type and returns **true** if the condition is met.

```
bool is_neg(int n) { return n < 0};
. . .
int arr[8] = {10, 20, 30, 40, 50, -60, -70, 80 };
int *p = find_if(arr, arr + 8, is_neg);
if (p == arr + 8) {
     cout << "Neg. num not found.";
} else {
     cout << "Neg. found @ position " << p – arr;
     cout << endl;
}
```

▶ **find_if_not(*beg*, *end*, *condf*)**

C++11 specific. Returns an iterator pointing to the first element in the range (*beg*, *end*) that fails to fulfill a specified condition. Returns *end* if no such element is found. Both iterators are input iterators. The *condf* argument is a Boolean function that takes one argument of the base type and returns **true** if the condition is met.

```
bool is_neg(int n) { return n < 0};
. . .
int arr[8] = {-10,-20, 0, 40, 50, -60, 70, 80 };
int *p = find_if_not(arr, arr + 8, is_neg);
if (p == arr + 8) {
   cout << "Nonneg. num not found.";
} else {
   cout << "Nonneg. num found @ position ";
   cout << p – arr << "."endl;
}
```

These statements, when executed, print:

```
Nonneg. num found @ position 2.
```

▸ **for_each(*beg*, *end*, *fnct*)**

Repeats an action for each element in the range (*beg*, *end*), each time passing the value of the element to the function *fnct*. This function has **void** return type and takes one argument of the base type. The iterators are both input iterators.

```
void output_f(int n) {cout << " " << endl; }
. . .
arr[5] = {5, 100, 27, 33, -44 };
vector<int>  iVec(arr, arr + 5);
for_each(iVec.begin(), iVec.end(), output_f);
```

This example prints:

```
5 100 27 33 -44
```

▸ **generate(*beg*, *end*, *gen_f*)**

Assigns a value to each element in the range (*beg*, *end*), by calling the function *gen_f*, which is a function that takes no arguments and returns a value of the base type. The iterators *beg* and *end* are forward iterators.

```
int gen_fnct() {
     static int i = 0;
     return ++i;
}
. . .
vector<int>  my_vec(10, 0);
generate(my_vec.begin(), my_vec.end(), gen_fnct);
```

After these statements are executed, the contents of my_vec are:

```
1 2 3 4 5 6 7 8 9 10
```

▸ **generate_n(*beg*, *n*, *gen_f*)**

Performs the same action as the previous version of **generate**, except that the range is specified as starting with *beg* and being *n* elements long.

```
vector<int>  my_vec(10, 0);
generate(my_vec.begin(), 10, gen_fnct);
```

▸ **includes(*beg*, *end*, *beg2*, *end2* [, *less_than_f*])**

Returns **true** if the sorted range (*beg*, *end*) contains all the values in the sorted range (*beg2*, *end2*): That is, every element in the second range is also an element of the first range. Both ranges should be presorted. The iterators are all input iterators. (For *less_than_f*, see the beginning of this section.)

```
int big[10] = {1, 2, 3, 4, 5, 6, 11, 12, 13, 14};
int tiny[3] = {6, 11, 12};
if (includes(big, big + 10, tiny, tiny + 3)) {
      cout << "big contains tiny." << endl;
}
```

▸ **`inner_product(`*`beg`*`, `*`end`*`, `*`beg2`*`, `*`init_val`*` [, `*`op1`*`] [, `*`op2`*`])`**

Requires the <numeric> header rather than <algorithm>.

Default behavior is to multiply each element in the range (*beg*, *end*) with the corresponding element in the range beginning with *beg2* and return the sum. The first three arguments are input iterators. For each pair of corresponding elements, the algorithm performs the following operation:

```
init_val = init_val + (elemFirstRange * elemSecondRange)
```

The optional *op1* and *op2* arguments may specify functions. (They can be function addresses, lambdas, or function objects.) If these are specified, the algorithm does the following for each pair of corresponding elements.

```
init_val = init_val op1 (elemFirstRange op2 elemSecondRange)
```

For example, the following statements total 1*2 + 3*4 + 5*6, producing 44:

```
#include <numeric>
. . .
int arrA[3] = {1, 3, 5};
int arrB[3] = {2, 4, 6};
// Print 44.
cout << inner_product(arrA, arrA+3, arrB, 0);
```

The last statement above could have been written as:

```
cout << inner_product(arrA, arrA+3, arrB, 0,
   plus<int>(), multiplies<int>());
```

▸ **`inplace_merge(`*`beg`*`, `*`middle`*`, `*`end`*` [, `*`less_than_f`*`])`**

Merges two adjacent, presorted ranges: (*beg*, *middle*) and (*middle*, *end*). The first range consists of elements up to but not including the element pointed to by *middle*; the second begins with the element pointed to by *middle*, up to but not including the element pointed to by *end*. The effect of this function is to create one sorted range. The first three arguments are bidirectional iterators. (For *less_than_f*, see the beginning of this section.)

```
int arr[9] = {1, 3, 5, 7, 9, 2, 4, 6, 8 };
inplace_merge(arr, arr + 5, arr + 9);
```

The array now contains these contents:

```
1 2 3 4 5 6 7 8 9
```

▸ **`iota(`*`beg`*`, `*`end`*`, `*`val`*`)`**

C++11 specific. Requires the <numeric> header rather than <algorithm>.

Initializes the first element in the range (*beg*, *end*) to the specified value (*val*). Then each element is set to 1 plus the previous element. *beg* and *end* are forward iterators.

```
#include <numeric>
. . .
int arr[5];
iota(arr, arr + 5, 100);
```

The array now contains these elements:

```
100 101 102 103 104
```

- **is_heap(***beg*, *end*, [, *less_than_f*]**)**

C++11 specific. Returns **true** if the range (*beg*, *end*) is ordered according to the rules for a "heap" described in Section 18.6.4, "Heap Algorithms." (For *less_than_f*, see the beginning of this section.)

```
int arr[6] = {1, 100, 50, 75, 2, 3};
vector<int> iVec(arr, arr+6);
make_heap(iVec.begin(), iVec.end());
if(is_heap(iVec.begin(), iVec.end())) {
     cout << "iVec is now a heap." << endl;
}
```

- **is_heap_until(***beg*, *end*, [, *less_than_f*]**)**

C++11 specific. Returns an iterator pointing to the first element in the range (*beg*, *end*) that breaks the requirements for a "heap"—according to the rules described in Section 18.6.4. If the entire range qualifies as a heap, *end* is returned. The first two arguments are random-access iterators. (For *less_than_f*, see the beginning of this section.)

```
int arr[6] = {1, 100, 50, 75, 2, 3};
vector<int> iVec(arr, arr + 6);
make_heap(iVec.begin(), iVec.end());
iVec.push_back(200);
iVec.push_back(300);
cout << "The heap consists of the first ";
cout << is_heap_until(iVec.begin(), iVec.end())
        - iVec.begin();
cout << " elements only." << endl;
```

These statements, when printed, reported that the heap consists of the first six elements only.

- **is_partitioned(***beg*, *end*, *condf***)**

Returns **true** if the range (*beg*, *end*) is entirely partitioned by the *condf* function: All the elements fulfilling a specified condition must precede all the elements not fulfilling that condition. The *condf* argument is a function that takes a value of the base type and returns **true** if it meets the condition. The first two arguments are input iterators.

```
bool is_pos(int n) {return n > 0;}
. . .
int arr[7] = {5, 1, 9, 0, -3, 0, -20 };
if (is_partitioned(arr, arr + 7, is_pos)) {
     cout << "Array is partitioned by ";
     cout << "positive / not positive." << endl;
}
```

▸ **is_permutation(***beg*, *end*, *beg2* [, *less_than_f*]**)**

C++11 specific. Compares the range (*beg*, *end*) to a range of equal size beginning with *beg2*; returns **true** if the two ranges are permutations (rearrangements) of the same set of values. The first three arguments are forward iterators. (For *less_than_f*, see the beginning of this section.)

```
int arrA[4] = {1, 2, 3, 4};
int arrB[4] = {4, 1, 3, 2};
if(is_permutation(arrA, arrA + 4, arrB)) {
     cout << "The arrays are permutations of";
     cout << " each other." << endl;
}
```

▸ **is_sorted(***beg*, *end* [, *less_than_f*]**)**

C++11 specific. Returns **true** if an array is sorted in order from lowest value to highest value. Elements that are considered equal can be in any order relative to each other. The first two arguments are forward iterators. (For *less_than_f*, see the beginning of this section.)

```
int arrA[4] = {1, 2, 3, 4};
int arrB[5] = {4, 1, 3, 2, 2};
if (is_sorted(arrA, arrA + 4)) { // This is true.
     cout << "arrA is sorted." << endl;
}
if (is_sorted(arrB, arrB + 5)) { // But not this.
     cout << "arrB is sorted." << endl;
}
```

▸ **is_sorted_until(***beg*, *end* [, *less_than_f*]**)**

C++11 specific. Returns an iterator pointing to the first element in (*beg*, *end*) that breaks the pattern of a sorted arrangement—that is, the first element that is less than its predecessor. The template returns *end* if the entire range is sorted. The first two arguments are forward iterators. (For *less_than_f*, see the beginning of this section.)

```
int arr[5] = {10, 20, 30, 25, 50};
cout << "The first ";
cout << is_sorted_until(arr, arr + 5) - arr;
cout << " elements are sorted." << endl;
```

▸ **iter_swap(*iterA*, *iterB*)**

Swaps the elements pointed to by iterA and iterB, two forward iterators.

```
int arr[5] = {0, 10, 20, 30, 100};
iter_swap(arr, arr + 4);
```

The array now contains these contents:

```
100 10 20 30 0
```

▸ **lexicographical_compare(*beg*, *end*, *beg2*, *end2* [, *less_than_f*])**

Compares the range (*beg*, *end*) to the range (*beg2*, *end2*) and returns **true** if the first range is "less than" the second. The template compares the first pair of corresponding elements; if they are equal, the template compares the next pair of elements, and so on, until one range is less than another. This algorithm is similar to the less-than operation (<) for the **string** class. The first four arguments are input iterators. (For *less_than_f*, see the beginning of this section.)

Note that if the one range matches the other but is shorter, the shorter range is "less than":

```
int a1[5] = {'B', 'r', 'i', 'a', 'n'};
int a2[6] = {'B', 'r', 'i', 'a', 'n', 'O'};
if(lexicographical_compare(a1, a1+5, a2, a2+6)) {
     cout << "First range precedes the second ";
     cout << "in lexicographical order." << endl;
}
```

▸ **lower_bound(*beg*, *end*, *value* [, *less_than_f*])**

Returns the lower bound of *value* in the range (*beg*, *end*); returns *end* if no such element is found. The lower bound is an iterator pointing to the first element in the range that has a value equal to or greater than *value*. *beg* and *end* are forward iterators. (For *less_than_f*, see the beginning of this section.)

```
int arr[5] = {10, 20, 30, 40, 50};
int *p = lower_bound(arr, arr + 5, 40);
if (p == arr + 5) {
     cout << "No element >= 40 found." << endl;
} else {
      cout << "First element >= 40 is in pos. ";
      cout << p – arr << endl;
}
```

▸ **make_heap(*beg*, *end* [, *less_than_f*])**

Reorders a range of a random-access container (array, vector, or deque) into a virtual binary tree, or "heap," as described in Section 18.6.4. The first two arguments are random-access iterators. One of the qualities of such a heap is that the first element always has the highest value—or rather, it is not less than the highest value. (For *less_than_f*, see the beginning of this section.)

```
int arr[10] = {1, 1, 2, 3, 3, 4, 4, 4, 5, 6};
make_heap(arr, arr + 10);
cout << "Highest value is " << arr[0] << endl;
for (int i = 0; i < 10; ++i)
    {cout << arr[i] << " ";}
```

This example prints:

```
Highest value is 6
6 5 4 4 3 4 2 1 3 1
```

- **max(*a*, *b* [, *less_than_f*])**

Returns the maximum of two values, which must have the same base type. For *less_than_f*, see the beginning of this section.

```
int i = 100, j = 200;
cout << max(i, j);   // Print 200.
```

- **max_element(*beg*, *end* [, *less_than_f*])**

Returns an iterator pointing to the greatest element in the range (*beg*, *end*). *beg* and *end* are forward iterators, as is the return value. (For *less_than_f*, see the beginning of this section.)

```
int arr[5] = {50, 10, 20, 555, 3};
// This next statement prints 555...
cout << *max_element(arr, arr + 5) << endl;
```

- **merge(*beg*, *end*, *beg2*, *end2*, *dest* [, *less_than_f*])**

Merges two presorted ranges together and copies the results to a destination range beginning with *dest*; the destination range should have a length at least as great as the sum of the sizes of the two input ranges. The first four arguments are input iterators, and *dest* is an output iterator. (For *less_than_f*, see the beginning of this section.)

```
int arr1[4] = {10, 30, 50, 70};
int arr2[3] = {20, 40, 60};
vector<int>  v(10, 0);
merge(arr1, arr1 + 4, arr2, arr2 + 3, v.begin());
```

After these statements are executed, iVec contains the following values:

```
10 20 30 40 50 60 70 0 0 0
```

- **min(*a*, *b* [, *less_than_f*])**

Returns the minimum of two values, which must have the same base type. For *less_than_f*, see the beginning of this section.

```
int i = 100, j = 200;
cout << min(i, j);   // Print 100.
```

▸ **`min_element(`***`beg`***`, `***`end`*** `[, `***`less_than_f`***`])`**

Returns an iterator pointing to the lowest element in the range (*beg*, *end*). *beg* and *end* are forward iterators. For *less_than_f*, see the beginning of this section.

```
int arr[5] = {50, 12, 10, -20, 155};
// Print -20.
cout << *min_element(arr, arr + 5) << endl;
```

▸ **`minmax_element(`***`beg`***`, `***`end`*** `[, `***`less_than_f`***`])`**

C++11 specific. Returns a **pair** object in which the **first** member is an iterator pointing to an element in the range (*beg*, *end*) with the lowest value, and the **second** member is an iterator pointing to the greatest value. The first two arguments are forward iterators. (For *less_than_f*, see the beginning of this section.)

```
int arr[7] = {50, 1, 10, 255, 20, 12, 155};
pair<int*, int*> rv;
rv = minmax_element(arr, arr + 7);
cout << "Pos. of min. is " << rv.first – arr;
cout << endl;
cout << "Pos. of max. is " << rv.second – arr;
```

These statements, when executed, print the following (using zero-based positions):

```
Pos. of min. is 1
Pos. of max. is 3
```

▸ **`mismatch(`***`beg`***`, `***`end`***`, `***`beg2`*** `[, `***`eq_f`***`])`**

Compares the range (*beg*, *end*) to a range of equal size beginning with *beg2* and finds the first mismatch—that is, the first pair of elements in which the two ranges do not match each other. The first three arguments are input iterators. (For *eq_f*, see the beginning of this section.)

The return value is a **pair** object, in which the **first** element is an iterator pointing to the first mismatched element found in the first range, (*beg*, *end*), and the **second** element is an iterator pointing to the mismatched element in the second range.

```
int arr1[6] = {10, 20, 5, 30, 100, 200};
int arr2[6] = {10, 20, 5, 30, -100, -200};

typedef  pair<int*, int*>  return_type;
return_type rv = mismatch(arr1, arr1 + 6, arr2);
cout<<"First mismatch in arr1: " << *(rv.first);
cout << endl;
cout<<"First mismatch in arr2: " << *(rv.second);
```

These statements print:

```
First mismatch in arr1: 100
First mismatch in arr2: -100
```

▸ **move(*beg*, *end*, *beg2*)**

C++11 specific. Transfers data in the range (*beg*, *end*) to a range of equal size beginning with *beg2*. The first two arguments are input iterators and the last is an output iterator. Returns an iterator pointing to the first element not overwritten in the destination.

A move operation is not the same as a copy! A "move" transfers data ownership from one place to another, presumably leaving the source nulled out or otherwise unusable. This is safe only if the source is a temporary object or is about to be assigned a new value. Where complex objects are involved, moves are potentially more efficient than copying, as explained in Appendix A, "A Painless Introduction to Rvalue References (C++11)."

This template function enables data transfers of overlapping ranges. This is done in a forward direction, so use **move** when copying a range forward within the same container. To move an overlapping range in a backward direction, use **move_backward** instead.

The following example moves the string data "John" and "Paul" two positions forward within the vector. The first two elements do not retain their values.

```
string a[4]={"John", "Paul", "George", "Ringo"};
vector<string> v(a, a + 4);
move(v.begin(), v.begin() + 2, v.begin() + 2);
```

After these statements are executed, the vector contains "John" and "Paul" in its last two elements, and the first two elements no longer have these values.

Simply put, a move is a destructive transfer of data (not a copy) that does not preserve the value of the source objects. Move operations are potentially much faster than copy operations.

▸ **move_backward(*beg*, *end*, *end2*)**

C++11 specific. Transfers data in the range (*beg*, *end*) to a range of equal size ending with *end2* (that is, the destination range should include elements up to but not including end2 itself). All three arguments are bidirectional iterators. This is a version of **move** that should be used when copying an overlapping range backward within the same container.

See the description of **move** for more information. Note that a move is not the same thing as a copy.

The following example moves the string data "George" and "Ringo" two positions backward within the vector. The last two elements do not retain their values.

```
string a[4]={"John", "Paul", "George", "Ringo"};
vector<string> v(a, a + 4);
move_backward(v.begin() + 2, v.begin() + 4,
     v.begin() + 2);
```

▸ **next_permutation(***beg***,** *end* **[,** *less_than_f***])**

Rearranges elements in the range (*beg*, *end*) so that they form the next permutation of elements. The first two arguments are bidirectional iterators. (For *less_than_f*, see the beginning of this section.)

A permutation is a unique arrangement of N elements. For the integer array {1, 2, 3}, {1, 2, 3} is the lowest permutation and the next permutation is {1, 3, 2}. For any given arrangement, the **sort** algorithm should produce the lowest possible permutation.

If the elements are already arranged in the highest possible permutation, this function returns **false** and does not change the order. It returns **true** otherwise.

```
int arr[3] = {1, 2, 3};
do {
     for (int i = 0; i < 3; ++i) {
          cout << arr[i] << " ";
     }
     cout << endl;
} while (next_permutation(arr, arr + 3));
```

When run, this example prints:

```
1 2 3
1 3 2
2 1 3
2 3 1
3 1 2
3 2 1
```

▸ **none_of(***beg***,** *end***,** *cond_f***)**

C++11 specific. Returns **true** if none of the elements in the range (*beg*, *end*) fulfill a specified condition; returns **false** otherwise. A value of **true** is returned for a range of zero elements. The *cond_f* argument is a function that takes an argument of the base type and returns **true** if the condition is fulfilled.

For example, the following statements test each of two arrays (arrA, arrB) to see if none of the values in the array are negative. (Only the second statement is printed in this case.)

```
bool is_neg(int n) { return n < 0;}
. . .
int arrA[5] = {10, 15, 77, -10, 3};
int arrB[4] = {1, 5, 2, 100};
if (none_of(arrA, arrA + 5, is_neg)) {
     cout << "None of arrA is negative." << endl;
}
if(none_of(arrB, arrB + 4, is_neg)) {
     cout << "None of arrB is negative." << endl;
}
```

▸ **nth_element(***beg*, *nth_iter*, *end* [, *less_than_f*]**)**

Rearranges a container so that the nth greatest element (pointed to by iterator *nth_iter*) is placed so that all elements to its left are lower and all elements to its right are higher. The first three arguments are all random-access iterators—so the container must be an array, vector, or deque. (For *less_than_f*, see the beginning of this section.) In the process, the rest of the container may be sorted, but there is no guarantee it will be.

```
int arr[7] = {50, 3, 2, 1, 103, 102, 101};

nth_element(arr, arr + 3, arr + 7);
for (int i = 0; i < 7; ++i) {
     cout << arr[i];
}
cout << end;
```

After these statements are executed, the value 50 will be in the fourth position (arr + 3). The rest of the array may or may not be sorted.

▸ **partial_sort(***beg*, *middle*, *end* [, *less_than_f*]**)**

Rearranges a container in such a way that the subrange (*beg*, *middle*) contains the N lowest elements, in sorted order, from the larger range (*beg*, *end*), where N is the size of (*beg*, *middle*). The remaining elements are left unsorted. The first three arguments are all random-access iterators—so the container must be an array, vector, or deque. (For *less_than_f*, see the beginning of this section.)

```
int arr[6] = {30, 3, 20, 2, 10, 1};
partial_sort(arr, arr + 3, arr + 6);

for (int i = 0; i < 6; ++i) {
     cout << arr[i] << " ";
}
cout << endl;
```

These statements print:

```
1 2 3 30 20 10
```

▸ **partial_sort_copy(***beg*, *end*, *beg_dest*, *end_dest* [, *less_than_f*]**)**

Sorts elements in the range (*beg*, *end*) and copies them to the range (*beg_dest*, *end_dest*). If the destination range is smaller than (*beg*, *end*), only the first N elements are copied, where N is the length of (*beg*, *end*). The first four arguments are all random-access iterators—so the container must be an array, vector, or deque. (For *less_than_f*, see the beginning of this section.) This function, despite the similarity of names, does not work like **partial_sort** but produces different results.

```
int a[6] = {30, 20, 10, 15, 30, 25};
vector<int>  v(6, 0);
partial_sort_copy(a, a + 3, v.begin(), v.end());
```

After these statements are executed, the vector will contain:

```
10 20 30 0 0 0
```

But if the vector is initialized to have only two elements, it will contain:

```
10 20
```

- **`partial_sum(`*`beg`*`, `*`end`*`, `*`dest`*` [, `*`op`*`])`**

Requires the <numeric> header rather than <algorithm>.

Default behavior is to copy values to a destination range beginning with *dest* as follows: After execution, each element will contain the sum of the corresponding elements in the range (*beg*, *end*) up to that point. The first three arguments are input iterators. The optional *op* argument can specify an operation other than addition; this argument contains a function address, lambda, or function object.

The first element in the destination will contain the element pointed to by *beg*. The second element in the destination will contain the sum of the first two elements in (*beg*, *end*). The third element in the destination will contain the sum of the first three elements in (*beg*, *end*). And so on.

```
#include <numeric>
. . .
int arrA[5] = {1, 1, 1, 1, 1};
int destA[5];
partial_sum(arrA, arrA + 5, destA);
int arrB[4] = {2, 4, 6, 8};
dest destB[4];
partial_sum(arrB, arrB + 4, destB);
```

After these statements are executed, the arrays destA and destB will contain:

```
destA: 1 2 3 4 5
destB: 2 6 12 20
```

- **`partition(`*`beg`*`, `*`end`*`, `*`condf`*`)`**

Rearranges the range (*beg*, *end*) so that all the elements that satisfy a specified condition are placed before those that do not. The function returns an iterator pointing to the beginning of the second group (the elements not fulfilling the condition).

The *beg* and *end* arguments are random-access iterators (so the container must be an array, vector, or deque). The *condf* argument is a function that takes two arguments of appropriate type and returns **true** if the condition is satisfied.

For example, the following code places the odd numbers at the beginning of the array.

```
bool is_odd(int n) { return n % 2 == 1; }
. . .
int arr[8] = {10, 15, 5, 20, 25, 50, 35, 40 };
partition(arr, arr + 8, is_odd);
```

Now the array contains:

```
15 5 25 35 10 20 50 40
```

▸ **`partition_point(`*`beg`*`, `*`end`*`, `*`condf`*`)`**

C++11 specific. Returns an iterator pointing to the beginning of the second part of a partition based on the *condf* function. The range (*beg*, *end*) is assumed to be a partition: All the elements that satisfy the condition precede all the elements that do not. The *condf* argument is a function that takes an argument of the base type and returns **true** if the condition is met. The *beg* and *end* arguments are forward iterators.

```
bool is_odd(int n) {return n % 2 != 0;}
. . .
int a[6] = {10, 15, 20, 25, 30, 35};
partition(a, a + 6, is_odd);
int p = partition_point(a, a + 6, is_odd) - arr;

cout << "First part of partitioned array: ";
for(int i = 0; i < p; ++i) {cout << a[i] << "  ";}
cout << endl;
cout << "Second part of partitioned array: ";
for(int i = p; i < 6; ++i) {cout << a[i] << "  ";}
cout << endl;
```

These statements produce the following output:

```
First part of partitioned array: 35 15 25
Second part of partitioned array: 20 30 10
```

▸ **`pop_heap(`*`beg`*`, `*`end`*` [, `*`less_than_f`*`])`**

Removes the element at the front of a heap (pointed to by *beg*) and moves it to the last position in the range (this position is *end*-1). The remaining elements are then ordered into a heap of size N-1, where N is the old size. See Section 18.6.4 for more information on heaps. The first two arguments are random-access iterators. (For *less_than_f*, see the beginning of this section.)

```
int arr[10] = {1, 1, 2, 3, 3, 4, 4, 4, 5, 6};
make_heap(arr, arr + 10);
pop_heap(arr, arr + 10);
cout << "Second biggest element is " << arr[0];
```

▸ **`prev_permutation(`*`beg`*`, `*`end`*` [, `*`less_than_f`*`])`**

Rearranges elements in the range (*beg*, *end*) so that they form the previous permutation of the elements. The first two arguments are bidirectional iterators. (For *less_than_f*, see the beginning of this section.)

A permutation is a unique arrangement of N elements. For the integer array {1, 2, 3}, {1, 2, 3} itself is the lowest permutation and the next permutation is {1, 3, 2}.

For any given arrangement, the **sort** algorithm should produce the lowest possible permutation.

If the elements are already arranged in the lowest possible permutation, this function returns **false** and does not change the order. It returns **true** otherwise.

```
int arr[3] = {3, 2, 1};
do {
     for (int i = 0; i < 3; ++i) {
          cout << arr[i] << " ";
     }
     cout << endl;
} while (prev_permutation(arr, arr + 3));
```

When run, this example prints:

```
3 2 1
3 1 2
2 3 1
2 1 3
1 3 2
1 2 3
```

▸ **push_heap(***beg*, *end* [, *less_than_f*])

Creates a heap in the range (*beg*, *end*), assuming that the range (*beg*, *end*-1) is already ordered into a heap. The last element in (*beg*, *end*) is inserted into this new heap. Items are reordered so as to preserve the rules of the virtual top-down binary tree. See Section 18.6.4 for more information on heaps. The first two arguments are random-access iterators. (For *less_than_f*, see the beginning of this section.)

```
int arr[10] = {1, 1, 2, 3, 3, 4, 4, 4, 5, 7};
vector<int>  my_heap(arr, arr+10:
make_heap(my_heap.begin(), my_heap.end());
my_heap.push_back(6);      // Add 6 to the vector.

// Now fold the new element (6) into the heap...
push_heap(my_heap.begin(), my_heap.end());
```

▸ **random_shuffle(***beg*, *end* [, *rand_f*])

Randomly rearranges elements in the range (*beg*, *end*). The first two arguments are random-access iterators (so the container must be an array, vector, or deque).

You can optionally supply a randomization function, *rand_f*; otherwise, by default, **random_shuffle** calls the **rand** function from the C standard library. Regardless of which function is used, you should set a random seed unless you're willing to have the program produce the same "random" results each time it is run.

The following example creates a virtual deck of cards consisting of numbers of an array of 52 elements, in which each element has a value from 0 to 51. These values can, if you choose, be associated with the 52 possible values in a standard deck of playing cards. (For example, values 0 to 12 can be associated with the 13 spades from 2, 3, 4, on up to Q, K, A; values 13 to 25 can be associated with the 13 hearts, and so on.)

```
#include <cstdlib>
#include <ctime>
. . .
srand(time(NULL));    // Set random seed
vector<int>  cards;
for(int i = 0; i < 52; ++i) { // Generate 0 to 51
     cards.push_back(i);
}
random_shuffle(iVec.begin(), iVec.end());
for(int i = 0; i < 5; ++i) {  // Print 5 cards
     cout << iVec[i] << " ";
}
```

A sample output is:

```
12 33 3 16 48
```

- **remove(*beg*, *end*, *value*)**

Removes all elements from the range (*beg*, *end*) having the specified *value* and then copies the results to the beginning of the range, overwriting existing elements. The algorithm returns an iterator one past the position of the last element overwritten in this way. The first two arguments are forward iterators. For example, the following statements remove all elements from iVec equal to 0.

```
int arr[6] = {10, 0, 20, 0, 30, 0};
vector<int>  iVec(arr, arr + 6);
remove(iVec.begin(), iVec.end(), 0);
```

After this call to **remove**, the first three elements of iVec are:

```
10 20 30
```

To print these values—printing only the results after 0 is removed—it's necessary to use the return value, as in the following code.

```
vector<int>::iterator it, it_end;
it_end = remove(iVec.begin(), iVec.end(), 0);
for (it = iVec.begin(); it != it_end; ++it) {
     cout << *it << " ";
}
```

- **remove_copy(*beg*, *end*, *dest*, *value*)**

Copies elements from the range (*beg*, *end*), except for any elements having the specified value. Elements are copied to a destination range beginning with the element pointed to by *dest*, overwriting existing contents. It's assumed that the destination is large enough to hold the results. The two arguments are input iterators; *dest* is an output iterator. The algorithm returns an iterator pointing to one position past the last element written to.

```
int arr[6] = {5, -1, 10, -1, 15, -1};
vector<int>  iVec(6, 0);
remove_copy(arr, arr + 6, iVec.begin(), -1);
```

After the call to **remove_copy**, iVec contains:

```
5 10 15 0 0 0
```

Alternatively, you can start out with an empty container and use one of the insertion template functions to insert new data rather than overwriting existing values.

```
#include <iterator>
. . .
int arr[6] = {5, -1, 10, -1, 15, -1};
vector<int>  v;
remove_copy(arr, arr + 6, back_inserter(v), -1);
```

After these statements are executed, the vector contains:

```
5 10 15
```

- **remove_copy_if(*beg, end, dest, condf*)**

Copies elements from the range (*beg, end*) to a range of equal size beginning with *dest*; but an element is not copied if it meets a specified condition. *condf* is a function taking one argument of the base type and returning **true** if this condition is met. The two arguments are input iterators; *dest* is an output iterator. The algorithm returns an iterator pointing to one position past the last element written to.

For example, the following statements copy only the even numbers from arr.

```
bool is_odd(int n) { return n % 2 == 1; }
. . .
int arr[6] = {5, 10, 15, 20, 25, 30};
vector<int>  v(6, 0);
remove_copy_if(arr, arr + 6, v.begin(), is_odd);
```

After the call to **remove_copy_if**, the vector contains:

```
10 20 30 0 0 0
```

Alternatively, you can start out with an empty container and use one of the insertion template functions to insert new data rather than overwriting existing values.

```
#include <iterator>
. . .
int arr[6] = {5, 10, 15, 20, 25, 30};
vector<int>  v(6, 0);
remove_copy_if(arr, arr + 6, back_inserter(v),
   is_odd);
```

After these statements are executed, the vector contains:

```
10 20 30
```

- **`remove_if(`*`beg, end, condf`*`)`**

Performs the same action as **remove**—copying elements to the beginning of the range—except that elements are not copied if they meet a specified condition. *condf* is a function taking one argument of the base type and returning **true** if this condition is met. The algorithm returns an iterator pointing to one position past the last element to be overwritten this way (that is, the new end of the range). For example, the following statements copy only the even numbers from iVec:

```
bool is_odd(int n) { return n % 2 == 1; }
. . .
int arr[6] = {5, 10, 15, 20, 25, 30};
vector<int>  iVec(arr, arr + 6);
remove_if(iVec.begin(), iVec.end(), is_odd);
```

After the call to **remove_ if**, the first three elements of iVec are:

10 20 30

- **`replace(`*`beg, end, old_val, new_val`*`)`**

Replaces each occurrence of *old_val* with *new_val*, in the range (*beg*, *end*). The first two arguments are forward iterators; *old_val* and *new_val* are values of the base type.

```
int arr[8] = {1, 0, 0, 0, 2, 3, 0, 0};
replace(arr, arr + 8, 0, 10);
```

After the call to **replace**, the array contains:

```
1 10 10 10 2 3 10 10
```

- **`replace_copy(`*`beg, end, dest, old_val, new_val`*`)`**

Copies the values from the range (*beg*, *end*) to a destination range beginning with *dest*, overwriting existing elements, but copying *new_val* to the destination every time it finds an occurrence of *old_val*. The destination range is assumed to have as many elements as the range (*beg*, *end*). The first two arguments are input iterators; *dest* is an output iterator.

```
int arr[8] = {1, 0, 0, 0, 2, 3, 0, 0};
vector<int>  iVec(8, 0);
replace_copy(arr, arr + 8, iVec.begin(), 0, 99);
```

After the call to **replace_copy**, iVec contains:

```
1 99 99 99 2 3 99 99
```

Alternatively, you can start out with an empty container and use one of the insert operators to insert new data rather than overwriting existing values.

```
#include <iterator>
. . .
int arr[8] = {1, 0, 0, 0, 2, 3, 0, 0};
vector<int>  iVec;
replace_copy(arr, arr + 8, back_inserter(iVec),
   0, 99);
```

- **replace_copy_if(*beg*, *end*, *dest*, *condf*, *new_val*)**

  Copies the values from the range (*beg*, *end*) to a destination range beginning with *dest*, overwriting existing elements, but copying *new_val* to the destination every time it finds an element that meets a specified condition. *condf* is a function taking one argument of the appropriate type and returning **true** if this condition is met.

  The destination range is assumed to have as many elements as the range (*beg*, *end*). The first two arguments are input iterators; *dest* is an output iterator.

  For example, the following statements copy even numbers from an array, while copying negative one (-1) for each position in which it finds an odd number.

```
bool is_odd(int n) { return n % 2 == 1; }
. . .
int a[8] = {1, 2, 3, 4, 5, 6, 7, 8};
vector<int>  v(8, 0);
replace_copy_if(a, a + 8, v.begin(), is_odd, -1);
```

  After the call to **replace_copy**, iVec contains:

```
-1 2 -1 4 -1 6 -1 8
```

- **replace_if(*beg*, *end*, *condf*, *new_val*)**

  Finds each element in the range (*beg*, *end*) that meets a specified condition and replaces it with *new_val*. *condf* is a function taking one argument of the base type and returning **true** if the condition is met. The first two arguments are forward iterators. For example, the following statements replace each odd number in an array with zero.

```
bool is_odd(int n) { return n % 2 == 1; }
. . .
int arr[8] = {1, 2, 3, 4, 5, 6, 7, 8};
replace_if(arr, arr + 8, is_odd, 0);
```

  After the call to **replace_copy**, the array contains:

```
0 2 0 4 0 6 0 8
```

- **reverse(*beg*, *end*)**

  Reverses all the elements in the range (*beg*, *end*). Both arguments are bidirectional iterators.

```
int arr[5] = {10, 20, 30, 40, 50};
reverse(arr, arr + 5);
```

After the call to **reverse**, the array contains:

```
50 40 30 20 10
```

- **reverse_copy(*beg*, *end*, *dest*)**

Copies the elements from the range (*beg*, *end*) in reverse order. The destination is a range beginning with the element pointed to by *dest* and assumed to be large enough to hold all the elements copied. All three arguments are bidirectional iterators.

```
int arr[5] = {10, 20, 30, 40, 50};
vector<int> iVec(5, 0);
reverse_copy(arr, arr + 5, iVec.begin());
```

After the call to **reverse_copy**, iVec contains:

```
50 40 30 20 10
```

- **rotate(*beg*, *middle*, *end*)**

Rotates elements in the range (*beg*, *end*) so that the element pointed to by *middle* becomes the new first element. Elements that were in front of *middle* get rotated to the back of the range. All three arguments are forward iterators.

```
int a[6] = {91, 92, 95, 11, 12, 13};
for(int i = 0; i < 6; ++i) {cout << a[i] << " ";}
cout << endl;

rotate(arr, arr + 2, arr + 6);   // Rotate 2 pos.
for(int i = 0; i < 6; ++i) {cout << a[i] << " ";}
cout << "    (rotated 2 to left)" << endl;

rotate(arr, arr + 1, arr + 6);   // Rotate 1 pos.
for(int i = 0; i < 6; ++i) {cout << a[i] << " ";}
cout << "    (rotated 1 more to left)" << endl;
```

These statements print:

```
91 92 95 11 12 13
95 11 12 13 91 92      (rotated 2 to left)
11 12 13 91 92 95      (rotated 1 more to left)
```

- **rotate_copy(*beg*, *middle*, *end*, *dest*)**

Performs the same action as **rotate**, except that the new arrangement is copied to a range of sufficient size beginning with *dest*; the elements in the range (*beg*, *end*) itself are unaffected. The first three arguments are forward iterators, and the last argument is an output iterator.

```
int arr[6] = {91, 92, 95, 11, 12, 13};
vector<int>  iVec(6, 0);
rotate_copy(arr, arr + 3, arr + 6, iVec.begin());
```

After the call to **rotate_copy**, iVec contains:

```
11 12 13 91 92 95
```

- **search(*beg*, *end*, *beg2*, *end2* [, *eq_f*])**

Searches for an occurrence of the range (*beg2*, *end2*), in order and in its entirety, within the range (*beg*, *end*). If successful, **search** returns an iterator to the beginning of the subrange found; otherwise, it returns *end*. The first four arguments are forward iterators. (For *eq_f*, see the beginning of this section.)

```
int arr[8] = {1, 2, 3, 4, 5, 6, 7, 8 };
int sub1[3] = {2, 3, 4};
int *p = search(arr, arr + 8, sub1, sub1 + 3);
if (p != arr + 8) {
      cout << "sub1 was found." << endl;
}
int sub2[3] = {4, 5, 3};
p = search(arr, arr + 8, sub2, sub2 + 3);
if (p != arr + 8) {
      cout << "sub2 was found." << endl;
}
```

The result of this example is that subrange 1 is found but subrange 2 is not.

- **search_n(*beg*, *end*, *n*, *val* [, *eq_f*])**

Searches the range (*beg*, *end*) for *n* consecutive occurrences of the specified value. The *beg* and *end* arguments are forward iterators. (For *eq_f*, see the beginning of this section.)

```
int arr[8] = {5, 5, 2, 3, 5, 5, 5};
int *p = search_n(arr, arr + 8, 3, 5);
if (p != arr + 8) {
      cout << "5-5-5 was found in position ";
      cout << p - arr << "." << endl;
}
```

This example prints out:

```
5-5-5 was found, starting in position 4.
```

- **set_difference(*beg*, *end*, *beg2*, *end2*, *dest* [, *less_than_f*])**

Compares two sorted ranges: (*beg*, *end*) and (*beg2*, *end2*). Values that are in the first range but not in the second comprise the "difference" set. The contents of this resultant set are copied to a range beginning with the element pointed to by *dest*. This third range is assumed to be sufficiently large to contain the results. The first four arguments are input iterators, and the *dest* argument is an output iterator. (For *less_than_f*, see the beginning of this section.)

The algorithm returns an iterator pointing to one position past the last element written to.

```
int arr1[5] = {100, 150, 200, 250, 300 };
int arr2[3] = {150, 250, 350 };
vector<int>  iVec(5, 0);
set_difference(arr1, arr1 + 5, arr2, arr2 + 3,
     iVec.begin());
```

After these statements are executed, iVec contains the following values:

```
100 200 300 0 0
```

- **set_intersection(***beg*, *end*, *beg2*, *end2*, *dest* [, *less_than_f*] **)**

Compares two sorted ranges: (*beg*, *end*) and (*beg2*, *end2*). Values that are in both ranges comprise the intersection. The contents of this resultant set are written to a range beginning with the element pointed to by *dest*. This third range is assumed to be sufficiently large to contain the results. The first four arguments are input iterators, and the *dest* argument is an output iterator. (For *less_than_f*, see the beginning of this section.)

The algorithm returns an iterator pointing to one position past the last element written to.

```
int arr1[5] = {100, 150, 200, 250, 300 };
int arr2[3] = {150, 250, 350 };
vector<int>  iVec(5, 0);
set_intersection(arr1, arr1 + 5, arr2, arr2 + 3,
     iVec.begin());
```

After these statements are executed, iVec contains the following values:

```
150 250 0 0 0
```

- **set_symmetric_difference(***beg*, *end*, *beg2*, *end2*, *dest* [, *less_than_f*] **)**

Compares two sorted ranges: (*beg*, *end*) and (*beg2*, *end2*). Those values that are in either range but not both comprise the symmetric-difference set. The contents of this resultant set are copied to a range beginning with the element pointed to by *dest*. This third range is assumed to be sufficiently large to contain the results. The first four arguments are input iterators, and the *dest* argument is an output iterator. (For *less_than_f*, see the beginning of this section.)

The algorithm returns an iterator pointing to one position past the last element written to.

```
int arr1[5] = {100, 150, 200, 250, 300 };
int arr2[3] = {150, 250, 350 };
vector<int>  iVec(8, 0);
set_symmetric_difference(arr1, arr1 + 5, arr2,
     arr2 + 3, iVec.begin());
```

After these statements are executed, iVec contains the following values:

```
100 200 300 350 0 0 0 0
```

▸ **set_union(***beg*, *end*, *beg2*, *end2*, *dest* [, *less_than_f*] **)**

Compares two sorted ranges: (*beg*, *end*) and (*beg2*, *end2*). Values that appear in either or both ranges comprise the union. The contents of this union are copied to a range beginning with the element pointed to by *dest*. This third range is assumed to be sufficiently large to contain the results. The first four arguments are input iterators, and the *dest* argument is an output iterator. (For *less_than_f*, see the beginning of this section.)

The algorithm returns an iterator pointing to one position past the last element written to.

```
int arr1[5] = {100, 150, 200, 250, 300 };
int arr2[3] = {150, 250, 350 };
vector<int>  iVec(8, 0);
set_union(arr1, arr1 + 5, arr2, arr2 + 3,
     iVec.begin());
```

After these statements are executed, iVec contains the following values:

```
100 150 200 250 300 350 0 0
```

▸ **sort(***beg*, *end* [, *less_than_f*] **)**

Sorts the range (*beg*, *end*) into ascending order. The first two arguments are random-access iterators—so the container must be an array, vector, or deque. (For *less_than_f*, see the beginning of this section.) For example, the following statements sort an array from lowest to highest values:

```
int arr[9]={10, 0, 50, 20, 30, -80, 60, -70, 40};
sort(arr, arr + 9);
```

After these statements are executed, the array contains the elements in this order:

```
-80 -70 0 10 20 30 40 50 60
```

This next example uses a comparison function to ignore negative signs when sorting:

```
#include <cstdlib>
bool comp_abs(int a, int b)
    { return abs(a) < abs(b); }
. . .
int arr[9]={10, 0, 50, 20, 30, -80, 60, -70, 40};
sort(arr, arr + 9, comp_abs);
```

After these statements are executed, the array contains the following elements, in this order:

```
0 10 20 30 40 50 60 -70 -80
```

▸ **sort_heap(***beg*, *end* [, *less_than_f*] **)**

Sorts the range (*beg*, *end*), which must already be ordered as a heap as described in Section 18.6.4. The first two arguments are random-access iterators. (For *less_than_f*, see the beginning of this section.)

```
int arr[10] = {1, 1, 2, 3, 3, 4, 4, 4, 5, 7};
vector<int>  my_heap(arr, arr+10):
make_heap(my_heap.begin(), my_heap.end());
my_heap.push_back(6);      // Add 6 to the vector.
// Now fold in the new element (6) into the heap.
push_heap(my_heap.begin(), my_heap.end());
// Finally, sort this heap from low to high.
sort_heap(my_heap.begin(), my_heap.end());
```

After **sort_heap** is called for the container, my_heap, the new order of the elements is:

```
1 1 2 3 3 4 4 4 5 6 7
```

- **stable_partition(*beg*, *end*, *condf*)**

Performs the same action as the **partition** template but preserves the relative order of the elements. This algorithm places all elements fulfilling a specified condition at the beginning of the range and places the remaining elements to the right of the first group. The *beg* and *end* arguments are bidirectional iterators.

```
bool is_odd(int n) { return n % 2 == 1; }
. . .
int arr[6] = {20, 1, 7, 40, 30, 5};
partition(arr, arr + 6, is_odd);
```

After executing these statements, the array contains:

```
1 7 5 20 40 30
```

- **stable_sort(*beg*, *end* [, *less_than_f*])**

Performs the same action as **sort**, but the relative order of elements with an equal value is preserved. (Usually this won't matter, but it's conceivable that it could matter if you were, for example, doing case-insensitive comparisons of words.) The effect is to sort elements in ascending order. The first two arguments are random-access iterators—so the container must be an array, vector, or deque. (For *less_than_f*, see the beginning of this section.)

The following example performs a case-insensitive sorting of an array of strings, while preserving the relative order of the strings considered equal: Abc, ABC, and ABc.

```
#include <string>
#include <cstring>
#include <cctype>
bool comp_strs(string s1, string s2) {
     for (unsigned i = 0; i < s1.size(); ++i)
          { s1[i] = tolower(s1[i]); }
     for (unsigned i = 0; i < s2.size(); ++i)
          { s2[i] = tolower(s2[i]); }
     return strcmp(s1.c_str(), s2.c_str()) < 0;
}
```

```
. . .
string strs[5] = {"Abc","ABC","ABc","Aaa","zzz"};
stable_sort(strs, strs + 5, comp_strs);
```

After these statements are executed, the array contains strings in this order:

```
Aaa Abc ABC ABc zzz
```

▸ **swap(*a*, *b*)**

Exchanges the values of its two arguments, which must have the same base type.

```
int big_val = 100;
int small_val = 1;
swap(big_val, small_val);
cout << "big_val is now " << big_val << endl;
cout << "small_val is now " << small_val << endl;
```

This example prints:

```
big_val is now 1
small_val is now 100
```

▸ **swap_ranges(*beg*, *end*, *beg2*)**

Exchanges elements in the range (*beg*, *end*) with a range of equal size beginning with *beg2*. All three arguments are forward iterators. The ranges may or may not be part of the same container but must not overlap.

For example, the following statements exchange the first three elements of an array with the last three elements.

```
int arr[9] = {1, 2, 3, 10, 10, 10, 77, 77, 77};
swap_ranges(arr, arr + 3, arr + 6);
```

After these statements are executed, the array contains:

```
77 77 77 10 10 10 1 2 3
```

▸ **transform(*beg*, *end*, *begDest*, *unary_fnct*)**

Transforms elements in the range (*beg*, *end*) by applying the unary function given as the fourth argument; the results are copied to a range of equal size beginning with the element pointed to by *begDest*. The first two arguments are input operators, and the third is an output iterator. The *unary_fnct* argument is a function taking a single argument of the base type and returning a value of the same type.

```
int to_neg(int n) {return -n;}
. . .
int arr[5] = {10, 10, 20, 20, 15};
vector<int> iVec(5, 0);  // Init with 5 zeroes.
transform(arr, arr + 5, iVec.begin(), to_neg);
```

After these statements are executed, iVec contains:

```
-10 -10 -20 -20 -15
```

- **transform(*beg*, *end*, *beg2*, *begDest*, *binary_fnct*)**

  Transforms elements in the range (*beg*, *end*), along with a range of equal size beginning with *beg2*, by applying the binary function given as the last argument. The results are copied to a third range of equal size beginning with *begDest*. The first three arguments are input operators; *begDest* is an output iterator. The *binary_fnct* argument is a function taking two arguments of the base type and returning a value of the same type.

  This function is called for each pair of corresponding elements in the two input ranges. For example, the first transformation applies the binary function to the elements pointed to by *beg* and *beg2*, storing the result in the element pointed to by *begDest*.

  The following statements apply the formula 100 * (a + b) to each pair of corresponding elements in the two arrays, copying the results to iVec.

```
int twice_diff(int a, int b){return 100 * (a + b);}
. . .
int a1[5] = {1, 2, 3, 4, 5};
int a2[5] = {1, 1, 2, 2, 3};
vector<int> v(5, 0);   // Init with 5 zeroes.
transform(a1, a1 + 5, a2, v.begin(), twice_diff);
```

  After these statements are executed, the vector contains:

```
200 300 500 600 800
```

- **unique(*beg*, *end* [, *eq_f*])**

  Removes elements from duplicate sequences within the range (*beg*, *end*), so there are no occurrences of the same value twice in a row, and copies the results to the beginning of the range, overwriting existing elements. The algorithm returns an iterator pointing to one position past the last element overwritten in this way.

  The first two arguments are input iterators. (For *eq_f*, see the beginning of this section.)

  For example:

```
int arr[9]={10, 10, 20, 20, 10, 10, 40, 40, 40};
vector<int> iVec(arr, arr + 9);
unique(iVec.begin(), iVec.end());
```

  After these statements are executed, the first four elements represent the state of the vector with consecutive duplicates removed:

```
10 20 10 40
```

  To print just these values—the ones that represent the results—use the algorithm's return value, as in the following statements:

```
vector<int>::iterator it, it_end;
it_end = unique(iVec.begin(), iVec.end());
```

```
for (it = iVec.begin(); it != it_end; ++it) {
     cout << *it << " ";
}
```

- **unique_copy(*beg*, *end*, *dest* [, *eq_f*])**

  Performs the same action as **unique**—removing duplicate sequences so there are no occurrences of the same value twice in a row—but instead of overwriting the original range, it copies the results to a range beginning with an element pointed to by *dest*. This destination range is assumed to be large enough to contain the results. The first two arguments are input iterators and *dest* is an output iterator. (For *eq_f*, see the beginning of this section.)

  This algorithm returns an iterator pointing to one position past the last element written to.

```
int arr[9]={10, 10, 20, 20, 10, 10, 40, 40, 40};
vector<int>  iVec(9, 0);
unique_copy(arr, arr + 9, iVec.begin());
```

  After these statements are executed, iVec contains:

```
10 20 10 40 0 0 0 0 0
```

- **upper_bound(*beg*, *end*, *value* [, *less_than_f*])**

  Returns the upper bound of *value* within the range (*beg*, *end*); returns *end* if no such element is found. *beg* and *end* are forward iterators. (For *less_than_f*, see the beginning of this section.) The upper bound is an iterator pointing to the first element in the range that is greater than *value*.

  For example, the following statements find the subrange consisting of values of 20; the pair returned consists of a pointer to the first occurrence of 20 (lower bound) and a pointer to the first occurrence of a value greater than 20 (upper bound).

```
typedef pair<int*, int*> return_type;
int arr[6] = {10, 20, 20, 20, 30, 50 };
int *lower = lower_bound(arr, arr + 6, 20);
int *upper = upper_bound(arr, arr + 6, 20);
for(int *p = lower; p != upper; ++p) {
     cout << *p << " ";
}
```

  These statements print the range of values found, made up of three copies of 20:

```
20 20 20
```

Chapter 19

C++11 Randomization Library

The goal of most software is to make things more predictable and reduce risk; life is risky enough as it is. But some computer programs need to introduce randomization rather than eliminate it. Such programs include games and computer simulations.

For many years, programmers have used the C-library **rand** function to get a random number. This function still works in C++, and I have used it in previous chapters.

But randomization is a subtle and tricky subject. The new C++11 specification provides more reliable, more versatile, and less-biased random-number generation. To explain why the C++11 specification is superior in this area, I first need to discuss general issues in randomization.

19.1 Issues in Randomization

The C-library **rand** function is usable and, for the most part, adequate for some situations. But it has its limitations. Problems with randomization include

- Biased distribution
- Pseudorandom sequences
- Getting a seed

19.1.1 The Problem of Biased Distribution

One of the most common needs—one that's arisen in this book—is to generate a random number from 1 to N or from 0 to N. The easiest way to do that is to use the modulus operator:

```
int r = rand() % n;        // Generate random 0 to N.
```

To get a random number from 1 to N, add 1 to this number:

```
int r = rand() % n + 1;
```

The result is guaranteed to be in the range 1 to N. But are all values in this range equally likely? Consider what happens if n is 5:

```
int r = rand() % 5 + 1;
```

The problem is that the range of values returned by **rand** is not a multiple of 5. Therefore, the number of ways that "rand() % 5" can yield 4 is slightly less than the number of ways it can yield 1. Consequently, there is a bias toward smaller numbers, although this bias is tiny for small values of N.

But as N grows, the bias produced by "rand() % n" becomes worse. In the most degenerate case—N two-thirds the size of RAND_MAX—the bias is severe, for you can then expect lower numbers to be produced twice as often as higher ones.

An alternative approach is to divide by RAND_MAX, producing a floating-point number in the range 0 to 1, and then multiply this result by N. But this approach is highly inefficient—using floating-point math—and does not eliminate bias entirely.

```
double x = static_cast<double>(rand()) / RAND_MAX;
int r = static_cast<int>(n * x);
```

19.1.2 The Problem of Pseudorandom Sequences

A random number generator is really a pseudorandom generator: All it does is take a number and apply a transformation to get another number. Although it's possible to analyze the pattern of numbers and determine the next one, such prediction is intended to be extremely difficult.

The complexity of the transformation depends on the randomization *engine;* some sequences are harder to crack than others, and there are tradeoffs in terms of size, quality, and speed.

Every engine, no matter how complex, has a finite number of states; it must therefore repeat the same sequence of numbers eventually unless that state is periodically reset with a new seed. This is the problem of repetition, but the more sophisticated engines produce a very large number of values before degenerating into a state of repetition.

Another concern is that of "spectral characteristics": unevenness that may creep, ghostlike, into a distribution of a sequence of numbers.

19.1.3 The Problem of Getting a Seed

Yet another problem is that of getting a *seed:* No matter how good the sequence of pseudorandom numbers is, a program will yield the same set of numbers every time it is run—unless you begin the sequence with a different initial value each time the program starts up. But how do you do that?

The obvious solution is to get this initial value—the seed—from an external source. The C++11 randomization library does not alleviate the need to do that. The most convenient technique is to get the system time, as this ensures a different seed each time the program is run.

```
#include <ctime>
unsigned long  seed = time(NULL);
```

Note that compilers compliant with the C++11 specification support the **nullptr** keyword as a superior alternative to the use of NULL. The **nullptr** keyword has the advantage of being a genuine keyword rather than a symbol defined by headers. The rest of this chapter therefore uses **nullptr** in place of NULL.

```
unsigned long  seed = time(nullptr);
```

19.2 A Better Randomization Scheme

When you use the C++11 randomization library, you need to make a series of choices.

- Choose an engine. An engine generates raw pseudorandom numbers. Some engines provide better simulations of randomness than others, but as mentioned earlier, there are tradeoffs in terms of size (amount of memory taken up by the engine) and speed.
- Choose an initial seed unless you are debugging and therefore don't mind seeing the same "random" numbers every time. For best results, you should usually work with a single engine chosen just once.
- Choose a distribution. The STL randomization distributions are optimized to produce numbers in the desired range as efficiently as possible and with bias eliminated. A distribution takes input from the underlying randomization engine and transforms it into a number in the target range and probability function.

Before using any of these classes, include <random>. Also include <ctime> if you want to use the C-language **time** function. Note that all the symbols declared in the <random> header are, as usual, part of the **std** namespace.

```
#include <random>
#include <time>
```

The following example uses the default database engine and uniform integer distribution to get a random number from 1 to 6. It then simulates two dice rolls.

```
time_t seed = time(nullptr);
std::default_random_engine eng(seed);
std::uniform_int_distribution<int> dist(1, 6);
cout << "Die roll: " << dist(eng) << endl;    // Roll a die!
cout << "Another:  " << dist(eng) << endl;    // Roll a die!
```

Let's deconstruct this. The first thing this example does is to choose a seed and create a randomization engine.

default_random_engine *engine_name*(*seed_value*)

The name **default_random_engine** can be replaced by one of the other engines listed in Section 19.3, "Common Engines." The effect of this statement is to create an engine and initialize the sequence of pseudorandom numbers with the specified seed.

Next, the example creates a distribution. This object takes raw output from the randomization engine and translates it into the desired range: in this case, 1 to 6.

uniform_int_distribution<*type*> *dist_name*(*first*, *last*)

The name **uniform_int_distribution** can be replaced by one of the other distributions listed in Section 19.4, "Common Distributions." Because this distribution is used to generate integers, the type must be integral, but it can be any integer type, not just **int**. The arguments *first* and *last* specify the upper and lower bounds, respectively.

Finally, to get a random number, make the following function call:

dist_name(*engine_name*)

As another example, consider the task of producing 11 numbers, each of which is a random number 0 to 9:

```
time_t seed = time(nullptr);
std::default_random_engine eng(seed);
std::uniform_int_distribution<int> dist(0, 9);
for (int i = 0; i < 11; ++i) {
     cout << dist(eng) << " ";    // Generate 0 - 9.
}
```

Sample output for these statements might be:

```
6 4 9 5 0 1 7 0 3 2 5
```

While continuing to use the same engine, you might then produce a couple of random numbers from 1 to 1,000, inclusive:

```
std::uniform_int_distribution<int> dist2(1, 1000);
std::cout << dist2(eng) << ", ";         // Generate 1-1000.
std::cout << dist2(eng) << std::endl;    // Generate 1-1000.
```

Sample output for these statements might be:

```
218, 797
```

When generating random numbers, you should keep using the same engine unless you have a good reason for creating a new one. If you start with a new instance of the same engine, you get the same sequence of numbers. Calling the **time** function is unlikely to get a new seed unless significant time has passed (more than a second); so, if you create two instances of the same engine, you are liable to get duplicate results.

If you must create a second instance of the same randomization engine (usually not a good idea), then at minimum you should alter the seed in some way. For example:

```
time_t seed = time(nullptr);
std::default_random_engine eng(seed);
. . .
std::default_random_engine eng2(++seed);
```

If you need to create a new randomization engine—because you need a higher quality of random simulation for some parts of the program—it's a good idea to increment the seed, as just shown.

But one engine is usually sufficient, because you can reuse it without different distributions. For example, the first engine created—eng in this case—can be reused with a real-number distribution, producing a floating-point number in the range 0.0 up to but not including 1.0.

```
std::uniform_real_distribution<double>  rdis(0.0, 1.0);
using std::cout;
using std::endl;
cout << rdis(eng) << endl;    // Produce random 0.0 to 1.0.
```

Before moving on, you should take note of another use of randomization engines. The **random_shuffle** algorithm described in Chapter 18, "STL Algorithms," optionally takes a third argument specifying a randomization engine. For example, consider an array of numbers initialized as 0 to 51, corresponding to the 52 cards in a standard deck of playing cards.

```
std::vector<int>  cards(52, 0); // Init 52 cards to 0 each.
for (unsigned i = 0; i < 52; ++i) {
     cards(i) = i;              // Assign nums 0 to 51.
}
std::random_shuffle(cards.begin(), cards.end(), eng);
```

The effect of the **random_shuffle** algorithm should be to produce a thoroughly shuffled deck, in which the numbers 0 to 51 can be assigned to the different possible playing cards.

19.3 Common Engines

The C++11 randomization library provides a wide choice of randomization engines in the form of templates: These require you to specify a series of parameters affecting various aspects of the transformations. For convenience, the library also provides a number of engines that are specializations of the various templates, freeing you from having to worry about the details. Of this latter group, the most commonly used engines are listed here.

- **`default_random_engine`**

  This is the default engine provided by the randomization library. Because the choice is implementation-dependent, you may get different results on another platform or with another compiler. However, this engine is a good choice for casual programming.

  ```
  std::default_random_engine  eng(seed);
  ```

- **`minstd_rand`**

  This is a version of the **linear_congruential_engine**. This engine is fast and takes up little space in memory. Because it has a small state, it is liable to go into a repeating sequence (thus duplicating behavior) sooner than some of the more sophisticated engines, but it is adequate when you need no more than a few thousand random numbers.

  ```
  std::minstd_rand  eng(seed);
  ```

- **`minstd_rand0`**

  This engine is similar to **minstd_rand**; it is usually just as fast but provides slightly better results.

  ```
  std::minstd_rand0  eng(seed);
  ```

- **`ranlux24_base`**

  This is a version of the **subtract_with_carry** engine, which performs with reasonable speed even on simple processors but takes up more space than **minstd_rand**.

  ```
  std::randlux24_base  eng(seed);
  ```

- **`mt19937`**

  This is a version of the **mersenne_twister** engine. This is a high-quality, high-speed engine that produces 2 to the 19937th – 1 values before repeating. It's therefore an excellent solution where repetition is a concern, but its internal state takes up significantly more space in memory than some other engines. Another disadvantage of this engine is that, given a seed of 0, it takes several iterations before the results appear suitably random. However, it performs well when given a good seed value.

  ```
  std::int19937  eng(seed);
  ```

- **mt19937_64**

  This is similar to the **int19937** engine, but it operates on 64 bits rather than 32; it will be slower on a 32-bit architecture.

  ```
  std::int19937_64  eng(seed);
  ```

- **knuth_b**

  This is a complex adaptation that applies the **shuffle_order_engine** to shuffle the results of a **linear_congruential_engine**. This is a very high-quality engine, but it is slower than most other engines, and it takes up more space.

  ```
  std::knuth_b  eng(seed);
  ```

19.4 Common Distributions

A great many distributions are available, including some that are exotic and have extremely specialized uses. The distributions listed here are the ones with the widest application. In each case, the distribution templates have been optimized to provide results in the desired range and/or probability distribution, with systematic bias removed (that is to say, if there is any bias it is due to the underlying engine only).

Remember to include the <random> header. The names of all distributions and engines are part of the **std** namespace. Due to space considerations, the examples in this section assume **using namespace std**. However, most of the time you should consider applying the **using** statement more selectively.

```
#include <random>
using namespace std;  // Use only if space is a problem!
```

Detailed descriptions of the more common distributions follow.

- **uniform_int_distribution**<*type*> *name*(*first*, *last*)

  Produces integers of the specified integer *type* (such as **int**, **short**, or **long**) in the range from *first* to *last*, inclusive, with equal likelihood for each number. For example, argument values of 1 and 6 simulate the roll of a single die.

  ```
  uniform_int_distribution<int>  die_dist(1, 6);
  cout << "You rolled a " << die_dist(eng) << endl;
  ```

  This next example produces a random decimal digit: that is, a number from 0 to 9.

  ```
  uniform_int_distribution<int>  d10_dist(0, 9);
  cout << "A random digit: " << d10_dist(eng);
  cout << endl;
  ```

- **uniform_real_distribution**<*type*> *name*(*lower*, *upper*)

  Produces floating-point numbers of the specified *type* (usually **float** or **double**) in the range beginning with *lower*, up to but not including *upper*. The results should, over time, reflect roughly equal distribution throughout the range. The following statements produce a floating-point number from 0.0 to 1.0, but never 1.0 itself.

```
uniform_real_distribution<double> urd(0.0, 1.0);
cout << urd(eng) << endl;
```

- **bernoulli_distribution** *name*(*prob* = **0.5**)

  Produces **true** or **false** (1 or 0), with **true** having the specified probability. The default value of this argument is 0.5. The following statements simulate the flip of a fair coin.

```
bernoulli_distribution  fair_coin;
if (fair_coin(eng)) {
    cout << "It's HEADS!" << endl;
}
```

  Or, with a weighted coin, deliberately biased (75 percent chance) toward heads:

```
bernoulli_distribution  cheater_coin(0.75);
if (cheater_coin(eng)) {
    cout << "It's HEADS!" << endl;
}
```

- **binomial_distribution**<*type1*, *type2*> *name*(*n*, *prob*)

  Produces the sum of *n* Bernoulli trials: In other words, this distribution simulates *n* trials in which each trial has the stated probability (*prob*) of succeeding. The number returned by this distribution is the number of successes. The arguments *type1* and *type2* are the types of *n* and *prob*; these are typically **int** and **double**.

  For example, the following statements, which simulate 100 flips of a fair coin, will tend to produce a number close to 50.

```
binomial_distribution<int, double> dist(100,0.5);
cout << "Number of heads in 100 trials: ";
cout << dist(eng) << endl;
```

- **exponential_distribution**<*type*> *name*(*rate*)

  Produces a floating-point number of specified *type*, typically **double**. This distribution simulates the wait time for an event that happens at the average *rate* (a floating-point number) during one unit of time—assuming these events are random and independent of each other.

  For example, suppose a web site gets, on average, ten hits an hour. What is the wait time until the next hit? This is not necessarily the average wait time (which would be 0.1). Instead, this distribution is a random simulation of the wait time: It might be close to 0.1, but it might be higher or lower. Extremely long waits are possible but unlikely.

```
exponential_distribution<double>  exp_dis(10.0);
cout << "Time to next hit: " << exp_dis(eng);
```

- **geometric_distribution**<*type1*, *type2*> *name*(*prob*)

  Returns an integer (having type specified by *type1*) based on *prob*, a probability having type specified by *type2* (typically **double**). This distribution simulates the number of Bernoulli trials that fail before an event of probability *prob* occurs. This number may be as low as 0. It theoretically has no upper limit.

  For example, Bob is an out-of-work programmer. His odds of getting a response to any given resume is 1/50, or 0.02. How many of his resumes get ignored before he gets a response? You'd expect this number to be around 50, but it may be higher or lower.

  ```
  geometric_distribution<int, double>  geo(0.02);
  cout << "Congrats, Bob, you only had to send ";
  cout << "out " << geo(eng) + 1 << " resume(s) ";
  cout << "before getting a response." << endl;
  ```

- **normal_distribution**<*type*> *name*(*mean* = **0.0**, *std_dev* = **1.0**)

  Produces a number—of the specified *type*, which should be floating point—from a "normal," or Gaussian distribution. This distribution has the specified mean (average) and standard deviation. These arguments take default values of 0.0 and 1.0, respectively.

  For example, suppose you want to simulate a normal distribution with an average value of 100 and standard deviation of 10, meaning that about two-thirds of the time, values will fall into the "bulge" of the curve consisting of values from 90 to 110. Outliers are always possible but grow increasingly unlikely as they get farther from the mean. The following statements simulate such a probability curve and produce eight sample values:

  ```
  normal_distribution<double>  norm(100.0, 10.0);
  for (int i = 0; i < 8; ++i) {
       cout << norm(eng) << endl;
  }
  ```

  If you decrease the standard deviation from 10.0 to 2.5, you can expect that results will tend to be significantly closer to 100.

- **poisson_distribution**<*type*> *name*(*rate*)

  Takes a number, *rate*, of the specified type (usually **double**) and produces an integer simulating number of events per unit of time. This distribution is similar to the exponential distribution except that instead of producing wait time, it produces number of events. The *rate* is the average number of random events in a given unit of time. (Note: This number may be less than 1.0 but it must be positive.)

For example, suppose a web site gets, on average, 7.5 hits an hour. The Poisson distribution simulates the number of hits per time period. If you produce many such numbers, the average value will of course tend to be equal to this specified rate, 7.5.

```
poisson_distribution<double>  psn_dis(7.5);
cout << "# hits over next ten hours: ";
for (int i = 0; i < 10; ++i) {
     cout << psn_dis(eng) << " ";
}
```

Other distributions supported, though not elaborated on here, include the following:

- **gamma_distribution**
- **weibull_distribution**
- **extreme_value_distribution**
- **chi_squared_distribution**
- **cauchy_distribution**
- **fisher_f_distribution**
- **student_t_distribution**
- **discrete_distribution**
- **piecewise_constant_distribution**
- **piecewise_linear_distribution**

19.5 Operations on Engines

In the descriptions that following, *engine* is the name of a previously declared randomization engine.

- *engine_template<params> engine*
- *engine_template<params> engine*(*seed_value*)

  Constructors. If *seed_value* is not specified, the engine is set to a default initial state.

- *engine*.**seed()**

  Resets an engine to its default initial state.

  ```
  eng.seed();
  ```

- *engine*.**seed(***seed_value***)**

  Sets a new seed value for an existing engine. This can be useful if you want to reset the state of an engine from time to time so that no behavior is ever duplicated. For best results, you need to access some external source to get a new seed in a nondeterministic way. In the following example, a time value is added to the value returned by **clock**, which measures time, in microseconds, since the program began. But this value is nondeterministic only if a variable amount of time has passed since the last time the seed was set.

  ```
  eng.seed(time(nullptr) + clock());
  ```

- *engine***()**

  Gets raw output from the engine. This is a pseudorandom number not filtered by a distribution.

  ```
  cout << "Here is raw output: " << eng() << endl;
  ```

- *engine*.**discard(***n***)**

  Advances the random-number sequence through *n* values, ignoring them all.

  ```
  eng.discard(10);
  ```

- *ostream_obj* << **engine**
- *istream_obj* >> **engine**

  Perform serialization: That is, these operations read or write the internal state of the engine in text form. You can print to the console if you like; if you do, you'll see a series of numbers. You might do this for debugging purposes, or (for example) to save the internal state of a game program.

  ```
  file_out << eng;    // Save state of the engine.
  ```

19.6 Operations on Distributions

In the descriptions that follow, *engine* is the name of a previously declared randomization engine and *dist* is the name of a distribution.

- *dist***(***engine***)**

  Produces a pseudorandom number from the distribution, using the specified engine. This is the principal way of producing random numbers.

  ```
  uniform_int_distribution dist(1, 6);
  cout << "Die roll: " << dist(eng) << endl;
  ```

- *dist*.**min()**

  Returns the minimum number the distribution can produce. In the case of some distributions—such as a normal distribution—this number may theoretically be negative infinity; in that case, the function returns the lowest number you can actually get. (This is likely determined by the range of the data type involved.)

```
int n = dist.min();
```

- *dist*.**max()**

Returns the maximum number the distribution can produce. In the case of some distributions—such as a normal or geometric distribution—this number may theoretically be infinite; in that case, the function returns the greatest number you can actually get. (This is likely determined by the range of the data type involved.)

```
int n = dist.max();
```

- *ostream_obj* << **engine**
- *istream_obj* >> **engine**

Perform serialization: That is, they read or write the internal state of the distribution in text form. You can print to the console if you like; if you do, you'll see a series of numbers. You might do this for debugging purposes, or (for example) to save the internal state of a game program.

```
file_out << dist;
```

19.7 Sample App: Dice Game

The following sample program plays out the dice game described at the end of Chapter 5, "Functions," using the new C++11 randomization library. The engine and distribution are created at the beginning of the program. The goal is to roll a 7 or an 11, or to note the "point" rolled and then roll it again before rolling a 7.

```
#include <iostream>
#include <random>
#include <ctime>
#include <string>

using std::cout;                // Alternatively, you can use
using std::cin;                 //  using namespace std;
using std::endl;
using std::default_random_engine;
using std::uniform_int_distribution;

void play_out_game(int point);
int roll_dice();

time_t seed = time(nullptr);
default_random_engine  eng(seed);
uniform_int_distribution<int>  dist(1, 6);
```

```
int main() {
     int r = roll_dice();
     switch(r) {
     case 2:
     case 3:
         cout << "You lose!" << endl;
         break;
     case 7:
     case 11:
         cout << "You win!" << endl;
         break;
    default:
         play_out_game(r);
         break;
     }
     cout << "Press ENTER to exit game.";
     cin.ignore();   // Wait for user to press ENTER.
     return 0;
}

// Play Out Game function:
// Roll dice until 7 or the point is rolled.
void play_out_game (int point) {
     cout << "The point is now " << point << endl;
     while (true) {
          cout << "Press ENTER to roll... ";
          cin.ignore();   // Wait for user to press ENTER.
          int r = roll_dice();
          if (r == point) {
               cout << "You win!" << endl;
               return;
          } else if (r == 7) {
               cout << "You lose!" << endl;
               return;
          }
     }
}

// Roll Dice function.
// Roll two dice, print results, and return the total.
int roll_dice() {
     int n1 = dist(eng);      // Roll a die (1 to 6).
     int n2 = dist(eng);      // Roll another.
     cout << "Roll is: " << n1 << " " << n2 << ", ";
     cout << "for a total of " << n1 + n2 << "." << endl;
     return n1 + n2;
}
```

Exercises

1. Rewrite the program so that it prompts the user to play again. Keep a running total of wins and losses, and print these totals just before terminating the program.
2. Rewrite the game so that it uses weighted—that is, unfair—dice. One die should produce the number 3 twice as often as a fair die; the other die should produce the number 4 twice as often. Use a combination of Bernoulli and uniform-integer distributions to achieve this effect. (For extra credit, make this weighted factor easy to adjust.)
3. Write a program to use the **clock** function, described in Chapter 12, "Math, Time, and Other Library Functions," to measure the relative performances of all the engines listed in Section 19.3. For each engine, find the number of microseconds passed while rolling a die 222,000 times. (Do not, however, print out the rolls.)
4. Use the serialization operations described in Section 19.5, "Operations on Engines," to examine the sizes of the states of the common engine types. Then answer these questions: Which engine is the fastest? Which is the slowest? Which engines take up more space in memory than others do?

CHAPTER 20

C++11 Regular-Expression Library

Applications such as Microsoft Word have long supported pattern-matching, or *regular-expression,* capabilities. Using C and C++, it was always possible to write your own regular-expression engines, but it required sophisticated, complex programming—and usually a degree in computer science. Now C++11 makes these capabilities directly available to you, without your having to write a regular-expression engine yourself.

Regular expressions are of practical value in many programs, as they can aid with the task of *lexical analysis*—intelligently breaking up pieces of an input string—as well as tasks such as converting from one text-file format (such as HTML) to another.

I've found that when the C++11 regular expression library is explained in a straightforward, simple manner, it's easy to use. This chapter doesn't describe all the endless variations on the regex function-call syntax, but it does explain all the basic functionality: how to do just about anything you'd want to do.

20.1 Overview of C++11 Regular Expressions

Before using any regular-expression functions, include the <regex> header.

```
#include <regex>
```

A regular expression is a string that uses special characters—in combination with ordinary characters—to create a text pattern. That pattern can then be used to match another string, search it, or identify a substring as the target of a search-and-replace function.

For example, consider a simple pattern: a string consisting only of the digits 0 through 9, and nothing else. A decimal integer, assuming it has no plus or minus sign, fulfills this pattern.

With the C++11 regular-expression syntax, this pattern can be expressed as:

```
[0-9]+
```

In this regular-expression pattern, only the "0" and "9" are intended literally. The other characters—"[", "]", "-", and "+"—each have a special meaning.

The brackets specify a range of characters:

[*range***]**

This syntax says, "Match any one character in the specified range. The following examples specify different ranges.

```
[abc]          // Match a, b, or c.
[A-Z]          // Match any letter in range A to Z.
[a-zA-Z]       // Match any letter.
```

The other special character used in this example is the plus sign (+).

expr+

This syntax says, "Match the preceding expression, *expr*, one or more times. The plus sign is a pattern modifier, so it means that *expr+*, taken as a whole, matches one or more instances of *expr*.

Here are some examples:

```
a+            // Match a, aa, aaa, etc.
(ab)+         // Match ab, abab, ababab, etc.
ab+           // Match ab, abb, abbb, abbbb, etc.
```

Notice what a difference the parentheses make. Parentheses have a special role in forming *groups*. As with braces and the plus sign (+), parentheses are special characters; they have to be "escaped" to be rendered literally—that is, you have to use backslashes if you want to match actual parentheses in the target string.

You should now see why "[0-9]+" matches a string that consists of one or more digits. This pattern attempts to match a single digit and then says, "Match that one or more times." Again, the plus sign is a pattern modifier, so it matches [0-9] one or more times *instead of* matching it just once, not one or more times *in addition to* matching it once (which would've meant a total of two or more times overall).

The following statements attempt to match this regular-expression string against a target string. In this context, *match* means that the target string must match the regular-expression string completely.

```
#include <regex>
#include <string>
#include <iostream>
. . .
```

```
std::regex  reg1("[0-9]+");
if (std::regex_match("123000", reg1)) {
     std::cout << "It's a match!" << std::endl;
}
```

You can test a series of strings this way:

```
using std::cout;
using std::endl;
using std::regex;

regex  reg1("[0-9]+");
string str1("123000");
string str2("123000.0");

bool b = regex_match(str1, reg1);
cout << str1 << (b ? " is " : " is not ");
cout << "a match." << endl;

b = regex_match(str2, reg1);
cout << str2 << (b ? " is " : " is not ");
cout << "a match." << endl;
```

These statements print out:

```
123000 is a match.
123000.0 is not a match.
```

The string "123000.0" does not result in a match because **regex_match** attempts to match the entire target string; if it cannot, it returns **false**. The **regex_search** function, in contrast, returns **true** if any substring matches. Therefore, the following function call returns **true**, because the substring consisting of the first six characters matches the pattern specified earlier for reg1.

```
std::regex_search("123000.0", reg1)
```

Generally speaking, every regular-expression operation begins by initializing a **regex** object with a pattern; this object can then be given as input to **regex_match** or **regex_search**. Creating a regex object builds a regular-expression engine, which is compiled at runtime (!), so for best performance, create as few new regular expression objects as you need to.

Here are some other useful patterns:

```
using std::regex;
regex reg2("[0-9]*");            // Match 0 or more digits.
regex reg3("(\\+|-)?[0-9]+");    // Match digit string with
                                 //  optional + or - sign.
```

reg2 uses an asterisk (*) rather than a plus sign (+). The asterisk modifies the regular expression to mean, "Match zero or more copies of the preceding expression." Therefore, reg2 matches an empty string as well as a digit string.

reg3 matches a digit string with an optional sign. The "or" symbol (|) means match the expression on either side of this symbol:

```
"a|b"     // Match a or b but not both.
```

Putting "a|b" into a group (using parentheses) and then following it with a question mark (?), makes the entire group optional.

The following expression means, "Optionally match a plus sign or a minus sign, but not both."

```
"(\\+|-)?"
```

Because the plus sign (+) has special meaning, it must be "escaped" by using backslashes. More about that in the next section.

Note

There's a more concise way to write the expression in this case. Most symbols lose their special meaning inside brackets and do not need to be escaped. Even the minus sign (-) does not need to be escaped unless it occurs in between two other characters, indicating a run of characters (as in "[a-z]"). So the pattern just shown could be more concisely expressed as:

```
"[+-]?"
```

The limitation of a range, however, is that it is used just to match a single character, so the range syntax, [], is less general than "or" (|).

20.2 Dealing with Escape Sequences (\)

Escape sequences are a little tricky in C++ regular expressions, because they occur in two contexts.

- C++ assigns special meaning to the backslash within a string literal and requires it to be escaped to be read as an actual backslash: To represent a single backslash, it's necessary to place double backslashes (\\) in the source code. (Exception: Raw literals, supported by C++11, remove the need to escape characters.)
- The regular-expression interpreter also recognizes a backslash as the escape character. To render a special character literally, you must precede it with a backslash (\).

Consequently, if you want to render a special character literally, then, within a C++ literal string, you must precede the character with *two backslashes,* not just one.

For example, suppose you want to specify a pattern that matches an actual plus sign (+). The pattern is specified in source code this way:

```
std::regex  reg("\\+");
```

When the C++ compiler reads the literal, "\\+", it interprets \\ as an escape sequence that represents a single backslash. The actual string data that gets stored in memory is therefore:

```
\+
```

This is the string read by the regular-expression interpreter. It interprets "\+" as an actual plus sign (+).

Consider the following regular-expression pattern:

```
std::regex  reg("\\++");
```

Notice what's going on here: The first three characters (\\+) represent a literal plus sign (+). The fourth character (+) has its usual—and special—meaning; this second plus sign modifies the overall pattern to mean, "Match one or more copies of the preceding expression." The string as a whole therefore matches any of the following:

```
+
++
+++++
```

How do you represent a literal backslash, should you ever need to do that? That is, what is the regular-expression pattern that matches a target string consisting of one or more backslashes? The answer is that you need *four* backslashes.

```
using std::regex;
regex  reg("\\\\+");    // Matches one or more backslashes.
```

This regular-expression object, reg, would match any of the following:

```
str1[] = "\\"         // Represents "\".
str2[] = "\\\\"       // Represents "\\".
str3[] = "\\\\\\"     // Represents "\\\".
```

Note that if you use raw-string literals, supported by the C++11 specification, you don't have to deal with C literal-string escape conventions, so this example would be coded as:

```
regex  reg(R"\\+");     // Matches one or more backslashes.
str1[] = R"\"           // Represents "\".
str2[] = R"\\"          // Represents "\\".
str3[] = R"\\\"         // Represents "\\\".
```

The use of **R** does not change the format of the strings (which is still **const char***); it merely changes how literal text inside the quoted string is interpreted.

20.3 Constructing a RegEx String

The previous two sections provided an introduction to regular-expression patterns. The next several sections summarize the syntax rules, beginning with the syntax for matching individual characters.

This chapter adopts the default grammar used by the C++11 regular-expression library, which is a modified ECMAScript grammar. Although it's possible to use variations, the C++11 default is more versatile and expressive than the alternative grammars.

20.3.1 Matching Characters

The following special expressions match an individual character belonging to a group, such as letters or digits. This section also describes special conditions such as beginning-of-line or word boundary.

In the following list, a *range* may be a list of characters (not separated by spaces or commas, which themselves are characters). A *range* may optionally use a dash (minus sign) to indicate a run beginning with one character, up to and including another. Characters are ordered according to their underlying numeric (ASCII) value. For example, "[a-z]" matches all lowercase letters.

- `.`

  Matches any one character other than a newline. For example, the following pattern string matches almost any single character:

  ```
  "."
  ```

- `[`*range*`]`

  Matches any one character in the specified range. For example, the following pattern string matches any single letter in the range "a" to "m". It also matches "z".

  ```
  "[a-mz]"
  ```

  Most characters lose their special meaning inside the brackets. The minus sign gains special meaning to indicate a run of characters as in the example just shown, but only if it appears between two other characters inside the range. The following expression matches any one of the characters "+", "*", "/", or "-". None of these need to be escaped.

```
"[+*/-]"
```

- **[^*range*]**

  Matches any character *not* in the specified range. For example, the following pattern string matches any single character *other* than "a", "b", or "c":

  ```
  "[^abc]"
  ```

- **\n**

  Matches a newline. When using this in a C++ literal string meant to be part of a regular-expression pattern-matching string (as opposed to an actual embedded newline), remember that two backslashes must be used. For example:

  ```
  "\\n"
  ```

- **\t**

  Matches a tab character.

- **\f**

  Matches a form feed.

- **\r**

  Matches a carriage return.

- **\v**

  Matches a vertical tab.

- **\x*hh***

  Matches a character specified as a hexadecimal code. For example:

  ```
  "\\xf3"
  ```

- **\u*hhhh***

  Matches a Unicode character specified as a hexadecimal code. For example:

  ```
  "\\u02f3"
  ```

- **\d**

  Matches any digit character. This is equivalent to:

  ```
  [0-9]
  ```

- **\D**

  Matches any character other than a digit. This is equivalent to:

  ```
  [^0-9]
  ```

- `\s`

  Matches any whitespace character.

- `\S`

  Matches any character other than a whitespace character.

- `\w`

  Matches any digit, letter, or underscore.

- `\W`

  Matches any character other than a digit, letter, or underscore.

- `\b`

  Matches a word boundary. A word must begin or end at this position, or there is no match. Words are made up of alphanumeric characters and are delimited by whitespaces and punctuation. For example, the following string matches any word beginning with "c" and ending with "t", such as "cat" or "containment". It does not match "caution".

  ```
  "\\bc[a-zA-Z]*t\\b"
  ```

- `\B`

  Not a word boundary. For example, the following pattern matches a portion of a word beginning with "a." It will match "at" embedded in "cat", but it will not match "at" if it occurs as a stand-alone word.

  ```
  "\\Ba[a-zA-Z]*"
  ```

- `^`

  Beginning of line: The next character is matched only if it is the first character in the text to be examined or occurs just after a newline.

  ```
  "^Barney"
  ```

- `$`

  End of line: The previous character matched (if any) must be the last character in the line of text.

20.3.2 Pattern Modifiers

Regular-expression pattern matching becomes more interesting when you modify a pattern to indicate possible repetitions. This feature, as much as anything else, makes the regular-expression technology a powerful and versatile tool for searching and replacing text.

In the following list, *expr* is an expression. For example, in the string "[0-9]+", "[0-9]" is an expression and the + operator modifies its meaning.

An operator associates with the character closest to it, except where brackets or parentheses are used, in which case the operator refers to the whole range or group that precedes it.

- *expr**

  Matches zero or more instances of *expr*. For example, the following string matches an empty string or a digit string:

  ```
  "[0-9]*"
  ```

- *expr+*

  Matches one or more instances of *expr*. For example, the following string matches a digit string of length one or greater.

  ```
  "[0-9]+"
  ```

- *expr?*

  Matches either one or zero instances of *expr*. The *expr* thereby becomes an optional item that can appear at most once. For example, the following string matches a minus sign or an empty string.

  ```
  "-?"
  ```

- *expr1|expr2*

  Matches *expr1* or *expr2*, but not both. For example, the following regular-expression string matches "aa" or "bb" but not "aabb".

  ```
  "(aa)|(bb)"
  ```

  This expression can be made optional by placing it in a larger group and then using the ? operator. In that case, "aa" may appear, "bb" may appear, or they may both be omitted.

  ```
  "((aa)|(bb))?"
  ```

- *expr*{*n*}

  Matches exactly *n* instances of *expr*. For example, the following pattern string matches a target string containing exactly ten copies of capital "A".

  ```
  "A{10}"
  ```

- *expr*{*n*,}

  Matches *n* or more instances of *expr*. For example, the following pattern string matches a target string consisting of three or more digits.

  ```
  "[0-9]{3,}"
  ```

- *expr*{*n*,*m*}

  Matches at least *n*, but no more than *m*, instances of *expr*. For example, the following pattern string matches a digit string no more than seven digits long.

  ```
  "[0-9]{1,7}"
  ```

- (*expr*)

  Forms a group. *expr* is considered as a unit when modified by other special characters, as in (*expr*)+, (*expr*)*, and so on. For example, the following pattern string matches "AbcAbcAbc" in the target string:

  ```
  "(Abc){3}"
  ```

  Another important effect of parentheses is that they cause the expression inside to be "tagged," as explained in the next section.

20.3.3 Recurring Groups

Much of the power of regular expressions comes from the ability to look for repetitions of a group. The syntax:

n

refers to a previously tagged group. The expressions \1, \2, and \3 refer to the first three groups. Remember that C++ string literals use the backslash as an escape character, so the expressions "\1", "\2", and "\3" must be rendered as \\1, \\2, and \\3, and so on, in C++ source code (unless you're using raw string literals).

For example, the following expression—expressed as a string literal—matches aa, bb, and cc:

```
"(a|b|c)\\1"
```

This expression first matches a, b, or c. Whatever is matched is *tagged*. The regex pattern must then immediately match this tagged character again if it is to match the overall expression.

It will therefore match aa and bb, but not ab.

The next example is more practical: It finds a repeated word, in which a single space separates the two words:

```
"([A-Za-z]+) \\1"
```

This expression says, "Match a series of one or more letters. Tag the characters in this group. Then match a space. Finally, match an exact recurrence of the tagged characters." The following strings would therefore be matched:

```
"the the"
"Monday Monday"
"Rabbit Rabbit"
```

20.3.4 Character Classes

The C++11 grammar also provides a series of character classes that can be used to help specify a range. For example, the following expression specifies a range consisting of any letter:

```
[[:alpha:]]
```

This is equivalent to:

```
[A-Za-z]
```

The following expression specifies a range consisting of any letter or punctuation character:

```
[[:alpha:][:punct:]]
```

Descriptions of the character classes follow.

- **[:alnum:]**
  Any letter or digit.
- **[:alpha:]**
  Any letter.
- **[:blank:]**
  A space or tab character.
- **[:cntrl:]**
  Any control character. (These are not printable.)
- **[:digit:]**
  Any decimal digit.
- **[:graph:]**
  Any printable character that is not a whitespace.
- **[:lower:]**
  Any lowercase letter.
- **[:print:]**
  Any printable character, including whitespaces.

- **[:punct:]**

  Any punctuation character.

- **[:space:]**

  A whitespace character, such as a blank space, tab, or newline.

- **[:upper:]**

  Any uppercase letter.

- **[:xdigit:]**

  A hexadecimal digit: This includes digits, as well as uppercase and lowercase letters.

20.4 Matching and Searching Functions

This section summarizes the syntax for the matching and searching functions. Don't forget to include the <regex> header. Also, remember that regex symbols are part of the **std** namespace, so either include a **using** statement or identify each name with its **std** prefix.

```
#include <regex>
using std::regex;
```

Next, you need to specify a regular-expression pattern by creating a **regex** object:

```
regex  name(pattern_string [,flags])
```

This regex constructor includes an optional *flags* argument. The most useful flag is **regex_constants::icase**, which turns off case sensitivity.

regex objects are unusual in that they are compiled and built at runtime, not compile time. Consequently, you want to create as few **regex** objects as possible, because creating many such objects impacts runtime performance. You should make your **regex** objects global variables, or pass them by reference if you need to.

After constructing a **regex** object, you can perform matching and searching by calling the **regex_match** and **regex_search** functions. Each of these returns a Boolean value. The **regex_match** function returns **true** if the *target_string* matches the pattern stored in *regex_obj* exactly: That is, the entire *target_string* must match the pattern completely.

```
regex_match(target_string, regex_obj)
```

The **regex_search** function returns **true** if the target string contains any substring that matches the pattern stored in *regex_obj*.

regex_search(*target_string*, *regex_obj***)**

For example, consider the task of finding a repeated word in the sentence:

```
The the cow jumped over the the moon.
```

The following statements execute this search:

```
#include <regex>
#include <string>
#include <iostream>
using std::string;
using std::cout;
using std::endl;
. . .
std::regex reg1("([A-Za-z]+) \\1");
string target = "The the cow jumped over the the moon.";
if (std::regex_search(target, reg1)) {
     cout << "A repeated word was found." << endl;
}
```

The call to **regex_search** failed to find the first repeated-word occurrence ("The the") because the first word was capitalized and the second was not. That did not matter in this instance, because there was another repeated-word sequence ("the the"). However, sometimes you are interested in getting the position of the first match, so it can matter.

To find the position of the first substring found, it's necessary to include another argument:

regex_search(*target_string*, *match_info*, *regex_obj***)**

The *match_info* argument is an object of type **cmatch**, **smatch**, or **wmatch**, corresponding to the following formats: C-string, **string** object, and wide-character string. The format must match the type of *target_string*; in this case, the **string** class is used for the target string, so *match_info* must have type **smatch**.

For example:

```
std::smatch sm;
std::regex reg1("([A-Za-z]+) \\1");
std::string target="The the cow jumped over the the moon.";
bool b = std::regex_search(target, sm, reg1);
```

The *match_info* object (sm in this case) can be used to obtain information about the search, as follows:

```
match_obj.str()          // Return the matched string
match_obj.position()    // Return the position of the matched string
```

For example, the following call finds the position of the first repeated word:

```
std::smatch sm;
std::regex reg1("([A-Za-z]+) \\1");
std::string target="The the cow jumped over the the moon.";
bool b = std::regex_search(target, sm, reg1);
cout << "Match found at pos. " << sm.position() << endl;
cout << "Pattern found was: " << sm.str() << endl;
```

These statements print:

```
Match was found at pos. 24
Pattern found was: the the
```

Turning off case sensitivity causes a match to be found at position 0 instead.

```
std::regex reg1("([A-Za-z]+) \\1", regex_constants::icase);
```

You can also obtain information about groups—patterns enclosed in parentheses—within the matched string. This information only applies to groups within the *first* substring found; **regex_search** finds only one substring and then it stops searching. (The next section describes how to find multiple substrings.)

```
match_obj.str(n)        // Return nth group within the matched substring
match_obj.position(n)   // Return position of nth group
```

For example, you can use *match_object* (sm in this case) to get information on the group found *within* the first matched substring.

```
cout << "Text of sub-group: " << sm.str(1);
```

Assuming case sensitivity is turned off, this prints:

```
Text of sub-group: The
```

20.5 "Find All," or Iterative, Searches

When searching for substrings, you typically want to find all the matching substrings rather than just the first one. The easiest way to do this is to use an iterative search.

This technique involves creating two iterators: one that iterates through a target string and is associated with a **regex** object, and another that is simply an "end" condition.

```
sregex_iterator  iter_name(str_obj.begin(), str_obj.end(), regex_obj);
sregex_iterator  end_iter_name;
```

This second declaration—the one that creates *end_iter_name*—should strike you as something new: an uninitialized iterator that has a use. This is different from other STL containers, which require a call to their **end** function to get an end-position iterator. Not so with regex iterators: An uninitialized regex iterator automatically represents the ending position—one position past the end of the string.

The **sregex_iterator** type is an adapter that uses a template, **regex_iterator**, with the **string** class. You can build iterators upon other string types.

With these two declarations in place—providing an iterator and an end position—it's then an easy matter to iterate through all the substrings found. For example:

```
#include <regex>
#include <string>
using std::regex;
using std::sregex_iterator;
using std::string;

regex reg1("([A-Za-z]+) \\1", std::regex_constants::icase);
string target = "The the cow jumped over the the moon";
sregex_iterator it(target.begin(), target.end(), reg1);
sregex_iterator reg_end;
for (; it != reg_end; ++it) {
     std::cout << "Substring found: ";
     std::cout << it->str() << ", Position: ";
     std::cout << it->position() << std::endl;
}
```

These statements print:

```
Substring found: The the, Position: 0
Substring found: the the, Position: 24
```

This next example finds all words beginning with an uppercase or lowercase "B". Case sensitivity must be turned off in order to find "Barney" as well as "bat" and "big". In addition, the word-boundary character (\b) is used to ensure that the only patterns found are those in which the letter "B" comes at the beginning of the word.

```
regex reg2("\\bB[a-z]*", regex_constants::icase);
string bstr = "Barney goes up to bat with a big stick.";
sregex_iterator it(bstr.begin(), bstr.end(), reg2);
sregex_iterator reg_end;
for (; it != reg_end; ++it) {
     std::cout << "Substring found: ";
     std::cout << it->str() << ", Position: ";
     std::cout << it->position() << std::endl;
}
```

These statements print:

```
Substring found: Barney, Position: 0
Substring found: bat, Position: 18
Substring found: big, Position: 29
```

20.6 Replacing Text

One of the most powerful regular-expression capabilities is to selectively search-and-replace patterns within a string of text. Here's one possible use (out of zillions): to transform a target string by replacing each repeated pair of words with just one word.

For example, given this text:

```
The cow cow jumped over the the moon.
```

it would be useful to produce a string consisting of:

```
The cow jumped over the moon.
```

The **regex_replace** function performs this task by returning the transformed string. It has the following syntax:

`regex_replace(``*target_string*, *regex_obj*, *replacement_pattern_str*`**`);`**

The *replacement_pattern_str* is a string that can contain the following special sequences (in addition to ordinary characters).

- **$&**

  Refers to the entire matched string.

- **$*n***

  Refers to the nth group within the matched string. For example, "$1" refers to the first group of characters tagged by the regex object; "$2" refers to the second group of tagged characters (if there is one), and so on. The example that follows should clarify.

- **$$**

  A literal dollar sign ($).

The following declarations set up a search-and-replace designed to fix the repeated-word pattern, replacing it, where found, with one copy of the word.

```
using std::regex;
using std::regex_replace;
using std::string;
```

```
regex reg1("([A-Za-z]+) \\1");   // Find double word.
string replacement = "$1";       // Replace with one word.
```

With these objects defined, the following statements execute search-and-replace on the string shown earlier.

```
string target = "The cow cow jumped over the the moon.";
string result = regex_replace(target, reg1, replacement);
std::cout << result << std::endl;
```

The output is:

```
The cow jumped over the moon.
```

which is what we wanted.

Let's review how this works. When the text "cow cow" was matched by the regular-expression object, the first occurrence of "cow" was tagged because it matched the expression inside the parentheses: "([A-Za-z]+)". The rest of the expression, " \\1", indicated that the regex object then needed to match a space, followed by a recurrence of the tagged characters, to match the overall expression. Therefore, "cow" gets tagged and "cow cow" matches the entire regular expression.

The replacement pattern, "$1", causes the matched text—"cow cow"—to be replaced by "cow", the tagged group. Suppose the replacement pattern were "XX$1YY$1ZZ$1". Then the replacement text would have been "XXcowYYcowZZcow" and *that* would have replaced "cow cow".

Characters not matched by the regex object, reg1, are just copied into the result as they are. So, for example, the words "jumped over" are copied without being transformed.

Here's an example of another regex object and replacement-pattern string: When used with the call to **regex_replace** shown earlier, these result in the switching of two words separated by an ampersand (&). For example, "boy&girl" would be replaced by "girl&boy" and vice versa.

```
regex reg1("([A-Za-z]+)&([A-Za-z]+)");   // Find word&word
string replacement = "$2&$1";            // Switch order.
```

The **regex_replace** function is particularly convenient. It isn't necessary to iterate through the target string. Instead, **regex_replace** carries out replacements on all the substrings matching the pattern in the regex object, while leaving the rest of the text alone.

20.7 String Tokenizing

Although the functionality in the preceding sections can perform nearly any form of pattern matching, C++11 also provides string-tokenizing functionality that is a superior alternative to the C-library **strtok** function. Tokenization is the process of breaking a string into a series of individual words, or *tokens*.

To take advantage of this feature, use the following syntax, in which *str* represents a **string** object containing the target string:

```
sregex_token_iterator  iter_name(str.begin(), str.end(), regex_obj, -1);
sregex_token_iterator  end_iter_name;
```

As with **sregex_iterator**, **sregex_token_iterator** is an adapter built on top of the **string** class; you can use the underlying template, **regex_token_iterator**, with other kinds of strings.

sregex_token_iterator performs a range of operations, most of which are similar to what the standard iterator does, as described in Section 20.5, " "Find All," or Iterative Searches." Specifying -1 as the fourth argument makes the function skip over any patterns matching the *regex_obj*, causing the iterator to iterate through the tokens—which consist of text between each occurrence of the pattern.

For example, the following statements find each word, in which words are delimited by any series of spaces and/or commas.

```
#include <regex>
#include <string>
using std::regex;
using std::string;
using std::sregex_token_iterator;
. . .
// Delimiters are spaces (\s) and/or commas
regex re("[\\s,]+");
string s = "The White Rabbit,  is very,late.";
sregex_token_iterator it(s.begin(), s.end(), re, -1);
sregex_token_iterator reg_end;
for (; it != reg_end; ++it) {
     std::cout << it->str() << std::endl;
}
```

These statements, when executed, print the following, ignoring spaces and commas (except as to recognize them as delimiters):

```
The
White
```

```
Rabbit
is
very
late.
```

20.8 Catching RegEx Exceptions

Catching exceptions can be important when working with regular expressions, especially if you build a new regular-expression string at runtime or let the end user specify a pattern.

Remember that a regular expression object is compiled at runtime. If the pattern is ill-formed, the program throws an exception, causing abrupt termination unless the exception is caught. Catching the exception enables you to terminate more gracefully, or even—if you choose—continue execution after taking appropriate action (such as reporting the error to the user).

Regular-expression errors belong to the **regex_error** class, which is declared in the <regex> header and is part of the **std** namespace.

```
#include <regex>
using std::regex_error;
```

The **regex_error** class supports a **what** function, which returns a text string, and a **code** function, which returns an integer. The following example (which assumes the appropriate **#include** directives and **using** statements have been given) responds to a poorly formed **regex** object.

```
try {
     regex re("*\\bW[a-z]*");
     string s = "The White Rabbit is very late.";
     if (regex_search(s, re)) {
          cout << "Search string found." << endl;
     }
} catch (regex_error e) {
     cout << e.what() << endl;
     cout << "CODE IS: " << e.code() << endl;
}
```

When these statements are run, the program prints:

```
regex_error(error_badrepeat):
One of *?+{ was not preceded by a valid regular expression.
CODE IS: 10
```

The error is thrown as soon as there is an attempt to build a bad regular expression (because the regular-expression object, remember, is compiled at runtime).

```
regex re("*\\bW[a-z]*");   // Throws an exception!
```

Here you should be able to see the problem. The first use of the asterisk (*)—which means to repeat the preceding expression zero or more times—was not preceded by any expression; it was therefore not a meaningful use of regular-expression grammar. This is duly reported as a "badrepeat" error as long as exception handling is provided as just shown.

20.9 Sample App: RPN Calculator

In C++ *Without Fear,* 2nd Edition (Prentice Hall), I presented a Reverse Polish Notation (RPN) calculator as one of the more advanced examples. In this section, I present a superior version of that app.

An RPN calculator lets the user enter arbitrarily long arithmetic expressions in postfix notation. For example, to add 3 and 4, you specify not "3 + 4" but:

```
3 4 +
```

This might at first seem counterintuitive until you realize it's an elegant notational system that does away with the need for parentheses. For example, the RPN expression:

```
3 4 + 10 1.5 + *
```

is equivalent to the following standard (infix) expression:

```
(3 + 4) * (10 + 1.5)
```

With RPN, an operator always applies to the expressions that precede it. In this case, the asterisk (*) applies to the expressions "3 4 +" and "10 1.5 +", which produce 7 and 11.5, respectively. Multiplication is finally applied to produce 80.5. The RPN grammar can be summarized as:

```
expression  <=  number
expression  <=  expression expression op
```

Calculations: The stack mechanism, described in Section 16.3, "The stack Template," is what powers this application. When the program reads a number, it pushes that number onto the stack. When the program reads an operator, it pops the top two values off the stack, performs a calculation, and pushes the result back onto the stack.

Lexical analysis: It's easy enough to interpret a line of input in which spaces separate operators as well as numbers. The more challenging problem is to recognize operators as both tokens *and* separators so that some of the spaces are optional. For example, it would be desirable to interpret:

```
3 44*5  1.2+/
```

as if it were written as:

```
3 44 * 5 1.2 + /
```

The **strtok** function is inadequate for this task. So is the **regex_token_iterator** function. The solution is to use a **regex_iterator** and search for sequences of characters that constitute either of the following:

- A number, consisting of consecutive digits with or without a fractional portion, such as "3", "44", or "100.507"
- Any of several operators: +, -, *, or /

With this approach, it's not necessary to have spaces on either side of an operator, although spaces are freely permitted. The following will work just fine:

```
3 4+ 1 2+*
```

The code for the application follows.

```
#include <iostream>
#include <string>
#include <cctype>
#include <regex>
#include <stack>

using std::cout;          // Alternatively, you can use
using std::cin;           //  using namespace std;
using std::endl;
using std::string;
using std::regex;
using std::sregex_iterator;
using std::stack;

void process_token(string s);
stack<double> st;

main() {
     string instr;
     string num_pattern("[0-9]+(\\.[0-9]*)?");
     string op_pattern("[+*/-]");
```

```
     regex re(num_pattern + "|" + op_pattern);
     while (true) {
         cout << "Enter expression (or ENTER to exit): ";
         getline(cin, instr);
         if (instr.length() == 0) { break; }
         sregex_iterator it(instr.begin(), instr.end(), re);
         sregex_iterator it_end;
         for (;it != it_end; ++it) {
              process_token(it->str());
         }
         if (!st.empty()) {
              cout << "The value is: " << st.top() << endl;
         }
     };
     return 0;
}

void process_token(string s) {
     // If s contains any char that is NOT an op,
     //  consider it a number by default.
     if (s.find_first_not_of("+*/-") != s.npos) {
          st.push(atof(s.c_str()));
     } else {
          double op2 = st.top(); st.pop();
          double op1 = st.top(); st.pop();
          switch(s[0]) {
          case '+': st.push(op1 + op2); break;
          case '-': st.push(op1 - op2); break;
          case '*': st.push(op1 * op2); break;
          case '/': st.push(op1 / op2); break;
          }
     }
}
```

This program illustrates a couple of important features of regular-expression grammar. First, as mentioned earlier, special characters such as "*" and "+" do not need to be escaped when they occur inside brackets (although brackets themselves would need to be escaped to be treated literally, of course). Also, the minus sign (-) does not need to be escaped, because it does not occur between two other characters.

```
     string op_pattern("[+*/-]");
```

Another interesting feature is that order is potentially significant. The **regex** object in this application searches for a digit string first and *then* for an operator. This order makes Exercise 2 possible.

Exercises

1. The following string pattern almost works but fails to separate numbers from operators in some cases. (Fortunately, the sample application contains the correct pattern.) Without looking at the application, determine what's wrong with the following regular expression:

   ```
   [0-9]+(.[0-9]*)?
   ```

2. Add support for a leading minus sign so that "-100", for example, is interpreted as a negative number. Ambiguities arise if the minus sign (-) is simply a unary operator in addition to being a binary operator (which it already is). But if you make the minus sign an optional part of a digit string, the user can add spaces for clarity as needed. Questions: Why does this exercise depend on the **regex** object looking for a digit string first and operators second? What would happen if it looked for operators first?

3. In the sample application, numbers of the form "33" and "33.03" are both accepted; "0.333" and "3." are also. However, strings with no integer portion and no leading zero—such as ".333"—are not accepted. Revise the expression for number_pattern so that it accepts digit strings such as ".333" in addition to the other formats.

4. Extend the floating-point format even further, to accept the following scientific-notation formats:

   *digits*E*digits*
   digits.*digits*E*digits*

5. Each time an operator is processed, the application assumes there are at least two values on the stack. If there are less than two, the user has entered too many operators. Revise the application to handle this situation by reporting the error and then continuing rather than incorrectly popping the stack (which causes program failure if you let it happen). Hint: Check the size of the stack.

6. Add other operators, such as a binary ^ operator, to perform exponentiation: "2 3 ^" should produce 2 to the 3rd power. Also add the tilde (~) as a unary operator to perform arithmetic negation (multiplying by -1). Finally, add the == and != operators to perform test-for-equality and test-for-inequality. These operators, which are Boolean, should each return either 1 or 0.

7. As a *really* advanced exercise (not for the faint of heart), enable the RPN calculator to read symbols and assign values by using a single equal sign (=) as an assignment operator. Build a symbol table by using the **map** template. Whenever a symbol—that is, a name—appears in any context other than the left side of an assignment, look up its value in the map.

APPENDIX A

A Painless Introduction to Rvalue References (C++11)

Programming with rvalue references is a technique for optimizing the speed of your programs. It's closely related to *move semantics,* which replaces copying of data with data transfers. Think of how much faster a piece of code can be if it lets an object steal ownership of data rather than copying that data out. (If it isn't immediately clear how this can speed up your programs, don't worry. This appendix explores the concept in greater depth.)

C++11 builds support for rvalue references into the STL, which can cause your programs to run faster even if you don't know about this feature. Adding support for rvalue references to your own code can optimize your programs further, sometimes making them significantly faster.

A.1 The Trouble with Copying

Many of the classes in the C++ library involve deep copying. For example, when you create a **string** object and assign its value to another object, the destination gets its own copy of the string data.

```
#include <string>
using std::string;
string s1("rabbit");
string s2 = s1;
```

The assignment "s2 = s1" uses *copy* rather than *move* semantics, causing s2 to get its own copy of "rabbit". In other languages, such as Java, C#, and Visual Basic, assigning an object causes a reference to be copied, not the contents; you have to use a "clone" function to perform a copy.

But in C++ (this applies not only to **string** objects but to any kind of object), a basic principle is that you can manipulate objects just like primitive data. Therefore, "s2 = s1" doesn't just cause s2 to have the same value; it causes s2 to get its own copy of the data, not bound to the old copy. The “r” in “rabbit” can then be capitalized in s2 without affecting the contents of s1.

```
s2[0] = 'R';                       // Capitalize s2.
std::cout << s2 << std::endl;     // Print "Rabbit"
std::cout << s1 << std::endl;     // Print "rabbit"
```

So far, this is well and good. It means that object variables work like primitive data in C++. After all, programmers are used to copy semantics when it comes to simple data such as an integer. Why should objects be different?

Figure A.1 gives some idea of the work involved in copying out a piece of data. And this is just for a string; some objects involve copying a good deal more data than this.

But sometimes copying is unnecessary. Consider the following statements. They create a temporary string made up of “Elvis ” and “Presley”. The result is copied into the destination. For a brief moment, there are *two* copies of “Elvis Presley”: the temporary string (created on the right side of the statement) and the one that ends up in “name”.

```
string name = string("Elvis ") + "Presley";
```

Another example occurs when you create a temporary string and push it onto a vector.

```
#include <vector>
using std::vector;
vector<string>  vec;
vec.push_back("Elvis Presley");
```

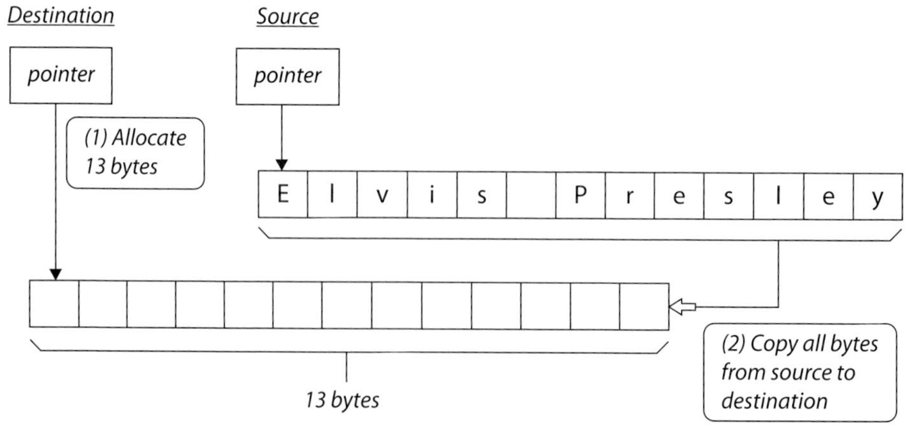

FIGURE A.1 Copy semantics

The action of the last statement in this example is to create a temporary string. The contents are then copied to a location inside the vector. But it would be more efficient to just transfer ownership of the data to the destination, avoiding a copy operation. Such a transfer is a *move*. A move is a destructive data transfer that doesn't need to preserve the source.

Figure A.2 illustrates move semantics. If we can be assured that the source object is temporary and does not need to be preserved (or if the source is going to be assigned a new value afterward), we can let the destination object just steal the resource—in this case, the string data—and null out the pointer in the source object.

Note how allocation is avoided as well as a copy operation. A deallocation is also avoided. Because the source object's internal pointer is nulled out, the data is not deleted when the source object is destroyed. The string data is alive and well but its ownership has been transferred. This is far more efficient.

After this operation, the source object no longer contains a valid reference to string data. But that's okay; the source is a temporary object and is about to be destroyed anyway.

To summarize, move semantics improves efficiency in three ways.

1. The destination no longer does a memory allocation.
2. The destination no longer copies the underlying data.
3. The source string's pointer is nulled out, preventing a deallocation later.

Only 13 bytes are involved in this case, but in other cases, the object creation-destruction process may be more involved. Furthermore, in cases in which an object owns a unique resource such as a file handle, copy semantics may not even be possible.

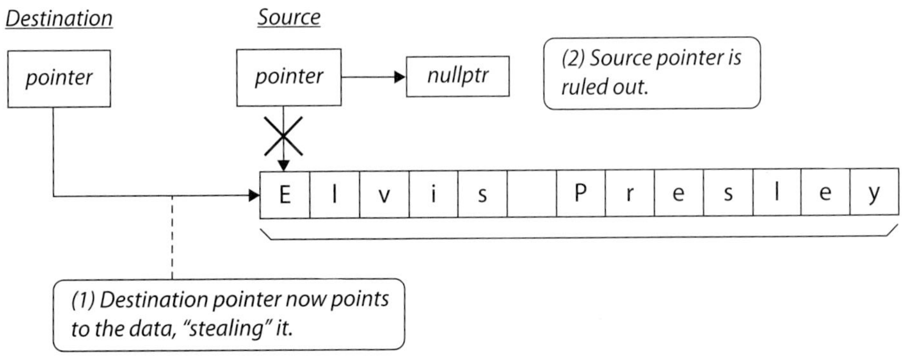

FIGURE A.2 Move semantics

So far, this gain in efficiency may seem small, but it can become significant. Consider a case in which you create a vector made up of a thousand strings.

```
#include <vector>
#include <string>
std::vector<std::string> svec;
// Load svec with a thousand strings.
```

What happens when you sort this vector?

```
sort(svec.begin(), svec.end());
```

The **sort** algorithm proceeds to carry out a large number of swaps. Each and every swap is expensive, as it involves three complete copy operations.

```
void swap(Type &A, Type &B) {
     Type temp = A;
     A = B;
     B = temp;
}
```

This is a lot of work, particularly if it has to be done thousands of times. It would be far more efficient to tell the compiler, "During each of these swaps, transfer ownership of data between A and B." For string objects, this would mean that A and B swap pointers.

In Section A.3, I'll show how this works by developing a primitive string class.

A.2 Move Semantics: C++11 to the Rescue!

In C++11, the standard library supports move semantics. Whenever a temporary object occurs on the right of an assignment, the compiler automatically executes a move (that is, a transfer of data ownership) rather than a copy operation.

How does the compiler know the source object is disposable? This is critical. The compiler invokes move semantics when the source is an *rvalue*. The basic principle is that an rvalue is anything that is not an lvalue. In practical terms, an rvalue is usually a temporary object.

A temporary object goes out of scope as soon as the statement terminates. Examples of temporary objects include the following.

- Any numeric or string literal. For example: 100, "John", "Elvis Presley", 3.14159265.
- Any expression consisting of more than one lvalue. For example, in the expression "x + y", "x" is an lvalue and "y" is an lvalue, but the expression "x + y" itself is a temporary object.

The second point above is a little subtle and deserves elaboration. Take the case of string objects again. Suppose you have strings making up the first and last names:

```
string first_name = "Elvis";
string last_name = "Presley";
string name = first_name + " " + last_name;
```

The variable first_name is an lvalue. It must be preserved. last_name is also an lvalue.

But the expression `first _ name + " " + last _ name` is not a persistent object. It is an expression without a name, and once its value is used, the program throws it away.

The value of `first _ name + " " + last _ name` is a new string containing "Elvis Presley". For a brief moment, a copy of this data exists on the right of the assignment (=) and also on the left. It would be much more efficient to *move* this data—to transfer ownership but not perform a copy.

In C++11, the compiler does just that. You don't need to make any changes to your programs to get this optimization for standard library classes.

Of course, the compiler does not use move semantics (sticking instead with copy semantics) when the source object is an lvalue, as in the following statement:

```
string name = first_name;
```

Sometimes it's useful to force an lvalue to be treated as an rvalue, although this must be done with care.

The **std::move** function causes its argument to be interpreted as an rvalue; **std::move** is really a cast. The effect is to force move semantics. This is extremely useful in the case of the **swap** template function, which C++11 implements as:

```
void swap(Type &A, Type &B) {
     Type temp = std::move(A);
     A = std::move(B);
     B = std::move(temp);
}
```

Note that A and B are not rvalues; on the contrary, they must be lvalues, because each is the target of an assignment.

But in each of these assignments, there's no need to preserve the source data because each time, the source is either temporary (in the case of temp) or about to be assigned a new value in a subsequent statement. All that's needed, then, is to transfer ownership to the destination. The effect of **std::move** is to treat A and B as rvalues within these statements; as a consequence, the **swap** function just moves around pointers

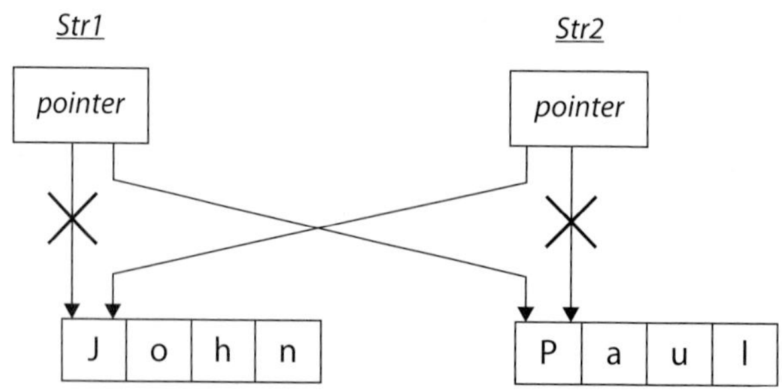

FIGURE A.3 Swapping strings using move semantics

(and also length data, but that's just an integer) instead of allocating, copying, and deallocating string data. This is a big win.

Prior to C++11, if you wanted this kind of efficiency when sorting a container of objects, it was necessary to create an array of pointers and then sort this container based on the values pointed to. The gain in efficiency sometimes justified all the extra programming involved. But it involved an extra data structure, and it was a lot of work!

In C++11, you get this gain in efficiency for free.

Figure A.3 illustrates what happens when two objects are swapped using move semantics. Consider the task of swapping two strings, Str1 and Str2, containing the data "John" and "Paul", respectively. As the figure shows, it's much more efficient to swap pointers than to do a series of copy operations.

Although all the classes, templates, and objects in the C++11 standard library are optimized to take advantage of move semantics, you don't get this benefit for your own classes unless you write new code. In the next section, I explain how to enable your own classes to support move semantics by using rvalue references.

A.3 Rvalue Refs in a User's String Class

C++11 introduces a new syntax—rvalue reference—which (with rare exceptions) should really only be used within function arguments, principally within constructors and assignment-operator functions. The syntax says, "This argument is an rvalue reference."

```
type&& name
```

This new operator (&&) is used in the same contexts in which you'd use & to declare a reference argument.

Consider the case of a primitive string class. You normally would not write this class, because the STL provides a powerful string class already. However, writing your own string class is a good exercise, and it illustrates many of the basic issues involved.

To keep things simple, I provide two members and a few constructors. Most of the time, it would make sense to declare some of the members private, but I'll make everything public here for ease of use. Also, to keep things simple, I've written this class to keep track of length and to use a terminating null, so you can print one of these strings by using the expression "string->ptr".

```
#include <cstring>  // To support memcpy.

class MyString {
public:
     char *ptr;
     int n_length;

     MyString() {
         ptr = new char;
         *ptr = '\0';
         n_length = 0;
     }

     MyString(const char *cstr) {
          int n = n_length = strlen(cstr);
          ptr = new char[n + 1];
          memcpy(ptr, cstr, n + 1);
     }

     MyString(const MyString& other) {
          int n = n_length = other.n_length;
          ptr = new char[n + 1];
          memcpy(ptr, other.ptr, n + 1);
     }

     ~MyString() {
          if (ptr) {delete ptr;}
     }
};
```

Look how much work the copy constructor has to do. It has to allocate new memory and then copy all the data from its source.

To improve performance, you can overload the constructor with a version that uses an rvalue reference; this creates a *move constructor.* The compiler determines which constructor to call, because it knows whether or not an operand is an rvalue.

```
MyString(MyString&& other) {    // Move constructor.
     ptr = other.ptr;
     n_length = other.n_length;
     other.ptr = nullptr;
}
```

All these statements do is transfer an integer and a couple of pointer values. This constructor (that is, the move constructor) uses an rvalue reference, so the compiler invokes it only when the source object is an rvalue: for example, when the object is a temporary one.

Note that the ptr member in the source object must be nulled out. This is necessary to prevent the MyString destructor from deleting the string data as soon as the source object goes out of scope. The string data itself is still valid; it simply gets a new owner. So it must be preserved.

In addition to providing a move constructor, rvalue references can be used to overload the assignment operator (=), invoking move semantics as appropriate for assignments.

The following example shows the standard assignment-operator function and the rvalue-reference version, side by side.

```
MyString& operator=(const MyString& other) {
     if (ptr) {
          delete ptr;
     }
     int n = n_length = other.n_length;
     ptr = new char[n + 1];
     memcpy(ptr, other.ptr, n + 1);
     return *this;
}

// Rvalue-ref version of assignment op.
MyString& operator=(MyString&& other) {
     ptr = other.ptr;
     n_length = other.n_length;
     other.ptr = nullptr;
     return *this;
}
```

Note the contrast in function signatures. The standard (lvalue-reference) version uses **const** in the declaration of the source argument. The rvalue-reference version must not use **const**, because one of the things it does is null out the pointer in the source object.

A.4 Verifying Runtime-Performance Improvement

There are a number of ways to verify that C++11 is actually using the overloaded rvalue-reference functions. For debugging and demonstration purposes, you can print diagnostic messages. For example:

```
MyString(MyString&& other) {    // Rvalue-ref version.
     ptr = other.ptr;
     n_length = other.n_length;
     other.ptr = nullptr;
     std::cout << "I'm in MyString&& constructor!\n";
}
```

The added statement verifies that the rvalue-reference version of the constructor is being used. This constructor will (for example) be invoked by the following statement, because the right side of the assignment creates a temporary string object.

```
MyString s = MyString("White Rabbit"); // Rvalue involved.
```

If you're like me, you want to verify that rvalue-reference member functions actually make real improvements to performance. You can do this by temporarily commenting out the rvalue-ref versions and then running test code—with and without rvalue references.

Note

If rvalue-reference functions (the move constructor and overloaded assignment operator) are not provided, the "standard" versions of these functions—that is, the lvalue-reference versions—are always used, even if the right side of an assignment is a temporary object. The converse, however, is not true: The compiler will never treat an lvalue as an rvalue—unless **std::move** is applied—because an lvalue must be preserved and cannot be nullified without bad consequences.

I ran the following test code to see how fast it performs with and without rvalue references—in the latter case using **#ifdef** and **#endif** directives to comment out the rvalue-ref versions of the member functions. After pushing 5,000 strings onto a vector, this test code shuffles the vector, which causes a great many swap operations to take place.

```
int t1 = clock();  // Include <ctime> to support this.
vector<MyString> vec(5000);
for(int i = 0; i < 5000; ++i) {
     vec.push_back(MyString(
          "Happy days are here again...!"));
}
random_shuffle(vec.begin(), vec.end());
int t2 = clock();
cout << "Elapsed time was: " << t2 - t1 << endl;
```

What I found is that on my computer, the version enhanced by rvalue references takes about 34 clock ticks—34 microseconds. The version without rvalue references takes about 100 clock ticks. That's a ratio of 3:1, or a speed enhancement of 200 percent.

If you run this test code, by the way, you'll want to first remove any diagnostic messages; otherwise, you'll be printing out thousands of strings.

A.5 Rvalues and Contained Objects

Although the **std::move** function (which is really a cast) must be used with care, there are other situations in which it is useful. Suppose you have a class that contains objects:

```
class FullName {
public:
     MyString first_name;
     MyString middle_name;
     MyString last_name;
};
```

Again, I've deliberately kept this declaration simple for the sake of illustration.

You might think that because the MyString class was enabled to use move semantics (as the STL string class already is, by the way), the FullName class is also. However, to get this optimization, you need to give FullName its own rvalue-reference functions. For example, you could write the following move constructor for the class:

```
FullName(FullName&& other) {
     first_name = std::move(other.first_name);
     middle_name = std::move(other.middle_name);
     last_name = std::move(other.last_name);
}
```

To fully optimize a class, you need to enable move semantics for each individual member that would benefit from such optimization.

A.6 References Reconsidered: Rvalues and Lvalues

In Chapter 6, "Pointers, Arrays, and References," I discussed references, the kind that are declared with a single ampersand (&), as in the following:

```
MyString(const Mystring& other) {...}
```

Now that we're dealing with rvalue reverences, it becomes necessary to be more specific; the first kind of reference (the kind mentioned in Chapter 6) is more correctly spoken of as an *lvalue reference*. In C++11, the language recognizes both kinds: lvalue and rvalue references.

It's worth taking another look at precisely what is an lvalue and what is an rvalue. In the simplest terms, an lvalue is a variable—although it can also be a number of similar things, such as an array element or a dereferenced pointer. An rvalue is most often a temporary value of some kind. These are not precise definitions, but they are a good starting point.

Although I don't generally recommend it, you can declare both lvalue and rvalue references directly. For example:

```
int n;
int &lval = n;          // Ok; n is an lvalue.
int &&rval = n + 1;     // Ok; n + 1 is an rvalue.
int &&rval2 = 12;       // Also Ok.
```

These last couple of statements are instructive in helping to understand what an rvalue is. The declarations just shown are permitted, but the compiler would never allow either of the following:

```
int &lval = n + 1;      // ERROR! Cannot bind to an rvalue!
int &lval2 = 12;        // ERROR! Cannot bind to an rvalue!
```

The point is that lvalue references can bind to variable names but they cannot bind to expressions such as "n + 1" or to literals. But rvalue references do bind to these.

We need a more precise definition. The one suggested by Stephan T. Lavavej (note his initials; yes, these are absolutely real!), Microsoft's resident guru on all things STL, including rvalue references, is:

An lvalue is anything that has a name. An rvalue is anything that doesn't.

If you think about it, this makes sense. If something has a name, you can assign data to it. But how can you assign data to something that doesn't have a name?

To this definition, we need to add some qualifiers. (Not to contradict Mr. Lavavej; he knows all this better than I.) Mr. Lavavej means, of course, that any *single entity* that has its own name is an lvalue. So "x" and "y" are both lvalues, but "x + y" is not.

Mr. Lavavej also understands that some complex expressions can be lvalues, such as a dereferenced address expression, such as the following:

```
*(ptr + i + 5);
```

Yet even with the ifs, ands, and buts, this definition—*anything that has a name is an lvalue*—is still useful. Note that whether something is an lvalue or rvalue is a property of an expression, not the object it refers to. This is important.

And here we're confronted with a fine point that is nonetheless critical. Suppose you want to leverage your code by having your move constructor call your assignment operator:

```
MyString(MyString&& other) {
     *this = other;    // ERROR! This won't work.
}
```

This code fails. But it's instructive to consider why. We know that "other" refers to something that was an rvalue at the time of the function call. It might seem reasonable, then, to conclude that move semantics will be used, resulting in a call to operator=(MyString&&).

But within the function, "other" has a name. Paradoxically, then, even though "other" refers to something that was formerly expressed as an rvalue, "other" is an lvalue within the context of the function! (Remember that whether something is an rvalue is a property of expressions, not objects.) To write the function correctly, it's necessary to use **std::move**, forcing this argument to once again be treated as an rvalue.

```
MyString(MyString&& other) {
     *this = std::move(other);   // This works.
}
```

We've finally arrived at the deepest and subtlest aspects of C++11. In Chapter 1, "C++ Fundamentals," I presented C++ as a language that can be approached about as easily as BASIC or any other language. And in fact, when learning C++ you can focus for a time on syntax that does simple things, like get input, perform some loops, and produce output.

But to become a real C++ programmer is to consider issues such as performance, implementation, and fine points of syntax. To truly master the language is to think about these matters in a whole new way from how you might have as a C or Fortran programmer. This task can be challenging, but the reward is a deep understanding of programming and computers. The White Rabbit and I wish you the thrill of the journey and the joy of discovery.

APPENDIX B

Summary of New Features in C++11

This book describes the great majority of new features in C++11. In the rare instance the book does not cover a new feature, it's usually because that feature is not implemented on most of the new compilers yet. The book does not cover the topic of multithreaded applications (except by mentioning the **thread_local** keyword), but that may be a topic for a future edition. Otherwise, the most important aspects of C++11 are covered.

This appendix summarizes four major areas:

1. Improvements in object construction (classes)
2. Other core-language enhancements
3. New keywords
4. Extensions to the C++ library

B.1 Improvements in Object Construction

C++11 provides improved techniques for declaring classes and writing constructors.

Inherited base-class constructors: C++ programmers have long wanted the ability to inherit all the constructors of a base class. See Section 7.7.3, "Inherited Constructors (C++11)."

Default member values: This is another ability C++ programmers have long wanted. You can initialize data members as they are declared, giving them default values. Constructors can still override these values. See Section 7.3.6, "Default Member Initialization (C++11)."

Delegated constructors: A delegated constructor invokes another constructor to do some or all of its work. This enables you to leverage programming, resulting in less duplication of code. See Section 7.3.5, "Delegated Constructors (C++11)."

The override keyword: This feature prevents C++ from creating an unwanted new function member due to your attempting to override an inherited function but misspelling the name. See Section 7.7.7, "Override Keyword (C++11)."

The final keyword: This keyword prevents a function from being overridden by derived classes of the class in which it's applied. See Section 5.3, "Complete Function Declaration Syntax."

Uniform initialization: All data items—including instances of a class (that is, object)—can now be initialized by using curly braces instead of parentheses. For example: "Point pt1{0, 1};". The old ways of initializing data are still supported, but this uniform use of curly braces makes syntax of declarations more consistent.

B.2 Other Core-Language Enhancements

In addition to improving class and object syntax, C++11 provides these other improvements to the language.

Range-based for loops: This is an alternative syntax of **for** loops, which is frequently more concise and easier to write. Moreover, it is less error-prone as it uses a container's own knowledge of where it begins and ends rather than requiring you to set boundaries explicitly. See Section 4.7, "Range-based for Statements (C++11)."

The long long int type: This is an extra-long integer type, usually 64-bits. See Section 2.2, "Primitive Data Types."

Lambda functions: A lambda function is an unnamed function, typically defined right at the point of usage. This feature is especially useful when working with containers and algorithms in the Standard Template Library, where you may often need to provide just a short function definition "on the fly." See Section 5.7, "Lambda, or Anonymous, Functions (C++11)" and Section 18.2, "Using Lambda Functions (C++11)."

Move semantics and rvalue references: Move semantics can significantly speed up program performance by replacing copy operations, where appropriate, with simple transfers of data ownership. Rvalue references, in turn, enable you to implement move semantics in your own classes. See Appendix A, "A Painless Introduction to Rvalue References (C++1)."

Strongly typed enumerations (enum): This is a feature that increases the type checking performed for types declared with the **enum** keyword, making them type-safe. See Section 2.8, "Enumerated Types."

Smart pointers: The new **shared_ptr** and **unique_ptr** types (replacing **auto_ptr**, which is now deprecated) provide an improved implementation of smart pointers, which automatically release dynamic memory when they go out of scope. This helps prevent memory leaks. See Section 6.6, "Smart Pointers (C++11)."

Raw string literals: Quoted (that is, literal) strings in C++ have an escape sequence convention, so "\n", for example, is treated as a newline rather than as a literal backslash followed by "n". This can be inconvenient in some situations, such as when specifying regular expressions (see Chapter 20, "C++11 Regular-Expression Library"). C++11 provides an R prefix indicating that no escape sequences are to be recognized. See Section 2.6.5, "Raw String Literals (C++11)."

Static assertions: The **static_assert** keyword provides a way to flag errors at compile time when a necessary condition is not met. This is particularly useful when working with templates. See Section 8.5, "Predefined Macros."

Variadic templates: This feature enables you to write templates that take any number of arguments. See Section 9.7, "Variadic Templates (C++11)."

Improved handling of right-angle brackets: Prior to C++11, two consecutive right-angle brackets (>>) were misinterpreted as a right-shift operator when used within nested template instantiation, as in "vector<list<int>>". This behavior has now been fixed.

B.3 Other New Keywords

This section lists new keywords in the language, in addition to the ones mentioned already.

auto: When a variable is declared as **auto**, it directs the compiler to infer the type from context. (Note that this is not the same thing as a variant data type, which can hold data in different formats at different times.) This is often a great convenience, especially with complex declarations. See Section 2.9.2, "The auto and decltype Keywords (C++11)."

constexpr: This keyword causes a variable to be treated as a compile-time constant. The advantage of such constants is that they are fully calculated before the program runs, so program performance is not hindered at runtime. Compile-time constants can also be used to initialize fixed-length arrays and template parameters. (See Section 2.7, "Data Declarations: The Complete Syntax.") The **constexpr** keyword can also be used with functions, subject to several restrictions. (See Section 5.3.)

decltype: This keyword returns the type of an expression; the result can be used just like a type name, to declare variables, arguments, or a return-value type. See Section 2.9.2.

nullptr: This keyword can be used to set pointers to "point nowhere" or to test them against; this is a superior alternative to the old NULL macro because it is a true keyword and does not rely on being provided by a header file. See Section 6.3.6, "Pointers and Memory Allocation."

thread_local: This keyword gives a variable thread-local storage class so that in multithreaded programs, each thread gets its own copy of the variable. See Section 2.7.

B.4 Extensions to the Standard Library

As significant as anything else are the new facilities that C++11 brings to the standard library.

List initialization of STL containers: STL containers can now be initialized directly from aggregate lists (enclosed in curly braces) just as arrays can. This eliminates the need to call **push_back** over and over just to initialize a container. See Section 15.3.3, "List Initialization (C++11)."

Randomization library: The new randomization library replaces the old C-library **rand** and **srand** functions, although these are still supported for backward compatibility. This new library provides a choice of randomization engines—each providing a different tradeoff between speed and quality—and also a large choice of distributions. Each distribution is optimized to produce a random number in the target range and according to a particular probability function. See Chapter 19, "C++11 Randomization Library."

Regular-Expression library: This library provides a set of powerful search-and-replace capabilities for analyzing and manipulating strings of text. These are useful for lexical analysis (breaking down the input in a string), tokenization, translating between one text-file format and another, and many other uses. See Chapter 20.

Unordered (hash-table-driven) containers: The new unordered **map** and **set** containers are variations on the **map** and **set** containers in Chapter 17, "STL Associated Containers (map, set)," each of which provides a convenient data dictionary, or rudimentary database, taking a key value and quickly finding the associated element. The advantage of the unordered versions of these containers is that they provide faster lookup times by using a hash-table technology. However, they have some limitations as well. See Section 17.6, "Unordered Containers (C++11)."

Additional algorithms: Prior to C++11, the STL contained a large set of algorithms, which can operate on arrays as well as other containers, to perform a number of standard programming tasks. C++11 supports all these algorithms but adds even more. See Chapter 18, "STL Algorithms."

The tuple template: This is a predefined variadic class template that can store any number of data items of any type. See Section 9.7.3, "Tuples."

Other new types: Although not all compiler vendors support all these types as of this writing, they will eventually be a standard part of C++11 compilers. These include **chrono**, **ratio**, and **complex** interfaces, which support time measurement (overlapping with the old C-library time functions, but more extensive), rational numbers (fractions), and complex numbers, respectively.

Overall, these improvements to C++, both in the core language and in the libraries, are important and innovative—although some of these improvements respond to requests that programmers have had for a long time. It's well worth your effort to master these features. Although it may at times feel like a burden to have to periodically learn new ways to do things, I find that this challenge helps keep the field of programming interesting. May it always be so, and may you live in interesting times.

APPENDIX C

ASCII Codes

This appendix presents ASCII codes according to decimal value, hexadecimal value, and corresponding character. Hexadecimal codes can be used to embed values into a string, as described in Chapter 2:

```
cout << "Hex code 6f is " << "\x6f" << endl;
```

Some nonprintable characters have special meanings:

- NUL: null value
- ACK: acknowledgment signal (used in network communications)
- BEL: bell
- BS: backspace
- LF: linefeed
- FF: form feed (new page)
- CR: carriage return
- NAK: no acknowledgment
- DEL: delete

Table C.1 gives the standard ASCII codes.

TABLE C.1 Standard ASCII Codes

DEC	HEX	CHAR	DEC	HEX	CHAR	DEC	HEX	CHAR	DEC	HEX	CHAR	DEC	HEX	CHAR
00	00	NUL	26	1a		52	34	4	78	4e	N	104	68	h
01	01		27	1b		53	35	5	79	4f	O	105	69	i
02	02		28	1c	FS	54	36	6	80	50	P	106	6a	j
03	03		29	1d	GS	55	37	7	81	51	Q	107	6b	k
04	04		30	1e	RS	56	38	8	82	52	R	108	6c	l
05	05		31	1f	US	57	39	9	83	53	S	109	6d	m
06	06	ACK	32	20	space	58	3a	:	84	54	T	110	6e	n
07	07	BEL	33	21	!	59	3b	;	85	55	U	111	6f	o
08	08	BS	34	22	"	60	3c	<	86	56	V	112	70	p
09	09		35	23	#	61	3d	=	87	57	W	113	71	q
10	0a	LF	36	24	$	62	3e	>	88	58	X	114	72	r
11	0b	CR	37	25	%	63	3f	?	89	59	Y	115	73	s
12	0c		38	26	&	64	40	@	90	5a	Z	116	74	t
13	0d		39	27	'	65	41	A	91	5b	[	117	75	u
14	0e		40	28	(	66	42	B	92	5c	\	118	76	v
15	0f		41	29	)	67	43	C	93	5d	]	119	77	w
16	10		42	2a	*	68	44	D	94	5e	^	120	78	x
17	11		43	2b	+	69	45	E	95	5f	-	121	79	y
18	12		44	2c	,	70	46	F	96	60	`	122	7a	z
19	13		45	2d	-	71	47	G	97	61	a	123	7b	{
20	14		46	2e	.	72	48	H	98	62	b	124	7c	|
21	15	NAK	47	2f	/	73	49	I	99	63	c	125	7d	}
22	16	SYN	48	30	0	74	4a	J	100	64	d	126	7e	~
23	17		49	31	1	75	4b	K	101	65	e	127	7f	DEL
24	18		50	32	2	76	4c	L	102	66	f			
25	19		51	33	3	77	4d	M	103	67	g			

Table C.2 lists extended ASCII codes; note that these are somewhat implementation dependent. They are most likely to be correct for computers of American manufacturers running Windows.

TABLE C.2 Extended ASCII Codes for American Equipment Manufacturers

DEC	HEX	CHAR	DEC	HEX	CHAR	DEC	HEX	CHAR	DEC	HEX	CHAR	DEC	HEX	CHAR
128	80	Ç	154	9a	Ü	180	b4	┤	206	ce	╬	232	e8	Φ
129	81	ü	155	9b	¢	181	b5	╡	207	cf	╧	233	e9	Θ
130	82	é	156	9c	£	182	b6	╢	208	d0	╨	234	ea	Ω
131	83	â	157	9d	¥	183	b7	╖	209	d1	╤	235	eb	δ
132	84	ä	158	9e	₧	184	b8	╕	210	d2	╥	236	ec	∞
133	85	à	159	9f	ƒ	185	b9	╣	211	d3	╙	237	ed	φ
134	86	å	160	a0	á	186	ba	║	212	d4	╘	238	ee	ε
135	87	ç	161	a1	í	187	bb	╗	213	d5	╒	239	ef	∩
136	88	ê	162	a2	ó	188	bc	╝	214	d6	╓	240	f0	≡
137	89	ë	163	a3	ú	189	bd	╜	215	d7	╫	241	f1	±
138	8a	è	164	a4	ñ	190	be	╛	216	d8	╪	242	f2	≥
139	8b	ï	165	a5	Ñ	191	bf	┐	217	d9	┘	243	f3	≤
140	8c	î	166	a6	ª	192	c0	└	218	da	┌	244	f4	⌠
141	8d	ì	167	a7	º	193	c1	┴	219	db	█	245	f5	⌡
142	8e	Ä	168	a8	¿	194	c2	┬	220	dc	▄	246	f6	÷
143	8f	Å	169	a9	⌐	195	c3	├	221	dd	▌	247	f7	≈
144	90	É	170	aa	¬	196	c4	─	222	de	▐	248	f8	°
145	91	æ	171	ab	½	197	c5	┼	223	df	▀	249	f9	∙
146	92	Æ	172	ac	¼	198	c6	╞	224	e0	α	250	fa	·
147	93	ô	173	ad	¡	199	c7	╟	225	e1	ß	251	fb	√
148	94	ö	174	ae	«	200	c8	╚	226	e2	Γ	252	fc	^{n}
149	95	ò	175	af	»	201	c9	╔	227	e3	π	253	fd	^{2}
150	96	û	176	b0	░	202	ca	╩	228	e4	Σ	254	fe	■
151	97	ù	177	b1	▒	203	cb	╦	229	e5	σ	255	ff	
152	98	ÿ	178	b2	▓	204	cc	╠	230	e6	µ			
153	99	Ö	179	b3	│	205	cd	═	231	e7	τ			

Index

Symbols

A

C

D

E

M

P

Q

R

T

U

Take the Next Step to Mastering C++

978-0-321-54372-1

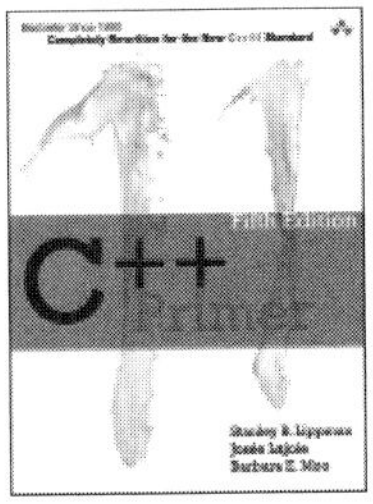

978-0-321-71411-4

978-0-321-56384-2

978-0-321-62321-8

978-0-321-11358-0

978-0-321-33487-9

978-0-201-63371-9

978-0-201-74962-5

978-0-321-32192-3

978-0-201-73484-3

978-0-13-704483-2

978-0-13-343985-4

978-0-13-267326-6

978-0-321-41299-7

978-0-321-13354-0

978-0-201-76042-2

978-0-201-61562-3

978-0-201-70434-1

978-0-201-70431-0

978-0-201-70353-5

Addison Wesley · PRENTICE HALL · informIT · Safari Books Online

For more information on these titles visit informit.com